# Britain, India, and the Arabs, 1914–1921

# Britain, India, and the Arabs, 1914-1921

*by*

BRITON COOPER BUSCH

UNIVERSITY OF CALIFORNIA PRESS
*Berkeley, Los Angeles, London*
1971

University of California Press
Berkeley and Los Angeles, California
University of California Press, Ltd.
London, England

Copyright © 1971, by
The Regents of the University of California

Library of Congress Catalog Card Number: 71–132421
International Standard Book Number: 0–520–01821–4
Printed in the United States of America

Acknowledgment is due to the following for permission
to quote from their works: Geoffrey Household and Michael Joseph, Ltd., for *A Watcher in the Shadows*; Desmond Young, Harper & Row, and Hamish Hamilton,
Ltd., for *All the Best Years*; and Lawrence Durrell, Faber
& Faber, Ltd., and E. P. Dutton & Co., for *Balthazar*.

*for my children*
PHILIP BRITON BUSCH
*and*
LESLIE COOPER BUSCH

# Preface

The history of international relations in the Middle East in the era of the First World War is notoriously complex. With this book I am afraid I have tried to make it more so. My thesis, however, is simple in itself: it is that British policy in this important era and area cannot adequately be understood without giving consideration not only to Anglo-French, Anglo-Arab, and Anglo-Zionist relations, but also equally to the conflict between British authorities in London and British authorities in India (with apologies to my Indian friends, "India" henceforth should be taken to mean the British Government in and of India). This conflict is not always readily discernible, because Indian influence came not from a single drive or position but rather from the sum of the parts of interference in the Hijaz or Aden or Iraq, and it was often fought out on the secondary level of London's subordinates in Cairo and India's deputies in Baghdad. Nevertheless, I believe that, taken over-all, Indian influence and intervention substantially limited the possibility of the creation of a coherent and unified policy for the entire British Empire towards the Middle East.

I must state several limitations in advance. First, I make no claim that this thesis is new, and indeed my debt to the several scholars who have worked in the history of Anglo-Arab relations will be clear even where no citation is made. I do claim, however, that India's role has never received the separate treatment its influence warrants. Second, since it is often necessary to follow closely the details of India's policy, less than adequate consideration is given to such subjects as French policy in Syria or Turkish nationalism in Anatolia, though I have no intention of belittling the importance of these issues in the formation of British policy. Finally, the work is based almost entirely upon British sources. Aside from private papers, I have principally used four documentary collections: Foreign Office and Cairo Residency records (both in the Public Record Office, London), India Office records in the India Office Library, London, and the records of the Indian Government in the National Archives of India, New Delhi.

Naturally I have incurred numerous obligations. My greatest debt is to the two foundations which so generously supported my research: the National Humanities Foundation, for research in England in 1968, and the Joint Committee on the Near and Middle East of the Social Science Research Council, for work in India and England in 1969. The Research Council of Colgate University provided supplemental assistance for the purchase of microfilm and the preparation of maps in the text. Second, I am indebted to the three libraries mentioned above and to the following for assistance over and above the normal demands of the researcher: The Middle East Centre, St. Antony's College, Oxford; The School of Oriental Studies, Durham University; the Departmental Record Office, Ministry of Power, London; The Royal Central Asian Society, London; and the United States Military Academy, West Point, New York.

It is small repayment, but at least I may mention those individuals who helped along the way. To Elizabeth Monroe of St. Antony's, George Rentz of the Hoover Institute, and Charles S. Blackton of Colgate University, all of whom read and commented upon the manuscript and saved me from some of my errors, my special thanks. Those who assisted in other ways include Dvorah Barzilay, Edgar Buckley, Jackie Cheetham, Georgianne Ensign, Professors Christina and David Harris, Matthew King, Jr., Sir John Richmond, K.C.M.G., and my hospitable colleagues in India, above all Professor Girija K. Mookerjee whose experience and wisdom so enriched my stay in New Delhi. To my wife, who despite earlier experiences of the same sort once again volunteered to type and edit the manuscript, for the second time, thanks.

Finally, I would like to express my gratitude to the several institutions and individuals who permitted quotation from their works. Unpublished Crown-copyright material in the India Office Library and India Office Records appears by permission of the Secretary of State for Commonwealth Relations; from other official documents, the bulk of which are from the Public Record Office, by permission of the Controller of H. M. Stationery Office; and from the Lloyd George Papers, by permission of the Director of the Beaverbrook Library, London.

B.C.B.

*Hamilton N.Y.*

# Contents

# MAPS

# PART ONE

# India and the Arab War

# I

# India's Campaign in Mesopotamia, 1914–1915

Generals are chosen, I am told,
For being very, very old.
And no exception to the rule
Was General Augustus Moore O'Toole,
Who'd lived retired from Public Scrutiny
Since just before the Indian Mutiny.
In ancient days, as I have heard,
He'd led the gallant umpty-third
To somewhere in Afghanistan
—Where they'd been butchered to a man.
Since then he had not been employed:
Whene'er the General was annoyed
Throughout the club they heard the tale
—The very waiters' hearts would quail
To hear his voice explaining more of his
Grievances against the War Office.

*Desmond Young,* ALL THE BEST YEARS

On 31 October 1914, Sir Louis Mallet, British Ambassador in Constantinople, reluctantly requested his passports from the Ottoman government and ordered the withdrawal of British consuls in Ottoman territory. No state of war between Britain

and Turkey yet existed, and Mallet even hoped this last desperate diplomatic measure might yet save the situation; but while he was bidding farewell, the Admiralty in London was ordering the commencement of hostilities against Turkey. Turkish ships, it was reported, had raided the Russian port of Odessa; by the time Turkey had offered regret for the incident, a new front was opening in Mesopotamia.[1]

Three days after the Admiralty's signal, the battleship *Ocean* with six other ships carrying a brigade and supporting units (some 5,000 men) appeared in the Shatt al-'Arab, the confluence of the Tigris and Euphrates rivers at the head of the Persian Gulf. On 5 November, war was officially declared.[2] On the 6th, these forces, working with the three British ships already waiting off the Shatt, cleared Turkish fortifications at Fao at the mouth of the river. On the 22nd, the town of Basra, 75 miles upriver, was formally entered. India was now in occupation of Ottoman territory, for India had provided the men, the means, and the initial control for this venture. From these first limited operations, unknown and unimportant to the

[1] Mallet telegrams to Sir Edward Grey, nos. 1097 and 1100, and Buchanan (Petrograd) telegram to Grey, 31 October; Grey telegram to Bertie (Paris), 3 November; Roberts (Odessa) telegram to Grey, 29 October 1914: Public Record Office (London), Foreign Office files, series 371, vol. 2145 [hereafter *FO* 371/2145]. Principal sources for the Mesopotamian Campaign used here are Brig.-Gen. F. J. Moberley, *The Campaign in Mesopotamia, 1914-1918*, 4 vol., *History of the Great War Based on Official Documents* (London, 1923-27); and A. J. Barker, *The Neglected War: Mesopotamia 1914-1918* (London, 1967), published in a revised edition as *The Bastard War: The Mesopotamian Campaign of 1914-1918* (N.Y., 1967). The first is the official history and the second the most recent scholarly account of the campaign, which includes a useful bibliography.

[2] War was declared on Turkey by the simple expedient of extending the existing Order in Council to cover the Ottoman Empire; it was signed by King George on 5 November (*FO* 371/2145), but local governments in India had been informed that war had broken out on 1 November: National Archives of India (New Delhi), Home Department, Political Proceedings, November 1914, nos. 1–27, Part A [hereafter *India Home Poli.* November 1914, 1–27, Part A].

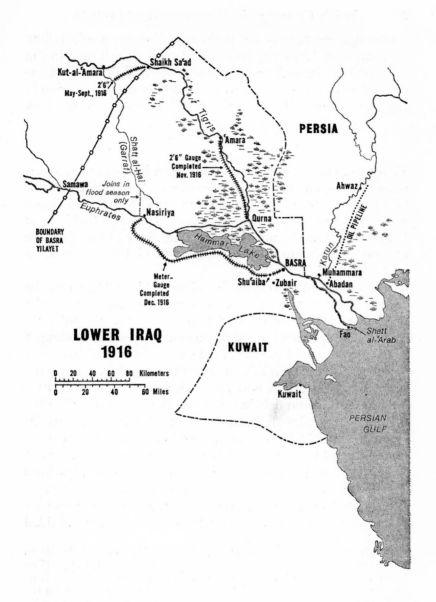

Kut-al-Amara
2'6"
May-Sept., 1916
Shaikh Sa'ad

PERSIA

Shatt al-Hai (Garraf)

Tigris

Amara

2'6" Gauge
Completed
Nov. 1916

Ahwaz

Samawa
Joins in
flood season
only

Euphrates

Nasiriya

Qurna

OIL PIPELINE

Karun

BOUNDARY
OF BASRA
YILAYET

Hammar Lake

BASRA

Muhammara

Meter-
Gauge
Completed
Dec. 1916

Shu'aiba · Zubair

Abadan

**LOWER IRAQ
1916**

KUWAIT

Fao    Shatt
al-'Arab

| 0 | 20 | 40 | 60 | 80 | Kilometers |
| 0 | 20 | 40 | | 60 | Miles |

Kuwait

PERSIAN
GULF

armies fighting bitterly for position in Europe, would follow complications involving nearly a million British and Indian soldiers, huge expenditures, and issues of Britain's Middle Eastern policy that would occupy considerable world attention in the years to come. This book is a study of those complications.

1

While expeditions may be decided upon in a moment, a moment will not suffice for their preparation. Yet "Force D," as it was known, needed only to sail up to the Shatt from Bahrain when the Admiralty order was issued. The ships had been at Bahrain, without disembarking the men, since 23 October; the Cabinet's decision to send the force to the Gulf had been taken on 2 October.[3]

The initial orders to Brigadier-General W. S. Delamain, the force's first commander, were to occupy Abadan Island in the Shatt (and in Persian territory) to protect the oil tanks, refinery, and pipe lines located there; to cover possible landing of reinforcements; and to assure the local Arabs of British support against Turkey. Ostensibly, at least, the main objective was the protection of oil; there was a great deal of oil to protect. Production of the main field in southwest Persia, at Masjid-i Sulaiman, some 25 miles southeast of Shustar, began in commercial quantities in 1908. In the year ending in March 1914, the pipeline running 130 miles to Abadan carried some 275,000 tons of crude oil. The Admiralty, by the conversion of its ships from coal to oil and by its long-term agreement with the Anglo-Persian Oil Company, had insured a permanent British interest in this oil before the war, and the British government had aided

---

[3] Moberley, *op. cit.*, I, pp. 80–91; Capt. T. H. Keyes (Bahrain) to Knox (Acting Resident, Persian Gulf), 4 November 1914, India Office Library (London), Political Department, Political and Secret files, Regular Series, vol. 86, no. 4923 of 1914 [hereafter, in accordance with the India Office system, *L/P&S/11*, vol. 86, no. 4923/14]. See also Lt.-Col. C. C. R. Murphy, *Soldiers of the Prophet*, (London, 1921), pp. 44–55.

the company in its negotiations with the semi-independent lord of southwest Persia, Shaikh Khaz'al of Muhammara in Arabistan (Khuzistan) province, with the chiefs of the Bakhtiari tribe through whose territory the pipe line ran, and with the Persian government itself.[4]

It is difficult to conceive precisely how Delamain's force was to protect the length of the pipe line—the Bakhtiaris were subsidized for just this purpose—but Abadan was certainly exposed to Turkish attack if war came. As early as mid-August the local representatives of the company were understandably nervous about the obvious danger to their property; in England, the Admiralty had let it be known by the end of that month that it attached great importance to Abadan and desired early action to secure it. The Foreign Office view was that the Admiralty should protect an Admiralty interest, but it was clear that the ships on the East Indies Station, already involved in escort and other duties, were insufficient. As reports began to arrive in September and early October of Turkish military reinforcements in the area and harassment of British ships and subjects, the danger became more and more real.[5]

These developments alarmed both naval and military authorities. Over and above the danger to oil production, to say nothing

[4] Sir Arnold T. Wilson, *Persia* (N.Y., 1933), p. 92; Briton C. Busch, *Britain and the Persian Gulf, 1894–1914* (Berkeley, Calif., 1967), pp. 380–81; Moberley, *op. cit.*, I, p. 14.

[5] Viceroy telegram to Secretary of State for India [SSI], 21 August, Admiralty to India Office [I.O.], 25 August, Hirtzel note for Gen. Barrow; (Military Secretary, I.O.), 29 August, Foreign Office [F.O.] to I.O., 25 August, Hardinge private telegram to Crewe (SSI), 1 September 1914, India Office Library, Political Department, Political and Secret Subject files [hereafter *L/P&S/10*], file 3136 of 1914, nos. 3305, 3340, 3344, and 3356 of 1914. Barrow memorandum, 24 August 1914, and other correspondence summarized in "Precis of Correspondence regarding the Mesopotamian Expedition: Its Genesis and Development," War Office files (Public Record Office), *WO* 106/877. Reports on Turkish military forces in *FO* 371/2138-42. Winston Churchill, at the Admiralty, argued that the Persian oil could be replaced from other sources, but he was under strong pressure from Admiral Slade, his ad-

of Britain's commanding commercial interests in Mesopotamia and a recently agreed upon share in the southern section of the unfinished Baghdad Railway, there was a possibility that the unchallenged establishment of a fortified Turkish base and harbor in Basra and the Shatt would seriously jeopardize British trade and communications in the Persian Gulf and perhaps the Indian Ocean beyond. The scare provided by the German raider *Emden* operating in the Indian Ocean in September was symptomatic; what if Basra should host a fleet of such ships, or even submarines?[6]

Such possibilities were remote, for Turkey would be engaged elsewhere in war; the incomplete nature of rail communications and the scarcity of available local military resources would make the development of a fortified harbor in the Basra area difficult at best. But Turkish agents would be active in the Gulf and beyond, perhaps as far as India and Afghanistan, and should a *jihad* (holy war) be proclaimed, there was some doubt as to the response of Indian Muslims. If Britain took steps to uphold her established position in the Gulf, and perhaps expand it, such seditious activity would be less likely to be of real significance.

It was this issue of "face," coupled with the possible benefits of a small, victorious campaign in Mesopotamia, that emerged

---

visor on Middle Eastern affairs, Moberley, *op. cit.*, I, p. 82, and minute by Shuckburgh (Assistant Secretary, Political Department, I.O.), 9 September 1914, *L/P&S/10* 3136/14, no. 3496/14.

[6] See Moberley, *op. cit.*, I, pp. 71–72, 91; naval operations may be followed in Sir Julian S. Corbett, *Naval Operations*, 5 vols. in 9, *History of the Great War Based on Official Documents* (London, 1920–28). H.M.S. *Ocean* was in fact attached to the expedition specifically because of the *Emden*; see National Archives of India, Foreign Department Proceedings, Secret, War [hereafter *India Sec. War*], February 1915, 31–100. On British commercial interests in Iraq, see Busch, *Britain and the Persian Gulf*, pp. 35ff., 315–17, 335f., 385, and bibliography; Philip Willard Ireland, *'Iraq: A Study in Political Development* (London, 1937), ch. II.

as the main cause for the campaign in the first instance—and for much of subsequent policy both civil and military. Sir Arthur Hirtzel, Political Secretary in the India Office in London, was one of the first to urge this motive, in a memorandum of 2 September: ". . . the political effect in the Persian Gulf & in India of leaving the head of the Gulf derelict will be *disastrous*, & we cannot afford, publicly, to acquiesce in such a thing for an indefinite period while the main issues are being settled elsewhere." There had already been some discussion on the chances of influencing Arab sentiment within the Ottoman Empire in case of war. These chances, noted Hirtzel, would be reduced if the Shaikh of Kuwait, long in friendly relations with Britain and for all practical purposes independent of the Turks, were sacrificed—for surely the Turks, if given half a chance, would move against him to make good their old claims. There was, too, the postwar situation to be considered (like others, Hirtzel still thought of a short war): ". . . if in the meantime we leave the Turks in possession of points that have always been regarded as strategically & politically of the utmost importance to India, we shall not be in a strong position to turn the situation to our advantage when the final settlement comes." [7]

Hirtzel was not the only official to consider Arab sentiments. Lieutenant-Colonel S. G. Knox, Acting Resident in the Persian Gulf, had predicted in a letter of 20 August that Britain would have no trouble with the Arab chiefs of the Persian Gulf region, who might rise against the Turks even without British intervention. If Britain should act to take Basra, however, it ". . . would

[7] Hirtzel memorandum, 2 September 1914: *L/P&S/10*, 3136/14, no. 3439/14; quoted in Lt.-Col. Sir Arnold T. Wilson, *Loyalties, Mesopotamia, 1914–1917: A Personal and Historical Record* (London, 1930), p. 4. For previous discussions see Mallet telegram to Grey, 27 August 1914, *FO* 371/2138; Crewe private to Hardinge, 14 August 1914, *Hardinge Papers* (all Hardinge papers cited are located in Cambridge University Library, unless it is specifically indicated that the reference is to a supplemental Hardinge collection in the Kent County Archives, Maidstone).

be the sign for a general insurrection along the river Tigris and also for an attack on Baghdad and for the probable capture by the Kurds of Aleppo and the demolition of [the] Baghdad Railway. This in addition to diversions created by Egypt in Syria and the Hedjaz would certainly have a demoralising effect on mobilisation by Turkey and would wreck the Empire." [8] Knox had little experience of Mesopotamia, and his predictions were to prove exceedingly overoptimistic, but he was accurate with regard to the position of the Gulf shaikhs; given the preservation of at least existing British strength there, they would prove loyal to their British connections. Some had good reason to do so. Shaikh Mubarak of Kuwait, for example, a perpetual problem to Ottoman authorities, could expect serious trouble; he wasted no time in giving expression of his loyalty to the local British agent and urging an attack on Basra, which town, he said, would gladly open its doors to British occupation.[9]

Mubarak might prove useful; so too might his friend and rival to the south, 'Abd al-'Aziz ibn Sa'ud, head of the Wahhabi state. Prewar policy in the Gulf had tended to shy away from close relations with Ibn Sa'ud, and although there were no outstanding Anglo-Saudi issues of importance, Ibn Sa'ud was not as securely in the British sphere of influence as Mubarak. There was worry, by late September, that he might be persuaded to side with the Turks. To forestall his subversion, the India Office had proposed to send an emissary, Captain W. H. I. Shakespear, an official with Gulf experience who had first met Ibn Sa'ud in Kuwait in 1910. By 2 October—the day the Cabinet

[8] Knox to Secretary, Foreign Department, Government of India [FSI], 20 August 1914, *L/P&S/10*, 3136/14, no. 3683/14.

[9] Memorandum by G. W. Grey (Agent, Kuwait), 22 August 1914, on his talks with Mubarak on the 21st, *FO* 371/2144; A. H. Grant (FSI) demi-official to Hirtzel, 19 November 1914, enclosing Mubarak to Cox (Political Officer, "Force D," formerly Persian Gulf Resident, and, in 1914, briefly FSI), 14 October, *L/P&S/10*, 2182/13, no. 4813/14. Letters to and from rulers of Kuwait, Bahrain, Qatar, and Muscat, *India Home Poli.* January 1915, 235, Part B, and *India Sec. War* March 1915, 1–576.

sanctioned the Gulf expedition—the decision to send Shakespear was definite. It was a plan which met with little opposition; even the cautious Mallet in Constantinople supported the scheme of using Ibn Sa'ud and Mubarak against the Turks if war came.[10]

Nor did the British-controlled Gulf shaikhs exhaust the list of possible allies. In Muhammara, the Persian port upriver from Abadan, Khaz'al had long been a staunch friend. In the hinterland of Mesopotamia, the powerful Muntafiq tribes had before the war made overtures, rejected at the time, to British officials.[11] And from Basra itself appeared a powerful political figure, Sayyid Talib Pasha ibn Sayyid Rajab, member of the family of the Naqib al-Ashraf (Marshal of the Nobles) of Basra, former holder of government positions, nationalist leader, and virtual feudal lord of Basra's 60,000 inhabitants. On 7 October, Talib, fearing loss of his influence if Turkish military forces took serious control of Basra, sounded out the British consul there. By the end of the month, Talib had asked to be recognized as Shaikh or Amir (Prince) of Basra under British protection. He was told that nothing could be promised in writing; his eventual position would depend upon the degree of his influence and the extent to which he exerted that influence in Britain's favor—a hint of rewards to come. Talib could not wait and fled to Kuwait before the British captured Basra. At Kuwait, he attempted to reopen negotiations on 12 November, but he no longer had anything to offer. Receiving no comfort from the British agent at Kuwait, he rode off to see Ibn Sa'ud, far inland at Buraida. A powerful and possibly dangerous man ("dangerous scoundrel," said Hirtzel; "notoriously

[10] Cheetham (Egypt) telegram to Grey, 21 September 1914, and other documents in *L/P&S/10*, 2182/13, nos. 3705/14ff.; G. R. Clerk (F.O.) and Crewe minutes, 2 and 3 October, and Mallet telegram to Grey, 4 September 1914, *FO* 371/2139. On Saudi-British relations and Shakespear's earlier meetings, Busch, *Britain and the Persian Gulf*, pp. 318 n., 340.

[11] *India Sec. E.* [External] May 1912, 100–1.

untrustworthy and slippery," added Mallet), Talib will be encountered again.[12]

The presence of possible allies, like fears of Turkish advances, danger to oil production, and prestige in general, played a role in the organization of a British effort in the Persian Gulf in October 1914. Another motive had been hinted at only: possible ambitions of an imperial nature in Mesopotamia. To officials in the Gulf or in London who for two decades and more had had the responsibility of putting up with constant Turkish pinpricks and the ambitions of various European powers in the Gulf, the possibility of war with Turkey gave rise to visions of solutions undreamed of only months earlier, and even greater dreams were to be born of the quick success of "Force D."

But vague desires to cooperate with the Arabs and strike at Turkey were not enough to send the expedition on its way. Forces must be provided, and, before the expedition was dispatched to the Gulf, agreement must be reached on the overall desirability of the expedition. The Admiralty could urge its concern, Knox telegraph from the Gulf, and Hirtzel worry about prestige, but it was still necessary to convince the Government of India on certain points and to decide upon the precise objectives to be obtained, for India controlled relations with the Gulf and would have to provide the force.

Lord Hardinge of Penshurst, Viceroy since 1910, was not particularly enthusiastic about the logic leading to action in the Gulf, even though initiative for the expedition appeared to come from several directions at once. It was not that he objected

[12] Viceroy telegrams to SSI, 9, 28, and 31 October and 30 November, and minutes; Hirtzel's remark, 1 December minute; Mallet's in telegram to Viceroy, 29 October 1914: *L/P&S/10*, 3136/14, nos. 4184, 4244, 4683, and 4658/14. For other, similar remarks: T. E. Lawrence, *Seven Pillars of Wisdom: A Triumph* (Garden City, N.Y., 1936), p. 46; Wilson, *Loyalties*, p. 18; Lord Birdwood, *Nuri as-Said: A Study in Arab Leadership* (London, 1959), pp. 21–22; Elie Kedourie, *England and the Middle East: The Destruction of the Ottoman Empire, 1914–1921* (London, 1956), pp. 204–5; Shakespear note for Hirtzel, 26 June 1914, *L/P&S/10*, 94/15, no. 2964/14.

to the idea of British control of Basra, or closer association with Mubarak, Ibn Sa'ud, or Khaz'al; rather, he was hesitant lest Britain prematurely force Turkey into war and by so doing assume the odium and responsibility for the conflict. India was concerned with Indian Muslim opinion and was not certain how that opinion should best be conciliated. In August, Indian authorities had asked London for an authoritative statement on the growing rupture with Turkey, in order not to spring a Turkish war suddenly on India (most Turkish news was being kept from release by government censors), but had then decided that the statement should not be issued until war appeared inevitable, for it would only unsettle loyal Muslims. On Hardinge's initiative London was next asked for—and granted—permission to issue an entirely different statement that, if Indian pilgrims to holy shrines in Arabia and elsewhere were undisturbed, the holy places and Jidda, the main Red Sea pilgrim port, would be immune from British attack. The declaration was issued, in India, on 2 November.[13]

Hardinge was also alarmed about encouraging a rebellion which Britain could not sufficiently support by force of arms. While fully willing to guarantee immunity to Mubarak and the others, and even "recognition of independence of principality of Koweit under British protection," as he telegraphed on 4 September (the obvious contradiction in terms is explained by the peculiar prewar status of Kuwait, long the subject of Anglo-Ottoman discussions), still he foresaw one sizable

[13] Hardinge private telegrams to Crewe, 21 and 26 August; Crewe private telegram to Hardinge, 25 August; Secretary to Government of India, Home Department, telegram to all local governments, 2 November 1914: *India Home Poli.* November 1914, 1–27, Part A. Hardinge private telegram to Crewe, 30 August, Crewe private telegram to Hardinge, 2 September 1914, *India Sec. War* May 1915, 453–87. Hardinge note of 28 August 1914, *ibid.* March 1915, 1–576. See also Knox's view from the Gulf in telegrams to FSI, 9 and 11 October 1914, *ibid.* February 1915, 31–100. Kitchener similarly advised caution on Muslim opinion; see Asquith's diary, 17 August 1914, Earl of Oxford and Asquith, *Memories and Reflections, 1852–1927* (Boston, 1928), II, p. 32.

stumbling block: ". . . it is impossible for us to say at present whether we should be in a position at any particular juncture to spare sufficient troops for the seizure of the place in the face of armed Turkish opposition," and by "we" he meant India.[14] Two weeks later the Viceroy was more specific. Fao and Basra could be taken; but if the Turks could bring up a corps in opposition, a full division from India would be necessary—and all available divisions had been allotted to Europe or Africa. If Gulf operations were to be undertaken on a major scale, either the Sixth (Poona) Division, now destined for Europe, must be retained for the Gulf or, alternatively, internal and frontier Indian troops would have to be cut below tolerable levels.[15]

Lack of forces, however, was not the sole reason for Hardinge's caution. Until the last minute, he continued to urge privately to Lord Crewe, Secretary of State for India, that until war actually broke out, for the sake of Indian Muslim opinion, Britain must not appear the aggressor. "I cannot help thinking that Winston Churchill is at the bottom of this proposal in his anxiety for the safety of the oil wells at Abadan . . . ," he wrote his friend Valentine Chirol. With Hardinge's lack of enthusiasm Crewe agreed; the oil was not absolutely essential as far as the India Office was concerned, and the effect on the tribes was the main thing.[16]

Hardinge's warnings forced a decision in England. On 2 October India was told to use the Sixth Division, although initially only a part of the unit would be sent to occupy Aba-

[14] Hardinge private telegram to Crewe, 4 Septembeer 1914, *FO* 371/ 2139; the same conclusion was reached by General Barrow in the I.O.: minute, 8 September 1914, *L/P&S/10*, 3136/14, no. 3496/14. On Kuwait, Busch, *Britain and the Persian Gulf*, chs. III, VII, X; and "Britain and the Status of Kuwayt, 1894–99," *Middle East Journal*, 21 (Spring 1967), 187–98.

[15] Hardinge private telegram to Crewe, 19 September 1914, *FO* 371/ 2143.

[16] Hardinge private to Crewe, 8, 15, and 29 October, and to Chirol, 8 October; Crewe private to Hardinge, 9 October 1914: *Hardinge Papers*.

dan. India's protests that such an action would be a violation of Persian neutrality, and therefore offensive to Muslim opinion generally as well as allowing the Turks to seize Persian territory inland, resulted only in halting the force at Bahrain as a useful temporary staging post until war broke out. Until war did come, furthermore, the presence of the force in the middle of the Gulf clearly strengthened Britain's hand with respect to the various Gulf rulers. When hostilities opened on the 31st, however, the destination was clear: the brigade was ordered to the Shatt to cooperate with the naval authorities already there in an immediate attack upon Fao. But Fao became the Shatt and the Shatt Basra: in less than a month's easy campaigning, a substantial foothold in Mesopotamia had been taken, and major decisions on future British intentions were required.[17]

2

Protection of British interests and cooperation with the Gulf Arabs were very compatible aims, particularly given the magnitude of British influence in the Gulf. Larger ambitions, however, such as those implicit in Hirtzel's memorandum of 2 September, were not necessarily compatible with the aspirations of the Arabs of Mesopotamia or the Arab world in general or with the sensibilities of the still larger body of Muslim opinion.

Initially, concern for Arab and Muslim sympathies had the upper hand in both India and London, as exemplified by the pledge on the holy places and a statement to Gulf rulers that only the protection of British interests—and no aggressive action—was intended. Hardinge had already approved a number of special pledges to Mubarak and the other Gulf shaikhs and would suggest a cautious statement that Britain would not be

[17] Crewe private telegram to Hardinge, 2 October 1914, *L/P&S/10*, 63/13, no. 3832a/14; Hardinge private telegrams to Crewe, 4 and 5 October, *FO* 371/2143, and 7 October 1914, *WO* 106/877; Viceroy telegram to SSI, 13 October 1914, *L/P&S/10*, 3136/14, no. 4166/14; see also *WO* 106/877, and Moberley, *op. cit.*, I, pp. 81–83.

sorry to see the holy places redeemed from the hands of the Turks ". . . owing to notorious misgovernment and spoliation of pilgrims which at present prevails under their *régime*." But India opposed—again in the name of Muslim opinion—the wider promise of support for Arab aspirations being discussed in London, where general Arab opinion had been a further motive for the expedition in the first place, just as it had been, to a lesser extent, a motive for the mission to Ibn Sa'ud and the pledges to the Gulf shaikhs.[18] It was increasingly evident, however, that the Gulf expedition was going to have to be associated with some move toward the Arabs in general.

In the Foreign Office, Assistant Under-Secretary Sir Eyre Crowe noted on 26 September that while the expedition's landing might have a steadying effect on the Turks—it was still not war—or at least check Turkish troop movements from Mosul toward Egypt, in any case "it would almost certainly prevent the Arabs from throwing in their lot with the Turks."[19] Crowe had not been closely associated with policy toward the Middle East and, like many who were to be called upon for advice, had no personal experience there. It would be some time before the ambiguity of the term "Arabs" became clear in London.

The early success of the expedition reinforced India's caution regarding further promises. Sir Milne Cheetham, Acting High Commissioner in Cairo, had proposed a British declaration that no action would be taken in Arabia save in the Arabs' own interests, that is, in aid of their achieving independence or in defense against Turkish aggression.[20] Hardinge was still unwilling to approve any definite statements that might become embarrassing later, and Lord Crewe agreed: Britain's

[18] SSI telegram to Viceroy, 26 October 1914, *WO* 106/877; Grey telegram to Mallet and F.O. to I.O., 1 September, and Hardinge private telegram to Crewe, 19 September 1914, *FO* 371/2138, 2139, and 2143.

[19] Eyre Crowe memorandum, 26 September 1914, *FO* 371/2139.

[20] SSI telegram to Viceroy, 15 November 1914, *India Sec. War* March 1915, 745–862.

hands should not be tied more than "political exigencies make necessary."[21] Then came a report from Lieutenant-General Sir Arthur Barrett (who had superseded Delamain with the arrival of other units of the division) that Sir Percy Cox, Chief Political Officer with the expedition, had issued a proclamation of annexation during the course of the occupation of Basra —which would indeed have tied Britain's hands. Actually, Cox had only said, "No remnant of Turkish Administration now remains on this region. In place thereof the British flag has been established . . . ," which was not exactly annexation, but Cox followed with a request for permission to declare permanent occupation.[22]

Hardinge, an early victim of success, concurred with this request. On 2 December, he wrote to Crewe that Britain "ought never to give up Basrah again"; he understood that no open declaration of possession could be made, but if Crewe could only give him an assurance in private, "that will be quite sufficient for me." It made some difference, after all, in the kind of administration to be established. On 7 December, he sent a telegram reiterating that, while he recognized that the statement might cause inconvenience, it would facilitate administration of the area, settle once and for all the question of Gulf supremacy, insure the safety and development of Abadan, secure the position of Khaz'al and Mubarak, and end the issue of the Baghdad Railway terminus. Further, it would pay in the long run, ". . . as Basrah and surrounding country are capable of enormous commercial development." Finally,

To abandon Basrah after a short operation would be to betray all those Arabs and tribes who are now in friendly cooperation with

[21] Viceroy telegram to SSI, 20 November, and SSI telegram to Viceroy, 22 November 1914, L/P&S/10, 3136/14, no. 4511/14.

[22] Barrett telegram to SSI, 24 November, and Cox telegram to SSI, 27 November 1914, WO 106/877. Cox telegram (dated 22 November) quoted in Wilson, Loyalties, p. 311, and in Philip Graves, The Life of Sir Percy Cox (London, 1941), p. 182. Hirtzel minute, 24 November 1914, L/P&S/10, 3136/14, no. 4573/14.

us. . . . We believe that the indications of the permanence of our rule are likely to stop possibility of intrigues and encourage population to settle down quickly, and we anticipate no local difficulty if the occupation is to be permanent.[23]

Lord Crewe now faced the rather difficult task of dampening the Viceroy's newfound ardor. In a letter of 10 December, he pointed out that there were serious disadvantages to moving too quickly, and much remained uncertain. "Assume, as I am willing to do, that in the final settlement we definitely hold on. Is it not difficult to say at this moment what form of control, over what area, and under or through whom, ought to be permanently instituted? It is not India, or much like any part of India; and much examination and reflection may be needed in establishing a new government there."[24] Actually, Crewe was saying in muted terms what Hirtzel had minuted three days earlier:

It will probably be admitted that the administration (temporary or permanent) must be undertaken by the G. of I.; but it is by no means certain that it will eventually prove advisable to take an Indian district as the model for it, if we want contentment among people accustomed to a widely different system of administration. It will be remembered that even in the N.W.F.P. [North-West Frontier Province] discontent has been caused by the revenue system. It will probably be necessary to go very gently at first, & some admixture of personnel accustomed to dealing with different kinds of people seems advisable.

Presumably there can be no question of H.M.G. sharing the cost & (eventual) profit. Nothing will ever be done if the Treasury are imported into the administration.[25]

[23] Hardinge private to Crewe, 2 December 1914, *Hardinge Papers* (partly quoted in Barker, *Neglected War*, p. 100), and Hardinge private telegram to Crewe, 7 December 1914, *FO* 371/2144.

[24] Crewe private to Hardinge, 10 December 1914, *Hardinge Papers*; see also Crewe's worried note to Grey, 8 December 1914, *Grey Papers* (Public Record Office), *FO* 800/96.

[25] Hirtzel minute on Viceroy telegram to SSI, 7 December 1914, *L/P&S/10*, 4097/14, no. 4726/14.

There were other pressures for positive action. Lord Inchcape, shipping magnate with important commercial interests in the Gulf and Mesopotamia, wrote to Sir Edward Grey and spoke to Eyre Crowe in early December urging that now was the time for permanently securing the Baghdad-Basra section of the railway and ridding the Gulf of nominal Turkish suzerainty once and for all. His goal was ". . . a British Protectorate . . . over Mesopotamia from Baghdad to the sea . . ." The population would be loyal, "and there are enormous developments possible there if the country is properly and honestly administered." Crowe, at least, was convinced; there was the further point that France and Russia would certainly have their postwar claims in Ottoman territory, and Britain should secure Mesopotamia as its share while the opportunity lasted. Cox should be asked, Crowe said, to draw up a memorandum on the best way ". . . of establishing British influence definitely in these regions." Perhaps a formal protectorate was not the best approach. "But that it would be good policy to let it be understood that we will not allow the Turk to return, and will if necessary stay in order to prevent this, I feel convinced." Lord Kitchener, Secretary of War, added simply that it was 500 miles from the Gulf to Baghdad, and so far only 50 of those miles had been covered.[26]

Sir Edward Grey came down against annexation, however; it was contrary to principles of Allied cooperation, and the occupation could only remain provisional until the war ended.[27] A consideration no doubt present in Grey's mind—if less evident to Indian authorities—was the annexation of Cyprus on

[26] Inchcape private to Grey, 3 December 1914, with minutes by Crowe and Kitchener, *FO* 371/2144. Inchcape letter quoted in Hector Bolitho, *James Lyle Mackay, First Earl of Inchcape* (London, 1936), pp. 121–22. Crowe's views were shared by Grant in India: note, 25 November 1914, *India Sec. War* June 1915, 47–50.

[27] Grey minute, undated (but 7 December), on Viceroy telegram to SSI, 5 December 1914, *FO* 371/2144; F.O. to I.O., 15 December 1914, *L/P&S/10*, 4097/14, no. 4887/14.

5 November and the approaching declaration of the formal protectorate over Egypt and the deposition of Egypt's Khedive on 18–19 December.[28] Too many such protectorates and annexations would arouse the gravest suspicions among Britain's allies during a war which, it was increasingly clear, could not end as quickly as some had thought. Grey and Prime Minister Asquith, too, found such a policy decision all the easier for their own lack of sympathy with the more grandiose expansionist plans,

... and this not from a merely moral and sentimental point of view. Taking Mesopotamia, for instance, means spending millions in irrigation and development with no immediate or early return, keeping up quite a large army in an unfamiliar country, tackling every kind of tangled administrative question, worse than any we have ever had in India, with a hornet's nest of Arab tribes, and even if that were all set right having a perpetual menace on our flank in Kurdistan.[29]

On 16 December India was told:

His Majesty's Government desire that no declaration of permanent annexation should be made, as it would arouse French and Russian suspicions and would be contrary to the principle that occupation of conquered territory by allies is provisional pending final settlement at close of war.[30]

Hardinge did not give up easily. He wrote to Lord Crewe; he wrote to Valentine Chirol of *The Times* (at the moment semi-officially responsible to the Foreign Office for eastern news); he wrote to Lord Curzon; he wrote to Sir Arthur

[28] Cyprus: SSI telegram to Viceroy, 5 November 1914, *FO* 371/2144; Egypt: F.O. to I.O., 17 and 18 December 1914, *L/P&S/11*, vol. 86, nos. 4907 and 4946/14.

[29] Oxford and Asquith, *op. cit.*, II, pp. 81–82. This statement, like Cox's telegram advocating advance, is often quoted: some examples are Ireland, *op. cit.*, p. 72; Kedourie, *England and the Middle East*, p. 33; Wilson, *Loyalties*, p. 83.

[30] SSI telegram to Viceroy, 16 December 1914, *FO* 371/2144.

Nicolson, who had succeeded Hardinge as Permanent Under-Secretary in the Foreign Office; he wrote to Sir Reginald Wingate, Governor-General of the Sudan and Sirdar (Commander-in-Chief) of the Egyptian Army. Each time, he urged permanent retention of the Basra vilayet—as he wrote to Nicolson, it could be "a second Egypt"—and "perhaps some kind of autonomous province at Bagdad more or less under our protectorate." And as each week passed, Hardinge's, and India's, ambitions grew in direct ratio to military success. Most of his correspondents responded in kind; but Nicolson, with an eye to foreign relations, urged Grey's point of interallied cooperation—although nothing precluded eventual annexation.[31]

Like his Secretary to the (Indian) Foreign Department,[32] A. H. Grant, Hardinge had assumed that the Government of India would administer occupied Mesopotamia, but there was also confusion on this question. In October Crewe had done little more than cable unhelpfully that, while India would manage the expedition, ". . . instructions as to scope of operations will of course come from me." In December the instructions were to maintain as much of the prewar local administration as possible. "No attempt should be made at present to trans-

[31] Hardinge private to Chirol, 2 December; to Crewe, 10 December; to Curzon, 14 December 1914; to Nicolson, 6 January and 4 February; and to Wingate, 28 March 1915, *Hardinge Papers*; to Nicolson, 31 March 1915 (quoted), *Nicolson Papers* (Public Record Office), *FO* 800/377. On Chirol's function with the F.O., Chirol demi-official to Hardinge, 18 August 1914, *India Home Poli.* November 1914, 33–34, Part A. See also the discussion of administration in *India Sec. War* March 1915, 577–606.

[32] The Foreign Department came under the direct supervision of the Viceroy and was concerned with (and had substantial responsibility for) India's relations with her neighbors, notably Arabia, the Persian Gulf, Persia, Afghanistan, and Tibet. It should be kept in mind that the whole of the British Government of India, including the Viceroy and the Foreign Department, were subordinate to the British Government in London; it is equally fair, however, to note that the question of the extent of the Viceroy's initiative in the area of foreign relations was of long standing. See, for example, Busch, *Britain and the Persian Gulf*.

form vilayet into an Indian district."[33] But some thoughts were turning in precisely this direction. The clearest expression is a private letter from Captain Arnold Talbot Wilson—who will play a major role in the events to be discussed—newly assigned to Cox's staff after service on the prewar Turko-Persian boundary commission: "I should like to see it announced that Mesopotamia was to be annexed to India as a colony for India and Indians, that the Government of India would administer it, and gradually bring under cultivation its vast unpopulated desert plains, peopling them with martial races from the Punjab . . ." Certainly this would mean greater responsibilities for India, but India would then require no other colonial claim, and it might relieve her population pressure.[34]

So long as political officers on the spot were thinking in this direction, it was easier to make a decision against annexation than to enforce it, from a practical administrative standpoint. On 12 December Hardinge cabled privately to Cox that H.M.G. could not, for international reasons, make an announcement of permanent occupation of Basra, "but we ought, I think, to base our administration on that hypothesis."[35] This remark ran counter to the intent of London's instructions—but to Cox, and to Hardinge, and to many others, it was unthinkable in 1914 that the future had something rather different in store than permanent British possession of Mesopotamia. And if there was some question in London, the necessity for

[33] SSI telegrams to Viceroy, 5 October and 16 December 1914, *FO* 371/2143–44. Grant's view (India must be prepared to govern Mesopotamia "like an Indian province"): note, 25 November 1914, *India Sec. War* June 1915, 47–50.

[34] A. T. Wilson private to Col. C. E. Yate, 28 November 1914: copies in *L/P&S/10*, 3136/14, no. 4717/14; *FO* 371/2482; *Bonar Law Papers* (Beaverbrook Library, London), 35/3/77. Maj. Sir Hubert Young, *The Independent Arab* (London, 1933), notes (p. 40) that most of the officers shared the same view.

[35] Hardinge private telegram to Cox, 12 December 1914, *Hardinge Papers*.

British and Indian administration for some time to come would be made quite clear by a further advance to Baghdad.

3

Thoughts of a possible advance beyond Basra had, of course, arisen with the initial success of the expedition. Hardinge wrote privately to Crewe on 5 November that after Basra was taken there would be time enough ". . . to consider what further action we can take in the direction of Baghdad."[36] By the 16th, when it was clear that operations were going well, Hirtzel and General Sir Edmund Barrow, Military Secretary in the India Office, discussed a possible telegram to the Viceroy urging a quick advance, but decided that Cox could be trusted to put the strongest case possible for the political advantages of forward movement.[37] Cox had been Resident in the Persian Gulf from 1904 to 1913, and subsequently Secretary of the Foreign Department in India, and had accompanied the expedition as its Chief Political Officer at his own request; his views could be expected to have considerable influence.[38]

Cox, well aware of the fact that discussion of "Mesopotamia" involved more than Basra and Fao,[39] had pressed for military advance at the same time as he pressed for annexation, just as Hirtzel and Barrow had surmised he would. On 23 November,

[36] Hardinge private to Crew, 5 November 1914, *ibid.*
[37] Minutes, 16 November 1914, *L/P&S/10*, 3136/14, no. 4446/14.
[38] Graves, *Cox*, p. 179; see also *India Sec. War* March 1915, 1–576.
[39] Prewar usage for lower Iraq was "Turkish Arabia," but the commonly used historical term was "Mesopotamia," which included the Basra and Baghdad vilayets. Subsequent occupation of the Mosul vilayet rather complicated problems of definition, both of "Mesopotamia" and of "Iraq," both officially and in popular usage. "Mesopotamia" and "Iraq" will be used interchangeably here to include approximately the boundaries of modern-day Iraq, a usage justified only by the similar wartime confusion of the terms before "Iraq" became generally accepted in the 1920's.

the day after formal entrance into Basra, he was telegraphing his reasons for an advance. Baghdad, whose population had always been friendly to Britain, would no doubt fall into British hands "very easily," as the Turks were unlikely to put up much opposition. Aside from the over-all importance of the city, British captives were being held there (roughly thirty). And if allies were needed, Shakespear had already been sent to bring Ibn Sa'ud north. All in all, it was difficult to see ". . . how we can well avoid taking over Baghdad."[40]

Despite Hardinge's support of Cox, the home authorities would sanction only an advance to Qurna, some 50 miles north of Basra on the Tigris (where it joined the old channel of the Euphrates). Baghdad was still far distant, and the future uncertain, for retirement in the face of superior Turkish forces was a very undesirable possibility. London opposed any action that would force Allies or Arabs to consider the ultimate settlement regarding Turkey and the rest of the Ottoman Empire. For the time being, Britain could only reassert its claims and powers at the head of the Gulf—and this had already been achieved by the capture of Basra.[41]

General Barrow was perhaps the most persuasive advocate of the advance to Qurna, and his reasons were revealing from the standpoint both of Mesopotamia and of small, independent campaigns generally. In the first place, as he stated in a minute of 27 November, ". . . a policy of passive inactivity is to be deprecated if we are to continue to impress the Arab and Indian world with our ability to defeat all designs against us."

[40] Cox telegram to Viceroy, 23 November, enclosed in Hardinge private telegram to Crewe, 25 November 1914: quoted in Moberley, *op. cit.*, I, pp. 133–34; Graves, *Cox*, pp. 181–82; Kedourie, *England and the Middle East*, p. 176. On the Turkish-held prisoners: Cox telegram to SSI, 12 November 1914, *L/P&S/10*, 3136/14, no. 4445/14.

[41] Hirtzel and Barrow minutes on F.O. to I.O., 9 December 1914, *L/P&S/11*, vol. 87, no. 4786/14; SSI telegram to Viceroy, 27 November, and Crewe private telegram to Hardinge, 30 November 1914, *WO* 106/877.

While it was premature now to embark on something so ambitious as the occupation of Baghdad (as Cox would have it), Qurna was a most desirable objective. Strong opposition seemed unlikely, and the flanks were "practically unassailable" marshes and river areas. The town commanded the area of rich agricultural production stretching southward to the sea, it covered Persian Arabistan (the area of the oilfields), and the "moral effect on the Arabs" of such an advance would be great. Then, of course, ". . . it will be time enough to consider whether we should go further," for by then the attitude of Ibn Sa'ud and other Arab leaders would be clear; ". . . but let nothing be done in haste. Time is on our side. It would be unwise to decide on going to Baghdad till we can frame a policy for the future. . . . But whatever we do, let us not stand still."[42]

Within a week of the occupation of Basra, in other words, arguments for a steady forward movement were being advanced, and some, like Cox, were already thinking of Baghdad as a feasible objective. Certainly there were some words of caution. General Sir Beauchamp Duff, Commander-in-Chief, India, wrote Hardinge privately on the same day that Barrow was penning his minute that he himself would not wait to advance if the troops were available: but what of the long lines of communication? Could the Arabs be trusted to hold them? And Baghdad was hard to defend against an attack from the north.[43] Yet as George Clerk, a junior Foreign Office official, minuted on 29 November, "The important thing is the decision to move on. Personally I should welcome a decision to go for Bagdad, as I am a fierce believer in the respect Orientals pay to hard facts, but the Persian Gulf operations are not isolated and must fit in more or less with the general

---

[42] Barrow minute, 27 November 1914, *FO* 371/2143; Moberley, *op. cit.*, I, pp. 136–37. Some of these "advantages," wrote Field-Marshal Sir William Robertson, were advantages "only by a stretch of the imagination," *Soldiers and Statesmen, 1914–1918* (N.Y., 1926), II, p. 27.

[43] Duff private to Hardinge, 27 November 1914, *Hardinge Papers*.

mosaic." Grey was more cautious; it all depended on whether, once taken, Baghdad could be held.[44]

As Barrow had noted, time enough after Qurna, but Qurna was taken on 9 December,[45] which made discussion of further advance all the more pressing. On 2 December Hardinge had written privately to Crewe that he had already reached the conclusion, after consultation with Duff, that Baghdad was impossible now, for it would require at least two divisions. Furthermore, while helpful to British prestige, possession of Baghdad would bring greater political and military responsibilities, among which would be counted, in all probability, a long frontier with Russia once the Ottoman Empire was partitioned.[46] On the other hand, Sir Henry McMahon, recently Foreign Secretary of India, now in London preparing to assume his new position as High Commissioner in Egypt in succession to Kitchener, wrote Hardinge in private that he was trying to disarm opposition at home to an advance on Baghdad. His own advice was simply to take the city and then base policy on the resulting situation.[47]

Hardinge was unlikely to take so much independent action —and he was no great admirer of McMahon in any case[48]—but he was rapidly succumbing to the lure of Baghdad, provided the military said it could be done and the home authorities approved. By 17 December, he wrote Crewe that he was now

[44] Minutes on Viceroy telegram to SSI, 25 November 1914 (advocating advance but noting that, once the advance was made, the positions gained must be retained), *FO* 371/2143.

[45] Barrett telegram to SSI, 9 December 1914, *FO* 371/2144. Barker, *Neglected War*, p. 55, is in error in giving surrender of Qurna as 19 November; *The Bastard War*, p. 38, gives the altered (and equally erroneous) date of 19 December.

[46] Hardinge private to Crewe, 2 December 1914, *Hardinge Papers*; partly quoted in Barker, *Neglected War*, p. 100.

[47] McMahon private to Hardinge, 11 December 1914 and 2 February 1915, *Hardinge Papers*. Technically Kitchener had been British Agent; McMahon was the first to hold the title of High Commissioner.

[48] See below, p. 65.

thinking of a further advance to Nasiriya, 70 (air) miles west of Qurna, on the main channel of the Euphrates, whose possession would enable Britain to "protect" and influence the powerful Muntafiq tribes nearby.[49] Cox, on the other hand, was thinking of 'Amara, 60 miles (90 by river) north of Qurna on the Tigris. 'Amara had been under Basra's prewar administration, and its control would fill out, as it were, the Basra vilayet. It was also the closest point on the Tigris to the Persian frontier (30 miles) and would thus facilitate protection of Arabistan; it offered control of new tribes and of new land susceptible to irrigation. When the advance was delayed by necessary regrouping after a Turkish attack and the need to make a decision on the direction of advance, Cox maintained that the Basra situation was deteriorating since no further British successes could be used to counteract Turkish *jihad* propaganda—a point matched by that of Grant in India: more advance and more success would more probably increase the spirit of *jihad*. Duff, the Commander-in-Chief, further objected to advance having only political, and not military advantages.[50]

While discussion continued, Hardinge decided to see for himself. Accompanied by Chirol, he sailed from Bombay on 25 January 1915 for his first visit to Iraq. In Basra he toured the hospitals and was quite satisfied, an interesting point in the light of the later medical scandal associated with this campaign.

[49] Hardinge private to Crewe, 17 December 1914, *Hardinge Papers.*
[50] Cox telegrams to FSI, 20 December 1914 and 3 January 1915, *FO* 371/2482; Viceroy telegram to SSI, 20 January 1915, *L/P&S/11*, vol. 87, no. 276/15; see also Graves, *Cox*, p. 186. Grant note, 16 January 1915, and Duff note, 22 December 1914, *India Sec. War* February 1915, 101–19.

Information on distances and physical conditions has beeen taken from (in addition to the standard accounts of Moberley and Barker) Great Britain, Admiralty, Naval Intelligence Division, Geographical Handbook Series, *Iraq and the Persian Gulf* (Oxford, 1944), a lengthy and useful compendium of information, and Harvey H. Smith, et al., eds., *Area Handbook for Iraq* (Washington, D.C., 1969).

He addressed the troops at Shaiba (Shu'aiba), a few miles southwest of Basra, and he viewed the Turks from advance positions at Qurna. In under two weeks he was back in Bombay, much impressed with all he had seen and in no way dissuaded from the idea that Basra must be kept—although, as he wrote Nicolson, to keep Basra quiet a further advance on the Tigris and Euphrates would be required.[51]

On the whole, the visit had only the negative value of encouraging the Viceroy. Conditions in the campaign were still tolerable, as there had not been really serious fighting for some time. Hardinge went away optimistic, and to his optimism, wrote Arnold Wilson later, "he clung long after any sort of justification had ceased to exist." On the other hand, as Wilson freely admitted, "the fact that the Viceroy, burdened as he was with innumerable cares, had undertaken the long journey to Basra to make personal contact with those on the spot was highly appreciated. It is to be regretted that his example was not followed by the Commander-in-Chief in India or any of his principal staff officers for more than two years."[52] For the time being, the troops were heartened, and some hoped that the visit meant new action; there had been little to lighten spirits since Qurna two months earlier. What Cox had said

[51] Hardinge private to Crewe, 4 February 1915, *Hardinge Papers,* and to Nicolson, 4 February; Chirol private to Nicolson, 2 February 1915, *Nicolson Papers, FO* 800/377. See also *India Sec. War* September 1915, 217–29; Lord Hardinge of Penshurst, *My Indian Years, 1910–1916: The Reminiscences of . . .* (London, 1948), pp. 112–13; "Black Tab," *On the Road to Kut: A Soldier's Story of the Mesopotamian Campaign* (London, 1917), p. 44.

Hardinge's comment on the wounded: "They all seemed comfortable and cheery, and the hospitals well run. I gave orders that no expense was to be spared to make the men comfortable . . . " Hardinge had a very personal interest in the wounded; in December his eldest son had died of wounds in France (and, it should be added, his wife had died a few months before). *Indian Years,* pp. 108–9, 112–13.

[52] Wilson, *Loyalties,* pp. 32–33; on Duff, see Sir George Buchanan, *The Tragedy of Mesopotamia* (London, 1938), pp. 91–93, and below, p. 37—38.

before of the uncertainty produced upon the Arabs by inactivity applied equally well to the Army, who, as one member commented, "had still no clear idea as to whether a further advance was contemplated."[53]

But a further advance was contemplated. A new commander, General Sir John Nixon, was sent out to supersede Barrett, who had not proved to be a particularly inspiring leader, in early April. Nixon's appointment was based mainly on seniority, but it was soon realized that he was not a man to sit quietly while images of glittering prizes shimmered in the desert air. And Nixon had his orders from Duff, orders provided apparently without reference to either Hardinge or the home military or civil authorities. He was told that his force was intended to hold the lower portion of Mesopotamia, ". . . comprising the Basra Vilayet and including all outlets to the sea, and such portions of the neighbouring territories as may affect your operations." He was to submit a plan for the effective operation of the Basra vilayet and one for a "subsequent advance" on Baghdad.[54]

As Nixon interpreted these instructions, they meant forward movement. Soon he had issued orders to the Sixth Division (Major-General C. V. F. Townshend: the expeditionary force was now a corps of two divisions) to move on 'Amara. London approved the orders provided Nixon felt certain he could hold 'Amara against any attack that might be made in the summer, for there was no prospect of reinforcements; Mesopotamia was a poor third in priority to Suez and the newly opened Gallipoli campaign.[55] Clearly the political objective now took precedence over the military. "The first ques-

[53] Capt. H. Birch-Reynardson, *Mesopotamia 1914–15: Extracts from a Regimental Officer's Diary* (London, 1919), p. 92.

[54] Nixon orders, 24 March 1915, are quoted in Public Record Office, Cabinet files [*CAB*] 19/2; see also Barker, *Neglected War*, p. 79; Moberley, *op. cit.*, I, pp. 194–95. On Nixon and Barrett from Hardinge's viewpoint, see *Indian Years*, pp. 120–21.

[55] Barker, *Neglected War*, pp. 83–84.

tion to be settled," later wrote Sir William Robertson (soon to be Chief of the Imperial General Staff), "was not whether Amara could be garrisoned after being occupied, but whether, having regard to our war plans as a whole, its occupation would be consistent with sound strategy and administrative possibilities."[56]

Austen Chamberlain, who replaced Crewe as Secretary of State for India on 27 May, was in a dilemma: Mesopotamia could command few British war resources, yet the campaign not only had a life of its own but its commanders seemed confident that there would be no setbacks. In any case, Crewe had approved the advance just before leaving office (to become Lord President of the Council).[57] 'Amara fell on 3 June, and within a week Nixon announced that Nasiriya, on the other river, was the next goal. In the absence of any answer from London to Hardinge's request for approval of this next step, Nixon was told to move on. Nasiriya fell on 25 July.

Optimism now prevailed everywhere, rising (to paraphrase Winston Churchill) in direct ratio to the distance from the front lines. But by now the Turks, alarmed at Mesopotamian developments, were concentrating at Kut al-'Amara, 90 miles north of 'Amara (125 miles by river) and only 100 miles south of Baghdad (but as usual far longer by river, 213 miles in this case). Nixon, nothing loath, was eager to press on. Alarmed by lengthening lines of communication and requests for reinforcements, India rejected his request until September. Then the advance pushed on in grand style: Kut fell on 29 September, and on 3 October Nixon let it be known that his force was strong enough to take Baghdad.[58]

There was, not surprisingly, considerable division of opin-

---

[56] Robertson, *Soldiers and Statesmen*, II, p. 32.

[57] Chamberlain private to Hardinge, 25 July 1915, quoted in Sir Charles Petrie, *The Life and Letters of the Right Hon. Sir Austen Chamberlain, K.G., P.C., M.P.* (London, 1940), II, pp. 34, 35–37; Hardinge, *Indian Years*, p. 121.

[58] Barker, *Neglected War*, p. 116.

ion. Barrow urged on 4 October that without two more divisions and more cavalry Baghdad was an unjustifiable risk. Even if the city were taken, a major Turkish attack might bring an Arab revolt behind the lines, and Baghdad would be difficult if not impossible to hold.[59] Townshend, too, objected to an immediate advance, although his objections made no visible impression upon India and none upon Nixon, who later denied that Townshend had even made them.[60] But the War Office and the Admiralty both urged caution. The Turks could, after all, reduce their armies in Palestine, Syria, the Caucasus, and even Gallipoli to shore up their Mesopotamian units, and Kitchener could not guarantee to provide the necessary reinforcements from other fronts. While it might be desirable to hold Baghdad if India—the responsible party—could do the job (especially if in doing so India could make use of troops which could not be profitably employed elsewhere), still, as a joint War Office-Admiralty memorandum of 19 October urged, it would be very wrong to divert troops from the main theater of war ". . . for the purpose of conducting a campaign which cannot appreciably influence the decision as between the armies of the Allies and those of the Central Powers."[61]

[59] Minute, 4 October 1915, *WO* 106/893.

[60] Barker, *Neglected War*, pp. 107, 117, 119–20, and *Townshend of Kut: A Biography of Major-General Sir Charles Townshend, K.C.B., D.S.O.* (London, 1967), pp. 154–55. See also Maj.-Gen. Charles Vere Ferrers Townshend, *My Campaign* (N.Y., 1920), vol. II; and Erroll Sherson, *Townshend of Chitral and Kut* (London, 1928). But see Hardinge private to Chamberlain, 26 November 1915 and 25 March 1916, *Hardinge Papers,* and, for Nixon's denial, *CAB* 19/8, p. 510 (the evidence of the Mesopotamian Commission). Further discussion, not used by Barker, may be found in the papers of Austen Chamberlain, particularly Chamberlain private to Curzon, 11 April 1916, Arnold Wilson to Chamberlain, 5 March 1931, and Chamberlain to Wilson, 11 March 1931, *Chamberlain Papers* (University of Birmingham Library), 47/1/9, 46/7/43, 46/7/47.

[61] General Staff memorandum, 6 October, Lt.-Gen. A. J. Murray (C.I.G.S.) and H. B. Jackson (First Sea Lord) memorandum, 19 October, Hardinge private telegram to Chamberlain, 21 October, and SSI

The argument was obviously not simply political vs. military officials. Nixon had been urging the advance since late August, and Lieutenant-General Sir Percy Lake, Chief of the Indian Staff, found his arguments persuasive, provided London found the reinforcements India could not provide. Hardinge, in his communications home, supported this view and was similarly worried about additional troops.[62]

The most persuasive point, however, made by Cox and Hirtzel (himself subject to occasional doubts), and eventually accepted by the Foreign Office and tacitly by the entire Cabinet, was the relatively simple matter of the sheer prestige of the capture of Baghdad, comparable only to the fall of Constantinople. To Cox, predictably, a halt to the advance now would be seen as a weakness: Persia would be convinced that it had nothing to fear from British retaliation if it joined the Central Powers; and, if this came to pass, the Amir of Afghanistan might give way to the pressures upon him, proclaim a *jihad*, and set ablaze the entire North-West Frontier. As Chamber-

---

telegram to Viceroy, 5 October 1915, *WO* 106/893; Moberley, *op. cit.*, II, pp. 24–25.

One interesting possibility which was discussed was requesting the forgotten ally, Japan, to send a division to Mesopotamia. To India, this idea overlooked the entire question of prestige and popular sentiment in the east, to say nothing, Hardinge admitted privately, of simple prejudice. The documents relating to this issue were not considered by the Mesopotamian Commission in 1916, for they were not handed over to that Commission. The scheme is discussed in SSI telegram to Viceroy, 5 October, and private telegram, 7 October 1915, *WO* 106/893; Chamberlain private to Hardinge and Hardinge private to Chirol, 7 October 1915, *Hardinge Papers*. See also Cabinet discussion of 21 October 1915, *CAB* 42/4. The failure to supply documents is mentioned in Lucas (I.O.) private to Hardinge, 16 December 1916, *Hardinge Papers*. On larger fears of Japan in 1916, see William Roger Louis, *Great Britain and Germany's Lost Colonies, 1914–1919* (Oxford, 1967), pp. 11, 48–49.

[62] Nixon telegram to C.G.S., India, 30 August, Lake memorandum, 5 October, Hardinge private telegram to Chamberlain, 21 October 1915, *WO* 106/893; and Hardinge private to Chirol, 23 September and 9 November 1915, *Hardinge Papers*.

lain put it in a telegram of 22 October, the prospects in Gallipoli were uncertain, the Arabs and Persians were wavering, and some striking success was necessary—even, as will be seen, if this meant a reduction in British ambitions by way of further promises to the Arabs.[63]

So confused had the issue become that, in early October, the Prime Minister appointed an interdepartmental committee under Sir Thomas Holderness, Permanent Under-Secretary of the India Office, to consider the advance. The committee had little authority and less military expertise. It decided the obvious: Baghdad was a desirable objective if it could be held. The decision was of little importance, but it added weight to the viewpoint eventually responsible for rejecting another alternative: a gigantic raid on Baghdad to destroy its military utility, followed by subsequent withdrawal.[64]

The committee's arguments and the supporting documents —above all those which made Nixon's self-confidence so clear —were persuasive, and the Cabinet (more precisely, the Dardanelles Committee) in its meetings of 14 and 21 October was inclining toward permanent, rather than temporary, advance.[65] For the most part, those like Churchill and Kitchener in favor

[63] Political Department, I.O., memorandum, 6 October 1915, *WO* 106/893; Shuckburgh Memorandum B.220, "Advance to Baghdad. Political Considerations," 6 October 1915, *L/P&S/11*, vol. 87, no. 276/15; F.O. memorandum, 7 October, with L. Mallet minute, and Chamberlain private telegram to Hardinge, 22 October 1915, *WO* 106/893.

[64] Memoranda of committee meetings, 11 and 16 October 1915, *CAB* 42/4; Holderness private to Hardinge, 22 October 1915, *Hardinge Papers*.

[65] Dardanelles Committee, 14 and 21 October 1915, *CAB* 42/4. On the rather confusing governmental changes during the war, see Paul Guinn, *British Strategy and Politics, 1914 to 1918* (Oxford, 1965), the best survey of the subject; Lord Hankey, *Government Control in War* (Cambridge, 1945) and *The Supreme Command, 1914–1918* (2 vols., London, 1961); for more on the politics behind the changes, Trevor Wilson, *The Downfall of the Liberal Party, 1914–1935* (Ithaca, N.Y., 1966), and, as the most recent scholarly general account, Sir Llewellyn Woodward, *Great Britain and the War of 1914–1918* (London, 1967).

of continued pressure at Gallipoli, where evacuation was already a strong possibility,[66] urged that such pressure would at least keep the Turks from sending major reinforcements to Mesopotamia. The opposite argument—that a mere holding operation in Mesopotamia would release Turkish troops for other operations—was not used, although Hardinge, viewing these events from another standpoint, had argued that Mesopotamian pressure might ease the Gallipoli situation.[67] Since Kitchener was never a partisan of a Mesopotamian advance, his intervention was indecisive. Curzon (Lord Privy Seal), similarly in favor of Gallipoli, was also much less enthusiastic about Baghdad and eventually advised against advance. But, as Bonar Law (Colonies) pointed out, there were risks in staying as well as in advancing, and Grey and Chamberlain again urged the advantages of Baghdad from the Foreign Office and India Office viewpoints. In the end, no definite decision was taken, except to ask India again for its views.

India had by now fairly sufficient grounds for assuming favorable Cabinet opinion. Chamberlain, at least, noted in his private correspondence that only the problem of the necessary reinforcements was holding up approval—that and the War Office's general hostility to the plan. After the meeting on the 21st (Chamberlain, not normally a member of the Dardanelles Committee, had been specially invited), he cabled privately that the authorities were so convinced of the necessity of taking Baghdad that, unless India saw the chance of eventual withdrawal as decisive, the advance would be sanctioned. Although the reinforcements were not on their way, it was expected that they would be available later, the idea being to return Indian units fighting in France to the Middle Eastern theater.[68]

[66] See Trumbull Higgins, *Winston Churchill and the Dardanelles: A Dialogue in Ends and Means* (N.Y., 1963), particularly pp. 223–24 and references given there.

[67] Hardinge private to Nicolson, 23 September, and Nicolson private to Hardinge, 7 October 1915, *Nicolson Papers, FO* 800/379–80.

[68] Chamberlain private to Hardinge, 7, 8, 13, 22, and 29 October 1915,

When this news was forwarded to Nixon, the General, disregarding reports of heavy Turkish reinforcements, ordered the advance of Townshend's apparently invincible division. But Townshend was not invincible. In mid-November, his 14,000 men fought a hectic battle at Ctesiphon, 20 miles south of Baghdad, and were sufficiently mauled and overextended to find it necessary to fall back on Kut to rest and await reinforcements. Townshend had lost 4,600 in killed, wounded, and missing. By the first week in December, the rest camp had turned into a trap where Townshend was to remain besieged for five dreary months. The end, in April 1916, was the bitter pill of surrender.[69]

### 4

The responsibility for the advance, and the failure, cannot be laid upon one individual, or even one department. The Cabinet, caught up in the issue of prestige, was influenced by the Indian urging of strategic and political considerations, but then India knew as little of the larger war situation as the War Office knew of Mesopotamia. Kitchener had opposed the advance; but he did not control this campaign, and he had his own pet project in Alexandretta Bay.[70] The latter was unfortunate, for otherwise Kitchener's military standing and his personal experience in the east might have influenced the Cabinet the other way. It is questionable, however, whether the War Office and

---

*Hardinge Papers.* Chamberlain private telegram to Hardinge, 22 October 1915, *WO* 106/893. Chamberlain's letter of 8 October is quoted in full in Petrie, *Austen Chamberlain,* pp. 36–38.

[69] Based on Wilson, *Loyalties,* pp. 112ff.; Hardinge, *Indian Years,* pp. 120–25; Robertson, *Soldiers and Statesmen,* II, pp. 35–39; Barker, *Neglected War,* pp. 79–100, and *Townshend,* ch. IX; Guinn, *op. cit.,* pp. 105–17; Buchanan, *op. cit.,* pp. 22–23; Richard Coke, *The Heart of the Middle East* (London, 1925), pp. 148–50; Lovat Fraser, "The Responsibility for Baghdad," *Edinburgh Review,* 226 (October 1917), 386–406; and Moberley, *op. cit.*

[70] See below, p. 115–17.

the Admiralty should, under the circumstances, have even offered their opinion (a point subsequently made by Sir William Robertson).[71]

The authorities in India were to be blamed as well: Duff for his lack of information and his independent orders to Nixon, and Hardinge for his over-all responsibility as Viceroy and his own subsequent enthusiasm. Certainly it appeared to the Mesopotamian Commission, sitting in December 1916, that India, and therefore the Viceroy, should shoulder its share of the responsibility. The Commission was to blame others, however, and others deserved blame.[72] Cox in Mesopotamia, Hirtzel in London: many had responded to the appeal of Baghdad. Certainly much of the odium must rest upon Sir John Nixon, who was, after all, the field commander. The home authorities had given him the responsibility of deciding whether his force was sufficient for the job, and, unwisely, Nixon took that responsibility—and the gamble—and lost.

Responsibility for the military aspects of the decision to advance is best left to military historians. But the speed of the advance and the confusion associated with it—notably the confusion of political and military objectives—had much to do with the nature of political and administrative policy in southern Iraq, and therefore India's policy toward the occupied Arab area. The continued increase in Anglo-Indian military forces there, and the policy confusion, meant that by necessity and by default initial administrative responsibility was in the hands of the Indian Army, working through attached but subordinate political officers under Sir Percy Cox. And over and above policy problems, the Indian Army had some serious problems of its own which go far toward explaining the military disaster as well. "In India," wrote a later commander in Mesopotamia,

[71] Robertson, *Soldiers and Statesmen*, II, pp. 35–48.

[72] Printed evidence of Mesopotamian Campaign Inquiry, *CAB* 19/8; see also *WO* 106/893 for the best summary of the events leading to the advance.

"everything tends to go upside-down as soon as you have put it straight and your back is turned. . ." [73]

In the first place, the Indian Army was a separate institution, under the control, in the final analysis, of the British Cabinet and Parliament. But this control functioned through the Indian government and the India Office in London, and not through the British Army and the War Office, even though some 70,000 British troops were a part of this Army. Until 1916, therefore, when important changes took place, the Mesopotamian campaign was not under the control of the principal British military authorities. In actual fact, Kitchener exchanged telegrams with Duff in the early days of the war, but Crewe urged that this practice be stopped on constitutional grounds. [74]

Given the constitutional position, much depended upon the character of the Indian Commander-in-Chief, and unfortunately Sir Beauchamp Duff was more administrator than field general. It should be said in his defense that the system of com-

[73] Lt.-Gen. Sir George MacMunn, *Behind the Scenes in Many Wars: Being the Military Reminiscences of* . . . (London, 1930), p. 85.

[74] Robertson, *Soldiers and Statesmen*, I, pp. 158–59, and Guinn, *op. cit.*, p. 33. Information on the Indian Army in this section is based upon Robertson; Guinn; Moberley, *op. cit.*, I, pp. 52–74; Barker, *Neglected War*, pp. 28–33; Wilson, *Loyalties*, pp. 21–22; MacMunn, *op. cit.*, pp. 58–61; F. C. Beatson, "Mesopotamia, I: The Recent Military Policy of the Government of India," *Nineteenth Century and After*, 82 (July–December 1917), 260–75; Lord Birdwood of Anzac and Totnes, *Khaki and Gown: An Autobiography* (London, 1941), pp. 143–44; Maj. R. Evans, "The Strategy of the Campaign in Mesopotamia, 1914–1918," *Journal of the Royal United Service Institution*, 68 (1923), 254–69; Cyril Falls, "The Army," *Edwardian England, 1901–1914*, ed. by Simon Nowell-Smith (London, 1964), pp. 517–44; Sir Wolseley Haig, "The Indian Army, 1858–1918," *The Cambridge History of the British Empire, V: The Indian Empire 1858–1918*, ed. by H. H. Dodwell (Cambridge, 1932), pp. 395–402; Hardinge, *Indian Years*, pp. 85–86, 103; Philip Magnus, *Kitchener: Portrait of an Imperialist* (N.Y. 1959), pp. 221, 226; Lt.-Gen. G. N. Molesworth, *Curfew on Olympus* (N.Y., 1965), pp. 12–14; Gen. Sir O'Moore Creagh, *Autobiography* (London, [1924]), pp. 254–70; and Gen. Sir Horace Smith-Dorrien, *Memories of Forty-Eight Years' Service* (N.Y., 1925), pp. 72, 313–32.

mand within India left him little scope for close personal involvement in conducting a distant campaign such as Mesopotamia or East Africa. Before the war, in 1904-1905, a major controversy had arisen between the Commander, Kitchener, and Curzon, the Viceroy.[75] The controversy was involved, and personalities played a considerable role; essentially, the victory of Kitchener in this struggle resulted in a system which placed an intolerable burden on the Commander-in-Chief when war actually came, even though the system had worked well enough in Kitchener's day. The alternatives then became those of activity in the field at the cost of administration or vice versa. Duff chose administration, but short of total reform of the system any choice he made would have been invidious. Hardinge, who had little confidence in Duff, might have exerted some salutary influence, but he did not, fearing repetition of the pre-war controversy and respecting the authority of the Commander's position.

Kitchener had also introduced other reforms, primarily as a result of military experience gained in the Boer War; but his successors, O'Moore Creagh and Duff, had not followed up. Again, this was not entirely their own fault. The reforms had been designed for Indian military efficiency in any conflict with Russia, and the Anglo-Russian accord of 1907 had removed a good deal of the incentive for reform, coming, as it did, on the heels of the destruction of Russia's military strength (and, more important, reputation) in the Russo-Japanese War. The Indian principle of economy first had once more gained the upper hand. As a result, the Indian Army in 1914 had little in the way of mechanical transport; its equipment was outmoded or designed, as in the case of artillery, for operations on the North-West Frontier; its medical facilities were below standard; it had almost no equipment reflecting modern technical advances (light machine guns, for example); and it was considerably

[75] See, on this controversy, Busch, *Britain and the Persian Gulf*, p. 269, n. 112, for a convenient list of sources.

oversupplied with cavalry. Officer reserves were negligible; in any case a considerable number of officers nominally serving in India had been taken by the home authorities for operations in Europe. Rather ironically, Kitchener himself saw that reform was necessary. As he wrote to Crewe in April 1915, ". . . I cannot help thinking that when the war is over, the Army System in India will have to go into the melting pot for drastic and radical improvement." [76]

It was already agreed before the war that India would be responsible for operations in the Gulf area, and a plan of 1912 had even foreseen the occupation of Fao and Basra in certain contingencies. In 1910-1911 the Indian staff had made plans as well for the possible use of the Indian Army in Europe. But when an attempt was made to follow up these discussions, India was told to concentrate on its own Indian affairs. [77] As a result, no plans, no maps, no information on Mesopotamia were available to the military authorities in actual command of the expedition. Much had been done by political officers, but the military men demonstrated a fine reluctance to consult them. Hubert Young, like Arnold Wilson to play a major role in British Middle Eastern policy, gives an interesting account of his 1913 travels through the area. Before leaving London he had asked the War Office if there was anything on which he might usefully collect information,

. . . and had been told that Iraq fell within the sphere of the Intelligence Department at Simla. They in their turn told me that they did not think there was anything I could do which would be of any use, and that what struck them most was that I should be able to get permission to travel there at all just then. This shows how little it was foreseen that exactly a year later an Indian expeditionary force would be waiting at Bahrein for the declaration of war . . . [78]

[76] Kitchener private to Crewe, 1 April 1915, *Kitchener Papers* (Public Record Office), *PRO* 30/57/69.

[77] *India Sec. E.* April 1912, 141–61; Moberley, *op. cit.*, I, p. 73; MacMunn, *op. cit.*, p. 84.

[78] Young, *op. cit.*, p. 33.

Even in its own affairs, India had been remiss: there existed no general plan for mobilization of troops and resources. No one there or in England had foreseen a European war in which India, dependent for officers and so much of its military equipment upon Britain, would have to fight a major campaign of its own and, at the same time, for practical supply purposes be cut off from Europe. For these deficiencies many men would lose their lives and not a few their reputations, because this was the army that had not only to conduct a difficult and overextended campaign but also to administer an occupied area, an area, moreover, whose administrative future was undecided, for the military advance had done nothing to settle this issue.

5

The problem, simply stated, was that the British Cabinet faced a considerable dilemma in Mesopotamia. The original "demonstration" had obviously gotten out of hand, and from the strictly military view alone there was real question whether Mesopotamia was the proper place for application of strength. Some, like Lloyd George (still Chancellor of the Exchequer), wished the Mesopotamian forces to be withdrawn and used where they were most needed in the east—at the Dardanelles. Others, like Churchill (Admiralty), felt that at least the Basra area now under British control should remain in British hands.[79] But one discussion was insufficient to settle this difficult issue; the visit of Lord Hardinge to Iraq and the change in the Mesopotamian command had given rise to a spate of memoranda on both civil and military policy.

On 14 March 1915, Hirtzel wrote a lengthy note, the main burden of which was that future British interests in the area would require a forward policy. Britain clearly needed control of the Shatt for trade; whoever held Baghdad controlled British

[79] War Council, 24 February 1915, *CAB* 42/1; David Lloyd George, *War Memoirs of* . . . (Boston, 1933), II, p. 237.

trade with Persia; whoever held Basra must control irrigation to the north of it, and so on. In short, Britain required Baghdad. Of course, for the development of the area, labor would be necessary, and if local Arabs could not do the job good men from the Punjab would be suitable. Immigration would at once reward India's war effort and remove any excuse for immigration into "white man's colonies"; the colonists would, further, provide the means for defense. A moral basis for controlling the area was clearly to be found in centuries of Turkish misrule. But how much of Mesopotamia should be controlled? Inclusion of the Mosul vilayet to the north would be too much and would raise problems regarding its Kurdish population; the line should rather be somewhere to the north of Baghdad. Basra and the Shatt alone were untenable, for Basra was only the gateway to Mesopotamia and was commanded by Baghdad. At least Qurna and Nasiriya should be held to define the limit of the minimum viable territory.

Hirtzel also dealt with the form of regime to be established. There would be resistance to annexation, if Arab spokesmen like 'Aziz 'Ali al-Misri were to be believed. None of the alternatives—independence, a British protectorate or puppet ruler, or Persian annexation (the survival of the Ottoman Empire was obviously out of the question)—could be satisfactory. No real basis existed for an independent state; and a protectorate in the normal Aden or Persian Gulf form of treaties with the local shaikhs would only reduce Mesopotamia to "the condition of Arabia." As Egypt proved, rule by a puppet, assuming a proper candidate could be found, was not the best possible form of government. Against some sort of dual control with Persia, the Sudan was a case in point. The most obvious course was incorporation in the Indian Empire, for India was the most concerned British-controlled area, but this would raise administrative problems. Mesopotamia could not expect to receive the close attention that would be the main justification for subordinating Iraq to an already subordinate government; India might well have constitutional changes in her own postwar future; and in any case the Indian type of rule was not wanted here. The only feasible method of control, concluded Hirtzel, was to create a governor-general, with a small executive council, working under the Foreign Office in London. The sole stumbling block would be finance; "There can be no doubt that its requirements would be more intelligently and more liberally met by the Government of India than by the Treasury." [80]

Hirtzel's memorandum is revealing, for it was the first official paper to discuss, although only to reject, the possibility of Mesopotamia as a colony for India, and it illustrates the sweep of ambition four months after the campaign began. Hirtzel made other points concerning the Arabian Peninsula; the result of his over-all policy would be a British protectorate "over half the Syrian wilderness and the whole of Arabia." Hirtzel knew some would object to this, but Britain would find it essential to push its frontiers up to the areas which would be held by other powers, and to possess control of a Mediterranean-Persian Gulf land communications route.

In writing this note, Hirtzel did not have available Lord Hardinge's memorandum of 24 February, mailed home on 3 March in a private letter to Crewe, pointing out that although the Gulf could be secured by Basra alone, provided the vilayet was under complete and permanent control, Basra, ". . . when it has passed permanently into our possession . . . ," would depend for much of its trade, irrigation, oil, and sheer safety on Baghdad. Eventually the Turks must surrender there and Britain occupy all Iraq. In contrast to Hirtzel, Hardinge maintained that India clearly was the logical choice as controller: "The interests concerned, strategic, commercial, political and religious alike, are mainly Indian." Iraq would be conquered by India; Indian troops would garrison it; it would prove attractive for colonization, and so on.[81]

[80] Hirtzel note, 14 March 1915, *CAB* 42/2 and 27/1.
[81] Hardinge private telegram to Crewe, 15 March 1915, summarizes

At the moment, the problem of who would control was subordinate to that of what was controlled. Hirtzel had gone further than Hardinge by mentioning the need for possession of part of Syria and Alexandretta, a block of territory reaching from the Gulf to the Mediterranean. Barrow voiced his fears of such vast territorial holdings from the standpoint of defense, financial liability, and possible racial animosity and Muslim suspicion. He would himself annex only the Basra vilayet and make Baghdad an autonomous province with a British administration in the name of the Sultan, similar to prewar Egypt. This would aid Turkish rehabilitation, conciliate Arabs and Muslims, calm Franco-Russian jealousy, and leave a buffer between British and French and Russian areas. Hirtzel replied that he had not proposed that Alexandretta actually be annexed, that he thought the reverse of rehabilitation was desired in the case of Turkey, and that Barrow's proposal would leave control of the migratory tribes to the Turks; prewar relations at the head of the Persian Gulf should serve as an object lesson against working with the Turks on such problems.[82]

Actually, the supplementary issue of Alexandretta was due mainly to Kitchener, to whom the area was a key strategic center; he had already advocated a landing in the bay as a means of shortening the war in the Middle East, but had been overruled. Still, he felt that Alexandretta would have to be controlled in the future. For Alexandretta, Mesopotamia was necessary— and for Mesopotamia, Alexandretta. It was a nice strategic argument, and to it Kitchener added the agricultural potential of Iraq, possible Indian settlement, oil, Persian Gulf interests, and the prestige of controlling Iraq's holy places and the future

---

contents, *Nicolson Papers, FO* 800/377; memorandum on the future status and administration of Basra of 24 February 1915, with Hirtzel and Crewe notes, *Hardinge Papers*, Kent County Record Office, UR5; *CAB* 27/1; and *Nicolson Papers, FO* 800/377.

[82] Barrow note, 16 March, Hirtzel note, 17 March 1915, *Nicolson Papers, FO* 800/377.

land route to India. If Britain did not take this area, sooner or later Russia would—and *that* possibility raised all the old pre-war ghosts of Russian designs on the Persian Gulf. If all this meant more immediate responsibility for Britain, still, in time, the area would become self-sufficient; if there were problems over French claims to Alexandretta, Alexandretta was really outside Syria, and no legitimate French claim there could be made.[83] To this comprehensive vision the Admiralty added a memorandum equally in the proper spirit of things: Alexandretta-Mesopotamia would provide an inexhaustible supply of oil where it was needed at a point far from home bases.[84]

With all of these somewhat contradictory documents but Hardinge's at hand and with current discussions with France and Russia over the fate of Turkey in mind, the War Council met to discuss future policy on 19 March 1915. All the arguments were repeated, with the addition of Sir Edward Grey's Foreign Office view. Grey at least recognized the strong feeling in the Muslim world that Islam should have a political as well as a religious existence, and that only Syria-Arabia-Mesopotamia was available for this purpose (given already existing partition plans for Turkey). To leave the whole matter in abeyance was impossible because of French and Russian claims. The decision, for the time being, was to tell Russia that some sort of Muslim entity, including Arabia, was Britain's first desire after the Straits had been forced, and that it was premature to discuss a partition in detail.[85] What Petrograd was not told was that this position was adopted because Britain could not make up its own mind.

[83] Kitchener memorandum, 16 March 1915, *CAB* 42/2. See also A. S. Klieman, "Britain's War Aims in the Middle East in 1915," *Journal of Contemporary History*, 3 (July 1968), 241. On the Russian danger, Busch, *Britain and the Persian Gulf*, chs. IV, VIII, XI.

[84] Admiralty memorandum, 17 March 1915, *CAB* 42/2.

[85] War Council, 19 March 1915, *ibid.* See also Crewe private to Hardinge, 19 March 1915, *Hardinge Papers*; and Klieman, *op. cit.*, p. 242.

In the light of Cabinet disagreements and, more importantly, the pressure of Allied claims, Asquith decided that an interdepartmental committee should study the question, making use of all available documents and any further material which any ministry wished to provide. The committee was chaired by Sir Maurice de Bunsen (formerly ambassador in Vienna) and included George Clerk (Foreign Office), Holderness, H. B. Jackson (Admiralty), Major-General C. E. Callwell (War Office), H. Llewellyn Smith (Board of Trade), Sir Mark Sykes, and Sir Maurice Hankey from the Cabinet Secretariat, with other members as necessary from time to time.[86]

The committee began its sittings in the second week of April 1915, and one point of controversy, at least, was settled before the meetings began, the internal friction in the India Office. Neither Barrow nor Hirtzel was a member of the committee, Crewe happily reported to Hardinge, for they were the ends of the spectrum. Holderness, by implication, occupied a middle position but, wary of increasing political responsibilities unless absolutely essential, he leaned more toward Barrow, agreeing that Basra required direct control and in Baghdad Britain should have only "some sort of controlling influence," for if more were taken, India, which would have the responsibility, would have to provide men and cash.[87] The India Office position, therefore, as represented in the committee, did not represent the more extreme views held by some in that office—and in India itself.

To facilitate the discussions, various individuals and departments now added to the already bulky documentation on "British Desiderata in Turkey in Asia." Hirtzel, for one, had found added justification for his maximalist program in Hardinge's paper of February, particularly the point of needing Baghdad for defense of the oilfields. On the other hand, he remained a

[86] "Report of the Committee on Asiatic Turkey," 30 June 1915, *CAB* 27/1; also in *L/P&S/11*, vol. 105, no. 1745/16.

[87] Crewe private to Hardinge, 2 April, Holderness private to Hardinge, 8 April 1915, *Hardinge Papers*.

consistent opponent of Indian administration in Mesopotamia, objecting even to Hardinge's idea of a transitional period in which Indian control would be replaced. Far better, Hirtzel felt, to begin immediately with personnel and methods borrowed from Egypt.[88] Crewe was cautious, as usual: nothing, he hoped, would be taken that was not absolutely essential, and that from the standpoint of what others should not be allowed to possess rather than what Britain hoped to possess for itself. It was tempting to think of loose control over Baghdad—but what then would remain for Turkey in Asia? A settlement with France in this area would be difficult; Arab opinion, too, would have to be considered, "even to the sacrifice of some efficiency." [89]

The Board of Trade added a plea for the importance of British commercial interests in Mesopotamia and pointed out why the Baghdad vilayet was the most important area of Iraq commercially. The India Office added afterthoughts on trade, the obligation imposed by promises already made to the population of Basra and the Arab shaikhs, the requirements of an open Red Sea, the end of the arms traffic, the requirement of peace in the Gulf, and the necessity for protecting Kuwait from central Arabian problems—all supporting a position that by now was clear to all.[90] The committee had, too, the essential outline of a plan for the partition of the Palestine-Syria-Mesopotamia area into spheres of influence (to become famous as the Sykes-Picot Agreement), presented by Mark Sykes at the fourth meeting on 17 April. Because of, or perhaps despite, this mass of ideas and material, the committee was ready to present its report at the end of June.

Important desiderata for British policy, the committee indicated, were preservation of Britain's Gulf position, fulfillment of the pledges made to the Arabs (in Basra and the Gulf), de-

[88] Hirtzel note on Hardinge note, 30 March 1915, *CAB* 27/1.

[89] Crewe note of 6 April 1915, *ibid.*

[90] Board of Trade memorandum, 8 April, I.O. memoranda, 21 and 26 April 1915, *ibid.*

velopment of "a possible field for Indian colonisation," and protection of the holy places, both Christian and Muslim.[91] Britain's Persian Gulf position dominated her policy requirements and compelled her, for good or ill, to claim a share in the disintegrating Ottoman Empire—in place of the prewar policy of linking that position with *maintenance* of the Ottoman Empire. Given these desiderata, the committee moved on to consider the alternative means of achieving them.

Four choices were available. The Ottoman Empire could be limited to Anatolia, with the rest divided among the powers; it could be reduced in size; or it could be nominally preserved, with spheres of influence allotted to the powers. Alternatively, by combining the first three solutions, some sort of a federal system could be shaped. Whichever choice was made, if Britain limited herself to the area on which it had made assurances—principally Basra and the Arabian Peninsula—it was safe to hazard that the other powers would expand to fill the remaining space. Thus, if Britain halted at Qurna, France or Russia would soon be found at Baghdad, and the committee was forced to recognize the persuasive argument that Baghdad did, indeed, control Basra; in Iraq, defensible frontiers would best be found in the hills north of Mosul. Oil and Mediterranean communications were other points in favor of the larger British claim.

On the other hand, the decision to divide Ottoman territory, either wholly or partially, or to delimit spheres of influence, would most probably mean fighting on into the heart of the Empire in circumstances in which Britain had stressed its war against Germany, not Turkey. Muslim feeling, particularly in India, responsibilities, costs, all militated against the larger claim. Decentralization and federalization, however, offered the chance of less cost and military responsibility and more development of the nationalities within the Empire. Under such

[91] *Ibid.*; the nine desiderata are conveniently summarized in Klieman, *op. cit.*; the maps accompanying the report are reproduced in Jukka Nevakivi, *Britain, France and the Arab Middle East, 1914–1920* (London, 1969), pp. 20–21.

circumstances it might not be necessary to hold Basra, although Arabia, a separate problem, would have to be under British protectorate or, at least, "negative" sphere of influence, one excluding the influence of all other powers. The conclusion, then, was that given the desiderata noted above and the desirability of the survival of the Ottoman Empire (if only to avoid extended, new direct frontiers with Russia and France) the best choice was decentralization.

The committee thus produced a flexible program aimed at the nominal preservation of the Ottoman Empire, with some sort of autonomous development of the various non-Turkish provinces. All this was vague and idealistic and took little account of the specific claims of the other powers. It did not facilitate a decision even on the area to be claimed by Britain, except that, by agreeing that the Mosul frontier was the most defensible for a necessarily united Iraq, it encouraged the forward military advance; and as the report was issued, Nixon was pushing on to Nasiriya. Nor, finally, did it convince the annexationists like Sir Arthur Hirtzel, who saw the issue, as he stated in a memorandum for the new Secretary of State for India, Austen Chamberlain, as one of Indian defense above all, not the Mediterranean links that the committee had been so concerned with. Moreover, Britain's responsibility would only be the greater if there were no annexation, for it then must participate in every quarrel involving the other powers sharing in the territory to be divided.[92]

Hardinge, who was shown the report by Mark Sykes when the latter passed through India in August, reserved comment, as the larger questions were outside his sphere. He was feeling rather slighted in any case, since his supply of Foreign Office printed documents had, for unexplained reasons, recently been cut off. Pressed by Sykes for an opinion, Hardinge replied—or so he wrote Nicolson—only that he would be happy with ". . . any system by which we may be assured of a friendly ad-

[92] Hirtzel memorandum, 14 July 1915, *Chamberlain Papers*, 19/2/4.

ministration at Baghdad, under British control of some kind, which will not create difficulties for us at Busrah." [93] Hardinge could assume, no doubt, that he need not object too strenuously, for there seemed every likelihood that the capture of Baghdad would be ordered and that Baghdad would fall. It would be most improbable that policy decisions would force a withdrawal later. And, indeed, Baghdad was ordered; but a check at Ctesiphon became a retreat, and a retreat became a disaster; long-range policy discussions were necessarily suspended while the army in Mesopotamia struggled simply to hold the Basra vilayet. Hardinge wrote in late 1915, before the need for surrender at Kut was realized, that perhaps the check was a blessing in disguise, for a serious blow had been given to the Turks, and Britain had not actually had to retreat from Baghdad itself —and, as Hardinge, Duff, and Chamberlain were all now quick to agree, the war would not be won in Mesopotamia.[94] Townshend's surrender would not be dismissed so easily.

6

The policy discussions, as inconclusive as the military discussions, were in abeyance, but administration of that area remaining under British control necessarily continued and made necessary the first tentative steps in the elaboration of a policy for the Arabs of Mesopotamia, perhaps the most decisive issue of all. The prewar organization of Iraq cannot be discussed in detail here; it will suffice to note that though under the control of local valis (governors) the various vilayets of the Empire were administered directly from Constantinople in many fields, including military affairs, courts, land records, posts and telegraphs, education, and various financial affairs (aside from local

[93] Hardinge private to Nicolson, 19 August 1915, *Nicolson Papers, FO* 800/379.

[94] Hardinge private to Chamberlain, 31 December, and to Nixon, 17 December 1915; Chamberlain private to Hardinge, 13 January 1916; and Duff private to Hardinge, 17 December 1915: *Hardinge Papers.*

accounts and collection of revenue). The vali was responsible for relations with local tribes and, to some extent, local relations with foreign powers. It was a complicated system, managed to a considerable degree by personal relationships, and it collapsed almost immediately when the campaign began.[95] If there was to be any administration at all, the armed forces would have at least initial responsibility. Given these conditions, it was only natural that the Indian Army and the Indian Political Service officers who accompanied it would turn to Indian methods in their need. Although there was little choice at the time, it must be said that the confident expectation that India would permanently control the Basra area meant that there was little serious search for an alternative.

Within a week of the occupation of Basra, an Indian-modeled civil police had replaced the military police. Similarly, Indian currency was introduced, again a necessary step in the light of the rapid depreciation of Turkish paper currency. A judicial system had to be established, and it, too, was essentially Indian, for few Turkish judges remained, and the elaborate system leading to higher Constantinople courts was hardly satisfactory. With exceptions, the Turkish civil law was to be applied; but as Philip Ireland—himself well-versed in later Iraqi administration—put it, most cases were exceptions. The overall impression given was that, regardless of some of the valid justifications for many of the Indian administrative patterns introduced, ". . . the most cogent reason was the underlying desire to pave the way for the painless absorption of lower Mesopotamia to India." [96]

But as noted above, within less than a month of the capture of Basra the Indian government had been told that it should neither declare annexation nor transform the Basra vilayet into an Indian province administratively. Hardinge and the Indian

[95] Based on Busch, *Britain and the Persian Gulf*, pp. 34–35, and references cited there in notes 79 and 80; Ireland, *op. cit.*, chs. II, IV.
[96] Ireland, *op. cit.*, pp. 83–85.

authorities hoped that all this was temporary, and certainly Hardinge encouraged Cox to continue in his present policies. The Viceroy was willing to cooperate with London so long as no absolute commitment was made that India would *not* take Basra if conditions permitted it. Shortly before his own conversations with Cox in Basra, Hardinge wrote Holderness that he was "anxious to see that the lines of administration are not laid down on too hard and fast a basis . . ." [97] On many issues, there was little choice. Indigenous laws and courts could hardly be retained when the whole system and its personnel had simply disappeared; as Cox suggested, it was vital to have law and order—and the Indian civil and penal codes were the most ready to hand (and, it should be pointed out, were already administered by British officials in the Persian Gulf in their consular judicial capacities). [98]

While these steps were allowed, there being no alternative at the moment, the essential underpinning—recognition of future amalgamation with India, at least administratively—could never be sanctioned. The authorities in Iraq were thus quite naturally in doubt, and the resulting government was one which was always temporary at best. Given the simultaneous uncertainty on over-all military and political aims, and the military insecurity (or at least hesitation) after Ctesiphon, it is hardly to be wondered that the regime became an unsatisfactory compromise. As one commentator has succinctly put it:

Advantage might have been taken of military domination to reorganize the civil administration on a permanent basis, but this would have implied a degree of permanent British control incompatible with Allied declarations and intentions. On the other hand, deliberately to leave the wreckage of a broken-down machine standing with only such repairs as to ensure its working momentarily with a certain minimum of efficiency was to invite trouble

[97] Hardinge private to Holderness, 6 January 1915, *Hardinge Papers.* See also Viceroy telegram to SSI, 7 December 1914, and Hirtzel minute, *L/P&S/10,* 4097/14, no. 4726/14.
[98] Viceroy telegram to SSI, 26 January 1915, *FO* 371/2482.

as soon as the exigencies of war ceased to demand the presence of large numbers of troops. The middle course . . . neither succeeded in preventing trouble nor in avoiding commitments which Great Britain was ill-disposed to bear. The degree of direct administration introduced on the Anglo-Indian model was sufficient to make Arab nationalists believe that the promises of the war were to be disregarded, while at the same time the administration was not strong enough to crush the dissatisfaction of which it was in a measure the cause.[99]

The promises had already been made, up to a point, by the end of 1914 (although the reference is to more sweeping pledges of a later date), at least to the Persian Gulf shaikhs and by implication to Basra. It must be remembered that the effect on the Arabs was a primary motive for the campaign in the first place. And yet the British and Indian forces had done the fighting in Iraq, and not an allied Arab army. However nicely distinctions might be drawn between Iraqi Arab and Turk, the actual fact was that most Arabs in Iraq were either fighting in the Turkish Army or defending their own interests. While the educated nationalists of Basra or Baghdad might have larger visions of the future, the "up-country" Arab saw little to distinguish between Briton and Turk and tended to loot the supplies and casualties of both with gleeful impartiality, respecting only forceful prevention. The guiding rule for most of the Army for most of the war was simple: "upstream of us, hostile; downstream, friendly." [100] That was the official rule, but many soldiers would have shared the judgment of one of them on the "Buddoos": "We had been long enough in Mesopotamia to know that the only friendly Arab we should ever meet would be a dead one." [101]

Relations with the tribes in general, in the first months of the war, depended upon success at arms. To that extent, Cox's

[99] J. de V. Loder, *The Truth about Mesopotamia, Palestine, and Syria* (London, 1923), p. 46.

[100] Brig.-Gen. A. W. Money to I.O., 22 January 1916, *FO* 371/2770.

[101] P. W. Long, *Other Ranks of Kut* (London, 1938), p. 31. See also

point on the dangers of delay was well taken: some improvement, to give one example, was noted in relations with the Euphrates tribes after the initial capture of Kut by the British.[102] But British successes were not going to be perpetual. Some sort of open declaration was the only possible hope for full Arab cooperation, and even then was no guarantee. Yet here the continuing hopes of annexation, or colony, or disguised control, created a paradoxical situation in which most British authorities in Iraq—with the exception of a number of political officers—could view the Arabs they encountered only as assassins, thieves, and mutilators of the dead, while at the same time, the same authorities were unable and unwilling to attempt to correct the situation by making long-range, serious promises to the Arabs as long as the aims of policy were undecided in every respect.[103]

The Mesopotamian campaign had been a haphazard affair

---

Wilson, *Loyalties*, p. 54; Barker, *Neglected War*, p. 61; and Edmund Candler, *The Long Road to Baghdad* (London, 1919), I, p. 68, on his trials as an official "eye-witness" who encountered objections to the term "friendly Arab" (for it implied that some were not) and consequently shifted to "marauder in Turkish pay" and later, the best term of all, "Kurds and others." Candler's book is an interesting account which makes a number of intelligent criticisms. Its appearance so soon after the war was the result of Candler's failure to submit his manuscript to the official censor in Mesopotamia: see W.O. (M.O.2.a.) note, 20 July 1918, *L/P&S/11*, vol. 138, no. 3698/18, with I.O. notes.

[102] Nixon telegram to FSI, 19 November 1915, *FO* 371/2770.

[103] See Chamberlain private telegram to Hardinge, 22 October, and Assistant Private Secretary to Viceroy telegram to Private Secretary to Viceroy, 24 October 1915, *WO* 106/893, and various documents (especially Nixon telegram to FSI, 9 November 1915) in *India Sec. War* June 1916, 315–52, for a discussion of a proclamation to be issued on the capture of Baghdad (which, as it happened, was not to occur until 1917). London outlined a statement declaring that Britain favored the creation of an Arab state and would be prepared to consider the further disposition of Baghdad in this connection, but India objected to anything more than a pledge to respect the holy places and, at the very most, the Arab administration of the province under British protection or suzerainty on the lines of a native state.

from start to finish. A demonstration had become an invasion; a successful advance had become a humiliating military setback. Policy toward administration, toward Iraqi Arabs, toward the Allies in the Middle East, toward even the step-by-step movements of the troops themselves, remained unresolved from the start. The result was that Britain controlled a sizable portion of Mesopotamia but knew not whether she would retain it, name it independent or protectorate, or simply abandon it to the Turks or other interested parties. The only certainties were that the military was likely to control the administration as long as the fighting continued; that, since there had been no cooperation with the Arabs from the start, there was mutual distrust from the start; and that this distrust was likely to continue.

Only one consistent thread emerges, and that only after the taking of Basra: the desire of Indian officials to receive their due, India's due, for sacrifices made in Mesopotamia.[104] They were great sacrifices, if made for the wrong reasons; at the very least, any settlement would have to take into account the fact that Mesopotamia was India's war, India's frontier, and,

[104] Indian officials were not alone in possessing dreams of a developed British Iraq. For some similar statements, see Sir William Willcocks, "Two and a Half Years in Mesopotamia," *Blackwood's*, 199 (1915), 304–23; A. B. Taylor, "The River Tigris from the Sea to Baghdad," *Journal of the Central Asian Society*, 4:3 (1917), 72–90; Canon Joseph T. Parfit, *Mesopotamia: The Key to the Future* (London, 1917), p. 28: "In less than two years British occupation has transformed lower Mesopotamia into something approaching a paradise," and *Marvellous Mesopotamia: The World's Wonderland* (London, [1920]); Lt.-Col. A. C. Yate, "Baghdad and Gaza—and After," *Nineteenth Century and After*, 82 (July-December 1917), 1276–86, and "Britain's Buffer States in the East," *Journal of the Central Asian Society*, 5:1 (1918), 3–23; Sir Theodore Morison, "A Colony for India," *Nineteenth Century and After*, 84 (July-December 1918), 430–41 (hostile to Indian possession of Iraq, but favoring East Africa), which is answered by Lord Sydenham of Combe, "The Future of India, I: India as a Colonising Power," *ibid.*, 762–70; Birch-Reynardson, *op. cit.*, p. 48 (". . . for three years we have shown the people what it is to live under honest administration, and taught them to rely on justice, and have begun to make the desert blossom as the rose . . ."); Capt. H. B. Usher, "Mesopotamia's Claim

with any luck, India's reward. If this should mean the sacrifice of local nationalistic aspirations, now or in the future, so be it; there could hardly be much sympathy for such aspirations in a Mesopotamia where Arabs were considered hostile until proven otherwise.

But, unfortunately for India and her plans for Iraq, Mesopotamia was not the only Arab Middle Eastern area involved in the war, nor was India the only overseas center contributing to Britain's policy in that part of the world—for in Cairo a different set of officials was elaborating a different policy and a different future for the Arab world.

---

on Britain," *Contemporary Review*, 120 (July-December 1921), 332–38; [C. C. Garbett], "Turkish Rule and British Administration in Mesopotamia," *Quarterly Review*, 232 (October 1919), 401–23; and A. T. Wilson, "Mesopotamia, 1914–1921," *Journal of the Central Asian Society*, 8:3 (1921), 144–61. Some official statements: [Iraq, British Occupation Administration], *The Arab of Mesopotamia* (Basra, n.d.); [India], *The Last Week of War in Mesopotamia* (Delhi, 1919).

# II

# Cairo's Arab Revolt, 1914–1916

> Pursewarden: "When the English feel they are in the wrong, their only recourse is to cant."
> Keats: "Am I to understand that you are criticizing British policy?"
> Pursewarden: "Of course not. Our statesmanship is impeccable."
>
> *Lawrence Durrell*, BALTHAZAR

1

To the Indian government, the word "Arabs" meant, in 1914, the somewhat carefree and occasionally obstreperous inhabitants of the Persian Gulf and south Arabia—backward, perhaps, but they were quite capable of cooperating in peaceful relations with the protecting British raj as long as they were administered with the proper mixture of carrot and stick. To the administrators of Egypt, on the other hand, "Arabs" had a rather different meaning; while the same elements of superiority might enter into their definition, Egyptian proconsuls had experience with educated intellectuals and advocates of nationalism. Most Arabs were also Muslim, and in Cairo "Muslim opinion" tended to mean "Arab opinion." To Indian officials, however, "Muslim" meant primarily an important section of India's population, and they were cautious of offending that section; that most Arabs were also Muslims simply complicated matters in the Middle East by insuring that anything that affected the faith in that area would probably have a subsequent effect on Indian Muslims. These differences in definitions and attitudes were apparent in the very early days of the war and were to become crucial as time passed.

The difference in the Egyptian view, to begin with, meant that Egypt was rather more attuned in 1914 to the idea of cooperation with the Arabs against the Turks. This was due partly to internal Egyptian problems and partly to the fact that Arab subjects of the Ottoman Empire were in touch with Cairo before the European war broke out in August. The first tentative contacts with the nationalist movement in Syria dated back to 1912, but a much more important overture occurred in February 1914 when Amir 'Abdullah, son of Sharif Husain, guardian of the holy places of Mecca and Medina—an important post both politically and religiously—spoke with Kitchener, then Consul-General in Cairo. Kitchener made no promises, but he certainly had in the back of his mind 'Abdullah's remarks on the likelihood of an approaching Arab-Turk clash.[1] In April 'Abdullah met with Ronald Storrs, Kitchener's Oriental Secretary; according to Storrs he did not really get down to the business of expressing his desires and aims and once again obtained nothing definite. Kitchener, while agreeing with other authorities that caution in such talks was essential so as not to wound Turkish susceptibilities, was convinced that Britain should not alienate the Arabs, if only because of its own

[1] G. P. Gooch and Harold Temperley, eds., *British Documents on the Origins of the War, 1898–1914*, vol. X, part II (London, 1938), pp. 824–32, particularly Kitchener to Grey, 6 February 1914; also *FO* 141/460.

interest in Muslim opinion and pilgrimages to the Hijaz in which Husain was so influential.[2]

Negotations remained at this point until September, when Sir Edward Grey let it be known to all concerned departments that should Turkey join Germany Britain would urge the Arabs to possess themselves of the holy places; within a few days Mallet in Constantinople agreed that the Arab movement would serve as a useful weapon. In these circumstances, Kitchener, now in London, telegraphed to Cairo on 24 September, ordering that 'Abdullah (and by implication, Husain) be approached once more on possible cooperation; this was done in early October.[3] By the end of the month London was assuring 'Abdullah that if the Arabs aided in the war Britain would not intervene in their internal affairs and would give all possible aid against external aggression. Before he could have received this message, 'Abdullah had returned by messenger a guarded but friendly reply to Kitchener's first approach, giving at least a hint of future cooperation.[4]

Nor was the Sharifal faction the only interested Arab party. A secret Arab society, al-'Ahd (The Covenant), founded before the war and composed of Arab officers in the Ottoman

[2] Kitchener to Grey, 4 April, and private to Sir W. Tyrrell (F.O.), 26 April, and Storrs memorandum, 19 April 1914, *FO* 141/460 and *British Documents*, X:2, pp. 830–31; see also Sir Ronald Storrs, *Memoirs* (N.Y., 1937), p. 135.

[3] F.O. to I.O., 1 September 1914, *FO* 371/2139; Grey (from Kitchener) telegram to Cheetham (for Storrs), 24 September 1914, *FO* 141/ 460, discussed in A. L. Tibawi, "Syria in the McMahon Correspondence: Fresh Evidence from the British Foreign Office Records," *Mid-East Forum* (Beirut), 42:4 (1966), 7–8. Tibawi's interesting article covers much of what follows here on the McMahon correspondence, but it is of little help to the researcher because it fails to cite specific sources.

Storrs, *op. cit.*, p. 163, claims that Kitchener's intervention resulted from Storrs's own urging, as approved by Lt.-Col. Gilbert F. Clayton (Director of Intelligence, Egyptian Army); there is apparently no record of this in either the F.O. files, the Egyptian Archives, or Kitchener's own papers.

[4] Grey telegram to Cheetham and Cheetham telegram to F.O., 31 October 1914, *FO* 141/460. Cheetham's telegram, with Grey minute, also in *Grey Papers, FO* 800/48.

Army, had several leaders of some merit. Although the extent and intentions of the group were little known to the British, these leaders had made contact with the Cairo administration by August 1914. Chief among them was Major 'Aziz 'Ali al-Misri, an influential ex-officer and a founder of the society, who had survived Turkish arrest and trial and had made his way to Cairo in April. He made it clear to the officials concerned that he was deputed by his group to ascertain Britain's attitude toward the formation of a united Arab state, with possible British tutelage and control of foreign policy.[5] Nothing could be promised until war had broken out with Turkey, of course, but in November events began to move more quickly.

On 13 November Cheetham cabled Grey that various Arab leaders in Cairo were voicing suspicion of British intentions to annex Arabian territory and occupy Red Sea ports. A definite statement that Britain had no such aims, and that any military or naval action that might be taken would be only for the protection of Arab interests against Turkish or other aggression or in support of the Arabs' own movement to free themselves from Turkish rule, would have an excellent effect. Al-Misri, he added, was talking of the possibility of organizing a revolution in Iraq and had suggested two Iraqis who might be approached for this purpose. Without consulting the India Office, Grey gave approval for both the assurance and the use of al-Misri, to whom £2,000 could be provided if he proved useful for this purpose.[6]

---

[5] On Misri: Majid Khadduri, " 'Azīz 'Alī al-Miṣrī and the Arab Nationalist Movement," *Middle Eastern Affairs*, No. 4, ed. A. Hourani (Oxford, 1965), 140–63. On al-'Ahd, Misri, and prewar Arab nationalist activities in general, George Antonius, *The Arab Awakening: The Story of the Arab National Movement* (London, 1938), ch. VI. On the negotiations: Cheetham telegram to Grey, 9 August, and R. E. M. Russell (Intelligence Dept., Cairo) note on conversation with Misri, 17 August 1914, *L/P&S/10*, 53/15, nos. 3136 and 3510/14; *FO* 371/2140.

[6] Cheetham telegram to Grey, 13 November, and Grey telegram to Cheetham, 14 November; Cheetham to Grey, 15 November, reporting Clayton conversation with al-Misri of 26 October; and Cheetham to

The suggestion of rebellion in Iraq—where still Basra had not been captured—involved India, and when, five days after Grey's cable to Cheetham, Hirtzel was able to comment on this exchange, he noted that it was "a very dangerous proceeding," and that Hardinge and Cox should be consulted. Hardinge had been told that the "pan-Arab" leaders in Cairo had dispatched several agents, including two destined for the Persian Gulf, and India now became aware of the al-Misri project, although not of the negotiations with 'Abdullah.[7]

These plans found a cold reception in India. The introduction of agitators was hardly to be viewed with eagerness by an Indian administration with more than enough agitators of its own (Hardinge himself had narrowly escaped death from a bomb thrown in 1912). Al-Misri had not only advanced a risky plan; he had also suggested that Britain contact Sayyid Talib— and Hardinge was well aware of Talib's reputation. The other man, Nuri as-Sa'id, was a better possibility. Cox, Hardinge reported, had interviewed Nuri and had found him a "highly Europeanised delicate Arab, aloof, about 25, apparently a visionary socialist. Ultimate aim of his party is to raise Arab nature to better things which they think will be more easily achieved under the liberality of British rule." But Hardinge had little hope of an organized rising among officers in the Turkish Army and less for one among the tribal shaikhs who were "too backward to listen to 'Young Arab' propaganda." The one serious possibility as leader of a spontaneous rising, if it ever occurred, was Ibn Sa'ud. If and when the rising came, it should be aided with British funds, but until the situation was clearer action along this line was premature.[8]

---

Grey, 13 December 1914, on al-Misri's conversation with Robert Graves of *The Times*: *FO* 371/2140; *L/P&S/10*, 53/15, nos. 4463/14 and 53/15.

[7] Hirtzel minute on Grey telegram to Cheetham, 14 November 1914, *ibid*; SSI telegram to Viceroy, 31 October 1914, *L/P&S/11*, vol. 95, no. 635/15, and file of documents in *India Sec. War* June 1915, 225–45.

[8] Viceroy telegram to SSI, 8 December 1914, *L/P&S/10*, 53/15, no. 4780/14.

Nuri, a Baghdadi, was indeed an experienced officer despite his youth, for he had served in several branches of the Army and in the Balkan Wars. An 'Ahd member, he had married the sister of Ja'far al-'Askari, who, like Nuri, was to play a prominent role in the Arab revolt and in postwar Iraq. Cox had been able to talk to Nuri for the simple reason that Nuri had been in a Basra hospital with lung trouble when the city fell to the British. Unfortunately for his immediate utility to the Arab revolt, Nuri had few clear plans (and, as yet, little command of English) and was damned by his own military knowledgeability and his earlier contacts with Talib. In January 1915, Nuri was packed off to India, where he was held in open arrest (no formal charges were ever levied) until allowed to proceed to Cairo in December.[9]

So far, India's response had been less than enthusiastic, not only because of the reasons given as explanation to London but also because of the conviction—held particularly by Grant, India's Foreign Secretary—that such aid as was contemplated would in the long run prove very embarrassing. If the revolt failed, the effort would have been wasted; but if it succeeded ". . . we shall have created a Frankenstein Monster which may be an infinite source of trouble hereafter."[10] The India Office shared this view; the Mesopotamian situation was fully complicated enough, the Foreign Office was told, without the added difficulty of the "introduction of any factors from outside." This, in turn, was a milder expression of Hirtzel's views, for he thoroughly distrusted the whole project; the plan was ". . . entirely irreconcilable with our military operations, & was intended by El Masri to be so."[11]

The India Office officials were concerned with another aspect as well, the logical result of Arab control of the holy

[9] Based on Maj. C. C. R. Murphy (Intelligence, "Force D") memorandum for Chief of Staff, India, 19 January 1915, *India Sec. War* June 1915, 52–119, and file in 225–45; and Birdwood, *Nuri*, pp. 1–27.

[10] Grant note, 5 December 1914, *India Sec. War* June 1915, 225–45.

[11] Hirtzel minute, 10 December, on Viceroy telegram to SSI, 8 December, and I.O. to F.O., 11 December 1914, *L/P&S/10*, 53/15, no. 4780/14.

places, namely, an Arab Caliphate. As Crewe informed Hardinge in private, Kitchener, the advocate of the Arab Caliphate, refused to see that the spiritual leadership of the Ottoman Sultan, in his alternate role as Caliph of the Muslim world, remained unshaken by any actions of his Young Turk ministers. While Muslim India might sanction the initiation of an Arab Caliphate, it certainly would not tolerate any change associated with outside intrigue.[12] Sweeping remarks on what Indian Muslims would tolerate—particularly remarks by those with little direct experience in India—were only beginning.

India's reaction echoed that of the India Office. Grant minuted that meddling with the Caliphate was unwise from the standpoint of Muslim opinion and, more important, the creation of a powerful Arab Caliphate was definitely not in Britain's interest. "What we want is not a United Arabia: but a weak and disunited Arabia, split up into little principalities so far as possible under our suzerainty—but incapable of co-ordinated action against us, forming a buffer against the Powers in the West." With support for Grant's opinion arriving from Cox and the governors of Aden and Bombay, Hardinge had little inclination to put up a different view. The India Office was given Grant's memorandum, essentially, as India's considered judgment.[13]

Meanwhile the negotiations with 'Abdullah and his father were proceeding. How unknown these communications were in India is revealed by an Indian suggestion of December 1914 (actually emanating from Aden, which was under India's administration) that Husain be approached by Britain, and, in return for aid, that he be given a pledge of protection of his

[12] Crewe private to Hardinge, 4 and 18 December 1914, *Hardinge Papers*.

[13] Crewe private telegram to Hardinge, 12 November, with Grant minute, 28 November; Hardinge private telegram to Crewe, 29 November; Secretary to Bombay Government private to FSI, 18 November; Resident, Aden, telegram to FSI, 19 November; and Cox private to Grant, 25 November 1914: *India Sec. War* May 1915, 433–52.

and his family's possession of their hereditary rights and privileges.[14] Within a few days of this suggestion, copies of the Cairo correspondence of the preceding months were on their way to India with Crewe's comment that it was not desirable to address the Sharif via Aden under the circumstances. The Foreign Office had apologized to the India Office for its failure to keep them informed of what Hirtzel termed "a very dangerous correspondence,"[15] but this hardly sufficed to quiet the alarm with which hints of Husain's assumption of the Caliphate and a pledge against foreign aggression—a pledge which appeared most difficult to fulfill if a test ever came—were received in the India Office.

For the time being, no significant statements were made (aside from what may have been said to al-Misri), and there was no Arab rising which would force their issue. While Cairo's negotiations with Husain continued in desultory style, India's attention was focused primarily upon discussions of Mesopotamian policy—with a brief diversion over the two pan-Arab agents sent by Cairo to the Persian Gulf, which ended with the simple expedient of having them arrested when they reached Bushire in February 1915. There were, naturally, explanations: the agents had corresponded with Talib, they were suspected of Turkish connections, and they were pan-Islamic and anti-Christian (a point which hardly came as a surprise)—all of which was enough to make their release in Basra undesirable. If Cairo wished them back, they would be sent to Bombay as prisoners of war and could then proceed back to point of origin. In the end, one was allowed to go to Zubair in Iraq (his home town) and the other to Bombay. The

[14] Viceroy telegram to SSI, 11 December 1914, *L/P&S/10*, 53/15, no. 4854/14.

[15] Hirtzel minute, 12 December, on Cheetham telegram to Grey, 31 October, and SSI telegram to Viceroy, 14 December 1914; see also Hirtzel, Holderness, and Crewe minutes of 9, 11, and 12 January 1915, respectively, on Cheetham telegram to Grey (on Misri discussions), 13 December 1914: *ibid.*, nos. 4855/14 and 82/15.

incident could not be said to have endeared Cairo's nationalists, and especially Rashid Rida, whose disciples they were, to the Indian administration. As the agents had not been acting in any official capacity as far as Cairo or London or Delhi was concerned, however, no official repercussions followed.[16]

2

But India was not to be let off so easily. The year 1915, in fact, was to be an important one for negotiations with the Arabs—even negotiations on Mesopotamia—and for interdepartmental discussion as well.

In charge now of Arab negotiations was Sir Henry McMahon, who had at last arrived in Egypt to replace Kitchener as High Commissioner, and who was, somewhat surprisingly, from the Indian Political Service (his last post had been Secretary of the Foreign Department, 1911–1914), which fact alone gave Crewe cause for hope.[17] But McMahon, like his Foreign Office superiors in London, fully intended to continue and if possible bring to a successful conclusion the negotiations with Husain. His Indian experience had not made him an opponent of Arab aspirations; it had, however, as his private correspondence with Hardinge reveals, given him an awareness of the likelihood of difficulties with India. Hardinge was obviously worried about British interference in Muslim religious affairs; he was equally concerned about the secular nationalists, for papers sent him by Wingate in Khartoum showed that they would wish Britain to evacuate Mesopotamia eventually. To India, such an eventuality was as objectionable as withdrawal

[16] High Commissioner, Cairo, telegram to FSI, 9 February; Viceroy telegram to High Commissioner, 16 February; Political Officer, "Force D" [Cox], telegram to High Commissioner, 18 March; and Cox telegram to FSI, 11 July 1915: *L/P&S/11*, vol. 95, nos. 635, 1660, and 2891/15. On Rashid Rida and his role in the Arab nationalist movement, see Albert Hourani, *Arabic Thought in the Liberal Age, 1798–1939* (London, 1962), ch. IX.

[17] Crewe private to Hardinge, 18 December 1914, *Hardinge Papers*.

from the Persian Gulf or the Sudan; the sole result of cooperation with such demands would be anarchy.[18]

Hardinge was not only hostile to the policy as it seemed to
be taking shape; he was also hostile to McMahon. This resulted
in part from London's failure to consult the Viceroy on another post for his own Foreign Secretary and in part from
Hardinge's personal knowledge of the new High Commissioner. As early as January 1915, he wrote to Nicolson in the
Foreign Office that "He is a very nice man and his opinions
are generally sound though somewhat reactionary." His main
fault was that he was very slow. "I could have shaken him over
and over again when he was my Foreign Secretary, but I am
very fond of him as he is a very straight little man." Hardinge's
view did not improve as time passed. Again to Nicolson, in late
May: "I had nothing to say to it [McMahon's appointment]
and would not have advised it if my opinion had been asked.
He is a nice man and I like him very much, but his ability is
of a very ordinary type, while his slowness of mind and ignorance of French must be two very serious drawbacks to him."[19]

Hardinge's attacks on McMahon, however nicely qualified,
were not finished but rather depended for their regularity and
urgency upon utterances from Cairo on the Arabs and the
Caliphate. Nor was Hardinge alone in his view, for it was
shared by his friend Sir Ronald Graham in the Egyptian Ministry of Interior, who wrote in 1916, "We can none of us
understand your little McMahon—he is pleasant and shrewd,

[18] McMahon private to Hardinge, 4 April, and Hardinge private to
McMahon, 21 April 1915, *ibid.*; McMahon private to Grey, 14 May,
Wingate private to Grey, 15 May (seen by Asquith, Chamberlain,
etc.), with Grey minute, 13 June 1915, *FO* 371/2486. Wingate, as Sirdar, was also responsible for intelligence in Egypt, and this, plus his
own inclinations, was in turn responsible for his early role in the Arab
negotiations.

[19] Hardinge private to Nicolson, 6 January and 25 May 1915, *Nicolson Papers, FO* 800/377–78. See also Hardinge's private letters to Crewe,
31 December 1914, R. Graham, 27 January 1915, and Chirol, 6 May
1915, *Hardinge Papers*; and Hardinge, *Indian Years*, p. 115.

but it is impossible to make him take a decision of any kind, and he effaces himself so completely and is so reluctant to see anyone that he has allowed Maxwell [Lieutenant-General Sir J. Maxwell, Commander on the Egyptian front] altogether to usurp his position."[20]

This sort of criticism was to have its effect, but for the moment Hardinge was more concerned with London than Cairo, for in August Sir Mark Sykes arrived in India on a mission of education—for both himself and those with whom he met. Hardinge thus received his first intimation of the plans elaborated by the de Bunsen committee in June and of the reasons for the construction of that committee in the first place, including the even more important problem of Britain's relations with her wartime allies.

In early 1915 the British attack on the Straits had sufficiently alarmed Russia on the possible nightmare of British possession of Constantinople so that the Russian government had asked for, and had received, an agreement (the "Constantinople Agreement")[21] which assured Russian participation in the future division of the Ottoman Empire (specifically, the Straits) and in return assigned to Britain the so-called "neutral" zone of Persia, a buffer district dividing British and Russian spheres as delineated by the Anglo-Russian accord of 1907. This first partition plan of 1915 was the beginning of a series of such agreements, as each ally became nervous about its share and each worry led to further demands. First to voice concern after the Anglo-Russian agreement was, logically

[20] R. Graham private to Hardinge, 1 March and 22 August 1916, *Hardinge Papers*; see also Hardinge note to Grey, 9 September 1916, *Grey Papers, FO* 800/96. Wingate, it should be added, carried on a private correspondence with Hardinge as well, in which he attempted to smooth India's feelings, with some good effect: see Hardinge private to Wingate, 10 June 1915, *Hardinge Papers*.

[21] J. C. Hurewitz, ed., *Diplomacy in the Near and Middle East: A Documentary Record* (Princeton, N.J., 1956), II, pp. 7–11; Harry N. Howard, *The Partition of Turkey: A Diplomatic History, 1913–1923* (N.Y., 1966), ch. IV.

enough, France, and in late March the French suggested Anglo-French discussions of other Asia Minor questions. Grey was forced to agree, but, as he pointed out to Bertie, the ambassador in Paris, while Britain had told Russia that there should be some sort of Muslim independent political unity, naturally centered on the holy places and including Arabia, there was as yet no definite decision on whether the state should include Mesopotamia, or whether "we should put forward a claim for ourselves in that region."[22]

The de Bunsen committee was instructed to decide this question, but, until its work was done, no serious discussions could be held with France. When its report was submitted, there was still India to be considered. Sykes was given the job of sounding out Hardinge, whom he had never met. Mark Sykes was a most unusual man, a man of fertile imagination and visionary plans and schemes and the ability to argue persuasively in their favor at any given moment. He was well-traveled, experienced in politics (as a Conservative M.P.), witty, artistically inclined (both with his pen and in his ability to mime), and, until his death in 1919, a figure of considerable influence behind the scenes of Middle Eastern policy. Yet there was a flaw in his character which led him to hasty generalizations and to hasty advocacy of causes only half-defined. As T. E. Lawrence put it, "He saw the odd in everything, and missed the even."[23]

Hardinge was a completely different sort of person—the

[22] Grey to Bertie, 23 March 1915, FO 371/2486.

[23] Lawrence, Seven Pillars, p. 58. See also Wilson, Loyalties, p. 152; Elizabeth Monroe, Britain's Moment in the Middle East, 1914–1956 (London, 1965), p. 41; Stephen Hemsley Longrigg, Syria and Lebanon under French Mandate (London, 1958), p. 56, n. 4; P. M. Holt, Egypt and the Fertile Crescent, 1516–1922: A Political History (Ithaca, N.Y., 1966), p. 269; Sir Stewart Symes, Tour of Duty (London, 1946), p. 33. The standard, though inadequate, biography is Shane Leslie, Mark Sykes: His Life and Letters (London, 1923); a briefer but more useful characterization may be found in Christopher Sykes, Two Studies in Virtue (N.Y., 1953), pp. 173–76.

most unlikely sort, in fact, to be drawn by Sykes's magnetism. And Sykes had already aroused suspicion by the simple appointment of his mission, which was ostensibly as liaison for the Director of Military Intelligence in London, collecting information in Egypt and Mesopotamia. When asked to extend full facilities to Sykes for his work, India replied that, while glad to do so, it wished more information on his status and the scope of his mission. If it was to be entirely separate and independent, cabled Hardinge, there was the "grave risk of friction and duplication of work." Since Sykes would have no executive duties, replied the War Office, but would only study some of the questions raised by the de Bunsen committee, there would be no question of duplication or friction; he would be only a visitor.[24]

In June Delhi had been further perturbed to hear from General Nixon of a proclamation made by Cairo that Britain would take "not one foot" of territory in the Arabian Peninsula. "I have seldom read a more stupid proclamation," commented Hardinge in India.[25] As it turned out, the proclamation was no proclamation at all, being an unsigned leaflet dropped on the Hijaz coast and elsewhere as an attempt to counter German *jihad* propaganda; but McMahon had said, regarding the Arabian Peninsula, that Britain intended to annex not "one foot of land in it, nor suffer any other Power to do so," and general authority for the statement had been given by Grey.

[24] Shuckburgh note for Hirtzel and SSI telegram to Viceroy, repeated to Aden and Cox, 2 June; Viceroy telegram to SSI, 7 June; I.O. to W.O., 10 June; W.O. to I.O., 12 June 1915; *L/P&S/11*, vol. 93, no. 2059/15.

The mission is outlined in *India Sec. War* August 1915, 209–14. Sykes was technically operating under the Director of Military Intelligence until May 1916, at which point he was transferred to Hankey's Cabinet Secretariat: Committee of Imperial Defence [Hankey] to F.O., 22 May 1916, *FO 371/2777*.

[25] Minute, 22 June, Nixon telegram to FSI, 16 June, FSI telegram to Nixon and Viceroy telegram to SSI, 22 June 1915, *India Sec. War* May 1916, 304–10.

The document was not a happy production, grumbled Nicolson; but the Foreign Office did not consider Basra part of the Arabian Peninsula, and anyway nothing in the statement barred treaties with states there. India was told that the leaflet need not be issued in Mesopotamia,[26] and the controversy was settled—but, like the al-Misri scheme and statements on the Caliphate before it, it left a legacy of distrust in Delhi.

By July Sykes was in Cairo, telegraphing home various projects for cooperation with Iraqi Arabs, using captured Arab prisoners of war, and so on; by August he was in India, by which time Hardinge had already termed his several proposals "absolutely fantastic" and "perfectly fatal."[27] Hardinge subsequently wrote Nicolson that he had made no commitments in the discussions that followed; but in a letter to Chamberlain, now Secretary of State for India, he was franker. While not strenuously objecting to the de Bunsen document itself, Hardinge urged that Britain could not take the initiative on the Caliphate and, as far as Mesopotamia was concerned, Sykes's vision of representative government was, to say the least, premature. Obviously communication between Hardinge and Sykes had been most difficult; Sykes, wrote Hardinge, "did not seem to be able to grasp the fact that there are parts of Turkey quite unfit for representative institutions." Sykes was an interesting man, it was true, he wrote Chirol, who "takes himself very seriously. He knows a good deal, but seems unduly impressed with the importance of the Syrian Arabs."[28] To Sykes,

[26] Grey telegrams to McMahon, 19 May and 26 June, McMahon telegram to Grey, 30 June, with Clerk and Nicolson minutes, I.O. to F.O., 6 July 1915, *FO* 371/2486; Hardinge private to Chirol, 24 June 1915, *Hardinge Papers*; SSI telegram to Viceroy, 21 July, and FSI telegram to Nixon, 24 July 1915, *India Sec. War* May 1916, 304–10.

[27] McMahon (for Sykes) telegram to Grey, 2 August 1915, *FO* 371/2486; Hardinge private to Chamberlain, 6 August 1915, *Hardinge Papers*.

[28] Hardinge private to Nicolson, 19 August, *Nicolson Papers, FO* 800/379; to Chamberlain, 27 August, to Chirol, 19 August, and to McMahon, 20 August 1915, *Hardinge Papers*.

on the other hand, India refused to see the Mesopotamian expedition from anything but "a purely Indian point of view and not as an Imperial question."[29] The gap between the two men revealed by these few remarks was enormous.

In September Sykes was in Mesopotamia itself. Here too the impression he left was unfavorable, if Arnold Wilson may be believed.

He had an intense hatred of injustice and a thoroughly English compassion for the under-dog, but he was too short a time in Mesopotamia to gather more than fragmentary impressions. He had come with his mind made up, and he set himself to discover facts in favour of his preconceived notions, rather than to survey the local situation with an impartial eye. Whatever we were doing to change the Turkish régime, or to better the lot of the Armenian, Jew, and Sabaean minorities, had his cordial approval—for the rest, we must do justice to Arab ambitions, and satisfy France![30]

Sykes was back in England by December; he had seen much, learned a great deal, and planned great plans—but in India and among Indian administrators of Mesopotamia he had served only to alarm. As another M.P. and associate of the Cairo authorities, Captain George Lloyd, wrote during his own subsequent visit to Iraq, Sykes "seems to have been amazingly tactless, and not only to have rather blustered everyone but also to have decried openly everything Indian, in a manner which was bound to cause some resentment."[31] The mission, it may safely be concluded, was worse than a failure.

[29] Sykes private to Robert Cecil, 4 October 1915, *Sykes Papers* (St. Antony's College, Oxford).

[30] Wilson, *Loyalties*, p. 152.

[31] G. Lloyd private to Clayton, 27 May 1916, *FO* 882/4 (Arab Bureau Papers). Sykes's own reports are in telegram to W.O., 23 October 1915, *L/P&S/10*, 53/15, no. 4259/15, and letter to D.M.O., 23 October 1915, *FO* 371/2491. See also Sykes to D.M.O. (Callwell), 15 November 1915, *FO* 882/13. General Callwell, who had sat on the de Bunsen committee and was Director of Military Operations at this time, was also Director of Military Intelligence, as the positions were as yet unseparated: Field-Marshal Sir William Robertson, *From Private to Field-Marshal* (Boston, 1921), pp. 250–51.

3

While Sykes was explaining himself in India and Mesopotamia, events were moving ahead in the Sharifal negotiations. By late August 1915, an Anglo-Arab alliance (or at least Anglo-Hijazi Arab alliance) seemed a real possibility. The terms, as put forward by Husain, would require British recognition of the independence of the Arabs and approval of an Arab Caliphate. McMahon proposed a favorable reply, but wished to add that discussion of boundaries, as desired by Husain, was premature.[32]

This time, the India Office was informed with more dispatch and, predictably, there was some disagreement. Hirtzel remained cynical: if Britain took Constantinople that winter, there would be no need for the Sharif's aid; if she did not, the Sharif would have no incentive to action. The more time passed, the more the Sharif was likely to reduce his demands, which now included Arab control of those areas which the de Bunsen report had proposed as British and French spheres. On the other hand, some alternative Muslim center was perhaps necessary; it was, in short, difficult to know how to proceed. Holderness was clearer in his own mind: the Sharif was aiming at an Arabian kingdom, and "We have no intention of helping him to this, and we ought not to hold out even a vague hope of negotiating an agreement on this basis. Betw$^n$ our views & his there is more difference than unity." At least the India Office staff agreed that the answer McMahon proposed was likely to put Husain off, although, of course, agreement with the Sharif's terms was impossible in the light of the existence of other, rival Arab chiefs, a position the India Office had already expressed in June. The best line to follow now, the Foreign Office was advised, was to invite a Sharifal representative to Cairo to negotiate a preliminary agreement, perhaps on

[32] McMahon to Grey, 20 August, and telegram to Grey, 22 August 1915, FO 371/2486 and L/P&S/10, 53/15, nos. 2061 and 2455/15.

the Hijaz and the Caliphate, although no specific terms were suggested.[33] In Khartoum, Wingate was already thinking along similar lines, and his memorandum of 25 August, which he forwarded to Grey and Hardinge, outlined a future confederation of "semi-independent" Arab states under some form of British protectorate.[34]

The India Office's criticism prompted Grey to suggest that the points it raised be included in McMahon's next letter to Husain. McMahon, on his own authority, refused to suggest any preliminary agreement to the Sharif on the grounds that this was premature and that the Sharif's position might be damaged if such an agreement later became public knowledge. As a result, and as the India Office had predicted, Husain found McMahon's August letter cold and hesitant and made this clear in his response of 9 September. It was now fairly obvious that if Husain's cooperation was to be won something more was required from the British side.[35]

As the autumn passed, new ingredients were added. The most notable of these was the influence of a young (24) Iraqi, Muhammad Sharif al-Faruqi, who as a Turkish lieutenant had deserted to the British at Gallipoli and had asked to be taken to Egypt. Al-Faruqi was an 'Ahd member, but he had little experience and equally little English. General G. F. Clayton, head of Intelligence in Cairo (and therefore Wingate's subordinate), talked with al-Faruqi in Egypt in October and reported that he urged action now, warning that if there was none the Arabs would throw in their lot with the Turks. There was a chance,

[33] Hirtzel and Holderness minutes on McMahon telegram, *ibid.*; I.O. to F.O., 24 June and 24 August 1915, *FO* 371/2486; "eminently sound," Nicolson minuted on the June letter.

[34] Wingate note, 25 August 1915, *FO* 371/2486; Wingate private to Hardinge, 26 August, *Hardinge Papers,* and private to Grey, 7 September 1915, *FO* 371/2486.

[35] Grey telegram to McMahon, 25 August, McMahon telegram and letter to Grey, 26 August, and Husain to McMahon, 9 September 1915, *FO* 371/2486.

too, that Husain's position simply represented his maximum demands and would be subject to modification in negotiations with Britain. But Maxwell, for one, felt that the Arabs would continue to demand Syria and the rest of Mesopotamia (beyond British-held Basra) and, interestingly, predicted that they would insist on keeping the Syrian towns of Damascus, Homs, Hama, and Aleppo. The discussions with al-Faruqi and a reference to Mesopotamia in Husain's September letter gave every indication of the truth of Maxwell's remarks.[36]

On 18 October the Foreign Office received a summary of Husain's letter. George Clerk, first to wrestle with the issues involved, noted that the initial question was whether Britain wanted an independent Arabia. The answer clearly was yes, although there would have to be limits to this state in the light of both British interests in Iraq and French claims in Syria. "But we cannot win the Arabs unless we can reconcile French and Arab claims, and the position must be clearly understood from both the French and the Arab side from the outset, or we shall be heading straight for serious trouble." What was required was an agreement among all the Allies, and it did not seem impossible that some solution might be found which would at once preserve British interests and provide for Arab independence. There might, of course, be some cost; if necessary, Britain might have to resign Mesopotamia in order to insure French resignation of Syria. It was time that McMahon tell Husain: Britain is ready to discuss frontiers. Nicolson was less optimistic, for it was not so simple to discuss the conflicting clams of Ibn Sa'ud and other leaders; he now drafted a tele-

<hr />

[36] Clayton memorandum, 11 October 1915, *ibid.*; Maxwell telegram to Kitchener, 16 October 1915, *L/P&S/10*, 53/15, no. 3849/15; Tibawi, "Syria . . . ," pp. 19–23; Antonius, *op. cit.*, p. 169; Birdwood, *Nuri*, p. 33. Al-Faruqi was to stay on as Husain's Cairo representative—not the best man for the job as it happened, for he had a habit of reporting fictitious conversations to Husain: E. Kedourie, "Cairo and Khartoum on the Arab Question 1915–18," *Historical Journal*, 7:2 (1964), 289.

gram beginning "The questions raised will receive immediate consideration, but we shall have to consult the French. . ."[37]

The same afternoon (19 October) a private telegram from McMahon was received. Further conversations with Faruqi, McMahon reported, showed that immediate assurances were necessary if the Arabs were not to be lost to the Allied cause, and the Arabs would not accept less than a clear statement of support for independent Arab authority within the limits set by Husain and "in so far as England is free to act without detriment to the interests of her present Allies . . . ," meaning France. Although Britain would help in the establishment of a suitable form of government and provide the necessary advisors and officials "as may be necessary to ensure sound administration," the Arabian Peninsula itself would remain under its own chiefs. The Arabs would have to be assured possession of the "purely Arab districts of Aleppo Damascus Hama and Homs, whose occupation by the French they would oppose by force of arms," but Faruqi accepted the fact that British interests "necessitate special measures of British control in Basrah Vilayet."[38]

McMahon had pleaded urgency and did so again in another telegram of the 20th.[39] Grey therefore hastened to collect the basic approval of Kitchener and Chamberlain and then telegraphed to McMahon that evening. The outline proposed was approved, with the qualification that remarks on British guidance "should not be included unless it is necessary to secure

[37] McMahon telegram to Grey, 18 October, and Clerk and Nicolson minutes, 19 October 1915, *FO* 371/2486. Tibawi, "Syria . . . ," p. 23, notes that McMahon deliberately kept the text of the Sharif's letter back, but it is not clear precisely when the translation was in McMahon's hands.

[38] McMahon private (unnumbered) telegram to Grey, 18 October 1915 (received 1:10 P.M., 19 October), *FO* 371/2486. See also Emile Marmorstein, "A Note on 'Damascus, Homs, Hama and Aleppo,'" *Middle Eastern Affairs*, No. 2, ed. by A. Hourani (London, 1961), pp. 161–65, tracing the phrase, ultimately, to Mark Sykes.

[39] McMahon telegram to Grey, no. 627, 20 October 1915, *FO* 371/2486.

Arab consent, as this might give rise to impression in France that we were not only endeavouring to secure Arab interests, but to establish our own in Syria at expense of French." The reservations on the northwestern boundaries and Mesopotamia were essential, however; and "As regards Mesopotamia proposed sphere of British control, namely, Basra Vilayet, will need extension in view of special interests in Bagdad province and area actually in our occupation. Our treaties with Arab chiefs will of course stand." The most vital clause was that giving McMahon freedom of action: "But the important thing is to give our assurances that will prevent Arabs from being alienated, and I must leave you discretion in the matter as it is urgent and there is not time to discuss an exact formula."[40]

The only major modification of McMahon's draft, therefore, was that extending the Mesopotamian area and upholding the legitimacy of the Persian Gulf (and Aden) treaties, and this had been taken, word for word, from a note by Holderness. The India Office had given approval to the basic terms offered Husain, for Chamberlain (the Secretary) had been responsible for inserting the modification drafted by Holderness (the Permanent Under-Secretary).[41]

On 25 October, McMahon sent off the most important letter of the entire "Husain-McMahon correspondence," outlining the area in which Britain would give support for Arab independence, essentially as he had cabled the Foreign Office earlier and as Grey had approved. The territorial reservations were somewhat differently phrased, however: "The two districts of

[40] Grey's handwritten draft of telegram to McMahon (no. 796, dispatched 20 October), on which Grey's *Lord Kitchener. Will this do? E.G.* is followed by "Yes, I think it might start 'You can give warm assurances' K." Inserted between the pages of Grey's draft is a note dated 20 October from T. W. H. [Holderness] addressed to S/S [Chamberlain] and giving the text of the Mesopotamian clause. *Ibid.*

[41] It is not clear whether Hirtzel was consulted on this precise document; the evidence seems to indicate that he was not; a note he wrote for Holderness on the 26th showed that he saw no need for panic: Hirtzel note for Holderness and Holderness minute, 26 October 1915, L/P&S/10, 53/15, no. 3894/15.

Mersina and Alexandretta and portions of Syria lying to the west of the districts of Damascus, Homs, Hama and Aleppo cannot be said to be purely Arab, and should be excluded from the limits demanded." The second qualification read, "without prejudice to our existing treaties with Arab chiefs. . . ."

On Mesopotamia, McMahon's draft letter had said only, "With regard to the Vilayets of BAGHDAD and BASRA, the Arabs will recognize the vital economic interests of Great Britain and will guarantee to safeguard them." But on receipt of Grey's telegram of the 20th, he had amplified this clause to read, in the final version:

With regard to the Vilayets of BAGHDAD and BASRA, the Arabs will recognize that the established position and interests of Great Britain necessitate special measures of administrative control in order to secure these territories from foreign aggression, to promote the welfare of the local populations and to safeguard our mutual economic interests.[42]

The actual words were of McMahon's own choosing, and he made no further reference home after his telegram of the 20th. As Clayton remarked in one of his frequent private letters to Wingate, McMahon had come out of the whole business quite well,

. . . in taking the responsibility upon himself of replying to the Sherif without further reference. The F.O. telegram certainly gave

[42] The draft, with handwritten revisions, is in *FO* 882/19. The text: McMahon to Husain, 25 October, enclosed in McMahon to Grey, 26 October 1915, *FO* 371/2486. This letter may be found in Hurewitz, *op. cit.*, II, pp. 14–15; Antonius, *op. cit.*, pp. 419–20; and Great Britain, *Parliamentary Papers*, 1939, Misc. No. 3, Cmd. 5957: dated 24 October. The text given in these places, however, gives "special administrative arrangements" for "special measures of administrative control" as in McMahon's original letter to Grey. According to *Parl. Papers, op. cit.*, and Antonius, *op. cit.*, p. 420, n. 1, the former is closer to the original Arabic, but original copies of the Arabic texts sent to Husain are not available in the F.O., Egyptian, or Arab Bureau records; see, for the search for the Arabic original, *FO* 141/654, 710, and 825 and *FO* 371/5067.

him a free hand but, in their usual way, they left several openings for making a scapegoat in the event of necessity, and there is many a man who would have funked it, and referred his proposed reply for approval.[43]

The effect of McMahon's letter was dramatic. To Hirtzel, already hostile to the moderate de Bunsen committee conclusions, McMahon's pledges had gone far beyond, and were in fact incompatible with, these conclusions. British annexation of Basra had been a basic assumption throughout, and was a *sine qua non* of the Indian government. The only hope was that this would be covered by the reference to "special" administrative measures. Holderness and Chamberlain agreed, and within a day Chamberlain had spoken to Grey; but "the best comfort he could give me was that the whole thing was a castle in the air which would never materialize . . ."[44]

Hardinge, needless to say, was appalled—although it is interesting to speculate how much more so he would have been without Holderness's addition. While Hardinge realized, with regret, the urgency of the case, or so India telegraphed officially, McMahon had exercised his discretion "without due regard to Indian interests, by the inclusion of provinces of Bagdad and Bussorah in the proposed independent Arab state . . . ," since he had reserved only some special sort of administration there. India had always opposed such a state if it was to be outside the area of British control as "a not unlikely source of ultimate trouble . . ." It was not that the Viceroy opposed ties with the Arabs, if London felt that these would help win the war (by implication, Hardinge did not), but he most certainly opposed the grounds upon which they were based. "We have

[43] Clayton private to Wingate, 27 October 1915, *Wingate Papers* (Durham University Library, Oriental Section), box 135; copies of Clayton-Wingate correspondence are also in the smaller *Clayton Papers* collection in that library.

[44] Hirtzel, Holderness, and Chamberlain notes of 27 October on McMahon telegram to Grey of 26 October 1915 (outlining text of letter to Husain), *L/P&S/10*, 53/15, no. 3935/15.

always contemplated as a minimum eventual annexation of Bussorah vilayet," and, in addition, some form of native administration at Baghdad "under our close political control." Now McMahon's guarantees apparently put annexation out of the question, and out of simple justice to India the formula had to be changed. "By surrendering Bussorah vilayet to Arab Govt. of any kind, we shall not only be preparing trouble for ourselves at the head of and along southern littoral of the Gulf, but shall be giving up main fruits of hard won victories in Mesopotamia." [45]

McMahon, to whom Hardinge's objections were repeated, was quick to strike back. The Mesopotamian formula was deliberately designed to give Britain "everything short of definite and open annexation," but certainly a monopoly of administration. McMahon fully shared, he added gratuitously, in Hardinge's fears of a strong Arab state, but the elements for this as yet hardly existed. [46]

For Hirtzel this was not enough. McMahon, Kitchener, and the others all urged the vital necessity of Arab cooperation, but no one had as yet bothered to explain *why* it was so vital. Certainly it was better to have the Arabs for, rather than against, Britain, but this was hardly evidence for the supreme importance of the revolt. Aubrey Herbert, another of the Cairo school, had talked wildly in his memoranda of the danger of Indian Muslim sympathy for the Arabs, but as far as he, Hirtzel, knew the probability was in the opposite direction: Muslim hostility for revolt against the Caliph. Anyway, what could the Arabs do if they were hostile to Britain? There was not a single shred of evidence that the various Arab factions could combine. From Hirtzel's point of view, the explanation was simple: McMahon, as he had heard from private sources, was

[45] Viceroy telegram to SSI, 4 November 1915, *FO* 371/2486; and Hardinge private to Chamberlain, 5 November 1915, *Hardinge Papers.*
[46] McMahon telegrams to Grey, 5 and 7 November 1915, *FO* 371/2486.

being rushed by his military advisors and had thrown off all his "habitual prudence & sagacity." There was no question that the India Office would have to take an official position on this, and its letter of 6 November to the Foreign Office expressed most of the main lines of Hirtzel's criticism.[47]

Chamberlain, hard pressed by his own advisors, expressed himself even more forcefully. He circulated a strong memorandum on the negotiations with Husain, expressing his view that Grey had gone further than he, Chamberlain, had approved, and McMahon further than Grey had intended. McMahon's assurances would cause much disappointment in India —although, of course, Britain must abide by her promises—and Chamberlain had serious reservations about Husain; ". . . my information is that the Grand Shareef is a nonentity without power to carry out his proposals . . ." The Arabs had little chance of achieving unity and, in short, he disbelieved in the "reality and efficacy" of an Arab revolt. All that was left, however, was to attempt to safeguard the Mesopotamian position and interests "as far as is still possible after McMahon's pledges."[48] The Foreign Office gave little argument to all this, for both Nicolson and Grey agreed that the Arab movement was a dubious proposition; but as Nicolson pointed out Britain had had to respond to the overtures.[49]

Meanwhile, Hardinge, as a result of the letters to Husain and with Grant's support, was expressing his view in direct correspondence with McMahon. As he wrote on 9 November, he would not object to the inclusion of Baghdad in an Arab state if Britain retained some sort of political control. But Persian Gulf and oil interests made it vital that Basra's control be pre-

[47] Hirtzel minute on McMahon telegram of 5 November 1915, *L/ P&S/10*, 53/15, no. 4068/15; I.O. to F.O., 6 November 1915, *FO* 371/ 2486. On Herbert, see below, p. 104.

[48] Chamberlain memorandum, 8 November 1915, *FO* 371/2486; but see more moderate remarks in private to Hardinge, 5 and 10 November 1915, *Hardinge Papers*.

[49] Nicolson minute, 9 November 1915, *FO* 371/2486.

served absolutely, "and this can only be obtained by annexation," an attitude Hardinge had already expressed to London. "You may imagine, therefore, my surprise," he wrote McMahon, "when I read that you had given away this policy to the Arabs with absolutely nothing to show in return." India had been fighting both Turks and Arabs in Iraq and saw little justification for McMahon's actions.[50]

The letter was a strong one, but not as strong as Hardinge's private expressions to Nicolson. Nothing but trouble, he wrote on 15 November, would come from these "fatuous proceedings." There could not have been much difficulty in obtaining Arab approval of British Mesopotamia; but while McMahon was careful to get for France all that she wanted, he completely forgot India. Hardinge could be thankful for only one thing: he had had nothing to do with McMahon's appointment!

I devoutly hope that this proposed independent Arab State will fall to pieces, if it is ever created. Nobody could possibly have devised any scheme more detrimental to British interests in the Middle East than this. It simply means misgovernment, chaos and corruption, since there never can be and never has been any consistency or cohesion amongst the Arab tribes. Had it not been for opposition from India Cairo would months ago have appointed a new Khalif! I cannot tell you how detrimental I think the interference & influence of Cairo have been.

Excuse a good grumble on my part.[51]

Kitchener and Grey might have defended McMahon, but the influence of both was declining: Kitchener was soon to be sent off to Russia (and unfortunately killed on the way) and Grey to resign from ill-health. And even McMahon had doubts

[50] Hardinge private to McMahon, 9 November, *Hardinge Papers*; and private to Wingate, 25 November 1915, *Wingate Papers*, box 135. Grant's views: minute, 31 October, on McMahon telegram of 26 October 1915, *India Sec. War* March 1916, 195–265.

[51] Hardinge private to Nicolson, 15 November; see also same of 12 November and 9 December and Nicolson private to Hardinge, 11 and 16 November 1915: all *Nicolson Papers*, FO 800/378 and 380; and Hardinge private to Graham, 8 December 1915, *Hardinge Papers*.

about the Arab movement, doubts which go far to explain the
looseness of language he employed. He had done his best for
India in Mesopotamia, he replied to Hardinge—in any case the
probable future of the Arab areas was to be another Balkans,
but under one tutelary power.

> I find myself at the moment in the difficult position of having to
> give in great haste such assurances in respect to a nebulous state of
> affairs, both present and future, as would satisfy a somewhat neb-
> ulous community and prompt them into taking sides with us instead
> of the enemy. . . . This on our part is at present largely a matter of
> words and to succeed we must use persuasive terms and abstain
> from academic haggling over conditions—whether about Baghdad
> or elsewhere. . .[52]

It was not a satisfactory explanation, and Hardinge was relent-
less in his criticism of McMahon and his policy.[53] But very
shortly the Viceroy had something new to worry about, as did
all personnel involved in the Anglo-Arab negotiations: discussions with France.

4

In late October 1915, tentative Anglo-French discussions began. Some would have preferred to see the question of Baghdad, among others, settled before the conversations opened, but
Kitchener was anxious to consult France at once. The preliminary discussions went slowly, since France had not yet been
told of the Husain negotiations (Britain nevertheless had some
suspicion that the French were aware of them, if only in a general way).[54] For the formal meetings, France designated

[52] McMahon private to Hardinge, 4 December 1915, *ibid.*

[53] See letters to various individuals, *ibid.* Further discussion of the
Husain-McMahon correspondence may be found in Antonius, *op. cit.*,
pp. 157–58, Tibawi, "Syria . . . ," and Monroe, *op. cit.*, pp. 35–36. Tibawi
and Monroe are two of the few authors to recognize the great importance of the Indian role.

[54] McMahon telegram to Grey, 26 October, with Kitchener and Grey
notes; Nicolson note for Crewe (Lord President of the Council; Crewe

Georges Picot, French Counselor in London and formerly French representative in Beirut, with whom the respective British and French positions would have to be worked out.[55]

Before Picot arrived, Grey, even though he had India well in mind, told Paul Cambon, French Ambassador in London, that the British government was "naturally reluctant to let Busra and Bagdad be included in the boundaries of an Arab State," but that even this would be done if it meant dividing Arab from Turk. Cambon's reply was interesting and indicative of France's future attitude: France had no intention of yielding up Syria. Britain, said Cambon, would still dominate Mesopotamia even if she surrendered formal control, yet she asked France to give Syria to the Arabs, when France's connection with Syria was ancient and she "really regarded Syria as a dependency." There had, the Ambassador added, "been too much talk in Cairo," although he too was willing to grant the importance of dividing the Arabs and Turks.[56]

Obviously the negotiations were going to be difficult. On 13 November, an interdepartmental conference, including Nicolson, Clerk, Holderness, and Hirtzel, decided that when the meetings with Picot began he should be told of the Arab negotiations and of the dangers of the situation—but that all promises to the Arabs depended upon their giving "serious proof" of their separation from Turkey. Also, France should be willing to resign its immediate hopes of Damascus, "just as we were ready to give back Basra &c., if the Arabs came in." [57]

Mark Sykes now proved to occupy a key position. He was

---

usually acted for Grey in 1915–16 when the latter was away), on talks with Cambon, 30 October; Crewe and Grey minutes, 30 October and 2 November, on McMahon telegram of 26 October; Grey telegram to Bertie, 30 October; and, on French knowledge, McMahon telegram to Grey, 28 October 1915; *FO* 371/2486.

[55] F.O. to I.O., 9 November, Grey to Cambon, 17 November 1915, *ibid*.

[56] Grey to Bertie, 10 November 1915, *ibid*.

[57] Clerk minutes of conference, 13 November 1915, *ibid*.

fresh from India and Mesopotamia and was shown the Arab correspondence to date by Cheetham in Cairo in November and was therefore the only one with anything like a comprehensive picture at the moment. His answer to the puzzle of an agreement satisfactory to Arabs and French alike lay in Anglo-French recognition of a provisional wartime government or governments in the vilayets constituting Syria and the Hijaz, with further agreements on concessions and the like after the war. Sunnite-Shiite religious divisions made Mesopotamia incapable of self-government at this time, and it might be agreed that Britain would administer Baghdad and Basra on the Arabs' behalf, allocating certain sums to the local exchequer (a polite way of saying "subsidy"). When the time came for British evacuation, religious and financial problems would make the Sharif's government ready to allow Britain to stay. It was hardly a practical hope upon which to base a policy, although it showed that Sykes had absorbed something of the attitude of Mesopotamian officials on the problems of Iraqi administration. But, in the long run, "Indian and Arab civilisation and mentality are poles asunder, and I am of opinion that the introduction of Indian methods and Indian personnel should be merely temporary, and should form no part of our future scheme." What Britain wanted, Sykes concluded in his report to the War Office, was really an external protectorate over the Arabian littoral from Kuwait to Hudaida in the southern Red Sea, and an internal and external protectorate over part of Mesopotamia, with an area of French influence to the north.[58]

Sykes's advice had not arrived too soon, for on 23 November the negotiating committee met with the French in London and began with an attempt to obtain concessions leading toward independence in Syria. Picot was uncompromising and held out no hope at all; no French government, he said frankly, would

[58] McMahon (from Sykes) telegrams to Grey (for D.M.O.), 19 and 21 (two of date) November, and Sykes report to D.M.O., 15 November 1915, *ibid.*

stand a day if it yielded French claims here. To Major-General Sir C. E. Callwell, Director of Military Operations, present at the meetings as War Office representative (and the initial recipient of Sykes's advice), the French view was explained only by the fact that Picot knew that the Syrians much preferred British to French, and France would consequently find the going much easier if the area was treated as theirs from the very first.[59]

In further meetings, in December, Britain was forced to give way, and the lines of what was to be known as the Sykes-Picot Agreement were hammered out. There would be an Arab state or states, divided into administrative and commercial spheres of influence for Britain (zone "B") and France (zone "A"). Special reference was made to the areas of possible direct administration: Lebanon for France ("Blue" zone) and Mesopotamia for Britain ("Red" zone). Roughly, the lines of demarcation paralleled the modern Syria-Iraq frontier with the exceptions of Palestine and the Mosul vilayet, both of which fell initially into the French sphere. Palestine was a special problem. Although under the Ottomans Palestine was administratively part of Syria, it was clear that Jerusalem would require some sort of special status; in the final agreement, Palestine was made a "Brown" zone for a future international regime.[60]

The French had struck a hard bargain, for neither Picot (a "notorious fanatic" on Syria, said McMahon) nor Cambon was

[59] Callwell memorandum, 29 November, Clerk and Nicolson memoranda, 27 November 1915, *ibid.* Another file of documents on these discussions is at *FO* 608/93 (Paris Conference records).

[60] F.O. memorandum on 21 December 1915 meeting, *FO* 371/2486. The agreement may be found in Hurewitz, *op. cit.*, II, pp. 18-22. The discussions may be followed in Great Britain, Foreign Office, *Documents on British Foreign Policy, 1919-1939*, ed. Rohan Butler, J. P. T. Bury, and E. L. Woodward, First Series (London, 1947-67) [hereafter *DBFP*], IV, pp. 241-51 (introductory note to 1919-20 discussions quoting 1916 documents); Nevakivi, *Britain, France and the Arab Middle East*, ch. II; and Antonius, *op. cit.*, ch. XIII.

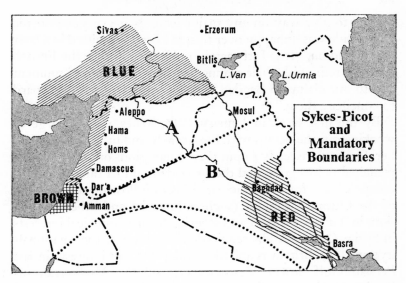

Sivas • •Erzerum

**BLUE**

Bitlis•
L. Van       L. Urmia

•Aleppo          Mosul

Hama          **A**

Homs

•Damascus          **B**

Dar'a          Baghdad

**BROWN**

•Amman          **RED**

Basra

**Sykes-Picot
and
Mandatory
Boundaries**

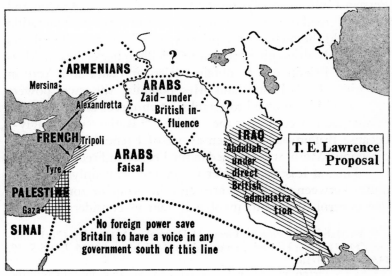

**ARMENIANS**          **?**

Mersina          **ARABS**
                 Zaid – under
Alexandretta     British in-
                 fluence          **?**

**FRENCH** Tripoli          **IRAQ**
                            Abdullah
Tyre          **ARABS**      under
              Faisal         direct
**PALESTINE**                British
Gaza•                        administra-
                             tion
**SINAI**

No foreign power save
Britain to have a voice in any
government south of this line

**T. E. Lawrence
Proposal**

willing to give way on any major issue. Not everyone on the British side was unhappy over this; as Hirtzel admitted in a later memorandum, "It is fortunately quite certain that the French will not relinquish their claims, or there wd. be an imminent risk to our claims to Bagdad & Basra being thrown overboard to conciliate them." [61]

By the first week in January 1916, Sykes, given charge of working out the details with the French, and his opposite number, Picot, were ready to put their conclusions on paper. Three principal points governed the agreement: (1) France required compensation for her anticipated losses following the breakup of the Ottoman Empire (such as financial and other concessions in Turkey proper) and security for her historical interests in Syria; (2) the Arabs required recognition of their nationality; and (3) Britain required security for her interests in the Persian Gulf, lower Mesopotamia, and the Mediterranean-Persian Gulf route. To meet these requirements, France and Britain agreed to recognize and protect an Arab confederation but would themselves have priority of influence in the spheres as outlined—although, in return for yielding her claims to Alexandretta, Britain was to obtain outlets at Haifa and Acre in Palestine. In Lebanon and Mesopotamia, the two powers ". . . should be allowed to establish such direct or indirect administration or control as they desire." [62] Rather surprisingly—because Britain had not been aware of French desires in this direction—Mosul was retained in the French indirect zone. This was done, at least as the War Office saw it, mainly to keep a buffer between the British area and the probable zone of Russian control. It was to involve Britain in considerable head-

[61] McMahon telegram to Grey, 11 December 1915, with Clerk minute, FO 371/2486; Hirtzel memorandum, 14 February 1916, L/P&S/10, 53/15, no. 540/16.

[62] Sykes memorandum, n.d. (received 5 January in F.O.); Capt. W. R. Hall (Intelligence Division, Admiralty) to Nicolson, 12 January 1916: FO 371/2767.

aches later; Hirtzel, at least, was immediately sensitive to the importance to Mesopotamia of this lost vilayet.[63]

Anglo-French agreement was not enough for Allied peace of mind. Russia too must be consulted; although Sazonov (Russian Foreign Minister, 1910-1916) had given blanket approval to the agreement without knowing of its details, it was considered necessary to dispatch Sykes and Picot to Russia in March.[64] By the 17th, Russia had given basic approval to the Anglo-French division of the Arab area, after some modification of the proposed frontier in Armenia. Detailed discussions continued into April, and by mid-May the final agreement had been initialed—with the interesting proviso, on Britain's part, that it would stand ". . . provided that the co-operation of the Arabs is secured, and that the Arabs fulfil the conditions and obtain the towns of Homs, Hama, Damascus, and Aleppo." [65]

The agreement was to be modified later in some important particulars, but its outlines remained a permanent feature of wartime and postwar Allied relations. Because the sense of urgency in Britain gave the French the upper hand, France had achieved a great deal. It has never been established whether Picot had at hand the details of the Husain-McMahon negotia-

[63] Brig.-Gen. G. M. W. Macdonogh to Nicolson, 6 January, and Holderness to Nicolson (mentioning Hirtzel's view), 13 January 1916, *ibid.* Surprise at French claims to Mosul: Holderness private to Hardinge, 25 November, and Hardinge private to Holderness, 29 December 1915, *Hardinge Papers.* See also Holderness, Hirtzel, and Barrow minutes of 15 and 16 March 1916, *L/P&S/10,* 53/15, no. 953/16, further criticisms expressed in minutes of conference, 21 January, Hirtzel note to Nicolson, 23 January, Sykes to Nicolson, 24 January, Nicolson note to Grey, 2 February 1916, *FO* 371/2767.

[64] Nicolson for Grey and Cabinet minute, 4 February, Buchanan telegrams to Grey, 10 and 19 February, Grey telegram to Buchanan, 23 February, Nicolson note for Grey, 16 February 1916, *ibid.*

[65] Grey to Cambon, 16 May 1916, *FO* 371/2768; circulated as *CAB* 37/147 and reprinted with the other official exchanges in *DBFP* and Hurewitz, *op. cit.;* the Russian negotiations may be followed in *FO* 371/2767–68.

tions, but certainly Sykes did; and it is clear that Britain considered it essential to work out the French settlement before completing the Arab negotiations. Thus the Sykes-Picot Agreement was contracted by Britain not only to avoid Anglo-French conflict over claims in the Ottoman Empire, but also to avoid a conflict between these inevitable discussions and those in progress with the Arabs. From this standpoint, it was necessary to delineate—and wherever possible reduce—French claims so that Britain could support an Arab state in the remaining territory.

It is also clear, finally, that although Britain worked in haste —too much haste, as was to become self-evident later—she had tried, if only tentatively and briefly, to urge France to drop her claims to Syria and, at least in Grey's mind, was herself prepared to sacrifice Mesopotamia to achieve the French denial. Since France refused—and it must be said that Syria to France was only a claim, while British occupation of much of Mesopotamia was a reality (for by mid-1916 a new advance was taking place)—the British objective had then been to limit rather than eliminate French claims. Unfortunately, to Britain's later cost, the requirement of a speedy settlement went far to offset the desire to limit France's sphere of interest.

Few diplomatic documents have suffered the odium heaped upon the Sykes-Picot treaty, from Arnold Wilson's "counter to every sound principle" or George Antonius's "shocking document . . . greed at its worst . . . a startling piece of double-dealing" to Lloyd George's "a fatuous arrangement judged from any and every point of view," but the intentions as well as the effects should be borne in mind when this agreement, born in an age of agreements, is considered.[66]

[66] Wilson, *Loyalties*, p. 153; Antonius, *op. cit.*, p. 248; Lloyd George, *War Memoirs*, IV, p. 86. See also Holt, *op. cit.*, p. 269, which makes the point that McMahon's negotiations also served to limit French claims; Monroe, *op. cit.*, pp. 32–33; A. P. Thornton, *The Imperial Idea and Its Enemies: A Study in British Power* (Garden City, N.Y., 1968), pp. 184–88; Zeine N. Zeine, *The Struggle for Arab Independence:*

5

The Anglo-French discussions were paralleled throughout by the continuing Cairo-Hijaz negotiations, each serving as counterpoint, with occasional dissonance, to the other. Sykes, the principal liaison officer, was preoccupied with the larger French contract and, at least while in Petrograd, cut off from developments in Cairo. London thus had for its edification only McMahon's reports (until McMahon was replaced by Wingate on the first day of 1917), which were not always as comprehensive as they might have been.

In mid-November 1915, the Sharif's answer to McMahon's 25 October letter was received. Husain proved reluctant to accept Britain's total outline of the future Arab territories: while Alexandretta might be excluded, Beirut and Aleppo were Arab and must be part of the new state. Mesopotamia, too, was Arab. Britain admittedly had special interests there and it might for the time being be left out of the discussions without prejudice to the claims of either party. In the meantime, Husain would require a subsidy for the Arab kingdom; implicitly, at least, this subsidy would be something like a rental fee for Britain's occupation of Iraq.[67] As Wingate, still an interested spectator, pointed out, it was a shrewd argument; Husain needed money, and this was a way for Britain to provide it. But future negotiations must be handled with great caution.

The agreement as to our retention of the Baghdad and Basra Vila-

---

*Western Diplomacy and the Rise and Fall of Faisal's Kingdom in Syria* (Beirut, 1960), pp. 198–99; and, for Edward Grey's view, Curzon to Lloyd George, 17 February 1919, enclosing Grey to Balfour, 9 September 1918, *Lloyd George Papers* (Beaverbrook Library, London), F/12/1/43, and Viscount Grey of Fallodon, *Twenty-Five Years, 1892–1916* (N.Y., 1925), II, pp. 236–37.

[67] McMahon telegrams to Grey, 14, 16, and 17 November, SSI telegram to Viceroy (repeating McMahon's information), 19 November 1915, *FO* 371/2486.

yets and the entire freedom of our administrative and commercial control therein, should be very specifically stated, but we should have an entirely free hand as to time-limit. If the Arab negotiators insist on a definition of the period of occupation, it would be quite reasonable for us to say that such period must necessarily depend on the measure of success which attends their efforts to make good their new State and give it a sound foundation on which we—as its guarantors—can rely, in order that the vital interests of India in these localities shall not suffer when we eventually hand over the districts in question to the Arab Government.[68]

Cairo and London agreed that the best approach to the Sharif on Mesopotamia was to point out that conditions did not now permit full consideration of this subject. McMahon's reply to Husain therefore made no mention of the "rent" for Mesopotamia, but according to McMahon's own account he hinted orally to the messenger who delivered his letter to the Sharif that the cash already provided (£20,000 had been sent off as an earnest of Britain's good intentions) showed that some such agreement might be worked out.[69]

If, as McMahon had written earlier, the entire exchange was largely verbiage, certainly this was even more true of a British position that the High Commissioner would not even commit to paper. The feeling persists after examination of the documents that British negotiators felt that nothing really mattered if the Arabs made no significant contribution to the war, and if the revolt actually came to pass—which many doubted—then there would be time enough to work out a more realistic settlement with which the Arabs would no doubt have to agree. Such a settlement would not include a powerful, united Arab state. Clayton in Cairo, an influential advisor to Wingate in these matters, made this quite clear in commenting on India's attitude:

[68] Wingate private to Clayton, 15 November 1915, *FO* 882/12.

[69] McMahon telegrams to Grey, 28 and 30 November, and letter, 14 December, and Grey telegram to McMahon, 10 December 1915, *FO* 371/2486.

It is curious how they cling to their fear of a strong united Arab state on the flank of the road to India. I should not have thought that anyone who knew anything about the Arabs or Arabia (as they wish to have it) would have ever dreamed of such a possibility. I have never personally felt that there would be a danger to our position in Mesopotamia for the very reasons which Lord H[ardinge] gives, viz: that the majority of the people there have no connection with the Sherif . . .

This was really a safeguard against a politically powerful Arab Caliphate, as opposed to a mere spiritual authority, for "an Englishman would naturally avoid producing such a 'Frankenstein.'" [70] On this, at least, Cairo and Delhi were in agreement —even to the image such a scheme brought to mind.

The Foreign Office, if Nicolson is any example, shared the general skepticism. "I said from the first that an independent Arab State was an absurdity and was an impracticable proposal," he wrote in mid-December 1915; and two months later, "I do not myself believe that they [the negotiations] will ever fructify into anything really definite." [71] The goal, and the urgency, was to forestall Arab-Turk cooperation, and this was a more realistic aim, for the achievement of which London had resigned the smaller details to McMahon. To the "western Arabians," [72] India's attitude was simply another hurdle to be overcome; as Sykes put it, "the best plan is to show it every consideration and carry on." [73]

But India too had goals and saw at once that Cairo's commitments would make fulfillment of its own objectives impossible. Moreover, the India Office, having only McMahon's letters by which to judge, feared that Cairo did indeed aim at the creation of a strong and unified Arab state. Hirtzel was sufficiently con-

[70] Clayton private to Wingate, 6 January 1916, *Wingate Papers*, box 136.

[71] Nicolson private to Hardinge, 16 December 1915 and 16 February 1916, *Nicolson Papers*, FO 800/380–81.

[72] The term is Elizabeth Monroe's, *op. cit.*, p. 36.

[73] Sykes private to Clayton, 28 December 1915, *FO 882/2*.

cerned about this to state his mind clearly, although only for internal India Office consumption, in late February:

A strong Arab State might be more dangerous to Christendom than a strong Ottoman State, & Lord Kitchener's policy of destroying one Islamic State merely for the purpose of creating another, has always seemed to me disastrous, from the point of view no less of expediency than of civilisation. The justification of the policy of H.M.G. lies mainly in the fact that the Arabs have shown themselves incapable of creating or maintaining such a State; &, inasmuch as it will be to the joint interests of France, Russia & ourselves to prevent them from doing so in fact—while enabling them to present a suitable facade to the world—the policy is probably also sufficiently free from practical danger. The danger of it, to my mind, lies in its disingenuousness.[74]

At the same time, Hardinge in India had begun to temper his remarks. Possessed of no new faith in the Sharif, he was at least willing to recognize, once the army in Mesopotamia had been checked at Ctesiphon, that if the revolt did take place the military participation of the Arabs might yet prove useful.[75] Thus India's opposition toward the Hijaz negotiations was not pressed more strenuously for several (admittedly contradictory) reasons: the possible utility of the revolt to the Mesopotamian campaign, the belief—shared nearly universally—that the revolt would come to nothing, and the preoccupation with Cairo's ultimate aims if the revolt succeeded.

Sharif Husain was a wily diplomat himself, and his replies to McMahon show that he and his advisors had reservations of their own about the future. In January 1916, he replied to McMahon that the area assigned to France, and Mesopotamia, could be left for later discussion—but he made it very clear that the Arabs would never acquiesce in French control of any or

---

[74] Hirtzel minute, 23 February, on *Arabian Report*, week ending 16 February 1916; also Holderness and Chamberlain minutes of 25 and 28 February: *L/P&S/10*, 705/16, no. 705/16.

[75] Hardinge private to Wingate, 28 November 1915, *Hardinge Papers*.

all of Syria once the war was over.[76] Husain may well have been much more alarmed about Syria than Mesopotamia, and in any case the British had already made some statements on the future Arab connection with the latter. Husain, like the British, was interested in getting on with the revolt and probably had a rather different vision of where the war's end would leave the Arab forces; hence his willingness to put off these issues. To all this, Grey could only minute, "The Arab question is a regular quicksand." [77]

While the desirability and extent of aid to Husain were being considered, other suggestions were being put forward for facilitating an Arab revolt. The fertile mind of Sykes continued active while he was in Russia. One telegram, for example, suggested that, considering the setback in Mesopotamia and the promise of the Hijaz revolt, Arab and Kurdish prisoners of war should be sent to Egypt for Clayton to use. A declaration should also be prepared in case of a Mesopotamian crisis stating that Britain intended only to maintain an administration in the Sharif's name until the Arab confederation was capable of good government and proved this in the areas assigned them in the Allied agreements ("A" and "B" zones). "Out of the question," Hirtzel flatly declared. "The whole thing is such a muddle of improbabilities and impossibilities that the less we say to anybody the better." As usual with Sykes's projects, the India Office was thinking as one. "It seems to me," said Chamberlain, "that the time has come for us to sit still & for someone else to move. This would be a very admirable change of roles between us & the Grand Sherif!" Even the War Office, while favoring the use of prisoners and recognizing the need for declaring Mesopotamian policy when Husain acted, objected to any intimation to the Iraqis that they were going to come under the

[76] McMahon telegram to Grey, 24 January, and Sharif to McMahon, 1 January 1916, FO 371/2767. Sharif's letter in Hurewitz, op. cit., II, pp. 15–16.

[77] Grey minute on McMahon telegram, ibid.

Sharif's jurisdiction.[78] All this was academic, really, for, with Townshend locked up in Kut amid seriously deteriorating conditions, it was hardly the time for statements on the future government of Baghdad.

McMahon also had a suggestion. The Sharif was close to action, but future unity of the Arabs was going to be difficult. To set the stage in Iraq, therefore, it might be useful to send al-Misri and al-Faruqi to make contact with their secret-society brethren there. The Foreign Office approved the plan. Although Hirtzel complained that by dealing separately with other factions Britain might be making it more difficult for the Sharif and laying herself open to the charge of undermining him (to which Holderness replied that the position would be even more difficult if Britain were forced to deal with other factions only through Husain), the scheme was passed to India labeled as already approved by the home authorities.[79]

The India Office protested that Grey had failed to consult it and predicted, correctly, that India would be hostile. As Lieutenant-General Sir Percy Lake, newly arrived in Mesopotamia to replace the discredited Nixon, explained, the agents could hardly pass through the lines to Turkish-held territory, and even if they could, of what use would they be? "From the political standpoint it appears to us that their political views and schemes are much too advanced to be safe pabula for the communities of occupied territories and their presence in any of the towns of Irak would be in our opinion undesirable and inconvenient." If they could reach Turkish-held territory by another route, well and good—but as Lake knew very well,

[78] Buchanan (Petrograd) telegram (from Sykes) to Grey, 13 March 1916, with Hirtzel and Chamberlain minutes, L/P&S/10, 53/15, no. 988/16; and FO 371/2767 (where Oliphant minuted, "I cannot conceal my skepticism as to the success of this scheme . . ."); W.O. (M.I.2) to F.O., 16 March 1916, and minute, ibid.

[79] McMahon telegram to Grey, 21 March, and Grey telegram to McMahon, 22 March 1916, ibid.; Hirtzel and Holderness (24 March) and Chamberlain (27 March) minutes, L/P&S/10, 53/15, no. 1076b/16.

there was hardly an alternative except via Turkish-held Arabia or the Turkish lines in Egypt.[80]

McMahon had no choice but to stop the al-Misri mission. He recognized, he told Grey, the force of Lake's reasoning, but al-Misri's new confidence, resulting from the Sharifal negotiations, would be increased if he could be given a practical job to do in Iraq. The negative decision would give rise to rumors of British distrust of Iraqi Arabs' loyalty, ".... or to our unwillingness, if not inability, to carry out our assurances ..." and might adversely affect Husain as well. Actually, McMahon had not intended that al-Misri should pass to the Turkish side to stir revolt but had rather imagined that his presence behind British lines would prove to the Arab element in the Turkish Army (it was not clear how) that Britain was working in good faith. This would also improve relations with the local Arabs in British-held territory.[81]

The India Office, of course, challenged McMahon's views. Of what use would al-Misri and al-Faruqi be if they did not pass across the lines? Anyway, as Chamberlain told Grey, the India Office was unaware of any significant influence possessed by either man in Iraq; so what were they supposed to achieve? More importantly, McMahon had damned himself. He predicted an end to the patience of those among whom Britain had raised such high expectations, but who, if not McMahon himself, had raised them? Britain had by now given money and

[80] SSI telegram to Viceroy, 24 March, I.O. to F.O., 28 March 1916, FO 371/2768; Viceroy telegram to SSI, 30 March 1916, with minutes, L/P&S/10, 53/15, no. 1181/16; Lake telegram to SSI, 30 March, enclosed in I.O. to F.O., 31 March, and Viceroy telegram to SSI, 31 March 1916, FO 371/2768. See also John Presland [Mrs. Gladys Skelton], Deedes Bey: A Study of Sir Wyndham Deedes, 1883–1923 (London, 1942), pp. 251–54, and Kedourie, England and the Middle East, pp. 109–10 (essentially repeating Presland).

[81] McMahon telegram to Grey, 1 April 1916, FO 371/2768; Dirmilint (Director of Military Intelligence, W.O.) telegram to Intrusive (Clayton), 18 April, and Intrusive telegram to Dirmilint, 20 April 1916, FO 141/736.

arms and promised more; the Sharif had done nothing; and now McMahon was saying ". . . that it is we who fail to fulfil the expectations we have raised!" McMahon must be made to realize that there were two sides to every bargain, and that Britain was as important to the Sharif as he to Britain. "I am very uneasy," Chamberlain concluded, "about the whole handling of the question, by Egypt." Faced with this strong and rather justified criticism, Grey could only repeat its main points to McMahon.[82]

Grey had other more crucial problems to worry about during these months of spring 1916, for he was aware of the growing disparity between what was being said to Husain and what was being said to the French. If he had any doubts on this score, the India Office removed them. On 14 February, Hirtzel minuted that he questioned even the possibility of continuing the Allied negotiations without informing the French and Russians of what Husain had said, evidence that he, at least (and he was a member of the interdepartmental committee on French negotiations), was under the impression that France had not been told. "Altogether," he added, "these negotiations rest on a very insecure basis, & if we are not very careful we shall lay ourselves open to charges of bad faith from all parties"—a prophetic remark.[83]

Holderness agreed; the impossibility of satisfying both Arab and French demands should be pointed out to the Foreign Office at the very next meeting. Even Chamberlain shared this view, "& I would add that Sir H. McMahon's 'gush' seems to me to lower British prestige & to be of a character to confirm the Grand Sherif in his impression that he is more important to us than we are to him." [84] In its letter of 28 February to the

---

[82] Chamberlain memorandum for Grey, 3 April, Grey telegram to McMahon, 5 April 1916, *FO* 371/2768.

[83] Hirtzel minute, 14 February, on McMahon telegram to Grey, 24 January 1916, *L/P&S/10*, 53/15, no. 540/16.

[84] Holderness and Chamberlain minutes, 17 February 1916, *ibid.*

Foreign Office, the India Office asked that France be told that the Arabs would be unlikely to accept the sort of administration that would satisfy French aspirations. The request was made, Hirtzel minuted, so that when Britain got what it wanted while the French had trouble later, "we may not be under the suspicion of having instigated it"—a suspicion which Britain was to get in full measure in any case.[85] The French at least were told, by March, that after the war Husain planned to ask restitution to the Arabs of any areas assigned to France on the coast and in Beirut—to which Cambon replied, ". . . the Sherif would not be an Arab if he did not say something of that kind." [86]

Husain had not been given the full list of French desiderata either. Until early 1916 there was still some hope of reducing French claims, but by February it was certainly clear that France would not give way. Some further indication to the Sharif of the area to be under French control and influence might have been advisable—not to facilitate the Arab revolt, for it would more probably have had the opposite effect, but to avoid later, very damaging repercussions. Also by February, McMahon had received clear indications of Husain's utter unwillingness to treat directly with the French on Syria.[87] But apparently there was no one in a position to urge, with success, frank admissions to Husain; certainly the India Office was far more concerned with inter-Allied relations than with the Sharif, whom they distrusted as much as they distrusted those in Cairo who made plans for him.

By the first of March McMahon had received another communication from Mecca: the Sharif was willing to act now and asked £50,000 and arms and ammunition. McMahon, like

[85] I.O. to F.O., 28 February 1916, and Hirtzel minute, *ibid.*

[86] Nicolson note to Grey, 2 March 1916, *FO* 371/2767.

[87] And of a hint that Husain wished to assume the Caliphate—for Husain, too, had more than one ambition. McMahon to Grey, 7 February 1916, *ibid.*

Kitchener, urged that these requests be granted.[88] He was convinced that the Sharif would act in late April or May and was concerned that nothing be said or done to interfere with the revolt he had so carefully nurtured. A precise danger lay in premature revelation to the Sharif of the detailed plans for the future of the Middle East (of which McMahon was still unaware);[89] the longer a final Arab commitment was delayed, the more chance that Arabs and Turks would come to some sort of understanding. The Arab Bureau in Cairo, a new institution now largely responsible for intelligence on Arab affairs and, so far as anyone could be said to be, for coordination of Middle Eastern policy, tended to support McMahon's position. After all, a Bureau memorandum pointed out, Husain had not yet indicated any agreement to the territorial terms McMahon had outlined, while Britain had neither promised to recognize Husain as the only Arab chief nor set any definite terms for holding Iraq—and any one of these terms could give rise to difficulties.[90]

To Sykes, however, fresh from his Russian negotiations, the main problem was still France, and he pressed for a meeting of some Arab Bureau official with Picot to spell out the details of mutual relations with the Arabs.[91] It was an unpalatable suggestion. Nicolson in the Foreign Office—whose faith had never been McMahon's—saw little point in such discussions until the Arabs actually revolted. Clayton in Egypt also balked on the ground that raising issues of Arab-French relations, and particularly Syria, might well divert the course of the rising. Clay-

[88] McMahon telegram to Grey, 1 March, and Kitchener to Nicolson, 4 March 1916, *ibid.*

[89] McMahon private to Grey, 16 April 1916: "I am yet in the dark as to the mission of Mark Sykes and Picot to Petrograd, and I know nothing of what their mission was, what they have done, or with what authority." *Grey Papers, FO* 800/48.

[90] McMahon telegram to Grey, 12 April, and letter of 19 April 1916 (enclosing undated memorandum), *FO* 371/2768.

[91] Clerk minute, 3 May 1916 (explaining Sykes's view), on McMahon letter, *ibid.*

ton was willing, however, to have Sykes come to Egypt to be told the Egyptian view and to explain the details of the Anglo-French-Russian negotiations. His indication of unfamiliarity with these negotiations resulted in his being cabled the essential outline of that agreement on 27 April, including French "absolute freedom to annex or exercise control" in Lebanon. These details only confirmed the opinion already held by both Clayton and McMahon: it was best not to tell the Arabs at present—they might misinterpret(!) the meaning; they could be told later with much less risk.[92]

And so the position remained. France was not officially given the details of the Sharifal negotiations, and the Sharif was not given the details of the Sykes-Picot Agreement, although it is fairly clear that both parties had a good inkling of the opposite negotiations. From both sides, however, no real problem would arise until one final ingredient was added—and that was introduced in June 1916, when Husain, Sharif of Mecca, raised the standard of revolt against the Ottoman Empire.

## 6

The Arab revolt brought a new element into Middle Eastern politics; for with the entrance of Husain and his forces into the war in a meaningful way (in the political sense at least), it was clear that not only the problem of definitions and fulfillment of promises made, but also the need for coordination of British Arab and Middle Eastern policies could no longer be postponed. The latter requirement had been obvious for some time —above all to Sir Mark Sykes, to whom the contradictions of London and Paris and Cairo and Delhi were more painfully clear than to any other individual. In October 1915, while in the Middle East collecting the views of these various policy-

[92] McMahon telegram (from Clayton) to Grey (for Sykes), 20 April, McMahon telegrams to Grey, 22 April and 4 and 30 May, Nicolson minute, 24 April, Grey telegrams to McMahon, 27 April and 6 and 29 May 1916, *ibid.*

making centers, Sykes had suggested that some sort of special bureau be established with the task of coordination specifically assigned to it, and that Cairo would be the best location. Nicolson in the Foreign Office saw the utility of this suggestion, but once more the India Office and India had to be asked their opinions.[93] In this way, one more issue was raised which could be—and was—used as a vehicle for expressing the conflicting views already so obvious in discussions of Mesopotamian and Sharifal policies.

The bureau, the plan specified, would be under Sykes himself, responsible to the High Commissioner in Egypt and through him to the Foreign Office, and would deal only with Muslims outside India. The India Office was further told that the bureau would deal with Mesopotamia only through the political officers under the control of the Indian authorities there in questions such as propaganda, and it would throughout correspond directly with the Secretary of the Foreign Department in India.[94] It was India's reaction that mattered, and this was not so much against the bureau as against Sykes himself. As Grant wrote, ". . . we were not favourably impressed in India with his attitude generally towards the Indian Administration, or with the practicality of his schemes" when he was in India. Lake, Chief of Staff, agreed: Sykes's reports ". . . are so visionary and strategically unpractical that we should not have recommended him for the work." Hardinge could not quite put this forward as an official opinion, however, so India simply urged the need of tight control of any liaison officers, policy toward such questions as the Caliphate, and so on.[95]

[93] Sykes to D.M.O., 9 October 1915, with Nicolson minute, *FO 371/2491*; formal proposal made in Sykes memorandum, 23 December 1915, I.O. copy in *L/P&S/10*, 4744/15, no. 4744/15; Sykes private to R. Cecil, 4 October 1915, *Sykes Papers* (Oxford).

[94] SSI telegram to Viceroy, 10 December, and Hirtzel private to Grant, 31 December 1915, *India Sec. War* March 1916, 195–265.

[95] Grant and Lake minutes, 14 and 20 December 1915, *ibid.*; Viceroy telegram to SSI, 24 December 1915, *L/P&S/10*, 4744/15, no. 4744/15.

The plan had been received with mixed feelings in London as well. At a meeting on 7 January 1916 of Hirtzel, Lancelot Oliphant (Foreign Office, at that time mainly concerned with Persian questions), General Macdonogh (War Office, Intelligence), Sykes, Hankey, and Admiral Hall (Naval Intelligence), it was decided to approve the bureau, but as a part of military intelligence in Cairo and not as a separate institution. War Office, Foreign Office, and India Office for once were in agreement. Most important of all was the reconstruction: "Mark Sykes drops out," Hirtzel wrote—no doubt with relief —to Grant. Further relief was provided by Chamberlain after talking to Sykes; it was not intended, the Secretary wrote Hardinge, to impose upon India in creating this bureau, and Sykes had also agreed that interference with the Caliphate was undesirable.[96]

The basic plan remained. McMahon considered the institution important to avoid jurisdictional disputes and erroneous impressions of policy decisions made by such free-lance operatives as Sykes himself. He wanted it made clear that the bureau would serve to process and filter various schemes; already he feared opposition to the bureau from those who mistakenly regarded Sykes's schemes as his own.[97] There was the further problem—which McMahon did not mention and which is only surmise—that McMahon, somewhat sensitive to the criticism against him, might have feared that the bureau, connected as it was with Intelligence, would be more under Wingate's control than his own; he was shortly to be involved in a controversy with the Sirdar on just this sort of matter. In February the interdepartmental group drew up general instructions for the bureau's operations; McMahon was told to work out the details

---

[96] Minutes and report of meeting, 10 January 1916, *ibid.*; Hirtzel private to Grant, 7 January 1916, *India Sec. War* March 1916, 195–265; Chamberlain private to Hardinge, 18 January 1916, *Hardinge Papers.*
[97] McMahon private to Grey, 25 January, and Hankey note to F.O., 7 February 1916, *FO* 371/2771.

in cooperation with Clayton and that all reports from the bureau were to go to the Foreign Office (an order which leads to the conclusion that there may have been some conflict over which London department was to have final authority for this bureau).[98]

Hardinge in India, now that Sykes was out of the picture, was meanwhile more concerned to obtain a definite commitment that his political officers in Mesopotamia would not have to work at the direction of the bureau, and this was agreed. As Hardinge explained to Nicolson, in the first real indication London apparently received of Delhi's underlying attitude, Indian officials had primarily opposed the composition of the bureau, ". . . for we have no confidence in Mark Sykes . . . ," but now that the bureau would be under Clayton things would be different and India would delegate a good officer to Cairo as its representative. Lake, in command in Iraq, would cooperate fully, Hardinge reported[99]—although even as he was reporting this view some awkwardness was arising in Mesopotamia involving two men closely associated with the work of the Arab Bureau: T. E. Lawrence and Aubrey Herbert.

Early in April 1916, the two men arrived in Mesopotamia with the mission of bribing the commander of the Turkish forces besieging Kut, which was now close to surrender. The mission was at first unknown to the Indian authorities, for it was given out that Lawrence and Herbert were to obtain intelligence, particularly for the compilation of maps in Cairo. As it turned out, Lake approved the attempt, but a number of generals, and Sir Percy Cox, objected—Cox going so far as to have nothing to do with it. Khalil Pasha, the Turkish commander, refused £1 million, then £2 million—fortunately, in a way, for

[98] Grey telegram to McMahon, 17 February, and D.M.I., Cairo, to F.O., 14 January 1916, *ibid.*

[99] Viceroy telegram to SSI, 15 February, and SSI telegram to Viceroy, 2 March 1916, *ibid.*; Hardinge private to Nicolson, 18 February 1916, *Nicolson Papers*, FO 800/381; Viceroy telegram to SSI, 9 April 1916, FO 371/2771.

the sum was not then available in Mesopotamia and it was not clear who was to pay it or to what uses it would be put if handed over (for example, to buy military supplies to be used against Britain?). Khalil, nephew of the powerful Enver Pasha, hardly needed the cash and would have found it most embarrassing if the facts had escaped, as they were sure to do—unless, of course, the bribe was made public, which would have drawbacks as well.[100] It was, all in all, a desperate effort with no chance of success. Although all news of the attempt was stifled in Allied areas, the Turkish propaganda apparatus made considerable capital out of the methods of the "nation of shopkeepers." Lawrence and Herbert, in the end, were able to obtain only the release of some sick and wounded prisoners in return for healthy Turks in British hands—but on 29 April over 13,000 British and Indian officers and men became Turkish prisoners.[101]

Even more unfortunate than the bribery attempt was the inevitable exchange of impression and counterimpression of the

[100] For a hostile view of Khalil, see Rafael de Nogales, *Four Years Beneath the Crescent* (N.Y., 1926), pp. 23–24, 104-7, an interesting account by a soldier of fortune.

[101] Account based on Graves, *Cox*, pp. 199–203; Presland, *op. cit.*, pp. 250–52; Robert Graves and B. H. Liddell Hart, eds., *T. E. Lawrence to His Biographers* (Garden City, N.Y., 1963), pp. 82–83, and part II, 61–62; B. H. Liddell Hart, *"T. E. Lawrence" in Arabia and After* (London, 1935), pp. 99–101; Charles Edmonds, *T. E. Lawrence* (London, 1935), pp. 35–37; Wilson, *Loyalties*, pp. 97–99, 154–55; Robert Graves, *Lawrence and the Arabs* (London, 1927), pp. 85–88; Sir Ronald Wingate, *Not in the Limelight* (London, 1959), p. 62; Lady Wester Wemyss, *The Life and Letters of Lord Wester Wemyss, G.C.B., C.M.G., M.V.O., Admiral of the Fleet* (London, 1935), p. 298; Suleiman Mousa, *T. E. Lawrence: An Arab View* (London, 1966), p. 10; Richard Aldington, *Lawrence of Arabia: A Biographical Enquiry* (Chicago, 1955), pp. 149–51; "An M.P." [Aubrey Herbert], *Mons, Anzac and Kut* (London, 1919), pp. 226–35; David Garnett, ed., *The Letters of T. E. Lawrence* (N.Y., 1939), pp. 202–10; Phillip Knightley and Colin Simpson, *The Secret Lives of Lawrence of Arabia* (London, 1969), ch. 4; Young, *op. cit.*, pp. 72–73; Lt.-Col. W. F. Stirling, *Safety Last* (London, 1953), pp. 67–68. See also Summary No. 2, Arab Bureau, 12 June 1916, *FO* 371/2771.

Cairo representatives and the Mesopotamian officers. Lawrence's contempt for Mesopotamian military methods was made painfully clear, and his supplementary intention, which he later described as assessing the possibility of cooperation "on national lines" of Arabs and English, he found an impossible task. Cox and "T. E." so thoroughly misunderstood each other that their positions later had to be clarified by telegraph.[102] It was fortunate, in fact, that Aubrey Herbert had accompanied Lawrence, for he made a much better impression in Iraq. A man of many qualities—"half-poet, half-politician, and as pro-Turkish at heart as Mark Sykes was the reverse," said Arnold Wilson—Herbert had managed, despite extremely weak eyesight, to make a fascinating career as Oriental traveler and linguist and, since 1911, M.P. He had, among other things, served in the Guards at Mons and was the principal model for one of John Buchan's Imperial heroes, Sandy Arbuthnot. In Iraq, Herbert was unwell (he was to succumb to blindness and death in 1923). While his ease in relations with his fellow man and his fund of good humor made him a number of friends, he, like Lawrence, was appalled by Mesopotamian conditions, and he found himself smuggling information past the rigorous Indian censorship, if Vice-Admiral Sir Rosslyn Wemyss (later Lord Wester Wemyss), Commander-in-Chief, East Indies Station, who accompanied Herbert and Lawrence to Mesopotamia, is to be believed.[103]

The whole affair was unfortunate from first to last and, like

[102] Graves, *Cox*, pp. 200–4; see Lawrence telegram to Intrusive ("There is no Arab sentiment and for us the place is negligible."), 9 April 1916, *FO* 141/161.

[103] Wemyss, *op. cit.*, p. 298. On Herbert, see Wilson, *Loyalties*, p. 154 (quoted); Janet Adam Smith, *John Buchan: A Biography* (London, 1965), pp. 206–7; John Buchan, *Mountain Meadow* (Boston, 1941), p. vii (intro. by Howard Swiggett); Herbert, *op. cit.*, and *Ben Kendim: A Record of Eastern Travel* (2nd ed., N.Y., 1925); John Marlowe, *Late Victorian: The Life of Sir Arnold Talbot Wilson, K.C.I.E., C.S.I., C.M.G., D.S.O., M.P.* (London, 1967), p. 110.

Sykes's earlier visit to India and Iraq, did little to endear the Arab Bureau or its representatives to the Indian or Mesopotamian authorities. It was fortunate that Ronald Storrs, similarly engaged on Bureau work, arrived in June and was able to make some repairs in relations while on his way to an abortive mission to Ibn Sa'ud.[104] Storrs, like Herbert, was better than Lawrence at concealing his emotions.

The Arab Bureau was only beginning; and while its relations with Mesopotamia were to handicap it from the outset, the organization nevertheless began to take shape in Cairo. McMahon was nominally responsible, and Clayton, as Director of Intelligence, was ex officio its director. For practical purposes, however, the first director was Lieutenant-Commander D. G. Hogarth (the naval rank was honorary), another from Britain's rich fund of experienced orientalists. Hogarth collected the staff and papers and library of "Arbur," as the Bureau was known, in three rooms in Cairo's Savoy Hotel, and went to work with considerable energy. Cornwallis of the Sudan, Deedes Bey of the Turkish gendarmerie, A. B. fforde from India, and P. and R. W. Graves formed the nucleus, later supplemented by Lawrence and others. Soon Arbur was taking on the tasks previously done by Military Intelligence, which could now revert to its proper functions for the military campaign being waged by Egypt.[105]

Hogarth supervised the various publications of the Bureau and in so doing was careful to bear in mind the problems that had surrounded Arbur's birth. He wrote to McMahon:

I have so drafted the report [Arab Report No. 2] as to meet Indian objections, so far as I understand these, i.e., I have tried to show that the Bureau has not acted as a "mouthpiece of H.M.G.'s pol-

---

[104] Wilson, *Loyalties*, pp. 304–5.

[105] Hogarth first report, 1 May, McMahon to Grey, 10 May, F.O. to McMahon, 13 July 1916, *FO* 371/2771. The Bureau's costs, incidentally, were in the neighborhood of £4,000 per annum.

icy," but has confined its energies to collecting & distributing Arab Intelligence, & giving advice on Arab matters.[106]

Wingate, to whom this information was forwarded, appreciated the Indian view, but too much of such caution could be risky. ". . . I earnestly trust that those responsible at home for deciding on the policy to be adopted will not be seriously disturbed by Indian alarms," he wrote Hogarth, for if the revolt failed, the repercussions would be worst in India. But Wingate, like McMahon, had other interests; he was currently writing Sir William Robertson, the new Chief of the Imperial General Staff, on the advantages to be gained by controlling British relations with the revolt from Khartoum.[107]

The last word had not been heard from the other side of the Arabian Peninsula. In April, Hirtzel, worried lest Lake misinterpret earlier assurances on the political officers' independence from the Bureau, had defined the Bureau's function as ". . . the central organ through which His Majesty's Government will lay down principles and policy in respect of Arab propaganda in the East, and . . . the General Staff in Mesopotamia must therefore work in strict conformity with the indications received from the Bureau." Lake now cabled that it would be far better if special officers arriving in Mesopotamia would automatically come under Cox's authority upon arrival; this would avoid confusion and coordinate whatever efforts had to be made. London was eager to get the Bureau off to a good start and quickly agreed. Cox, moreover, would still bear responsibility for central Arabia and the Gulf. So far, so good, and Sykes was sufficiently encouraged to minute on Lake's remark that Lawrence's visit had left a different impression of the Arab

---

[106] Hogarth private to McMahon, 28 June 1916, *FO* 141/738.

[107] Wingate private to Hogarth, 5 July, and to Robertson, 9 July; Robertson private to Wingate, 11 July and 8 August 1916: *Wingate Papers,* boxes 138–39. On Wingate's wartime activities, see Sir Ronald Wingate, *Wingate of the Sudan: The Life and Times of General Sir Reginald Wingate, Maker of the Anglo-Egyptian Sudan* (London, 1955), chs. VI–VIII.

Bureau than that previously held in Mesopotamia and that Mesopotamia and Cairo now "understand one another better." It was true, but not quite in the sense meant by Sykes.[108]

India was told that the Iraqi branch of the Bureau would operate as a section of Lake's own intelligence for purposes of distributing Cairo's propaganda. If the "policy and principles" to which London had referred meant only propaganda, countered Lake, well and good; but if this meant larger policy, then the matter would have to undergo further discussion, for Cairo's view and Iraq's view were not necessarily the same. Every attempt so far made to handle Iraq's affairs from Cairo had proved most unfortunate: McMahon's pledges, the al-Misri-al-Faruqi visit, the Lawrence mission, proposed overtures to Talib, and so on. Lake and Cox could hardly be asked, therefore, to accept a situation in which decisions would be taken on Mesopotamia without consulting them—and that via Cairo.[109]

Obviously, some clarification was required. On 14 June, Chamberlain cabled India that "policy and principles" meant policy toward Arabs in general; Lake would decide, after consultation with India, to what extent he would use the materials provided by Cairo. The Bureau, moreover, was meant simply to be an informing agency; the *policy* would be decided in London and naturally India would be consulted before a decision was taken on any relevant subject. It was indeed the differences between Cairo and Iraq that required closer cooperation and coordination for policy to be effective, and this was the purpose of the change. "Given loyal co-operation in all quarters, on which they confidently rely . . . ," London thought the plan would work, and the conference of Iraqi and Egyp-

---

[108] Hirtzel minute, 11 April, I.O. to F.O., 12 April 1916, *L/P&S/10*, 4744/15, no. 1342/16; Lake telegram to Viceroy, 8 May, SSI telegram to Viceroy, 27 May, Viceroy telegram to SSI, 28 May 1916, with Sykes minute, *FO 371/2771*. The Viceroy's telegram of 28 May suggested that Gertrude Bell be the Bureau's corresponding member in Iraq.

[109] Grey telegram to McMahon, 2 June, and Lake telegram to FSI, 11 June 1916, *ibid.*

tian officers which India had suggested, and which would be most difficult to arrange, would not be necessary.[110] India, and Lord Chelmsford—who had replaced Hardinge as Viceroy in the spring of 1916—still balked. Better, the Viceroy cabled, if the Bureau did propaganda only, for as the mouthpiece of British policy, it was difficult to tell at that distance the authority behind any of the Bureau's communications.[111]

The position was exasperating. "This telegram is only one of the usual kind," wrote an agonized Sykes; "for similar telegrams see any in which there is any question of common policy . . ." But now Hardinge had, in an unprecedented step, resumed the post he had left in 1910 to become Viceroy: Permanent Under-Secretary in the Foreign Office. "As experience has shown," Hardinge minuted, the Government of India was right in reserving liberty of action. Hardinge's new position was a most unfortunate one from Sykes's view, for the ex-Viceroy was fresh from hostile India and was not a man to rush at fences in any case. In the end, India was simply told once more that Lake would have freedom to judge the applicability to local conditions of Bureau propaganda, and any major decisions would come via the India Office from London.[112]

The limitation of Arbur's functions to propaganda only, as far as Iraq was concerned, did little to facilitate coordinated control of Middle Eastern policy—rather the contrary, for Arbur was now one more center for the production of plans and schemes for the future of the area. Many individuals, par-

[110] SSI telegram to Viceroy, 14 June 1916, *ibid.* Compare Storrs's later remark (Storrs, *op. cit.*, p. 210): "I have no doubt whatever that if the officers behind the Arab Campaign in the Hejaz had been allowed to exchange awhile with, or even to meet their colleagues from the Persian Gulf, well before instead of long after the Arab Revolution, they could have effected an intense concentration of purpose and a sure economy of many thousands of pounds."
[111] Viceroy telegram to SSI, 20 June 1916, *FO* 371/2771, and, with Hirtzel minute, *L/P&S/10*, 4755/15, no. 2379/16.
[112] Sykes and Hardinge minutes on Viceroy telegram of 20 June, and SSI telegram to Viceroy, 28 June 1916, *FO* 371/2771.

ticularly in London and Cairo, fully appreciated the need for some central control. Gertrude Bell, soon to play an influential role herself in Mesopotamia, concluded that one head in London should be responsible (her own choice was Hardinge, or so at least she wrote to him)[113] for something like a department within the Foreign Office. Sykes, too, had a separate department in mind, but, with his "Eastern Bureau" now a considerably watered-down "Arabian Bureau," it seemed that even his fertile mind was at a loss as to how to proceed.[114] Even from the purely military standpoint, India stood as an obstacle to every plan—for Robertson's demand for War Office control of all Imperial forces was rejected on the ground that India alone could deal with Indian internal problems.[115]

Sharifal policy, Mesopotamian policy, coordination of policy —all had provided considerable difficulty for those responsible for formulation and implementation. There can be no question that the persistent defense by India (and her officers in Iraq) of what was righteously conceived to be her own best interests —including those involving Arabs—was one of the obstacles, and perhaps the most important one, to London and Cairo's desires in all three areas. That India was only a part of the Empire, and her activities only a part of the over-all war effort, was a vital consideration which, seen from London or Cairo, was often lost sight of in Delhi or Basra. From this awkward situation there might have been no escape but for two events: disaster in Mesopotamia and success in the Hijaz.

[113] Bell private to Hardinge, 9 April 1916, *Hardinge Papers*.

[114] Sykes private to R. Cecil, 4 October 1915, had mentioned such a plan, *Sykes Papers* (Oxford); for later uncertainty, see series of complaining notes—without any positive suggestions—introducing Arabian Reports for 28 June and 16 August 1916, *L/P&S/10*, 705/16, nos. 2511 and 3311/16.

[115] Chamberlain private to Chelmsford, 5 June, enclosing Robertson note, 12 May, Chamberlain note, 26 May, and Chamberlain private to Robertson, 4 June 1916, *Chelmsford Papers* (I.O. Library), Eur. Mss. E.264.

# III

# Britain's War in Iraq, 1916–1918

L. Is the Loot we hope we shall seize—
Wives and wine and bags of Rupees,
When the mayor of Baghdad hands over the keys
To the British in Mesopotamia.

*Ferdinand Tuohy*, THE CRATER OF MARS

1

In December 1915 the hopes and plans of total victory in Iraq had first been undermined, then destroyed, by Townshend's retreat and the siege of Kut al-'Amara. Every relief attempt failed, and in April 1916 Townshend's men marched into captivity, many never to be heard from again. The story is a gruesome one of incompetence and overoptimism, and survivors' accounts bear witness to near-criminal negligence in matters of supply, transport, and medical facilities. Kut's surrender had only one virtue: it made it perfectly clear that India was incompetent to conduct an overseas campaign of this scope.[1]

[1] In addition to the works of Moberley, Barker, and others already cited, later stages of the Mesopotamian campaign may be followed in Lt.-Col. A. H. Burne, *Mesopotamia, the Last Phase* (Aldershot, 1936),

In February 1916, when there was still hope of relieving Townshend, the War Office and its chief, General Sir William Robertson, assumed charge of the "Mesopotamian Expeditionary Force," for "Force D" was a thing of the past. Nixon went too, to be replaced by Lake, but Lake was already in his sixties and tainted by his association with the Indian Staff and with Duff. Lake had not the drive to match his conscientiousness and sympathy, nor the ability required to overhaul the Mesopotamian military machine and effect the necessary reforms, with the result that in August he was replaced by a considerably stronger and younger man, Major-General (later General Sir) Stanley Maude. Maude, son of a Crimean general and V.C., an Etonian and Guardsman, was cold and meticulous and possessed a reputation for efficiency and an addiction to paper work (he was "Systematic Joe" to the 14th Brigade in France). He had been severely wounded on the Western Front and had served in both the Dardanelles and Mesopotamia—and he was the man to get the job done, as Robertson, whose personal choice he was, knew very well.[2]

---

and Lt.-Col. Sir Arnold T. Wilson, *Mesopotamia 1917–1920: A Clash of Loyalties. A Personal and Historical Record* (Oxford, 1931). These standard sources supply lengthy bibliographies which include unit histories and the like. Some of the less obvious firsthand accounts are Wingate, *Not in the Limelight*; Hesketh Pearson, *Thinking it Over: The Reminiscences of . . .* (N.Y., 1938) and *Hesketh Pearson by Himself* (N.Y., 1965); Field-Marshal Sir William Slim, *Unofficial History* (N.Y., 1962). The literature on the Kut prisoners is considerable; a few samples of book-length works: Capt. E. O. Mousley, *The Secrets of a Kuttite: An Authentic Story of Kut, Adventures in Captivity and Stamboul Intrigue* (London, 1922); Maj. E. W. C. Sandes, *In Kut and Captivity with the Sixth Indian Division* (London, 1919); Maj. C. H. Barber, *Besieged in Kut and After* (Edinburgh and London, 1917); and Dorina L. Neave, *Remembering Kut: "Lest We Forget"* (London, 1937).

[2] Maj.-Gen. Sir C. E. Callwell, *The Life of Sir Stanley Maude, Lieutenant-General, K.C.B., C.M.G., D.S.O.* (London, 1920), p. 140, for nickname; Wilson, *Loyalties*, p. 112; Barker, *Neglected War*, pp. 224–26, 317–19; Guinn, *op. cit.*, p. 157; Buchanan, *op. cit.*, p. 70; Elizabeth Burgoyne, *Gertrude Bell, from Her Personal Papers, 1914–1926*

India, too, saw significant changes. Hardinge was gone in April, and Viscount Chelmsford became Viceroy. Chelmsford (Frederic John Napier Thesiger) was something of a surprise choice, for his experience was mainly Australian (Governor of Queensland, 1905-1909, and New South Wales, 1909-1913); he was an unknown quantity from the Indian standpoint. In October, Duff was replaced by General Sir Charles Monro as Commander-in-Chief of Indian forces. Monro, like Maude, was an Irish gentleman and a Sandhurst product. He, too, had served in France, as well as in South Africa and on the Indian frontier, although he had not been in India for twenty-odd years. No paper shuffler, he was before the war primarily known for the "Monro Doctrine" of fire and movement as preached at the musketry school at Hythe. More recently, he had been responsible for recommending the evacuation of Gallipoli ("He came, he saw, he capitulated," said Churchill unfairly). Monro was to correspond directly with the Chief of the General Staff in London (a change introduced in February) on all military affairs, although matters of internal Indian security and general political questions still passed to the Viceroy and from him to the India Office. In July 1916, Monro was made directly responsible to the Army Council in London for the provision of supplies, personnel, and matériel.[3]

---

(London, 1961), p. 44. Robertson's friendship for Maude: Callwell, *Maude*, pp. 236-37; Eleanor Franklin Egan, *The War in the Cradle of the World: Mesopotamia* (N.Y., 1918), pp. 289-92. Mrs. Stuart Menzies, *Sir Stanley Maude and Other Memories* (London, 1920), is a laudatory work but of some utility nevertheless, admitting, for example (p. 34), that Maude was unpopular with his own staff.

[3] Gen. Sir George Barrow, *The Life of General Sir Charles Carmichael Monro, Bart., G.C.B., G.C.S.I., G.C.M.G.* (London, 1931). Robertson, *Soldiers and Statesmen*, II, pp. 58-60; Lt. Col. C. à Court Repington, *The First World War, 1914-1918: Personal Experiences of . . .* (London, 1920), I, pp. 317-18 and 285 (where Repington claims he proposed Monro to Lloyd George). Monro in Gallipoli: Robert Rhodes James, *Gallipoli* (N.Y., 1965), pp. 321-24 (quoting Churchill). Monro's later career did not live up to earlier expectations, for he was

It was naturally hoped that after such a clean sweep the conditions and conduct of the campaign would show consequent improvement, but after the fall of Kut and the piecemeal exhaustion of every available reserve in unsuccessful relief attempts there could obviously be no more hope of Baghdad for the time being. What, then, was to be the role of the campaign? Was Britain to withdraw and suffer the humiliation of a second evacuation within less than a year after Gallipoli? Sacrifices already made, Indian determination to preserve the position in Basra and the Gulf, and the failure of the Turks to press on after Kut, all combined to make an evacuation as unnecessary as it was unthinkable. Nevertheless, some definition of the campaign's function was vital—and definition still implied some consensus on general objectives in the Middle East.

From India's point of view, one of the drawbacks to War Office control of the Mesopotamian campaign was that this theater was likely to come under more serious scrutiny in its relation to the war as a whole and to become a part of the larger controversy on strategic policy between "Easterners" and "Westerners" over whether available force should be concentrated in the Western Front or elsewhere—"To attack the strong or to attack the weak," as Churchill put it in yet another misleading remark.[4] The disagreement is sometimes represented

blamed for persecuting General Dyer, author of the Amritsar massacre: Hugh Thomas, *The Story of Sandhurst* (London, 1961), p. 143.

[4] Quoted in Samuel J. Hurwitz, "Winston S. Churchill," *Some Modern Historians of Britain: Essays in Honor of R. L. Schuyler,* ed. Herman Ausubel, et al. (N.Y., 1951), p. 316.

The following discussion is based on: B. H. Liddell Hart, *The War in Outline, 1914–1918* (N.Y., 1936), pp. 87, 143–46; Robertson, *Soldiers and Statesmen,* I, pp. 83–84; Victor Bonham-Carter, *The Strategy of Victory, 1914–1918: The Life and Times of the Master Strategist of World War I: Field-Marshal Sir William Robertson* (N.Y., 1964; publ. in Britain as *Soldier True* . . . ), pp. 107–8, 169, 286f.; Lord Beaverbrook, *Men and Power, 1917–1918* (N.Y., 1956), pp. 157–73; Winston S. Churchill, *The World Crisis* (London, 1923–29), II, pp. 31, 93, 168, 508–11, and *The Unknown War: The Eastern Front* (N.Y., 1931), pp. 284–86, 304; Magnus, *op. cit.,* pp. 309–20; Higgins, *op. cit.,* pp. 100–4,

as one of civilians ("Frocks") against the military ("Brass Hats") but, while it took on this aspect from time to time, more was involved. The "Westerner" group did include most of the higher ranks of professional soldiers, most of whom had gone immediately to France when the war broke out and who had come quickly to the conclusion that the principal enemy was Germany and that the war would be won or lost on the Western Front (although of course Russia had its role to play in the east). Any scheme that detracted from Allied strength on that front was therefore likely to prolong the war—or worse. The "Easterners," on the other hand, had various motives for urging proposals involving the Balkans (Salonika), the Straits, or elsewhere in the Ottoman Empire. Their arguments, sometimes conflicting, rested on such points as the failure to break through in the west, the need to utilize Britain's overwhelming naval strength and strategic mobility, the unacceptability of continued hideous casualty figures in the west, or the great advantages to be won from the capture of Constantinople: cooperative Balkan states, free access to Russia, and so on. Both groups could be wrongheaded and naively optimistic, but the

---

135–36, 245–51. Guinn, *op. cit.*, furnishes the best over-all survey of the problem of British wartime strategy.

The views of individual generals and Cabinet members, in addition to works by or on Churchill, Kitchener, and Robertson already noted, may be found in Basil Collier, *Brasshat: A Biography of Field-Marshal Sir Henry Wilson*, pp. 210–11, 223; Grey, *op. cit.*, II, pp. 187ff.; Ian Colvin, *The Life of Lord Carson* (N.Y., 1937), III, p. 80; Blanche E. C. Dugdale, *Arthur James Balfour, First Earl of Balfour, K.G., O.M., F.R.S., etc.* (N.Y., 1937), II, p. 91; A. M. Gollin, *Proconsul in Politics: A Study of Lord Milner in Opposition and in Power* (N.Y., 1964), pp. 299–306, 448–51, and John Evelyn Wrench, *Alfred Lord Milner: The Man of No Illusions, 1854–1925* (London, 1958), p. 337; Lloyd George, *War Memoirs*, I, pp. 322–28,IV, pp. 66–101, V, pp. 9–10, 371; Roy Jenkins, *Asquith* (London, 1964), pp. 392–97. See also Maj.-Gen. Sir. Frederick Maurice, "The Eastern and Western Controversy," *Contemporary Review*, 114 (July-December 1918), 623–30; Correlli Barnett, *The Swordbearers: Supreme Command in the First World War* (N.Y., 1964).

principal difference, as L. C. B. Seaman has written, was that "The soldiers looked at maps of France; the amateurs looked at maps of the world." [5]

The controversy, as Lord Beaverbrook rightly remarked, has been overstressed on occasion, for power was essentially in the hands of the "Westerners."[6] Still, the "Easterners," because of both force of circumstance and their own influence, were able to implement some of their plans for breaking the war's deadlock. Early in 1915, in particular, an appeal for aid from Russia combined with ideas already in the air to provide the necessary final incentive for operations in the Dardanelles. Alexandretta, chosen for the third landing against the Turks (for India's separate war had already begun), was at this time by-passed, but that project never suffered the test of reality of Mesopotamia or Gallipoli or Salonika and therefore was never dead so long as the war lasted. Kitchener had favored it, and Lord Fisher at the Admiralty—who could produce some wild schemes of his own—envisioned a waterway from Alexandretta to the Persian Gulf, complete with locks and dams and barges carrying heavy guns.[7]

France received the Alexandretta plan coldly: ". . . just as the British were nervous about the possibility of the war in Europe being won entirely by the French, so the French were nervous at the prospect of seeing the British revert to their traditional habit of using great European wars as an opportunity to extend their power outside Europe."[8] In return for French

[5] L. C. B. Seaman, *Post-Victorian Britain, 1902–1951* (London, 1967), p. 68.

[6] Beaverbrook, *Men and Power*, pp. xxxix–xl.

[7] Fisher to Kitchener, 11 March 1915, quoted in Magnus, *op. cit.*, p. 314 (and see pp. 309–15, 364–65).

[8] Seaman, *op. cit.*, pp. 66–67. The statement has been made that the failure to land at Alexandretta prolonged the war—for example, Lt.-Gen. Sir. Gerald Ellison, *The Perils of Amateur Strategy as Exemplified by the Attack on the Dardanelles Fortress in 1915* (London, 1926), p. 27, and Henry H. Cumming, *Franco-British Rivalry in the Post-War Near East: The Decline of French Influence* (London, 1938), p. 109;

participation at the Straits, the Alexandretta plan was dropped. Kitchener and Fisher wanted Alexandretta; but the Straits and Constantinople were also desirable and had the advantage that an Anglo-French victory here might possibly prevent future Russian expansion in this direction. Alas, Russia had the same thought and, in March 1915, quickly opened the negotiations already discussed.[9]

But Constantinople was not captured. In November 1915, Kitchener revived the idea of a landing at Alexandretta as a means of relieving the pressure at Gallipoli and facilitating the defense of Egypt—for the current policy of defending Egypt and the Suez Canal just at the line of the Canal he considered doomed to eventual failure. Kitchener seemed to think, according to one of his biographers, that if Gallipoli were not offset by Alexandretta the Allies would lose the war. The Cabinet, unfortunately, was already in revolt against "K," and it was only six months until his mission to Russia and death in the North Sea.[10] One failure was enough, and qualified "Westerners" like Asquith saw that while Gallipoli had had some promise it was the only eastern scheme which did.[11]

Recognition of failure in the Straits was probably delayed by the theory that the mere presence of this expedition eased pressures in Mesopotamia. Conversely, when the Gallipoli failure was recognized, the advance on Baghdad was hurried

it would certainly have been a great strain on resources: Maj. Gen. Sir F. Maurice, "The Campaign in Palestine and Egypt, 1914–1918 . . . ," *Army Quarterly*, 18 (1929), 21. For a useful review of Kitchener's thinking, see Jukka Nevakivi, "Lord Kitchener and the Partition of the Ottoman Empire, 1915–1916," *Studies in International History*, ed. K. Bourne and D. C. Watt (Hamden, Conn., 1967), pp. 316–29.

[9] Ch. II above; see also W. W. Gottlieb, *Studies in Secret Diplomacy During the First World War* (London, 1957), pp. 81–87.

[10] Magnus, *op. cit.*, pp. 363–65; Barker, *Neglected War*, pp. 471–73; Corbett, *op. cit.*, IV, pp. 207–16.

[11] J. A. Spender and Cyril Asquith, *Life of Herbert Henry Asquith, Lord Oxford and Asquith* (London, 1932), II, pp. 163, 193.

on to relieve pressure in the Dardanelles. And so it went; the side shows, expensive in any case, multiplied and grew larger in order to offset each other's failures. And as they multiplied, so too did their critics; as generals like Robertson would have it, it was necessary not to yield to the temptation of dispersal of effort simply because this was facilitated by mobility. Each such effort must have real objectives and be considered primarily in relation to the general conduct of the war.[12]

Still, however, the "Easterners" lived on, secure in their burrows in Whitehall, though the "Westerners" remained dominant through the winter of 1915–1916. "The soldier squareheads," wrote Admiral Corbett, "have got hold of the war solid & refuse to do anything except on the Western Front, damn it!"[13] But Alexandretta was resurrected in 1916 (with the relief of Kut as the primary motive) and again in 1917, this time in a most unlikely form: unused troops in France were to be shipped out for a winter's work on the Syrian coast and returned in the spring—but the first troops would be returning to France as the last of the six divisions planned was leaving![14] Alexandretta remained only a dream—French hostility would probably have insured that it remain so in any case—and it died a natural death when the tide turned in the Middle East and the Palestinian and Mesopotamian campaigns moved rapidly to absorb the Arab portions of the Ottoman Empire.

Viewed against the background of this larger struggle and the dismal history of the war in Iraq in its own right, there appeared not one single point to be urged in favor of a forward policy in Mesopotamia, always assuming the army there had the capacity to mount one. Robertson, for one thing, was a

[12] Maj.-Gen. Sir F. Maurice, *British Strategy: A Study of the Application of the Principles of War* (London, 1929), pp. 82–83.
[13] Quoted in Arthur J. Marder, *From the Dreadnought to Scapa Flow: The Royal Navy in the Fisher Era, 1904–1919*, II (London, 1954), p. 420.
[14] Robertson, *Soldiers and Statesmen*, II, pp. 175–77.

convinced "Westerner" and held little brief for a campaign which he considered ". . . the worst that ever was run. . ."[15] And, though he had control of the Mesopotamian campaign, India had nicely forestalled his control of its internal forces on the grounds of the constitutional prerogatives of the Secretary of State for India and the Viceroy and the dangers of over- looking local needs and aspects, or, as General Macdonogh put it, the War Office ". . . knew nothing of dhoolies, and coolies, and ghi."[16]

But when Robertson informed the Commander in India on 30 April that the policy was now to be defensive, the debate resumed. Robertson cabled, ". . . we do not attach any im- portance to the possession of Kut or the occupation of Bagh- dad." If it were only a question of Iraq, he added, he would order withdrawal to 'Amara or even Qurna; but it was im- portant to minimize the effect of Kut's fall and desirable to give Russia all possible aid to her Caucasian campaign. The policy was thus to keep as far forward as possible without incurring heavy losses.[17]

Hirtzel applied his heaviest brand of sarcasm to these instruc- tions, which were, he minuted on 2 May, tantamount to saying Britain did not care what was going to happen to India or Persia. Why then did she not just make peace? The War Office's natural instinct to run away was not going to aid Russia, or India's northern frontier. Both Holderness and Chamberlain pointed out that for the moment there was no alternative to the policy the War Office had set, but Hirtzel was unwilling to leave the issue without further comment. In a memorandum of 8 May he urged—without sarcasm—his own

[15] Robertson private to General Murray (Egypt), 15 August 1916, *Robertson-Murray Correspondence* (British Museum), Add.Mss. 52463.

[16] Repington, *op. cit.*, I, p. 278. Macdonogh was the W.O.'s expert on eastern affairs and succeeded Callwell as D.M.I.

[17] C.I.G.S. telegram to Commander-in-Chief, India, 30 April 1916, *L/P&S/11*, vol. 105, no. 2400/16.

view of the wider war: Turkey could never be merely a side issue for either Britain or Russia, or it would hardly have been worth Germany's while to bring Turkey in. Britain, as a semi-Asiatic power with 70 million Muslim subjects, could not afford to be beaten by the Turks; but she had been. The War Office wanted peace with Turkey, even if it had to be bought, but peace without victory would mean a serious fall in British prestige. That the collapse of Germany would mean the subsequent collapse of the Ottoman Empire might be true, but in the east a mere diplomatic defeat would not be enough. It was not Verdun, for example, but the Russian victories at Erzerum and Trebizond that kept Afghanistan so quiet. While these were political considerations, military decisions were being made which impinged upon the political aspect. India would still have to be governed after the war, and unless Turkey were beaten, and soundly, the Arab policy now being pursued would mean only problems for Britain.[18]

Hirtzel's memorandum was a good representation of the war as seen from India but once more Holderness and Chamberlain tried to maintain a broader view. Reinforcements were unavailable now; in the light of the wider war Mesopotamia was low in priority; and although the effects of Kut were deplorable and would have to be neutralized by the end of the war, the struggle in the west could not be jeopardized. But Chamberlain did agree on the importance of the Turkish role to British interests and with the suggestion that this should be put to the Cabinet.[19]

The India Office's "Easterner" attitude was similar to that

[18] Hirtzel (2 May) and Holderness and Chamberlain (3 May) minutes, *ibid.*, and Hirtzel memorandum, 8 May 1916, *ibid.*, no. 1745/16. The remark on Germany bringing Turkey into the war represents the standard view held at the time, but see the excellent revisionary work by Ulrich Trumpener, *Germany and the Ottoman Empire, 1914–1918* (Princeton, N.J., 1968). See also Y. T. Kurat, "How Turkey Drifted into World War I," *Studies in International History . . . ,* ed. Bourne and Watt, pp. 291–315.

[19] Holderness, Islington (Parliamentary Under-Secretary, I.O.), and

of the Cairo authorities—India's bête noire—in that both agreed on the importance of the Middle Eastern operations. For this view, Sykes was a persuasive advocate, and one with perhaps more influence in the Cabinet than even Chamberlain. To Sykes, who took as usual an extremist position, the Ottoman Empire could even be seen as the main arena of conflict. As he put it in a June 1916 memorandum titled "The Problem of the Near East," even if Alsace and Poland and Serbia were lost it would nevertheless be a considerable achievement if Britain could preserve her Middle East role.[20] It could be pointed out, of course, that Britain had never managed to add Alsace, Poland, or Serbia to the Empire—but still, the picture painted by Sykes of German domination in the east should Britain fail was a grim one.

Such arguments meant that with the arrival of Maude and Monro, when the Turks looked weak and British reorganization was accomplished, Robertson began to hint at a possible future advance. Maude's orders were to maintain Basra, but London added that H.M.G. wished, when it became possible, to establish itself in the Baghdad vilayet, and the War Office sanctioned further railway construction to facilitate an advance when the time came. By October limited operations were approved to increase control over local tribesmen and to demonstrate Britain's fortitude. It was agreed at a meeting of the Prime Minister, Grey, Balfour, Chamberlain, and General Staff representatives that, when available, the Indian division in France would be sent to Iraq.[21] Yet this compromise on military matters did nothing to settle the by-now insoluble question: What did Britain wish to do with, and in, Mesopotamia?

---

Chamberlain minutes on Hirtzel memorandum, 8 May 1916, *L/P&S/11*, vol. 105, no. 1745/16.

[20] Sykes memorandum, 20 June 1916, *FO* 371/2774.

[21] Robertson memorandum, 12 May, Barrow note, 25 June, Islington memorandum, 26 May, Robertson private to Chamberlain, 11 July 1916, *Chamberlain Papers*, 20/7; Robertson, *Soldiers and Statesmen*, I,

2

Perhaps because he agreed with India about the importance of the Middle East, Sykes continued his attacks on Indian methods there through the summer of 1916: "The cooperation of the Indian Government with that of Egypt seems to lack enthusiasm, and Indian political internal policy to act as a drag on operations." In particular, he added in still another memorandum, little attempt had been made to gain political capital from the Mesopotamian position; a little ingenuity and dexterity should produce a sizable effect on Arabs both in and outside Iraq. What was wanted was not declarations forswearing annexation but a policy for the Arab race. Propaganda, newspapers circulated in the area, as the French ("although most repressive in their administration") knew so well how to do—that was the sort of thing needed. It was ignorance of British intentions that blocked Anglo-Arab cooperation.[22]

In early July, Sykes presented his position directly to the War Cabinet: India was just not capable of running a pro-Arab policy in a satisfactory manner. Arabs were easily divided; with such a race it was vital not to have two separate policy-making centers, ". . . and if you work from India you have all the old traditions of black and white, and you can not run the Arabs on black and white lines." Cox and his staff in Mesopotamia, therefore, should be under the Foreign Office.[23]

---

pp. 170–74; Wilson, *Loyalties*, pp. 184–209. See also Hardinge private to Nicolson, 11 January 1916, *Nicolson Papers, FO* 800/381; Chamberlain private to Chelmsford, 5 June 1916, enclosing memoranda, *Chelmsford Papers*. On later stages: Guinn, *op. cit.*, pp. 157–58; Barker, *Neglected War*, pp. 321–23; Chamberlain private telegram to Chelmsford and note, 9 October 1916; *Chamberlain Papers*, 46/1/13.

[22] Sykes memoranda, 19 June, *CAB* 17/175, and undated (but late June 1916), with Grey minute, *FO* 371/2774.

[23] Memorandum on Sykes evidence to Cabinet, 6 July 1916, *Sykes Papers* (Oxford).

Sykes was referring to a common view of India's administration, a view that stemmed both from widely held assumptions about India itself and from the nature of the first administrative steps taken in Basra. To those with visions of Arab
freedom and Arab equality (but not necessarily Arab unity),
India's paternalistic approach would not do; they would continue to hold this conviction as long as India remained responsible for Iraq's government (it should be added that the change
in military control had not directly affected the political officers). Hogarth, Arbur's first director, clearly had India in mind
when, in 1920, he described the British administrator as:

... the Protector of the Poor, and his view is apt to be bounded by
the material well-being of those he protects. So long as he is spending the best of his bodily and mental vigour on his people, he feels
no need to justify his own superior position, being, by force of
tradition, training, and function, an Imperial Whig. He is the
Father, they are the Children. . . . The British *raj* is the best form of
human government; and the best government makes for the happi-
ness of the greatest number. Therefore to fail to impose it wherever possible is to fail in one's duty to mankind.[24]

Views like those of Sykes and Hogarth were often justified.
The justifications can best be found in the period after 1918,
when there existed relative leisure and an opportunity to concentrate on forms of administrative development; but even in
1916 there were critics within the Mesopotamian administration, the most important of whom was that rarity in Britain's
official eastern Empire—a woman. Gertrude Bell found her way
to Mesopotamia by a chain of circumstances which involved
her own background as a prewar traveler and writer of some
eminence, her long-standing personal friendship with Hardinge, and her mission to Cairo and India to gather information
much in the same way as (but not in the manner of) Sykes before her. She got along with Hardinge in a way which Sykes

24 D. G. Hogarth, "Present Discontents in the Near and Middle
East," *Quarterly Review*, 234 (April 1920), 414.

found impossible. Through the Viceroy's good graces, she turned up in Basra in March 1916 to aid in the intelligence service, and, with the establishment of the Arab Bureau, to be Arbur's official correspondent in Mesopotamia.[25]

When Miss Bell arrived in Mesopotamia—fiftyish, long and thin and Edwardian and intelligent ("remarkably clever woman with the brain of a man," said Hardinge)[26]—she shared the views of some who had gone before her. India could not run Mesopotamia, though no change could be made while the war continued. There should be some central office in London controlling British Middle East interests—or, at least as she wrote T. E. Lawrence, failing London, Egypt.[27] Gertrude Bell was not above changing her mind, or, for that matter, suiting her correspondence to the recipient, but on India's incompatibility with Iraq she never varied. She found Cox very congenial: as far as she could tell, he had no desire to Indianize Mesopotamia; he was not, for example, in favor of establishing Indian legal codes there. These views prepared Lawrence, no doubt, to find a fellow spirit in Cox, and when he arrived in April he cabled Cairo that "Cox disassociates himself from

---

[25] Remarks on Gertrude Bell, and her friendship with Hardinge, based on Burgoyne, *op. cit.*; Hardinge, *Indian Years*, p. 136; Ronald Bodley and Lorna Hearst, *Gertrude Bell* (N.Y., 1940), pp. 26, 149; Gerald de Gaury, *Three Kings in Baghdad, 1921–1958* (London, 1961), pp. 19–22; C. J. Edmonds, "Gertrude Bell in the Near and Middle East," *Journal of the Royal Central Asian Society*, 56 (October 1969), 229–44. Clayton in Cairo, interestingly, claimed that Miss Bell had been sent on partly at his instigation, and he clearly banked on both her friendship with Hardinge (and with Hardinge's friend Chirol) and her pro-Arab views: Clayton private to Wingate, 28 January 1916, *Wingate Papers*, box 136. This view was not entirely accurate: see Bell to F. B. [Frank Balfour], 27 April 1916, Lady Bell, ed., *The Letters of Gertrude Bell* (London, 1927), I, pp. 374–75.

[26] Hardinge private to Duff, 11 February 1916, *Hardinge Papers*. Hardinge's remark corresponds to Robert Vansittart's, "There may have been more remarkable women, but I never met one.": Lord Vansittart, *The Mist Procession: The Autobiography of . . .* (London, 1958), p. 204.

[27] Bell private to Lawrence, 18 and 25 March 1916, FO 882/13.

India very clearly; he does not know how Cairene he is." Cox wanted to help the Arab movement; he was "entirely ignorant of Arab Societies and of Turkish politics," but he had an open approach and "will change his mind as required." Cox was the only one who counted in Iraq, and his instincts were good.[28]

But Cox did not have the entirely free hand reported by Lawrence; he was responsible in the first instance to the Commander in Mesopotamia, and then to the Foreign Department and Viceroy in India. Further, any hope placed in him by Lawrence and Cairo was blasted by the failure of an Arab Bureau attempt in the fall of 1916 to make use of Sayyid Talib of Basra in the Arab movement. To this Cox was strongly opposed, at least if it meant that Talib would turn up in Basra; while Cox's mind might be open on other matters, it was completely closed on Talib, and he objected to any discussion of Talib's role in postwar Mesopotamia even if the man should be used in Cairo, as Arbur suggested. Talib, now residing in Bangalore as a "guest" of the Indian government, agreed to serve in return for nothing more than generous treatment. Given Cox's implacable hostility, however, Cairo decided that Talib would be a liability. Talib did not leave India until September 1917, and then as a private citizen traveling to Cairo for his health and the education of his sons—but Mesopotamia was to hear of him again.[29]

Somehow India was not entirely disassociated from Cox, or Cox from India, and the connection boded ill for Sykes, who by now saw India as the principal obstacle to an effective Arab policy. By late 1916 Chelmsford had moved to the offensive,

[28] Lawrence telegrams to "Intrusive" (Clayton), 8 and 9 April 1916, FO 882/15.

[29] Resident, Persian Gulf, telegram to FSI, 23 October, FSI telegram to Egypt, 14 November, A. T. Wilson to Arab Bureau, 23 December 1916; Egypt telegram to FSI, 10 February, FSI telegrams to Egypt, 2 March and 12 May, Egypt telegrams to FSI, 10 May and 29 July, Bombay telegram to FSI, 20 September 1917: FO 371/3048.

making a direct attack on Sykes's plans. The Viceroy freely admitted that India desired no more responsibility, but how, in the final analysis, could India cut herself away from Iraq? From what other place would come the necessary reinforcements or garrison? Of course the form of administration was different from that of India, but so was that of Burma, or the North-West Frontier; and India would in fact *prefer* an administration which was in large measure independent, subject only to the control of those external relations which might involve India militarily.[30]

One of the things that made India's position so difficult was that, even to the India Office, preservation of Mesopotamia for Britain simply did not mean the preservation of Indian administration there. There was no strong advocate in the India Office of a firm Iraqi-Indian connection. Hirtzel, in a December memorandum, made light of Chelmsford's argument. Indeed, India ruled diverse peoples; but none were Arabs. Indeed, Britain required a watch over the Persian Gulf; but in the future, if Basra were secure, this would mean only local police functions and not questions of high policy. Persia, not Iraq or Arabia, was India's natural sphere of interest and activity. The issue of Iraq's administration had to be faced. Already there were some tendencies "to rapid systematisation which is not of very good omen"; if steps were not taken now, sooner or later the whole Indian system would follow. Chelmsford's argument of loose control would be very difficult to translate into action, and there was always the question of costs, for the power which would take shares in the Ottoman Empire "makes itself morally responsible to humanity and civilisation for their reclamation and development." Holderness, in full agreement, added simply that it would not be possible to control external relations only,

[30] Chelmsford private to Chamberlain, 18 October 1916, *Chelmsford Papers*; printed extract, B.246, with Sykes memorandum, 19 March 1917, *FO* 371/3051.

for even this limited role would imply problems of taxation and so forth. The logic of the situation required total separation of India from Iraq.[31]

By early 1917, the position had advanced no further than that of 1914, for India was righteous in its defense of its Mesopotamian interests. Chelmsford's position was more flexible than Hardinge's had been, but both men, like viceroys before them, had embraced the outlook of India's bureaucracy. The administration, in any case, was going to last the war. Beyond that was anyone's guess, for the Meccan negotiations had complicated matters as much as Kut al-'Amara. (The Sykes-Picot Agreement may be said to have done the same, but not in Cox's view: he was not informed of this agreement until later that year.)[32] One point only had been learned: the India Office and India both now showed caution on making pronouncements—learned, perhaps, from Cairo's lack of it. To Curzon's suggestion, for example, that it be spread about in Basra "that *we meant to stay there*," Chamberlain could only reply, after consulting his staff, that "Our pledge to the Shareef, given very much against my wishes, as well as our relations with our Ally, make it, I fear, impossible to go further." He might have added, as did Hirtzel in a note to Chamberlain, that it was still not known whether Britain would annex or protect; if the first, the Sharif would object, and if the second, it would be necessary to spell out the details of the form of administration.[33]

Chamberlain was right; everything militated against a statement by the Cabinet. Assuming that a policy could be agreed upon (a risky assumption), the war had yet to be won in Iraq, the administration secured, the Arabs sounded out, and the

---

[31] Hirtzel note, 30 December 1916, Holderness memorandum, 9 January 1917, *ibid*.
[32] Sykes private to Cox, 23 May 1917, *Sykes Papers* (Oxford); Wilson, *Loyalties*, p. 154.
[33] Curzon private to Chamberlain, 4 December, Chamberlain note for Curzon, 15 December, and Hirtzel note, 16 December 1916, *L/P&S/11*, vol. 115, no. 5336/16.

future of Turkey planned by the Allies. The Arab revolt, too, had yet to prove its worth. There was one other consideration which must have given considerable cause for doubt to precisely those individuals most clearly associated with the Mesopotamian campaign: in mid-1916, an inquiry into its conduct had begun in England.

3

The Mesopotamian Commission was, perhaps, inevitable, for Britain had a habit of official inquiries into military disasters dating, in modern times, from the Crimean War. The double fiasco of Gallipoli and Kut would sooner or later have led to Parliamentary pressure for an examination of the respective circumstances of the two campaigns; but it was not inevitable that the examination would occur when and in the form it did.

Even before Gallipoli had come to an end, there had been pressure for publication of relevant papers; the Government refused all requests. On 2 May 1916, however, after Kut's fall, it was announced that papers would be laid on the subject, and on 30 May some preliminary documents dealing with Townshend's appreciation after Britain's initial capture of Kut were made public. This was an error, for it was now urged that, if such a step could be taken regarding the still-continuing Mesopotamian campaign, it could certainly be done on Gallipoli. On 1 June, Bonar Law (Leader of the House) conceded this principle. It was a brave decision, considering the history of other governments which had submitted to inquiries, but it also might prove to be a foolish one. As Sir Maurice Hankey has written:

It would be difficult to find a better example than this of the faulty system under which we were still working, whereby the last word in the Supreme Command in War lay in the hands of a purely civilian Cabinet, which was not attended by any professional advisors. Whether the subject was really discussed in Cabinet at all [in 1916], Heaven alone knows, for in those days the Cabinet kept no records. That it was not discussed adequately is highly probable when it is remembered that the incident occurred at that supreme moment when the news of the battle of Jutland was trickling in. . . . The decision was taken by politicians on political grounds alone. The rich experience of the past in such matters was unknown to those responsible for the decision. And if history was over-looked, the effect of the publication of papers on current operations was ignored. It was a decision that could only have been taken by a body working without an Agenda paper, and without any systematic documentation.[34]

The dangers were real: dissension in the Government, and possibly even its fall; diversion of effort needed for conducting the war to the job of "raking over the ashes of a dead past"; injury to morale; and the lowering of the prestige of the Supreme Command.[35] Hankey, and others including Chamberlain, resisted an inquiry, but their position was weak. An independent commission sent out to Iraq by Hardinge under Sir William Vincent and Major-General Sir Alfred Bingley showed in its June 1916 report on medical arrangements that there were considerable grounds for suspicion on at least this aspect of the campaign. The report was secret until the Mesopotamian Commission issued its own document, but the results were known to the higher authorities; from the standpoint of conscience, at least—which Chamberlain had in full measure—it was hard to resist further investigation.[36]

Any attempt to resist an inquiry, in any case, would quite probably have been defeated in both houses of Parliament, with the result that each would probably have then conducted its own investigation. The Government therefore moved first and offered to set up two small bodies to inquire into operations, supply, treatment of wounded, and so on, respectively for Gallipoli and Mesopotamia. Both inquiries would be secret. The Mesopotamian Commission which thus came into being

[34] Hankey, *Supreme Command,* pp. 517–18.
[35] *Ibid.,* pp. 521–24.
[36] Hardinge, *Indian Years,* pp. 134–35; Buchanan, *op. cit.,* p. 205; Petrie, *Austen Chamberlain,* p. 70; Guinn, *op. cit.,* pp. 128–29; Barker, *Neglected War,* p. 461.

began the first of more than sixty meetings on 21 August 1916.[37] It included men of standing and prestige, though no one of great eminence. The chairman was Lord George Hamilton, former Secretary of State for India (1895–1903). The seven other members were Lord Donoughmore, an influential Irish peer; General Sir Neville Lyttelton, the only member who had ever served in India (and that, according to Hardinge, only as a subaltern); Admiral Sir Cyprian Bridge; Lord Hugh Cecil, M.P. (late Lord Quickswood); Sir Archibald Williamson (late Lord Forres); (ex-)Commander Josiah Wedgwood (later Baron Wedgwood of Barlaston), historian, naval architect, and an avid questioner on eastern affairs in Parliament, who was to present his own minority report; and John Hodge, M.P. An ex-Secretary, four M.P.s, a general, an admiral—but little Indian experience or knowledge. Only Hamilton had serious knowledge of Indian administration, and he had only taken the job, as he wrote *The Times* in July 1917, when told (by Lord Lansdowne, Minister without Portfolio) that it was essential in order to avert a political crisis.[38]

Much criticism has been leveled at the work done by these men—they failed to visit India; they failed to interview India's Quarter-Master General; they failed, in their examination of a hundred witnesses, to observe the normal rules of evidence—justified criticisms, no doubt, but the principal figures—Duff, Hardinge, Barrow, Hirtzel, Chamberlain—not only testified but had the opportunity to present documentary evidence and written testimony on their own behalf. The details of the Commission's work and findings go beyond the scope of this book, involving as they do much technical military and administrative procedure, but very few individuals directly involved in the

---

[37] Petrie, *Austen Chamberlain*, p. 71; evidence (both printed and in longhand), documents, and report in *CAB* 19. The printed evidence—22,577 questions—occupies 1,176 closely printed pages, *CAB* 19/8.

[38] Hardinge, *Old Diplomacy: The Reminiscences of . . .* (London, 1947), p. 215; Wilson, *Loyalties*, p. 172; Lord G. Hamilton memorandum, 18 July 1917, *Asquith Papers* (Bodleian Library, Oxford), vol. 32.

campaign escaped contamination or condemnation in the report.[39]

When the report was first circulated to Cabinet members, it was immediately clear that the dust of Kut had not cleared. The enormity of the breakdown and incompetence was at least partially revealed, and the activities of the commission uncovered a world of political intrigue and personal animosities. "I regret to have to say," wrote Curzon to his colleagues, "that a more shocking exposure of official blundering and incompetence has not in my opinion been made, at any rate since the Crimean War. . ." Undesirable as it was to publish the report in wartime—here he agreed with Robertson—it had to be done in this case in the light of Parliament's interest, the precedent of the already released Dardanelles Commission report, and the necessity for dealing rapidly with some of the questions raised.[40] He might also have added the fact that Hamilton was likely to stand up in the House of Lords and attack the Government if his report was pigeonholed.[41]

Through June and July the Cabinet wrestled with the problem of what to do with the results, a struggle that occupied two full Cabinet meetings and considerable time in half a dozen more. As one commentator put it, "never did our politicians fall into so deep a pit of ineptitude as when they discussed the

[39] Buchanan, *op. cit.*, pp. 205–7; Barker, *Neglected War*, pp. 101–2, 458–64; Petrie, *Austen Chamberlain*, pp. 39–41, 72–73; Oxford and Asquith, *op. cit.*, II, p. 103; Robertson, *Soldiers and Statesmen*, II, pp. 64–65. Hamilton opposed traveling to India so that, as he put it, he would not be the recipient of every gossip and complaint and impair the job of government: Hamilton private to Chamberlain, 22 September, enclosed in Chamberlain private to Chelmsford, 25 September 1916, *Chelmsford Papers*. Hamilton did correspond with individuals in India, however: see, for example, Marquis Willingdon (Governor of Bombay) to Hamilton 7 October 1916, *Willingdon Papers* (I.O. Library), Eur.Mss. F.93.

[40] Curzon memorandum, 4 June 1917, *CAB* 1/24.

[41] War Cabinet 160, 11 June 1917, *CAB* 23/3.

findings of their own Commission."[42] Balfour and Carson (Foreign Office and Admiralty) were brought to agree with Curzon on the desirability of publication, and Chamberlain was hardly in a position to oppose a report on deeds for which he had some responsibility. Personally, he found the report "heartrending," especially in the light of his view a year earlier that, since both he and Hardinge had done their best, the inquiry "can be only to our advantage." But when it appeared—and blamed the Secretary at the least for excessive reliance on private communications with Hardinge for passing matters of official interest—Chamberlain regarded it as ". . . the saddest and most appalling document that I have ever read," not for the blame cast on him, but for the other revelations: ". . . not only was the expedition ill-found from the first, but . . . high-placed and responsible officers deliberately concealed the truth and reported falsely in reply to my enquiries."[43]

These officers to whom Chamberlain referred could not be punished by the Commission, which had no legal power; but publication of the report, together with changes already made (such as Duff's removal), was already a step in this direction.[44] When the report was published on 27 June (without the supporting documents), the newspaper comment, notably in the Northcliffe papers, made it clear that publication was not going to be enough. The debate in Parliament began on 3 July, and it was necessary for Lloyd George's Government to rise in

[42] "Musings Without Method," *Blackwood's*, 202 (1917), 272. Cabinet meetings: War Cabinet 160 (11 June), 161 (12 June), 162 (13 June,) 169 (23 June), 175 (4 July 1917); and see also 180–83, 189: *CAB* 23/3. On political aspect, see also Hardinge private to Chelmsford, 19 July 1916, *Chelmsford Papers*.

[43] Chamberlain memorandum, 5 June 1917, *CAB* 1/24; Chamberlain private to Curzon, 5 June 1917, *Chamberlain Papers*, 48, and to Hardinge, 21 July 1916, *Hardinge Papers*; Petrie, *Austen Chamberlain*, p. 81.

[44] Note on meeting, 18 June 1917, Curzon, Barnes, Derby, Chamberlain, *Lloyd George Papers*, F/63/2/2.

defense at least of the civilian authorities involved—in their interest and in the interest of the survival of the Government.[45]

Chamberlain, however, was in an awkward position. As the minister technically responsible, he had now come to the conclusion that it was his duty to resign. When he learned that the Cabinet intended to establish a court of inquiry to review the report and the individuals cited by name—a trial of a sort—he made his decision. As he wrote to the Prime Minister, a minister who might find his acts called into question before a judicial tribunal at any moment ". . . cannot possess the authority which is necessary for the discharge of his duties. . ." It was, as he wrote Chelmsford, a matter of principle: a minister had to defend his subordinates. The House, for this reason, should deal only with the executive, that is, with the Secretary. In the debate in the House, Chamberlain spoke for over an hour to a full audience and some cheers; he paid tribute to Nixon and Hardinge and then announced his resignation.[46]

For Chamberlain it was a bitter blow. "Well," he wrote to his sister, "there's an end of my ambition to do big work for India and for the Empire in that sphere. . . . It *was* a sacrifice to give it all up, but it was clearly right and I can swallow down my regrets. . ."[47] Some regretted his departure—notably Asquith (out of office since December 1916), who had also opposed the inquiry.[48] Chamberlain was a trusted and respected man, although neither a dynamic leader nor a notable administrator. "It was one of the finest things in his career," said one biographer, but perhaps Lord Birkenhead made the aptest

[45] Chamberlain private to Chelmsford, 14 and 28 June and 5 July 1917, *Chelmsford Papers.*

[46] Petrie, *Austen Chamberlain*, pp. 87–92 (quoted); Chamberlain private to Chelmsford, 18 July, Holderness private to Chelmsford, 19 July 1917 (noting that the Viceroy's telegram attempting to dissuade Chamberlain from resigning had arrived on the 18th and Chamberlain was out on the 17th), *Chelmsford Papers.*

[47] Petrie, *Austen Chamberlain*, pp. 93–94.

[48] Spender and Asquith, *op. cit.*, II, pp. 294–96.

remark: "Austen always played the game, and he always lost it."[49]

Chamberlain was not alone in responsibility. Hardinge, now back in the Foreign Office, was both a witness before the Commission and a blameworthy party in the Commission's report. Three times in June and July he offered his resignation, but Balfour each time refused it, despite Curzon's attempt to persuade Hardinge to go (the two ex-viceroys were not the best of friends, a relationship which was to be of considerable importance when Curzon became Foreign Minister in 1919 and had to deal directly with Hardinge as Permanent Under-Secretary). Hardinge was given the opportunity, rather rare for a permanent official, to intervene in his own defense in Parliamentary debate (made possible in this case because he was a peer), and his reputation was vindicated in the end.[50]

The revelation of Indian incompetence was to have even greater effect than the question of reputations and personal relations. The natural desire to avoid still another disaster speeded reinforcements to Palestine in 1917. More important was the fact that England's confidence in India's government was, as Chamberlain put it, "profoundly shaken," and not only in military affairs. Chelmsford, in India, fully realized the disastrous effect of the report, coming as it did at a time of considerable political agitation. He could only hope that India would not be pushed into major reforms which would be most awkward in the middle of a war. But the changes, both civil and military,

---

[49] Sir Charles Petrie, *The Chamberlain Tradition* (N.Y., 1938), p. 176. Birkenhead is quoted in Beaverbrook, *Men and Power*, p. xiii, but see the favorable remark in Earl of Birkenhead, *Contemporary Personalities* (London, 1924), p. 70. Christopher Addison, *Politics from Within, 1911–1918. Including Some Records of a Great National Effort* (London, 1924), II, p. 170.

[50] Hardinge, *Old Diplomacy*, pp. 215–19, 243–44; Balfour private to Lloyd George, 9 July 1917, *Lloyd George Papers*, F/3/2/23; Dugdale, *op. cit.*, II, pp. 177–78; Hardinge private to Grant, 28 August 1917, *Grant Papers* (I.O. Library), Eur.Mss. D.660.

were to come in time. They cannot be considered here, for certainly more was involved than the Mesopotamian campaign—yet Mesopotamia certainly played a considerable role.[51]

Chelmsford had to deal in these matters with Chamberlain's successor, Edwin Montagu. Montagu had had no intimation before Chamberlain's resignation of his approaching responsibility for Indian affairs (in fact, he had been designated for the Ministry of Reconstruction), but he had participated in the Mesopotamian debate in the House. In his remarks (12 July) he had characterized the Indian government, as revealed in the report, as ". . . too wooden, too iron, too inelastic, too antediluvian to be of any use for the modern purposes we have in view": the whole system of executive control in Whitehall and India would have to be overhauled and more responsibility given to the people of India. It was an ominous portent to those who found fault only with individuals and not with the system. Up to a point, the Government was now handicapped by the assumption that Montagu's appointment lent official sanction to his Parliamentary remarks; for that reason both Balfour and Curzon opposed his appointment.[52]

Montagu distrusted the Indian governmental system and desired reform. India had lost considerable public respect for its conduct of operations in Mesopotamia. "Side shows" as a whole had fallen out of favor. These simply stated effects of the pub-

---

[51] Chamberlain private to Chelmsford, 5 July, and Chelmsford private to Chamberlain, 7 July 1917, *Chelmsford Papers*. Some indications of the reception given the Mesopotamian report may be gained from Everard Cotes, "Mesopotamia, II: The Tragedy of an Impossible System," *Nineteenth Century and After*, 82 (July-December 1917), 272–82; G. M. Chesney, "The Mesopotamian Breakdown," *Fortnightly Review*, 108 (1917), 34–44; Lovat Fraser, "Problems of Indian Administration," *Edinburgh Review*, 227 (January 1918), 166–87; Repington, *op. cit.*, I, pp. 599–600, 605–8; and Wilson, *Loyalties*, pp. 170–83. See also S. R. Mehrotra, *India and the Commonwealth, 1885–1929* (N.Y., 1965), p. 101; and, for a discussion of military changes resulting from the report, Barrow, *op. cit.*, pp. 239–48.

[52] S. D. Waley, *Edwin Montagu: A Memoir and an Account of His Visits to India* (N.Y., 1964), pp. 127–29.

lished Mesopotamian Commission report were to have far-reaching consequences, and not least for India's achievement of her goals regarding both the administration of Mesopotamia and Arab policy in general.

4

To some extent, the impact of the muddy political and personal waters stirred by the Mesopotamian report was offset by the fact that between the fall of Kut and the debate on the report a sweeping victory had occurred in Mesopotamia: Baghdad itself had been captured. Both Maude and Monro had been anxious to move on, once regrouping and reorganization had reached a suitable point; and in December 1916, a force four times the size of Townshend's of a year earlier began a second Mesopotamian advance.

This time there was no check; "a sledge-hammer was used to crush a flea—and the flea escaped being crushed," said Liddell Hart,[53] for no major defeat was inflicted on the Turks. In February 1917, Kut fell a third time, and Maude was ordered to press on. On 11 March, Baghdad was entered by the British Thirteenth Division. The capture might have come earlier but for soul-searching prompted by fear of repetition of 1915 and the knowledge that Baghdad offered no defensible position and the advance would not be able to stop there. But it was difficult to reject so easy a prize, and the virtually unopposed capture was indeed a success worthy of such enthusiasm and publicity as it generated. Yet it was a hollow victory; the east seemed little impressed, and the unpublicized motive for the advance—forestalling Russian occupation of Baghdad (for Russian forces were acting in nominal cooperation with Britain in the Persian theater)—was rendered meaningless by the Russian revolution and consequent military collapse. The victory also served to stir further debate on policy, most notably in the matter of an

[53] Capt. B. H. Liddell Hart, *The Real War, 1914–1918* (Boston, 1930), p. 267.

announcement or declaration to be made on the entrance into Baghdad.[54]

The discussion began in early March, when capture seemed imminent, and Cox was told to draft a statement. Cox's draft briefly reviewed the causes of the conflict, remarked upon the excellent quality of the British administration, and advised the local inhabitants to cooperate with Britain and with the Sharifal movement—this last point having been insisted upon by London. India had no corrections to suggest, but the sole response from London was to order that no proclamation be issued until London gave approval.[55]

It seemed that considerable excitement had been generated by the opportunity for the first proclamation of this sort since early in the war; it would have to be planned carefully, for many parties would give it careful study. To Hirtzel, Cox's draft simply told the Arabs, "Mind your own affairs and leave the governing to us." Insofar as H.M.G. had a policy, this was not it. Britain was irretrievably committed to Husain and to her allies, and she had made no claim for special administrative rights in Baghdad (a claim the Sharif would not have approved earlier and would certainly not approve now). Basra was different, if only because Britain had occupied it before the Sharifal negotiations had begun. Hirtzel was forgetting his own remarks on McMahon's pledges and McMahon's letter of Oc-

[54] Barker, *Neglected War*, chs. XV–XVII; Graves, *Cox*, pp. 209–12; Barrow, *op. cit.*, pp. 163–66; Repington, *op. cit.*, I, pp. 594–99, II, pp. 112–14, 118–24 (Repington was corresponding with both Monro and Maude); Robertson, *Soldiers and Statesmen*, II, pp. 72–77; Guinn, *op. cit.*, pp. 217–20; Wilson, *Loyalties*, pp. 225–27; Callwell, *Maude*, pp. 270–78; Brig.-Gen. Sir James E. Edmonds, *A Short History of World War I* (London, 1951), pp. 387–91; Moberley, *op. cit.* An early expression of the Russian role: Hardinge private to Nicolson, 18 February 1916, *Nicolson Papers*, FO 800/381.

[55] SSI telegrams to Viceroy, 6 and 9 March, Cox telegrams to SSI, 8 and 9 March, Viceroy telegram to SSI, 9 March 1917, *FO* 371/3042, and *L/P&S/10*, 978/17, no. 1019/17, with Hirtzel notes and unsent draft reply to Cox.

tober 1915—but in a general sense he was right, for the Sykes-Picot Agreement described this vilayet only as being in Britain's sphere of interest.[56]

Mark Sykes, meanwhile, was preparing his own draft, and he was in communication with Hirtzel on the subject. *His* draft was very different from Cox's, bearing, as Arnold Wilson remarked, the full mark of Sykes's "ebullient orientalism" in its flowery references to the Arab past and future.[57] Britain had come as liberator, freeing the Arabs from the ancient tyranny of strangers since the days of "Halaka" (the Mongol conqueror Hulagu was meant). Since those times, "your palaces have fallen into ruins, your gardens have sunken in desolation, and your forefathers and yourselves have groaned in bondage." Promises of reform had been made again and again, but without result, and while others like Husain and Ibn Sa'ud had won their freedom Iraq continued to suffer.

Therefore I am commanded to invite you, through your nobles and elders and representatives, to assume the management of your civil affairs in collaboration with the political representatives of Great Britain who accompany the British Army, so that ~~when peace comes~~ in due time you may be in a position to unite with your kinsmen in North, East, South, and West in realising the aspirations of your race.[58]

Even Sykes, this corrected draft makes clear, thought better of specific commitments.

A key passage advised the Iraqis to prepare the way "so that

[56] Hirtzel note, 9 March 1917, *ibid.*

[57] Wilson, *Loyalties*, p. 237. Wilson was considerably kinder than Sir Ronald Wingate, speaking at St. Antony's College in 1965, who, having read Wilson, described the proclamation as ". . . a farrago of nonsense composed by presumably some 'ebullient orientalist' such as Sir Mark Sykes based on the Arabian Nights, the play of Kismet which had been a great success before the War, and Flecker's 'Hassan.' ": typescript, 2 March 1965, St. Antony's Library, Ds.46.1.

[58] Sykes undated draft proclamation, *FO* 371/3042, no. 56627. Original draft corrected as shown.

the British people may when the time comes give freedom to those who have proved themselves worthy to enjoy their own wealth and substance under their own institutions and laws." Holderness and Chamberlain both objected to going so far, and Chamberlain's substitute passage made reference only to the fact that the Arabs of Iraq would in future be free from oppression and enjoy their wealth and substance under "institutions and laws congenial to them." The amendment, responded Sykes, meant the British would rule, while his draft made them equal partners with the Arabs. "I am certain if we take the line of trying to rule Arabs as we rule Indians we shall fail. We shall introduce the social colour distinction and antagonise the whole Arab movement; we shall have the intellectuals against us from the very start. . ." And, as Hirtzel had already pointed out, such a declaration would force the hand of France in Syria, for the French would not be left behind in declarations pointing to close control (Sykes was already thinking of modifications of the Sykes-Picot arrangement); at any rate, while there were dangers, ". . . if we are courageous, we have every prospect of being supreme in region (B), and beloved in region (A)." [59]

On 12 March, the day after Baghdad fell, the War Cabinet considered the matter and the opposing memoranda of Sykes and Chamberlain. It approved the Sykes draft in principle and appointed a subcommittee of Curzon, Milner, Chamberlain, and Hardinge to work out the final details. The text, with modifications, was cabled out to Cox the same day and given retroactive Cabinet approval on the 14th. Also on the 12th, in another telegram, Britain's policy was set out for the edification of authorities in the east: a sound administration was essential in the Baghdad vilayet, but for the time being H.M.G. was not

[59] *Ibid.;* Hirtzel to Sykes and Sykes memorandum, 10 March 1917, *Sykes Papers* (Oxford); Sykes memorandum also appended, with Chamberlain memorandum of 10 March, to Cabinet discussion, W.C. 94, 12 March 1917, *CAB* 23/2.

prepared to sanction the extension of direct British administration to that province. Until the war was over, "... the predominant considerations in Bagdad must be political rather than administrative." Existing machinery must be preserved, with only the substitution "of Arab for Turkish spirit and personnel." In other words, while remaining under martial law, the vilayet should have an Arab façade, and British officials "should not be multiplied unnecessarily." [60]

Maude, in whose name the proclamation would have to be issued, and Cox were unwilling to accept these instructions without protest. The security problem was important now, cabled Maude, and it was essential to establish an administration simply to avoid considerable trouble from and with the local inhabitants—and by administration he meant British-run, as in Basra. As for the proclamation, it would hardly serve locally since a sizable percentage of the population (a majority, said Maude) was Jewish, and they had not been mentioned. This telegram produced some exasperation owing to a curious accident. It happened occasionally that a cable was garbled and mistranslated at the receiving end—indeed, one wonders why it did not happen more often—and Maude's of the 16th was one such case. As deciphered, it read that, while the war continued, the problem of administration had to be dealt with "primarily from standpoint of security and essential needs of this force and secondly from aspect of local bazars." "Bazars" should have read "possibilities," but this apparently sarcastic remark was not corrected until the 29th, rather late to alter first impressions. But Maude had left no doubt on his views: he would be glad to use any suitable Arab personnel, but the Turkish administration had ceased to exist,

... and local conditions do not permit of employing in responsible positions any but British officers competent to deal with Military authorities and with people of the country. Before any truly Arab

[60] War Cabinet discussion, *ibid.;* SSI telegrams to Cox and Viceroy, 12 March 1917, *FO* 371/3042; W.C. 96, 14 March 1917, *CAB* 32/2.

facade can be applied to edifice it seems essential that foundation of law and order should be well and truly laid.[61]

No appeal was permitted. The proclamation was intended for general consumption, both India and Iraq were told, and would have to be adhered to carefully. Some supplemental proclamation might be issued, provided it did not suggest the incorporation of the Baghdad vilayet into the Empire.[62] The language of the telegram brooked no quarrel, for Baghdad had been under British occupation for nearly a week. The home authorities, apparently, shared Hirtzel's fears of an unchecked Military-Indian administration.

If we do not intend to introduce British rule we must say so & put our foot down, from the start. If, even after a week of British occupation, the inhabitants would be "dismayed" at the thought of anything else (which I do not for a moment believe, except as regards a few rich Jews), after a month or a year—or whatever period the war may last—we shall be told that withdrawal is impossible. And that, no doubt, is what G.O.C. [General Officer Commanding, i.e., Maude] and Sir P. Cox want to make it.[63]

The proclamation was finally issued, amid general hilarity, on 19 March. Who were those "noble Arabs"? it was asked. "It's officialese for *beastly Buddoos*," explained Edmund Candler, the writer, who was "Eyewitness" with the Mesopotamian armies. Few, if any, of the authorities in Mesopotamia—civil or

[61] Maude telegrams to FSI, 16 (X.1309 and X.1310, latter quoted) and 29 March 1917 (such telegrams were repeated, of course, to London), *L/P&S/10*, 978/17, no. 1116/17, and *FO* 371/3042. The point about the Jewish population was also made by Chaim Weizmann: Leonard Stein, *The Balfour Declaration* (N.Y., 1961), pp. 378–79.

[62] SSI telegram to Viceroy and Maude, 17 March 1917, with minutes, *L/P&S/10*, 978/17, no. 1116/17, and *FO* 371/3042, showing that it was drafted in the Foreign Office. In India, Grant knew the situation was virtually hopeless; see minute of 17 March 1917, *India Sec. War July* 1917, 1–132.

[63] Hirtzel note, 17 March 1917, with minutes by Hardinge, Curzon, and Milner, *L/P&S/10*, 978/17, no. 1116/17.

military—believed that either Cox or Maude was responsible.[64]
The whole discussion, however, had raised the problem of Mesopotamian policy in the most acute form. The issues were deemed complex enough to require the consideration of a committee, this time a standing one. On 16 March the War Cabinet created the Mesopotamian Administration Committee under Curzon's chairmanship and including Chamberlain (replaced in July by Montagu), Lord Milner, Hardinge, Hirtzel, Holderness, and others from the Foreign Office, with Sykes as secretary. On the 19th, the committee held the first of nine meetings under this title and for the moment managed to agree upon a tentative policy. Basra was to be British; Baghdad was not, but it was premature to fix the precise form of its Arab government (meaning there was no India Office–Foreign Office agreement on this). Iraq would have a special government service, drawn not from the Indian Civil Service but from the Levant and the Sudan, the details to be worked out by a subcommittee of Curzon, Milner, Hardinge, and Chamberlain. Most important, for the duration of the occupation, the India Office in London, and not India, would be responsible for Iraq's administration (India was left with responsibility for the Gulf and south Persia through the Gulf Resident at Bushire).[65] By 27 March the subcommittee had done its work and had, among other things, recommended that the Iraq legal code, as patterned on India and established in Basra, should not be extended to the Baghdad vilayet.[66]

[64] Candler is quoted in Edward Thompson, *These Men, Thy Friends* (N.Y., 1928), pp. 268–69. Candler, *op. cit.*, II, pp. 114–17, quotes the proclamation and notes that Maude was not blamed but does not make this particular remark. Moberley, *op. cit.*, III, pp. 404–5, and Wilson, *Loyalties*, pp. 237–38, also quote the proclamation; also Memorandum B.253, *L/P&S/10*, 978/17, no. 1146/17.

[65] War Cabinet 98, 16 March 1917, *CAB* 23/2; Mesopotamian Administration Committee (M.A.C.) minutes, 19 March 1917, *CAB* 27/22 and *FO* 371/3051; also summarized in Chamberlain private to Chelmsford, 22 March 1917, *Chelmsford Papers*.

[66] Memorandum B.254, report of subcommittee, 27 March 1917,

On the 29th the larger conclusions of the committee and the details worked out by the smaller group were telegraphed officially to India. Basra would be British; Baghdad would be "an Arab state with local ruler or Government under British Protectorate in everything but name," or so at least had the India Office interpreted the conclusions. "Behind Arab façade," the cable continued, "Bagdad to be administered as an Arab Province by indigenous agency and in accordance with existing laws and institutions as far as possible." Local systems would be preserved, including the legal system, with "Arab" for "Turk" as the only change. And, if all this were not sufficiently clear, "employment of Indians in any branch of administration is to be strictly discountenanced as inconsistent with above principles . . ." Finally, insofar as possible, the same principles should be applied in Basra.[67]

It was only to be expected that India and Baghdad would comment. India had already indicated that, whatever the eventual plan, it would be necessary to overhaul and replace the collapsed Turkish structure and set in motion the work of the various civil departments; and since suitable Arabs were just not available, the job must be done for the time being by British officers. This particular issue of "suitable Arabs" was to lead to much discussion, not only on the question of their availability but also on whether the Indian political officers were themselves "suitable" substitutes—a point on which Hardinge, after a year in London, now had his doubts.[68] But Cox, because of his position, was best placed to offer detailed criticism, and in a telegram of 7 April (to both the India Office and India,

---

*L/P&S/10*, 978/17, no. 1146/17, and draft report of M.A.C., 10–11 April 1917, *FO* 371/3042; Chamberlain private telegram to Chelmsford, 30 March 1917, *Chelmsford Papers*.

[67] SSI telegram to Viceroy, 29 March 1917, *FO* 371/3042 (quoted in Kedourie, *England and the Middle East*, p. 176, and Ireland, *op. cit.*, p. 96); Balfour telegram to Wingate, 31 March 1917, *FO* 371/3051.

[68] Viceroy telegram to SSI, 26 March, *FO* 371/3042; Hardinge private to Grant, 24 April 1917, *Grant Papers*.

increasingly the common practice) he set out his objections. Cox could not comment on the principle of London's, rather than India's, responsibility, for this was high policy. But who was to rule this Arab state in Baghdad? He himself had no candidate. As for the law codes, some substitute was still essential for the Constantinople High Court and appellate (Ottoman) Privy Council jurisdiction. Most important, grave difficulties would arise if Basra and Baghdad were not to be similarly administered, although it would be possible to make a technical distinction between the two areas. With other points raised by the committee, and with the policy as a whole, Cox expressed general agreement. He himself, he added, would be happy to be the High Commissioner who would control the structure created by this plan, but India already was aware of his personal opposition to remaining in the area after the war—and it would be better in any case if the structure got a new start under a new man. For the present, he would carry on, but he urged that a committee of first-class men be sent out to examine the problems on the spot. "Premature conclusions," he added, "arrived at now may do irreparable damage, and it is submitted that only greatest emergency can justify hasty decision by War Cabinet before His Majesty's Government are in possession of complete facts and details regarding Baghdad Vilayet." [69]

To these comments, the Viceroy added that the vilayet was after all not secure yet militarily, and there would be substantial confusion if an attempt were to be made now to introduce a civil administration under the aegis of martial law. One other point attracted particular Indian attention: India's expenditure in the Mesopotamian war and her legitimate interests in Iraq meant that any attempt to bar Indians from Iraq, either as immigrant civilians or as administrators, would excite "bitter and legitimate resentment." [70]

[69] Cox telegram, 7 April 1917, and minutes, L/P&S/10, 978/17, no. 1435/17.
[70] Viceroy telegram to SSI, 27 April 1917, ibid., no. 1762/17.

These criticisms raised serious doubts in London. Sir John Shuckburgh, Assistant Secretary of the Political Department of the India Office, for example, recognized the difficulty in finding an Arab ruler. Sykes advocated a member of the Sharifal family, but there was no evidence that such a candidate would find local acceptance, and certainly expansion of Sharifal influence would raise suspicions in the mind of Ibn Sa'ud. As for Indians in Mesopotamia, it would appear that they would at least be necessary as laborers (and indeed, noncombatants from India provided by far the greatest labor force for the Anglo-Indian army), and any eventual total exclusion must initially be applied in moderation. Hirtzel had misgivings on all this. Cox was sincere, he thought, but it was only natural that in his need for administrative personnel his thoughts turned to India. If this was to be the result of the free hand Cox desired, it could only mean future trouble: Baghdad would be developed to a suitable level of efficiency, and this in turn would be used after the war as an argument for staying on. London must be firm and Indians used only where no other service could provide the staff—or else the level of efficiency would become so high that no indigenous Arab personnel would ever qualify. Surely all that was necessary was to keep the Turkish machine going, without undertaking reforms. Once more, Holderness and Chamberlain took a more moderate view, realizing, as Chelmsford had pointed out, that Cox's position was difficult, ordered as he was to establish civil government in a situation of martial law.[71]

The home view, as put privately to Chelmsford, was only mildly in disagreement with India. It was never intended, said Chamberlain, to establish in wartime the form of government intended for Iraq in the future. As for immigration, it was not desirable to close off Iraq to India, but the rights of the Arabs

---

[71] Minutes on Cox telegram, 7 April: Shuckburgh, Hirtzel, and Holderness and Chamberlain, 9, 11, and 12 April 1917, *ibid.*, no. 1435/17.

had also to be protected.[72] These remarks represented the conclusions of a Mesopotamian Administration Committee meeting of 8 May: temporize now and do nothing that would prejudice the future. But Baghdad was still to be administered separately from Basra—a point upon which Curzon had been insistent—although Chamberlain, considering Cox's remarks, questioned the practicality of this edict, which would complicate matters enormously.[73]

Chelmsford's reply of 25 May showed that India was becoming hardened to her inevitable separation from Iraq. Doubtless, said India, there would be resentment in some quarters, considering strong religious ties, commercial interests, and wartime losses; everything in Britain's power should be done to mitigate the effects of this by offering compensation elsewhere—such as the primacy of Indian interests, or at least "most favoured nation" status, in East Africa. Yet even eventual exclusion of Indians from Iraq was acceptable, as long as it was recognized that this was impossible now; publication of orders for the discharge of Indians already there, particularly, would be most impolitic. This step must be taken gradually; and it must be borne in mind that Britain could not then call upon India for aid in other directions—such as elaborate irrigation projects. In other words, India must have a *quid pro quo* if it was to continue to make sacrifices in Mesopotamia.[74]

The principal conclusion to emerge from a study of the discussions of March, April, and May 1917 is this: Occupation of the Baghdad vilayet had forced renewed consideration of a

[72] Chamberlain private to Chelmsford, 8/9 May 1917, *Chelmsford Papers*.

[73] M.A.C. minutes, 2nd meeting, 8 May 1917, *CAB* 27/22; SSI telegram to Viceroy, 10 May 1917, *L/P&S/10*, 978/17, no. 1854/17 (drafted by Shuckburgh, with Chamberlain and Curzon approval).

[74] Viceroy in Council to SSI, 25 May 1917, *L/P&S/10*, 2571/17, no. 2571/17; the letter was drafted before receipt of Chamberlain's 10 May telegram but sent after that telegram had been considered. On East Africa and India, see Louis, *op. cit.*, pp. 113–14.

Mesopotamian policy and, at least tentatively, London had managed to outline such a policy. That policy presaged not only the possible removal of Baghdad from direct British control (although few would have admitted so at the time), but also the end of India's rule over Mesopotamia, including the province of Basra. The reasons for this decision are fairly clear. The introduction of Indian administrative techniques was alarming, particularly to those who were supporters of future Arab independence, which India had never advocated. The blunders of the Mesopotamian campaign carried over into political and administrative affairs, and it was logical to assume the need for London's political as well as military responsibility. The Mesopotamian Commission report only appeared in June, after these decisions were made, but the "shaken faith" was already present. Finally, Britain had, for better or worse, introduced Iraq into the negotiations with Husain, and McMahon's pledges acted as a check upon Mesopotamian policy nearly as much as Mesopotamian policy had limited McMahon's statements.

All these decisions were tentative; they had yet to be applied in practice. After May, higher policy discussions were superseded by consideration of the Mesopotamian Commission's report and Chamberlain's resignation. Moreover, it seemed unnecessary for the moment to discuss the problem further, for both India and Cox had acquiesced in the general policy. Unfortunately, the decisions on civil government only served to amplify a considerable difference of opinion in Mesopotamia itself on the nature of the administration, a difference of opinion that was to culminate in a crisis in the relations between Cox and Maude.

5

At its second meeting, the Mesopotamian Administration Committee had agreed that the special study commission to visit Mesopotamia which Cox had suggested should be sent, if possible, in the next cold weather season to investigate administrative problems in detail; meanwhile, Cox had the new general guidelines upon which to base his practices.[75] The guidelines—notably the division of the two vilayets and the prohibition against more than the absolute minimum of Indian administration—and the fact that the campaign, like the martial law, still continued now bound Cox's hands.

These difficulties were compounded by instructions sent to Maude on 16 May by the War Office, at Sykes's urging. It was not enough, cabled the C.I.G.S., to mark time on the issue of Arab cooperation; Maude should consult with Cox on the possibility of making use of friendly Arab tribes, the idea being, of course, to organize a Mesopotamian equivalent to the Hijaz revolt.[76] Maude's reaction, not surprisingly, was unenthusiastic. As he cabled on 1 June, peace and quiet were the most desirable Arab attributes at the moment, with the administration friendly to those who were friendly and repressive to those who were hostile. To Maude, the Arabs had little fighting value—and they had too many weapons as it was, obtained by various means, without being given more through official channels. A number of shaikhs were already receiving subsidies for which little return could be seen. And, if the Arabs had to be used, careful organization would be required. Although Cox later reported that something might be done with a tribe or two, the home authorities could do little in the light of Maude's attitude; no significant effort was made.[77] It seemed in London that Cox and Maude had agreed on this question, but, unfortunately, there were other issues.

The difficulties were, in the first instance, personal. Cox was

[75] M.A.C. minutes, 2nd meeting, 8 May 1917, *CAB* 27/22.
[76] C.I.G.S. telegram to Maude, 16 May 1917, *L/P&S/11*, vol. 123, no. 2052/17; Wingate telegram to F.O. (Sykes private for R. Graham), 12 May 1917, *FO* 371/3056; Sykes urged that Maude not be told the origin of the idea.
[77] Maude telegrams to C.I.G.S., 1 and 24 June 1917, *L/P&S/11*, vol. 123, nos. 2324 and 2664/17; Wilson, *Loyalties*, pp. 260–62.

a man of vast experience, which had included many years of independent local power, first in Muscat, then in the Persian Gulf. He had his orders, he had his administrative concepts, and he had determination—but he was now subordinate to a commander who had equally determined views, a taste for administrative detail, and superior authority. Above all, Maude was convinced that the defeat of the enemy must take precedence over any extension of British influence in the Baghdad vilayet. So strained had relations become that Cox had cabled to Chelmsford privately on 25 May that he had been facing difficulties with Maude ever since the latter's appointment. Maude, he said, saw only the military side of things and being without any significant eastern experience was rather unsympathetic to local problems. Cox was ready to resign; the alternative was that he must have the freedom to send reports directly to the higher civilian authorities and not only through Maude.[78]

This clash had obviously to be solved. Hirtzel, when the news reached him, was quick to telegraph privately to Cox that, while disposal of the issue would take time, everything would be done which could make Cox's position a satisfactory one. India's reaction was to suggest that Cox come for a visit to explain in person what appeared to be a vaguely stated problem. The invitation came from Chelmsford but in fact had been worked out by Grant and Monro as a means to get Cox away from Maude for a month or so—during which time, Grant minuted, Maude would probably see how valuable Cox was to him. Cox demurred, on the ground that much time would be necessary to reach Simla (where the government was located in summer) and return; it would be a demanding trip through the Gulf in the height of the hot season (the hottest summer then on record, incidentally—temperatures were already over 120° in Baghdad); most important, it would be dangerous to leave a subordinate officer in charge in the interim, that is, the

[78] Cox private telegram to Viceroy, 25 May 1917, *L/P&S/10*, 978/17, no. 2146/17.

subordinate would be less able to defend the civil administration against Maude.[79]

The problem in India and London was understanding the disagreement. Both Cox and Maude were certainly strong men, but what were the issues? The answer appears to be, over and above personality, primarily the question of policy toward the Arabs. Cox was no more eager to arm the tribesmen than Maude, but he was anxious to see a pacification program extended to the outlying areas. This would require garrisons in locations of dubious strategic value. In particular, he wanted to garrison the Euphrates, where major military actions had not taken place; but Maude refused to see his troops scattered on the ground that he feared Turkish preparations for an attack on the British position in Baghdad. As it was, the Commander already felt that he was forced to lock up too many of his troops on his lines of communication, mainly for the purpose of dealing with troublesome tribes; there was no great incentive to a "civilising mission" on the part of Mesopotamian officers who had been fighting these same Arabs for three years.[80]

Nor was Arab tribal policy the only bone of contention.

---

[79] Hirtzel private telegram to Cox, 1 June, Chelmsford private telegrams to Chamberlain, 29 May and 9 June, and Storrs (Basra) private to R. Graham, 3 June 1917, *ibid.* Cox-Chelmsford exchange quoted in Graves, *Cox*, pp. 223–25. Grant note, recording his discussion with Monro, 28 May, and private to Cox, attempting to explain the maneuver, which Cox had misinterpreted as a hostile one, 13 June 1917, *India Sec. War* June 1919, 183–303; temperature: Barker, *Neglected War*, p. 411.

[80] Lt.-Gen. Sir William Marshall, *Memories of Four Fronts* (London, 1929), pp. 249–50; the Turkish offensive, "Yildirim," is discussed in Barker, *Neglected War*, pp. 413–15, and Burne, *op. cit.*, pp. 56–59. Some Arab levies were formed in Iraq as early as 1915 to patrol river banks, etc., but these tended to weaken the authority of the shaikhs over their own tribes and thus conflicted with another British policy, that of dealing with the tribes through the shaikhs. It was also urged that without a policy declaration there would be little response; still, there were some 4,800 men in this force by April 1920: Wilson, *Mesopotamia*, pp. 69–70; Brig. J. Gilbert Browne, *The Iraq Levies, 1915–1932* (London, 1932), gives a history of the movement.

Some appointments had also created trouble, such as Maude's posting of Brigadier-General C. J. Hawker as Military Governor in Baghdad; Hawker's recent experience was with the Turkish gendarmerie, he knew no Arabic, and, most important, he was not a political officer and therefore not responsible to Cox. Administrative responsibility was another issue, as in the Department of Local Resources, formed to collect local supplies, which had come under military rather than political control by the accident that this essentially political scheme was presented to Cox as a military plot to put a further burden of work upon his department, so that he opposed it. By the time of the armistice, this department had nearly as many officers, mostly in the field dealing directly with the inhabitants, as Cox had political officers. Friction was inevitable. There were, in fact, many similar problems. They may be traced in works dealing in detail with the administration of Mesopotamia, but it is more important here to consider the outcome of the conflict, which was to give more power to Cox and, therefore, to his views.[81]

Revelations of the depth of the quarrel prompted serious thought on the division of authority in Iraq. The War Office thought that it was premature to alter the Commander's position, especially in the light of the anticipated Turkish attack; but the Mesopotamian Administration Committee had already agreed in June that Cox's authority should be strengthened and leaned toward Cox's own suggestion that he (or someone in his stead) be made "High Commissioner" of the area, directly responsible to some political authority and by-passing Maude altogether, similar to the wartime structure in Egypt. In the absence of more detailed information on the quarrel, the committee did not issue any strong recommendation at that time.

[81] Wilson, *Loyalties*, pp. 240–43; see also Young, *op. cit.*, p. 79, for a good example of the general military attitude toward politicals. Wilson, *Loyalties* and *Mesopotamia*, and Ireland, *op. cit.*, both give detailed coverage of administrative problems.

By July, after consultation with General Robertson, a compromise was reached: Cox was to be "Civil Commissioner" (Chamberlain's phrase) instead of "Chief Political Officer," and would submit reports on the political and economic situation directly to London; but Maude would still have the higher authority, and the reports would still pass through his hands.[82]

To that extent, it was a small victory for Cox, and under other circumstances he might have taken some satisfaction in the support given him in both London and India. But the problems of implementation of policy remained, as did the strained relations with Maude, until the General died of cholera in November and was replaced by Lieutenant-General Sir William Marshall, with whom Cox was on much better terms.[83] In the midst of the difficulties, Cox had also been showered with honors: Honorary Major-General in June, Grand Commander of the Order of the Indian Empire in August. These rewards hardly offset Cox's weariness, the day-to-day problems of creating an administration, the necessity for continued policy discussions, or—greatest blow of all—the death of his only son in France in August (and, it should be added, of his daughter-in-law, in childbirth, in early 1918).[84]

6

The last year of the war in Mesopotamia was one of advance and consolidation militarily and confusion politically. To the

[82] W.O. to I.O., 25 June 1917, *L/P&S/10*, 978/17, no. 2546/17; M.A.C. minutes, 3rd meeting, 12 June, 5th meeting, 3 July, and SSI telegram to Viceroy, 4 July 1917, *CAB* 27/22.

[83] Wilson, *Loyalties*, pp. 275–78; Marshall, *op. cit.*, pp. 260–61; Callwell, *Maude*, ch. XV; Burne, *op. cit.*, pp. 56–59; Barker, *Neglected War*, pp. 431–33; Egan, *op. cit.*, pp. 340–41.

[84] Graves, *Cox*, pp. 232–34; Storrs, *op. cit.*, p. 233, remarks on Cox's tiredness in May, as does Frank Balfour private to Wingate, 24 October 1917, *Wingate Papers*, box 146.

War Office, the Russian collapse and the failure of the Turkish offensive to develop dictated a reduction of military strength in Mesopotamia and Palestine. On the other hand, these same circumstances created a vacuum in Persia and the Caucasus which it seemed advisable to fill. General Marshall's flank units were established in Persia, and General Dunsterville prepared to mount a campaign which led him on the long road to Baku on the Caspian. Marshall objected strenuously to the expenditure of his resources on "Dunsterforce" and on absorbing as much of Iraq as the home authorities seemed to desire; he grumbled on about 700 miles of communications to the Caspian—and what that sort of problem had meant for Napoleon—but in October 1918 the Turks were broken; on the 30th, Turkey and Britain concluded an armistice.[85]

The Caucasian and Persian operations considerably hampered military policy in Mesopotamia, and continued to do so as long as there were British troops in either area, by introducing extraneous considerations of the supply and protection of such extended units. Marshall's troops were involved from both standpoints, for it was his force which occupied Mosul shortly after the armistice. These problems changed the environment in which Mesopotamia was considered at a time when developments of world-wide significance were forcing reconsideration of political questions which all assumed had been settled in 1917. Both the Russian revolution and American entrance into the war were significant, but for Iraq the most important developments were statements made in early 1918

[85] Marshall, *op. cit.*, pp. 286–87, 303; Wilson, *Mesopotamia*, pp. 2–4; Barker, *Neglected War*, pp. 383–453; Burne, *op. cit.*, pp. 77, 86–90, Guinn, *op. cit.*, pp. 310–21.

Caucasian and Persian operations may be followed in: Firuz Kazemzadeh, *The Struggle for Transcaucasia (1917–1921)* (N.Y., 1951); Maj-Gen. L. C. Dunsterville, *The Adventures of Dunsterforce* (N.Y., 1920) and *Stalky's Reminiscences* (London, 1928); Sir Clarmont Skrine, *World War in Iran* (London, 1962); Christopher Sykes, *Wassmuss*, "*The German Lawrence*" (London, 1936); C. H. Ellis, *The British Intervention in Transcaspia, 1918–1919* (Berkeley, Calif., 1963).

by President Wilson and Prime Minister Lloyd George which called into question even the ambitions of 1917, reduced as they were from earlier plans.

Particularly alarming was Lloyd George's speech to the Trades Unions on 5 January 1918 stating that the various areas of the Ottoman Empire, including Armenia, Arabia, Syria, Palestine, and Mesopotamia, were "entitled to a recognition of their separate national conditions," although the Prime Minister provided no details of what this was to mean.[86] Taken in conjunction with President Wilson's Fourteen Points, this speech seemed to cast doubt upon even the commonly accepted future annexation of Basra. As Hirtzel noted on 11 January, the Prime Minister's speech raised a number of questions. Was Mesopotamia to be seen as one unit for purposes of self-determination? And, if so, what bodies would do the self-determining? Even veiled annexation, as contemplated in the Sykes-Picot Agreement, appeared to be out of the question; the Arab façade, in short, would have to be more than façade. Perhaps it was time to revive Cox's idea of a visiting commission, postponed in August 1917 owing to Maude's position on political and administrative questions. "It is clear that somehow or other we must retain predominating influence in Mesopotamia. By what means?"[87]

Hirtzel saw the problem, but Sykes saw the answer and set it out in a memorandum entitled "The Position in Mesopotamia in Relation to the spirit of the Age." By prewar standards, he wrote, the position in Mesopotamia was sound: the forces held their own and the administration was thriving; but now protectorates and spheres and such would have to be "consigned to

<hr />

[86] Quoted in Lloyd George, *War Memoirs, V*, pp. 63–73; *CAB* 23/5 (W.C. 314).

[87] Hirtzel note, 11 January 1918, Memorandum B.277, *L/P&S/10*, 2571/17, no. 617/18. SSI telegram to Cox, 22 August, and minutes, Cox telegram to SSI, 24 August, Viceroy telegram to SSI, 26 August 1917, *L/P&S/11*, vol. 126, nos. 3377 and 3435/17.

the Diplomatic lumber-room." If Britain was to stay, it would be to develop the country with the cooperation of the inhabitants; a provisional government would have to be elaborated, trade encouraged, and an Arab political party and a nationalist press begun. Twenty-five years of provisional control (with United States approval) incorporating trusteeship and the open door—that was the answer.[88]

The idea did not commend itself to Hirtzel; ". . . we don't want any more schemes evolved from the inner consciousness of Sykes or others without any contact with the facts on the spot (which are very imperfectly known to us)." For the moment, he wrote, all that should be done was to tell Cox what the situation was and ask his views, but, he added in private, "I suspect that there will be a great deal of difficulty in getting Sykes to put before the C$^{me}$ things with which he personally does not agree."[89] Shuckburgh and Hirtzel worked out a draft telegram to Cox reviewing the various pledges to the Arabs and statements on self-determination. But Basra would be British in all essentials, whether annexed or not; rewards for British blood and sterling were not to be discarded so easily. The only difference now was that the principle of self-determination would have to be put into effect "(speciously, at any rate)," and the means to accomplish this should be discussed.[90]

Curzon objected strenuously to this draft and insisted that the question be held over for consideration by the Middle East Committee, the newly expanded version of the Mesopotamian Administration Committee.[91] Curzon's view—and some re-

[88] Sykes memorandum, 16 January 1918, *Sykes Papers* (F.O. collection), *FO* 800/221.
[89] Hirtzel note, 22 January 1918, on Memorandum B.277, n. 87 above.
[90] Shuckburgh to Sykes, 29 January 1918, *Sykes Papers, FO* 800/221.
[91] In August 1917 the Administration Committee recommended to the Cabinet that its name be changed to "Middle East Administration Committee" as more suitable for the expanded area of its discussions. The Middle East Committee ("Administration" was dropped out in general usage) continued to number its meetings consecutively with

thinking by the India Office under Holderness's prompting—produced a more devious, if not more moderate, memorandum for the committee. The probability of a negotiated peace, the "autonomous development" mentioned by President Wilson, and the "separate national conditions" of Lloyd George made the likelihood of Basra's annexation very small. The British position would then be that of a candidate for advisory power, rather than that of ruler over subject. And, unless the constituency was nursed in advance, it was not at all certain that Britain would win the necessary votes. "Is it possible so to handle the local population, or the elements in it that count, as to ensure that, if and when the moment for 'self-determination' arrives, they will pronounce decisively in favour of continuing the British connection?" Cox should be consulted; but time was fast running out, and it was decided that he should be asked to travel to Cairo or England, or, failing that, a high-ranking representative should be sent out to him to discuss policy.[92]

Cox had suggested some form of personal contact more than once, and his own favored idea of a committee to visit Mesopotamia had been rejected. Later, Cox had himself rejected a trip to Simla to explain his quarrel with Maude, no doubt wisely considering the outcome of that quarrel.[93] Now, however, Cox was asked to visit Cairo, and soon his absence from

---

the M.A.C. until January 1918. In March 1918, the Cabinet amalgamated the Middle East Committee (now including Balfour and General Macdonogh, but excluding Milner by his own request of July 1917) with the F.O.'s committee on Russia and an interdepartmental committee on Persia. Curzon was assigned the task of working out the details of the amalgamation and reconstruction of the new "Eastern Committee." War Cabinet 363, 11 March 1918, *CAB* 23/5; M.E.C. 11th minutes, 12 January 1918, *CAB* 27/22.

[92] I.O. memorandum, 31 January, and M.E.C., 3rd minutes, new series, 2 February 1918, *CAB* 27/23.

[93] Another suggestion of December 1916, that Wingate, now in charge of Hijaz operations, should meet Cox at Aden, was rejected because of a crisis in Hijaz affairs: *L/P&S/11*, vol. 115, file 5320/16.

Iraq was prolonged by instructions to proceed to London. He was gone nearly seven months, leaving Captain Arnold Wilson as Officiating Civil Commissioner.[94] With him on his journey went the hopes of Mesopotamia's administrators, not that Cox would return with information on world conditions, but that he would leave the home authorities with an accurate understanding of the needs of Mesopotamia. As Gertrude Bell wrote to her friend Hardinge, "Things look so black now that the fact that we cannot abandon this country to its fate needs insisting upon." Great strides had already been made, but they had imposed a heavy responsibility on Britain for continuing the progress. The population was satisfied, and "The stronger the hold we are able to keep here the better the inhabitants will be pleased. What they dread is any half measure." No one, she concluded, could conceive of an independent Arab government.[95]

By late March Cox was in Cairo, talking with Wingate, Clayton, Hogarth, and others, mainly on problems of the Arabian Peninsula but also expressing the Mesopotamian view of the Mesopotamian future. In mid-April he was in London. He talked to Shuckburgh and Lord Islington (Parliamentary Under-Secretary for India, acting for Montagu who was in India); he spent the weekend at Hackwood with Curzon; he attended the War Council and the Eastern Committee (another reorganization had removed the word "Middle"); he was received at Windsor. In early June he was in Paris, talking with Sykes and Robert Cecil (Minister of Blockade); by the middle of the month he was in Cairo discussing Ibn Sa'ud; in late July he was in Simla; and finally by late August he was

[94] SSI telegram to Cox, 9 February 1918, *CAB* 27/23; Graves, *Cox*, pp. 235–47. Cox, most unusually for him, kept a diary in this period, to which Graves had access, and discussion of Cox's journey is based on this and various documents in *FO* 371/3401.

[95] Bell private to Hardinge, 22 February 1918, *FO* 371/3406; quoted in Burgoyne, *op. cit.*, pp. 78–79.

back in Baghdad—but this too was only a stopover, for Cox was badly needed as Minister to Persia. It was a hectic trip, and Cox did his best both to explain and to understand.

Before Cox reached England, an effort had been made to prepare a position for discussion with him; the effort showed only that it was going to be up to Cox to advise. As Shuckburgh wrote in a memorandum of 3 April, it should still be possible, even considering the new situation, to keep Basra in British hands. But was the policy now being pursued the right one? He did not mean to imply criticism of Cox, but which of the various elements in Iraq should be strengthened? What machinery existed for the establishment of local government? Could any Arab authority be discovered which would command general support?[96]

Curzon felt that this sort of pessimistic talk would give Cox the wrong impression. A better plan than facing Cox with such a document was for Curzon himself to talk privately with him, along with Balfour and Islington, and explain the problems. The real question was this: How much was the existing form of government in consonance with Arab ideas? How much Turkish, and how much Indian, role could there be? Would the administration still require the presence of British officers? Positive questions were wanted. Islington had no objections; Shuckburgh's memorandum had, after all, been meant for the committee, where some—notably the newly joined General Smuts—had only a hazy idea of the situation.

But Cox still had to provide the principal explanations. In a lengthy memorandum of 22 April he set out what appeared to him to be the situation now and the requirements for the future. Cox made it clear he understood the changed conditions; ". . . it is recognised that the question of annexation has become ex-

---

[96] Shuckburgh memorandum B.281 (not signed), 3 April, Curzon note, 3 April, Islington undated note for Curzon, and I.O. Political Department note B.283, 12 April 1918, *L/P&S/10*, 2571/17, no. 617/18.

ceedingly difficult *vis-à-vis* the President of the United States . . . ," and Britain must be prepared to accept something less. Still, considering the money spent on development and other sacrifices, a strong case for control of Basra could, he believed, still be made.

As far as the administration was concerned, he did not believe that homogeneous administration of the vilayets of Baghdad and Basra was necessarily incompatible with separate administrative status, nor did the Arab façade present insurmountable problems. The best solution would be a High Commissioner aided by a council. The main thing was to preserve British control of foreign relations, which would make the area a practical protectorate; if the Allies would not agree to this, then the establishment of a titular native ruler would become a necessity, and then the problem would be finding the right man. The Sharifal family could be eliminated, for there was neither justification nor necessity for involving them in Iraq; Cox had always opposed even discussing the area with Husain. It might be possible to pay him deference as titular head of a confederation, or Sharif of the holy places—even, if necessary, to pay him a subsidy from Iraqi revenues; but no actual control. In fact, Cox had a candidate: the Naqib of Baghdad, head of the Gilani family and, though elderly, a man of much social and religious prestige (he was head of the Qadiri order of dervishes). The Naqib had little political ambition, and he had so far proved cooperative. He would engender considerable support in Iraq and in India—but the important point that emerged from these considerations was Cox's hostility to any Sharifal candidate.

Yet another issue was the use of Arabs in the local administration. Qualified Arab staff simply did not exist; while suitable for subordinate positions, they could not yet fill the top jobs, saturated as they were with Turkish methods and "evil traditions." The substitution of local levies for British and

Indian troops would also take time. The main task, still, was winning the loyalty of the locally powerful—landlords, shaikhs, merchants, and the like—and this raised the question of asking Iraqi public opinion its view on the British connection.

> If it becomes a question of obtaining public expression of feeling in favour of British control, it can be done; but I think the subject would have to be handled cautiously. The intelligent inhabitants of Iraq at the back of their minds are possessed by the apprehension that Mesopotamia may conceivably be restored to the Turks at the Peace Conference, and as long as this nightmare is present with them we should merely emphasize it by asking them which Government they would prefer. By so doing we should be clearly putting them in a very unfair position because they know well that if they elect for British control and if nevertheless the Turks were ultimately to return, all those who had declared for us would receive short shrift.[97]

Two days after this was written the Eastern Committee met to discuss Iraq, with Cox as a visitor. All of Cox's points were discussed, and some others, and the committee was generally quite sympathetic. Balfour even soothed some fears of American reaction; he thought (and Balfour had been in Washington before replacing Grey in the Foreign Office) that President Wilson did not seriously foresee the application of his formula outside Europe, but rather meant that no civilized country would be under another; the President would probably accept an Arab state under British protection if it were shown that the Arabs could not stand alone. Cox still urged that nothing in the form of a plebiscite be held in Iraq, for it was unsuited to the local population and would excite lively misgivings. Balfour

---

[97] Cox memorandum, 22 April 1918, B.284, *ibid.*, no. 1604/18. Not all Cox's staff agreed on the Naqib; Gertrude Bell, for one, objected to his age, lack of heir, and religious standing, for the Shiite Muslims would not relish a Sunnite religious leader as amir. But she had no concrete alternative. Bell private to Hardinge, 25 May 1918, *FO* 371/3407. Miss Bell's letters had a habit of turning up in official places—which fact was to cause her some pain later.

left the impression that this would perhaps not be necessary. As for the Arab ruler, Cox again pleaded that no negotiations be conducted on this subject with Husain.[98]

When Cox left the committee, it was with the conviction that it had sanctioned his policy to date and, further, had given approval to continued development along the lines already laid down. How much in tune with Cox the committee was is shown by its discussion of a possible proclamation annexing Basra, or, since Sykes opposed the word "annexation," announcing a "perpetual lease" or "enclave" or something of the sort, although no decision was taken on this, or on the Arab ruler.

Back in Iraq, however, Cox's attention was focused on a rather different matter, for it was apparent that in his absence the War Office had attempted to intervene in civil affairs by sending to Mesopotamia on its own behalf precisely the commission that had been denied Cox. Wilson had perceived one way to stop the Army's inquiry, and in September he revived Cox's request for a special commission. His own rather sudden elevation to the post of Civil Commissioner when Cox was sent to Persia served as one justification for this request. Still another was that Wilson had taken it upon himself to run the whole of Mesopotamia from Baghdad, for he saw no justification for continued separation of the Basra and Baghdad vilayets. This measure he considered consistent with the Eastern Committee's earlier instructions to Cox that, where administrative differences existed, the system as applied in Baghdad rather than that of Basra would be preferred, on the grounds that practical distinctions—over and above technical separation—were not desirable. As Wilson pointed out, the earlier difference of Basra being at peace while Baghdad was at war was now removed. To the India Office, all this seemed reasonable, including the commission—for the rapid approach of the end of the war and the necessary peace conference made it desirable

[98] E.C. 5th minutes, 24 April 1918, *CAB* 27/24.

that a substantial case on Mesopotamia be prepared in advance.[99]

The spectacle of rival visiting commissions was forestalled by the Foreign Office, and particularly by Lord Robert Cecil, now responsible in that department for eastern affairs, who thought that little purpose would be served by a commission until the general principles of policy were agreed upon—although some had thought this was already the case. Shuckburgh had already prepared instructions for the proposed three-man committee (one each from military and political sides and one with Egyptian experience), but the draft, while corresponding to Cecil's idea of the main purpose, was, as Holderness pointed out, not at all the sort of document Wilson had had in mind. He had asked for a commission to give advice on administrative questions, but now it was to consider such issues as annexation, possible Arab ruler, and so on—all questions which Holderness felt were incapable of any solution until a peace was concluded and these points ironed out. If it were done now, it would all have to be done again.[100]

The confusion was not aided by Montagu's support of, and Chelmsford's opposition to, the plan—the latter on the grounds that the commission would be discussing issues vital to India without consulting India. On 29 October, the day before the Turkish armistice, the Eastern Committee discussed the matter, and the view held by Curzon and Smuts carried the day: to Smuts, a commission in Iraq could not work out a policy which must be decided in London; to Curzon, the commission would bring Allied suspicions and questions in Parliament,

[99] *L/P&S/10*, file 3156/18 (on W.O. attempt); Wilson telegram to FSI/SSI, 27 September, I.O. Political Department (Shuckburgh) minute, 21 October 1918, *L/P&S/10*, 2571/17, nos. 4252 and 4424/18. Wilson technically remained Officiating Civil Commissioner, replacing Cox, who was to return to Iraq after his stint in Persia, but with no time limit on his tenure his freedom to act was much greater.

[100] Shuckburgh draft, 22 October, Holderness minute, 23 October, Cecil for Montagu, 28 October 1918, *ibid.*, no. 4677/18.

and would more hinder than help Britain at the peace conference. Tempers flared, for Cecil, who like Montagu favored the
commission (although on his own, not Wilson's terms), was
convinced that the committee was here intervening in a departmental executive question rather than laying down the lines of
larger policy as was its legitimate function.[101]

But the decision stood. With the commission rejected, it
appeared to Mesopotamia and to India that policy questions,
administrative and otherwise, would have to await the peace
conference. As it happened, discussion of policy was not to
await the great gathering at Paris but was to commence within
a week of the Eastern Committee's decision against the commission. For on 7 November Britain and France jointly issued
a policy declaration which came as a shock to a considerable
number of Britain's imperial representatives in the Middle East
—but consideration of that declaration and its effects first requires discussion of the later stages of the Arab revolt.

The war in Mesopotamia was over; it is difficult to call it a
glorious campaign. Seldom has a British military effort under-
gone more criticism, from Lloyd George's "a gruesome story
of tragedy and suffering resulting from incompetence and slov-
enly carelessness on the part of the responsible military authorities" to Cyril Falls's considered conclusion: "The Mesopotamian campaign was, in fact, not a contribution to winning the
war so much as a contribution to its dreary and bloody prolon-
gation."[102] Whatever the judgment, the cost cannot be denied:
nearly 100,000 casualties in all, of which 30,000 had been killed
or had died of wounds or disease—and a ration strength at the
end of the war of over 400,000 troops.[103]

[101] E.C. 37th minutes, 29 October 1918, *CAB* 27/24; Montagu private
to Chelmsford, 22 October 1918, *Montagu Papers* (I.O. Library),
Eur.Mss. D.523; Viceroy telegram to SSI, 6 October 1918, *FO* 371/3387;
Cecil private to Curzon, 30 October, Curzon private to Cecil, 31 October 1918, *Cecil Papers* (British Museum), Add.Mss. 51077.

[102] Lloyd George, *War Memoirs*, II, p. 238; Cyril Falls, *The Great
War* (N.Y., 1961), p. 179.

[103] J. Edmonds, *op. cit.*, p. 393; Barker, *Neglected War*, p. 457.

And yet, perhaps the cost would be worth it to the Empire—
for that Empire now stretched from Egypt through Palestine
and Syria (where British troops were still in occupation) into
Persia and the Caucasus and Central Asia and down the Persian
Gulf, and so on to India and the Far East; "from the left bank
of the Don to India is our interest and preserve," wrote the
C.I.G.S.,[104] as British ships sailed the Black Sea and roamed the
Caspian. In Palestine, Mesopotamia, and Mosul, Britain controlled nearly 200,000 square miles of additional territory and
several million inhabitants.

Mesopotamia itself had been a difficult problem in administration, and dealings with the Arabs had not been easy. Indeed, there had been some serious outbreaks in the holy cities
of Najaf and Karbala in late 1917 and early 1918, but they
were now quiet.[105] As Cox wrote later,

> By the end of the war the people of Mesopotamia had come to
> accept the fact of our occupation and were resigned to the prospect
> of a permanent British administration. . . . Throughout the country
> there was a conviction, which frequently found open expression,
> that the British meant well by the Arabs, and this was accompanied
> by a frank appreciation of the increased prosperity which had fol-
> lowed in the track of our armies and, no doubt, by a lively sense of
> favours to come, in the way of progress and reform.

It is the idealistic picture of hindsight, and it was written with
an eye to later events. "But," as he added, "with the Armistice,
and the Anglo French declaration by which it was immediately
followed, a new turn was given to the native mind."[106] The
nature of the "new turn" was to be vital for British Middle East
interests, and it depended to a considerable extent on events on
the other side of the Arabian Peninsula.

[104] Guinn, op. cit., p. 321.
[105] Wilson, Loyalties, pp. 226–27; Marlowe, op. cit., pp. 128–129;
Burgoyne, op. cit., p. 84.
[106] Bell, op. cit., II, p. 523.

# IV

# The Arabs and the
# Allies, 1916-1918

. . . beyond this we dimly glimpsed black-coated
figures in far-away London, the shoulders of their
coats worn with shrugging away responsibilities. Fog
stained their windows and darkened their office lights.
"Passed to you," they wrote, hoping the cup of decision might pass for ever. "The Treasury," they
breathed, coughing in the fog, "will never stand for
this. . ."

*Lord Belhaven*, THE UNEVEN ROAD

1

The Arab revolt came as a considerable surprise to India, even
to those who knew of the negotiations leading to the revolt, for
they had consistently dismissed the possibility of actual rebellion as a pipe dream, having only Cairo's reports and no
firsthand information on Arab attitudes (other than in Mesopotamia) on which to judge. It came as a surprise, too, to
Indian opinion—particularly Muslim opinion—because the Indian public had been told nothing about the negotiations and,
indeed, very little about the war itself.

The Indian government had issued a statement on the sanctity of the holy places, but no other pronouncements had been made, partly to preserve calm and partly to avoid making any commitments on future policy. In general, it had been decided that as little news as possible would be given out on the Turkish war, particularly the Russo-Turkish conflict which it involved; instructions in that sense were given orally—deliberately, nothing was sent out in writing—to all subordinate Indian governments.[1] By 1915 it had been decided, in connection with the first advance to Baghdad, that local celebrations of victories over the Turks should be avoided. There was some debate on this policy, for it seemed to belittle India's war effort, and after the fall of Baghdad in 1917 local governments were allowed to decide for themselves about victory celebrations, provided they consulted with Delhi.[2]

Obviously there was fear in India of hostile Muslim reaction. There was fear too of the dangers of using Muslim troops against the Turks, although this proved generally unfounded. Such incidents as occurred—a Baluchi infantry mutiny, a Muslim unit's bloody rising in Singapore—proved exceptions to the rule. The biggest problem, in fact, was not religious feeling so much as an unwillingness to serve in the conditions prevalent in the Middle East; at one point in 1916, the Indian authorities even discussed, but happily discarded, the introduction of the death penalty for self-inflicted wounds.[3] In general, it was true to say, as did Hardinge, that Indian Muslim troops had no qualms about shooting at Arabs in Mesopotamia.[4]

Religious reasons for rigorous censorship were soon superseded by reluctance to bombard the Indian public with news

[1] Grant note, 1 December 1914, *India Home Poli.* December 1914, 27; files in *India Sec. I.* [Internal] June 1916, 1–28, and *India Home Poli.* November 1914, 35, deposit.
[2] *India Home Poli.* May 1917, 4, deposit.
[3] *Ibid.* October 1916, 2, deposit.
[4] Hardinge private to General Birdwood, 1 July 1916, *Hardinge Papers.*

of the conditions in Mesopotamia once serious fighting began, conditions among the wounded became intolerable, and serious general setbacks occurred. But for those who governed India, the problem of religion was still a real one, and there was (curiously, in the light of later events) a feeling that Hindus might gloat over Muslim reverses and thereby increase Hindu-Muslim friction. Nothing should be done that would upset the equilibrium, and for this reason, for example, another proposal was rejected—again in 1916 and again wisely—to try to substitute the name "King-Emperor" for "Caliph" in Muslim prayers (it rankled that supposedly loyal Muslim subjects still prayed openly for the head of an enemy state).[5]

The Arab revolt required more substantial information for the public. On 23 June 1916 news of the revolt was released in India, although all news of Britain's sponsorship was carefully suppressed. As Grant put it, ". . . officially to identify Government with an unsuccessful venture of this kind [for he was certain it would fail] could only serve to excite religious odium and lower our prestige. . ."[6] At first, news of the revolt was received quietly, for many Muslims disbelieved it and others saw it as a short-lived eruption which would doubtless be quickly suppressed. When sections of the English-language press began to publish more detailed reports, some protests did arise.

On 26 June the Council of the All-India Muslim League, meeting at Lucknow, made known its "abhorrence" at the action of the rebels, which might well jeopardize the safety and sanctity of the holy places—a resolution that, in its turn, the India Office wished to censor from the press. Concern for the centers of pilgrimage, rather than reverence for the Caliph, seems to have been the dominant reaction. There is no evidence

[5] India Home Poli. November 1914, 35, deposit, and December 1916, 20, deposit; India Sec. War December 1917, 378–400.

[6] India Home Poli. July 1916, 441–45; Grant demi-official to all local governments, 4 July 1916, ibid. April 1919, 31, deposit.

that news of the revolt interested, let alone disturbed, the majority of Indian Muslims; it was, after all, far away, and God
orders such things for reasons best known to Him.[7]

But there were sufficient indications of concern from La-
hore, Cawnpore, Poona, and Quetta to prompt the Indian authorities to instruct local governments to issue no public pronouncements—for it would be better to let the Muslim
community gradually become accustomed to the situation—
and to guide influential Muslims to the proper sort of interpretation of these events through individual discussion, pointing
out in particular that to be pro-Turk was, of course, to be anti-
British. Above all, nothing should be said about Britain's role
in the revolt. In private, doubtless a number of India's rulers
shared the attitude expressed by Grant: the revolt might
"quietly fizzle out," although he knew that support of the
revolt was official policy and "we must not wish that." Most
important, as he wrote Hardinge, his superior until only a few
months earlier, it was vital that no troops under alien (that is,
Christian) officers be sent to aid Husain in the Hijaz. He only
wished, he continued, that Hardinge was still there to give
guidance on a course to be steered "between the Scylla of HM's
govt's arab policy and the Charybdis of Moslem feeling in
India and Afghanistan."[8]

Officially India reported that the news had come as a bomb-
shell, and a profound sensation had been caused just at a time

[7] *Ibid.* July 1916, 441–45, particularly Criminal Intelligence Depart-
ment report, 8 July 1916; Abstract of Intelligence, United Provinces, 1
July 1916, *ibid.* April 1919, 31, deposit. I.O. opposition: SSI telegram to
Viceroy, 29 June 1916, L/P&S/10, 2100/16, no. 2501/16.

[8] Grant private to Hardinge, 1 July 1916, *Hardinge Papers* (and see
also 12 July); see also Chamberlain private to Chelmsford, 22 June, and
Chelmsford private to Chamberlain, 30 June and 7 July 1916, *Chelmsford Papers.* The Indian reaction, and connection, is discussed briefly
in Antonius, *op. cit.*, pp. 204–5; Monroe, *op. cit.*, p. 36; Thornton, *op.
cit.*, p. 184; and Sir Michael O'Dwyer, *India as I Knew It, 1885–1925*
(London, 1925), p. 181. See also Ludwic W. Adamec, *Afghanistan
1900–1923: A Diplomatic History* (Berkeley, Calif., 1967), p. 100.

when all had seemed relatively peaceful. It was thus advisable to remain quiet about the revolt so as not to be associated with an unpopular movement. By the first week in July, India admitted that the situation was in hand but warned that if Britain took any action at Jidda it might prove impossible to keep it so. Care should be taken before ". . . we drift into action which may permanently estrange 70,000,000 Indian subjects. . ."[9]

The surprise and hostility voiced in India came, in turn, as a surprise to the home authorities, who did not know how little Indian public opinion had been prepared for the revolt, or how little information was released generally; the rigorous censorship had been one of the main difficulties even they had encountered in obtaining information of any accuracy on conditions in Mesopotamia. India was told in no uncertain terms that Muslims in India must be brought to see which side of the war they were on—but no landing of British troops was intended in the Hijaz.[10]

But what Valentine Chirol termed the "stagnant pools of Simla" (incidentally using a term of Gertrude Bell's)[11] did not respond in a particularly enthusiastic manner, for they had no assurance that the revolt would succeed (and, indeed, premature release of information might, they said, have revealed the Sharif's plans); first reports on operations were not of a character to inspire confidence. Hardinge, now in the Foreign Office but still sharing India's doubts, wrote that "chaos" seemed to reign in the Hijaz: ". . . there appears to be no policy at all, everything being allowed to drift according to the Shereef's will & pleasure. The latter seems rather hopeless. He does not know what he wants, but continues to make fantastic de-

[9] Viceroy telegrams to SSI, 29 June, 1, 6, and 7 July (quoted) 1916, *L/P&S/10*, 2100/16, nos. 2506, 2542, 2661, and 2678/16.

[10] SSI telegram to Viceroy, 30 June 1916, *CAB* 17/175; F.O. to I.O., 7 July, Hirtzel draft and Chamberlain minute, 12 July, SSI telegram to Viceroy, 13 July 1916, *L/P&S/10*, 2100/16, nos. 2677 and 2692/16.

[11] Chirol private to Hardinge, 7 July 1916, *Hardinge Papers.*

mands."[12] There was not even enough certainty for London to force India to issue the proclamation and explanation of the revolt that was published in Cairo's sphere of action.[13]

Considering the doubts held by India Office personnel on the future of the rising, it was not surprising that some, like Holderness, agreed with Chelmsford that even the one public declaration already made was a mistake and it was not desirable to excite public opinion by further releases—a major reason, the Viceroy added, why the ground had not been prepared in India in the first place. India also requested that the declaration, a general one of support, not even be issued in Mesopotamia.[14] There were two reasons for this. One, unspoken, was a natural unwillingness to have policy on such matters dictated (by Sykes, for example) to the India Office and India.[15] Another, more acceptable in public, was the fact that the revolt had excited little response in Iraq and the Persian Gulf. Any propaganda, reported General Lake, would be likely to produce the wrong impression, although a proclamation from the Sharif himself for circulation in Iraq might, as Chelmsford agreed, be acceptable. Both Lake and the Viceroy were concerned that Britain's connection be deemphasized, but by the end of July, with Muslim opinion satisfactorily quiet (primarily due to muzzling of meetings and censorship of news), the Viceroy

[12] Cornwallis to Arab Bureau, 8 July 1916, and undated Hardinge minute, *FO* 371/2774. Viceroy telegram to SSI, 3 July 1916, *India Sec. War* September 1916, 248–441, makes the point about premature revelation of plans.

[13] Clayton memorandum, 5 July, Viceroy telegram to SSI and McMahon telegram to Grey (with minutes showing I.O. would not press India), 13 July 1916, *FO* 371/2774.

[14] Holderness private to Chelmsford, 13 July, Chelmsford private to Chamberlain, 14 July and 25 August 1916, *Chelmsford Papers*; Grant private to Hardinge, 2 and 30 August 1916, *Hardinge Papers*; and SSI telegram to Viceroy, 19 July, and clipping of *The Times* (giving text of declaration), 28 July 1916, *FO* 371/2774.

[15] See Holderness memorandum on Sykes's interest in Indian affairs, 31 July 1916, *L/P&S/10*, 2100/16, no. 3093/16.

had become confident that Muslim opinion would come around to accept the *fait accompli* if the revolt actually succeeded.[16]

It was difficult to press India so long as home authorities were divided themselves. Hardinge, for example, continued to see an air of unreality about the revolt even in August. By October he was willing to admit that it might have been better had India taken a "broader line" from the start; the revolt's success and a few months in the Foreign Office were altering his attitude. Sykes saw from the first that India was going to be uncooperative. The question was less propaganda for Indians and more education for Indian officials, who, he claimed, were fighting problems of their own making, chiefly the fallacious concept that the revolt was nothing more than the result of Cairo's intrigue and the Sharif's ambition to proclaim himself Caliph. India attached too much importance to the Caliphate in any case. Hardinge was not impressed: Sykes, he wrote, "inundates the War Committee with a terrible lot of rubbish . . . ," and when Sykes actually testified before that body, "talked a great deal of nonsense to the amusement of everybody." Chamberlain, too, was skeptical of Sykes's visions—not so skeptical, however, that he could not be persuaded by Sykes's argument that history justified the Sultan's future loss of the title of Caliph. It was Chamberlain, prompted by Sykes, who originated the "King-Emperor" plan—one more plan gone awry.[17]

With its own arguments, and with disagreement at home, India had so far managed to stave off any major measures in

[16] Lake telegram to SSI/FSI, 25 July, Viceroy telegram to SSI, 27 July 1916, *FO* 371/2774; Maj. A. P. Trevor (Persian Gulf) demi-official to Grant, 31 July 1916, *India Sec. War* March 1917, 1–175.

[17] Chamberlain to Prime Minister, 16 August, Sykes to Chamberlain, 21 August 1916, *L/P&S/11*, vol. 113, no. 4851/16; Hardinge private to Chirol (quoted), and to Grant, 3 August 1916, *Hardinge Papers*; Hardinge private to Grant, 4 October 1916, *Grant Papers*; Chamberlain private to Chelmsford, 6 September, Chelmsford private to Chamberlain, 27 November 1916, *Chelmsford Papers*.

support of the revolt—or, indeed, any official commitment to its support. The attitude it adopted and wished to maintain was one of simply waiting for the results to be forthcoming in Arabia—waiting, it must be said, with neither optimism nor enthusiasm. But this disassociation from events in the Middle East could hardly be maintained if Britain was to have one Arab policy, as India was soon to find to her own dissatisfaction.

2

The early weeks of the Arab revolt, once Mecca was captured, were not crowned with outstanding success. It began to appear, in fact, that the Turks might snuff out the revolt with superior forces. The obvious way to forestall this was for Britain to aid with more than money and guns and promises and to send troops to Sharif Husain. By early September 1916 such a plan was being studied closely.

The opponents were numerous. At their head stood General Robertson, who viewed a plan to land a brigade at Rabigh (roughly 100 miles north of Jidda on the Red Sea coast, Rabigh is one of the last feasible landing places—although the town is not itself directly on the coast—before the main Medina road turns inland) as another Gallipoli or Salonika or Mesopotamia; in short, "strategy gone mad." General Murray, commanding in Egypt, also saw the common logic of such campaigns: a few troops, then artillery, then a base, then doctors, and lawyers, and so on.[18] The Arab Bureau, for varying reasons, was opposed almost to a man. Clayton feared for the credibility of Britain's disinterest once the troops landed; T. E. Lawrence said that once the Arabs heard the British were in the field they

[18] Robertson private to Murray, 16 October (quoted), and Murray private to Robertson, 1 September 1916, *Robertson-Murray Correspondence*.

would probably go home themselves; Hogarth was worried about pledges given of noninterference in the holy places (already compromised to a point by the shelling of Turkish troops outside Jidda, although it was not strictly a "holy place") and the Sharif's existing suspicions of British intentions.[19]

There was little doubt, too, of India's position. Far better, said Chelmsford bluntly, to see the revolt go down to disaster than to let it be known among Indian Muslims that Britain was not only responsible but actively participating. In the India Office, Hirtzel shared this view, but Chamberlain was persuaded that the reverse was true: it was better to offend Indian Muslim opinion than to see yet another small ally go down. After all, Egyptian or Sudanese Muslim troops could be used, thereby at least forestalling any criticism that might arise simply because of Christian presence in the Hijaz.[20]

The principal supporters of Rabigh were Wingate and Mc-Mahon. Wingate in particular was the leading advocate; he assumed military control over Hijaz operations in October 1916, and political responsibility as well in November—and then, on 1 January 1917, became High Commissioner when McMahon was dismissed. In February he was also made General Officer Commanding, Hijaz, but on his own suggestion this appointment was not publicized; India, he said, would misunderstand. Wingate let his strong views on Rabigh color his objectivity; if aid was not given Husain, he urged in October,

[19] Clayton views mentioned in Murray private to Robertson, *ibid.*; Lawrence, *Seven Pillars*, pp. 62, 111–12; Liddell Hart, *Lawrence*, pp. 105–22. Lawrence report enclosed in Clayton private to Wingate, 23 November 1916, *Wingate Papers*, box 143a; Hogarth memorandum, 10 January 1917, FO 882/6. See also Robertson, *Soldiers and Statesmen*, II, pp. 153–63, and Robertson private to Wingate, 8 September 1916, *Wingate Papers*, box 140.

[20] Chelmsford private to McMahon, 16/17 September, Chamberlain private to Chelmsford, 21 and 30 September 1916, *Chelmsford Papers*; Hirtzel private to Lucas (Private Secretary to SSI), 20 November 1916, and Chamberlain private to G. Lloyd (Cairo), 1 February 1917, *Chamberlain Papers*, 20/5/20.

it would mean the "almost inevitable collapse of Sherif movement." [21]

Wingate's strong support and Chamberlain's indecision lent
the plan enough credence to be considered by the Cabinet.
Curzon and Chamberlain both argued that the local responsible
officials, McMahon and Wingate, should be entitled to have
their opinions respected in this. After a meeting of Curzon,
Chamberlain, and Grey in November, Robertson was forced to
spell out to the War Cabinet exactly what the requirements for
such an operation would be: at least two brigades of infantry,
artillery, engineers, and so on to a total of something on the
order of 16,000 men. Enthusiasm quickly dampened for a small
victorious campaign at Rabigh.[22]

Incredibly, the discussions were still kept alive, mostly by
unfounded rumors of a Turkish advance; and when Wingate
was put in full control in 1917 he sent off to Jidda, without
authority, news that the brigade of troops would land, although
in fact the Cabinet had already decided against the project (the
brigade never landed). Finally, Husain himself proved hostile
to the plan, for Husain had blown now hot, now very cold, on
the scheme; many British officials, in fact, now met for the first
time this particular feature of Sharifal diplomacy. But only
when the Sharif had made his position quite clear was Wingate
willing to give up a plan he had supported against the advice
of many of his subordinates. "It will not be so easy hereafter,"
wrote Hirtzel of Wingate, "to feel confidence in his judg-

[21] Sirdar telegram to High Commissioner, 13 October 1916, *FO* 141/
462.
[22] Discussions of Rabigh in the Cabinet: W.C. 1 (9 December), 2 (11
December), 12 (20 December 1916), 29 (8 January 1917), *CAB* 23/1;
Hirtzel noted on 13 October, however (on McMahon telegram to
Grey, 18 September 1916, *L/P&S/10*, 2100/16, no. 4115/16), that he
understood from the F.O. that Grey and Lloyd George had decided
that day not to send any troops to Rabigh. While indicative of the
attitude of the two men, this decision was not final, owing to Wingate's
representations.

ment." Wingate, in his turn, tended to blame India and the "poisonous propaganda" which it had absorbed for so long and which was responsible for its unrealistic objections.[23]

It was a curious affair, made no less curious by the overriding of their respective subordinates by Wingate and Chamberlain. Certainly India's persistent opposition had entered into the story, but the debate on this issue was as much "Easterner" vs. "Westerner" as Cairo vs. India, and even then Cairo was a house divided. Since India had not had to stand alone, its influence was not as clear in this question as it might have been, despite Wingate's attitude; nor had India applied as much pressure as it might have if it had ever been suggested that Indian troops be used for the landing. But there were other schemes, and some of them touched India more directly.

As already noted, from the time of the outbreak of war there had been considerable thought devoted to the use of Arab nationalists, and the bag of prisoners in Mesopotamia included a number of individuals who might fall into this category. Here Sykes was particularly involved, for use of Arab prisoners was one of his favorite projects. Attempts made to use prisoners in Iraq all encountered the insurmountable hostility of the Indian and Mesopotamian authorities, but with the coming of the revolt the Hijaz offered a new and fertile field for such activities. In July 1916, Egypt suggested that the sixty-odd prisoners it held be used with the Sharif.[24]

[23] On brigade landing: Arab Bureau telegram to Col. C. E. Wilson (Jidda), 6 January 1917, *FO* 686/53. On Husain: Wingate telegram to Balfour, 12 January, and Hirtzel minute (quoted), 15 January 1917, *L/P&S/11*, vol. 116, no. 243/17. Wingate's views on India: private to C. E. Wilson, 1 September (quoted) and 29 October, and to Clayton, 14 September and 16 October; also Clayton private to Wingate, 20 September 1916, *Wingate Papers*, boxes 140–41. C. E. Wilson, incidentally, also opposed the landing, on the ground that it would prejudice the Sharif's chances at the Caliphate: C. Wilson telegram to Arbur, 7 January 1917 (on receipt of Wingate's information of the coming landing), *FO* 141/736.

[24] Sykes reference to this: memorandum, 19 June 1916, *CAB* 17/175; W.O. to F.O., 20 July 1916, *FO* 371/2774. A few Indian officers, it

But if sizable forces were to be built up, Egypt's small supply of prisoners would not do. Aside from some notable persons who had joined Husain (or more properly his son and field commander, Amir Faisal) and who would play a considerable role in the story, some more significant effort would have to be made among non-Hijazi Arabs. Supporters of this sort of activity had one eye on eventual repercussions in Iraq, and it was to their advantage that some of Faisal's ablest lieutenants were Iraqis. Nuri as-Sa'id, when he was permitted to leave India; Nuri's brother-in-law, Ja'far al-'Askari, from the Kirkuk area in the Mosul vilayet, probably the only man in history to win both the German Iron Cross and the C.M.G., who later headed the regular units in Faisal's force; or others of lesser rank: Maulud Pasha al-Mukhlis, captured at Shaiba, and the first regular soldier to join Faisal, or Jamil Bey al-Midfa'i, artillery commander, who had escaped from Syria—all of these men could have influence over and above their military roles.[25] On the other hand, individuals were not enough.

The obvious recruiting ground for a force was India, where the majority of Arab prisoners were held. India had no real objection to handing over these prisoners to Egyptian responsibility (it would be, after all, a reduction in expenditure), and by December 1916 the first shipload had reached the Red Sea. By mid-1917 about 450 Arabs had been recruited for the cause, both in India and in Mesopotamia. But India handed them over with little courtesy—and handed over *all* available Arab prisoners without either informing them of their destination or making a selection of the most responsive or suitable. As a result, the prisoners arrived with little enthusiasm and, in some

should be added, did serve in the Hijaz, and for this Maj. N. N. E. Bray (attached to the Arab Legion for a few months in 1917) was largely responsible: Bray (then Capt.) to D.M.I., 19 October 1916, *L/P&S/10*, 2100/16, no. 4657/16, and *Shifting Sands* (London, 1934), pp. 61–72.

[25] Information on role of these individuals taken from Liddell Hart, *Lawrence, passim*; Lawrence, *Seven Pillars*, pp. 92, 164; Birdwood, *Nuri*, pp. 47–49, 60; de Gaury, *op. cit.*, pp. 49–50; Graves, *Lawrence, passim*.

cases, much bitterness. In Cairo, India was blamed for deliberately putting the recruits off: "The cause of this," said Sykes, "is want of a co-ordinated policy between India and Egypt. . ." But, said India, if Cairo had wanted the prisoners to be selected, why had it not said so? [26]

Despite this setback, Sykes forged ahead. By June 1917 he had managed to convince some people of the possibility of an "Arab Legion" of perhaps as many as 10,000 men, with France to contribute half the cost. Wingate supported the idea; the Foreign Office, the India Office, and the War Office all objected. Anglo-French relations in the Hijaz were not working particularly smoothly at this time (although that is another story), and the primary desire was to disentangle France from the Arab revolt altogether; yet here was a Sykes scheme that would result in exactly the opposite. Sykes had an answer to this as well: his opposite number, Picot, would be able to provide French funds without really consulting his government, and when the Legion was trained and ready the French officers would be withdrawn.[27]

But all this was very chancy, and Sykes's involvement of France did his project little good. Wingate was persuaded by Sykes that the force so created could serve as a nucleus not only for Hijaz operations but also, later, in Syria. It is not difficult to follow Sykes here; by mid-1917 he was already thinking of

[26] Viceroy telegram to SSI, 14 December, Lt.-Col. A. C. Parker (with the Arabs) to Arbur, 6 December 1916, Chelmsford in Council to Chamberlain, 23 February, Viceroy telegram to SSI, 1 August 1917, *L/P&S/ 10*, 81/17, nos. 5262/16 and 81, 1165, and 3122/17, and *FO* 371/3043, including Sykes minute (quoted) on A.C. Parker to Arbur; Sykes to Chief of Staff, Egypt, 28 April, Egypt telegram to F.O., 10 June, G. Lloyd to Wingate, 8 June 1917, *FO* 141/746.

[27] G.O.C., Egypt, telegram to W.O., 20 May, Wingate telegram to Balfour, 2 June, and undated Balfour note, *L/P&S/11*, vol. 123, nos. 2097, 2319, and 2981/17; F.O. to D.M.I., 6 June 1917, *FO* 371/3043. On French involvement, see, for example, Général Edmond Brémond, *Le Hedjaz dans la guerre mondiale* (Paris, 1931). A more general account is Eugène Jung, *La Révolte arabe* (2 vols., Paris, 1924).

how to counter the French hold on Syria as recognized in the
agreement that bore his name. But the home authorities looked
at shorter-term effects and the simple fact that the Legion
would involve France all the more deeply in Hijaz affairs. It is
a fascinating commentary on Sykes's character and the per-
suasiveness of his personality in a face-to-face situation that
Wingate, who really had no desire to see France involved in
Arabian affairs, only thought better of the plan after Sykes
had left Cairo and was on his way home.[28]

By July Sykes was arguing to a hostile audience in a War
Cabinet subcommittee that included Hirtzel, Shuckburgh,
Graham, and Army representatives; amazingly, his plan was
approved, but not necessarily for use in the Hijaz, and not
necessarily with joint Anglo-French responsibility. By the end
of the month Sykes had managed to obtain an even more favorable compromise: the force was to operate under the orders of
the Commander in Egypt for the defense of the Hijaz (and
while there was to be nominally responsible to Husain); if elsewhere, under dual Anglo-French control. In the last week of
July Balfour in Paris reached final agreement with France; on
the 30th, Sykes cabled to the officers of his legion, "O Arabs be
wise, be disciplined, be calm, be steadfast. . . . Look neither to
the right nor the left, beware of speculations and intrigues, beware of suspicions. . . . These words I send you from a distance,
would that I could speak them in your ears." [29]

But by the end of September the 10,000 yet remained only
500, in camp at Ismailia, and some of these, reported Clayton,
were useless. Morale was low, and the officers seemed more inclined to political intrigue than to military efforts. An aroused

[28] Lord Methuen (Malta) telegram to Balfour (from Sykes for Graham), 8 June, appealing for delay in consideration of his plan; Wingate
telegram to Balfour, 10 June 1917: *FO 371/3043*.
[29] Note on subcommittee, 5 July 1917, *L/P&S/11*, vol. 123, no. 2981/
17; Balfour telegram to Wingate, 13 July, and drafts; Bertie (Paris)
telegram to Balfour, 26 July; Balfour telegram to Wingate (from Sykes
to Arab Legion), quoted, 30 July 1917: *FO 371/3043*.

Sykes could only cable, again from a distance, ". . . say it is better to be cook in Arab legion than a wazir under the Turks say it and by God believe it if you are capable of belief for it is true." [30] Clayton hastened to report that this message was not necessary, as Nuri and Fu'ad al-Khatib (a primarily diplomatic advisor with the Sharifal forces) had visited the camp with an encouraging message from Husain. The Legion, however, was a failure, and despite Sykes's encouragement of Clayton ("Patience, enthusiasm, and determination surmount obstacles and make circumstances. Dimness of future can only be overcome by vision.") it was sent off to 'Aqaba, recently captured by Lawrence's forces, and absorbed into the regular unit under Faisal—a future Clayton had probably had in mind as soon as the Legion appeared unworkable some months before—and, it should be added, the suspicion of both Faisal and Husain toward this separate force was revealed.[31]

Again, India had played a minor role in the affair of Sykes's Ten Thousand, but when called upon it had responded in less than full measure. Neither India nor Cairo was pleased with the

[30] Wingate telegram to F.O. (from Clayton for Sykes), 30 September 1917, *L/P&S/11*, vol. 123, no. 2946/17; F.O. telegram to Wingate (from Sykes for Clayton), quoted, 9 October 1917, *FO* 141/746. Iraq got its share of similar Sykesian language. Perhaps the most outstanding example is his proposal to Cox, in May 1918, for an order to be called the "Noble Order of the Light of Iraq," with five divisions (the lamp of service, cities, waters, lands, and pastures) and five grades (squire, officer, knight, warden, chief) below the Grand Master (lamp of lamps). There would be an annual meeting of the chapter, with the public admitted to the gallery; the gallery room would be circular "in memory of the round city of Mansur." The banner of each member would be retired to a special room on his death, marked with his promotions, and so on. On a long file, full of scribbled designs for ribbons and shields and the like, Kidston (F.O.) minuted, much later, "interesting & characteristic." Sykes to Cox, 29 May 1918, with Kidston minute, 15 October 1919, *FO* 371/4210.

[31] Wingate telegrams to Balfour (Clayton for Sykes), 16 October and 15 December 1917, *FO* 141/746; Clayton private to Sykes, 15 December 1917, *Wingate Papers*, box 147; Sykes private telegram to Clayton, 15 December 1917 (quoted), *FO* 371/3043.

results, for which they had no hesitation in blaming each other. Unfortunately, there was another issue on which opinions also differed: the substantial subsidy paid to Husain. In the first instance, the Treasury, with the War Cabinet's sanction, approved £125,000 a month for four months in July 1916, to be charged to the Foreign Office accounts. The Treasury, as was the Treasury's wont, suggested that India be asked to pay half this sum. Negotiations were opened on the subject, and McMahon, who had originally suggested the four-month period, now objected that it would hardly be enough to get the revolt going, and Sir Edward Grey, without either Cabinet or Treasury approval, substituted "for the present" for "for four months." Within a day or two the India Office made it known —clearly known—that India had no intention of paying any, let alone half, of that sum from Indian revenues.[32]

The subsidy was continued until April 1917, at the original rate, at which point the Treasury at last discovered what was going on and demanded to know who had authorized the payment beyond the original four months. The Foreign Office apologized, and payment was at least made with official sanction after that date. But the cost of the revolt mounted steadily and, in the months May through August 1917, the fee had reached £200,000 per month, paid, it should be added, in gold sovereigns. Egypt's gold reserve dwindled so rapidly that by July there remained only some £1,600,000 to back the country's finances, and, other things being equal, within eight months more the entire reserve would be in the hands of Husain's hardy warriors. Gold was available in Britain, and Foreign Office funds were supposed to replenish Egypt's coffers, but the Treasury had never bargained on parting with its

[32] Treasury to F.O., 17 July, McMahon telegram to Grey, 14 August, Grey telegram to McMahon, 15 August, Hirtzel to Clerk, 18 August 1916, *FO* 371/2774. India did, however, pay half the cost of the (peacetime) Jidda mission: Hirtzel note, 27 July 1916, *L/P&S/10*, 3280/16, no. 2914/16.

own gold and refused to do so. The Foreign Office, familiar with this sort of problem, therefore told the Treasury that it was now a question of whether Britain would honor her agreements. Egypt, said the Treasury, equally adept at answering arguments, had doubtless not really made sufficient effort to find the money.[33] But by mid-July Wingate had only £30,000 with which to meet the subsidy, and the only recourse was to ask India to help.

The request raised a number of questions. One was the problem of what actually happened to the gold once it disappeared into bankless Arabia. Wingate thought he had turned up at least a partial answer when his investigations showed that some of the money was being exported to India from the Hijaz, although he did not specify why. The solution then appeared to be to get Husain to prohibit the export of gold and to persuade India to provide rupee notes and silver rupees in exchange for gold, presumably credited to India's account in London.[34] Eventually these steps were taken, and the crisis eased somewhat—although the further suggestion that Husain be paid in commodities raised the horrifying picture in the Hijaz of a glut of everything then available in Egypt, and the suggestion was totally rejected. It was necessary to turn to other expedients. Army funds were tapped, and finally the Treasury agreed to ship some gold in November 1917—only to find that the total cost of the revolt had now exploded to £500,000 per month, for the Sharif planned an offensive.[35]

Once more India had been marginally involved—this time, however, the involvement came close to the sensitive area of the Indian rupee and its silver backing. Perhaps more important were the financial lever given, however briefly, to India in the

[33] Waterfield private to Oliphant, 7 May, Balfour telegram to Wingate, 12 July, H. Nicolson note, 14 July 1917, and other documents, in FO 371/3048.

[34] Balfour telegram to Wingate, 18 August 1917, discussing W.O.-I.O.-F.O. conference on the matter, *ibid.*

[35] W.C. 275, 16 November 1917, *CAB* 23/4.

issue of the revolt and the revelation to any official studying the correspondence of just how much the revolt was costing: by August 1917, for example, over £2,200,000 had been paid out to the Sharif and his agents.[36] It was enough to dampen enthusiasm, scant enough in the first place and further reduced by the Rabigh project.

It was obvious that Britain was going to have its problems with Husain and that the issues of Rabigh and subsidy were only indicative of things to come. From the viewpoint of India, each of these affairs was of minor importance (although the financial matter might have become major under other circumstances), but together they did nothing to inspire confidence in India—or Mesopotamia—over future relations with the independent Arab movement. Above all, such differences of opinion served to hamper operations conducted from Cairo if only because the Indian view had each time to be considered. But if this statement stands for the Arab revolt itself, it is even more true of the conduct of Anglo-French negotiations on the future of the Arab Middle East.

3

The conclusion of the Sykes-Picot Agreement in the spring of 1916 temporarily—but only temporarily—settled the future of

[36] Figures in Wingate telegram to Balfour, 8 September 1917, *FO* 371/3048. A further problem, symptomatic of the views involved, was recognition of Husain's self-proclaimed title of "King of the Arab Nation" or "King of the Arabs" (both versions are cited), reduced, for the time being, to "King of the Hijaz" by the British. See various documents in *L/P&S/10*, 5235/16; Wingate telegram to McMahon, 2 November, and Reuters telegram, 26 December 1916, *FO* 141/679; Wingate private to Grey, 15 November 1916, *Grey Papers*, *FO* 800/48; McMahon private to Hardinge, 10 November 1916, *Hardinge Papers*; Grant note, 2 November 1916, *India Sec. War* March 1917, 241–342; and Cox telegram to FSI, 1 February 1917, *FO* 371/3044, reporting that Husain had styled himself "King of the Arabian Countries" in a letter to Ibn Sa'ud.

the Arab world between France and Britain with Russian approval. There was no question at that time of publication of a document dividing the Ottoman Empire among the Allies and giving the Arabs Christian rather than Muslim masters. Certainly both Turkey and Germany would stress such an interpretation. Finally, Britain realized, as France apparently did not, that France had a long way to go in reconciling Arab nationalist opinion to its hoped-for role in Syria.[37]

Despite the secret nature of the document, it was soon known in an unfortunate quarter, namely, the Italian government. Although Grey responded to the Italian inquiry about Italy's sphere if spheres were being handed out by saying that there would be time enough to discuss this when Italy entered the war, the time had arrived by the summer of 1916; while Russia returned a noncommittal answer to Italy, the French began quite quickly to discuss Italy's position in Asia Minor.[38] The negotiations that followed had little bearing upon either the Arab world or India, but the necessity of working Italy into future plans for Asia Minor, coupled with the need to see how the Arab revolt would actually develop, meant that no significant negotiations took place either among the Allies or between Allies and Sharif.

By the spring of 1917 it was obvious that the revolt was going to survive, if not more, and the problem of reconciling French with Arab commitments was no longer one that Britain could wave away. Wingate now suggested that the approaching April visit of Sykes and Picot to Husain—at the request of the latter—would be a good time to inform the "King" (as he now styled himself) of the general lines of the Anglo-French agreement. Sykes, who was traveling to Egypt to act as Chief Political Officer (in place of Clayton), had himself suggested

[37] Unsigned memorandum (by Clayton), 5 July 1916, *FO* 371/2774.
[38] Grey telegrams to Buchanan and Bertie, 12 July, Buchanan telegram to Grey, 14 July, Bertie telegram to Grey, 16 July, Crewe to Bertie, 26 July 1916, *ibid.*

that Picot accompany him as French representative, and that Sharifal representatives be added to the tour, as it now became.[39]

In the first week of May, Sykes met Husain. Sykes had been told by Wingate to clear up with the King questions on the French role in Syria, on the impossibility of imposing Husain's authority on any who did not wish it (that is, in the Arabian Peninsula), and, finally, on the fact that while Arab culture and prosperity would be promoted in the Baghdad area, ". . . we will retain that position of military and political predominance which our strategical and commercial interests require." No detailed and specific record of the conversation appears in the British archives, but Sykes cabled to Wingate and Wingate cabled to the Foreign Office, after the talks, "In accordance with my instructions I explained fully the agreement regarding Arab confederation or State." [40]

From Aden Sykes cabled further details. He had, he reported, an inconclusive interview with Husain. When Syria was mentioned, Sykes said he wished to withdraw to let Husain and Picot talk privately on this Franco-Arab question, but Husain asked him to stay. Husain again made it clear that he could not be a party to handing over Muslims to the direct rule of a non-Muslim state. At this point Sykes did leave, and Picot and Husain talked on for half an hour: when he returned, Sykes discussed the question of advisors for the Arabs.[41] Whether

[39] Wingate telegram to Balfour ("King" is not used), 27 April 1917, L/P&S/10, 3280/16, no. 1972/17; Hirtzel memorandum, 7 March, and Wingate telegram to Balfour (making the first suggestion: "King is not yet informed of S-P agreement"), 12 March 1917, L/P&S/11, vol. 119, nos. 989 and 1055/17. Clayton's memorandum of 3 April made the same point and added that it would be difficult to make explanations to Husain on the French role until approval was received from home to do so: FO 882/16.

[40] Wingate telegrams to Balfour, 28 April (circulated to Cabinet) and 7 May (for Sykes) 1917, L/P&S/11, vol. 119, no. 1947/17.

[41] Sykes (Aden) telegram to Wingate, 24 May 1917, FO 141/654, and also in L/P&S/10, 5235/16, no. 2121/17, which includes Cox tele-

Husain was given the details of the Sykes-Picot Agreement at this time remains an open question, but there can be no doubt that Syria was discussed, that Husain knew very well that France was to have a role there, and, finally, that Britain recognized the legitimacy of that role, for all this was fairly clear in McMahon's earlier letters.

There is also no question that Sykes was alarmed about the future of Syria by the time he visited Husain, and he used his obviously powerful persuasive abilities to get a commitment from Picot, and, he hoped, France, on future policy. For this reason he may well have been unwilling to spell out for Husain the full details of the Sykes-Picot Agreement, hoping that it would soon be modified. Sykes and Picot agreed in writing that the two powers should focus on the development of Arab institutions and unity. To this end, they should take as their administrative policy in both French and British zones the official use of the Arabic language and similar administrative, educational and legal patterns, at least on a local level. The King of the Hijaz would be head of the Arab movement, and he or one of his sons would rule in "A" and one in "B," ". . . provided always that such an agreement is fully in accord with the desires of the population of the respective areas." [42]

It was a document full of promises. To Sykes, the possibility of future Arab union was an essential part of the whole structure. "If we and the French intend to work towards annexation then I am certain that our plans will sink in chaos and failure . . ." given the fundamental change that had come over the

---

gram to SSI, 24 May, reporting that he had received a cable from Sykes that he had visited Jidda with Picot to give Husain "an outline of Anglo-French policy in regard to Arab area." But see C. E. Wilson to Cheetham, 31 January 1919, *FO* 141/431; Wilson talked at the time to Sykes: "at these meetings a great opportunity to 'clear the air' was lost. . . ."

[42] Joint Sykes-Picot note, with minute, 17 May, 1917, *L/P&S/11*, vol. 119, no. 2527/17; Nevakivi, *Britain, France and the Arab Middle East*, p. 60.

democratic world since the outbreak of the war. Nor was Sykes the only one who was concerned. Wingate, commenting on the assurances given by Picot—and Wingate, like T. E. Lawrence, understood that the same assurances had been given to Husain—welcomed the concept of an Arab facade for France in Syria such as that intended for Britain in Iraq. This promise would go far to reconcile Arab opinion, especially since it did not exclude the possibility of some sort of future Arab union.[43]

But Wingate's main concern was that the first Sykes-Picot Agreement had failed to cover the Red Sea and the Hijaz; Britain should obtain a preferential treaty with Husain and revise the French agreement in that sense. France seemed to ignore the fact ". . . that only by our support military as well as diplomatic, can they expect to realise their present aims . . ." in the Middle East. This was particularly true regarding Britain's good offices if an amicable settlement was to be reached on Syria. What Wingate particularly had in mind was amendment of the Sykes-Picot Agreement to eliminate the approximate boundary on the southern side of Britain's sphere, so as to include the whole of Arabia.[44]

Sykes's view that disguised control of the Sharif would be a disaster and there must be a free king in Mecca had again gone considerably beyond that of Wingate, but for once the India Office was sympathetic. As Hirtzel put it, Britain had a policy of supporting the independence of the Hijaz, and it could not deny to the Hijaz relations with the outside world. This might, of course, prove dangerous, for if Husain became Caliph he would have an important role regarding Indian Muslims, and it was vital that no other power dominate him. France, at least, seemed willing to recognize Britain's supremacy in Arabia, but

[43] Sykes note for M.A.C., 22 June; Wingate to Balfour, 11 June; and T. E. Lawrence to Wingate, 30 July, in Wingate to Balfour, 16 August 1917: *FO* 371/3054.

[44] Wingate telegram to Balfour, 3 June (quoted), Balfour telegram to Wingate, 5 June, and minutes, Wingate telegram to Balfour, 3 July 1917, *FO* 371/3056.

there were other interested parties—such as Italy with her concern for Yemen and 'Asir.[45]

Others, too, wanted a redefinition of the agreement. Hogarth pointed out that Russia's collapse and America's entrance into the war had altered the situation. France had been unduly favored in the Sykes-Picot treaty; she had, in particular, taken for herself the best Syrian harbors even before she was established in the Middle East. He did not see that it was either possible or desirable to exclude France from a Middle Eastern role, however, and with this Sykes agreed: all that was really necessary was to get France to "play up" to Arab nationalism. Sykes-Picot allowed annexation of "Red" and "Blue" zones, but Sykes maintained that formal annexation was quite contrary to current trends.[46]

As the summer passed, Sykes was increasingly anxious to press his view in every possible quarter and to urge that Picot do the same in France. Many were unconvinced, but despite the failures, Sykes as usual pressed on, for he had attached his customary enthusiasm for causes to self-determination. It is hard not to conclude, however, that in this case his own personal connection with the Anglo-French agreement, to which his very name had been attached, drove him all the harder.[47] It was not renegotiation of boundaries that was wanted—Sykes's feeling of hopelessness on that sort of approach comes through clearly—but frank discussion leading to the sort of policy which would be right, both morally and politically. The people were to be consulted, and so on—and in Sykes's mind was a prophetic fear of what would happen if the new revolutionary regime in Russia were to obtain a copy of the agreement as it now stood. Syria alone was not the problem; rather, the whole of Middle

[45] Hirtzel and Holderness minutes, 27 June and 2 July 1917, *L/P&S/ 10*, 3372/16, no. 2342/17.
[46] Hogarth memorandum, 10 July 1917, *ibid.*, 53/16, no. 2832/17.
[47] See, for example, Sykes private to Eric Drummond, 20 July 1917, *Sykes Papers* (Oxford).

Eastern policy, including the traditional views on "influence" in the Hijaz, had to be adjusted.[48]

Sykes's policy called for vast self-denial on Britain's part. As George Clerk in the Foreign Office put it:

> Throughout these Asia Minor and Arabian negotiations it has seemed to me that Sir Mark Sykes, while quite rightly endeavouring to reach an understanding with the French which shall be free from all suspicion and misunderstanding, has gone to work on the wrong principle. He appears to think that the way to get rid of suspicion is always to recognise what the other party claims and to give up, when asked, our claims.

And this, the minute continued, was exactly what Britain had done before the war. Hardinge agreed: "Thanks to the Sykes-Picot agreement our position is already a bad one in connection with Asiatic Turkey & Arabia, & for Heaven's sake let us not make it even worse." The more cautious Oliphant noted in the margin: "Note. Care must be taken that this paper is not sent at any time to Sir M. Sykes." [49]

The most the Foreign Office would do was to approach France on recognition of Britain's Hijaz sphere, which of course was not at all what Sykes wished. Britain, Ambassador Cambon was told, had no desire to extend its sphere of political influence in Arabia, still less to assume a protectorate there. Rather, Britain's policy was to reduce responsibilities by making it impossible for "these semi-civilised countries" to play off the powers against one another. "Nothing has produced a happier effect in the past than a strict delimitation of the spheres in which such Powers can legitimately exercise their influence. . ." Sykes, now in Paris, was given the task of working up a draft with the French; Britain was to be the power of influence in the

---

[48] Sykes memorandum, 14 August 1917, *L/P&S/10*, 53/16, no. 3256/17; Sykes private to R. Graham, n.d. (27 August 1917), *FO* 371/3044.

[49] Clerk minute, 28 August 1917, on Sykes to Graham (27 August), with Hardinge and Oliphant minutes, *ibid.*

whole of the peninsula except for the independent Hijaz, the limits of which were to be defined.[50]

In the fall of 1917, however, tentative negotiations begun toward this end had no immediate result, surprisingly in the light of the consummate energy with which Sykes approached most tasks given him, but not, perhaps, if Sykes's own attitude to this particular issue is kept in mind. It should also be remembered that a considerable number of problems were then occupying the attention of Foreign Secretary Balfour and of Sykes himself, not the least of which was the pledge to Zionist leaders in the Balfour Declaration of November 1917, in which Britain promised to support a national home for the Jews in Palestine.[51] There was the further problem that any negotiations on Arabia might be used as a lever by France for obtaining reconfirmation of its own Syrian sphere, if reconfirmation were needed. As a result, formal recognition of Britain's Arabian position would have to wait.

4

The issue of the Balfour Declaration brought in its wake some shift of attention on the part of those responsible for making Arab policy. General Clayton, for example, well aware that the Balfour Declaration would do nothing to calm Arab fears of Allied annexation plans, suggested that the Allies should publicly deny any such intentions. Such a statement, particularly by France on Syria, was of much more importance, he felt, than redefinition of Arabian boundaries. Sykes naturally picked up this proposal with alacrity, although he modified it somewhat—probably realizing that there was little likelihood of

[50] Robert Cecil to Cambon, 29 August (Balfour was out of London, but Curzon approved the draft), F.O. telegram to Bertie, 26 September 1917, *FO* 371/3056.

[51] Hurewitz, *op. cit.*, II, pp. 25–26. See also Stein, *op. cit.*; C. Sykes, *Two Studies in Virtue* (on Sykes); and Jon Kimche, *The Unromantics: The Great Powers and the Balfour Declaration* (London, 1968).

France sharing in such a declaration at the moment—into a plan to distribute a pamphlet, mainly for Turkish troops, making the same pledge, at least on Britain's part, and at least with regard to Baghdad becoming part of the Arab state.[52] It was the sort of plan which Sykes proposed more than once as a means of obtaining a similar pledge of action from France, apparently preferring this to direct negotiation with the French government.

But "Baghdad" and "declaration" were suspicious terms by now. Hardinge, still with Indian aspirations in mind, pointed out that a general declaration would prevent the annexation of Basra; this was too high a price to pay for such a "sentimental" declaration. Wingate too objected; vague statements would only further unsettle the Arabs, already thus affected by the Balfour Declaration, for Zionism had few Arab adherents. His suggestion, in January 1918, was that he be allowed to tell Husain that Britain would allow no permanent occupation of Palestine, Syria, or Iraq, excluding only Basra, and that foreign aid would be limited to assistance and protection.[53]

Wingate was not acting solely from conscience. In December Husain had told Colonel C. E. Wilson, British representative in Jidda, that he intended to predominate in his area of influence and that he resented Britain's treaty relations with other Arab leaders (meaning in particular Ibn Sa'ud). Wingate saw little real chance of Husain ever achieving the sort of control he desired and recommended only that Britain make it clear that she would take a dim view of any inter-Arab hostilities likely to interfere with the holy cities, and that Husain was superior to, but not predominant over, the other chiefs. On

[52] Wingate telegram to Balfour (from Clayton for Sykes), 28 November 1917, *FO* 371/3054; D.M.I. telegram to Clayton, 24 December 1917, *FO* 371/3380.

[53] Hardinge minute on Wingate telegram of 28 November, *FO* 371/3054; Wingate telegrams to Balfour, 31 December 1917 and 22 January 1918, *FO* 371/3380.

the other hand, Husain must be brought to understand that the Jews must be accepted in parts of Palestine to be determined by the peace conference. Details on the regimes in Damascus (where Husain and Faisal would have to consult the French) and Baghdad similarly would have to wait.[54]

With all this the Foreign Office tended to agree; Husain would have to recognize a special regime in Palestine, although Jewish immigration would continue only so long as it was compatible with the interests of the local population "both economic and political"—not at all the same qualification as the Balfour Declaration's provision that "nothing shall be done which may prejudice the civil and religious rights of existing non-Jewish communities." But now, with references to Baghdad, the India Office was also involved. As Shuckburgh minuted on 25 January, it was clear that the prevalent mood was likely to prevent British occupation of even Basra after the war, yet the India Office had never seen why commitments of this sort should be made to Husain, since the area was far from his own sphere, and he could not in the ordinary course of events ever hope to extend it so far. Britain had conquered Iraq at great cost, and some consideration had to be given to that:

I submit that we ought not to let ourselves be rushed by Sir M. Sykes & General Clayton (neither of whom, I suspect is much interested in Mesopotamia) into tying our hands more than we have done already, unless and until H.M.'s Gov$^t$ are really satisfied that there is no alternative open to them.

As an afterthought, Shuckburgh pointed out that the suggested declaration would satisfy neither Husain on Syria nor the Syrians on Husain (a reference to Syrian objections, real or

[54] Wingate to Balfour, 25 December 1917, *L/P&S/11*, vol. 131, no. 457/18, with Hirtzel minute that this was generally sound; Wingate telegram to Balfour, 31 December 1917, *FO* 371/3054; Wingate private to Sykes, 13 March 1918, *FO* 371/3403.

imagined, to Sharifal control) nor, finally, the French or the Zionists.[55]

From Cox in Mesopotamia came further criticism. If Husain was really that restless, then a statement could be made, but he very much hoped it would include no reference to Iraq, for the Baghdad proclamation had been quite enough. The more highly developed Iraq should not be used as a pawn in negotiations with the Sharif and with Cairo's "Young Arabs." Chelmsford agreed; any further statements on Iraq could only compromise Britain's position. If discussions with Husain were necessary, quite the other tack should be taken and an attempt made to modify McMahon's "unfortunate pledge"—a most impractical suggestion, of course.[56]

These representations were strong enough to force a Middle East Committee decision that no further announcement on Iraq would be made to King Husain. Wingate would send him a message thanking him for passing on messages from the Turks (attempting conciliation with the Hashimites on the basis of Allied betrayal) and pointing out that this was only an obvious Turkish ploy to divide the Allies. The Turks were wrong; Britain did not desire further territory, for "Liberation and not annexation is the policy. . ." But the Foreign Office draft was altered by Hardinge, who struck out "and not annexation" —and the policy became, simply, "liberation." [57]

Problems of Middle Eastern policy had been made no easier by publication of the Sykes-Picot Agreement by the Russians

[55] Balfour telegram to Wingate, 4 January 1918, *FO* 371/3054; Shuckburgh minutes, 25 and 29 January, on Wingate telegram of 22 January 1918, *L/P&S/11*, vol. 130, no. 322/18.

[56] Cox telegram to SSI, 25 January, and Viceroy telegram to SSI, 28 January 1918, *FO* 371/3380; I.O. memorandum, 31 January 1918, *CAB* 27/23; Shuckburgh minute, 30 January 1918, *L/P&S/11*, vol. 130, no. 434/18.

[57] M.E.C. 3rd minutes (new series), 2 February 1918, *CAB* 27/23; Balfour telegram to Wingate, 4 February 1918, *FO* 371/3380.

(and then by the Turks). On 16 June Wingate reported that King Husain had sent a rather violent message to his agent in Cairo ordering inquiries. "You will recollect," Wingate pointed out, "that King was never officially informed of Sykes-Picot agreement." Wingate told London that he, the High Commissioner, had told Husain that the Bolsheviks had merely found a record of an old conversation and a provisional, not a formal, undertaking—and that the stipulation of native consent and the Arab revolt itself had "for a long time past created wholly different situation." [58]

The differing opinions of Sykes and Wingate now became clear. "The King has frequently been given the outline and detail of the agreement in question," said Sykes, "both by myself, Monsieur Picot, Colonel Bremond and Commander Hogarth who was specially sent down for the purpose." Probably, he continued, the King was simply affected by rumors that Britain intended annexation in Iraq and that a Turkish presence in the Arab world was to survive the war—this and other factors such as recent military setbacks east of the Jordan and the Turkish intrigues had together prompted this response. Sykes pointed all this out in an Eastern Committee meeting on 18 June. He, at least, was certain that Husain knew the details and

[58] Wingate telegram to F.O., 16 June 1918, *FO* 371/3381. Jamal Pasha, Governor of Syria, made overtures to Faisal and Ja'far in late November 1917, and in early December he spoke publicly in Beirut outlining the Sykes-Picot treaty (from Russian-released information); the text of his remarks was subsequently published in several papers. Wingate telegram to Balfour, 24 December 1917, discusses the original letters; Joyce ('Aqaba) telegram to Arbur, 9 January 1918, notes that Husain wanted a refutation of Jamal's points: *FO* 141/430. Antonius, *op. cit.*, pp. 253–58, discusses the Jamal negotiations but gives the rather misleading impression that Wingate's telegram to Husain, which he quotes, was sent in February (p. 257) rather than in June; his Appendix C, pp. 431–32, quotes the February message (cited as Balfour to Wingate, 4 February, n. 57 above). The text of the June message was not provided by the F.O., as Antonius declares; see Balfour telegram to Wingate, 18 June 1918, answering his message of the 16th, *FO* 371/3381. See also E.C. 1st minutes, 28 March 1918, *CAB* 27/24.

was feigning indignation—but, oddly, he seemed to rely more on what Hogarth had told the King than on what he had said himself, although this rather undermines the point made in his own minute, quoted above.[59]

On how to assuage Husain's anger, feigned or real, opinions were divided. Sykes thought it was enough to tell him that the agreement was no longer in effect, subject to French concurrence; but Hardinge was not willing to go so far and wished to say that it was "temporarily in suspense." Smuts, on the other hand, opposed any statement on either Sykes-Picot or larger policy until France could be consulted; Husain should only be reminded that Britain's policy was as he had been informed in February.[60]

The first thing to be done, it was clear, was to persuade France. Sykes, who had been thinking along this line for some months, went quickly to work. In early July he spoke to Picot, urging upon him the facts of a changed situation in the light of the new democratic war aims. Picot was cautious; there would be violent objection from the French colonial party at any suggestion to abolish the agreement. Sykes replied that the agreement as it stood would already be open to the severe criticism of the "democratic" forces in the Allied camp, which would interpret it as "an instrument of Capitalistic exploitation and Imperialistic aggression," to say nothing of its effect on the

---

[59] Sykes minute on Wingate telegram, 16 June, *FO* 371/3381; E.C. 14th minutes, 18 June 1918, *CAB* 27/24. On Hogarth mission of January 1918, to calm King Husain, see Hogarth's record of conversation and notes, *Parl. Papers*, Cmd. 5964, Misc. no. 4 (1939); Nevakivi, *Britain, France and the Arab Middle East*, pp. 61–62; A.L. Tibawi, "T. E. Lawrence, Faisal and Weizmann: The 1919 Attempt to Secure an Arab Balfour Declaration," *Journal of the Royal Central Asian Society*, 56 (June 1969), 157; *FO* 371/3383. There is, of course, always Lawrence: "Fortunately, I had early betrayed the Treaty's existence to Feisal . . . ," *Seven Pillars*, p. 555. But see C. E. Wilson to Cheetham (n. 41 above) and Cheetham to Curzon, 9 February 1919 (*FO* 141/431), on Hogarth mission which left Husain with no illusions.

[60] Balfour telegram to Wingate, 21 June 1918, *FO* 371/3881.

Arabs. Picot concurred; the agreement could hardly be construed as in accord with President Wilson's policy.[61]

Again Sykes's powers of persuasion worked, and he and Picot drew up a statement not far different from that given at about this time to seven unnamed Arabs in Cairo and known, therefore, as the "Declaration to the Seven" (which document, although frequently cited by commentators, made little impression upon British officials at the time and was almost never referred to in the relevant documents). The new Sykes-Picot memorandum declared that (1) all territories freed by the inhabitants themselves would be sovereign and independent; (2) where captured by Allied action, territories would have a form of government based upon consent of the governed; but, (3) owing to the condition of such areas arising from prewar misgovernment, wartime conditions, and the like, a period of tutelage "must supervene before the inhabitants of these areas are capable of complete self government, and in a position to maintain their independence." The advising powers, however, must have the approval of both free governments and the governed. It was not very inspiring, and the India Office at least agreed that it would be harmless if it really was to go no further than the Declaration to the Seven.[62]

Sykes, of course, had more in mind. Within a week of his agreement with Picot, he had submitted to the Eastern Com-

---

[61] Sykes undated memorandum (2/3 July 1918), *ibid.*

[62] *Ibid.;* I.O. minutes on copy in *L/P&S/10,* 3372/16, no. 4586/18. Sykes himself made the point that the "Declaration to the Seven" was similar. On this declaration, see Nevakivi, *Britain, France and the Arab Middle East,* pp. 61–62; Antonius, *op. cit.,* pp. 270–74, and text of declaration, Appendix D, pp. 433–34; also printed along with the Hogarth message of January in Hurewitz, *op. cit.,* II, pp. 28–30. See also Wingate to Balfour, 7 May, enclosing the petition from the Seven; Balfour telegrams to Wingate, 7 and 11 June 1918, on reply: *FO* 371/3380. Lawrence, in his letter to *The Times* of 11 September 1919, erroneously gives the date of the declaration as 11 June 1917; quoted in Stanley and Rodelle Weintraub, eds., *Evolution of a Revolt: Early Postwar Writings of T. E. Lawrence* (University Park, Pa., 1968), p. 64.

mittee his draft for a proposed Anglo-French statement which would be a clear declaration of nonannexation and correspond rather closely to the terms he had worked out with Picot—which had not yet been approved by the French government. Another week followed, and Sykes submitted one more memorandum, which rounded out his proposed Middle East settlement. Britain would also recognize Husain by a title that gave him primacy in Arabia, but without suggesting suzerainty or spiritual authority; at the same time, a conference of various Arabian chiefs should take place on neutral ground, presumably to formalize this relationship.[63]

The Eastern Committee considered these proposals. On 18 July the idea of a nonannexation pledge raised the usual opposition, notably from Lord Curzon, when it was discussed. The chairman pointed out that from the very start Britain had reserved Basra, and it still might be decided that this had to be included in British postwar territory. It was quite gratuitous to volunteer pledges now for which no one had asked (a typical example of the insignificance of the "Seven," who had indeed asked); he advised against it. As for the revision of the 1916 agreement, there was little question that France would be hostile. It was pointed out, however, that this was precisely the motive for the nonannexation declaration, for by signing it France would virtually be abrogating the 1916 terms—an exceedingly optimistic interpretation, as it happened.

The India Office representatives, Montagu and Shuckburgh, objected to any statement which would involve France however remotely in Mesopotamia. The declaration as drafted might conceivably permit the French to demand a voice in the supervision of the application of the pledge to all areas involved. The document was recast to state simply that the areas would

[63] Sykes memorandum, 7 July 1918, *FO* 371/3383; undated memorandum (but 15 July) apparently by Sykes, with Hardinge minute objecting to proposed title; Wingate to Balfour, 25 June 1918, outlined a similar position on Husain: *FO* 371/3381.

not be disposed of in a way contrary to the views of the indigenous population (a revision which really was open to the
same objection).[64] Further revisions followed, and further discussions in committee—but the most useful development came
from Robert Cecil (now Assistant Secretary of State for Eastern Affairs in the Foreign Office). Cecil took working drafts
of a joint announcement produced by both Sykes and Hogarth
and joined them together to produce a document that pledged
the two powers to aid in the establishment of native governments (Sykes's modifier "independent" was stricken out) in
the Arab areas, excepting lower Iraq and Palestine—although
Cecil rather preferred to list those areas where the pledge would
apply than to make negative exceptions. Moreover, the Allies
promised not to annex, place under protection, or occupy
these areas unless asked to do so by the native government
(Sykes had written "majority of the inhabitants") or unless
that government should become unable or unwilling to prevent
annexation by another power.[65]

In the last week of September detailed negotiations were resumed with the French. On the 23rd, Balfour and Sykes had a
long conversation with Ambassador Cambon during which
France not only insisted upon the efficacy of the 1916 agreement but also asked a British pledge that French civilian officers
would administer the French zones. The British negotiators
were unwilling to go quite so far, but in a conference on the
30th (Sykes, Cecil, Picot, Cambon, and De Fleurieau, French
Minister and sometimes Chargé in London) a compromise was
worked out: Allenby would use a French representative as his
Chief Political Officer in the "Blue" zone on the Syrian-

[64] E. C. 21st minutes, 18 July 1918, *CAB* 27/24.
[65] E.C. 23rd minutes, 8 August 1918, *ibid*. Hogarth private to Cecil,
18 August, with corrections; Hogarth private to Graham, 9 August; G.
Lloyd memorandum (18–20 August 1918): *FO* 371/3881. Nevakivi,
*Britain, France and the Arab Middle East*, p. 81.

Lebanese coast. At the same time the negotiators recommended to the two governments that an anti-annexation declaration be issued.[66]

The basis for agreement with France was thus achieved, but, paradoxically, the goal of a propaganda statement was bought only at the price of the first actual steps of the French political and administrative control in Syria which the suggested declaration was designed specifically to avoid. Unfortunately for the stability of the new Anglo-French accord, while Allenby appointed French officers in "Blue" and "A" zones, he had also given over the administration of "A" to Faisal, and Faisal's men were everywhere opposing the assumption of jurisdiction by those same French officers.[67] The full effects of this tension were yet to come, and by 14 October the British Cabinet had before it a draft agreement negotiated in Paris by Cecil and Pichon and approved by the Prime Minister which confirmed the agreement reached in London on 30 September. The draft partitioned spheres of political authority in the area under General Allenby (excluding, therefore, General Marshall's command in Iraq) and agreed on the principle of a declaration—but the actual wording of that declaration was left to the Eastern Committee meeting of 16-17 October, where some disagreement ensued.[68]

Both Smuts and Montagu objected to the draft clause which would, at least by implication, permit annexation and occupation if the Arab state or states could not defend themselves against aggression. Crowe, speaking for the Foreign Office,

[66] Balfour to Cambon and to Derby, 23 September, Sykes memorandum for Crowe, 28 September, and Crowe draft, with Cecil minute; notes of conference, 30 September 1918: *FO* 371/3383. See also E.C. 34th minutes, 3 October 1918, *CAB* 27/24.

[67] Clayton telegrams to Balfour, 12 and 14 October, Allenby telegrams to W.O., 12 and 17 October 1918, *FO* 371/3384.

[68] Cecil to Pichon, 8 October, and W.C. 485, 14 October 1918, *CAB* 23/8; E.C. 35th minutes, 16–17 October 1918, *CAB* 27/24.

argued from his diplomatic experience: binding commitments could result in awkwardness, as in Muscat before the war where more than once Britain had been unable to act because of a similar Anglo-French declaration.[69] Curzon wished to limit the statement to Syria only; Cecil, no doubt with some exasperation, pointed out that this was impossible, for France would hardly approve a declaration that did not also apply to Mesopotamia. The draft was approved with the qualifying section on possible annexation removed. Now it remained only to obtain French agreement; the same day, Balfour wrote to Cambon.

The pace was now rapid. On the 18th, Cambon reported to Cecil that France was ready to sign the 30 September document. As for the draft joint declaration, France wished to extend the terms to all territories liberated from the Turks. Cecil could only reply that Britain would have to consider the suggestion, which raised problems in such matters as the international status of Palestine.[70] On the 21st, Cecil had the British position ready; the broad French suggestion could not be made, as it would include Palestine, Aden, and the like; therefore he suggested: "territories of Syria and Mesopotamia now in course of being liberated from Turkish yoke." There is no evidence that the India Office, the more junior staff, or the Eastern Committee was again consulted on the text after the 17th. France repeated its earlier proposal, but by the 31st the wording was agreed upon.[71] On 8 November, just over a week after the Turkish armistice, the declaration, published in Allied capitals the previous day, was released in Baghdad. It is important enough to quote here in full.

[69] See Busch, *Britain and the Persian Gulf*, chs. II, VI, IX.

[70] Cecil memorandum, 18 October, Balfour to Cambon, 19 October 1918, *FO* 371/3384; Balfour to Cambon, 17 October, French Embassy note to F.O., 19 October 1918, *FO* 371/3381.

[71] Cecil notes, 21 and 22 October 1918, *ibid.;* Cecil note, 25 October, and Balfour telegram to Barclay (British Chargé, Washington), 31 October 1918, *FO* 371/3384.

The end which France and Great Britain have in view in their prosecution in the East of the war let loose by German ambition is the complete and definitive liberation of the peoples so long oppressed by the Turks and the establishment of national Governments and Administrations drawing their authority from the initiative and free choice of indigenous populations.

In order to give effect to these intentions France and Great Britain are agreed to encourage and assist the establishment of indigenous Governments and Administrations in Syria and Mesopotamia, which have already in fact been liberated by the Allies, and in countries whose liberation they are endeavouring to effect, and to recognize the latter as soon as they shall be effectively established. Far from wishing to impose any particular institution on these lands, they have no other care but to assure by their support and effective aid the normal working of the Governments and Administrations, which they shall have adopted of their free will. To ensure impartial and equal justice, to facilitate economic development by evoking and encouraging indigenous initiative, to foster the spread of education and to put an end to the divisions too long exploited by Turkish policy—such is the rôle which the two allied Governments assume in the liberated territories.[72]

The declaration was received by some Arabs, at least, with enthusiasm—although Clayton, reporting on celebrations in Damascus, noted that questions were already being asked about the exclusion of Palestine.[73] Indeed, criticism was raised even before the declaration's issue by no less an Arabophile than T. E. Lawrence. Lawrence saw Cecil on 28 October and was shown the text. He admitted that the declaration was satisfactory, but he also was convinced that it was contrary to the Sykes-Picot Agreement, which it did not, after all, formally abrogate. Lawrence urged upon Cecil the fact that Faisal and the Arabs—"(to whom he always referred as 'we')"—could have taken Damascus at any time since November 1917 and

---

[72] Ireland, *op. cit.*, pp. 459–60 (see also p. 136); Wilson, *Mesopotamia*, p. 102. Also quoted, with slightly different texts according to translations from the original French, in Hurewitz, *op. cit.*, II, p. 30, and Antonius, *op. cit.*, pp. 435–36.

[73] Clayton telegram to Balfour, 16 November 1918, *FO* 371/3385.

come to a very favorable settlement with the Turks. "He denounced in unmeasured terms the folly (or, as he called it, the levity) of the Sykes-Picot Agreement, the boundaries of which were, he said, entirely absurd and unworkable." Lawrence also had a word to add on Mesopotamia; this, he said, should be put under an Arab government, and he suggested 'Abdullah, son of Husain, partly, at least, because he distrusted the Naqib of Baghdad, Cox's candidate, as too weak to keep the nefarious Sayyid Talib from influence.[74]

Iraq's criticism, on the other hand, focused on the actual wording of the declaration, for which neither India nor Mesopotamia had responsibility. But the pious hope that the declaration meant alteration of the Sykes-Picot Agreement was centered in London, and to a certain extent in the India Office—not in India or Mesopotamia, where there was some satisfaction with the treaty terms as they stood. That satisfaction was only relative, and an event occurring simultaneously with the armistice brought the Iraqi authorities to desire major revision as well, for reasons very different from those of Sykes. At the very end of the fighting, British and Indian troops pushed forward to occupy Mosul and the vilayet of the same name. Naturally, Iraq wished instructions on how the area should be treated, urging that it should be dealt with in the same manner as Baghdad. Even more than Mosul was involved, for A. T. Wilson urged that his officers be permitted to move further into Kurdistan, which was linked to Mosul as Mosul was to Baghdad; greater Mesopotamia, in short, was inseparable.[75]

Wilson dismissed the fact that all this had been assigned to France by stating that the French had only religious (that is, missionary) interests in the area; but those reading the cor-

[74] Cecil note, 28 October 1918, *FO* 371/3384.
[75] Wilson telegrams to SSI, 16, 18, and 27 October 1918, *FO* 371/3384. "Kurdistan" refers to the indefinitely bounded area inhabited by Kurds which today falls in Turkey, Iraq, and Iran. The mountainous areas of the Mosul vilayet of the Ottoman Empire were heavily Kurdish.

respondence knew that Britain was sufficiently concerned with French interests in Mesopotamia to make it difficult if not impossible for French representatives to travel into the various occupied Iraqi areas.[76] The India Office backed Wilson, but the Foreign Office objected to anything more than simple military administration, for it wished to avoid raising this particular question at the moment. The India Office claimed that the Anglo-French agreement applied only to Allenby's sector—for commitments had been made only on this in the recent Paris discussions—but Balfour pointed out that the basic treaty applied throughout until altered. Wilson was told that as the joint declaration was being issued shortly the whole issue would have to wait.[77]

The war was over, and the Allies had pledged a policy of nonannexation; but as discussions on positions to be adopted at the peace conference began in real earnest, the Sykes-Picot Agreement still hung around Britain's throat. Sykes and Wingate and Lawrence and Clayton and Cecil had all of them done their best, but France was immovable. There was always a hope that France would awaken to the difficulty of imposing its will upon Syria and Lebanon, but it was a faint hope. The negotiations for revision, too, had come late and perhaps were not pressed as strongly as they might have been, in part due to the common failure to recognize the new era of "self-

[76] In 1916, for example, an offer of French troops for Mesopotamia was most definitely refused; Bertie telegram to Grey, 9 January, General Barrow to F.O., 23 January, and I.O. to F.O., 29 January 1916, *FO* 371/2769. In 1917 the French Consul-designate for Iraq was prevented from moving north of Basra; F.O. to Cambon, 20 September 1917, and other documents in file, *L/P&S/10*, 3000/17, no. 3845/17, and *India Sec. War* March 1918, 1–169. It was, as Cox pointed out, rather unusual for a government to appoint a representative to an area still under martial law—but then the French could argue that their consul was simply returning to his prewar post; Cox demi-official telegram to FSI, 23 July 1917, *ibid.*

[77] I.O. to F.O., 29 October, F.O. to I.O., 2 November, *FO* 371/3384; SSI telegram to A. T. Wilson, 5 November 1918, *FO* 371/3385.

determination," but in a more specific sense because the diplomats and administrators still worked toward what they saw as Britain's real interests: recognition of Britain's Arabian position (originated in Cairo) and possession of at least Basra, with influence in Baghdad and Mosul beyond (originally an Indian objective, but now pursued primarily from Baghdad itself). Both objectives hampered the negotiations.

Many questions remained unanswered. Above all, how would the Sykes-Picot Agreement be implemented to take into account various pledges made to the Arabs, and in particular the joint declaration of 7 November? It appeared that Basra could not be annexed; but if France insisted upon her pound of flesh in Syria; would the attitude on Basra change? What actually was Britain's Middle Eastern policy, over and above vague and general statements? And, finally, who was to decide that policy? This latter question, in particular, was a vexing one, and the declaration of the Arab revolt in mid-1916 had in no way provided an answer.

No sooner had Britain embarked upon an Arab policy than questions were raised about the management of that policy. The problem was not acute, however, until the disparity of "occupation" in Iraq and "alliance" in the Hijaz became obvious in 1916. Despite India's disgust with McMahon's pledges, there had always been hope that the revolt would come to nothing, and coordinating efforts or interfering projects had been sidestepped or so watered down as to be little or no danger. The "Islamic Bureau" in particular, Sykes's pet brain child, had been changed into an "Arab Bureau" which produced useful results in its own sphere of operations but had little influence in Iraq, the Gulf, or India. Not a coordinating body at all, it rather became another advisory group adding to the chorus offering solutions to Middle Eastern problems and was therefore regarded with suspicion in the further east.

Obviously, workers for coordination had to turn to other projects altogether. In May 1916, for example, Hankey attached Sykes, who had not managed to become the Bureau's director, to the Committee of Imperial Defence. The body was virtually defunct in wartime, but in making this association Hankey was including Sykes in the small but important Cabinet secretariat of which he was also the chief (technically, he was only Secretary of the C.I.D.). Sykes therefore had quick access to the Cabinet, to any other departments or individuals who might be of use, and to information exchanged at the highest level. This was really the reason for the appointment, although the justification presented to Sir Edward Grey was the need for interdepartmental cooperation, particularly in relating military operations to political circumstances.[78]

Within a short time Sykes was urging the need for unified control, while at the same time doing his best to undermine India's influence in Arab affairs. Sykes's freedom to comment on the various reports coming from the Arab Bureau in Cairo and destined for Cabinet circulation proved an excellent medium for this task. "The cooperation of the Indian Government with that of Egypt," he wrote on one such report in mid-June, "seems to lack enthusiasm, and Indian political internal policy to act as a drag on operations. The Indian Government has done nothing with Arab prisoners, objected to the blockade of the Hejaz, has no Arab policy in Mesopotamia, and has not done much to bring about good relations between Ibn Saud, or Idris of Asir and the Sherif." Another sample, from September 1916, on a remark in an Arabian Report that in Muscat they hardly believed the revolt had occurred:

Of course, allowance must be made for the fact that the C.P.O., Basra [Chief Political Officer, i.e., Cox], had assumed that the idea of a confederation of Arab states was defunct; it naturally follows that there could not be much enthusiasm in pushing what was supposed to be an abandoned idea.

The coldness shown by the Government of India towards the

[78] Hankey private to Grey, 4 May, and C.I.D. to F.O., 22 May 1916, *FO* 371/2777.

Arab movement since its inception will always prove a deadening influence in the Persian Gulf, and must naturally act as a damper on the keenness of our political officers there.

Repetition is hardly necessary, but perhaps one more example, this time from a Foreign Office minute by Sykes, from December, will demonstrate the harassment which the India Office and India must have felt:

. . . we have suffered, are suffering and shall continue to suffer owing to the fact that political control in Arabia is divided between India and Egypt; that Egypt being Arabic speaking and akin to Arabia has naturally a different policy to India which has laws, customs and traditions entirely alien to those existing in any Arabic speaking country.[79]

In July Sykes had testified before the War Committee, heavily criticizing India's whole attitude and recommending that much more freedom be given Cox, whose attitude Sykes then considered more favorable than that of his chiefs. Sykes urged that much more be done in the direction of obtaining Arab cooperation, although it has already been demonstrated how such suggestions fared in Iraq. In August, Hankey, on behalf of Prime Minister Asquith, found it necessary to write to Chamberlain to find out if anything had actually been done in this direction. Hirtzel managed to mislay this inquiry for another two weeks and then noted that all necessary steps had been taken—for while India and Iraq had been urged to act in a pro-Arab manner, they could not really be given orders to do so, "because no instructions will infuse a spirit. The G. of I. believe that they are going to administer Mesopotamia permanently; & so long as they believe that, they will administer it on Indian

[79] Sykes minute, 19 June 1916, on Arabian Report (undated), *CAB* 17/175; minute on Arabian Report, n.s., XI, 27 September 1916, *L/ P&S/10*, 705/16, no. 4121/16; Sykes minute on Wingate to Balfour, 20 December 1916, *FO* 371/3043.

lines—naturally." [80] The India Office, under pressure from Sykes, was unwilling to exert the same pressure upon India, and the result was that Sykes could not bring to bear the overall influence that he saw was required.

It must have been an exasperating situation for Sykes: a position of influence, Cabinet approval for his policy, but inability to put it into effect. India was, of course, not the only problem; and Sykes could only outline in gloomy fashion the incredibly complicated line of authority for the Middle East, to which Wingate's appointment added one further post. There were, in fact, a dozen and a half separate individuals who were advising on policy, and the list bears repetition. There were General Sir Archibald Murray, commanding the Egyptian theater; McMahon, the High Commissioner; Vice-Admiral Wemyss, Commander-in-Chief, East Indies Station; Hogarth and his Arab Bureau; Clayton, Director of Military Intelligence, Egypt, supposedly maintaining communications between McMahon and Murray but in fact rather more conscious of his own technical subordination to Wingate; Wingate in Khartoum as Sirdar, now also in charge of the Hijaz and corresponding with the Foreign Office, supposedly via McMahon; C. E. Wilson at Jidda and Colonel Parker at Rabigh; the Resident at Aden and the Bombay authorities to whom he was nominally responsible; Cox and Maude in Mesopotamia (who could hardly be said to be in agreement); Grant, the Foreign Secretary in India; the Viceroy; Chamberlain and Grey in the India Office and Foreign Office; and, finally, the French representative (political) and the French mission (military) in Egypt and the Hijaz. The total was eighteen and a system which insured continued passage "from crisis to inertia, and from coma to

[80] War Committee 99th minutes, 6 July 1916, appendix 99d, precis of Sykes evidence, *CAB* 42/16 (see also above, p. 121); Hankey to Chamberlain, 2 August, with Hirtzel minute, 18 August 1916, *L/P&S/10*, 2100/16, no. 2739/16.

panic; watching assets frittered away and opportunities missed." [81]

To Sykes, the answer was simple: one department in London controlling policy and two Chief Political Officers responsible to their local military commanders for operations and to London for policy, one in the Red Sea area and the other in the Persian Gulf area. Nothing, he minuted, was happening that required "either thought, decision, or action; . . . if there can be thirty telegrams a week about nothing, it would require a nice calculation to figure out how many telegrams would be necessary if something urgent were afoot." [82]

It must be stressed that the highest civilian and military officials in the British government had the opportunity to read Sykes's remarks, for the Arabian Report they introduced was circulated at Cabinet level in addition to being sent to relevant departments. The remarks are therefore indicative of Sykes's willingness to tread where angels dared not, propelled by his obvious conviction that unless decision came of confusion and action of lethargy it might be too late. But in the calmer rooms of the India Office, where tradition lurked in every corner, his impassioned appeals, while persuasive enough on the need for coordination, inspired no sympathetic enthusiasm. As Holderness put it, correcting the mechanics of control was not going to be enough, for example, to ease Ibn Sa'ud's fears for his independence: this particular instance was not, though Sykes saw it so, merely a case of a shrewd desert chief playing on Cox's hostility to Cairo. If the problem were really to be reduced to essence, it was that Sykes and the Arab Bureau were pursuing a will-o'-the-wisp. [83]

It was a paradox. The India Office and India would continue

[81] Sykes minute on Arabian Report, n.s., XIV, 15 October 1916, *ibid.*, 705/16, no. 4293/16.

[82] Sykes minute on Arabian Report, n.s., XV, 25 October 1916, *ibid.*, no. 4488/16.

[83] Holderness minute on Arabian Report, 15 October 1916, n. 81 above.

to discount the Arab movement until there was some visible concrete result; Sykes was convinced that no such result would be forthcoming so long as India discounted the movement. All that could be done was for each area to pursue its own policy and for Sykes and like-minded officials to marshal all possible pressure on India to conform to Egypt. That pressure was not always ineffective: while no central control was established in the Middle East, at least the Baghdad and Basra vilayets were separated, and Sykes got his Baghdad proclamation and the orders to Cox and Maude to encourage Arab cooperation; and in London it did prove possible to nudge the Cabinet into the creation of the Mesopotamian Administration Committee, in turn enlarged into the Middle East Committee, in turn enlarged once more into the Eastern Committee.[84]

The difficulty was that policy formed by a committee was by no means as satisfactory as policy formed by a single responsible ministry. Nor was Curzon the best of all possible chairmen, despite his eastern expertise, for his manner, at least to Montagu and Cecil, too often resembled that of a viceroy ordering his staff. "Curzon liked to preside," John Connell has written, "calmly and unbending, over a council or a committee who would agree, tranquilly and cheerfully, to the enlightened and reasonable proposals which he, Curzon, would from time to time lay before them." [85] One need only read through the

---

[84] See above, p. 141. In September 1917 a committee of Balfour, Curzon, and Milner held several meetings to discuss the future administration of Egypt, and in both meetings and report it was clear that there was general sentiment in favor of a department to be created after the war with larger responsibilities for the Middle East. The principal difficulty, it was recognized, was that the F.O. simply could not continue to administer Britain's foreign policy and sizable territories such as Egypt at the same time. Minutes, memoranda, and report (dated 20 February 1918) in *CAB* 27/12.

[85] John Connell, *The "Office": The Story of the British Foreign Office, 1919–1951* (N.Y., 1958), p. 33. See also Montagu private to Chelmsford, 31 May 1918, *Chelmsford Papers*; and Montagu memorandum, 5 July 1918, *CAB* 27/24.

minutes to discover how accurate a description this is, and many a committee member must have fidgeted under the strain of Curzon's lengthy opening remarks and situation reviews and summaries.

In early 1918 the situation changed slightly, for when the Middle East Committee was given wider scope of responsibility by the Cabinet it was decided both that the committee should meet weekly and that Sykes would now move to the Foreign Office as head of a Middle Eastern Department under Hardinge. Cecil, who announced the latter scheme, at the same time advocated the larger plan of creating a truly separate department with secretary, staff, and so on—but until this could be done, the Foreign Office would provide the staff from within its own organization. All this was really little more than a plot to do away with the committee and with Curzon's control of it. As Cecil wrote privately to Balfour, Curzon held tight rein on the committee, and its function seemed "mainly to be to enable George Curzon and Mark Sykes to explain to each other how very little they know about the subject. An attempt by me to smother decorously both Committees [Eastern and the Foreign Office's Persian Committee] was detected by George, and had to be abandoned. They are now to meet regularly on Saturday mornings: a time fixed with the hope that it may ultimately prove discouraging to their existence." [86]

But Sykes in the Foreign Office was still to be responsible only for Palestine and the Hijaz, and Clayton was still to be Chief Political Officer for both areas, responsible respectively to General Allenby in Palestine and Wingate in Khartoum. The central problem of coordination of all Arab policy was overcome only insofar as the committee itself was able to resolve various issues—indeed, even policy for the Hijaz was still

[86] M.E.C. 11th minutes, 12 January 1918, *CAB* 27/22; Cecil private to Balfour (quoted), 8 January 1918, *Balfour Papers* (British Museum), Add.Mss. 49738. See also Hardinge note for Cecil, 4 January 1918, welcoming Sykes's appointment, *FO* 371/3388.

complicated by the dual responsibility of Clayton and Wingate. In June 1918 a step was taken which went much further
toward a centralized ministry: Robert Cecil was appointed
Assistant Secretary of State for Eastern Affairs in the Foreign
Office. Cecil and Sykes had worked together fairly closely, and
Cecil's appointment was at a considerably higher level than
Sykes's before. But Cecil's new role raised the issue of the Eastern Committee's responsibility, as Curzon knew only too
well.[87]

In an August meeting of the committee, Curzon expressed
himself in favor of the idea of the committee of which he was
chairman obtaining the necessary staff to implement its decisions—but Cecil replied that a department could do this with
much more dispatch than a committee. Curzon was not over-
joyed to find that Cecil's view—and, it should be added, Montagu's view as well—of Cecil's position meant, as Curzon saw
it, no necessity at all for committee or chairman except to work
out occasional questions of high policy. Curzon was rather
logically offended by Cecil's justification for his new responsibility—that the committee's method of procedure had caused
unnecessary delays—and by the War Office's accusation that
the committee was overburdened in any case. Curzon thought
any delays were due to departmental failure to submit views. A
new department was necessary, he agreed, but not now. All, it
might be added, were agreed only on one point: the undesir-
ability of placing any new department under the India Office.[88]

Unfortunately, Cecil did not let the discussion drop there
but suggested that perhaps he could call together an informal
group of Oliphant of the Foreign Office (largely concerned
with Persian Committee affairs), Shuckburgh of the India Of-

[87] War Cabinet decision of 17 June 1918.
[88] E.C. 24a minutes, 13 August 1918; see also Montagu memorandum
of 5 July, Cecil, 20 July, Balfour, 27 July, and Curzon, 1 August 1918,
CAB 27/24; Balfour memorandum, 20 July, and Curzon's of 1 August,
CAB 27/29.

fice, and General Macdonogh of the War Office to meet with himself to discuss Middle Eastern questions. Curzon's reaction may be imagined: Where did that leave his committee? Obviously, this was designed only to undermine his own role. An icily polite private correspondence was conducted on this affair. By the end of October, Curzon's despair was sufficient to prompt him to write Cecil,

> . . . if my principal Colleague is to proclaim before the assembled Committee that the E. Committee is hated by all the Departments (as it cordially is by himself) & that he would like to move for a return of all the recommendations it has postponed (including, I may remark, a good many very unwise ones)—I confess that I feel little tempted to go on.[89]

For the time being, confusion reigned. If Cecil's new role was designed to simplify matters, it is most difficult to conclude that this aim was achieved. For some months to come various committee members and departmental officials were thoroughly uncertain of the lines of authority on Middle Eastern affairs, and this situation was not eased by Curzon's relations with Cecil or Montagu (or Hardinge, for that matter). Montagu in particular was uncertain. He did not strenuously object to transfer of authority for the area to Cecil in the Foreign Office, as it could not really be resisted and it would not lead to less attention being paid to Indian views; India, he wrote Chelmsford in private, would say that less attention was impossible, there being none now. Montagu's own project, which he advocated in the committee when discussion was on a rational level, was some form of joint Foreign Office-India Office cooperation through a separate official. In other words, he was not particularly happy about Cecil, and the Foreign Office, having the last

---

[89] Cecil private to Curzon, 1 (two of date), 5, and 27 August, and Curzon private to Cecil, 1, 3, and 25 August and 29 October (quoted); Montagu private to Cecil, 3 and 17 September, and Cecil private to Montagu, 13 September 1918: *Cecil Papers*, Add. Mss. 51077 and 51094.

word, nor did he understand what Cecil's responsibilities were really to be.[90]

Cecil himself was not happy, either. The committee was somehow still meeting, and Curzon was still in the chair. Also, Cecil was still negotiating for staff with all concerned. In particular, he was embroiled in a controversy with Hardinge over personnel. Cecil proposed Eyre Crowe for permanent head of the new department, and Hardinge wished Ronald Graham, now supervising Egyptian affairs as Assistant Under-Secretary in the Foreign Office, to be its head. Cecil preferred to see the scheme "dished" rather than let Graham control it. Sykes, on the other hand, naturally eager to serve in the new department, was reluctant to serve under Crowe (it would appear he had no particular grudge against Crowe, but rather thought that he, Sykes, would be better suited for the post proposed for Crowe). And Montagu refused to hand over Shuckburgh . . . It seemed as if there would never be a new department.[91]

As if the new department scheme was not enough, General Monro in India now suggested that the entire area east of Suez be treated as one in the military as well as the political sense, with India to be the headquarters (Monro was suggesting Monro). Monro was prompted by the problem not only of Arab areas and Mesopotamia but also of controlling operations in Persia and as far afield as Central Asia and the Caspian. Smuts, whose military opinion was valued and who still sat on

[90] Montagu private to Chelmsford, 5 and 25 September and 10 October 1918, *Montagu Papers.*
[91] Cecil private telegram to Balfour (in Scotland), 21 August, Balfour private to Cecil, 22 August, Cecil private to Balfour, 23 August 1918, *Balfour Papers,* Add. Mss. 49738; Montagu private to Cecil, 3 September, and Cecil private to Montagu, 5 September 1918, *Cecil Papers, FO* 800/207; Cecil private to Montagu, 13 September, Montagu private to Cecil, 17 September, Cecil to Sykes ("Mark"), 7 September, and Sykes to Cecil ("Bob"), 9 September 1918, *Cecil Papers,* Add. Mss. 51094; Graham private to Hardinge, 11 September 1918, *FO* 794/6A (Private Secretary office files); Cecil private to Balfour, 15 September 1918, appended to E.C. 32nd minutes, 18 September 1918, *CAB* 27/24.

the Eastern Committee, was in favor of the suggestion but advised that Monro be shifted to Baghdad and come directly under the War Office—at which Curzon in exasperation said that the War Office, too, would have its Middle Eastern Department.[92]

Incredible, said Chelmsford when the Smuts proposal was sent on; this meant that India would not have a say on operations based upon India. The whole scheme he saw as the result of prejudice stemming from the Mesopotamian Commission report of 1917. Officially, India was more restrained. Not only was there the question of a base for operations, but also of control of action against the enemies of India and Afghanistan, the interests of which were so closely linked in turn with Persia. Monro, Chelmsford cabled, had not intended his proposal to mean direct War Office control at all; he had meant the Commander-in-Chief, India, to become the Commander-in-Chief, Near East, or that a separate Middle Eastern commander would be appointed who would also have his base in India.[93] By the end of the war, no decision had been taken on the matter of military authority—but these suggestions clearly added to the confusion.

In sum, no unified control of Middle Eastern policy, in

---

[92] C.-in-C., India, telegram to W.O., 21 August, and Smuts memorandum, 16 September 1918, appended to *CAB* 27/24; Cecil private to Balfour, 15 September 1918, *CAB* 27/32; E.C. 31st minutes, 17 September 1918, *CAB* 27/24.

Smuts had himself declined to accept a proposal of 1917 to assume over-all command in Palestine; see W.C. 135a, 9 May 1917, *CAB* 23/13 (secret military minutes); Guinn, *op. cit.*, pp. 297-98; Brian Gardner, *Allenby* (London, 1965), pp. 166–67. Smuts's wartime activities may be followed in W. K. Hancock, *Smuts: The Sanguine Years, 1870–1919* (Cambridge, 1962) and Hancock and Jean van der Poel, eds., *Selections from the Smuts Papers* (III: 1910–1918) (Cambridge, 1966).

[93] Chelmsford private to Montagu, 30 September, and Montagu private to Chelmsford, 7 November, enclosing Hirtzel memorandum of 21 September, Chelmsford private telegram to Montagu, 1 October 1918, *Chelmsford Papers;* I.O. memorandum, 25 October 1918, *CAB* 27/35.

formulation or execution, civil or military, had been established by the time of armistice. Criticism of India's role, particularly by Sykes, had been unrelenting, but that criticism and the obvious confusion of policy direction had resulted in little more than the creation of an Arab Bureau in Cairo, an Eastern Committee in London, and an Assistant Secretary of State in the Foreign Office—all, perhaps, steps in the right direction but never the final and most essential creation of unified control. Many factors had contributed to this failure, but once again India's view had been important. India had lost control of the campaign in Iraq but, through the India Office and Cox and Arnold Wilson, still had substantial influence in policymaking.

India had, too, the intention of expressing her views on the Middle East where it was thought her interests were involved—and neither Kut nor proclamations in Baghdad nor promises to Husain altered this intention. Montagu, in discussing the proposed transfer of authority in September, had asked Chelmsford his view of how much, exactly, India could afford to cut herself away from the whole Middle East administrative and policy-making tangle. Chelmsford had replied that whatever the fate of Arabia India would continue to have a major share in Mesopotamian affairs from the standpoint of troops and supplies, and would therefore have to have a voice in policy there, to say nothing of Persia and the Gulf. While India had no objection to an India Office-Foreign Office condominium, the party supplying the military force must have a say in the policy that called for that force.[94] Indian withdrawal from Middle Eastern affairs, to put it another way, would mean withdrawal of responsibility for furnishing military matériel, and such a possibility was hardly attractive in late 1918 when lines were overextended in Central Asia and Indian troops made up the majority of British armies from Egypt to Persia. Indian interest thus would remain, and as long as Indian interest remained In-

[94] Montagu private to Chelmsford, 5 September, and Chelmsford private to Montagu, 19 November 1918, *Chelmsford Papers.*

dia would demand a voice in policy decisions—and in the policy aspects of the peace conference, the next item on the agenda.

But there was one further consideration: Indian involvement did not come only from Mesopotamian and Persian activities. It also came, and came very definitely, from questions of the Arabian Peninsula over and above Husain's revolt, ranging from Red Sea pilgrimage to Aden affairs to the Persian Gulf and, last but hardly least, to Ibn Saʻud. Since the beginning of the war the running dialogue that had continued on peninsular affairs had been one further important aspect of Indian involvement in Arab policy.

# V

# 'Asir, Yemen, Najd: The Rival Chiefs, 1914-1918

And as for the unbelievers,
Their works are a mirage in the desert.
The thirsty man thinks it water
Till, coming to it, he finds it nothing.

QUR'ĀN, 24:39

Britain's war against Turkey, beginning as it did after the principal conflict had already opened in Europe, was a war in which only limited resources could be used to harass the new enemy. The campaigns in Mesopotamia and Gallipoli went far to exhaust available men and material for the east; the policy in the area of the Suez Canal, for example, had necessarily to be one of defense for some time. More could be done by diplomacy, as the negotiations with Husain were to prove. In this direction the possibilities were virtually limitless, opening up vistas of the collapse of the entire Ottoman structure; from this collapse Britain might stand to gain much more than changes in the legal status of Egypt and Cyprus.

Initially, however, future collapse of the Turkish Empire

was a motive second in importance to the defense of already existing British interests: the position in Egypt, or the Persian Gulf, or the oilfields. There were other interests which specifically involved the Arabian Peninsula. On the west, Britain had a very real concern for traffic in the Red Sea and for the way station at Aden, a possession for nearly a century. On the east, there was the desire to insure the cooperation of the rulers of the entire Gulf region with the war effort, a desire that raised in particular the question of Ibn Sa'ud, the only real uncertainty in a situation generally settled in 1914. It is not surprising, therefore, that while Cairo conducted its revolt in the Hijaz and beyond and India fought on toward Baghdad, lesser, but nevertheless important, schemes were set afoot for consolidating and extending British influence and weakening Ottoman authority in the peninsula at one and the same time.

1

In August 1914, while Cairo was discussing plans for a revolt with al-Misri, and Kitchener in London was preparing to open negotiations with 'Abdullah, Lieutenant-Colonel H. F. Jacob, the Acting British Resident in Aden, suggested to India that if war with Turkey broke out the ruler of Yemen, Imam Yahya ibn Muhammad Hamid al-Din, should be encouraged to sever his dependency upon the Ottoman Empire. Jacob felt that cash, and the cooperation of 'Asir, the Red Sea coastal province on the northwest of Yemen, might prove a profitable approach. British forces could, of course, move inland from Aden, but this might have the serious disadvantage of alarming the tribes under British protectorate but outside Aden colony proper with fears of closer British control.[1] By 11 September Jacob

---

[1] Jacob telegram to FSI, 19 August 1914, *L/P&S/10*, 3086/15, no. 3290/14. Aden was technically subordinate to the Bombay government, but on important matters usually communicated direct to Delhi or Simla as well. On Jacob see H. F. Jacob, *Kings of Arabia: The Rise and Set of the Turkish Sovranty in the Arabian Peninsula* (London, 1923).

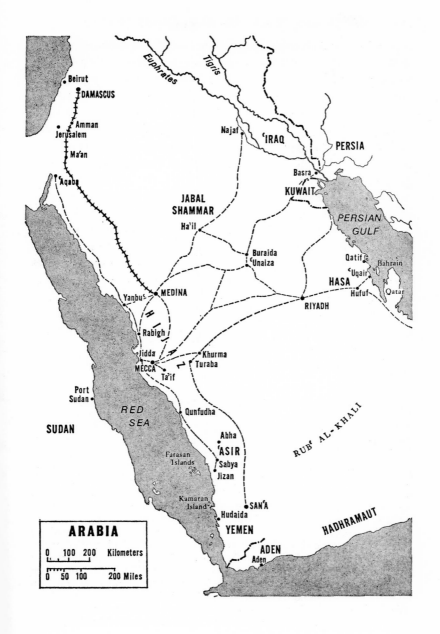

Beirut
DAMASCUS

Euphrates

Tigris

Amman
Jerusalem

Najaf

'IRAQ

PERSIA

Ma'an

'Aqaba

Basra

KUWAIT

JABAL
SHAMMAR

Ha'il

PERSIAN
GULF

Buraida
'Unaiza

Qatif
'Uqair

Bahrain

HASA

Qatar

Yanbu

MEDINA

Rabigh

RIYADH

Hufuf

Jidda
MECCA

Khurma
Turaba

Ta'if

Port
Sudan

Qunfudha

RED
SEA

SUDAN

Abha

Farasan
Islands

'ASIR

Sabya
Jizan

RUB' AL-KHALI

Kamaran
Island

SAN'A

HADHRAMAUT

Hudaida

YEMEN

ARABIA

0   100   200   Kilometers

ADEN

Aden

0   50   100   200 Miles

was able to add that an emissary from Sayyid Muhammad ibn 'Ali ibn Muhammad ibn Ahmad al-Idrisi, the ruler of 'Asir, had appeared in Aden, and Jacob wished to begin negotiations which might end the recurring 'Asir-Yemen controversy.[2] Al-Idrisi could be promised his autonomy, for example (although in fact he already had this to a considerable extent), and the promise could be driven home by the bombardment of Hudaida and Mocha (Mukha), the two principal Yemeni ports, so as to deny their use to the Turks.

In September the Foreign Office and the India Office considered all this premature, but as war approached it became clearer that the southern Red Sea area could not be entirely neglected, if only because the Turks were there. One rejected possibility was the seizure of Kamaran island (some 40 miles north of Hudaida off the Yemeni coast, used by the Turks as a quarantine station for pilgrims proceeding to Mecca and Medina), but this would require British assumption of the quarantine responsibilities and thereby might offend Muslim opinion as Christian interference in the *hajj*.

After some thought, it was decided in the India Office that

---

[2] Aden telegram to FSI, 11 September 1914, with Shuckburgh minute, *L/P&S/10*, 3086/15, no. 3539/14. Al-Idrisi was the great-grandson of Ahmad ibn Idris, a Moroccan religious leader who had founded the Ahmadiyya (or Idrisiyya) *tarīqa* (religious order or brotherhood), forerunner of the better-known Sanusiyya order of Libya (and should not be confused with Sayyid Muhammad al-Idris, in 1918 "Grand Sanusi" and later King Idris of Libya). The great-grandson, Sayyid Muhammad ibn 'Ali, was about 40 in 1914 and had carved out a petty state for himself since about 1906, for which reason he was also styled the Amir of Sabya (his capital, 25 miles inland from the port of Jaizan). He based his appeal on religious zeal and piety, although he claimed no divinity. He was a shrewd and interesting man, who had studied at the Muslim university of al-Azhar in Cairo and spent time in the Sudan before his arrival in 'Asir. His relations with the Turks had not been too difficult until the 1911 attempt by Yemen to break off from Turkish jurisdiction was ended by a compromise, at which point Yemen and the Sharif of Mecca both cooperated in reducing al-Idrisi's influence. This clash ended in stalemate, and in 1914 al-Idrisi's power extended over

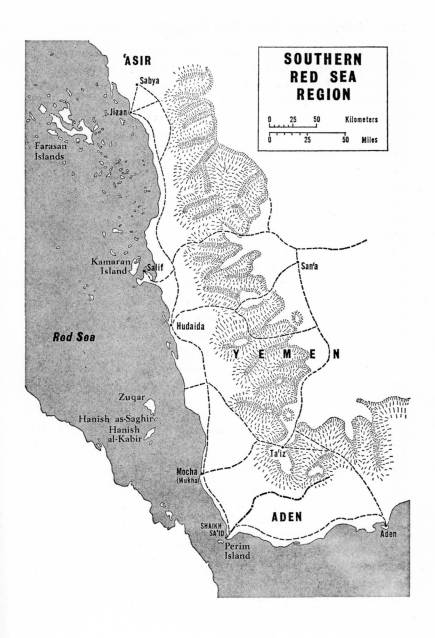

**SOUTHERN RED SEA REGION**

0   25   50   Kilometers

0   25   50   Miles

'ASIR

Sabya

Jizan

Farasan Islands

Kamaran Island   Salif

San'a

Hudaida

Red Sea

Y E M E N

Zuqar

Hanish as-Saghir
Hanish al-Kabir

Ta'iz

Mocha
(Mukha)

ADEN

SHAIKH SA'ID

Aden

Perim Island

the best line of policy to pursue in southwestern Arabia was a defensive posture in Aden coupled with an approach to the Imam with a promise of aid in his achievement of autonomy. Nothing else—certainly not interference in religious areas— would be ventured. The India Office was nervous not only about Muslim opinion but also about a possible Arab confederation—although in recommending its policy to the Foreign Office, Hirtzel's draft paragraph that made this point was wisely cut ("Panislamism is a danger that must be steadily borne in mind . . . a consolidated Arabia wd. be a far greater danger, alike in Africa & Asia, than the Jewish freemasons who now represent the Caliphate," the latter being a reference to the Young Turks). As for al-Idrisi, no commitments could be made which might be difficult to fulfill, such as mediation between that ruler and Imam Yahya. Al-Idrisi, however, could be given an assurance on the sanctity of the holy places and the security of ports under his control, together with a promise of British postwar support of autonomy. Finally, such arms and ammunition as could be spared might be furnished to him.[3]

While an approach was being made to al-Idrisi, further steps were being taken in the Red Sea. Early in November, the Ad-

---

most of 'Asir. Khartoum Intelligence report, December 1914, *FO* 141/ 527; N. W. Clayton (on mission to al-Idrisi) note, 22 February 1919, *FO* 141/432; G. S. Symes (attached to High Commissioner's office, Cairo) memorandum for General Clayton, 15 June, enclosed in Mc-Mahon to Viceroy, 25 July 1915, *India Sec. War* May 1916, 479–95; Antonius, *op. cit.*, pp. 123–24. See also Great Britain, Admiralty, Naval Intelligence Division, *Western Arabia and the Red Sea* ([Oxford], 1946), from which information on the whole region is taken. On Sanusi: Wingate, *Wingate of the Sudan*, pp. 172–73, and N. A. Ziadeh, *Sanūsīya. A Study of a Revivalist Movement in Islam* (Leiden, 1958).

[3] Viceroy telegram to SSI, 7 October, F.O. to I.O., 16 October, Viceroy telegram to SSI, 13 October, I.O. to F.O., 19 October (draft quoted, with Holderness and Crewe minutes), SSI telegram to Viceroy, 31 October, and Viceroy telegram to SSI, 1 November 1914, *L/P&S/10*, 3086/15, nos. 3792, 4051, 3935, 4206, and 4203/14.

miralty issued orders to local commanders to take action against Turkish shipping and to collect Arab dhows, although there was no more significant Turkish naval strength there than in the Persian Gulf. On the rapid intervention of the India Office, the orders were modified to insure that no anti-Turkish operations would be taken, at least in the southern Red Sea, without the approval of the Resident in Aden—the voice of India in the Red Sea. Further discussion was held on the possibility of laying claim to the Farasan islands, a group 75 miles north of Hudaida and opposite Jaizan, the principal port of 'Asir. This group might prove a useful counter in negotiations with al-Idrisi; since the islands were not garrisoned, it would not be necessary to occupy them with troops but only to hoist the British flag. Again, nothing was done for the moment.[4]

Such possibilities demanded interdepartmental consultation. On 16 November, Clerk of the Foreign Office, Hirtzel, and Admiral Slade decided that it was desirable to hold not only Kamaran and the Farasan group but also Hudaida itself, and that the local populations should be worked with wherever possible. Similarly, Shaikh Sa'id, the tip of the peninsula which juts into the Red Sea at the southern narrows (the straits of Bab al-Mandab), should be occupied to keep it from the Turks, for the 14,000 men or so in the Turkish garrison in Yemen might use it to mount an attack upon Aden or Perim island in the straits. One further reason for taking Shaikh Sa'id, interestingly, was to prevent any revival of a long-standing French claim to this spot. But occupation proved unnecessary; the Turkish post on the peninsula was raided by Indian troops from Aden almost as the committee was meeting in London. It was felt that a subsequent sea patrol would be sufficient protec-

---

[4] I.O. to Admiralty and Admiralty telegram to Senior Naval Officer, Red Sea, 4 November, Viceroy telegram to SSI, 7 November, F.O. to I.O., 16 November 1914, *ibid.*, nos. 4270, 4283, 5342, and 4469/14; Grant note, 28 November 1914, *India Sec. War* March 1915, 745–862.

tion, for the danger was heavy guns here; and the Turks could bring them in only by sea.[5]

All of these minor operations were designed to secure Britain's already virtually supreme position. Aden lies 1,500 miles southeast of Suez and seemed so distant even from the major theaters of the Turkish war that the conviction was firmly held by some—Hirtzel in particular—that Red Sea and Aden operations should be as limited as possible. India agreed; European, African, and Mesopotamian commitments were already more than sufficient, and since Aden was under Indian control any operations would require Indian resources. Farasan flags were one thing, but assaults on Hudaida or Shaikh Sa'id were something else. Not only would resources be expended and small units exposed to attack, but such actions might be premature. The attitudes of Yahya and al-Idrisi were unknown, and their reactions might be the reverse of what was desired, particularly since some of the measures planned could be interpreted as violations of Britain's pledge on the holy places.[6]

More promising by far were the diplomatic negotiations. The Imam, approached through Aden, had returned no more than a polite reply by the end of the year, but al-Idrisi sent his messenger to Aden to initiate negotiations for an alliance with Britain. Other feelers, unproductive in the long run, were extended to possibly dissident Yemeni tribal leaders. India was rarely enthusiastic about such projects, no matter how feasible

[5] Notes on meeting, 16 November 1914, *L/P&S/10*, 3086/15, no. 4502/14; Viceroy telegram to SSI, 17 November, SSI telegram to Viceroy, 22 November 1914, *India Sec. War* March 1915, 745–862; Secretary to Government of India, Marine Dept., telegram to Commander-in-Chief, East Indies Station [CinCEI], 3 December 1914, *ibid.*, 871–900.

[6] Hirtzel minute (undated) on SSI telegram to Viceroy, 22 November, and Viceroy telegram to SSI, 29 November 1914, *L/P&S/10*, 3086/15, nos. 4510 and 4666/14; Hardinge private to Crewe, 26 November 1914, *Hardinge Papers;* Jacob telegram to FSI, 24 November, and SSI telegram to Viceroy, 10 December 1914, *India Sec. War* March 1915, 745–862.

they appeared to Aden; added political and military responsibilities were hardly to be desired, although the temptation to achieve a major coup at the cost of a few rupees or rifles was usually too great to resist. Hardinge was generally only too correct: ". . . all these Arabs are slippery gentlemen, and I doubt if their co-operation will really amount to much," he minuted in India. Yet home authorities had a persuasive reason for such activities. Italy had long indicated a considerable interest in the 'Asir-Yemen area and could be warned off only by a locally strong British position; this, under the circumstances, could be secured by diplomacy only.[7]

Negotiations in southwest Arabia were of a paradoxical nature: the chiefs were naturally hesitant to act until Britain had shown some determination to provide military support; Britain wished to have these chiefs as allies partly to avoid large-scale military operations. The Aden garrison did not advance, and the Turks even managed to reoccupy Shaikh Sa'id. As Hirtzel minuted, the policy for Aden set in India was no reinforcements. If the home authorities wished for something more, they would have to provide—and, as has been seen, that was not even possible for a more important operation at Rabigh up the coast.[8]

Money was slightly easier to pry from Indian authorities, at least in a limited amount for subsidizing al-Idrisi. Early in February 1915, India sanctioned Rs. 25,000 in cash and Rs. 30,000 in arms (roughly £5,000 total) and gave Aden full authority to negotiate a treaty, provided only that nothing be included in the terms which would so alienate the Imam of Yemen as to

[7] Viceroy telegram to SSI, 20 December, Aden telegram to FSI, 17 December, I.O. to F.O., 20 December 1914, *L/P&S/10*, 3086/15, nos. 4721, 4903, and 4959/14; Hardinge minute (quoted), 18 December, and Grant notes, 18 December 1914 and 19 February 1915, *India Sec. War* March 1915, 745–862.

[8] Hirtzel minute, 22 January, Viceroy telegrams to SSI, 8 and 10 February 1915, with minutes, *L/P&S/10*, 3086/15, nos. 279, 522, and 547/15.

prevent cooperation with him as well—an important qualification, since Yahya and al-Idrisi had been determined enemies for some years.[9] Negotiation of a treaty, however, raised a question of authority for Red Sea operations and diplomacy, a question which appears, from hindsight, to be rather out of proportion to the effects achieved by the policy. As recently as July 1914, India had tried to rid itself of the rather embarrassing appendage of Aden, but Aden itself was naturally anxious to carry out negotiations with its neighbors, and so long as India was still paying the bill, it would insist on a policy voice.[10]

The problem was McMahon in Cairo, who logically felt that separate Aden negotiations might complicate his dealings with Husain (who was, it should be pointed out, no friend of al-Idrisi either; both he and Yahya had cooperated with the Turks against a prewar 'Asiri revolt). The need for a coordinated Arab policy, the High Commissioner wrote to the Foreign Office in January, and the 'Asiri-Egyptian connections—more important than those of Aden and 'Asir (from the standpoint of al-Idrisi himself, a valid point)—suggested that Cairo control these negotiations, although the Imam could legitimately be dealt with from Aden. The India Office had already proposed that Aden be the authority for both 'Asir and Yemen, although Hirtzel admitted in a minute that 'Asir had fallen to Aden more by default than for any legitimate reasons. Aden now appealed against McMahon, and the Foreign Office decided in its favor for the very good reason that al-Idrisi's agent was there and the negotiations were already in progress. McMahon agreed, as he had to—but according to Clayton he did not intend to let this decision stand permanently.[11]

Unfortunately, McMahon had also mentioned 'Abd al-'Aziz ibn Mut'ib ibn Rashid, perpetual enemy of Ibn Sa'ud in north-

[9] FSI telegram to Cairo/SSI, 5 February 1915, *India Sec. War* March 1915, 745–862.
[10] See on this *India Sec. E.* June 1916, 18–23.
[11] McMahon telegram to Grey, 24 January; SSI telegram to Viceroy,

ern Arabia and long considered to be in India's Gulf sphere, as another candidate for Cairo-directed overtures. This was a red flag to Indian authorities, who had no intention whatsoever of letting Cairo direct any future negotiations with Ibn Rashid and who now determined to keep a watchful eye on the Hijaz, assigned to Cairo, on the grounds that Indian Muslim opinion was clearly affected by such issues as interference in the holy places or the *hajj*—at the very least, Jidda, the major pilgrim port.[12]

Jurisdictional disputes did not stop at negotiations with 'Asir or Ibn Rashid. By January 1915, control of Red Sea operations was again at issue. As McMahon explained to London, the northern area, where Cairo held political sway (the Commander-in-Chief, East Indies Station, commanded the whole as far as the Admiralty was concerned), was pursuing a policy of cooperation with the Arabs and the revival of trade. In the south, however, Aden had brought trade to a standstill and was firing on Arab dhows. Aden replied in some heat to its Indian superiors that it had instituted no blockade except of such Yemeni ports as might supply the Turks. A few dhows had been sunk without authority, but the error had been corrected; as for the northern zone, the "cooperative" locals had a habit of firing on Cairo's ships—so much for the success of their policy. The answer to all this was to reiterate that no ship south of Jidda would take action without Aden's approval, upholding a line of demarcated spheres of authority. This, in fact, rather extended Aden's jurisdiction, for 'Asir hardly reached as far northward as Jidda, however indeterminate the Arab

---

28 January, with Hirtzel minute, 27 January; Aden telegram to SSI, 30 January; Grey telegram to McMahon, 8 February 1915: *L/P&S/10,* 3086/15, nos. 330, 375, and 521/15; Clayton private to Wingate, 3 March 1915, *Wingate Papers,* box 134.

[12] Grant minute, 14 February 1915, *India Sec. War* March 1915, 745–862; contents sent home in Viceroy telegram to SSI, 19 February 1915, *L/P&S/10,* 3086/15, no. 674/15.

political frontiers.[13] The issue was shelved for the moment, and it was hoped that coordination of military measures with diplomacy was achieved.

By 30 April 1915 an 'Asiri treaty had been concluded. Britain and al-Idrisi would cooperate against Turkey; Britain would furnish wartime aid, secure 'Asir's safety from the sea, and guarantee independence at war's end; and Britain gave further indication that it had no desire to enlarge its borders "on Arabian soil." It was the final link of Britain's treaty relationships with the coastal chiefs of Arabia (if Husain was included) from the Gulf of 'Aqaba to the head of the Persian Gulf—with the possible exception of a gap or two in the unimportant Hadhramaut—for as will be seen, final steps in the Gulf had already been taken.[14]

One change, however, had been made in India in the text of the executed but as yet unratified treaty: "on Arabian soil" was altered to read "in Western Arabia" on Hardinge's initiative, for it was not desirable to be held by a clause which might be construed to mean Basra or Hudaida or Shaikh Sa'id at some later date. It was indicative of India's worries, but not really of great importance, particularly since the original Arabic version read "in the Yemen"—but when India ratified the treaty in No-

[13] McMahon telegram to Grey, 24 January, SSI telegrams to Viceroy, 28 January and 9 February, Aden telegram to FSI, 30 January 1915, *India Sec. War* March 1915, 745–862. The entire issue was not helped by Admiral Wemyss's own attitude: ". . . I have personally such a contempt for the Government of India that I cannot bring myself to look upon any of their ideas with sympathy," he wrote in July 1916: Wester Wemyss, *op. cit.*, pp. 320–21, and see also pp. 277–78.

[14] Treaty quoted in Hurewitz, *op. cit.*, II, pp. 12–13; originals were enclosed in Maj.-Gen. D. G. L. Shaw, Political Resident, Aden (who signed the treaty on Britain's behalf), to FSI, 1 May; Hardinge in Council to SSI, 20 May; Maj.-Gen. Sir G. Younghusband to FSI (discussing Arabic version), 23 August 1915: *L/P&S/10*, 3086/15, nos. 1954, 2170, and 3075/15; see also *India Sec. War* August 1915, 102–77, and Rosita Forbes, "A Visit to the Idrisi Territory in Asir and Yemen," *Geographical Journal*, 62 (September 1923), 271–78, one of the few private accounts of this area before al-Idrisi's death in 1923.

vember there was no indication that al-Idrisi had been told of the alteration.[15]

With a treaty concluded, operations could get under way in a serious manner—perhaps. In February the Foreign Office had already approved occupation of Kamaran to forestall Italy, if Aden had the men to spare. India's countersuggestion that perhaps it could all be worked out by discussions with Italy was unequivocally rejected by the Foreign Office; the entire operation was designed specifically to avoid this, and it was certainly true that delicate negotiations for Italy's entrance into the war (which occurred in May) had only just been concluded. The Foreign Office now wished to recognize al-Idrisi's ownership of Kamaran on the condition that he agree not to surrender it to another power. Kamaran—but not the Farasan islands—was occupied in mid-June; the eight Turkish quarantine officials offered no resistance and were packed off to Aden.[16]

India had given way on Kamaran and had also compromised somewhat on the more important issue of the pilgrimage. As the season approached in May, India pressed strongly for allowing the *hajj* to take place—again in the name of the pledge already given—but the specter of lines of Indian Muslim princes and dignitaries proceeding to enemy territory did not appeal to London, especially since Britain was in no position to guarantee their safety or security. In the end, no official ban was issued, but a communiqué was released stressing the dangers and insecurity of the trip.[17]

[15] I.O. to F.O., 17 June 1915, L/P&S/10, 3086/15, no. 2170/15; Indian documents in *India Sec. War* August 1915, 102–77, keep-withs.

[16] F.O. to I.O., 25 February, Viceroy telegrams to SSI, 3 March and 30 May, Aden telegrams to SSI, 28 May and 10 and 15 June, F.O. to I.O., 2 June, SSI telegram to Viceroy, 4 June 1915, L/P&S/10, 3086/15, nos. 684, 1571, 1967, 2060, 2137, and 2224/15; Grant and Lake minutes, 28 and 29 May 1915, *India Sec. War* May 1916, 311–62, discuss approaching Italy. The Italo-Entente agreement of 26 April 1915 is reproduced in Hurewitz, *op. cit.*, II, pp. 11–12.

[17] Viceroy telegrams to SSI, 11 March, 12 May, and 13 June, SSI telegram to Viceroy, 7 June 1915, *India Sec. War* June 1916, 223–314.

India was also unhappy over Red Sea arrangements. Blockade of Turkish ports, Cairo's independent Hijaz negotiations, unwanted occupation of unwanted islands, disrupted pilgrimage—only the agreement on the need to keep Italy out preserved peaceful relations with Cairo. Military success might have engendered enthusiasm, but military success was an unapproachable mirage in southwest Arabia. When the Turks appeared to have occupied Lahj in British-protected Aden territory, for example, a column was sent out only to retreat in haste in what Hardinge called a "despicable performance" which resulted mainly from the General Officer Commanding being struck down by heat. The Turks wound up at Shaikh 'Uthman next to Aden itself, and the Aden garrison managed only to drive the Turks off Aden's principal water supply—a supremely fortunate maneuver in midsummer.[18]

If Aden found operations on its own doorstep difficult, conditions were even worse in the Red Sea. To hold waterless and mostly deserted islands was intolerable, and evacuation of Kamaran and nearby Hanish al-Kabir was approved. The evacuation was delayed so as not to be simultaneous with Italian entry into the war, although one might suppose Italy had other problems at the moment more worthy of consideration than Kamaran, and arrangements were set on foot to hire local Arabs to raise the British flag periodically.[19]

As far as al-Idrisi was concerned, nothing seemed to come of the cash and arms and treaty but some friendly discussions with Jacob, who had reverted to his usual position of First Assistant Resident to a rapidly changing series of major-generals. Jacob admired al-Idrisi for his polished manners and piety but found

[18] Hardinge private to Nicolson, 21 June, to Chirol, 15 July, and to Lt.-Gen. Sir J. Willcocks (in France), 4 August 1915, *Hardinge Papers*, and to Lord Willingdon (Bombay), 11 July 1915, *Willingdon Papers*. See also *India Sec. War* December 1915, 176–249.

[19] Aden telegram to SSI, 8 August, SSI telegram to Viceroy, 24 August 1915, *L/P&S/10*, 3086/15, nos. 2907 and 3047/15; and *India Sec. War* May 1916, 311–62.

him ambitious for political influence, distrustful of Husain, and
hostile to Yahya. Al-Idrisi promised much and asked in return
for considerable amounts of guns and ammunition (the latter
was hard to supply; 'Asir's prewar arms came from Italy, and
Italy was unwilling to give Britain several million cartridges to
pass on to an 'Asir increasingly in the British sphere). Even
Jacob had to admit that al-Idrisi was doing little, although all
who came in contact with him agreed that he was loyal and
that he was more important than the Imam—if only because
al-Idrisi had a seacoast, and Yahya, for practical wartime purposes, did not. India continued to agree to furnish the neces-
saries, for even keeping al-Idrisi neutral was a point gained, but
no significant action had come of all this by the time of Husain's
declaration of revolt in June 1916; and of the 6,000 rifles and
11,000,000 rounds authorized, only 3,000 guns and 200,000
rounds had actually been provided (the rest of the guns and
more ammunition were held at Aden).[20]

By mid-1916 neither al-Idrisi nor Yahya, nor the various
Yemeni chiefs, had made any noticeable impact on the war in
Arabia. On the other hand, it could be argued that the British
arrangements with 'Asir had created a situation of deadlock in
which al-Idrisi balanced Yahya, and that was, as India had admitted, something gained. Britain had also established its claim
to some of the Red Sea islands, although all that was left as
demonstration of this was a handful of Arabs, presumably
equipped with a British flag. At one point the India Office,
which had caught the spirit of the thing, suggested enthusias-
tically that one or two ships should be stationed off the Farasan

[20] Aden telegrams to FSI, 18 August and 25 November 1915, and 29
January, 19 March, 29 May, and 9 July 1916; Viceroy telegram to SSI,
12 July; SSI telegram to Viceroy, 7 July; and Aden to FSI, 27 January,
12 June, and 4 July 1916: *India Sec. War* September 1916, 442–589, and
*L/P&S/10*, 3086/15, parts 6–8 (especially Political Dept., I.O., memorandum, 25 November 1916, no. 5392/16). Arms figures are from June
1917: Maj.-Gen. J. M. Stuart to I.O., 22 June 1917, *India Sec. War*
September 1917, 317–67.

islands "with instructions to land & hoist the British and red Arab flags on the approach of an Italian ship." [21] British control of these islands required no such elaborate measures, however. How firm existing control was thought to be can be seen by an arrangement of the War Office and the India Office to halve the expenses and divide the revenue, for no department made that sort of commitment lightly.[22] So much, at least, had been achieved, by the advent of the Arab revolt. Meanwhile, British and Indian authorities in the Persian Gulf had not been entirely idle either.

## 2

World War I found Britain in virtually unchallenged control of the Persian Gulf. From Muscat to Kuwait the Arabian littoral was almost entirely under British influence, and the local Arab chiefs had bound themselves by treaties into an informal protectorate status administered by the Gulf Resident, Sir Percy Cox. It was not surprising that the several shaikhs hurried to congratulate Britain on the first Mesopotamian successes and to acknowledge the various explanatory communications issued by the Resident in the name of the Raj. Some had been given good cause for their loyalty: Mubarak of Kuwait, for example, was pledged perpetual tax-free possession of his date groves in Turkish territory and guaranteed the independence (as usual, "under British protection") which he had *de facto* exercised for nearly two decades.[23]

There were some gaps in the Gulf treaty system which for various reasons remained to be filled. The Qatar peninsula was one; Anglo-Ottoman disputes on minor jurisdictional points

[21] F.O. to I.O., 14 January, I.O. to F.O., 17 January, Admiralty to F.O., 20 January 1916, *L/P&S/10*, 3086/15, nos. 183, 288, and 360/16.
[22] SSI telegram to Viceroy, 6 July 1916, *ibid.*, no. 4256/16.
[23] Cox to Mubarak, 3 November 1914, *L/P&S/11*, vol. 169, no. 7474/20, and other documents in file; Hurewitz, *op. cit.*, II, p. 4.

and internecine family quarrels had combined to prevent formal addition of Qatar to the Trucial Coast, Bahrain, Kuwait, and (loosely) Muscat. The advent of war removed the problem of Turkish interests, and in October 1914—before declaration—authorization for Indian signature of a treaty was being discussed.[24] The actual negotiations took some time, for Sir Percy Cox, whose responsibility the Gulf was, had other duties, and the situation on Qatar was confused. By November 1916, however, the treaty was signed, the delay caused in part by Britain so Qatar negotiations would not conflict with those then proceeding with Ibn Sa'ud.[25] In the treaty, Shaikh 'Abd Allah ibn Qasim ibn Thani bound himself to the standard Gulf treaty clauses against slavery, piracy, the arms trade, concessions or territorial cessions to foreigners, maximum customs duties, and so on. 'Abd Allah received little in return, if British protection itself be discounted, except a few (300) rifles for his military force.[26]

Much more important than Qatar was the territory under the control of 'Abd al-'Aziz ibn Sa'ud. The House of Sa'ud had only recently recovered anything like its nineteenth-century position; it had entered into contact with Britain only in 1906 with a tentative (and rebuffed) overture, and to a larger extent in 1911 in the discussions between Ibn Sa'ud and Shakespear. Ibn Sa'ud's capture from the Turks of the Hasa district between Qatar and Kuwait in 1913 made him a Gulf coast ruler. It was not possible to open formal relations with him before the war (other than a few meetings with political officers, and those mainly on local affairs) because of Anglo-Ottoman relations. In fact, the Anglo-Ottoman settlement in the unratified treaty

---

[24] I.O. to F.O., 21 October 1914, *L/P&S/10*, 2182/13, no. 4042/14.

[25] Grant note, 30 April 1915, *India Sec. E.* February 1919, 4–100.

[26] Details on negotiations are in *L/P&S/10*, file 2182/13, part 3; treaty of 3 November in Hurewitz, *op. cit.*, II, pp. 22–23; see also Busch, *Britain and the Persian Gulf*, p. 346. The small Turkish garrison on Qatar was removed in August 1915; *FO* 371/2489 gives details.

of 1913 left Ibn Sa'ud rather unwillingly to Ottoman jurisdiction, but the war nullified that agreement.[27]

It has already been seen that, in October 1914, Captain Shakespear was recalled from leave and ordered to the Gulf to apply his influence and experience to the task of persuading the ruler of Najd—Ibn Sa'ud's main base of operations—to join sides with Britain if and when war came. It was hoped that Shakespear might reach Ibn Sa'ud before war broke out, but he arrived at Bahrain only on 7 November and then had to proceed not to the interior but to Kuwait in order to reach Ibn Sa'ud, who was reported at 'Unaiza, some 325 miles southwest of Kuwait. On the 18th, after conferring with Cox at Abadan and receiving instructions to remain as permanent emissary to Ibn Sa'ud in case the latter's help was required in Iraq, Shakespear was at Kuwait; there he found that the "notorious" Sayyid Talib had left two days earlier for the interior with fifty men. Talib was reportedly acting for the Turks and would try to persuade Ibn Sa'ud to remain loyal to his nominal sovereign (although Talib had denied this to the local British agent). Shakespear moved faster, however, reaching Ibn Sa'ud's camp east of 'Unaiza on the last day of the year; Cox reported that when Talib arrived to find Shakespear already there he departed, on 3 January. Talib was subsequently ordered off to exile in India by Cox, and the mission to Ibn Sa'ud could proceed.[28]

By 4 January Shakespear was in a position to report in detail on the Amir's views and plans. Ibn Sa'ud had already received several requests to participate in a *jihad* against the British, but

[27] Busch, *Britain and the Persian Gulf*, pp. 340–45.

[28] Account of Shakespear's journey is based on I.O. to Shakespear, 5 October, Viceroy telegrams to SSI, 24 November and 23 December 1914, and 2 January 1915, Cox to FSI, 29 November 1914, I.O. to F.O., 4 January 1915, Lt.-Col. W. G. Grey (Kuwait) to Resident, 16 November, and Shakespear to Resident, 20 November 1914: *L/P&S/10*, 2182/13, nos. 3832, 4578, 5002, 5089, and 5106/14 and 43 and 181/15; W. G. Grey to Resident, 27 October, Shakespear to Resident, 9 November, Cox telegram to FSI, 29 November 1914 and 13 January 1915, *India Sec. War* May 1915, 502–615.

he had steadfastly declined on the grounds that he could not leave Najd open to attack unless Ibn Rashid also left his home province of Jabal Shammar. Ibn Sa'ud had taken heart at Cox's letter of November promising guarantees against reprisals and recognition of independence, something Ibn Sa'ud had long desired, in return for aid against the Turks. He had already publicly read the declaration on the holy places and had ousted or otherwise contained the few Turkish agents in his territory. The problem was his lingering doubt as to how long the new British attitude would last, for only a few months earlier Britain had said it was unable to do precisely what it now proposed to do. The Amir, in short, wanted it all in writing, and he and Shakespear now sat down to work out a draft treaty. In forwarding the terms, Shakespear urged that the advantages to be gained were very great: the treaty would complete the Gulf network and, with clauses on arms trade and foreign interests, would considerably increase Gulf security.[29]

Unfortunately, Ibn Sa'ud was even then involved in a campaign against Ibn Rashid, and in a clash on 24 January Captain Shakespear was killed. A most promising career was cut short, for Shakespear had already revealed great ability.[30] It was also unfortunate for the continuation of a link with Ibn Sa'ud, for some time had now to elapse before a replacement with anything like the same ability and experience could be found and appointed; in any event, the draft treaty which Shakespear had luckily sent out before his death had to be considered in both

[29] Shakespear to Resident, 4 January 1915, *L/P&S/10*, 2182/13, no. 975/15.

[30] W. G. Grey to Cox, 17 February 1915, Persian Gulf files (I.O. Library), *R/15/1/53/10*. See also Douglas Carruthers, "Captain Shakespear's Last Journey," *Geographical Journal*, 59 (May–June 1922), 321–34, 401–17. Arnold Wilson's later remarks (in part quoting Philby) demonstrate the high regard in which Shakespear was held, and the hopes placed in his mission—although questionable as a historical judgment: had Shakespear lived, Lawrence and his Arab revolt would never have come to pass. And Wilson added his own view: "The world would have been deprived of an epic, and the British Treasury would

India and England. India had no hesitations and fully recommended signature. In London, the India Office pressed hard for an agreement which was more than a question of wartime aid; even if Ibn Sa'ud did not actively fight Turkey he was already at war with Turkey's loyal minion, Ibn Rashid, and this alone should insure preferential treatment. The likelihood of the disappearance of Ottoman power from postwar Basra also made it most desirable to cement relations now with an Ibn Sa'ud who would still be master of a considerable portion of central Arabia and the Persian Gulf coast.[31]

Wording of the draft presented some difficulties, for negotiations on this point had to be conducted via messengers passing to and fro to Ibn Sa'ud's headquarters, wherever they happened to be. But by July Ibn Sa'ud had given Cox a signed copy of the treaty. It required some revision, for Ibn Sa'ud had removed "unprovoked" from the clause requiring British aid against aggression and inserted "in all circumstances and in any place," which was unsatisfactory, to say the least. Further difficulty was encountered in the clause requiring the ruler to follow Britain's advice "unreservedly," which to Cox meant in problems of the sale or lease of territory but which Ibn Sa'ud interpreted as applying to his policy generally. Ibn Sa'ud therefore added a rider, which proved acceptable: ". . . provided that it be not damaging to his own interests. . ." Nor, finally, did

---

have been saved many millions of pounds sterling; the Sharifian family might never have emerged from the obscurity of the Hejaz and the arms of the Turks, with whom, until April 1916, they were in active negotiation; Palestine might have remained Turkish and Zionism a dream. In the event, however, it was left to the military authorities in Egypt to accomplish what, with better luck and more imagination, especially on the part of the Government of India, might have been accomplished with our assistance by Ibn Sa'ud." (*Loyalties*, p. 161.)

[31] Viceroy telegram to SSI, 29 January, I.O. to F.O., 30 January, and SSI telegram to Viceroy, 1 February 1915, *L/P&S/10*, 2182/13, no. 350/15.

Britain have the right of approval of the successor to the Saudi throne; the treaty provided only that the ruler not be antagonistic to Britain in any respect. The treaty was, therefore, the most flexible of the Gulf network when it was signed at a meeting of Cox and Ibn Sa'ud near Bahrain in December 1915 (and ratified in mid-1916).[32]

Several problems remained, notably the failure to designate any boundaries to Ibn Sa'ud's area, but the Amir of Najd was now a British ally. One important question regarding his contribution to the total war effort concerned his attitude toward Sharif Husain. As Shakespear had discovered, Ibn Sa'ud was hardly enthusiastic about the Sharif, whom he saw as weak and undependable. Given Husain's religious position as guardian of Mecca and Medina and the hostility of Ibn Sa'ud's Wahhabi warriors to the "orthodox" Sharif, this attitude was not unexpected, particularly in Cairo, where Hogarth wrote, for example, that the new treaty was all to the good—provided no pledge had been made to support Ibn Sa'ud against the Sharif. Similarly, McMahon and Wingate both were quick to urge Husain's superior claims to Arab leadership on the basis of both the prestige of his title and his central position at Mecca. But Grant in India replied that Cairo overrated the Sharif, and if predictions were to be made his was that nothing would come of the revolt.[33]

These views were indicative of the major controversy to come, for Ibn Sa'ud had indeed entered the lists on India's be-

[32] Viceroy telegram to SSI, 12 July, I.O. to F.O., 11 August, SSI telegram to Viceroy, 16 August 1915, Cox to FSI, 3 January, Chelmsford in Council to SSI, 28 July 1916 (enclosing ratified version), *ibid.*, nos. 2490, 2832, and 2966/15 and 668 and 3439/16. Text is in Hurewitz, *op. cit.*, II, pp. 17–18.

[33] G.O.C., "Force D," telegram to C.I.G.S., 5 January, McMahon to Grey (giving Wingate views), 29 February 1916, *FO* 371/2769; Hogarth private to Chelmsford, 11 April (enclosing 8 February memorandum), Chelmsford private to Chamberlain, 5 May (enclosing Grant memorandum of 28 April) 1916, *Chelmsford Papers.*

half. Both Cairo and India distrusted the other's man, and both intended to support Mecca and Riyadh respectively, providing arms and cash when necessary. India was never to supply Ibn Sa'ud on a scale equivalent to the aid provided Husain, and indeed had given nothing at all by the time of the June 1916 revolt, although 1,000 rifles and £20,000 had been approved.[34] India had now been responsible for agreements with two rivals of Husain, al-Idrisi and Ibn Sa'ud. It remained to be seen what contribution these two Arabian rulers would make to the revolt, and whether that contribution would be positive.

3

The Arab revolt meant problems for India—use of prisoners, landings at Rabigh, declarations—all of which raised issues of Muslim opinion, and all of which brought warnings or obstruction from India. On the other hand, India's policy in the Arabian Peninsula had not been notably successful as yet, for while treaties bound 'Asir and Najd, neither gave any real promise of actual military cooperation in the revolt declared by Husain. To the contrary, there was some danger that al-Idrisi might use his arms and ammunition on Husain.

Officials in Whitehall were also concerned that nothing had come of several approaches so far made to Imam Yahya of Yemen; it was to be hoped that the revolt might now prompt him to alter his essentially anti-British posture—but here once more India tended to disagree, for negotiations with Yemen might well precipitate British entrance into the quagmire of conflicting 'Asiri-Yemeni territorial claims. Aden was told to proceed with negotiations but to say nothing about territory or, for that matter, Britain's assumption of the rather substantial

[34] Viceroy telegram to SSI, 7 October, F.O. to I.O., 18 October 1915, *L/P&S/10*, 2182/13, nos. 3670 and 3820/15.

liability of Turkey's Yemen subsidy, which, the India Office calculated, ran to some £10–12,000 per annum, a sizable sum for a potential enemy.[35]

By mid-1916 British interest in an agreement with Yahya was as much due to Italy as to any possible aid against the Turks. Italy had put forward no formal claims, but at least Hirtzel was concerned that when the Italians came to study the Anglo-French-Russian contract such claims would be made. Hirtzel had already suggested unsuccessfully that those agreements include a restrictive clause on Arabia that would bar Italy; now the only recourse seemed to be treaties with 'Asir and Yemen that would perform the same function.[36]

India, informed of high-level discussion of this question, went even further in advocating an "Arabian 'Monroe Doctrine'" (Holderness's phrase) and in considering a military advance from Aden designed primarily to influence postwar events in the hinterland. Unfortunately, Yahya's uncooperative attitude suggested that this type of pressure would be less than effective in achieving a treaty. By December 1916, in fact, all were aware of the Imam's reply: he was unable to break with the Ottoman authorities out of loyalty to his legal sovereign and Caliph, although his clear recognition of British strength at least left the fairly safe presumption that Yahya would not take the offensive.[37]

[35] SSI telegrams to Viceroy, 7 and 14 July, Viceroy telegram to SSI, 12 July, Hirtzel minute, 18 July 1916, *L/P&S/10*, 2100/16, nos. 2630, 2700, and 2835/16.

[36] Hirtzel note for Nicolson, 23 January, and Holderness for Nicolson, 24 January 1916, *FO* 371/2767; Hirtzel note, 4 August 1916, *L/P&S/10*, 53/16, no. 3092/16; see also Rodd (Rome) private to Hardinge, 9 September, Chamberlain note for Grey, 14 September, Hardinge private to Rodd, 13 and 27 September 1916, *Hardinge Papers.*

[37] Hirtzel, Holderness, and Chamberlain minutes of 17, 20, and 21 September, on Rodd to Grey, 24 July 1916; Memorandum B.244, 22 September 1916, and B.247, 20 January 1917; Chelmsford in Council to SSI, 29 September 1916: *L/P&S/10*, 53/16, nos. 3777 and 4807/16 and

If the Imam could not be secured, the Red Sea islands could, and Italy, by "persistent inquiries" about the Farasan group, insured that attention again turned in this direction. As the Foreign Office wrote the India Office, Foreign Office records showed that in 1915 it had been proposed to recognize al-Idrisi's occupation of this group in return for a promise not to yield them to a third power—but the documents did not make it clear whether this had actually been done. It had not: al-Idrisi had been approached, Aden reported, but he had not replied and Aden had considered it impolitic to push the matter.[38]

Extraordinary as it seemed, no one in London had realized that the islands had not been flagged as British. The India Office was now quick to apologize and to suggest (in a letter drafted by Hirtzel) that ". . . the British flag sd. be hoisted at once on the islands & left there," and that Italy be told that all Red Sea islands belonged to the future Arab state and were covered by the Anglo-French agreement—in particular, that the Farasan islands belonged to al-Idrisi. In rapid succession, the Admiralty was asked to act and Jacob to visit al-Idrisi at once to get effective occupation of the islands, failing which the flag might be hoisted; only then would Italy be told. On 29 December 1916, even before al-Idrisi could be approached, a flag was hoisted on one island, and on 1 January another ship arrived with a military guard.[39]

---

1030/17. D. Bray minute, 7 October, and Grant note, 8 December 1916, *India Sec. War* September 1917, 317–67; Aden telegram to FSI, 4 December, and W.O. to I.O., 16 December 1916, *L/P&S/11*, vol. 111, nos. 5099 and 5339/16.

[38] F.O. to I.O., 18 December, with Hirtzel minute, 19 December, Aden telegram to SSI, 21 December 1916, *L/P&S/10*, 3086/15, nos. 5335 and 5433/16.

[39] I.O. to F.O., 23 December, F.O. to Admiralty and to I.O. and Viceroy telegram to SSI, 26 December, Aden telegram to SSI, 28 December, CinCEI (Ismailia) telegram to Admiralty, 30 December 1916, *ibid.*, nos. 5433, 5455, 5496, and 5508/16.

It was just as well that action had been taken, for al-Idrisi refused to grant Jacob an interview[40]—curious behavior for an
ally, perhaps, but al-Idrisi had a most legitimate grievance
against Britain dating from his one serious attempt to participate in the anti-Turk struggle. On 12 June 1916 al-Idrisi had
signified his intention of cooperating with British forces, and it
had been arranged that an assault would be made on the coastal
settlement of Qunfudha, midway between Jidda and Jaizan. On
the 18th British ships had shelled the Turkish garrison out of
their position, and although al-Idrisi was not quite enthusiastic
a garrison of his men was landed. Sharifal forces soon arrived
outside the town, to which they laid claim; Cairo and Khartoum both supported Husain, and the local tribes did not favor
al-Idrisi. To al-Idrisi's great disgust, the affair was concluded
by the evacuation of his forces in British ships; even worse, in
October the Turks reoccupied the town and held it until Husain regained control in May 1919. As was clear in India, al-
Idrisi had to go to the wall, but this was no surprise given the
importance of Husain compared to what Wingate termed "a
mere upstart" who had been brought in only as a counter to
Italy.[41]
    Al-Idrisi naturally had little interest in continuing a coopera-
tion that was going to mean Sharifal territorial and propaganda
victories.[42] To India, in fact, the only possible happy interpre-

---

[40] Aden telegram to SSI, 2 January 1917, *ibid.*, no. 34/17.
[41] Based on McMahon telegram to Grey, 3 August, Aden telegram
to H.M.S. *Fox* (Red Sea patrol), 4 August, McMahon telegram to
Aden, 5 August, Senior Naval Officer, Red Sea (Port Sudan) telegram
to Arab Bureau, 7 August, Aden telegrams to McMahon, 9 August and
12 September 1916, *FO* 141/161; Arab Bureau (note on phone conversation) to McMahon, 3 October 1916, *FO* 141/462; McMahon telegram
to Grey, 4 October 1916, *L/P&S/10*, 2100/16, no. 4109/16; D. Bray
note, 4 July 1916, *India Sec. War* March 1917, 1–175; and, on the 1919
reoccupation, High Commissioner of Egypt (Allenby) to Curzon
(F.O.), 24 June 1919, *L/P&S/10*, 1182/23, no. 3942/19.
[42] Al-Idrisi to Maj.-Gen. Stuart (Aden), 20 August 1916, *L/P&S/10*,
2100/16, no. 3925/16.

tation of the incident was that it further lessened the likelihood of an Arab confederation.[43] But when Britain approached al-Idrisi again on the Farasan islands in early 1917, the real meaning of Qunfudha was clear. After some delay, al-Idrisi replied that if the need ever came to hoist the British flag to ward off aggression against the islands by another power, it would be too late anyway, as British power would have vanished from the Red Sea. Such brutally clear logic was not the logic of imperialism, however. It was decided that Italy would be told that Britain was occupying the islands in al-Idrisi's name, and al-Idrisi would be pressed to conclude some sort of formal agreement. Although he clearly feared both Turkish reprisals and a commitment which would make any later dealings with Italy or France impossible, a British flag and guard on the islands persuaded al-Idrisi that a bad bargain was better than no bargain, for he had nothing on paper that guaranteed even his possession of the Farasans. The supplementary agreement on the islands was signed on 22 January; the flag and guard were removed on the next day.[44]

The treaty was not quite what London had planned, for while al-Idrisi was recognized as possessor of the Farasan islands in return for a pledge not to cede, sell, or lease, Britain promised to protect 'Asir from outside interference, to aid in postwar development, to exert every effort to replace al-Idrisi in control if he should be forced into exile (an obvious reference to his concern with the enmity of Husain and Yahya), and, finally, to supply military aid for an indefinite period. Jacob had found al-Idrisi a hard bargainer who had refused the noncession clause

[43] D. Bray minute, 11 September 1916, *India Sec. War* March 1917, 1–175.
[44] Aden telegrams to SSI, 3 (with minutes), 11, and 14 January, SSI telegram to Viceroy, 15 January, CinCEI telegram to Admiralty, 25 January, and Memorandum B.250 (agreement with al-Idrisi), 22 January 1917, *L/P&S/10*, 3086/15, nos. 34, 168, 241, 376, and 746/17. For text of the agreement, C. U. Aitchison, ed., *A Collection of Treaties, Engagements and Sanads Relating to India and Neighbouring Countries*, XI (5th ed., Delhi, 1933), pp. 178–79.

unless his own points were written into the treaty. India, admitting that in both Qunfudha and the occupation of the Farasan islands al-Idrisi had been treated rather cavalierly, recommended approval of the agreement without revision, on the understanding that postwar circumstances would no doubt provide the opportunity for revision[45] (the death of al-Idrisi in 1923 and the subsequent absorption of 'Asir into Saudi Arabia allowed for the agreement's total abrogation, as it happened).

The Farasan islands were secure, and just in time, for Italy returned to the issue by inquiring whether Britain had, as reported, actually raised its flag there. The Italian government was told that the action had been ordered in 1915 and only now executed, and that it was all done on al-Idrisi's behalf. Italy had no choice but to accept the explanation, but her continued interest in Arabian affairs and in 'Asir in particular was demonstrated by an offer to send a company of askaris to join the Allied contingents in the Hijaz and by some rather accusatory discussion of the problem of furnishing arms to al-Idrisi. Above all, Italy warned that she had no intention of holding herself aloof from events in the Hijaz which were of an international character, for Italy too was a Muslim colonial power and had, moreover, definite interests in the Red Sea. If occasion for reviewing the situation arose, Italy would want to participate. There things remained for the moment—but Italy was a factor to be borne constantly in mind when the Red Sea was mentioned.[46]

[45] Treaty with note by D. Bray, 14 February 1917, *India Sec. War* September 1917, 369–407; Jacob memorandum, 24 January 1917, *L/ P&S/10*, 3086/15, no. 748/17; and Jacob demi-official to Grant, 3 February 1918, *India Sec. War* October 1918, 1–170; Chelmsford private to Chamberlain, 19 January, and Chamberlain private to Chelmsford, 14 February 1917, *Chelmsford Papers*. Official Indian approval: Viceroy telegram to SSI, 17 February, and F.O. to I.O., 16 March 1917, *L/P&S/ 10*, 3086/15, no. 746/17.

[46] Balfour to Rodd, 29 January, Italian Embassy to Balfour, 28 February, Rodd to Balfour, 31 March, I.O. to F.O., 17 April, Imperiali (Italian Ambassador) to Balfour, 18 July, F.O. to I.O., 12 October, I.O.

By the end of the war, there had been no substantial change in the situation in the Red Sea, 'Asir, or Yemen from that of mid-1917, although an occasional minor naval action had augmented the continuing blockade. Al-Idrisi remained an ally and the Imam remained an enemy, but it cannot be said that either significantly affected the conduct of the war. On the other hand, the commitments to al-Idrisi and the existence of the Imam meant that there were two more Arab chiefs to be considered along with Ibn Sa'ud and Husain (and possibly Ibn Rashid) at war's end. The relations of al-Idrisi with Sharif Husain, in particular, had done a good deal to undermine dreams of an Arab confederation, for there was little hope of achieving even friendly communications between the two rulers. This rivalry, like that of Husain with Ibn Sa'ud, remained—and in both cases India had had primary responsibility for bringing the Sharif's rivals into the Allied fold.

Ironically, India would much rather have parted with responsibility for Aden—and therefore for 'Asir and Yemen—but by the end of the war no technical change in this relationship had been made. The need to coordinate military operations, proved in such costly fashion in Mesopotamia, had brought transfer of Aden military operations to the War Office and political authority to Cairo in July 1917, although neither change altered policy in any major way, but the issue of ultimate control of Aden remained for postwar consideration, and India's insistence that it could not continue to pay for operations not now under its control insured that reconsideration would take place at an early date.[47]

---

to F.O., 18 October, and Hirtzel minute, 16 October 1917, *ibid.*, no. 538/17, and 53/16, nos. 1030, 1478, 3116, and 4112/17; SSI telegram to Viceroy, 4 August 1917, *India Sec. War* October 1917, 398–407.

[47] Viceroy telegrams to SSI, 24 July and 15 August 1917, and 9 January 1918, Balfour telegram to Wingate, 24 July 1917, *L/P&S/10*, 3082/17, nos. 3082 and 3158/17 and 169/18; M.A.C. 9th minutes, 22 August, and W.O. memorandum, 6 July 1917, *CAB* 27/22.

At best, it could be said that Britain had up to a point been able to offset its failure to drive the Turks away from Aden by creating a system rather delicately balancing Sharif, al-Idrisi, Imam, and rebel Yemeni tribes, but it was a very murky relationship. Far more important to the concept of an Arabia under unchallenged British influence—and as has been seen, some concerned officials interpreted this to mean a balance of rival chiefs rather than a single state—the rather dangerous Italian interests had been kept away for the time being. All in all, the policy in southwestern Arabia could be termed successful in the short run. Whether the same could be said of relations with Ibn Sa'ud is another question, but the parallels of Saudi-Sharifal relations with those of 'Asir and Yemen are striking and not altogether accidental.

## 4

Sharif Husain's revolt meant, for al-Idrisi, the humiliation of Qunfudha and distrust of Britain's intentions. For Ibn Sa'ud, on the other side of Arabia, the revolt engendered similar fear, fear that in its zeal for Husain's cause Britain might go too far in recognition of the Sharif's primacy over the Arabs. In July 1916, and again in August, Ibn Sa'ud wrote to Sir Percy Cox expressing his concern and supporting his case with references to the long-standing hostility of the two rulers and Husain's perpetual desire to obtain a foothold in Najd. British references to "the Arabs" as if they were a whole had not encouraged him at all. When, therefore, Husain wrote to Ibn Sa'ud informing him of the capture of Mecca and urging cooperation, Ibn Sa'ud was willing—at least nominally—to furnish aid, but unwilling to unite himself with the Sharif unless the latter gave his solemn undertaking on the immunity of the subjects and territory of Najd.[48]

[48] Ibn Sa'ud to Cox, 20 July and 15 August 1916, FO 371/2776.

Britain's policy was naturally to urge Saudi cooperation, and Cox suggested that Ibn Sa'ud should be told that nothing in the Sharifal negotiations would prejudice the Anglo-Saudi treaty of 1915, the text of which should at the same time be given to Husain. The assurance to the Amir was acceptable, but London hesitated to give the treaty to Husain for the rather obvious reason that the Sharif might misinterpret both the intent of the treaty and the detailed clauses, notably that which promised aid against aggression.[49]

Assurances alone, however, would not help the war, and it was suggested that Ibn Sa'ud be encouraged to attack Ha'il (400 miles west-southwest of Kuwait), the stronghold of his old enemy Ibn Rashid of Jabal Shammar. Cox was of the opinion that Ibn Sa'ud was unlikely to attempt this without money and artillery (and the men to man it), and it was questionable in any case whether the result would be worth the effort. India similarly opposed pressing Ibn Sa'ud. If he moved against Ha'il on his own, well and good, but no guns could be spared; if he sent a detachment to aid Husain, this might result in embarrassing claims later, so that too should not be encouraged.[50]

It was not a very promising situation, and Cox could only suggest that he meet Ibn Sa'ud and discuss matters. In London, Hirtzel had some doubts about this, and about the entire policy toward Ibn Sa'ud. India wanted to do nothing, but the treaty had not been concluded so that Ibn Sa'ud could simply do nothing. Apparently Cox had suggested taking Ha'il, but it was not clear that this was necessary for containing Ibn Rashid or that the required guns would be available. On the strength of

[49] Cox to Arab Bureau, 8 and 9 (telegram) September, McMahon telegram to Grey, 13 September, I.O. to F.O., 15 September, SSI telegram to Viceroy, 19 September 1916; it is not clear that Husain was actually given the text, although Grey (telegram to McMahon, 23 September) ordered that this be done: FO 371/2769.

[50] Cox telegram to FSI, 27 September, Viceroy telegram to SSI, 30 September 1916, *ibid.*

this minute, India was told that while Ibn Sa'ud's military value against the Turks was doubtless small, he could still aid in controlling Ibn Rashid. If some munitions would produce a limited offensive against Ha'il, this was an acceptable price to pay.[51]

On 11–12 November Cox met Ibn Sa'ud at 'Uqair on the Gulf coast south of Qatif. Cox's conclusion, after the discussion, was that while Saudi cooperation with the Sharif was not practicable, a demonstration against Ibn Rashid might be achieved with limited material aid. As for Ibn Sa'ud himself, he was on his way to visit Kuwait and Muhammara and, Cox hoped, Basra, where the Resident wished to invest him with the dignity of Knight Commander of the Most Eminent Order of the Indian Empire (K.C.I.E.). On 20 November 1916 Ibn Sa'ud duly arrived at Kuwait on H.M.S. *Juno*. Here he met with the rulers of Kuwait and Muhammara in an impressive durbar, and many pleasantries and pledges of cooperation were exchanged. In his further discussions with Cox, Ibn Sa'ud was persuaded to send one of his sons and a handful of followers to the Sharif, if this was deemed desirable, although the Amir maintained that Husain had been discourteous and arrogant in his recent correspondence. Cox had to agree that the Sharif's attitude was at least offhand and patronizing and would do little to further the cause (a representation that resulted in a hint being passed to Husain to mend his ways).[52]

Ibn Sa'ud was also interested in military aid, for he had lost much in the fight with Ibn Rashid in which Shakespear had been killed and also had been forced to deal with the 'Ajman

[51] Cox telegram to FSI/SSI, 6 October, with Hirtzel minute, 17 October 1916, *L/P&S/10*, 2182/13, nos. 4131 and 4174/16; SSI telegram to Viceroy, 27 October 1916, *FO* 371/2769.

[52] Cox telegrams to FSI/SSI, 3 and 21 (three of date, nos. T56–58) November, and Grey telegram to Wingate, 25 November 1916, *ibid.* The K.C.I.E. had originally been planned in conjunction with Hardinge's trip. See also Bell, *op. cit.*, II, pp. 509–10 (a supplement written by Sir Percy Cox).

('Ujman) tribe, Ibn Rashid's ally and at that time Ibn Sa'ud's implacable enemy.[53] Ibn Sa'ud lacked the resources to repair his losses, since the camel trade to Syria, his main source of income at that time, was shut down due to the war. Britain had supplied £20,000 and 1,000 rifles, but the cash had gone for debts and the arms to his own guards. More of both was necessary, and some machine guns; it cost Ibn Sa'ud a rupee per day per man in the field, and any action had to be based upon this appreciation. Cox advocated the machine guns and a subsidy of £5,000 per month, convinced that this was modest cost for good value compared with what was being furnished to Husain.[54]

While Cox and Ibn Sa'ud were discussing these issues, the Amir had been persuaded without great difficulty to go to Basra, where he arrived on the 27th. He toured the various base depots and the lines at Shaiba, meeting the principal mili-

[53] The 'Ajman was a powerful tribe, normally influential in Hasa, but after Ibn Sa'ud's assumption of the control of that province in 1913 he and the 'Ajman were at odds and the tribe naturally allied with Ibn Rashid. In an attack upon the 'Ajman near Hofuf in July 1915, Ibn Sa'ud's brother was killed, and his hostility was now permanent. In September of the same year Ibn Sa'ud, in alliance with Mubarak of Kuwait, broke the 'Ajman in battle, but many of the 'Ajman subsequently took refuge in Kuwait, whence Ibn Sa'ud obtained their expulsion only after protracted and not very friendly negotiations with Kuwait. The rather curious reversal of Kuwait's position is explained by the fact that Mubarak died in November 1915, and his sons and successors—Jabir, who himself died in February 1917, and Salim, who survived until February 1921—had a rather different attitude toward Najd. Further details on the 'Ajman quarrel: Cox to Arab Bureau, 14 October 1916, *India Sec. War* June 1917, 197–229; Grey (Kuwait) to Resident, 25 November 1915, Wilson (Basra) to Cox, 25 July 1916, enclosing memorandum on the 'Ajman, and Capt. P. G. Loch (Kuwait) report, 3 September 1918, *R/15/1/53/10*. On Kuwait: *India Sec. E.* July 1916, 1–38, and August 1917, 44–62: Abdul 'Azīz ar-Rushaid, *Ta'rīkh al-Kuwait* (Beirut, n.d.), pp. 198ff.; and H. R. P. Dickson, *Kuwait and Her Neighbours* (London, 1956), pp. 150–53. The best discussion of the 'Ajman and Saudi relations is R. Bayly Winder, *Saudi Arabia in the Nineteenth Century* (N.Y., 1965).
[54] Cox telegram to FSI, 26 November 1916, *FO 371/2769*.

tary and political officers—guided about, for the most part, by Gertrude Bell, although it is doubtful whether he was at all flattered by this attention. "We took him in trains and motors," she wrote to her parents, "showed him aeroplanes, high explosives, anti-aircraft guns, hospitals, base depots—everything. He was full of wonder but never agape. He asked innumerable questions and made intelligent comments. He's a big man." Cox too was impressed; Ibn Sa'ud's curiosity was that of a man learning new things, not a man confused, even with such spectacular displays as a view of the bones of his own hand in an X-ray machine.[55]

It seemed that the visit was a success, all the more so when India approved the subsidy and 1,000 rifles, with a possibility of 2,000 more and some machine guns (although naturally the India Office noted that Imperial funds would have to bear the cost of all this in the end; the Treasury gave approval for six months from January 1917). When Husain sent telegrams to Ibn Sa'ud and to Mubarak's successor, Shaikh Jabir ibn Mubarak (who had also been offended) stating that the reported strain in the correspondence was all a misunderstanding, it appeared that a new day had dawned and that the Arab confederation had moved that much closer to realization.[56] But Ibn Sa'ud was a man who kept his own counsel, and the Sharif and Ibn Rashid were truer realities than the wonders of Basra.

That Cox was well aware of the basic, underlying tension in Anglo-Saudi relations is shown by his refusal, in May 1917, to write to the Amir suggesting that he give recognition to Husain as titular head of the Arab movement—although the

[55] Burgoyne, op. cit., p. 48 (quoted); see also Wilson, Loyalties, pp. 159–60; H. St. J. B. Philby, Arabian Jubilee (N.Y., 1953), pp. 46–47; Cox to SSI, 3 December 1916, L/P&S/10, 2182/13, no. 126/17, and telegram to SSI, 29 November 1916, FO 371/2769.

[56] Viceroy telegram to SSI, 7 December, I.O. to F.O., 11 December, Wingate telegram to Grey, 2 December 1916, ibid.; Memorandum B.251 by Arab Bureau, Iraq section, 12 January, and Treasury to F.O., 1 January 1917, L/P&S/10, 2182/13, no. 712/17, and 4931/16, no. 43/17.

fact that this was another Mark Sykes idea may have influenced Cox's attitude. Ronald Storrs, Oriental Secretary in Cairo, had been chosen to replace Shakespear, and it had been planned that Cox's appeal would be included in his letter introducing Storrs to Ibn Sa'ud. As a result of Cox's objection, Storrs was instructed only to try to get some such agreement once he got to know Ibn Sa'ud—a mission that needs no discussion since Storrs no sooner set out from Kuwait than he had to turn back because of heatstroke.[57] In fairness it must be said that Ibn Sa'ud was a difficult man to reach, and June hardly the month for such activities, but then Storrs was never really that kind of orientalist.

When fall arrived, Cox suggested another mission, this time possibly a joint Iraq-Egypt endeavor. Ibn Sa'ud was still not supplying any real help to the war; as Cox rightly pointed out on his behalf, the Amir's people were anti-Sharif and irritated by the trade restrictions of a long war. It would not be easy to persuade Ibn Sa'ud to attack Ha'il under the existing circumstances, if only because he was unable to compete with Husain in the payment of tribal subsidies. No officer was available in Egypt, but Storrs, in England in October, was willing to try again, and Cairo was willing to support his mission as an object lesson to a Sharif who seemed unconcerned with the necessity for winning Saudi cooperation.[58]

From his side Cox deputed Harry St. John Bridger Philby as political representative, Lieutenant-Colonel F. Cunliffe-Owen as military expert, and Lieutenant-Colonel R. E. A. Hamilton (later 11th Lord Belhaven and Stenton), Agent at Kuwait, to discuss such Kuwaiti matters as trade restrictions

---

[57] Cox telegrams to SSI, 24 May (includes text of Sykes telegram, 22 May), and 2 June 1917, *FO* 371/3054; Cox to SSI, 17 June 1917, and undated aide-mémoire for Storrs, *L/P&S/10*, 2182/13, nos. 2484 and 3661/17; Storrs, *op. cit.*, pp. 255–64.

[58] Cox telegram to SSI, 28 September, Wingate telegram to Balfour, 5 October, I.O. to F.O., 17 October 1917, *L/P&S/10*, 2182/13, no. 3959/17.

and the Saudi-Kuwaiti disagreement over the 'Ajman. The mission was now taking on formidable aspects. Storrs was to travel to Husain, then to Ibn Sa'ud, then back to Husain with a Saudi envoy in tow; unfortunately, Husain now withdrew permission for Storrs to pass through his territory, permission that had been obtained only with great difficulty in the first place.[59] The mission had encountered its first, but hardly its last, obstacle.

Not the least problem was the character of Philby. Philby simply was not cut out for a life of orders and files and dispatches. The very individualism that was to lead him to considerable fame as intrepid traveler, prolific author, and esteemed advisor to King Ibn Sa'ud also precipitated a trail of personality clashes that eventually drove him to leave Britain's service. He clashed in Basra with Arnold Wilson. Wilson wrote later, "He was one of those men who are apt to assume that everything they come across, from a government to a fountain-pen, is constructed on wrong principles and capable of amendment." He was to go on to similar clashes in Jordan, where W. F. Stirling and Norman Bentwich both knew him: "As an Irishman, he was 'agin' the Government, or indeed *any* Government, on principle," wrote Stirling, who admired his brilliance; ". . . a son of Ishmael, because his hand was against every man . . . ," said Bentwich, who did not.[60]

Wilson's difficulties with Philby were one cause for the latter's selection for the mission, according to Wilson's biographer,[61] and it was not the best of motives. Nor, given his character, was Philby the best man to aid Ibn Sa'ud's cause. From

---

[59] Cox telegram to SSI, 30 October, Balfour telegram to Wingate, 5 November, Wingate telegrams to Balfour, 9, 12, and 21 November 1917, *ibid.*, nos. 4356, 4489, 4541, 4552, and 4713/17.

[60] Wilson, *Loyalties*, p. 281; Stirling, *op. cit.*, p. 117 (Stirling served with Faisal, then under Clayton, then as C.P.O. himself); and Norman and Helen Bentwich, *Mandate Memories, 1918–1948* (N.Y., 1965), p. 120 (Bentwich served many years in the Palestine judicial service). See also Philby's *Arabian Days: An Autobiography* (London, 1948).

[61] Marlowe, *op. cit.*, pp. 114–17.

the very start, too, there was another conflict: Hamilton, the
Kuwait agent, was (if his son is to be believed) originally selected by Cox to lead the group—and certainly he had the requisite linguistic abilities and considerable seniority over Philby.[62] After private negotiations in Baghdad and Basra, at which
Hamilton was not present, Cox wrote Hamilton that it was
essential to have a new man on the job with fresh instructions,
so Hamilton was to represent only Kuwait's views to Ibn
Sa'ud. When Philby reached Riyadh, Hamilton was already
there. The two men failed to get along, and Hamilton returned
from the mission in a rage, leaving all duties to Philby and Cunliffe-Owen; his outspoken complaints on his return in effect
ruined his career. Philby's history was similar, but Philby became a man of influence in Arabia and Hamilton financial advisor to the Indian state of Jodhpur.

If the Iraqi delegation was hamstrung from the outset, the
Cairo mission of Storrs was unable even to begin, as Husain
refused to allow him to travel through his territory and advised
him to go via Kuwait. Philby had left Baghdad on 29 October,
arrived at Bahrain on 13 November, and reached Riyadh on
30 November. He wrote that Ibn Sa'ud, who was clearly upset
at Husain's title, would himself guarantee Storrs's safety once
he left the Sharif's territory, but this was not enough. Worse,
Husain refused even to send a delegation to meet with Ibn
Sa'ud or his representatives. In mid-December, as Philby's reports filtered out, and Storrs still sought a way to get in, it was
clear that Ibn Sa'ud was angry at the Sharif's conduct and
behavior and suspicious that behind all this was some sort of
secret understanding between Husain and Britain. For this
reason he asked more definite assurances on postwar spheres
and boundaries, together with more equitable financial assistance.[63]

[62] Lord Belhaven, *The Uneven Road* (London, 1955) pp. 22–26.
[63] Cox telegrams to SSI, 12 and 15 December, Wingate telegrams to
Balfour, 12 and 21 November and 18 December 1917, *L/P&S/10*, 2182/

Ibn Sa'ud saw, in short, that Allied victory would mean an all-powerful Sharif, while he himself would still be a Bedouin chief. Hamilton inferred from those discussions he attended in the few days he remained in Riyadh that if the Turks won Ibn Sa'ud would have the satisfaction of seeing Husain go down, and he had confidence in his own ability to negotiate terms with them. Above all, Ibn Sa'ud was concerned over the insidious undermining of his tribal authority by Husain's subsidy money, which he was unable to meet; and Hamilton felt that any further money paid to the Amir would be used to counter Husain's payments rather than to prepare an attack on Ibn Rashid.

To aid in taking Ha'il, Ibn Sa'ud wanted 10,000 rifles and artillery and £50,000 a month. There is little doubt that the size of the sum mentioned—ten times his ordinary subsidy—was partly calculated to offset the amount given Husain. Since Ibn Sa'ud admitted that action would be difficult as long as the 'Ajman problem remained (a number had taken refuge in Kuwait, and the new ruler, Salim ibn Mubarak, refused to expel them), since Britain was still paying £5,000 a month for which little result could be shown (the Treasury had temporarily lost sight of this drain and had not been told that the payment had continued after initial sanction had expired at the end of June), and since the chances were excellent that General Allenby in the Jordan Valley would soon bring off a major victory,

---

13, nos. 4552, 4713, 4968, 4993, and 5113/17; see also *FO* 371/3061. Remarks on Philby and Hamilton impressions taken from Philby's "Report on the Operations of the Najd Mission, October 29th, 1917, to November 1st, 1918," which covers 39 printed foolscap pages (*L/P&S/10*, 2182/13), and report by Hamilton (B.286), 1 February 1918, on November conversations at Riyadh, *L/P&S/11*, vol. 140, no. 4836/18. Philby's later account of his travels may be found in *The Heart of Arabia: A Record of Travel* (2 vols., N.Y., 1923) and (from June 1918 onwards) *Arabia of the Wahhabis* (London, 1928); brief and more general references are in his *Arabian Jubilee*, ch. IV, and *Sa'udi Arabia* (N.Y., 1955), ch. X.

there seemed little to justify the additional subsidy as far as London was concerned.[64]

Yet Philby continued to urge both the advantages of the capture of Ha'il and Ibn Sa'ud's financial difficulties. There was no doubt in his mind that if the Amir were promised recognition of his future status he would attack Ibn Rashid's capital.[65] Cairo and Delhi and Baghdad all remained unenthusiastic, and Philby was soon projecting a policy with no supporters anywhere. Wingate, for example, regarded the suggested level of aid as highly dangerous; although Husain had acted unwisely, at least his tribes would be easier to control than the Wahhabis. "A well equipped Nejd force of 15,000 men with a crowd of Wahabi zealots might sweep through Hedjaz to the confusion of our Arab and Moslem policies," he telegraphed London, a remark that showed little faith in Husain's might, but then Faisal's forces were operating well to the north. Cox in Baghdad rather saw Arabian politics from the traditional Indian view: there was considerable advantage to having Ibn Sa'ud to balance off Husain, but fresh and further assurances to the Amir would only excite further Hijazi suspicions.[66]

In India, too, the focus was on a balance of forces. The original idea of the joint mission, minuted Denys Bray, Deputy Secretary in the Foreign Department, had been to disarm mutual suspicion in Mecca and Riyadh and to obtain more Saudi cooperation in the war effort, but Philby was concentrating on the second goal to the considerable cost of the first; Britain must stay away from promises on the future. Early in January 1918, Grant met with General Monro and his Chief of Staff, General G. W. M. Kirkpatrick, and the three men decided that at least from the military standpoint there was

[64] Cox telegrams to SSI (nos. 6184 and 6185), 20 December, with Shuckburgh minute, 24 December 1917, *L/P&S/10*, 2182/13, no. 5131/17.

[65] Cox telegram to SSI, 21 December 1917, *ibid*.

[66] Wingate telegram to Balfour and Cox telegram to SSI, 23 December 1917, *ibid*., no. 5146/17.

nothing but a further drain on military resources to be gained from eliminating Ibn Rashid, who was no real threat to Britain's interests. From the political standpoint, on the other hand, there was much to be gained from a three-way balance of Husain, Ibn Rashid, and Ibn Sa'ud, for Ibn Rashid's existence would tend to dissuade the other two from attacking each other.[67]

The various policy-making centers had, separately, been driven to the same conclusion—except that Wingate thought in terms of a balance built around the essential sovereignty of Husain as *primus inter pares*.[68] The junior officials—Philby, Arnold Wilson, Lieutenant-Colonel G. E. Leachman (who had been touted as Shakespear's replacement),[69] and even Mark Sykes—all urged the elimination of Ha'il, but all were overruled by the higher authorities, invincible when in agreement. Only Philby refused to bow to the inevitable; Ha'il, once taken, would eliminate the need for the recently instituted blockade of Kuwait (to prevent supplies reaching the Turks through Jabal Shammar), and it would be unwise to call off Ibn Sa'ud now, having so long urged him to take action, for the Amir would clearly see this as the subordination of his interests to those of Husain. Finally, the existence of Ibn Rashid would only complicate any postwar settlement.[70]

Philby was not able to push his view personally. When he

[67] Bray minute, 24 December 1917, note on conference, 3 January 1918, *India Sec. War* October 1918, 1–170.

[68] Wingate telegram to Balfour, 28 December 1917, *L/P&S/10*, 2182/13, no. 5203/17.

[69] Leachman, a well-traveled Sandhurst product, had joined the cadre of Mesopotamian political officers in early 1915, temporarily moved to Cairo in 1917, and was in charge of Mosul from shortly before the armistice to late 1919; he was shot in the back by an Arab shaikh in August 1920. See Maj. N. N. E. Bray, *Paladin of Arabia: The Biography of Brevet Lieut.-Colonel G. E. Leachman, C.I.E., D.S.O., of the Royal Sussex Regiment* (London, 1936).

[70] Cox demi-official telegram to SSI, 28 December 1917, *FO* 371/3883; Hogarth note, 31 December 1917, *FO* 882/8; Viceroy telegram to SSI, 5 January, Wingate telegram to Balfour, 10 January, and letter 11

had heard that permission had been refused to Storrs, he and Ibn Saʿud agreed that Philby himself should travel overland to Jidda to disprove the dangers of the journey. On 9 December he left Ibn Saʿud (and Cunliffe-Owen in charge of the British mission) and set out for Taʾif, 40 miles east of Mecca (and over 450 air miles from Riyadh) in the hope that Storrs would be there. Storrs was not, and Philby rode on, reaching Jidda on 31 December after a pioneering trip. Early in January, Hogarth arrived from Cairo, and a few days later Husain, and a series of conversations ensued.

Philby entered the discussions with the view that (1) destruction of Ibn Rashid would be a useful blow against the Turks, (2) continuation of a three-way balance would only perpetuate Arabian strife, (3) there was a chance of a Sharifal-inspired Rashidi attack on Ibn Saʿud that might force Britain to comply with her treaty promise of aid against aggression, (4) a two-power balance would create a realistic situation in which neither ruler could attack the other, and (5) there was a danger, if a suitable compromise was not reached, of the end of any chance of cooperation by Ibn Saʿud. He found, however, that Husain, who described himself to Philby as "King of the Arab Nation," had other ideas. All Husain really wanted, Philby reported, was Saudi recognition of his own leadership, for which purpose a small body of men and a flag would be sufficient token. Basically, Husain feared a Wahhabi revival and was conscious of Ibn Rashid's utility in checking Ibn Saʿud. Philby's suggested solution to the dilemma of Mecca-Riyadh relations was pressure upon both men to compel respect for each other's position.[71]

---

January, and Shuckburgh memorandum (B.279), 10 January 1918, L/P&S/10, 2182/13, nos. 181, 192, and 618/18.

[71] Cox telegrams (nos. 385 and 387–89) to SSI, 14 January, and Wingate telegrams (nos. 81 and 83) to Balfour, 12 January 1918, *ibid.*, no. 192/18. Details of Philby's journey are taken from his "Report," cited in n. 63 above.

The reports that reached Wingate of the discussions—from Hogarth and Lieutenant-Colonel J. R. Basset of the Jidda mission, both present at the meetings—were that Philby had not made the best possible impression. As Basset put it:

His treatment of the subject has not always been as tactful as it might and on at least one occasion the King had been made really angry. A certain lack of respect in Mr PHILBY'S manner throughout the various interviews must inevitably have unfavourably impressed King HUSSEIN. I myself was much struck by it.[72]

Philby spent two weeks in Jidda and had some ten meetings with the King. Neither he, speaking for Ibn Sa'ud rather than for Britain, nor the King gave way. The mission if anything only added to the friction, as evidenced by Husain's absolute refusal to permit Philby to return to Saudi territory by land, despite the urgings of both Hogarth and Basset and the fact that Philby had (deliberately) left his heavier baggage at Ta'if. Philby returned to Cairo with Hogarth, departing for Iraq in mid-February by sea, arriving at Basra on 24 March—only to find Cox departed for England.

Philby's mission to Husain had failed. There was therefore little reason for either India or Cairo to alter the earlier plan to utilize Ibn Rashid as a counter in the game and to keep Ibn Sa'ud in play by judicious doles of assistance. At its meeting of 12 January, just as news of Philby's meeting with Husain was coming in, the Middle East Committee approved this policy, while recognizing that both Ibn Sa'ud and Philby would be disappointed. Cox, more out of loyalty to his deputy than conviction of the rightness of Philby's policy, protested that at least the authorities should await Philby's full report, and this was agreed. The delay did nothing to alter the verdict. As both India Office and War Office pointed out, the various reports

[72] Basset to Arab Bureau, 12 January 1918, *FO* 882/9; see also Hogarth report, 15 January, and Wingate telegram no. 83 to Balfour, 12 January 1918, *FO* 371/3883.

did not demonstrate that the capture of Ha'il would have any noticeable effect; Ibn Rashid himself, the War Office reported, had only 1,000 men to put in the field. Cunliffe-Owen, the War Office representative, shared Philby's views, but he too had failed to convince his superiors. Both men, concluded the War Office, had been "carried away by their local surroundings or gulled completely by the Wahabi Emir. . ." Officials in India agreed among themselves but kept out of this quarrel.[73]

Cox had not been a particularly warm supporter of Philby so far, and he now accepted London's decision. He still regarded Ibn Sa'ud as a useful and necessary counterweight to Husain, but Cox was at the moment thinking more of Iraqi pronouncements and other problems. He now suggested that Britain should tell Ibn Sa'ud that suitable artillery personnel were not available and the siege guns for which the Amir asked were unsuitable in the desert. In these circumstances, Britain would understand if Ibn Sa'ud did not wish to move against Ha'il. At the same time, Cox would authorize 1,000 more rifles, 100,000 rounds of ammunition, and an advance of two months' subsidy.[74]

Cox had a further opportunity to explain his views during his visit to Cairo and London, particularly at his Cairo meeting (on 23 March; Philby was still at sea on his way to Basra) with Wingate, Colonel C. E. Wilson, Clayton, Colonel Jacob, Cornwallis, and other concerned personnel. No obstacle, he saw, need be placed directly in the way of Ibn Sa'ud's attack on Ha'il because the Amir was not too keen on the idea himself.

[73] M.E.C. 11th minutes, 12 January, CAB 27/22. SSI telegram to Viceroy, 14 January; Shuckburgh minute, 16 January, and memorandum (B.280), 19 January; W.O. memorandum (B.270, quoted), 21 January; Shuckburgh note and SSI telegram to Viceroy, 28 January; and, for Cox's appeal, Cox telegram to SSI, 16 January 1918: L/P&S/10, 2182/ 13, nos. 192, 237, 337, and 337a/18. Indian views recorded in D. Bray note, 16 January 1918, India Sec. War October 1918, 1–170.

[74] Cox telegrams to SSI, 25 January, FO 371/3380, and 9 March 1918, L/P&S/10, 2182/13, no. 1009/18; and Philby telegram (from Cairo) to Cox, 11 February 1918, FO 882/9.

Cox went on to suggest—and to find Cairo in agreement—that al-Idrisi and Yahya and Ibn Sa'ud should not be forced to recognize Husain's temporal overlordship. On the other hand, a declaration by Husain of his assumption of the caliphal title just might win acceptance, and Britain in such a circumstance should remain noncommittal, saying only that Muslims must deal with this issue themselves.[75] As Cox proceeded to London the Arabian situation appeared to be developing favorably— but in July there occurred an unexpected Saudi-Hashimite confrontation.

5

In the summer of 1918 King Husain became alarmed at the occupation by Saudi followers of the village of Khurma, some 140 miles by road north and east of Ta'if. Husain had long considered Khurma to be in his territory, but several years earlier the disaffection of his own local governor had been responsible for the changed allegiance of the town; it was not clear to outsiders just how long the Saudis had been in occupation. Husain, worried, tired, and concerned with what he saw as dwindling British support, organized an expedition to retake the settlement. When news of this crisis arrived, it was decided to rush messages of conciliation to both rulers, at the same time attempting to obtain accurate information on the issues involved, principally from Philby.[76] Philby had left Basra to rejoin Ibn Sa'ud (with what he thought was London's approval of his own suggestions) and after talking with the Amir in April and finding the situation generally quiet and the

[75] Memorandum on meeting, Cairo Residency, 23 March 1918 (E.C. 180), *L/P&S/11*, vol. 135, no. 2142/18. See above, p. 156.
[76] Wingate telegrams to Balfour, 9 and 17 July, SSI telegrams to Viceroy, 13 and 22 July 1918, *L/P&S/10*, 2182/13, nos. 3124, 3176, and 3191/18; Col. C. E. Wilson to Wingate (on his talks with Husain, 16–21 July), 23 July 1918, *FO* 371/3381. On the Khurma dispute in the framework of the evolution of Saudi Arabia, see George Rentz, "al-Ikhwān," *The Encyclopedia of Islam* (2nd ed., forthcoming).

prospects of immediate action small had set off for a tour of exploration (lasting fifty days) to the southern border of Najd, returning to Riyadh at the end of June. He was in Riyadh in July, and here he could be reached.

While Philby was being contacted, the Khurma affair was revealing the complete futility of a policy—any policy—that overlooked the basic, ineradicable rivalry of Ibn Sa'ud and Husain. At the same time, this crisis again revealed the differing loyalties of Iraq on the one hand and Cairo on the other, with London caught in the middle and India as interested spectator. The Sharif, Wingate was instructed by London, should send the conciliatory message; he ought to be impressed with the fact that war with Ibn Sa'ud would impair all his prospects. Ibn Sa'ud's attitude, replied the High Commissioner, was going to lead to war over Khurma unless he was restrained by Britain. Ibn Sa'ud had so far shown considerable restraint in this business, cabled India ominously; Philby reported, added Baghdad, that Ibn Sa'ud was increasingly restless and that public feeling in Najd was turning against his pro-British policy.[77]

Whatever the rights of the case—and a very complicated one it was—there was no question that Husain had precipitated this particular crisis and therefore the burden of conciliation was upon him. Husain, however, had one card yet to play: on 31 July, Wingate reported that Husain had asked Britain to recognize his abdication, for it seemed that he was now an obstacle to the Arab movement and to Britain's policy. Husain had not actually abdicated, but London had to make a decision. So Khurma was recognized as in the King's sphere, if only because he could not be allowed to be distracted from more important activities. Curzon, Cecil, and Shuckburgh had agreed on this in an informal conference, and it was policy. Perhaps,

[77] Balfour telegram to Wingate, 27 July, Wingate telegram to Balfour and Viceroy telegram to SSI, 30 July, A. T. Wilson telegram to SSI, 7 August 1918, *FO* 371/3390.

however, Husain could ease the situation by declaring that he occupied the town only to preserve order there.[78] The policy bore little relation to reality. On 28 July Philby reported that Husain's forces had attacked Khurma and had been driven off with 200 dead. While the figures might be exaggerated, there could be little doubt that Ibn Sa'ud's forces had come off best. Yet despite the military verdict, Wingate still insisted that Husain's view be upheld: he was merely punishing a rebel governor and disclaimed any aggressive intention, after all, and was now sending the requested conciliatory message. According to Wingate, Philby was simply wrong in his pro-Saudi interpretation of the whole affair.[79] On this last point, at least, there was considerable agreement in London and India, for as Grant and the Indian military authorities agreed Husain was more dependent upon Britain than was Ibn Sa'ud. Hirtzel disagreed: "... from Bin Saud's point of view it is as though the French were to claim to restore order in Alsace without entertaining hostile designs against Germany." But, as Wingate had suggested, while Ibn Sa'ud was to be bought off with money and some arms, basically Husain would be supported in this issue.[80]

It was not clear whether Ibn Sa'ud would be satisfied with such obvious bribery, especially since some of the arms already furnished him had proven faulty, and when replacements were authorized a clerk's error had changed 1,000 guns to 100. London refused to correct the mistake, and in the end Ibn Sa'ud was told that the guns already received were the same as other

[78] Wingate telegrams to Balfour, 31 July, *ibid.*, and 1 August, SSI telegram to Cox and Balfour telegram to Wingate, 2 August 1918, *L/P&S/10*, 2182/13, no. 3327/18.

[79] A. T. Wilson telegram to SSI, 5 August 1918, *ibid.*, no. 3384/18; Wingate telegram to Balfour, 12 August 1918, *FO* 371/3390.

[80] Grant memorandum, 13 August 1918, *India Sec. War* December 1919, 191–317; Shuckburgh minutes, 12 and 14 August, and Hirtzel minute (quoted), 14 August 1918, *L/P&S/10*, 2182/13, no. 3565/18; Balfour telegram to Wingate, 16 August 1918, *FO* 371/3390.

weapons—all passed as serviceable—given to other Gulf shaikhs. This helped not at all. The question of money, too, would require considerable discussion.[81]

Meanwhile, another suggestion altogether had been received from Arnold Wilson in Baghdad: a commission to proceed to the area to examine and presumably to pass upon the boundary issues. The suggestion was received with grave doubts, partly, no doubt, because of its place of origin. But as the Arab Bureau pointed out, the problem was more than one of boundaries and was rather symptomatic of years of conflict on more basic issues. Both sides would probably oppose a commission—certainly Ibn Sa'ud could not afford over-close cooperation with Britain in view of the disaffection among his Wahhabi subjects —and in any case the commission would necessarily be without local knowledge. The India Office sided with Cairo on the ground that Britain should not become directly involved in internal Arabian affairs; responsibility for delimiting frontiers might become responsibility for maintaining them. Since Philby had reported that Khurma was a central point for communication and tribal control, the affair was likely to prove even more complicated than it already appeared. Ibn Sa'ud could not abandon his claims without alienating his followers; the local population was hostile to Husain—an excellent imbroglio to avoid.[82]

Only Philby seemed to have a clear policy in mind. Ibn Sa'ud would be encouraged to attack Ha'il, which would distract his attention from a possibly disastrous frontal clash with Husain, and, he repeated, only 5,000 rifles and £10,000 a month were

[81] Wilson telegrams to SSI, 8 and 17 August and 13, 14, and 15 September, Viceroy telegrams to SSI, 29 August and 2 September, SSI telegram to Viceroy, 31 August 1918, L/P&S/10, 2182/13, nos. 3565, 3660, 3391, 3862, 3931, 4079, and 4129/18.

[82] Unsigned Arab Bureau note, 31 August, for High Commissioner, sent as Wingate telegram to Balfour, 4 September 1918, FO 882/9; Shuckburgh and Hirtzel minutes, 10 September, on Baghdad telegram to SSI, 7 September 1918, L/P&S/10, 2182/13, no. 3931/18.

required. Despite every entreaty, the decision remained un-changed. There can be little doubt that lack of faith in Philby's impartiality had something to do with the decision—beyond the basic pro-Husain policy. Sykes, for example, urged Philby's replacement, calling for a "less anti-King of Hejaz" representative in Najd. Even Baghdad felt that Philby's six months in Arabia (in fact, the total time spent on Arabian soil by the time of his recall, by Philby's own account, was nine months, during which he traveled some 2,600 miles) was quite enough and suggested his replacement, a suggestion that found warm response in London. For the moment, however, Philby was only told that there would be no more rifles and that he was to play down ideas of an assault on Ha'il.[83]

Before London's final word (in a telegram of 13 September) could reach Philby, Ibn Sa'ud had actually mounted a raid on Ibn Rashid's capital, although the town was not taken. Philby, who had already made an unauthorized "loan" to the Amir of £20,000 (from money with which Philby had been provided for his mission and which was kept at 'Uqair), was not allowed to accompany the Saudi forces; Ibn Sa'ud worried about the fanaticism of his own Wahhabi followers and apparently feared a repetition of the unfortunate fate that had befallen Shakespear.[84] Outside Arabia, it was clear that the best face possible had to be put on this news; Ibn Sa'ud was to be congratulated and at last given his 1,000 guns. But Britain had meanwhile captured Damascus, and the war was nearly over; further operations were hardly necessary from Britain's standpoint.[85]

[83] Baghdad telegram to SSI, 7 September 1918, *ibid.;* also *India Sec. War* December 1919, 191–317, showing India's determination to stay out of this squabble. Sykes note, 11 September (quoted), and Baghdad telegram to SSI, 15 September 1918, with Sykes and Crowe minutes, *FO* 371/3390; E.C. 30th minutes, 11 September 1918, *CAB* 27/24; SSI telegram to Viceroy, 13 September, and Shuckburgh note, 22 September 1918, *L/P&S/10*, 2182/13, no. 4138/18.

[84] Philby, "Report," pp. 24–25, for which cf. n. 63 above.

[85] Wilson telegram to SSI, 11 October, and SSI telegram to Wilson/ Viceroy, 17 October 1918, *L/P&S/10*, 2182/13, nos. 4482 and 4585/18.

The question of Ibn Sa'ud's attitude was not so easily resolved, for Philby was only now receiving the earlier orders that no guns would be provided. Ibn Sa'ud, reported Philby, suspected a successful intrigue against him by Husain and "expressed himself bitterly disappointed at the treatment he had received from the British Government. . . " Khurma took on new and ominous overtones, and at the same time the Amir received congratulations from the Turks—and an offer of arms, ammunition, and funds—for his victory over Husain. "Who," Philby quoted Ibn Sa'ud as saying, "will trust you after this?" The Amir now demanded that Britain either cooperate actively in the alliance or, alternatively, guarantee him against the 'Ajman, Ibn Rashid, and Husain—clearly an impossibility in the latter case, for Ibn Sa'ud claimed that the King had three times assaulted Khurma already. "A year's work collapsed before my eyes . . . ," wrote Philby in his subsequent report. He decided to come out himself to the Gulf coast to appeal the orders and requested permission to go to Baghdad for consultation. Once in Kuwait (16 October) Philby discovered how complete the Allied victories were—and that Arnold Wilson had ordered the 1,000 rifles released to the Amir even before receiving home approval.[86]

Philby had made a mistake, however; the opportunity he had so conveniently provided to change the personnel of the Saudi mission was taken. Philby was told to proceed to Baghdad, but it was intended to send Leachman to replace him. As a military officer (Brevet Lieutenant-Colonel), Leachman was more suitable (particularly in London and Cairo) than an Indian Political Service officer like Philby; but he had his hands full in Mosul, and for the time being Ibn Sa'ud was left without a British representative at his side. The matter did not appear urgent; the Amir could hardly join the Turks, and more press-

[86] Philby, "Report," p. 25; also Wilson telegram to SSI, 16 October 1918, L/P&S/10, 2182/13, no. 4618/18.

ing problems occupied official attention in November 1918 than the rivalry of Arabian princes. Faisal was in Damascus, and the Allies—and the Hijaz—had won; Ibn Sa'ud, in his own interest, would have to trim his sails, or so it appeared.[87]

Although British policy-makers would soon discover that for Husain and Ibn Sa'ud the war had not really begun, perhaps the policy in Arabia could be termed a success up to that time. Britain had taken an undeveloped peninsula of warring tribes and left it an undeveloped peninsula of warring tribes—but her negotiations had prevented the various rulers from making much capital from the war. The intricate web of alliances had at least resulted in stalemate and deadlock, except for the flare-ups of Qunfudha and Khurma and Ha'il. Ibn Rashid had been prevented from damaging British interests, and so too had Yahya of Yemen, while Husain had proved a useful ally. That much could be termed success, and the success had cost only money. In the larger political view, however, nothing was settled: Husain, al-Idrisi, Ibn Sa'ud, Ibn Rashid—all had yet to work out their final destinies in Arabia, and it remained to be seen whether Britain could actually influence, or indeed would desire to influence, their respective futures.

Militarily, the Arabian "side show" must be termed a complete success with the sole exception of Aden. With small expenditure of resources, the Turks had been held nearly everywhere, and Britain had used well her three main resources: money, sea power (with which to raid a port, to blockade a coast, or to land supplies), and talented and spirited persons with eastern expertise, who for all their faults (and men like T. E. Lawrence and H. St. J. B. Philby must be forgiven a few faults) often succeeded brilliantly in the limited circumstances in which they operated.

Politically, however, the decision to support Husain as the

[87] SSI telegram to Wilson, 28 October, Wilson telegram to SSI, 15 November, and Shuckburgh minute, 22 November 1918, *ibid.*

leader of an idealistic confederation, never to develop, was a fateful one, and not only for Arabia. The doubters, in India or Iraq or Egypt, were right: in Arabia, the only meaningful settlement must come through the victory of one or another of the chiefs over the rest. Yet, given the basic desire for Arab cooperation in the war and the equally basic desire to aid the Arabs in the achievement of independence (which did not necessarily mean the achievement of unity) at the cost of the Turks, there seems now, as then, little choice save Husain. Would Ibn Sa'ud, if chosen as British standard-bearer against a Turkish-allied Husain, have had similar success? When Indian parsimony is remembered, and given the likelihood in such a situation of an active Husain-Ibn Rashid-'Ajman alliance, there must at least be substantial doubt.

But from the most important standpoint of all, Britain had managed to preserve a clear field in Arabia. French participation in the Hijaz mission had been limited (a story that falls beyond this work, as it never really concerned either India or Iraq); Italy had been warned off in the Red Sea; and it had even been possible in the midst of world war to handicap seriously Japanese commercial interests attempting to establish a foothold in the Gulf—a feat due primarily to the watchfulness of Sir Percy Cox.[88] The treaties with 'Asir, Qatar, and Najd obviously augmented the already strong British position on Arabia's seaboards to a point which was almost unchallengeable at war's end.[89]

[88] This rather peculiar story was due to the commercial opportunities of supplying the British armies in Mesopotamia, especially with such products as "Best Japanese Light Pilsener" beer. The competition, which might be damaging to British postwar commerce, was dealt with by publication of a regulation that all ships destined for Basra must have prior clearance before leaving their last British port of call—and such clearance was not intended for Japanese merchantmen. *India Sec. War* September 1917, 435–90; see also Wilson, *Loyalties*, p. 300.

[89] Even then it might have been stronger, for several opportunities were rejected, such as an advance from Aden, Mubarak of Kuwait's offer that Britain take control of his customs (*L/P&S/11*, vol. 70, file

Ironically, there remained one weak link: control of Britain's own policy. India, it is true, had gradually fallen out of the picture except where the Gulf itself was concerned, but where India hung back Aden and Baghdad and Philby in Riyadh pushed ahead. Naturally, when policy coordination was discussed, the Husain-Ibn Saʻud problem was the standard example of why coordination was needed. But each time the example was used, there was likely to come the reply that unless India (by which was often meant Baghdad now) had her separate voice and representation the same Husain-Ibn Saʻud rivalry showed that Indian interests would be sacrificed.[90]

Most concerned officials doubtless agreed with Shuckburgh's memorandum of September 1918:

There has been too much of a tendency in the past for the two rival chieftains—Bin Saud and King Husain—to find their respective champions in India and Egypt, and for the whole controversy between them to be reflected in a conflict of view between the two great administrations concerned. It is scarcely to be supposed that this aspect of the case, or the possibility of turning it to advantage, is lost upon the chieftains themselves.[91]

But how to achieve unanimity? That was precisely the difficulty, and as the war ended Robert Cecil was realizing the extent of the problem as he wrestled with India Office and Foreign Office and War Office in an attempt to establish one center for Middle Eastern policy. And it was not simply a question of rival departments and rival chieftains and rival overseas administrative centers, but also a matter of rival promises and pledges and commitments—to Ibn Saʻud, al-Idrisi, Hu-

---

618/14), and a chance to help the Sultan of Muscat expand the territory under his control (*L/P&S/10*, 4684/13, part 1).

[90] Wilson telegram to SSI, 7 September 1918, and notes containing draft points for Montagu private letter to Cecil, *L/P&S/10*, 2182/13, no. 3931/18.

[91] Shuckburgh memorandum, 22 September 1918, n. 83 above; also in appendix to E.C. 33rd minutes, 26 September 1918, *CAB* 27/24.

sain, the Baghdadis, the Gulf shaikhs, the French, the Zionists, the Arabs in general, and the world at large. It was a muddle to be muddled through—but what had served for four years of war no longer was enough. A solution was vital, perhaps desperately so, for it was time for peacemaking.

# PART TWO

# India's Legacy

# VI

# Peacemaking, 1918–1919

General Sir Thomas Pamellor: "Now then, *mon vieux*, I used to say, here's British policy! And I'd tell him. Here's French policy! And I'd tell him that, too. Then all we had to do was to go our own way and make the thing work."

*Geoffrey Household,* WATCHER IN THE SHADOWS

## 1

The Anglo-Turkish armistice which ended World War I in the Middle East brought to a close the most radical four years of change that area had witnessed in the memory of any living man. The Ottoman Empire was dead and gone—at least for practical purposes. In its place stood, technically, the victorious Allies—but in practice, Britain. British troops and British administrators held sway from Egypt to Central Asia, and for a moment it seemed as simple as that. But there were complications, complications so grave as to jeopardize quickly and seriously Britain's conquest of the Middle East.

In the first place, Britain had commitments to the Allies, particularly France and Italy. Russia had removed herself from the struggle for spoils under a new revolutionary regime, but the problems of dealing with that regime now intruded as much upon Middle Eastern affairs as dealing with a surviving Tsarist Russia might have done. Other commitments, in writing, had been made to the Arabs, singularly in the case of the various rulers and collectively in several instances. That these commitments were conflicting as they stood has often been argued; that they created a confusing situation is undeniable. Out of this confusion, and amid the welter of the still vaster problems of Germany and reparations and reconstruction and demobilization, proposals of some sort for the future of the Middle East had to be forthcoming in the few months between armistice and peace conference.

It was not that ideas were unavailable. On the contrary, a number of position papers and lists of desiderata had been prepared during the war. They had come from several quarters and included the report of the de Bunsen committee and several statements from the Indian government on Indian and Persian Gulf matters.[1] It was well known that India had long urged the retention of Basra as a principal policy goal, although even in India there was little hope in late 1918 of realizing this. Others thought of oil, or Palestine, or a Mediterranean-Persian Gulf line; but somehow all the paper work of the preceding four years seemed so much waste in the light of new conditions. A new start had to be made; in fact, one had already been made in the unsuccessful attempt to persuade France to alter the terms of the Sykes-Picot Agreement and the successful issue of a very general joint renunciation of annexationist aims. This, then, was the starting point: "Blue" and "Red" zones had to be assimilated to local interests; frontiers drawn along lines of national communities, if they could be found; and, hopefully, some sort of confederation established over-all. Only this kind

---

[1] I.O. Political Dept. memoranda, 20 April 1915 (B.239) and 4 December 1918, Viceroy telegram to SSI, 8 September 1916, *FO* 608/116 (Peace Conference files). See also Nevakivi, *Britain, France and the Arab Middle East*, ch. V.

of settlement would serve self-determination and yet end Otto-man sovereignty over the Arab world as both Lloyd George and President Wilson had pledged.

All of this was pointed out by Arnold Toynbee, working on peace problems in the Foreign Office, in a memorandum of 1 October 1918.[2] There was even a specific outline of how this general settlement might be applied, and T. E. Lawrence, whose brain child it was, was able to discuss it with the Eastern Committee only two days before the Turkish armistice.[3] To Lawrence, the key was total support for the Hashimite house through the construction of a viable confederation bound by blood, that is, by the use of Husain and his sons as its rulers. 'Abdullah would rule in Baghdad; Faisal, head of the revolt's forces, would remain in Damascus; Zaid, the youngest son, would head a third area in upper Mesopotamia and Mosul; Husain, King of the Hijaz, would be over-all head and religious leader.

The committee found a conclusion hard to reach. The real state of opinion in Mesopotamia was unknown, and whether Lawrence's plan, involving as it did the partition of Iraq, would find acceptance there was at least arguable. For this reason some support was given to an older suggestion recently revived by Arnold Wilson: a study commission to visit Iraq. The various London departments had approved the idea, and Robert Cecil, its strongest advocate, took the plan to the Eastern Commit-tee.[4] Wilson's suggestion had the merit that it would present substantive support for the proposals Britain would make at

[2] Toynbee memorandum, 1 October 1918, *FO* 371/3385.

[3] E.C. 37th minutes, 29 October 1918, *CAB* 27/24. A map on which the outlines of the three states are drawn, possibly by Lawrence him-self, is in *Milner Papers* (Public Record Office, London), *PRO* 30/30/20, and is given in outline in map on p. 85.

[4] A. T. Wilson telegram to SSI, 27 September 1918 (and draft in-structions to commission by Shuckburgh, 22 October), *L/P&S/10*, 2571/17, nos. 4252 and 4677/18. Viceroy telegram to SSI, 6 October 1918 (opposing the plan), and minutes by Sykes, Cecil, Crowe, etc., *FO* 371/3387.

the conference and thus influence President Wilson. It was naturally assumed that Britain would stay on in Iraq in one way or another, and that Mesopotamian opinion (or at least the recommendations of a study commission) would favor this; these assumptions even the most enlightened were as yet unwilling to challenge. Curzon, still managing the committee, objected to the commission, however, for it would stir opinion both at home and abroad and lead to Parliamentary question and Allied suspicion of the sort that he had already called up in imagination when expressing his opposition to other plans. For the time being, there would be no commission; Mesopotamia would have to proceed on its own, aided by such advice as London in its wisdom cared to give.

Already the discussions in the committee had mired on details. This was to be exactly the problem from the standpoint of the India Office, and India, and Iraq. Detailed consideration of this or that issue, often in London, and often in Curzon's committee, sometimes resulted in a policy decision, but a separate group under General Smuts was technically responsible to the Cabinet for preparing the British position at Paris. Such consultation as eventually occurred between that group and the officers with which this study is concerned was through these same Eastern Committee meetings.[5] Moreover, when the Paris conference assembled, Lloyd George further developed his habit of acting without reference to advisors or departments or prepared positions.[6] Few subjects offer more difficulty to the

[5] The War Cabinet had given the task of preparation of the Middle Eastern brief to Sir Erle Richards (whose main product was a draft Turkish treaty) under Smuts's direction and, on Curzon's representations, Smuts was told to consult the Eastern Committee, although not until late in November; W.C. 506, 22 November 1918, *CAB* 23/8.

[6] But the Prime Minister's position had been fairly clear, for those who paid attention, in a Cabinet meeting of early October. Lloyd George had said that the Sykes-Picot Agreement, on which he had just refreshed his memory, was "quite inapplicable to present circumstances, and was altogether a most undesirable agreement from the British point

historian than the attempt to trace a particular problem or government policy through the murky labyrinth of the conference's prolific documentation, often meaningless, and crucial decisions that went forever unrecorded. Seen from Baghdad, or the India Office, or even through the eyes of Montagu, who was often at Paris, it was usually impossible to understand the course of events.

But, until the British Government divided itself into the separate and unequal halves in Paris and London, there was continued discussion without resolution in the traditional manner. One illustrative problem was the question of the immediate policy to be pursued in Mosul. Mosul had been occupied on the point of armistice—in violation of its terms in the view of some, in accordance with them to others.[7] The Iraqi and Indian authorities, under the hopeful misapprehension that the Sykes-Picot Agreement was dead, fully intended applying their existing administrative pattern to this vilayet. The Foreign Office quickly put a stop to this procedure, for Mosul had been assigned to France, and until some definite decision was made on revision of the treaty the area would remain under military occupation only, Arab officers used wherever possible, and the "Arab flag" flown. These instruction were passed on to Baghdad, although reference to the "Arab flag" (which was taken to mean Sharifal green) was censored out by the India Office. Even if the area was still technically to go to France, no decision had been made on Sharifal control of Mosul; use of the

---

of view," and that Clemenceau might have to be sounded out on this. The meeting, however, had focused primarily on the Turkish armistice terms; W.C. 482a (Secret military minutes), 3 October 1918, *CAB* 23/14.

[7] Marshall, *op. cit.*, pp. 324–25; Wilson, *Mesopotamia*, pp. 17–21; Zeine, *Struggle*, p. 60, n. 1; Howard, *Partition*, pp. 210–12; see also W. R. Hay, *Two Years in Kurdistan. Experiences of a Political Officer, 1918–1920* (London, 1921), and C. J. Edmonds, *Kurds, Turks, and Arabs: Politics, Travel and Research in North-Eastern Iraq, 1919–1925* (London, 1957).

Sharifal flag would prejudice the decision.[8] In the meantime, the French Consul in Basra was not allowed to proceed to Mosul; he asked permission to look into French charitable interests there and was told that the British military authorities were doing all that was necessary. The unavailing French protest was one more minor irritation to be kept in mind when larger negotiations were begun.[9]

Control of Mosul simply reinforced India's hold over Iraq. More visionary individuals like Sykes and Toynbee argued that circumstances had changed entirely over those prevailing early in the war, but they were not aided by suggestions like that of T. E. Lawrence which appeared—at least to Hirtzel—to sacrifice tangible Mesopotamian interests for the nebulous freedom of Syria. "The material interests involved in Mesopotamia are far too great to be jockeyed away merely for the sake of diplomatic convenience," Hirtzel wrote. Lawrence had no real understanding of Mesopotamian conditions, for he proposed a solidarity of the entire area which did not exist now and which Britain had no interest in fostering. What was there, after all, to recommend 'Abdullah, or Zaid, as the stuff of which kings are made?[10]

In any case, Mesopotamia seemed to be pursuing its own line of policy, almost without control. In October Arnold Wilson had announced that he was amalgamating the Basra and Baghdad legal administrations (with Baghdad's system to prevail). In early November he reported that he was reviving the old local councils as a means of showing conformity with pledges made in Europe. In the middle of the month he announced that

---

[8] F.O. to I.O., 2 November, SSI telegram to Wilson, 5 November, Shuckburgh minute, 4 November 1918, *L/P&S/10*, 36/19, no. 4890/18.

[9] Wilson telegrams to SSI, 15 and 16 November, SSI telegram to Viceroy, 14 November, Hogarth memorandum, 11 November, Cambon to Balfour, 16 November 1918, *FO* 371/3385; I.O. memorandum (B.294), 3 November 1918, *L/P&S/11*, vol. 108, no. 4896/18.

[10] Toynbee memorandum, ca. 20 November 1918, *FO* 371/3385; Hirtzel memorandum (quoted), 20 November 1918, *CAB* 27/36.

he was occupying Sulaimaniya (160 miles northeast of Baghdad, near the Persian frontier) at the instance of a Kurdish delegation and that a swelling movement for self-determination under British auspices could be discerned among the Kurdish people. By the end of November Wilson was talking of an independent Kurdistan stretching to Lake Van.[11]

Wilson had also reacted rather violently to the Anglo-French declaration, which, he predicted, was likely to lead to difficulties as great as those resulting from McMahon's assurances; the letter might be adhered to, but not the spirit. The average Arab saw that every advantage lay with British rule, not Sharifal connections, a point that had little to do with the declaration but obviously worried him. In short, said Wilson, Iraq ". . . neither expects nor desires any such sweeping schemes of independence. . ." It was Britain's duty and high privilege to establish a government that would develop the country; if this were to be diverted by catchwords and the demands of "the handful of amateur politicians of Baghdad," British soldiers would have died in vain. The only truly satisfactory answer: declaration of a British protectorate. The India Office Political Department was in full agreement. As Shuckburgh put it, ". . . the enlightened and progressive Arab, in whom the enthusiasts ask us to believe, is a mere fiction as far as Mesopotamia is concerned." Others had a different view. "Incorrigible," said Toynbee, and even Curzon had to admit that Wilson had sent in a "rather remarkable sequence of telegrams," the language of which hardly seemed tempered by any recognition of the justice of the principles enunciated by his American namesake.[12]

London's response to Wilson's confident conviction was an outline of T. E. Lawrence's scheme to divide all Syria-

---

[11] Wilson telegrams to SSI, 21 October, *FO* 371/3403, 10 November, *FO* 371/3407, 16, 18, and 27 November 1918, *FO* 371/3385.

[12] Wilson telegram to SSI, 17 November 1918, with Toynbee minute, *ibid.*, and with Shuckburgh minute of 20 November, *L/P&S/10*, 4722/18, no. 5104/18; Curzon remark in E.C. 39th minutes, 27 November 1918, *CAB* 27/24; see also Ireland, *op. cit.*, pp. 136–39.

Mesopotamia into three parts. Wilson's reaction was no surprise: totally impracticable; ignorant of historical and geographical divisions; puppet rulers would only give more scope to extremists; if Britain had any intention of promoting the welfare of the population and valued adherence to the spirit of the Anglo-French declaration (an interesting change of approach, considering his earlier remarks on that document), she would exclude Mesopotamia definitely not only from any contemplated Sharifal settlement but from any further discussion in that connection. After further thought Wilson even objected to his own proposal of a study commission on the grounds that now his staff's full attention would be required by the task of ascertaining the "responsible indigenous opinion" to which the declaration had referred, the job being made so difficult, he implied, by the total lack of such opinion.[13]

The declaration had actually been meant more as a whip with which to flog the French from Syria. But French abandonment of Syria seemed so improbable to Hirtzel and to Arnold Wilson that they had to consider the declaration on other grounds, and in so doing they found that Britain would be throwing away her position in Mesopotamia for exactly nothing. In this view they were confirmed by the action of France herself, for on 18 November Ambassador Cambon in a note to Balfour made it very clear that France regarded the Sykes-Picot Agreement as valid and in force. All arrangements and discussions designed to achieve revision could now only be "consigned to the official paper basket," as Eyre Crowe wrote in disgust. British exasperation is clear from Balfour's injudicious reaction. Britain, he replied to Cambon, sincerely regretted the French decision and ". . . can only hope that the French Government may not on their part experience the embarrassment which an equally unaccommodating attitude on the part of their Allies

---

[13] SSI telegram to Wilson, 18 November, Wilson telegram to SSI, 20 November 1918, *FO* 371/3385; Wilson telegram to SSI, 23 November 1918, *FO* 371/3387; Ireland, *op. cit.*, pp. 156–59.

would be likely to cause." [14] Only Lloyd George could give effect to this threat of retaliatory pressure, but concerned departments were by now dangerously ill-informed of the Prime Minister's diplomatic activities.

## 2

The Eastern Committee was still charged with responsibility for outlining a general British policy. At a crucial meeting of 27 November, with Curzon, Smuts, Montagu, Cecil, Hirtzel, Shuckburgh, General Sir Henry H. Wilson (C.I.G.S.), and a number of others present, the attempt was made. [15] Curzon, as usual, opened with a summary of the situation as he saw it. He outlined the McMahon pledges ("embarrassing") and the Sykes-Picot commitment ("a millstone round our necks"), together with the conflicting suggestions so far made on Mesopotamia: the division of the vilayets, a Sharifal candidate, Cox's Naqib of Baghdad, and Wilson's commission. The latter, in particular, had been vetoed because "We [the committee] thought that our case, instead of being helped, might be hampered at the Peace Conference if we were suspected by our friends or rivals there of having stolen a march on them by creating a system of government in advance." Now the War Office had brought forward Lawrence's proposal, and Lawrence had presented it to the committee. But Arnold Wilson had set up local councils, and as Curzon saw it this important step would permit Britain to refer at Paris to already existing indigenous institutions. On the other hand, both Wilson and General Marshall had reacted negatively to both the Anglo-French declaration and Lawrence's outline, and now Wilson opposed even a study commission.

[14] Cambon to Balfour, 18 November, and Crowe and Hardinge minutes, and Balfour to Cambon, 26 November 1918, *FO* 371/3385.

[15] E.C. 39th minutes, 27 November 1918, *CAB* 27/24; see also Nevakivi, *Britain, France and the Arab Middle East*, pp. 86f.

Wilson had been asked his opinion of the Naqib of Baghdad and had replied that although public opinion had not formally been polled the population opposed either an unsupervised Arab amir or, the other extreme solution, British annexation. Most of Iraq wanted an Arab ruler, but with a British High Commissioner (Cox by preference) and with advice and assistance in the various ministries. On the identity of the amir opinions differed widely, but neither a Sharifal candidate nor the Naqib had a majority following. Wilson's own choice was no amir, Cox as High Commissioner, and British advisors for a breathing space of five years or so.[16] The question before the committee, therefore, was whether Wilson should be told to continue to ascertain local opinion, and what decision should be taken on the identity of a figurehead amir.

In the discussion that followed, each office proved to have a favorite candidate. Cecil, for example, backed 'Abdullah, although he was "a sensualist, idle and very lazy." Montagu agreed: "If Abdullah is the lascivious, idle creature he is represented to be, he is the ideal man, because he would leave the British administrator to govern the country wholly. If Abdullah is the person who would be welcomed by the population he is the ideal man." To Curzon, however, it was "presumptuous folly" for the committee to sit there and try to select the right man—the population would have to be asked.

But how? As Curzon put it, who was capable of finding the answers to the questions posed? And Cecil had a different warning: Britain must not give the appearance of anything opposing an Arab government or of a quarrel with King Husain.

The Americans will only support us if they think we are going in for something in the nature of a native Government, and there are signs—I do not want to say more about it here—that the Americans are not so friendly disposed to us as they were, certainly as we

---

[16] Wilson telegram to SSI, 24 November 1918, *FO* 371/4148.

hoped they would be in all these matters. Therefore, we have to be careful, for the position is a difficult one.

The administrators of Iraq must find out themselves—by asking—whether the population favored a state under British tutelage, and whether they wanted 'Abdullah as ruler. Curzon drew up the wording of the precise questions, and the cable to Arnold Wilson was sent off.[17]

The basic policy, and for once there was a basic policy, was to create a government which was both national and popular, in the sense of public approval. With those two conditions, Britain intended to establish the strongest and most settled government possible and was prepared to do her utmost in furnishing aid for this purpose. The absence of local leaders and the lack of qualified personnel, together with postwar conditions, meant that a large measure of British supervision would be required at the outset, including that of foreign policy. "But there will be no annexation, and as far as can be seen at present, no formal declaration of protectorate." The situation would more probably be similar to that of prewar Egypt. With this introduction, London now required to know: Did the population favor a single Arab state with British tutelage from Mosul to the Gulf? if so, should this state be under a titular head? and if so again, who was preferred? The greatest possible importance attached to these questions, and an answer was required —not any answer, but ". . . one which can fairly be placed before the world as unbiased pronouncement by population of Mesopotamia." [18]

[17] SSI telegram to Wilson, 28 November 1918, *ibid.*; Ireland, *op. cit.*, pp. 160–66.

[18] Balfour, who had missed the meeting, protested unavailingly against these decisions; see Balfour notes to Montagu, 7 and 10 December, Montagu to Balfour, 9 December (written by Hirtzel), Curzon minute, 20 December 1918, and Shuckburgh minute, 11 January 1919, *L/P&S/10*, 4722/18, no. 5435a/18.

On receipt of his instructions, Arnold Wilson sent out orders to all divisional political officers, dated 30 November, and enclosing a copy of the Anglo-French declaration. The introduction to the orders was rather different in tone from the committee's intention: "... it is our concern to ensure that such degree of support and effective assistance shall be given by His Majesty's Government, including an Army of occupation, as will ensure the strongest and most settled Government possible ..." subject always to the provision that the regime would not be calculated to arouse the dislike of the population. Although there would be no annexation, a high degree of British supervision would be required, and "it goes without saying" that this would include foreign policy. Wilson then listed London's specific questions and instructed the officers to sound public opinion. They were to offer, as alternative to the plan suggested in the questions, a vision of a separate Mosul state probably under British control but without commercial free relations and without the material benefits of British rule. "When public opinion appears likely, under the guidance of the persons whom you have consulted, to take a definitely satisfactory line ... ," the officers might call a public meeting; if, however, opinion was "sharply divided, or in the unlikely event of its being unfavourable," Baghdad was to be informed, and no meetings held. Where favorable decisions were reached, these were to be recorded in writing and sent in.[19]

The intention of Wilson's orders is clear: opinion was to be sounded, but the response was to be guided in the proper direction. Wilson had the honest conviction that there was no general public opinion unless it was framed by such suggestion. The population would tend to look for guidance to Britain; and if no guidance was furnished, there would be no verdict to report. Wilson's subordinates doubtless agreed—although not necessarily on Wilson's list of possible candidates, which had

[19] Wilson instructions to divisional officers, 30 November 1918, FO 371/4178.

not ranked the Sharifians highly among the Naqib of Baghdad and Egyptian and Turkish princes. Wilson's Deputy Commissioner, E. B. Howell, wrote privately to Shuckburgh:

> . . . you might just as well appoint, for example, the Archbishop of Canterbury or Lord French to go and be King of Australia. The project would have just as much chance of succeeding. The only person who would have a chance would be a son of the Sharif, & it is quite safe to say that Mesopotamia is so separate from the rest of the Arab world, that of themselves, they would not have thought of any such solution.[20]

It would take time, naturally, for the poll to be complete, and it was still only a pious hope that a clear answer would be forthcoming even then. Meanwhile, a position had yet to be found toward the French in Syria which could be maintained at Paris. As it was, France had already complained on 30 November about Britain's failure to live up to her agreements, principally by the continued refusal to allow French representatives to visit Mosul.[21]

To the Eastern Committee, meeting on 5 December to discuss problems of Anglo-French relations in the Middle East and apparently completely unaware that Lloyd George was in the process even then of working out this problem with Clemenceau,[22] the alternatives seemed to be agreement with the French or agreement with the Arabs—and Curzon, for one, preferred the Arabs. The best procedure would be British support for self-determination to the utmost, "because," said the chairman, "I believe that most of the people would determine in our favour." Cecil and Balfour agreed, but, as Balfour added, self-

---

[20] Extract from Howell private to Shuckburgh, 4 December 1918, *L/P&S/10*, 4722/18, no. 689/19.

[21] Cambon note, 30 November, with Crowe minute, 4 December 1918, *FO* 371/3385.

[22] E.C. 41st minutes, 5 December 1918, *CAB* 27/24. Lloyd George–Clemenceau agreement is discussed below, pp. 315–316. Nevakivi, *Britain, France and the Arab Middle East*, p. 91.

determination could not be applied prematurely in the more backward areas, nor could Britain afford to give France and Italy the impression that she wished to escape from her commitments. Not that these were so desirable: "I never quite understood the inception of the Sykes-Picot Agreement, I never thoroughly understood it, and do not understand it to this day," said the nominal author of the Balfour Declaration. As Cecil said, a treaty was a treaty, and all that could be done was to try to get France to let Britain off. For this there was really little hope: "Cambon himself is quite insane if you suggest it." At this point, unfortunately, Balfour insisted that temporarily no further stenographic notes be taken, and further remarks on France and French statesmen are forever lost.

In the end, nothing was decided on policy at this meeting, although some striking remarks were recorded, not the least of which was Curzon's condemnation of a Haifa-Baghdad railway (mentioned in the Sykes-Picot Agreement) as ". . . one of the wildest chimeras that ever entered into the brain of man. . ." The most interesting remark of all:

Self-determination has been a good deal talked about. I think it is a foolish idea in many ways. We might allow the people who have fought with us to determine themselves. People like the Mesopotamian Arabs, who have fought against us, deserve nothing from us in the way of self-determination. No doubt the situation will change again and again.

These words were from the mouth not of Lord Curzon, but of T. E. Lawrence. They might be discounted as spoken in one of Lawrence's fits of self-denigration, had he not already shown his view on Iraq in his tripartite division scheme. "There is nothing here for us," he had cabled Cairo from Basra in 1916,[23] and Lawrence had neither revisited Mesopotamia nor seen other evidence that might alter his views. His attitude would prove important in due course.

[23] See above, ch. II, n. 102.

If the members had not yet discovered that this committee was unlikely to reach common agreement, a further lesson was provided in the next meeting, four days later.[24] Montagu, missing on the 5th, was now present. He had studied the minutes and had been struck by the fact that so many objections had been raised to the presence of France here or the United States there that when all was said and done the committee would finish by earmarking everything for Britain. The Allies would not be happy. The pessimism of Montagu seemed to set the general tone. On the possibility of giving France some African territory in exchange for Syria, for example, Cecil could only say, with considerable justice:

I know that if Mr. Balfour or myself makes any proposition with regard to Africa, we shall be told that there is an aeroplane station, or a submarine base, or that it is the oldest colony, or it will bitterly offend some New Zealand politician if we do it, or something of the kind. It is always the same.

Curzon's final remark was equally justified: "We came here to-day with what turned out to be a vain hope, on my part, that we should arrive at something like a conclusion."

When the committee again assembled on the 16th it was obvious that the departments had individually considered the matter and were better able to express their views. It was not really too difficult to agree upon a general position: France could have Lebanon and Alexandretta, but Syria must be independent and under the control of Faisal in Damascus; France and Italy should be persuaded to recognize Britain's special position in Arabia. Finally, while it was not really worthwhile to interfere with Husain's self-proclaimed title of "King of the Arabs" (which had never been recognized), it was also unnecessary to concur in his pretensions. Some sort of treaty with the Hijaz, giving control of foreign relations, was desirable—although here the India Office, presenting India's view with the aid of

[24] E.C. 42nd minutes, 9 December 1918, *CAB* 27/24.

Grant, now in England for this express purpose, objected to any interference in Arabia and, with the pilgrimage mainly in mind, preferred some sort of internationalization.[25]

Two days later, the committee turned to Mesopotamia. Arnold Wilson had reported on the 14th his first impressions of Mesopotamia's answers to the committee's questions, for he had toured the country, visiting Najaf, Hilla, and Karbala. So far he found opinion favoring one united state including Mosul, but there was no consensus on an Arab amir—mainly because neither Sunnite nor Shiite was willing to accept a ruler of the other persuasion. The general impression he had gained was that the inhabitants did not wish to escape from Turkish tyranny only to undergo a new one, but that they did desire the continuation of the present administration, with more British officials.[26]

With this report in mind, the committee again found agreement on Wilson's rather satisfactory impressions, although some questions remained. What of Hijazi-Iraqi relations, for example? It was fairly clear that Husain might have some spiritual authority, but not political—even though it might be necessary to subsidize him from Mesopotamian revenues in his capacity as keeper of the holy places. What was most puzzling, however, was the issue of terminology. If, as Balfour asked, Britain was not to declare a protectorate, how could protection be given? How could Britain control the area and still claim to be supporting self-determination? It was the sort of problem Balfour enjoyed, but Cecil, more pragmatic, pointed out that the regime would simply amount to control of the administration for the time being.[27]

By the forty-seventh meeting of the committee, on the day after Christmas, the general outline of Britain's approach was settled; British goals in the Arab areas would include: (1) no

[25] E.C. 43rd minutes, 16 December 1918, *ibid.*
[26] Wilson telegram to SSI, 14 December 1918, *FO* 371/4148.
[27] E.C. 44th minutes, 18 December 1918, *CAB* 27/24.

Turkish restoration, (2) no Allied annexation, and (3) self-determination with some form of European advice and support; but (4) this would require cancellation of the Sykes-Picot Agreement; and, finally, (5) the precise future of Iraq was unclear. Only one further decision was called for regarding the conference: Britain would not herself raise the issue of recognition of her Arabian position, for there was no intention of submitting her long-standing relations with Arabian chiefs to the judgment of the assembled powers.[28] It was the most the committee could do, as Balfour and Cecil and Smuts and Montagu now proceeded to Paris and Curzon had his hands full as acting head of the Foreign Office in Balfour's absence. On 7 January the committee disbanded, on the understanding that Curzon would head an *ad hoc* interdepartmental committee when occasion for consultation arose.[29] It would now be up to the negotiators in Paris, and there were few illusions that it would be easy to persuade France to accept Britain's proposed settlement.

3

By January 1919 the conference had assembled. Britain's delegation, led by Lloyd George and Balfour, included an impressive group of foreign experts nominally headed by Hardinge as Permanent Under-Secretary of the Foreign Office but largely coordinated by Hankey. Cecil, Mallet, Sykes, Toynbee, Crowe, and Robert Vansittart (then a junior official in the Foreign Office) had special interest in Arab affairs, working in conjunction with Hirtzel, the India Office representative for this area. Experts with first hand knowledge were also on hand: Gertrude Bell and Arnold Wilson would both arrive in March, and T. E. Lawrence accompanied Faisal, though none knew "T. E." 's exact status in relation to either Britain or the Amir.

---

[28] E.C. 47th minutes, 26 December 1918, *ibid.*
[29] E.C. 49th minutes, 7 January 1919, *ibid.*

The more the experts multiplied, the more the confusion grew. The conference opened formally on 18 January, and by 8 February it was temporarily at a standstill with Lloyd George returning to London (President Wilson left on the 15th, and Clemenceau entered the hospital with an assassin's bullet on the 19th).

But if the experts were confused, Faisal, with Lawrence at his shoulder, was not. In a memorandum of 1 January he set out a moderate and reasonable position which won considerable sympathy from the British delegates. The Arabs desired unity, Faisal began, but recognized that it was impossible to constrain all Arab parts of the Ottoman Empire into one form of government. Syria, for example, was sufficiently advanced to manage her own affairs, although it would require foreign assistance—and that could be paid for in cash, but not in freedom. Iraq also needed supervision, and here Faisal asked only that the government be Arab at least in spirit. The Arabs could not be forced into a western mold; if the Allies desired gratitude, they must help the Arabs to choose what was best for themselves. It was a useful statement, and the Foreign Office officials saw that Faisal might be a positive influence on the conference in aiding the solution of the Syrian problem.[30]

By mid-January it was apparent that Faisal had found friendly auditors in the American delegation. Mallet reported that they had taken up his cause with enthusiasm and ". . . have expressed their intention of tearing up the Sykes-Picot Agreement, being confident of Col House's collaboration." A twenty-page report on Syria was prepared by the British delegation, concluding satisfactorily that the arguments for revision of the Agreement were unanswerable.[31] Unfortunately, British

---

[30] Faisal memorandum, 1 January 1919, with minutes by Mallet, Balfour, and Toynbee, FO 608/80; memorandum in Hurewitz, op. cit., II, pp. 38–39.

[31] Mallet minute (quoted), 19 January (and later additions), British delegation memorandum (Erle Richards), January 1919, FO 608/105.

logic was not French logic. On 31 January Foreign Minister Pichon handed Balfour a note listing grievances against General Allenby's administration in Syria: anti-French activities by British officers, newspaper attacks, active Sharifal propaganda, and the like. Faisal's supporters were terrorizing a settled population that had no desire to submit to nomadic Bedouin rule. The French plan that followed outlined all the historic and cultural and economic justifications for the French presence in Syria and modified the Sykes-Picot Agreement only in (1) ending the distinctions between "Red" and "Blue" zones on the one hand and "A" and "B" zones on the other, (2) including Mosul in Mesopotamia—provided France was given an equal share in that area's oil, and (3) implying a possible change in Kurdistan, although no details were provided.[32]

It was not what Britain had wanted; but as Mallet had already noted for Balfour and Lloyd George, what was the alternative? France still intended partition of the Arab areas, which Britain's own experts said could not be done without serious Arab resistance and an unfavorable effect on Iraq, to say nothing of being contrary to Britain's own pledges. In Mesopotamia, of course, "As we are wanted there by the population it will be easy to come to terms with the Arabs." Mallet's only suggestion was unrealistic in the circumstances: he would honestly accept President Wilson's principles and those of the Anglo-French declaration, even though this would work to the probable exclusion of France from Syria and the election of Britain as Syrian mandatory power. It would be a great obligation, but less of an obligation than attempting to cooperate with France in suppressing nationalism by force.[33]

On 6 February Faisal outlined his position to the Council of

---

[32] Pichon to Balfour, 31 January 1919, and undated French draft agreement (6 February), *FO* 608/107; Cecil to Lloyd George, 4 February 1919, *Lloyd George Papers*, F/6/6/5. See also Nevakivi, *Britain, France and the Arab Middle East*, pp. 116–25.

[33] Mallet minute, 4 February 1919, *FO* 608/105.

Ten. The Amir asked the independence of the Arabs and presented all possible arguments in justification, suggesting, finally, that perhaps a commission could go out and study these matters. Lloyd George, however, picked on Faisal's point of Arab wartime efforts: How many Arabs had taken to the field? Something over 100,000, said Faisal. And how many in Mesopotamia? asked the Prime Minister. Faisal had no trouble in following Lloyd George's direction and answered by making reference to the many Iraqis fighting in the Hijaz armies, fighting, he said, for vindication of their rights of self-government. The Council came to no decision at this meeting, nor in another of the 13th, although the Reverend Howard S. Bliss, President of the Syrian Protestant College (later the American University of Beirut), lent his not inconsiderable support to the idea of a study commission.[34]

This new turn of events permitted some hope, at least to Mallet, for a commission might result in a British mandate—it was increasingly clear that "mandates" would be the form of control—for all of Syria. In that case, Britain could deal with the Arabs in her own way. If, on the other hand, the French were allowed to keep Syria, they would have to use force, and Britain would have to dance to the same tune. To avoid that possibility, compensation elsewhere in exchange for Sykes-Picot revision was still the answer.[35] Mallet, however, had misinterpreted the French proposals on Mosul and Kurdistan,

---

[34] United States, Department of State, *Papers Relating to the Foreign Relations of the United States. The Paris Peace Conference, 1919* (13 vols., Washington, D.C., 1942–47 [hereafter *U.S. For. Rel., Paris*], III, pp. 888–94 and 1013–24. See also Bliss private to Balfour, 16 February 1919, *FO* 800/215, and British Empire Delegation meeting, 7 February 1919, *CAB* 29/28.

[35] Mallet memorandum, 12 February 1919, *Milner Papers, PRO* 30/30/10. It should be added that negotiations were then in progress on adjustments of Anglo-French relations in Egypt and Morocco, which might have served as a vehicle for discussion of compensation; R. Graham (London) to Mallet (Paris), 18 February, and F.O. telegram to Cheetham, 1 March 1919, *FO* 608/116.

which had not at all indicated a willingness to renegotiate the entire Agreement, but rather were concessions which France was willing to pay to keep the rest of the Agreement intact. Hirtzel saw clearly the hold Syria had on French opinion, and in his memorandum of 14 February he stressed the vital importance of avoiding a clash with France on the issue of Syria, although he admittedly differed on this point with Montagu. France insisted on Syria; nor could the Americans be relied upon, for the United States position was growing steadily less popular in Paris. Britain had paid the Sykes-Picot treaty as the price for French consent to major military activities in the Middle East. Faisal demanded to know why the pound of flesh must now be paid—but he would not be in Paris making such a demand without the Arab revolt, there would have been no revolt without British aid and advisors like Lawrence, and such aid would not have been possible without French consent. France had essentially stayed out of the Arab operations in order to fight at Verdun, and without Verdun Faisal would be dead or a loyal Turkish subject. It would be pleasant to escape from the treaty and uphold the 1918 declaration, but even T. E. Lawrence had called self-determination a foolish expression. Finally, the joint declaration could not be used against France, for France would never have agreed to it if the French had taken it to mean the abrogation of the 1916 treaty.[36]

Hirtzel's attitude was supported by news from London, for Curzon and his subordinates had had several discussions with

---

[36] Hirtzel memorandum, 14 February 1919, *FO* 608/107. Nevakivi, *Britain, France and the Arab Middle East*, p. 124, adds, "Hirtzel claimed to present only his personal opinion but he naturally represented the views of the India Office, in opposition to the Arab Bureau line of policy." Full cooperation with France, however, was not exactly the I.O. view, if France could be eased out of Syria and Mesopotamia still kept by Britain; in any case, Montagu, the Secretary of State, had quite a different view, which is precisely why Hirtzel claimed to give only his own viewpoint. Hirtzel's position that there would have been no revolt without advisors was commonly held—and has been heavily (but not entirely successfully) attacked by Suleiman Mousa, *op. cit.*

Cambon which demonstrated the growing feeling of distrust, particularly over Mosul.[37] In Paris itself, negotiations were becoming more and more bitter over several issues, and in a sense it was fortunate that the three principal individuals were in the process of leaving the discussions. On the issue of Syria, perhaps only the charismatic quality of Mark Sykes could have forced agreement—and even that is very arguable—but Mark Sykes died on 16 February, one of many victims to the raging influenza. It was a tragic loss, but there is no evidence that Sykes could have persuaded Clemenceau as he had persuaded Picot. Sykes, like others, might have found the only solution in the compromise of an American mandate, a solution much discussed in Paris in February and March for Palestine, or Kurdistan, or Armenia, or anywhere else where problems of administration seemed most likely. But as President Wilson himself was soon to learn, there was little chance of an American mandate anywhere in the Middle East.[38]

Mallet, Toynbee, Hirtzel, and the others who remained struggled on, drafting treaties with Turkey or clauses on the Ottoman Empire to be included in the German treaty, grandly referring to self-determination and supervising powers and assistance and the like—but all such plans, where they related to Syria, foundered on the rock of Sykes-Picot.[39] The more time passed, the clearer it became that whatever niceties of expression might be advanced to the contrary Britain had made three conflicting pledges—to the Arabs, the French, and the Zionists—and as General Clayton, still in the Middle East as Allenby's

[37] Curzon to Derby, 12 February 1919, on conversation with Cambon, *FO* 371/4178; Curzon to Balfour, 21 February 1919, on Graham-Cambon conversations, *FO* 608/107.

[38] An American mandate would not have been popular with many British officials either; see Clayton telegram to F.O., 28 February 1919, with Toynbee, Bell, and Hirtzel minutes, *ibid.*

[39] See various drafts of March 1919, *FO* 608/116, and Cecil to Balfour, 4 March 1919 (with minutes), *FO* 608/107; Milner to Lloyd George, 8 March 1919, on talks with Clemenceau, *Milner Papers, PRO* 30/30/10.

Chief Political Officer, put it clearly and simply and correctly, a solution that satisfied all three demands was not possible.[40] If only France would see the truth, how easy it would be; but every appeal, every reference to the incompatibility of the Sykes-Picot Agreement with France's pledged word in the joint declaration, was of no avail.[41] In desperation, an attempt was made to bring American pressure to bear, and Colonel House was given a persuasive memorandum by Gertrude Bell which argued that the French attitude jeopardized the entire Middle Eastern situation, for despite every warning France was "either dangerously unconscious of the hostility to themselves which exists in Syria or no less dangerously determined to ignore it." [42] The most the American delegation could achieve was British acceptance of a proposal made by President Wilson, now returned to Paris, that a commission proceed to the Middle East to study the situation. Syria and Mesopotamia, the President argued, would have to be consulted if the McMahon pledges and the 1916 treaty did not, taken together, provide a workable solution. Lloyd George agreed at once to this proposal, but Clemenceau postponed his decision.[43]

The Foreign Office in London, now advised by the delegation in Paris that a commission was to be sent, was seriously alarmed. Both the Foreign Office and the India Office felt that such a commission was likely to delay a Middle Eastern settle-

---

[40] Clayton memorandum, 11 March 1919, *Lloyd George Papers*, F/205/3/9.

[41] See, for example, Curzon to Derby, 12 March 1919, *FO* 371/4179.

[42] Bell memorandum, received 14 March, with E. G. Forbes Adam note, 19 March (initialed by Vansittart, Mallet, and Toynbee), that document given to House; also British Delegation to American Commission, 24 March 1919, citing 350 anti-French petitions given to Clayton: *FO* 608/105. Official pressure on France was also continued: Curzon to Cambon, 19 March 1919, *FO* 371/4178.

[43] The proposal was made in the Council of Four on 20 March: *U.S. For. Rel., Paris*, V, pp. 1–14; Hurewitz, *op. cit.*, II, pp. 50–59; see also Nevakivi, *Britain, France and the Arab Middle East*, pp. 129–47. Pichon argued in this meeting that France had never been informed of the

ment even more. The commission, moreover, was very likely to disrupt the situation in Iraq. Shuckburgh minuted that probably the Paris delegation had little choice in agreeing, but even that was in error, for, as Hirtzel later minuted in the margin, "We weren't asked!" [44]

It is a striking feature of these negotiations in Paris in the first three months of 1919 that, while Britain tried often and hard to push France into a change of policy, or even withdrawal, in Syria, one possible means—indeed the most likely—of achieving this had not been tried. With one exception, the possibility of British withdrawal from Mesopotamia had not been mentioned, and that single reference had come from President Wilson, not any British representative. [45] The reason is basically simple, for by March Britain at last appeared to be on the road to settlement of the Mesopotamian problem.

### 4

When the British delegation arrived in Paris, it was with the feeling that while France and Syria were going to be troublesome Mesopotamia itself should not prove of great difficulty. The general outline had been decided: one state, including Mosul; no annexation, but some form of British control. That much had been agreed upon, and Arnold Wilson was contin-

---

McMahon pledges. The British delegation and the F.O. both tried to refute this claim, but only vague intimations, and no definite proof, could be found; Forbes Adam to Toynbee, 24 March 1919, *FO 608/93*. Nevakivi, *Britain, France and the Arab Middle East*, p. 129, adds that Pichon had "deliberately forgotten" the December Lloyd George–Clemenceau agreement—but perhaps, like the F.O. officials, he was as yet unaware of it?

[44] Astoria (British delegation, Paris) telegram to F.O., 25 March, I.O. to F.O., 3 April, Shuckburgh minute, 28 March 1919, *L/P&S/10*, 786/19, no. 1722/19.

[45] Council of Ten, 30 January 1919, *U.S. For. Rel., Paris*, III, pp. 807–8.

uing the process of polling opinion, primarily on possible candidates for ruler.

This did not mean that individual officials in London were above putting forth their own candidates before the verdict was in. In December, for example, both Toynbee and Mallet had pushed for 'Abdullah (it was assumed by all that Faisal would remain in Syria). A Sharifal candidate might be able to play down Sunnite-Shiite differences and perhaps patch over the Husain-Ibn Sa'ud rivalry. Mallet had been a bit more cautious; his own Turkish experience led him to mistrust eastern public opinion, but mistrust of the views put to Arnold Wilson by the Mesopotamian elite only made it that much easier to support 'Abdullah should the verdict go against him. 'Abdullah was not so favored in other quarters, however. Shuckburgh and Hirtzel preferred to wait. To Hirtzel, this was simply a case of the Foreign Office supporting T. E. Lawrence's dangerous scheme, and Hirtzel very much mistrusted Lawrence: "I have a great admiration for Col. L., but the F.O. made a bad mistake when they handed themselves over to him—showed him all their papers & admitted him to their most secret deliberations." It was as if the old Cairo-Baghdad quarrel had simply been transferred to the issue of individual rulers, to be fought out in the departments in London. Cox, still in Teheran, still objected to any Sharifian and still supported the Naqib.[46]

By year's end, Wilson's reports were nearly complete. Kut, 'Amara, Qurna, and Basra had all been visited, and Wilson had found opinion there similar to that in towns already visited: generally against an Arab amir because no suitable candidate could be found. Mosul, with its sizable Kurdish population, not surprisingly had been opposed to the general idea of an Arab ruler. Only Baghdad remained unreported, although the Naqib

---

[46] Toynbee memorandum, 19 December 1918, *FO* 371/3385; Mallet memorandum, 24 December 1918, *CAB* 27/39; Cox telegram to Balfour, 24 December 1918, with Hirtzel minute (quoted), 6 January 1919, *L/P&S/10*, 4722/18, no. 26/19.

and the elders appeared opposed to a "Young Arab" or Sharifal government. The result was clear, as much as any result could be under the circumstances. Wilson's discussions with the various notables and people of influence, guided by his questions, had produced legitimate expressions of opinion. Wilson was unlikely to ask the view of the younger hotheads, and more established elders, particularly those as yet untouched by nationalist sympathies, would naturally be against any ruler, from inside Iraq or outside, until they knew their own relative standing with such a regime. It was also true that conditions were at that point relatively peaceful, and, from the administrative side, talks were proceeding on the transfer of various governmental departments from military to civilian control.[47]

It was too simple, too easy—as several incidents now revealed, one of which in particular was to have important repercussions. After the armistice in 1918 Wilson had acted to enlarge the area of his administration, and by the end of November was justifying the need of posting a political officer at Dair az-Zaur, a rather important settlement on the west bank of the Euphrates, roughly 400 (300 air) miles northwest of Baghdad. Since it controlled the chief river crossing in the Syrian Euphrates valley on the route to Mosul, it was an important communication center. The problem was that even on small-scale maps accompanying the Sykes-Picot Agreement, Dair az-Zaur was in the French zone of influence. London saw no reason for posting an officer there, and Wilson was told to send no officer farther upriver than Abu Kamal, 80 miles southeast of Dair az-Zaur and apparently just within the edge of Britain's zone (it was on the line on maps), for nothing should be done which might appear

---

[47] Wilson telegrams to SSI, 14, 22 (2), 26, and 29 December 1918, *ibid.*, nos. 5619, 5777, 5778, 5810, and 5856/18 (also *FO* 371/4147); Commander-in-Chief, India, telegram to W.O., 9 January, and W.O. to F.O., 28 January 1919, *FO* 371/4148. See, on the whole issue of constitutional decisions, Ireland, *op. cit.*, chs. X–XI.

to disregard the 1916 arrangement. Wilson argued that the presence in Dair az-Zaur of Armenian refugees, the availability of needed wool and wheat, and the probable unfortunate future results for whatever power was to control the area if no authority was established there now, all advised an officer's presence. The refugee argument proved particularly persuasive, and the India Office gave a somewhat grudging approval to what was to prove to be an unwise decision.[48]

On 19 December the officer was at Abu Kamal and found to his dismay that it was already occupied by Arab officials ostensibly connected with Faisal's Damascus government. While they offered no difficulties for the moment, they refused to leave until ordered to do so by their superior at Dair az-Zaur (which had been the capital of the Syrian vilayet of the same name). The India Office now took up the issue on Wilson's behalf, urging that such measures by Damascus were premature until the final boundaries were settled—but the conflict was rather interdepartmental than international, for General Allenby was supposedly still in charge of Syria. Inquiries showed that the Arab officials had acted without the knowledge of Faisal's government and against the orders of the military, and orders for their immediate recall were issued. For the time being, the matter was settled, although Wilson reported on 10 January that the Arab officer was still in Abu Kamal, claiming that his orders had not arrived. Disagreements on jurisdictional authority continued through the spring and early summer—

[48] SSI telegrams to Wilson, 9 and 13 December, Wilson telegrams to SSI, 24 November and 11 December 1918, *L/P&S/10*, 5202/18, nos. 5202, 5426, and 5570/18, and *FO* 371/3386. Information on Syria is taken from Great Britain, Admiralty, Naval Intelligence Division, *Syria* (Oxford, 1943). The serious refugee problem cannot be treated here, although, as in the case of Dair az-Zaur, it occasionally affected consideration of the extent and duration of occupied areas. In addition to general works on Iraq and Syria, see Brig.-Gen. H. H. Austin, *The Baqubah Refugee Camp: An Account of Work on Behalf of the Persecuted Assyrian Christians* (London, 1920).

both locally and in telegrams to and from London—and more was to be heard of Abu Kamal.[49]

For Wilson, the affair, small as it was, was an ominous portent of things to come if the Sharifal faction was given its head. As yet, the malcontents in Mesopotamia, the "Committee of Young Arabs" as he called them, could still be blamed on pro-Turkish influences centered in Mosul. The return of those Iraqis fighting with Faisal would increase the strength of this group; for the moment their feelings seemed more pan-Arab than anti-British, but Wilson left little doubt of his fears for the future.[50]

If Wilson's concern for the returned Iraqis was premature, his anxiety about changing attitudes was not. Telegrams sent to London in late January were indicative of this, for leaders of both Sunnite and Shiite communities in Baghdad turned out to want an Arab state without British protection—an attitude, Wilson explained, due to meetings in which inflammatory language had been used and the full pressure of religious sentiment brought to bear, and those who objected to such procedure had been threatened with political and religious ostracism. A few of the more wealthy and powerful individuals, including the Naqib (who expressed surprise that Britain had consulted opinion at all), held out for British protection. The majority of the fifty Muslims consulted, however, submitted a document asking for one unified state from Mosul to the Gulf under a

---

[49] Wilson telegram to SSI, 22 December, I.O. to F.O., 21 and 27 December, Balfour telegram to Wingate, 24 December 1918, F.O. to I.O., 3 January, I.O. to W.O., 10 January, Clayton (Cairo) telegram to F.O., 2 January, G.H.Q., Mesopotamia, telegram to Commander, Egypt, 10 January 1919, L/P&S/10, 5202/18, nos. 5779 and 5818/18 and 38, 195, and 231/19, and FO 371/3386. Further correspondence may be found in both files. See also on Dair az-Zaur, Bray, *Paladin*, pp. 369–76, Marlowe, *op. cit.*, pp. 178–80, Wilson, *Mesopotamia*, pp. 228–38, Laurence Evans, *United States Policy and the Partition of Turkey, 1914–1924* (Baltimore, 1965), p. 246, and Loder, *op. cit.*, pp. 69–70.

[50] Wilson telegram to SSI, 23 January 1919, FO 608/96; see also Bell private to Hardinge, 24 January 1919, *Hardinge Papers*.

son of the Sharif—with nothing said about British protection.
Wilson was quick to add that Jewish and Christian leaders de-
terminedly opposed such a scheme, and that as the document
became better known a revulsion of feeling against the petitioners was occurring in Baghdad and a counterdocument requesting a state under British protection with no amir was being
circulated.[51]

In Paris, the precise meaning of all this was most unclear to
the British delegation. To Toynbee, it meant that the politically
conscious element desired an amir but ". . . the much larger
non-political element has instinctively echoed the wishes of
Captain Wilson." Vansittart felt that no significant body of
pro-Arab opinion emerged from the telegrams, but Mallet concluded the opposite: it was just Wilson's first admission of the
existence of such a body. Hardinge preferred to believe Wilson: the bulk of opinion opposed an amir, and such sentiment
as existed to the contrary was due to the threats of the religious
leaders.[52]

Wilson next sent in a long report on "Self-Determination in
Mesopotamia," written by Gertrude Bell.[53] It recorded the
entire process of the consultation, and it was the Civil Commissioner's last word. He had already proposed, in fact, to send
Miss Bell to Europe (she was going on leave in the summer in
any case) to speak for him, for he felt himself at a disadvantage
compared to the direct contacts of Cairo and Damascus with
Paris and London. This was permitted, although she was urged
to make haste: a decision on Iraq might soon be taken.[54]

[51] Wilson telegram to SSI, 26 January 1919, FO 371/4148.

[52] Ibid., with Toynbee, Vansittart, Mallet, and Hardinge minutes,
FO 608/96. Toynbee was behind the times on one matter, for Wilson
had been gazetted Brevet Lieutenant-Colonel the previous fall when
Cox moved on to Teheran: Marlowe, op. cit., p. 131.

[53] Dated 22 February, received in I.O. 22 March and in F.O. September 1919. See F.O. copy and Young minute, FO 371/4150.

[54] Wilson private telegram to Montagu, 28 January, and SSI telegram to Wilson, 1 February 1919, FO 371/4148.

For two reasons Wilson's "last word" would not be so regarded. One was the necessity of reaching agreement with the Hashimites, and the other was the arrival in London, by slow sea mail, of a batch of orders and reports from Iraq. Among these documents was a copy of Wilson's orders to his political officers, dating from November, on how to conduct the poll. On 24 January, Hubert Young, who had himself served in Mesopotamia (1915-1917) and with the Arabs in Syria (1918) and had recently arrived in the Foreign Office as an advisor on Middle Eastern affairs, drew attention to the key passages. The instructions, he minuted, made it ". . . almost brutally clear that public opinion is not to be encouraged, or even allowed, to express itself in a sense contrary to Colonel Wilson's opinion."

Most officials agreed that the orders would certainly startle the conference, particularly President Wilson, but that there seemed little use in taking exception to them so late in the day. Curzon, however, was in charge in London, and Curzon, in a righteous mood, did not agree with his subordinates. "When the French do this sort of thing we are up in arms. But when our man does it, because it is marked 'Secret and Confidential', it is proposed that we should wink at it. Col. Wilson may have acted with the best intentions. But his intentions were not our orders and these it was incumbent on him to obey." The India Office would be taken to task.[55]

The India Office could only agree that, if published, the clauses in question might arouse some hostile comment, but the Iraqi situation was one that required great delicacy. Perhaps Arnold Wilson unconsciously overstepped his instructions ". . . in his anxiety to guide his officers in ascertaining the real drift of public opinion—a very intangible and uncertain factor in an oriental population. . ." His error was not, therefore, ser-

[55] Young minute, 24 January, and other comments, including Curzon's minute of 29 January, and F.O. to I.O., 3 February 1919, *FO* 371/4178.

ious, and the India Office would do no more than send copies of the current correspondence to Baghdad. "I like the idea of Col Wilson being in a state of unconsciousness when he overstepped his instructions," commented Curzon, but little could be done at the moment.[56] The memory remained, and it served to discredit Wilson and his inquiry just at the time when 'Abdullah was being touted as the best candidate. Embittered personal relations were to result as well; Young had begun this controversy, and Young, as a sympathizer with the Arab cause and with self-determination, now became a determined enemy of Wilson and all for which he stood, a position of which Wilson was not long to remain in ignorance.

While this discussion was taking place in London, Paris was cabling to ask the Foreign Office's opinion on 'Abdullah. The conference had not got around to discussing him officially, but Hirtzel, who drafted the telegram, wanted a statement in case Britain wished to put 'Abdullah's case to the conference. Curzon could only report that Lawrence had suggested him as ruler for one of the three states but that Baghdad had reported unfavorably on a Hashimite amir. Toynbee and Mallet, still 'Abdullah's staunchest supporters, urged that 'Abdullah had not had any chance to put forward his candidacy, that Lawrence had given his assurance that 'Abdullah had a large following in Iraq, and that whether the Eastern Committee recommended him or not he would in the end go there as titular king. Lawrence himself added a curious minute in Paris: "This question has now been much talked round, and I will not put it up again. The Syria question requires settling first. After that I will make up my mind whether I will put Abdulla up for Mesopotamia or not." It was a proper comment for a Foreign Secretary, but not for a junior advisor of indeterminate status, and Hirtzel's reaction was just what Lawrence had asked for:

[56] I.O. to F.O., 17 February 1919, with Curzon minute, *ibid.*

"I apprehend that H.M.G. are at liberty to do this whether or not Col. Lawrence makes up his mind." [57]

The problem had taken on a new aspect. Britain had decided on a poll of the population, and the decision had not favored 'Abdullah. If, then, the Amir was allowed to stump the country as Britain's candidate, Britain would be in a most embarrassing situation. This at least was Hirtzel's view, but within the India Office opinions differed. Shuckburgh could not believe that the conference really wished Britain to give up Iraq, and therefore it was a question of finding a pretext for Britain going her own way—and Arnold Wilson's report furnished just such a pretext. Once more Hirtzel disagreed, for France must be given no grounds for establishing a protectorate in Syria because Britain was doing the same in Mesopotamia. A regime must be established which would pass muster as an Arab government, which would be both politically and administratively workable, and which at the same time would not push the nationalist element completely and totally into hostility toward Britain.[58]

It was a paradoxical situation. All, even Hirtzel, agreed that the intrigues and demonstrations and counterdemonstrations would continue so long as no decision on Mesopotamia was reached.[59] But the government was unwilling to impose a solution upon Wilson which would run counter to the expressions of public opinion he had reported; that much faith had to be placed in him. Instead, while the conference muddled its way through, and it became increasingly apparent that no decision would be reached in Paris on this issue, Wilson was told that Britain would wait for Gertrude Bell before taking any inde-

[57] Astoria telegram to Curzon, 23 January, Curzon to Balfour, 26 January, Lawrence minute, 28 January, and Hirtzel minute, 29 January 1919 (also explaining why he drafted the telegram), *FO* 608/96; F.O. telegram to Astoria, 26 January 1919, *FO* 371/4148.

[58] Wilson telegram to SSI, 26 January 1919, with Shuckburgh (30 January) and Hirtzel (2 February) minutes, *L/P&S/10*, 4722/18, no. 551/19.

[59] Wilson telegram to SSI, 14 February 1919, and minutes, *FO* 608/96.

pendent action. In the meantime, Wilson was to prepare proposals for a constitution for the Arab state or states, using as a basis his reports on opinion and the necessity "of effective and indisputable British control." On the other hand, Britain was committed to the Anglo-French declaration, "and we must adhere to this in spirit as well as letter." The objective should be a flexible document, giving provision for increasing Arab participation in the government. These points admittedly "may not be any great guide to you," but they indicated the essential policy.[60]

It was a difficult assignment. Wilson was prepared to follow instructions, he replied, but he would also work on the assumption that there would be a British High Commissioner and not an Arab amir, and that the state would include both Mosul and Dair az-Zaur. Whatever the form of government, British control would be effective in practice. His conclusion, quickly reached, was that Iraq should be divided into five or six divisions, each with advisory council, all subordinate to the High Commissioner. Arabs would be included in positions of "executive and administrative responsibility," although they would be "selected Arabs of good birth and education belonging to 'Iraq by birth. . . ." This would mean a certain loss of efficiency, but Wilson was prepared to pay the price, even if it meant (and to him it clearly did) the rise of political discontent and greater nationalist demands for power. Finally, there would be no fixed constitution for the time being; it would be better to proceed slowly on this.[61]

No comment was called for from London or Paris, for Wilson was on his way to Europe for consultation. Leaving on 25 February, he was in Paris on 20 March, talking to Hirtzel, Gertrude Bell, Crowe, Mallet, and the more important leaders: Lloyd George, Balfour, Cecil, Faisal, Weizmann of the Zion-

[60] SSI telegram to Wilson, 14 February 1919, *FO* 371/4148.
[61] Wilson telegram to SSI, 20 February, and letter, 6 April 1919, *ibid.*; letter (B.317) is also in *L/P&S/10*, 2023/19, no. 2023/19.

ists. Among his contacts was Lawrence, whom he now met for
the first time and who ". . . seems to have done immense harm
and our difficulties with the French in Syria seem to me to be
mainly due to his action and advice," as he wrote Cox later,
describing the encounter.[62] In several interdepartmental meetings Wilson argued mainly for the extension of Mesopotamian
boundaries and the establishment of a northern fringe of autonomous Kurdish states. On 4 April he left for London, where
he remained almost a month. During this time he met on several
occasions with the more formal interdepartmental committee,
of which Hubert Young had just been appointed Secretary,
to discuss his proposals. The committee had been critical, but
Wilson had in his favor his own experience and expertise and
the fact that Paris had decided nothing; by the time of his departure, the committee had made no formal decision, but it was
clear that unless Paris acted immediately London's decision on
Wilson's proposals would be favorable.[63]

Shortly after Wilson's departure the India Office felt itself
competent to approve, without the committee's sanction, at
least the establishment of the councils Wilson had proposed; authority was telegraphed to Baghdad, reaching Wilson the day
after his arrival, by air, via Aleppo and Dair az-Zaur. Wilson
reported that the situation was generally quiet, although educated Baghdadis wished more governmental authority to pass
from the military to the civilian officials as soon as possible, and
that Sharifal propaganda was quite active, with marked anti-

[62] Wilson private to Cox, 9 May 1919, *Arnold Wilson Papers* (British
Museum), Add. Mss. 52455. Wilson's journey: Ireland, *op. cit.*, pp.
184–85; Wilson, *Mesopotamia*, pp. 115–16; Marlowe, *op. cit.*, pp. 147–
49; Wilson says he reached Paris on 20 March, but Marlowe puts the
date four days later.

[63] Interdepartmental Committee on Eastern Affairs [I.D.C.E.] minutes,
8 April 1919, *L/P&S/10*, 2249/15, no. 1858/19; 10 and 17 April, *FO*
371/4148–49; Young, *op. cit.*, pp. 285–86; Hirtzel private to Mallet, 26
April 1919, *FO* 608/95. See also Nevakivi, *Britain, France and the Arab
Middle East*, p. 136, and Burgoyne, *op. cit.*, p. 110.

foreign tendencies.[64] It was obvious that Wilson's alarm was growing; the councils might not be sufficient, but no more could be approved pending the results of the conference. Faisal had yet to come to terms with the French,[65] and, much more important for the future of Iraq, Anglo-French discussions had become thoroughly sidetracked on the issue of oil.

5

The issue of oil concessions in Mesopotamia had been a major problem of prewar diplomacy in Turkey, closely connected with railway development, financial projects, spheres of influence, and the like. In the spring of 1914, however, an agreement was reached in which the interests of William Knox D'Arcy, influential speculator and developer, were to receive a share of the controversial Turkish Petroleum Company for development of these resources. War intervened, but in early 1918 the D'Arcy Exploration Company requested that the prewar agreement be regarded as invalid and that it be given a full concession for Mesopotamia. From the first, the issue of such a concession was opposed by the military and civil authorities in Iraq, for it was in their interest to see that Iraq—and its temporarily British government—reaped the full benefit of Iraqi resources.[66]

The problem was complicated. D'Arcy was in effect part-owner of the Anglo-Persian Oil Company, in which the British

[64] SSI telegram to Wilson, 9 May 1919, L/P&S/10, 4722/18, no. 2023/19; quoted in Wilson, *Mesopotamia*, pp. 123–24, and dated the 10th (when Wilson received it); Wilson's dating is followed in Marlowe, *op. cit.*, p. 150. Wilson telegram to SSI, 13 May 1919, FO 371/4148.

[65] See, on the Arab French negotiations, Nevakivi, *Britain, France and the Arab Middle East*, ch. VII, and FO 608/93 and 371/4145.

[66] D'Arcy Exploration Co. to F.O., 16 May, F.O. to Army Council, 19 July, Petroleum Executive to F.O., 2 July, Wilson telegram to SSI, 16 September 1918, FO 371/3402.

government had a substantial interest. The A.P.O.C. as such, and not D'Arcy Exploration, had received the prewar share of 50 per cent of the T.P.C., with the remaining shares to be parceled out among Royal Dutch Shell, the Deutsche Bank, and (5 per cent) Nubar Gulbenkian.[67] At the end of the war the British Petroleum Executive—a special body established to control petroleum resources and acquisitions—recommended that the British government purchase the Deutsche Bank's 25 per cent, now held by the public trustee of enemy property, and thereby give British interests control of the T.P.C. (or its

[67] The Turkish Petroleum Company was established in 1912 to work the oil deposits of the Mosul and Baghdad vilayets. The Deutsche Bank, which arranged the establishment of the company, claimed that it had obtained a contract for this purpose from the Turkish Ministry of the Civil List (which controlled mineral rights) and which covered mineral rights adjoining the right-of-way of the Baghdad Railway. After considerable negotiation, the 1912 company was capitalized at £80,000. The £1 shares were distributed as follows: National Bank of Turkey, 40,000; Deutsche Bank, 20,000; Anglo-Saxon Petroleum Company (the holding company of the Royal Dutch Shell group), 20,000. In March 1914, the capital was doubled, and the further 80,000 shares were given to D'Arcy's interests to compensate for a claim to the same oil based on a totally different contract with the Turkish government (both agreements, incidentally, were denied at various times by Ottoman authorities). The National Bank of Turkey shares were divided between the Deutsche Bank and Anglo-Saxon, so that the position became: A.P.O.C., 50 per cent; Deutsche Bank, 25 per cent; Anglo-Saxon, 25 per cent; Gulbenkian's 5 per cent was to come from transfers of stock from A.P.O.C. (2½ per cent) and Anglo-Saxon (2½ per cent). A further complication was that the 1914 agreement had not actually been formalized, as Louis Mallet, who had handled the negotiations, well knew. The point of these details is that in actual fact Shell had a claim of its own to Mesopotamia's oil which Shell regarded as being as legitimate as D'Arcy's. See L. Evans, *op. cit.*, pp. 295–303; H. Woodhouse, "American Oil Claims in Turkey," *Current History*, 15 (March 1922), 953–59; E. M. Earle, "The Turkish Petroleum Company . . . ," *Political Science Quarterly*, 39 (June 1924), 265–79; Nubar Gulbenkian, *Portrait in Oil: The Autobiography of . . .* (N.Y., 1965), pp. 82–90; and, for general background, Benjamin Schwadran, *The Middle East, Oil, and the Great Powers, 1959* (2nd ed., N.Y., 1959).

heir). To do this, however, would require upholding the pre-war concession as valid.[68]

That side of the argument was supported by the fact that if Britain denied the validity of the existing concession a number of other claims might be staked, including that of the French government and of Royal Dutch Shell. There was another side, however. The British government wished to obtain control of Sir Henry Deterding's Shell company (then controlled outside Britain), and one excellent way to obtain that control was to offer a share of Mesopotamia's oil to Shell as an inducement—but that would require that the T.P.C. concession be treated as invalid. Upholding the concession's validity seemed the more satisfactory solution at first glance—it was rather more certain than the other proposal—but not only would it raise suspicions among the French, who would appear to be kept out of Iraq by this maneuver, but also it would set a very dubious prece-dent on the validity of prewar Ottoman concessions generally. For the moment, a compromise was reached. The Deutsche Bank shares were purchased by Britain, but in the name of a private individual; control was thus obtained, but flexibility on the validity of the concession was preserved.[69]

By the time of the Paris conference Anglo-French discus-sions had revealed that it would be far easier to persuade France to yield Mosul if the 1914 oil agreement was ruled valid. If

---

[68] W. Long to Balfour, 18 November 1918, and attached notes, *FO* 371/3402. The records of the Petroleum Executive would have proven invaluable for this discussion had they not been largely destroyed for reasons of space after the Second World War. I would like to express my thanks to the staff of the Record Department of the Ministry of Power, which allowed me to see the indexes and conducted an arduous search in my behalf for the few records remaining in existence, which they subsequently permitted me to consult. It was a notable effort on their part that proved without any doubt that the history of Britain's oil negotiations in this important era must be written without the files of the department principally concerned.

[69] Long to Balfour, 18 November 1918, *ibid.*

there was to be no struggle for new concessions, the French would have to be reconciled to the fact that they would have no share of the oil in Mosul, whoever ruled that vilayet. That France was working on the same assumption was demonstrated by its request for a share of this valuable property (after all, a sizable share had been held by the Germans before the war). The intimation was clear: if France was not given a share it would oppose the validity of the 1914 concession and quite possibly present obstacles to the necessary pipe-line facilities to the Mediterranean. It was no surprise that the Petroleum Executive wished to negotiate an agreement with France.[70]

The Paris delegation agreed, but Curzon and the London Foreign Office did not, feeling that the whole question of oil should be treated in conjunction with the revision of Sykes-Picot. Unfortunately for this view, Walter Long, Minister for Petroleum Affairs, was in Paris already negotiating with his French counterpart, Senator Henry Bérenger, Commissioner-General for Petroleum Products. Long, who had not worked out any common proposals with either Foreign Office or India Office, was in a hurry, for he was convinced that France was already in contact with the American Standard Oil Company and, if Britain did not come to terms, would enlist American pressure for an "open door" to Mesopotamian oil. Sir John Cadman, head of the Petroleum Executive (later Baron Cadman of Silverdale, director and chairman of A.P.O.C. and Iraq Petroleum Company), also in Paris, denied to Foreign Office representatives that any detailed (as opposed to general) agreement had been reached with Bérenger, for Cadman thought

---

[70] The proposed agreement was A.P.O.C., 34 per cent; Anglo-Saxon, 34 per cent; British government, 2 per cent; other interests, 30 per cent. Notes on interdepartmental meeting, 1 February (Paris), Mallet memorandum and Montagu to Long, 3 February, and E. Weakley memorandum, 14 April 1919, *FO* 371/4209; H. Payne memorandum, 13 February 1919, *FO* 371/4205; Weakley to Clarke, 11 December 1922, *Petroleum Executive Files* S/613.

the negotiations with Shell must be arranged before a settlement with France.[71] Foreign Office, Paris delegation, Petroleum Minister, Petroleum Executive—there were too many concerned and uncoordinated officials, and it was most difficult to untangle the course of events.

There were, it is clear, two separate issues involved: the allotment of shares by country and the allotment by each country of its shares to public or private concerns. Although the Shell negotiations insured that for Britain the two issues were interlocked, Long was principally concerned with France at the moment, and by mid-March he and Bérenger had reached an agreement in which 25 per cent of Mesopotamian oil would go to France (presumably all Mesopotamia and not merely Mosul, although this was not yet clear). The company or companies would be British-controlled, each side if necessary would yield 5 per cent to "native" interests, and France would provide royalty-free pipe-line facilities through territory under her control.[72] The agreement was approved, on the British side, by Balfour, for it insured French cooperation both in legitimizing the concession and, presumably, on yielding Mosul and keeping other interlopers out.[73] That the agreement was a step toward purchasing French claims on Mosul was clear; that such a purchase was also a step toward recognition and confirmation of the Sykes-Picot Agreement was rather lost sight of.

---

[71] Curzon to Balfour, 20 February 1919, *FO* 608/231, and 22 February; Cadman's denial recorded in E. Weakley minute, 21 February 1919, *FO* 371/4209. Both Standard Oil of New Jersey and Standard Oil of New York were involved in the pressure to secure an "open door," and it is unclear which is referred to here.

[72] Cadman to Mallet, 13 March 1919, *FO* 608/97; *Petroleum Executive File* S/60 deals with earlier discussions of the formation of a large British company, file 608 with Cadman's subsequent career.

[73] Balfour to Curzon, 17 March 1919, *FO* 608/231 and 371/4209; Cadman to Curzon, 30 April 1919, *FO* 371/4209, cites Balfour's initials on Mallet's memorandum of 3 February (n. 70 above) as authority for the French negotiations.

Curzon in London was more pessimistic than Balfour, pointing out that the remainder of the Sykes-Picot Agreement still stood, ". . . and the position would seem to be that their [French] assets for bargaining remain undiminished while we have given up a quarter share of our best asset for this purpose in exchange for no concrete advantage."[74] His view was supported by Arnold Wilson, now in London, in an interdepartmental meeting on 8 April at the India Office, with Foreign Office, Treasury, Department of Overseas Trade, Petroleum Executive, and A.P.O.C. representatives present. Wilson argued strenuously that oil was Mesopotamia's only asset, that it would be vitally necessary as security for the loans that would be required for her development, and that it should become the property of the Mesopotamian state despite any agreements—valid or invalid—to the contrary. With the Shell negotiations mainly in mind, he objected to handing over these immense potential riches to a small group of private shareholders.

Hirtzel and Montagu believed that Wilson had given his approval, in Paris, to the draft Long-Bérenger terms, but Wilson had now most definitely altered his view, as his minute on an India Office draft record of the interdepartmental meeting (written, to correspond to the report, in the third person) shows:

Colonel Wilson has since added that, as at present advised, and so far as he is the trustee of the interests of the future Iraq State, he would not feel able to give the facilities which the Turkish Petroleum Company desire and which His Majesty's Government have undertaken to use their influence to obtain.

It was a pompous remark, and Hirtzel, who liked to advise Wilson in a fatherly manner, felt he should expunge it from the record in Wilson's interest. "He is a little bit apt, being young, to adopt that tone, & it makes a bad impression. I spoke

[74] Curzon to Balfour, 2 April (drafted by Kidston), enclosing Cadman to Curzon, 13 March 1919, enclosing Bérenger agreement, *ibid.*

to him about it in Paris, & propose to do so again before he returns to Mesopotamia."[75]

Wilson's argument may have given pause for thought on yielding Mesopotamian oil to Shell, but it had no effect on the Long-Bérenger agreement, for that agreement was formally signed on 8 April, the day on which Wilson was arguing in London.[76] Wilson and the India Office could only watch their preserve against invaders, and these were not slow in coming. In May, Sir John Cowans, a British subject, traveled to Mesopotamia in the interests of Shell; it was a move calculated, in the India Office view, to establish a claim in case Shell's pending negotiations with Britain fell through. There was considerable fear, too, of similar American attempts, and Wilson was told to remain on his guard—superfluous instructions under the circumstances.[77] But Wilson was now to have, unknowingly, some strong allies: Clemenceau and Lloyd George. If the Foreign Office had difficulty following the oil negotiations, those negotiations now appeared to be totally unknown to the heads of state; at the very least, the implications of the agreement had so far escaped the Council of Four.

6

Since their discussion in March the principal negotiators had been unable to reach a decision on the problems of Syria and Mesopotamia, or on the Ottoman Empire in general, partly because of continuing (and abortive) negotiations between Faisal and Clemenceau. It was assumed that the area would be divided into mandates, and a visiting commission of inquiry had been organized to sound out the populations. Unfortunately,

[75] Weakley memorandum, 9 April, Kidston note, 12 April 1919, *ibid.*; I.D.C.E. minutes, 8 April 1919 (I.O. Memorandum B.322), with Wilson addition and Hirtzel minute (both quoted), *L/P&S/10*, 2249/15, no. 1858/19.
[76] *DBFP*, IV, pp. 1089–91.
[77] SSI telegrams to Wilson, 2 and 15 May 1919, *FO* 371/4209.

France refused to appoint delegates or proceed with the commission until her troops replaced those of Britain in Syria,[78] and this apparent lack of cooperation governed discussion of Middle Eastern issues when these were again taken up by the Council of Four on 21 May.

At a meeting at President Wilson's quarters Clemenceau made it clear that he was unable to cooperate in the commission, for, having given way on Mosul, France now found that Britain was putting up new suggestions for Cilicia and so on, including one for an American mandate. This could not be tolerated, for Britain could not bring America in in order to keep France out. Lloyd George, on the other hand, accused France of failing to carry out its commitment regarding the commission; and as for Mosul, Clemenceau had already agreed in London that Mosul would go to Mesopotamia. Clemenceau had also complained about a railway right of way in Syria—but this was part of the bargain for "half the oil of Mesopotamia. . . ." Lloyd George, obviously annoyed, insisted that the negotiations on a railway right of way were to the French advantage. "However, he must put a stop to those negotiations until the present misunderstanding was cleared up." The meeting was hastily adjourned, but later in the day Lloyd George wrote Clemenceau, formally confirming his remarks of that morning: since France found the railway and pipe line proposal to be a departure from the agreement of December 1918, Britain now withdrew from that agreement.[79]

[78] Paris delegation undated memorandum for Curzon (received 25 April), Curzon telegram to Clayton, 29 April, SSI telegram to Viceroy and Curzon memorandum, 18 April, Astoria telegram to F.O. (from Hogarth to McMahon), 20 May 1919, *FO* 371/4180; Mallet private to Hirtzel, 2 May 1919, *FO* 608/95; on the King-Crane Commission see Harry N. Howard, *The King-Crane Commission: An American Inquiry in the Middle East* (Beirut, 1963), and, in the larger framework of U.S. policy, L. Evans, *op. cit.*

[79] Council of Four, 21 May 1919, *U.S. For. Rel., Paris*, V, pp. 760–66; Cadman to J. T. Davies (secretary to Lloyd George), 24 July 1919, enclosing copy of Lloyd George to Clemenceau, 21 May, and request-

Had many members of the British delegation in Paris—let alone of the Foreign Office or India Office in London—read the minutes of this meeting, they would have been hopelessly confused. Clemenceau's reference to recent British proposals could be understood, perhaps, for Lloyd George had presented, on 21 May, a proposal on Turkey that had included a possible American mandate over Constantinople and the Straits or Anatolia.[80] But references by both Clemenceau and Lloyd George to French concession of Mosul in London in December would have been utterly unintelligible, for that agreement was not only unknown to subordinates but, as will be seen, was to remain so in general until July, and in terms of actual details forever—at least from the British side. Finally, Lloyd George had rather confused railway right of way with oil pipe line, but that at least was somewhat clarified when the Council of Four met again the next day.[81]

On the 22nd, Clemenceau announced that he had meant to complain only about railway negotiations then proceeding, which proposed moving Syrian frontiers too far to the north; the Long-Bérenger agreement, of which he, Clemenceau, had only learned that very morning, was not concerned. Lloyd George, however, insisted he had known nothing of the oil agreement and had canceled it when he learned of it. Long, who apparently had initiated the whole discussion, had never spoken of it to him. Now, unless the Mosul question was settled, the issues of France's position in Syria and in Mesopotamian oil would simply have to await the report of the commission of inquiry. But Clemenceau was not so easily moved. The Sykes-Picot Agreement still stood; yielding Mosul had not

---

ing explanation, *Lloyd George Papers*, F/33/2/66; Forbes Adam note for Hirtzel, with same enclosure, 18 July 1919, FO 608/96; see *DBFP*, IV, p. 1092.

   80 Lloyd George outline of settlement, 21 May 1919, App. III to CF-20A, *U.S. For. Rel., Paris*, V, pp. 769–70.

   81 Council of Four, 22 May 1919, *ibid.*, pp. 807–12. Nevakivi, *Britain, France and the Arab Middle East*, pp. 154–55.

meant any other changes in the treaty, he insisted, and no French commissioners would be sent unless the agreement was honored. "As for himself, he would say plainly that he would no longer associate in connection with the British in this part of the world, because the harm done to his country was too great." Lloyd George said only that until a decision was reached Allenby was in command in Syria, and Allenby would have a free hand—that is, to keep out the French. These positions remained unchanged, and neither power budged in the next similar discussions nine days later. As Lloyd George refused to send British commissioners unless French commissioners were also sent, the American commissioners, Henry C. King and Charles R. Crane, went alone.[82]

It was an exceedingly awkward situation, not the least because, once again, Britain's policy was hopelessly confused—John Bull, having stumbled into a swarm of bees, struck out blindly with all four limbs to escape a most embarrassing posi-

---

[82] Council of Four, 31 May 1919, *DBFP*, VI, pp. 132–33; Astoria telegram to Allenby, 2 June 1919, FO 371/4179. Why Lloyd George adopted this position has never been made clear. Apparently General Henry Wilson and Milner and Balfour all preferred the British representatives to go too, and this was strictly Lloyd George's personal decision. Lloyd George said later, "It might provoke further unpleasantness if we were to send out our representatives," since France already blamed British officials for stimulating anti-French feelings; the President's more impartial, purely American commission would be open to fewer suspicions of this kind. But was Lloyd George thinking also of the dangers of being bound by the commission's findings? There was not much doubt as to what the commission would discover about Syrian attitudes to the French; in view of the later complete disregard for the King-Crane Commission's report, certainly such a suspicion is not unfounded. See Maj. Gen. Sir C. E. Callwell, *Field-Marshal Sir Henry Wilson, Bart., G.C.B., D.S.O., His Life and Diaries* (N.Y., 1927), II, pp. 193–94, in which Wilson claimed support of Milner and Balfour in favoring British commissioners; Lloyd George, *Memoirs of the Peace Conference* (New Haven, Conn., 1939) II, p. 697 (quoted). Howard, *King-Crane*, pp. 74–83, does not treat Lloyd George's motives; Nevakivi, *Britain, France and the Arab Middle East*, p. 160, believes Lloyd George was attempting to meet France halfway because Clemenceau threatened to associate no longer with Britain in that part of the world.

tion. Lloyd George had little confidence in the ability of his Foreign Office personnel, and certainly not in Curzon, whom he had refused to take to Paris despite the urging of one as influential as General Smuts.[83] Balfour was in Paris, but Balfour was not a man to exercise great influence or strong control. Acting from irritation and acting in secrecy, the Prime Minister had created an incredible tangle. France reacted as she might have been expected to react. Conscious of the British desire to obliterate what she regarded as her just claims in Syria, aware of the pressure of French public opinion on these and other matters, the French government could not afford, as it did not desire, to be moved. As André Tardieu, member of the French delegation and staunch supporter of Clemenceau, put it to the Earl of Derby, Ambassador to France, in early June, "Whenever there was a question of asking for certain territories to be given to the French the answer given was that that was impossible as it was Arab property that was being dealt with and we must keep faith with them. Tardieu pointed out," continued Derby, "that while this argument held good when it was a question of giving up territory to the French it apparently was non-existent when it was a question of giving Mosul to the English." In any case, the issue could not be raised again until Clemenceau had quieted down—and, Tardieu might have added, Lloyd George as well.[84]

Yet this all occurred in a vacuum, in a sense, for London was still unaware of what Lloyd George had done until early June, and then only by rumor. It was not until the 12th, in fact, that Curzon was told by telephone about the whole business, and it was clear that the Prime Minister was still annoyed about the fact that neither he nor Clemenceau had been informed of the negotiations on the "Mosul Oil Works."[85] Now began a determined search, both in London and in Paris, to find out exactly

---

[83] Smuts to Lloyd George, 3 December 1918, Hancock and van der Poel, *op. cit.*, IV, pp. 24–25.
[84] Derby memorandum, 2 June 1919, *DBFP*, IV, pp. 1275–76.
[85] Young minute, 7 June, Kidston minute, 11 June 1919, *FO* 371/4209;

what had happened. As George Clerk of the Foreign Office re-
constructed events, oil discussions had begun, on French initiation, early in January (according to Long, however, 17 December), but Curzon, supported by another interdepartmental
group, had objected to discussions until the conference decided
the future of the areas involved. Britain could indicate general
willingness to bargain, so as to avoid French enlistment of
American aid, but that was all.

In February a different group altogether had discussed the
question in Paris, and as a result Cadman asked Balfour (3 February) for permission to tell France she could have 20 to 30
per cent of the oil in return for pipe-line facilities. Balfour
approved the minute. Cadman had not acted immediately but
had told E. Weakley (who had been commercial attaché in
Constantinople from 1897 to 1914, and was now responsible
for Foreign Office liaison with the Petroleum Executive and
the Foreign Office representative on the committee working
on the Shell negotiations) that no details had been discussed
with the French. On 15 March, however, the Petroleum Executive had sent over a draft of the Long-Bérenger agreement, and
private correspondence showed that Cadman was convinced
he had the approval of all concerned departments. Long said
that Balfour had approved the agreement in Paris, furthermore.
On 8 May, the Cabinet had approved the outline of the Shell
agreement, and with that problem out of the way the Long-
Bérenger agreement had been officially confirmed to the French
Ambassador on 16 May.[86]

The history of the oil negotiations was somewhat clarified,
but this did little to explain the present situation. The Petroleum
Executive, for example, was anxious to show the Americans

---

minute on telephone conversation, 12 June 1919 (quoted), *Lloyd
George Papers*, F/12/25.

[86] Clerk private to C. Kerr (private secretary to Prime Minister), 17
June 1919, *DBFP*, IV, pp. 1092–95; Long's correction is in Long to
Prime Minister, 4 November 1919, *Lloyd George Papers*, F/33/2/82.

the agreement (Standard Oil had asked about Rumania, also covered by Long-Bérenger), but it seemed that the Prime Minister had canceled what the Foreign Office had ratified. Could the Foreign Office please explain?[87] Only Lloyd George could answer that, and from Wales he replied simply that he had been surprised to hear of the agreement of which he should have been informed earlier; no such negotiation should have been concluded until the boundaries had been settled. The agreement had put Britain directly into French hands; Britain would have to have, now and in the future, direct access to the Mediterranean. Finally, agreements with the French should not be confused with negotiations in which private companies were concerned.[88]

But Lloyd George said nothing about the December 1918 agreement with Clemenceau, references to which were puzzling to all concerned. The agreement had been withdrawn, but what had the agreement been?[89] Lloyd George did not answer the question then, and his later record was not very much more satisfactory:

When Clemenceau came to London after the War I drove with him to the French Embassy. . . . After we reached the Embassy he asked me what it was I specially wanted from the French. I instantly replied that I wanted Mosul attached to Irak, and Palestine from Dan to Beersheba under British control. Without any hesitation he agreed. Although the agreement was not reduced into writing, he adhered to it honourably in subsequent negotiations.[90]

[87] Petroleum Executive to F.O., 2 July, enclosed in Curzon to Balfour, 4 July 1919, *DBFP*, IV, pp. 1097–98; F.O. memorandum, 4 July 1919, *Lloyd George Papers*, F/12/25, shows the F.O. was equally in the dark; nor did the Paris delegation have the necessary information: Kerr to E. Drummond, 21 May 1919, and minutes, *FO* 608/102.

[88] Lloyd George to Davies, 10 July, Davies to Curzon, 11 July 1919, *Lloyd George Papers*, F/12/25.

[89] Cadman to Davies, 24 July 1919, *ibid.*, F/33/2/66.

[90] Lloyd George, *Peace Conference*, II, p. 673; quoted in Nevakivi, *Britain, France and the Arab Middle East*, p. 91; see also Zeine, *Struggle*, pp. 55–56.

Not only was the agreement not "reduced into writing," but neither the Foreign Office nor the India Office nor the Mesopotamian administration was informed of this most important understanding. It was not the way to run a foreign policy, and months of confusion on both oil and Mosul resulted. But now, in May 1919, not only was the Lloyd George-Clemenceau agreement inoperable, apparently, but the Long-Bérenger agreement was similarly canceled. The future of Iraqi oil, like the future of Mosul, remained uncertain. Arnold Wilson was able to see to it that no private company established a firm foothold, but Britain became involved in rather serious negotiations with the United States over the resulting protests from American oil interests.[91] Wilson's policy remained firm throughout 1919, however; no action would be taken that would embarrass the future administration of the country until that administration was established.

7

If the many major problems of the Paris conference—League of Nations, European frontiers, reparations—insured that little attention could be given to the Ottoman Empire, the issues of oil and Mosul and the Sykes-Picot Agreement insured that such attention as was given produced nothing resembling a peace settlement. When the Versailles Treaty was signed, Faisal was still in Damascus, British troops were in Syria and Mosul, and the administration of Iraq was developing, or attempting to develop, along the lines suggested by Arnold Wilson. Wilson had argued strenuously for his views, and his influence was one further factor contributing to the indecision. India had little to say as such in these negotiations, although the India Office through Hirtzel had had a substantial role to play. India's voice on Mesopotamia had been relatively quiet for some time, in fact since London had assumed direct control. Arnold Wilson, and

91 See below, p. 352.

to some extent Sir Percy Cox in Teheran, were fully qualified
to stand in for what had been India's views; gradually, the
earlier London-India controversy had become a London-
Baghdad controversy.

This is not to say that India's voice went unheard in Paris,
though it was audible on the proposed general settlement with
Turkey rather than the Arab question. India had been involved
in the latter, but when India lost control of Iraq the original
motive for concern with Britain's Arab policy—Indian Muslim
feeling—once again became the dominant concern governing
attitudes toward the Middle East. It was easy to dismiss the
many Indian Muslim memorials to the government concerning
Turkey, as did Toynbee: "... I think we can take them calmly.
The danger-point was the outbreak of war with Turkey. Since
then the Moslems have let us fight her four years and beat her.
They will hardly take risks on her behalf now that her army is
broken and her prestige gone," he wrote in December 1918.[92]

Toynbee was wrong, for in the days following the end of
the war concern for Turkey—and above all for the Caliphate—
became a feature of the Indian nationalist movement and was
a prime factor in that most rare phenomenon, Hindu-Muslim
cooperation, which took the form of the "Khilafat" movement,[93] and which absorbed Montagu's and India's energies
throughout the Paris conference, in an attempt to exert sympathetic influence in any final settlement with Turkey. But Paris
produced no such settlement. In the Council of Four on 25
June Lloyd George had indeed appealed for a decision, since
the President was on the point of departure for the United

---

[92] Toynbee minute, 14 December 1918 (on memorial from Edinburgh Islamic Society), *FO* 371/3419.

[93] See, among other works, K. K. Aziz, *The Making of Pakistan: A
Study in Nationalism* (London, 1967), pp. 111–15; Ram Gopal, *Indian
Muslims: A Political History (1858–1947)* (N.Y., 1959), pp. 122–44;
R. P. Masani, *Britain in India: An Account of British Rule in the Indian
Subcontinent* (Bombay, 1960), pp. 120–25; O'Dwyer, *op. cit.*, pp. 264ff;
and Hugh Tinker, "India in the First World War and After," *Journal
of Contemporary History*, 3 (October 1968), 89–107.

States (he left immediately after the signing of the Versailles Treaty), and it hardly seemed reasonable to remain in a state of war with Turkey until his return. President Wilson agreed and suggested that perhaps Syria, Mesopotamia, and Armenia could be amputated and the treaty could provide that Turkey would accept any final disposition made of them by the Allies, with Allied troops to remain in these areas until the final settlement. Turkey, however, had submitted its own proposal for Turkish reconstruction, and it was clear that the treaty would require more discussion. On the 27th the Council agreed to suspend consideration until it could be ascertained whether the United States would be willing to assume a share of mandatory responsibility for Turkey. It was an indefinite postponement.[94]

In mid-1919 the Paris conference was over—and for Turkey and the Arab world there was no peace. Very little was clear: mandates—but where, and under what powers? France in Syria —but how much territory, how much authority? And what, after all, would be left to the Arabs? Whatever the rights and wrongs of the various departmental and individual positions presented in the period between the armistice and mid-1919, there can be no question that uncertainty about the future was a most unsettling factor in the Middle East. Many elements had contributed to the failure to reach a settlement, and the most important has not been considered here: the enormous difficulties of the European settlement in itself. But particular Middle Eastern considerations played a role. Not the least of these was Britain's continued pressure on France to abjure the Sykes-Picot Agreement while at the same time not only not offering to yield Mesopotamia but attempting to add Mosul to it, or so it seemed to France. Whatever the justice of France's Syrian claims, there was considerable justice in her conclusions on the meaning of British policy. Britain did wish to keep control of Mesopotamia and Arabia; she did not want Syria, if access to

[94] Council of Four, 25 and 27 June, Ottoman delegation note, 23 June 1919, *U.S. For. Rel., Paris*, VI, pp. 675, 691–94, 729.

the Mediterranean could be secured in pipe lines and communications, but she did wish to sever Palestine from the
French sphere. If France could be persuaded to abandon Syria,
no single British delegate would have had regrets.

Britain's position, finally, was firmly grounded on appeals
to self-determination and promises made to the Arabs; and for
many, such convictions were real and meaningful. It was ra-
tionalization, nevertheless. It was also British, not Indian, ration-
alization. India had really been removed from all but expression
of interest in the general treaty with Turkey or such special
details as pilgrimage or Caliphate. But India had left an important legacy in Mesopotamia, and the administration there,
despite all denials to the contrary, was based on Indian methods,
or at the very least the Indian concept of good government for
the people and by the wisdom of the governors, and this as eco-
nomically as possible in normal conditions. India itself had lost
control over Mesopotamia, but dual control was perpetuated
through the India Office's capacity to support Baghdad and
Arnold Wilson as a separate center of policy-making. This fact
was not really visible, except in individual instances of detail,
so long as the Paris conference had been unable to deal with the
precise nature of the government and future of Iraq. When
the conference was over, nothing was left to be done but to
press ahead as planned. Wilson in Baghdad, and Allenby in
Damascus, were the men of the hour.

# VII

## Trials and Errors, 1919

For forms of government let fools contest,
What'er is best administered is best.

Sir Michael O'Dwyer, INDIA AS I KNEW IT, 1885–1925

The failure of the Paris conference to resolve the contradictions and confusions of Allied promises was not surprising under the circumstances. Indeed, it should be put to the credit of the conference that it had agreed, seemingly, on the principles of mandatory supervision and consultation of the population through a commission of inquiry, however limited the membership of that commission. The conference technically remained in being in the summer of 1919, but in place of the heads of state there remained only subordinate delegates and ambassadors; until a conference of representatives with powers of commitment could reassemble to consider the King-Crane Commission's report, or the Middle East in general, and until a decision on American participation in a mandate system was forthcoming, Britain had to administer the area under its control as best it could.

The state of uncertainty, although a grave handicap, was hardly the sole difficulty. While Britain retained practical control, delegating powers to Faisal in inner Syria, negotiations between Faisal and the French had resulted only in tension and bitterness, and much the same could be said for Anglo-French discussions of Syria and Mosul. Furthermore, there was still no unified control of British policy; London remained a poorly informed arbiter between Allenby and Cairo on the one hand and Arnold Wilson and Baghdad on the other. Finally, Mesopotamian conditions depended largely upon British relations with Arab leaders, and these relations in turn depended upon Syria. But the question of Syria, and its solution, required, ultimately, the existence of mutual trust between Husain and Faisal and the British government—and of the various ways in which this trust was undermined none was more important than Britain's failure, from the standpoint of the Hijaz, to deal with the threat of Ibn Sa'ud.

1

The end of the war left Ibn Sa'ud a British ally, supplied with guns and money—though nothing equivalent to the aid furnished Husain—but without a British advisor or representative. Philby had been sent on leave and discussion of a possible replacement had come to nothing. But the end of the war had little significance in Arabia, particularly in the still unsettled Khurma dispute. As Colonel C. E. Wilson in Jidda reported the situation in December 1918, the tension was so great that Britain had only two choices: pressure Ibn Sa'ud to withdraw, which would imply some sort of Arabian suzerainty for Husain, or let the two rulers fight it out, which would lead to chaos. If Ibn Sa'ud were not deterred, Husain would be forced to put all his forces into the field; and if he lost, Ibn Sa'ud would, at the very least, be in Ta'if, only 40 miles from Mecca.[1]

The problem proved more than academic when Husain reported a Wahhabi advance; the information appeared so defi-

[1] C. E. Wilson to Wingate, 4 December 1918, *FO* 371/4144; Wingate telegram to Balfour, 10 December 1918, with Hirtzel and Shuckburgh minutes, *L/P&S/10*, 2182/13, no. 5547/18.

nite that Baghdad was ordered to stop Ibn Sa'ud's subsidy if he did not withdraw from west of Khurma. But Baghdad questioned the order altogether, based as it was on Husain's word alone. Arnold Wilson was willing to send an officer, Captain N. N. E. Bray, but would order him to deliver the ultimatum only if this seemed justified by the situation on his arrival. While Wilson was preparing to dispatch Bray, Faisal was asking for tanks from the War Office on Husain's behalf, with the obvious objective of Khurma in mind; as George Kidston in the Foreign Office noted, ". . . unless the Govt. of India supply Ibn Saud with poison gas or some other more modern death machine the provision of tanks ought to be effective."[2]

India had no such intention, fully realizing that Husain was the favored rival. Denys Bray, now Joint Secretary in the Indian Foreign Department (and soon to be sole Secretary), minuted in Delhi, ". . . our own interest and the interest of a vast majority of people weighs the scale overwhelmingly on the side of the Sheriff, whatever the rights in Khurma itself may be. It is this aspect of the case which Baghdad seems hardly to grasp in its entirety." India, he added, could only look on in any case.[3]

Bray's note shows how isolated Baghdad really was—but India's attitude was rather lost sight of in the process of filtration through the India Office, bound as it was to support Wilson, and the Foreign Office, where Husain's partisans were strongest. It made no difference, minuted Lawrence at the end of the year, what the loyalty of Khurma's population actually was: Khurma was a base of operations against the Hijaz in Saudi hands; surely England would object to a French-owned Dover even if Dover's population were French.[4] To some, the prob-

[2] SSI telegram to Wilson, 13 December 1918, *ibid.*; Wilson telegram to SSI, 27 December 1918, *FO* 371/4144; W.O. to F.O., 28 December 1918, with 6 January 1919 minute by Kidston (quoted), *FO* 371/3390.

[3] D. Bray minute, 30 December 1918, *India Sec. E.* June 1920, 1–152.

[4] Undated Lawrence minute (but 31 December 1918 or 1 January 1919), *FO* 371/3390.

lem could be solved if there was less attention paid to Saudi-Hashimite rivalry and more to differences between Lawrence and Philby, Cairo and Baghdad, War Office and India Office. As Kidston minuted, the War Office was in the process of supplying up-to-date military material to Husain to match the rifles given Ibn Sa'ud by the India Office. Robert Cecil agreed: "Unquestionably we should support Hussein. The I.O. are very obstinate."[5]

In the India Office, opinion was divided, as Wilson's objections forced reconsideration of the Bray mission. Shuckburgh would send the ultimatum to the Amir but insist only that he not be active west of Khurma; the town itself need not be evacuated. This would be a time-saving compromise, and, if fighting broke out anyway, past history showed that such clashes did not tend to be conclusive. Grant, fresh from India, urged that Britain should stand aloof and not identify with either party; the area should work out its own future; it might be argued that such a policy would diminish Britain's influence, but Britain's near presence in the Red Sea and the Gulf would permit her voice to be heard if and when necessary—a good representation of the traditional Indian viewpoint. Hirtzel once again saw somewhat further. He recognized that if Husain fell as a result of nonintervention Britain could be accused of responsibility, having urged revolt upon him and then left him so weakened as to fall victim to the Wahhabis. Hirtzel therefore wished Ibn Sa'ud's subsidy to be cut. Montagu, with the deciding vote, leaned toward Grant's nonintervention; Husain was not likely to see a simple ultimatum to the Amir as sufficient intervention in his own favor.[6]

On 14 January the interdepartmental group met under Curzon to consider the conflict, but could agree only that Cairo

[5] Kidston minute, 1 January 1919, and undated Cecil minute (quoted), *ibid.*

[6] Shuckburgh memorandum (B.308) and Grant and Hirtzel minutes, 7 January, and Montagu minute, 8 January 1919, *L/P&S/10*, 2182/13, no. 10/19.

and Baghdad would be asked to describe the current situation once again. In the meantime Curzon decided—on the next day, without again consulting the committee—that the ultimatum which Arnold Wilson had been told to send to Ibn Saʻud would be canceled for the time being, although it might have to be reconsidered if the Hijaz was further threatened. This meant, also for the time being, that Captain Bray's trip was unnecessary.[7] Almost by default, the policy had become nonintervention in the Arabian interior.

Disagreement continued on Ibn Saʻud's subsidy (£5,000 per month from January 1917), for Cairo insisted that it had to be stopped. It was absurd, telegraphed Sir Milne Cheetham, the Acting High Commissioner, that Husain claimed to be spending £12,000 per month for defense against a threat also subsidized from British revenues. Without further information, however, the most London could sanction was a message to both Husain and Ibn Saʻud that while Britain stood ready to adjudicate their quarrel, it had no intention of interfering, beyond furnishing aid "short of provision of troops" to Husain if the Amir moved further against the Hijaz.[8]

Cheetham was willing to send the King this message, but he wished C. E. Wilson to carry it personally to soften the blow when Husain learned that nothing would be done about Khurma. A day later Cheetham reported that Arnold Wilson, then in Cairo, recommended that Ibn Saʻud's subsidy—for which authorization had expired—not be renewed, although possibly some smaller figure might be given. The explanation would be, simply, that the subsidy had been paid for the war, and the war was over. Cheetham wished that Husain be told of the stoppage of Ibn Saʻud's money before the Foreign Office's last message was handed to him; obviously he wished to ease the impression

----

[7] I.D.C.E. 3rd minutes, 14 January, and F.O. telegram to Wingate, 17 January 1919, *FO* 371/4144.
[8] Cheetham telegram to F.O., 17 February, and F.O. telegram to Cheetham (quoted), 26 February, W.O. to F.O., 5 February 1919, *ibid.*

that message would convey. Although Cheetham's view was to be expected, it was a curious reversal of attitude for Arnold Wilson.[9]

Philby was in London and quite willing to speak his mind on Arnold Wilson's suggestion. Ibn Sa'ud, he said, would see through all talk of war's end and demobilization and the like and would fall back on his own resources. The backbone of the Amir's strength was the Ikhwan, or Wahhabi brotherhood, and Arnold Wilson asked the impossible when he suggested Ibn Sa'ud be persuaded to restrain them; Philby obviously had seen that ending the subsidy would also end any hold Britain had on Ibn Sa'ud. The only chance now, wrote Philby, was a meeting, perhaps of T. E. Lawrence and Faisal with himself, to talk these things out; Philby was on a year's leave, but he would happily put his services at the government's disposal for such a project.[10]

Philby's suggestion was not discarded out of hand, for it was now clear that the Foreign Office's last suggestion of identical messages to the two rulers had been received with scorn in Cairo. Cheetham had temporized in his reply, but General Clayton expressed himself very plainly on 4 March. The proposed messages, he advised London, were only "perpetuations of previous messages which were obviously of no effect or present necessity would not have arisen." Commitment to any international boundaries in Arabia would be dangerous. The Foreign Office wanted the same message to go to both rulers, and the message said plainly that Britain would not send troops to aid Husain. What then would Britain actually do? Far better, he concluded, to send no message at all.[11]

[9] Cheetham telegrams to F.O., 1 and 2 March, with Kidston minute of 4 March 1919, *ibid.*

[10] Shuckburgh minute (on discussions with Philby), 7 March, on Cheetham's telegram of 2 March, Philby to Lt. E. H. Jones (Secretary to I.D.C.E.), 2 March 1919 *L/P&S/10*, 2182/13, nos. 1254 and 1422/19; Philby to F.O., 2 March 1919, *FO* 371/4144.

[11] Clayton telegram to F.O., 4 March 1919, *ibid.*

Philby alone favored intervention through mediation to the extent of a boundary commission, but he had the advantage of being in London. As he pointed out in a memorandum of 6 March, there were three alternatives. One, nonintervention, had been favored by the interdepartmental committee. The second, a boundary commission, was Philby's choice and had once been Arnold Wilson's. The third, stopping Ibn Sa'ud's subsidy, was now suggested by Wilson. Philby was at a loss to explain Wilson's change of heart, but he surmised that Wilson was motivated by financial considerations, his fear of the possible Ikhwan danger to Iraq, and London's failure to consult him on nonintervention. Yet Wilson's policy had been rejected by the committee, and Philby could only add that £60,000 a year was not overmuch for a hold on Ibn Sa'ud. Philby did his best to appear reasonable, but obviously he was trying to demonstrate the serious flaws in a logic that would prompt a message to Ibn Sa'ud asking him to restrain his followers and at the same time informing him that his subsidy was stopped. All Philby asked was that the committee's decision would be adhered to and the two sides be left to fight out their conflict. If necessary, something might be done to protect the Hijaz proper—Philby offered no suggestions, for his heart was hardly in this remark—but Cairo would still be well advised to do everything possible to obtain the King's sanction of a boundary commission.[12]

The committee was in a quandary, from which it escaped through compromise. After its meeting of the 10th, Baghdad and Cairo were told that in deference to Cairo a stronger statement of support for Husain would be made. Ibn Sa'ud, on the other hand, would be informed that expansion beyond Khurma would be ill advised, for Britain was bound to defend the Hijaz, and the subsidy would be halved. These messages were ordered

[12] Philby memorandum, 6 March 1919, L/P&S/10, 2182/13, no. 1308/19. Ibn Sa'ud soon requested such a commission himself: Baghdad telegram to SSI, 26 March 1919, FO 608/92.

sent, and Husain was at least temporarily relieved when he received his in mid-April. By the end of the month, he was again threatening resignation, this time over money. He needed, he complained, £100,000 per month, a large sum, but less than the £120,000 he had demanded in December as compensation for Basra's occupation, said Cairo. The Treasury, rising to heights of magnanimity, agreed only to continue his subsidy at its current reduced rate of £75,000, and that only through September. By November it was to be cut to £25,000.[13]

There was no guarantee that cash would save Khurma or Husain's increasingly weak position. In late May Allenby cabled that Husain was again on the point of leaving the throne for lack of British aid. Allenby appealed for a peremptory demand to Ibn Sa'ud for withdrawal—he was reported to be on the move again—and, if he failed to comply, total stoppage of the subsidy.[14] The only new aspect to this appeal was that it came from Allenby, not Wingate or Cheetham or Clayton, and had the support of the War Office. Allenby's opinion carried considerable weight, for he was now "Special" High Commissioner of Egypt—Wingate had become embroiled in a controversy over the current and future policy to be pursued in Egypt and had not been allowed to return to Cairo after his departure in January 1919, although he technically remained High Commissioner until Allenby formally replaced him in October.[15] The Foreign Office was inclined to give in, although they were no clearer on how Ibn Sa'ud was to be evicted if he really took Mecca. Curzon, however, was working behind the scenes and managed to persuade the War Office to reverse its tentative

[13] F.O. telegram to Cheetham, 12 March, Allenby telegram to F.O., 21 April, FO 371/4145; SSI telegram to Wilson, 13 March, and Philby to Jones, 14 March 1919, L/P&S/10, 2182/13, no. 1308/19; Allenby telegram to F.O., 29 April 1919, and Wingate to Balfour, 19 December 1918, F.O. to Treasury, 6 June, Treasury to F.O., 23 August, 18 September, 12 November, and 8 December 1919, FO 371/4189.

[14] Allenby telegram to F.O., 27 May 1919, FO 608/80.

[15] Wingate, *Wingate*, p. 244.

approval to send off half a dozen tanks, for Curzon had the not illogical view that the French would be likely to think "Syria" and not "Khurma" when they heard of the armor.[16]

Such discussions were interesting but increasingly unrelated to Arabian reality. In late May it was reported that fighting had actually occurred some 45 miles east of Ta'if, and the Hashimite forces under 'Abdullah had been soundly defeated. If, as the signs seemed to indicate, the road to Ta'if and Mecca was open, a crisis had truly arisen.[17]

2

For once, the committee acted with speed and decision. On 30 May Baghdad was told to inform Ibn Sa'ud at once and by the fastest means that further operations would forfeit both British favor and subsidy. If he did not withdraw from Khurma and the Hijaz, his attitude would be regarded as definitely hostile and he would forfeit all advantages of the 1915 Anglo-Saudi treaty—a threat, however nicely phrased, of unilateral abrogation.[18] Within a few days, Allenby was further told that the Foreign Office was recommending the dispatch of T.E. Lawrence to aid Husain.[19] This was a valuable suggestion, except for the small detail that Lawrence had disappeared (he was unearthed in Crete in mid-June),[20] but the energy displayed was

[16] W.O. telegram to G.O.C., Egypt, 22 May, Kidston minute, 29 May 1919, *FO* 371/4145.

[17] Allenby telegrams to F.O., 27 and 28 May 1919, *ibid.* 'Abdullah, in his *Memoirs* (N.Y., 1950), p. 183, gives 7,000 Wahhabi dead; "This seems a very high estimate," remarked editor Philip Graves (n. 1).

[18] SSI telegram to Wilson, 30 May 1919 (drafted by Shuckburgh, approved for committee by Curzon), *L/P&S/10*, 2182/13, no. 2891/19.

[19] F.O. (Kidston) private telegram to Allenby, 5 June 1919, *FO* 371/4146.

[20] Allenby telegram to F.O., 6 June, F.O. telegram to Allenby, 7 June, British Consul, Canea, Crete, telegram to Allenby, 22 June 1919, *FO* 141/453.

enough to prompt a chill wind from the India Office. The India Office complained that it had always understood that the decision had been no troops—for troops, and a supply of airplanes, had all been proposed in the heat of the moment.[21]

It was up to Allenby to deal with the immediate crisis. In this he was seriously handicapped, for the one step which might really be helpful, that of advising Faisal to leave Damascus and return to help his father and brothers in the Hijaz, was impossible; Faisal would be very likely to misinterpret such advice considering the state of his negotiations with the French. Allenby, searching for expedients, suggested instead that Ibn Rashid might be loosed against Ibn Sa'ud. This the India Office viewed with alarm, although it was unlikely that Ibn Rashid could be brought in in time to affect the present crisis. The India Office's pressure was enough to modify the Rashidi project sufficiently so that Baghdad was told only that Britain might pay a small subsidy to Ibn Rashid (£500 per month) for security of the pilgrim traffic, but that such an offer should await the outcome of a new Philby mission to Ibn Sa'ud.[22]

Philby became involved because events had moved quickly in the Hijaz. C. E. Wilson had reported that Mecca was in a state of great alarm, and nothing stood in Ibn Sa'ud's way. Britain would have to intervene, hopefully with planes. Even aside from the question of military aid to Husain, there were some 11,500 Indian pilgrims whose safety would have to be considered.[23] It was an alarming situation, and while there was not much sympathy for Husain himself, British prestige was involved. As Robert Vansittart of the Foreign Office's Paris dele-

[21] I.O. to F.O., 5 June 1919, FO 371/4146.
[22] Allenby telegram to F.O., 1 June 1919, ibid., and 8 June, with Shuckburgh, Hirtzel, and Holderness minutes; SSI telegram to Wilson, 19 June 1919; L/P&S/10, 4929/18, no. 3161/19; F.O. to I.O., draft, not sent, FO 371/4146.
[23] Allenby telegrams to F.O., 10 and 11 June 1919, L/P&S/10, 2182/13, no. 3252/19.

gation minuted, ". . . we shall look fools all over the East if our puppet is knocked off his perch as easily as this. . ." [24]

On 13 June the interdepartmental conference assembled with the news at hand that Turaba, 50 miles southwest of Khurma on the Khurma-Ta'if road (Ta'if lay another 75 miles further west) had fallen and Ta'if was threatened. It was agreed that no troops (except for Lawrence) would be sent in support of planes; the real question, however, was Britain's response if pilgrim refugees poured into Jidda closely pursued by Ibn Sa'ud's Wahhabis. Curzon was of the opinion that the Amir would hold his hand if he found the port defended by Britain, but Gertrude Bell, who knew something of Ibn Sa'ud, was less optimistic: he would find it hard to control his followers under such conditions. Montagu, seeing where the conversation was leading, argued that Muslim troops would rebel if sent to the Hijaz to fight on the behalf of a rebel against the legitimate Caliph. Wrong, said Curzon; they would be fighting heretical Wahhabis. No policy was agreeable to all those present, and the committee temporized: the Ministry of Shipping would be asked about space for refugees, Egypt about available troops, and India (again) about its views. It was understood, however, that the message ordered for Ibn Sa'ud had already been delivered, from the Red Sea, although there was no clear information on this score. [25]

But delay was no answer; Husain was hysterical, and the danger to Mecca seemed real enough. On 14 June Allenby reported that a reply had been received from Ibn Sa'ud: Turaba and Khurma were his, and he now asked Britain to live up to her signature on the Anglo-Saudi treaty. If Britain wished him to withdraw she would have to guarantee that Hijazi forces would not reoccupy the area before the case was decided. The Amir obviously intended to be respectful and cooperative, but he

[24] Vansittart minute on Allenby telegram of 10 June, *FO* 608/80.
[25] I.D.C.E. minutes, 13 June 1919, *L/P&S/10*, 2182/13, no. 3233/19.

would obey no peremptory orders. Britain would have to go further if its influence was to be decisive.[26] In considering the proper policy London had the continued advice of India. While Indian Muslim opinion might support defense of the holy places against the Wahhabis, advised the Viceroy, such defense would naturally give Indian Muslims (assuming Muslim troops were used) a large voice on the Caliphate—it was advice calculated to dissuade London from any such action. Baghdad, too, added its view: military aid would simply increase the Iraqi conviction that Husain was merely a British puppet. When the Ministry of Shipping added (as could be expected) that no ships were available for refugees, the confusion in London was approaching the level of confusion in the Hijaz.[27]

Arnold Wilson, interestingly, was now clearly in favor of allowing Husain to abdicate. This would, in the long run, facilitate Iraqi and Palestinian regimes acceptable to local populations and Allies alike. The delegation in Paris was unimpressed by this parochial viewpoint, and Crowe clearly had increasingly less sympathy for Wilson's changes of mind, since the Civil Commissioner had quite recently been willing to stop Ibn Sa'ud's subsidy: "Colonel Wilson never seems to adhere to any line of policy for more than a few months." Allenby was equally annoyed; nothing Britain might gain from the King's abdication ". . . can compensate for loss of prestige we shall incur by throwing over a friend in time of need." [28]

The only hopeful possibility at the moment was the fact that by 17 June both Ibn Sa'ud and 'Abdullah (but not necessarily

[26] Allenby telegrams to F.O., 14 June 1919 (2 of date, nos. 969–70), *ibid.*, no. 3298/19.

[27] Viceroy telegram to SSI, 15 June, Arnold Wilson telegram to SSI, 14 June, Ministry of Shipping to F.O., 17 June 1919, *ibid.*, nos. 3298 and 3340/19.

[28] Wilson telegram to SSI, 14 June, with Vansittart and Crowe (quoted) minutes, 19 and 24 June 1919, *FO* 608/80; Allenby telegram to F.O., 16 June 1919, *FO* 371/4146.

Husain) had indicated a possible willingness to submit to arbitration; Arnold Wilson had agreed to delegate Philby (still on leave) as his representative.[29] On the same day the interdepartmental conference met, with Philby in attendance, but Philby argued (in opposition to Allenby and to C. E. Wilson in Jidda) against a face-to-face meeting of the two rulers. There was a much better chance of persuading Ibn Saʿud to pull back, said Philby, if he himself were sent alone. He was optimistic that he could persuade the Amir to retreat from Turaba, which was admittedly in the Hijaz. As Montagu pointed out, however, the controversy would hardly be resolved if this meant acquiescence in Saudi possession of Khurma. It was decided that Philby would go to Arabia, but only to try to bring an end to the fighting as an essential preliminary to arbitration. T. E. Lawrence, for the time being, would be held in reserve (he still had not been found).[30]

Fortunately, it seemed within a few days that Philby's urgent mission might not be necessary, for Ibn Saʿud claimed (in a letter to Allenby) to have retreated to Najd. C. E. Wilson reported that the Saudis had not abandoned either Turaba or Khurma, but at least the advance had stopped, and the Amir had in fact acted in response to the message which had reached him and been acknowledged via Jidda. Just in case, Husain was asked to permit Philby's passage through Hijazi territory—an error, for the King absolutely refused, and Arnold Wilson used this opportunity to urge, not for the first time, that the mission be canceled.[31]

[29] Wilson telegram to SSI, 17 June 1919, *L/P&S/10*, 2182/13, no. 3340/19.

[30] I.D.C.E., 17 June; SSI telegram to Wilson, 19 June, with details worked out by a committee of Philby, Shuckburgh, Young, and Kidston, and amended by Curzon: *ibid.*; similar instructions in F.O. telegram to Allenby, 18 June 1919, *FO* 371/4146.

[31] Allenby telegrams to F.O., 23 and 26 June, Col. J. L. French (acting C.P.O., Cairo) telegram to F.O., 28 June, Wilson telegrams to SSI, 23 June and 8 July 1919, *L/P&S/10*, 2182/13, nos. 3566, 3650, 3671, 3736, and 3896/19.

No sooner had the pressure eased than there came indications that Ibn Saʻud intended making a pilgrimage to Mecca, a sure way to bring further fighting. Cairo insisted that Philby be sent to persuade the Amir to cancel any such plans, even though Husain might abdicate if forced to allow Philby to travel via Taʼif.[32] The King's abdication was undesirable, but he lost further friends by his adamance—"a pampered and querulous nuisance," said Curzon. Philby, in the end, was told to return to London from Cairo, and Husain was told simply that Britain did not propose to take further action in the matter since he had refused arbitration.[33] Actually, Husain had not formally rejected arbitration, but he had regarded Philby's mission as so damaging to his own prestige that he could only abdicate if it was insisted upon.[34]

Ibn Saʻud had temporarily saved the day for Husain by retreating, well aware that every test of strength had so far gone in his favor and not wishing to force a confrontation with Britain by moving on to Mecca and Jidda. There was no mission by Philby, and there was no arbitration; in fact, it seemed also as if there was no policy. London, wrote Arnold Wilson privately to Cox, seemed inclined only to let things drift,[35] but under the circumstances this was likely to work to Ibn Saʻud's advantage. Husain had been unable to recover Khurma and Turaba; his forces under ʻAbdullah had been defeated; and for all this he was inclined to blame Britain's failure to give him sufficient support. The problem of Najd-Hijaz relations was thus a major concern throughout the summer of 1919, and it

[32] Allenby telegram to FSI, 9 July 1919, *India Sec. E.* August 1920, 141–200.
[33] Curzon minute (no. 97529, quoted), 5 July, G.O.C., Egypt, telegram to D.M.I., 18 July, F.O. telegram to Allenby, 25 July 1919, *FO* 371/4146; SSI telegram to Wilson, 16 July 1919, *L/P&S/10*, 4931/16, no. 4036/19.
[34] Allenby telegram to FSI, 10 July 1919, *India Sec. E.* August 1920, 141–200.
[35] Wilson private to Cox, 14 August 1919, *Wilson Papers*, Add. Mss. 52455.

must have been a concern for Faisal in Syria as well as Husain in Mecca; an ally which would not give aid to the independent Hijaz might well be untrustworthy in a Syria assigned to France. Nor was this the only issue, for at the same time another controversy had arisen between Faisal's administration in Damascus and Arnold Wilson's in Baghdad, and to this controversy, as to negotiations for the future of Syria, the Saudi conflict was a discordant background.

3

The Arab nationalists associated with Faisal's army, particularly those of Iraqi background, wished to see constructed in Mesopotamia an Arab administration at least as powerful as that of Faisal in Damascus. They also wished to go home, a desire intensified by occasional friction between them and the native Syrians. By the end of January 1919, the officers had already petitioned British authorities in Syria for permission to return home; it was clear these men would require careful handling if they were not to be pushed into active hostility. As Young in London minuted, if officers like Nuri as-Sa'id and Ja'far Pasha (neither of whom had been named in the petition) did return and concluded that Britain was not living up to her pledges they would make trouble. He suggested that Cheetham be permitted to respond by saying that Britain would fulfill its promises, but only a noncommittal reply was returned to the petitioners, for the danger of vague statements had been learned. "We have generally found," minuted Kidston, "that such promises either conflict with something that has been promised to somebody else or that subsequent developments make it impossible to fulfill them." [36]

The obstacles to the officers' return included more than dan-

---

[36] Cheetham telegram to F.O., 31 January 1919, and Paris delegation minutes, *FO* 608/94; same telegram (but recorded as 1 February), with F.O. minutes (Kidston's of 6 February quoted), *FO* 371/4148.

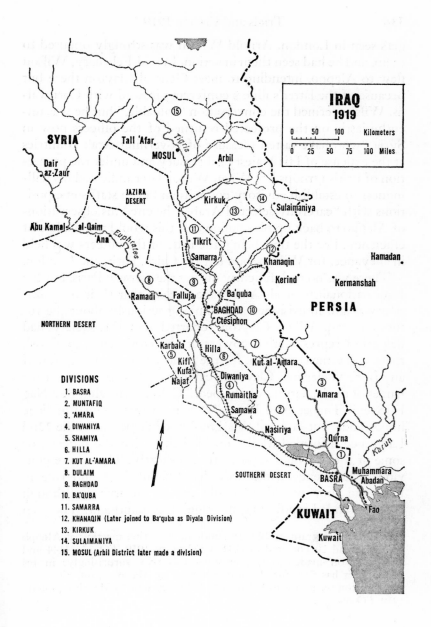

IRAQ
1919

0    50    100    Kilometers
0   25   50   75   100  Miles

SYRIA        Tall 'Afar.
                MOSUL        .Arbil
Dair
az-Zaur

JAZIRA
DESERT              Kirkuk.        ⑭
                           ⑬      .Sulaimaniya
Abu Kamal    al-Qaim
         'Ana              ⑪
                           .Tikrit
                     Samarra        ⑫              Hamadan .
                              Khanaqin
                        ⑧           Kerind°      °Kermanshah
                   Ramadi  Falluja   Ba'quba
NORTHERN DESERT         ⑨  ·BAGHDAD ⑩      PERSIA
                           Ctesiphon

                Karbala  Hilla
                   ⑤    ⑥      ⑦
DIVISIONS          Kifl      Kut al-Amara
                   Kufa
1. BASRA        Najaf  Diwaniya        ③
2. MUNTAFIQ            ④    'Amara
3. 'AMARA             Rumaitha
4. DIWANIYA          Samawa  ②
5. SHAMIYA            Nasiriya
6. HILLA                    Qurna
7. KUT AL-'AMARA                  ①
8. DULAIM
9. BAGHDAD       SOUTHERN DESERT  BASRA  Muhammara
10. BA'QUBA                           Abadan
11. SAMARRA
12. KHANAQIN (Later joined to Ba'quba as Diyala Division)   KUWAIT    °Fao
13. KIRKUK
14. SULAIMANIYA                    Kuwait
15. MOSUL (Arbil District later made a division)

gers seen in London. Arnold Wilson was strongly opposed to them, and he had seen them in action. In mid-February, Wilson flew to Aleppo, intending to meet General Clayton there but because of the latter's illness conferring instead with Cornwallis. Wilson termed the conversation "valuable," but he was unenthusiastic on the projected returned of the officers now in Syria "who have tasted pleasure of governing Arab countries at the expense of His Majesty's Treasury and under the protection of British troops." [37] When Wilson later indicated his willingness to establish advisory councils and even staff some positions with "carefully selected Arabs," he cited his observations of Aleppo to back up his opinion that this would mean a loss of efficiency. For the time being, the issue of the officers was held in abeyance, for Wilson soon left for Cairo, Paris, and London.

There was no real difficulty during the pause at Paris, but the Iraqi nationalists of al-'Ahd made it clear that their organization was still in existence and thinking seriously about the future of Iraq. When Clayton reported that the society had delegated representative powers at the conference to Faisal, there was some confusion, for the society was known to few if any British delegates. Clayton's cabled response to a request for names of the leaders hardly helped: "Colonel Mowlud Bey Nag El Sueidi Thabet Abd Elnur." [38] The matter seemed of little importance, but in April Faisal took the initiative. On the 22nd Lawrence informed Mallet on his behalf that the officers, or some of them, would want to return shortly. They were convinced, Lawrence continued, that 'Abdullah should rule in Iraq, and they would no doubt say so on arrival, although Faisal intended sending no message of commitment. The men

[37] Wilson telegrams to SSI, 18 (quoted; reporting meeting at Aleppo on 15th) and 20 (printed as B.317) February 1919, *FO* 371/4144 and 4148. Wilson made no reference to this trip, surprisingly, in his memoirs; it has therefore been overlooked by Marlowe, *op. cit.*

[38] Clayton telegrams to Balfour, 26 February and 10 March (quoted) 1919, *FO* 608/92.

could not be kept indefinitely in Syria, nor could they be kept silent; they had served loyally and were decidedly pro-British. Faisal only wished to know that the men would not be hindered and their views not be treated as seditious.[39] Faisal himself did not approach Britain directly; on the 23rd he left Paris, and on the 30th he landed in Beirut.

But Arnold Wilson was also in Paris and able to explain his attitude. He would not, he promised, take action, provided expression of the officers' views was made in private and not presented as Faisal's opinion. It was another of Wilson's jarring minutes:

I have no intention of repressing a popular movement nor of classing movements in favour of Abdullah as "seditious," but I hold that the people of the country have made their choice, district by district, in writing, and we cannot properly encourage nor officially countenance propaganda calculated to reverse their considered verdict.[40]

It was not only self-righteous, it was wrongheaded, for Wilson ignored both the nature of the "choice"—well known to those who had seen his instructions to his officers and Young's minute thereupon—and the influence of the Iraqis with Faisal. But Wilson had said he would not persecute the men if they behaved properly (by his definition) and were provided with proper credentials by British military authority; the Paris delegation passed the message that the officers could proceed.[41]

Once back in Baghdad Wilson changed his mind, deciding that his assent had been wrongly advised. Nuri as-Sa'id and some others were writing letters to announce their arrival, and the notables of Baghdad (identity unspecified, and later referred to as "he") objected that the return of Faisal's Iraqi supporters would appear to give the stamp of British approval to

[39] Lawrence for Mallet, 22 April 1919, *ibid*.
[40] Wilson note, 23 August 1919, *ibid*.
[41] Mallet to Curzon, 29 April 1919, *FO* 371/4145.

the movement for Arab unity under the Hashimites. Wilson concurred with his anonymous informants, adding that the officers, even though Iraqi, were now "totally out of sympathy with present inhabitants of Baghdad." [42] This impression had no doubt been gained by talks with several of them when he stopped over in Damascus on his return from Paris and was pushed strongly enough that for the time being no further steps were taken on this matter. [43]

A further difficulty was the Allied (more properly, American) King-Crane Commission, for Wilson was not only worried about its probable effect on local conditions but clear in his own mind that the Syrian Iraqis intended using its presence to make difficulties. The Commission, he reported on 30 May, was viewed in Iraq as a sign of Allied weakness and indecision. In Paris he had said that it was inexpedient but not dangerous, but he had changed his mind on this, too; by now Crowe was minuting that Wilson's opinions were "subject to somewhat violent fluctuations." But neither the delegation in Paris nor the Foreign Office really could say whether and when the Commission would arrive, and what it would do once in the Middle East. When it was decided on the 31st that it was definitely coming and would be American only, British officials worried that since the other Allies were not represented the Commission would be unable to decide which power would get which area. It could only make recommendations on the nature of the mandates, or else its mission would be simply to persuade the local populations to accept the inevitable. If the Commission merely reported that the Syrians opposed France and the Palestinian Arabs opposed Zionism, it would only create difficulties. Since Britain had already approved the inquiry in principle, it would

[42] Wilson telegram to SSI, 14 May 1919, *FO* 608/92.

[43] SSI telegram to Wilson, 15 May, Wilson telegram to SSI, 17 May 1919, *FO* 371/4145; Balfour telegram to Clayton, 2 May, I.O. to F.O., 26 May, Mallet minute, 2 June, Paris delegation to Curzon (advising no action), 6 June 1919, *FO* 608/92; Young, *op. cit.*, p. 286; Marlowe, *op. cit.*, p. 149.

be as impolitic to suggest cancellation now as it would be to suggest that the Commission not visit Iraq.[44]

Faisal must have had similar worries. He awaited the Commission in Syria, but he must have felt that if it visited Iraq, under Arnold Wilson's regime and without the presence of men like Nuri as-Sa'id and Ja'far, it might well carry away the wrong impression of Iraqi opinion. Faisal wrote to Allenby that Mesopotamian policy seemed to be alienating the population from the regime and that it was now time to end the military administration and fulfill the pledges of the joint declaration of 1918. An independent government might not be immediately possible, but Arab administrators should be appointed with British advisors. It was a moderate statement, too well written, really, for Young and Kidston were convinced that Lawrence's hand could be seen in its drafting.[45]

Faisal probably had in mind the fact that his own Iraqi officers were the most experienced candidates for administrative positions, but his letter did not produce the desired effective permission to return. The Foreign Office told the India Office in mid-June that no further delay was possible and that the officers must be allowed to proceed, but this instruction was seriously hampered by the qualification that General Clayton would confer with Wilson on each one, which of course gave Wilson veto power over any particular officer's return. Since Wilson was already blaming British officials in Syria for encouraging, or at least not discouraging, nationalist activity by the Iraqis, he was not likely to let his opinion of any individual be changed by the recommendations of those same British officials. The problem lost some of its urgency when Clayton reported on 20 June that the King-Crane Commission intended only quick visits to Jerusalem, Damascus, and Beirut and would

---

[44] Wilson telegram to SSI, 30 May, with Crowe minute, Balfour telegram to Allenby, 31 May, Forbes Adam undated minute (about 27 May 1919), *FO* 608/86.

[45] Clayton to F.O., 3 June 1919, and minutes, *FO* 371/4149; see also Nuri as-Sa'id to Lloyd George, 23 June 1919, *FO* 371/4181.

return to Constantinople in mid-July.[46] There was, of course, no assurance that the Commission would not wish to visit Iraq at a later date.

The fears of the Commission visit to Iraq were calmed for the moment, and nothing could be done further about the Iraqi officers. The principal problem, however, remained—the rise of nationalist activity in Iraq. Arnold Wilson tended to blame Faisal's Iraqis (and their British friends), but to Hirtzel the root of the trouble was closer to home. As he wrote privately to Curzon on 24 June (enclosing Wilson's complaint against the officers in Syria):

The propaganda originated with Feisal & Lawrence, & I am convinced that there will be no peace in the Middle East until Lawrence's malign influence is withdrawn. He is advocating & actively supporting a policy which is contrary to the policy of H.M.G. both in Syria & Mesopotamia, viz. a British or American mandate in the former, an Arab Amir in the latter; & he roams about Europe & Asia at his own sweet will, playing off one party against the other. Is it not possible to control him?[47]

The Foreign Office responded by cabling Clayton that Faisal's propaganda was causing alarm and that the India Office feared Clayton's juniors were encouraging it in the mistaken belief that Britain favored an uncontrolled Arab government in Iraq. The officers were to be instructed "to discourage the movement by all means in their power." [48]

The Foreign Office had backed the India Office and Arnold Wilson, and indeed such support was justified until Wilson was replaced or ordered to conform to a particular policy. But

[46] F.O. to I.O., 16 June 1919, *FO* 371/4146; Wilson private telegram to Hirtzel, 9 June 1919, *FO* 371/4149; I.O. to F.O., 19 June, and Clayton telegram to Balfour, 20 June 1919, *FO* 608/86.

[47] Hirtzel private to Curzon, with enclosure, 24 June 1919, *FO* 371/4149.

[48] F.O. telegram to Clayton, 24 June 1919, *FO* 371/4146; *DBFP*, IV, p. 296; partly quoted in Nevakivi, *Britain, France and the Arab Middle East*, p. 178.

in the Foreign Office second thoughts were beginning to find a hearing. In early July Wilson reported further propagandistic activities by Yasin Pasha al-Hashimi, Faisal's Chief of Staff, who had sent letters to Iraqi tribal chiefs announcing the impending arrival of the Commission and calling for canvassing of public opinion so as to insure a demand for a single, independent Arab nation with assistance, if needed, from a single power. The Foreign Office agreed that encouragement of the single state was ill advised, but so too was ignoring the Iraqi officers, who were spokesmen of an important element in Iraq who as yet had not had opportunity to express their views. Clayton should be permitted to advise them (as an answer to the unanswered petition) that the councils already established in Mesopotamia demonstrated British intent. When the mandate was actually given, a (British) commission would proceed to Mesopotamia to discuss the future form of government with the population. This statement, it was hoped, would remove any misconceptions.[49]

The India Office did not exactly object; after all, the idea of a commission, proposed some time ago by Cox, had already been approved in principle but had not been possible to carry out in practice. It was also true that the officers could not be ignored. Hirtzel was still worried about Lawrence's influence ("prompted by Col. Lawrence," he minuted beside a Foreign Office reference to Faisal's pan-Arab aspirations, which the officers shared), but like Shuckburgh he saw the need of winning their cooperation:

[49] Wilson telegram to SSI, 5 July 1919, *FO* 371/4149; F.O. to I.O., 8 July 1919, *L/P&S/10*, 4722/18, no. 3912/19. On the later career of Yasin Pasha and a number of other prominent Iraqis, see Stephen Hemsley Longrigg, *'Iraq 1900 to 1950: A Political, Social, and Economic History* (2nd ed., London, 1956); Ernest Main, *Iraq from Mandate to Independence* (London, 1935); Abid A. al-Marayati, *A Diplomatic History of Modern Iraq* (N.Y., 1961); and Majid Khadduri, *Independent Iraq, 1932–1958: A Study in Iraqi Politics* (2nd ed., London, 1960).

. . . for they are probably the best thing that Mesopotamia has produced yet & they are, I believe, many of them, well-educated men,
with western ideas. Whatever we may think of Pan-Arab aspirations, it is probably not an exaggeration to say that the success of
our régime in Mesopotamia depends upon our finding a proper
sphere for these men. Col. Wilson was quite of this opinion when
he was over here.

In a later minute, Hirtzel showed his awareness of Wilson's
true attitude; Wilson, he noted, had never faced up to the realization that an Arab state was necessary and inevitable and that
". . . the provincial and district councils are not an Arab State
—nor a state at all—but merely a British protectorate." [50]

Hirtzel had pointed this out in a private letter to Wilson
three months earlier, but Wilson answered by saying that sufficient native talent was not available in Iraq with which to form
a national government which would work (in his mind, Iraqi
government and Iraqi officers with Faisal were two separate
issues), and Britain had to fulfill its obligations to the local
population, by which he meant good government. Good government by Arabs meant, apparently, good government by
Arabs who were not associated with the movement for Arab
unity.[51] That Wilson was deliberately ignoring the officers in
order to preserve British control is an argument that cannot be
substantiated—but Wilson's regime was too parochial and paternalistic and too inclined to overlook the potency of postwar
Arab nationalism.

If there was any doubt about Wilson's position, it was removed in mid-July when Wilson had a chance to comment on
the petition from the Iraqi officers and the answer that had been
proposed. The signatories were "not now influential" in Iraq,

---

[50] Shuckburgh and Hirtzel (quoted) minutes, 10 and 11 July, on F.O.
to I.O., 8 July, and Hirtzel minute on Baghdad telegram to SSI, 9 July
1919, L/P&S/10, 4722/18, nos. 3912 and 4019/19.
[51] Hirtzel private to Wilson, 6 April, and Wilson private to Hirtzel,
8 July 1919, *Wilson Papers*, Add. Mss. 52455.

he commented; "They may compare to the Irish politicians in America graciously pleased to prefer to expound their territorial views on foreign soil." Wilson's contempt for the officers was not so great that he would let just any answer be returned to them. Rather, he advised that no answer should be sent, for it would only dignify their position, while a commission when Britain had the mandate implied a body with powers over the existing government, and that kind of promise would only add further difficulties. The officers were out of touch and wrong in their views of the situation in Iraq; if they wanted to know the truth, they were free to come to Mesopotamia to see for themselves (although Wilson said nothing about freedom to criticize what they saw).[52]

Even before Wilson's telegram, Hirtzel had offered further private advice on how to deal with Arab nationalism: ". . . to be frank, I do not feel that you are going the right way to work with it." Perhaps it was simply a case of badly drafted cables and the like (a thoroughly charitable suggestion), but "You appear to be trying, impossibly, to stem the tide instead of guide it into the channel that wd. suit you best." There was, in short, going to be an Arab state—"whether you like it or not, whether Mesopotamia wants it or not. . ." If the officers returned, took office, and resigned because they opposed British policies, Britain would have "another Egypt" on her hands—a reference to the serious problems caused by Egyptian nationalists in 1919. Building Mesopotamia into a model state under British control was simply a dead concept.[53]

But the chance of the officers reacting in such a way was remote, for Wilson was effectively keeping them out of Iraq by insisting on information on the political views of each prospec-

---

[52] SSI telegram to Wilson, 15 July, Wilson telegram to SSI, 19 July 1919, FO 371/4149.

[53] Hirtzel private to Wilson, 16 July, and answer in Wilson private to Hirtzel, 14 September 1919, Wilson Papers, Add. Mss. 52455.

tive returnee. Political officers in Syria and Cairo found this very hard to provide, for little was known of each Iraqi aside from the general nationalist sentiments held by all of them. London insisted that the regulation be upheld, however; it was undesirable to give official countenance to undesirable propaganda by facilitating the return of officers who might spread it. This was the sort of thing that drove T. E. Lawrence to distraction:

As they are all the men in Mesopotamia who had the courage to fight for their country, I regret that they are apparently going to be driven into opposition to our administration there. It is curious that men useful (indeed necessary) to Allenby in Syria should be "spreaders of undesirable propaganda" in Mesopotamia.[54]

Wilson would not have been convinced had this minute ever been passed to him (it was not), for he was even then experiencing the regrettable end of his one attempt to use an Arab administrator from Faisal's Iraqis.

Naji Bey as-Suwaidi, a Baghdadi of good family who had been a popular administrator in Najaf in the prewar regime and then served with Faisal, had returned to Iraq to accept a post from Wilson as Assistant to the Military Governor of Baghdad, Frank Balfour. According to Wilson, within a short time —too short a time—Naji Bey had submitted a proposal for municipal government in Baghdad. Wilson had given the proposal to a committee of four British officers for consideration and reported three days later that Naji Bey "finds the actual work of getting things going so onerous that I anticipate he will shortly resign." Three days later Naji Bey had indeed resigned and returned to Aleppo. Naji Bey claimed, according to Balfour, that he had resigned because his proposals had not been accepted, but in Balfour's own view his new subordinate had

[54] Col. French (Cairo) telegrams to F.O., 9 and 26 July, F.O. telegram to French, 17 July, Lawrence (Paris) minute, about 21–22 July 1919, *FO* 608/92.

made no effort to master his subject, had wasted much time on political projects, and was, in short, a failure.[55] Wilson in his report of the incident gave no sign that he regarded Naji Bey's resignation as any sort of disaster, but the affair made a very unfavorable impression in London. Hirtzel, who had done his best to defend Wilson and to guide him toward a more cooperative attitude, had warned of just such a result and now saw it all as a first-class misfortune, "which ought to have been avoided at almost any cost & I doubt if Col. Wilson appreciated the importance of it or indeed has the qualities necessary for dealing with people of this kind." Hirtzel's main conclusion: "It is becoming a matter of urgent necessity to get Sir P. Cox back to Mesopotamia as soon as possible." [56]

In the light of this experience, Wilson continued to raise objections to visits from Faisal's associates, as that discussed for Yasin Pasha when it was felt that his removal from Syria as a troublemaker was desirable. Wilson reported that Yasin Pasha was regarded in Baghdad as a dangerous fanatic who had in common with Wilson's informants (again unspecified) only the accident of Baghdadi birth. The visit would be satisfactory neither to Yasin Pasha himself nor to local opinion and should be discouraged. No government, said Wilson, not even a purely Arab one, could afford to employ a man of his caliber (Yasin Pasha was to be several times Finance Minister of Iraq and twice —1924 and 1935—Prime Minister). The answer to the whole difficulty was not visits by nationalist officers but for Britain to

<hr>

[55] Wilson telegram to SSI (quoted), 19 July 1919, *L/P&S/10*, 4722/ 18, no. 4208/19; Wilson telegrams to SSI, 24 and 28 July, Wilson to Judicial Secretary, Baghdad, 16 July (enclosing Naji Bey's proposals), Military Governor of Baghdad (F. C. Balfour) to Civil Commissioner, 22 July 1919, *L/P&S/11*, vol. 156, nos. 4312, 4491, 5446, and 5449/19. Naji Bey later told Philip Ireland (*op. cit.*, p. 190, n. 2) that he thought he had been invited to Mesopotamia to aid in the establishment of a national government. See also Birdwood, *Nuri*, p. 117; Wilson, *Mesopotamia*, has only a brief reference to the incident, p. 124.

[56] Hirtzel minute, 28 July, on Wilson telegram of 19 July 1919, *L/P&S/10*, 4722/18, no. 4208/19.

cut Husain's (and thus Faisal's) financial support and thus force reductions in his military establishment. Without Wilson's co-operation the visit would not work, and the Foreign Office was told that the India Office was not now prepared to force that cooperation.[57]

Obviously there was little chance of friendly association between Wilson and the Iraqi officers, and there was little point to discussion of either general personnel policy or individual cases until some major change took place. Such a change was not even being discussed in September 1919, although Hirtzel's minutes show that the idea of bringing Cox back from Teheran as soon as possible was in the air. But Wilson was fast losing friends in London, because of both his policy and his tendency to be rather annoying in the language of his official communications. There was still hope that the Mesopotamian situation could be eased, if only the problem of formal authority for the area could be resolved, if the Allies would agree among themselves on a treaty with Turkey and the formal distribution of mandates.

4

The signature of the Treaty of Versailles on 28 June and the disappearance of the principal negotiators from Paris left the future of the Middle East in confusion. The King-Crane Commission was proceeding to the area to assay opinion, but the Commission's authority, like its membership and itinerary, was most uncertain. Since the delegates awaited the Commission's report—and the even more important American decision

[57] Wilson telegram to SSI, 3 September 1919, *L/P&S/11*, vol. 159, no. 5464/19; Wilson telegram to SSI, 10 September, Hirtzel notes for Montagu, 7 and 15 September, SSI telegram to Wilson, 8 September 1919, *ibid.*, vol. 157, nos. 5501 and 5549/19; Weakley (F.O.) note for Young, 18 September 1919, *FO* 371/4150. See also Wilson telegram to SSI, 19 September 1919, on Yasin Pasha as leader of the Mesopotamian League, *L/P&S/10*, 4722/18, no. 5373/19.

on participation in mandatory responsibilities—it was not certain when discussion could resume on a Turkish treaty.[58] In the meantime, the Council of Five (the chief remaining delegates) might have worked upon the nature of the mandates, particularly those of class "A" (suitable for future independence), but France refused to discuss this problem until the areas themselves were allotted, and had gone to the extreme of neglecting to attend sessions on this subject. Article 22 of the Treaty of Versailles called for the provisional recognition of the independence of certain ex-Turkish areas subject to mandatory assistance, but obviously this clause was not going to be put into effect until an acceptable settlement among the powers was first arranged.[59]

The problem was aggravated by a growing press attack on British policy—on conflicting promises in the English press, and on Syrian policy in the French journals. *The Times* of 21 August carried a clear accusation of unwisdom, if not actual deceit, through the failure to inform the French of the Arab negotiations and the Arabs of the Sykes-Picot Agreement. Foreign Office officials in Paris were annoyed, and E. G. Forbes Adam (F. O.) wished to hint to *The Times* that printing inaccurate information was of little help, for the Sykes-Picot Agreement had been based upon the negotiations with Husain. In a sense he was correct, but so was Balfour: "It is rather dangerous to speak to the Times in this sense, unless we can reconcile our letters to Hussein of 1915 with the S.-P. agreement of 1916. *I cannot.* Can anyone else?" Mallet could only add that no docu-

---

[58] Drummond note to Balfour, 7 August (adding that the approaching French elections were also a factor), Milner private to Balfour, 8 August, H. Simon telegram to Milner, 4 August 1919, *FO* 608/152.

[59] Forbes Adam memorandum, 9 August, Vansittart memorandum, 11 August, *FO* 608/84, and C. J. B. Hurst memorandum, 22 August 1919, *FO* 608/152. Article 22 is quoted in Hurewitz, *op. cit.*, II, p. 62; this article served, as Hurewitz remarks, as the principal basis for later claims for independence of the mandated territories. Compare Vansittart, *op. cit.*, p. 245: "During the whole Conference I never heard anyone mention Article 22. . . ."

ment could be found which definitely proved that France had been told in so many words of what had been said to Husain, but that the Sykes-Picot terms showed French awareness of British commitments.[60]

Nobody had been told, but everybody knew. And it could be argued, as did T. E. Lawrence in *The Times* of 11 September, that there was no incompatibility between the various documents. This time it was the turn of the Foreign Office rather than the Paris delegation to comment; Young saw the article as self-justification on Lawrence's part, but Kidston pointed out that, while an unpardonable revelation from the official view, it might still do some good unofficially. Since Lawrence soon remarked that not only did he not consider himself a member of the British delegation any longer (Curzon hardly minded this, for he had never regarded him as a member), but also that he had written a number of articles (and could safely be assumed to be working on more), "T. E." might become more of a problem than a help.[61]

Meanwhile Balfour had turned his not inconsiderable reasoning powers to the Middle East situation. Clarity appeared to lie only in disregarding all the pledges and agreements and taking the League of Nations Covenant as a guide. But even Balfour was forced to admit that the inhabitants would have only "Hobson's choice": be they for or against France, the Syrians would have—France. In Palestine the inhabitants would

[60] Clipping of *The Times*, 21 August 1919, with Forbes Adam, Balfour (quoted), and Mallet minutes, *FO* 608/93; G. Grahame (Paris) to Curzon, 12 August 1919, *DBFP*, IV, pp. 349–51; see also Nevakivi, *Britain, France and the Arab Middle East*, p. 172, and Marlowe, *op. cit.*, pp. 162–67.

[61] *The Times*, 11 September 1919; clipping with Young, Kidston, and Curzon minutes, *FO* 371/4182. The letter is quoted in Weintraub, *op. cit.*, pp. 63–65; Lawrence—or *The Times*'s typesetter—erroneously gave the date of the Declaration to the Seven as 1917 rather than 1918, and it was easier to see no inconsistencies in a list of documents that failed to include the Balfour Declaration.

not be considered at all. To this the Foreign Secretary had no real objection: Zionism was "of far profounder import than the desires and prejudices of the 700,000 Arabs who now inhabit that ancient land." Such a policy was the larger justice, but how could it be harmonized with the joint declaration of 1918, or even the instructions to the King-Crane Commission? Only a compromise could serve. Syria and Mesopotamia would conform to Sykes-Picot spheres, but "Red" and "Blue" areas would lose their special distinctions and be absorbed into "A" and "B"; the Jews would have a national home in Palestine; France would take Alexandretta and Britain Mosul.

It was neat and logical, but to Kidston the easy proposals for Syria and Palestine would mean bloodshed and military repression if an attempt was made to carry them out. Hardinge concluded that Balfour's analysis was based on an estimate of Faisal's position as so much bluff—a view shared by Hardinge all alone—and the conviction that the Arabs would not seriously take up arms against the French. Hardinge's view was reminiscent of viceregal days: all things would work themselves out in the end. Faisal, he concluded, "is a clever Oriental who will make the best possible bargain, but he is not likely to burn his boats."[62]

Clichés and metaphors were not enough, and Lloyd George, who argued like Lawrence (and unlike Allenby) that there was no real incompatibility among the documents, had concluded that Britain must uphold her commitments, although the commitment he most probably had in mind was Clemenceau's of December 1918. But, said Allenby in a meeting with the Prime Minister at Deauville (9-11 September 1919), if "Blue" zone was to be handed over to France, Faisal from his base in "A" zone would have at them. The General advised

[62] Balfour to Curzon, 19 September, enclosing 11 August memorandum, with Kidston and Hardinge (quoted) minutes, *FO* 371/4183; *DBFP*, IV, pp. 340–49; see Nevakivi, *Britain, France and the Arab Middle East*, p. 181.

that Faisal should be brought to Europe to be given an explanation of why the coast had been turned over to the French. The
decisions were not entirely clear—Lloyd George for example
still wanted a British outlet on the Mediterranean—but one was
definite: France on the coast, Faisal in the interior.[63]

This was precisely what Balfour had argued against; as he
had pointed out in a memorandum of the 9th, "Blue" and "A"
zones would be impossible to separate: the whole area would
have to be given to one power. Worse, how could it be explained that there was to be more Arab independence in "A"
than Britain was prepared to concede in Mesopotamia? The
French would expect that their authority in Damascus would
not be less than Britain's in Mosul. Both powers really wanted
the same thing: full control of their respective areas, ". . . to
be exercised no doubt (at least in our case) in friendly and un-
ostentatious co-operation with the Arabs—but nevertheless, in
the last resort, to be exercised." Other problems were railways
and oil, for in all that he had heard it seemed that everyone
expected these to be entirely British when in fact the "open
door" would have to be applied in mandates.[64]

Lloyd George was undeterred and now advised Clemenceau
that he was coming to Paris to discuss the situation and that
Faisal, discouraged from leaving Syria in July, was coming to
London and Paris, a plan received unenthusiastically by
Clemenceau, who saw the problem as one of Anglo-French
military decisions only. Faisal came nevertheless. He made it
clear even before leaving Syria that there was likely to be
trouble, and trouble there would be, for in the Anglo-French
negotiations which followed, despite all Lloyd George's reser-

[63] Deauville meeting, minutes, 9–10 September 1919, *CAB* 21/153;
Hankey memorandum, 17 September 1919, *FO* 371/4182 (also *DBFP*,
IV, pp. 384–85); Nevakivi, *Britain, France and the Arab Middle East*,
pp. 188ff.

[64] Balfour memorandum, 9 September 1919, *FO* 608/106; *DBFP*, IV,
pp. 373–74.

vations on Arab areas and boundaries and railways and pipe lines, it was decided that the British were to withdraw from zone "Blue" and the French to assume responsibility for its occupation.[65]

Clemenceau was, of course, willing to move in troops, but he was not willing to let such a measure imply agreement with the remainder of Lloyd George's plan, particularly the continued and sole occupation by Faisal's forces of Homs, Hama, Aleppo, and Damascus. Quite the contrary, in fact; an exchange of memoranda and further military discussions showed that the French were very loath to remove the small French military representation already present in such towns as Damascus. These towns would be French; by mid-October the Foreign Office knew that the French wished British troops to remain in them until the French were ready to take over, thus avoiding independent Arab control and, as Curzon pointed out, making a stalkinghorse of the British.[66]

But Lloyd George, in conference with Allenby, had made his decision, with little help from the Foreign Office as was his wont by now. Syria, or at least "Blue" zone, would be left to France, or rather to France and the Arabs who would have to work out the future with each other. Many issues of detail remained, notably a vexing problem regarding the northern frontier of Palestine, and one large general problem: nothing had yet been agreed on an over-all policy to be pursued in common within the separate mandatory areas in such things as the institutions to be established and the like. It also remained,

[65] Lloyd George to Clemenceau and Clemenceau to Lloyd George, 11 September 1919, *FO* 608/106 and *DBFP*, IV, pp. 379–80; Paris delegation telegram to Arbur, 10 September 1919, *FO* 608/92; Balfour note, 13 September, *FO* 608/106, and Hankey note, 17 September, *FO* 371/4182 (and *DBFP*, IV, pp. 384–85), on Faisal talks.

[66] Nevakivi, *Britain, France and the Arab Middle East*, ch. IX, covers these negotiations in detail, fully citing the relevant published British documents. Curzon's remark is in a minute on Kidston to Curzon, 11 October 1919, *FO* 371/4183.

however, to explain the agreement to Faisal in several meetings in London in September and October.[67]

The Amir was hardly pleased, but Lloyd George was unwilling to accept Faisal's countersuggestion that the changeover in Syria await the peace conference's decision. President Wilson was ill; no American delegate had authority to make commitments on such a military question as Syrian occupation—the issue could not be postponed indefinitely. When Faisal left the meeting, it was with the knowledge that Allenby had set the date of evacuation for 1 November, and the decision was adhered to despite every further appeal from Faisal (including one to the Supreme Council of the Allied Conference in early November).[68]

Whatever the morality of the British withdrawal from Syria, or its positive political value to Britain in the light of subsequent events, in one respect, at least, Lloyd George was right: the way was now clear for further negotiations on suspended problems such as oil in Mesopotamia. Here the British had continued in difficulty, largely due to demands made by Standard and Shell Oil companies, but had persisted in the policy of not allowing commercial enterprises to operate until the peace conference determined the future of Iraq. The United States, under similar pressure, had suggested that a line be drawn between exploration and actual operations, but this, too, conflicted with established policy. The problem was more difficult than it appeared on the surface, for American demands were justified to the extent that the Iraqi authorities had permitted some development of oil production for the use of the military and some surveys of future pipe-line routes.[69]

[67] See notes on meetings, 19 and 23 September 1919, *FO* 608/106 and 109; *DBFP*, IV, pp. 395–404, 413–19.

[68] Minutes of conference, 13 October, and Faisal to Supreme Council, 6 November 1919, *FO* 608/106; *DBFP*, IV, pp. 458–60 and, for further details, 461–67.

[69] Wilson telegram to SSI, 29 September, Kidston minute, 1 October, Weakley note, 3 October, Davies (American Ambassador) to Curzon,

The obvious way to ward off American pressure was to revive the agreement reached with France at Paris but subsequently discarded by Lloyd George. Long suggested this approach to the Prime Minister in November, and it seemed that this would have to be done when, in December, the French asked for their share of Mesopotamian oil. The oil negotiations were linked with the pipe-line negotiations, the pipe line with railways, and railways with Palestine's northern frontier—it was most desirable to get this issue out of the way. By 21 December an agreement had been reached (the "Greenwood-Bérenger Agreement," negotiated by Bérenger and Sir Hamar Greenwood), closely resembling the Long-Bérenger agreement of earlier date. France was to receive 25 per cent of the Turkish Petroleum Company for the price of the cost of those (Deutsche Bank) shares to the British Treasury (plus 5 per cent), in return for railway and pipe-line facilities to be provided without royalties. Up to 20 per cent of the total capitalization was to be given to the native government or other native interests. The company would remain under permanent British control. It was not the end of controversy, particularly regarding possible American participation, but it was the basis of Anglo-French agreement, an agreement of the type that insured that the basic Sykes-Picot principle would stand, as modified in Mosul and Palestine.[70] It was only necessary that the two governments ratify the agreement.

Britain—more properly Lloyd George—had finally taken a stand on Anglo-French relations in the Middle East, and it was one of wide concession, in the sense that Syria had been yielded

---

31 October, and minutes, F.O. to I.O., 1 November, F.O. to Davies, 21 November 1919, *FO* 371/4209.

[70] Long to Lloyd George, 4 November 1919, *Lloyd George Papers*, F/33/2/82; Berthelot note, 12 December, Curzon to Derby, 17 December, notes on Anglo-French meeting, 23 December, Forbes Adam memorandum, 30 December, Greenwood-Bérenger agreement, 21 December 1919, *DBFP*, IV, pp. 577–89, 595–603, 607–9, 1114-17. For further discussions, *Petroleum Executive Files*, 606 (1921–22).

and Faisal forsaken. Lloyd George, of course, realized that Britain's commanding military presence in the Arab world and her formerly friendly relations with Arab nationalists might have permitted a satisfactory solution had not France been involved, but the Middle East could not be treated in a vacuum. Even if it could be divorced entirely from European problems (an obvious impossibility), the Prime Minister required French support for his Turkish policy alone. Other pressures too worked toward an accommodation with France: American interests in oil or Zionist requirements in Palestine were only two examples. Demobilization, expense—it was plain that Britain could not hold the entire Middle East against all comers, but only, it might be said, its majority.

Even then, Faisal might have carried the day had he spoken from a position of greater strength. But problems with his own followers in Syria (and Syrian-Iraqi disagreements) worked against him; much more important, Husain had never developed the position of primacy among Arab princes to which he aspired. If Ibn Sa'ud, al-Idrisi, and the others had looked to him for leadership, Britain might have had to think again. So far from being a leader, however, Husain was not even able to hold his own against Ibn Sa'ud. And, as the pressures had mounted, the King had only appeared to be more unreasonable and less cooperative. The more Husain refused negotiation and arbitration (justifiably, from his viewpoint), the more Britain was inclined to let him work out his own settlement with Ibn Sa'ud, whatever that settlement might be. Faisal had always to bear in mind that Arabian controversy, as he had to bear in mind the nature of developments in Iraq, as he carried on his own Syrian negotiations.

Several conclusions may be drawn from all this. In the first place, mutual distrust and suspicion between Britain and Faisal over Syria and Iraq steadily increased just at the time when the essential base of Faisal's power in the Hijaz was crumbling. Secondly, British policy had not been able to support Husain in any significant way, and for this the existence of Indian and Baghdadi contacts with Ibn Sa'ud must ultimately be blamed. Finally, problems in Syria and in Arabia left little time for consideration of Mesopotamia, where Arnold Wilson had certain aims which appeared to the Iraqi officers with Faisal to be hostile to their own aims and interests. But for Faisal and his officers immediate concerns had to take first priority, and this meant that in the second half of 1919 Arnold Wilson really had only to deal with the population in Iraq and his own superiors in London, for Husain's intervention was checked by Ibn Sa'ud and Faisal's by the French negotiations. Wilson might therefore have been able to establish in Iraq a regime on those sound but separate grounds which he desired. Such a solution depended upon London's approval, the cooperation of the Iraqis, both inside and outside the country, and a realistic policy that would insure the cooperation of those parties—a difficult set of requirements to fill.

5

In the summer of 1919 Arnold Wilson had a considerable number of handicaps to face in establishing his vision of the proper regime in Iraq. Some have been discussed above, such as the issue of the Iraqi officers or the annoyance of officials in London with his behavior. Wilson had been told with rare clarity that whether he liked it or not—such language implied that it was obvious he did not—an Arab state would be established in Mesopotamia. But there was another problem nearly as difficult: With or without "Arab" control, what areas would the state include? What, specifically, did Britain intend to do about Mosul and Kurdistan?

This particular point had been an issue since the occupation of Mosul at the armistice. The long delay in deciding Mosul's future as among the Allies, let alone institutionally, meant that Wilson found it most difficult to proceed there with the constitutional measures he had been ordered to initiate. Beyond Mosul, too, Wilson was concerned about the future of Kurdistan, and in June 1919 he advocated the establishment of the more southerly Kurdish vilayets as a state under British protection. Possibly they might be included in an American-controlled Armenia or even—although Wilson professed himself opposed to extension of authority—a British-controlled Armenia.[71]

The Foreign Office had not changed its view since 1918 and refused to sanction any measure which might prejudice a future decision on Mosul, either by the conference or in the negotiations with France. Wilson found it hard to press strongly for an active policy, for an active policy would require in the end the sort of rapid constitutional development to which he was opposed. In July he was still appealing, despite all London's warnings, for a more "virile" interpretation to be given to the joint declaration of 1918. "To install a real Arab Government in Mesopotamia is impossible, and, if we attempt it, we shall abandon the Middle East to anarchy." Wilson still wanted, in other words, effective British control without the sham trappings of ineffective Arab government or the chaos of independent Arab control, and the same principles applied to Mosul and the Kurdish areas.[72]

It was another of those exasperating remarks; a "masterly telegram on wholly wrong lines," minuted Denys Bray in India,

Wilson's policy would have been splendid half a century ago; it would be splendid now, if we could deal with the Mesopotamian

[71] Wilson telegrams to SSI, 7 and 13 June 1919, *FO* 371/4149 and 4192. On Armenia, which cannot be treated here, see, for recent discussions, James B. Gidney, *A Mandate for Armenia* (Kent, Ohio, 1967), and Richard Hovannisian, "The Allies and Armenia, 1915–18," *Journal of Contemporary History*, 3 (January 1968), 145–68, and *Armenia on the Road to Independence, 1918* (Berkeley, Calif., 1967).

[72] F.O. to I.O., 30 June, Wilson telegrams to SSI, 21 and 22 (quoted) July 1919, *FO* 371/4149; and I.O. minutes in *L/P&S/10*, 4722/18, no. 4282/19.

question *in vacuo* and ignore for instance the rest of the Arab world and the rest of the Great Powers. He talks of giving the November 8th pronouncement a more virile interpretation. . . . Does he seriously think that France, whose imperialism the war has so whetted that it would be a bold man who would hazard a guess at where it will stop, would content themselves with a less virile interpretation in Syria if we paint a greatly enlarged Mesopotamia one red?[73]

India and London were thinking alike, although it was London which had full responsibility for instilling in Wilson the realization of the world situation that India had already absorbed, on this issue at least.

The problem of controlling Wilson was magnified by the impossibility of disproving some of his predictions. In Kurdistan, for example, Wilson was afraid that the absence of a policy would create unrest which would find reflection in Iraq. As the India Office pointed out to the Foreign Office in August, while the status of Mosul was an issue that could not now be raised, and while Wilson's suggestions on Kurdistan would seriously increase British responsibilities, still somebody had to control the area or it would be a most troublesome neighbor.[74] Such an argument, curiously familiar in Whitehall—especially when coming from India's representatives—failed to convince other departments. In an interdepartmental meeting on 20 August Curzon took his usual delight in pointing out the inconsistency of the proposal then under discussion for extending the Army's Mesopotamian railway system to Sulaimaniya in order to control that area when the area's population was supposed to be friendly. To him, it was another North-West Frontier, and even the military members of the committee whose task it was to support the project had to agree. The railway extension was postponed, and Wilson was asked to explain why Sulaimaniya was essential.[75]

[73] D. Bray minute, 27 July 1919, *India Sec. E.* May 1920, 442–553.
[74] I.O. to F.O., 1 August 1919, *L/P&S/10*, 36/19, no. 4294/19.
[75] I.D.C.E., 20 August (and also 2 September) 1919, *ibid.*, no. 6123/19.

The difficulty in fact was a rising under the direction of a Kurdish leader, Shaikh Mahmud, which was thought by Wilson to be little more than nationalist anarchy designed to test Britain's ability to keep order in the district. Sulaimaniya, said Wilson, was a rich area which had been treated by the Turks as part of Mesopotamia, and which would be a problem similar to the North-West Frontier if left to its own devices: a point which showed the multiple use of analogies. Wilson argued that the Kurds really did want British rule but that no modern government could rule without some force behind it. Mahmud, captured and sentenced to death, was dealt with by the necessary force (he was in fact released in 1921).[76]

Wilson had more to contend with than Shaikh Mahmud, for he was at odds over Kurdistan with one of his own subordinates. Major E. W. C. Noel had been the officer in charge of Sulaimaniya in 1918, and he had been largely responsible for policy application in Kurdistan. Noel argued that if the area could not be independent it should be set up as part of Turkey with a wide measure of autonomy. Fully aware of traditional Kurdish-Arab hostility, he had no desire to see the Kurds, for whom he had conceived a considerable attachment, included in Wilson's Mesopotamia. Wilson, not unnaturally, had a different view, but he was perhaps less concerned about the future "Arab" state than Noel. Wilson sent Noel home in order to get him out of Kurdistan and because of his past association with Shaikh Mahmud, with the result that Noel was able to argue quite effectively for his policy in London, where opinion favored an autonomous Kurdistan in any case, so as not to

[76] Wilson telegrams to SSI, 23 and 29 August 1919, Bombay Government to FSI, 22 December 1921, *L/P&S/10*, 2879/19, nos. 5180 and 5283/19 and 257/22. In addition to Hay, *op. cit.*, and Edmonds, *Kurds*, see Hassan Arfa, *The Kurds: An Historical and Political Study* (London, 1966), pp. 111–15, which provides an interesting Persian viewpoint from a former Chief of Staff of the Iranian Army and an Ambassador to Turkey, whose personal experiences in Kurdistan are recorded in *Under Five Shahs* (N.Y., 1965).

extend British commitments into this area. Actually, most of the interdepartmental committee members would have preferred withdrawal from the Kurdish areas, but this was impossible given the uncertain future of Turkey, Armenia, and Kurdistan. By the end of 1919 no decision had been taken on the Kurds, so the area remained another problem for Wilson— and for the India Office, already rather upset to find that the Foreign Office was talking to the French about Mosul without any consultation with the responsible office.[77]

While the Mosul-Kurdistan problem was being thrashed out, discussion continued on the policy in Mesopotamia proper. To Wilson this was not a problem; the policy then underway was quite suitable. Home officials, who were again studying a collection of Mesopotamian reports, were not so certain. In this case the issue was another of Wilson's directives, or rather one from a subordinate, ordering some twenty students expelled from a Mosul school for wearing "Arab" colors; they were not to be readmitted without parental apology and public beating. London objected, but Wilson, who supported his subordinates with regularity, argued that the order was justified, as the colors were those of a political party. If permission was given for the display of Hijazi colors, ". . . it would be followed by Kurdish and Armenian flags and the Chaldeans would in self defense hoist French flag and the next development would probably be racial riots to which Mosul has always been prone." London had learned to doubt such predictions, and Wilson was told that the order was not in the spirit of the joint declaration of 1918. The incident was minor, but the expulsion of boys from primary-level schooling (twelve of the twenty were in the fourth year of primary education) was the sort of thing

[77] Noel memorandum, 27 September, SSI telegram to Wilson, 22 November, Wilson telegram to SSI and private telegram to Hirtzel, 27 November, Hirtzel memorandum for Montagu, 12 December, I.O. to F.O., 20 December, notes on meeting, 27 November, Hirtzel minute, 24 December, Montagu private to Curzon, 29 December 1919, *L/P&S/ 10*, 36/19, nos. 7328, 7495, 7701, 7707a, 8079, and 8345/19.

likely to stick in the minds of those reading the files—all of
which, fortunately for Wilson's reputation in the Foreign
Office, were in the India Office, for there is no record that the
affair was brought to the Foreign Office's attention.[78]

The incident, like Shaikh Mahmud's rebellion, was indicative of unrest in Iraq, and the India Office was moved by these
and other issues to ask the Foreign Office whether, in the light
of the indefinite postponement of a decision on Turkey and
ex-Turkish areas, some pronouncement might be made which
would remove the cause for unrest by assuring the permanence
of Britain's association with Iraq while at the same time not
contravening the spirit of previous statements. Such a declaration was no more possible in August 1919 than in previous
months. And statements were not going to reduce unrest when
the issue was basic policy. As Young put it, Wilson appeared
". . . to be somewhat out of touch with the policy of the Peace
Conference and to have little use for disinterested action towards encouraging native Governments to stand on their own
legs."[79]

It was unfortunate that Wilson was increasingly losing the
confidence of advisors at home—a long process which had
begun when he had replaced Cox in 1918. Young, in particular,
was a constant critic, a critic, moreover, who had the habit of
reading the detailed administrative reports sent home by sea
and singling out the more interesting passages for his superiors'
attention. The problem of the Iraqi officers particularly occupied his mind, for Wilson reported in September that Faisal's
supporters, realizing that Iraqi opinion was going against them,
were mounting an eleventh-hour propaganda campaign (a way

[78] Deputy Director of Education, Mosul, to Director of Education,
Baghdad, 20 May, Wilson telegram to SSI, 6 August (quoted), SSI
telegram to Wilson, 18 August 1919, *L/P&S/11*, vol. 154, nos. 3860 and
4709/19.

[79] I.O. to F.O., 19 August, with Young minute, 21 August (quoted)
1919, *FO* 371/4149, and, with Paris delegation minutes, *FO* 608/97; F.O.
to I.O., 26 September 1919, *FO* 371/4149.

of saying the agitation was mounting).[80] On a Baghdad police report of July, Young minuted, at the end of September:

It is lamentable that those very officers with whom Colonel Lawrence, Colonel Joyce, and myself, among others, lived in the closest possible touch, and who looked to the British Government as the mainstay of their revolt against the Turk, should be touring their own country *in disguise* [as the police report noted] with the object of obtaining signatures to anti-British manifestos. There is something very wrong somewhere.

Hardinge agreed; the sooner Cox returned to Iraq the better, for it was too big a task for such a young man (Wilson was then thirty-five), "much as I admire his ability." There was no doubt in Curzon's mind; Cox, he added, would return "the moment he considers that he can leave Persia with safety" (the state of affairs then prevailing in Teheran was rather delicate).[81]

Some of the India Office personnel were still willing to defend Wilson. In Hirtzel's case, at least, such defense was inspired as much by his deep distrust of Lawrence as by his loyalty to Wilson. Lawrence's proposals, he was convinced, were born as much of dislike for Wilson as of an appraisal of practical possibilities. "Lawrence told me months ago (the first time I ever met him, in fact) that he hates Wilson, and he practically admitted that his attitude towards Mesopotamian questions is coloured by this personal feeling." But even Hirtzel admitted that Wilson was not really the right man for permanent control of Iraq's administration.[82] The India Office was on safer ground objecting to false analogies between Syria or Palestine and Mesopotamia; conditions were different, and, in particular, the Syrians had long been active in the cause of their own freedom, while in Mesopotamia the British had had to bring first word of such ideas.

[80] Wilson telegram to SSI, 3 September 1919, *FO* 608/97.

[81] Baghdad Police Report for week ending 19 July 1919, Young (29 September), Hardinge, Curzon, and Cornwallis minutes, *FO* 371/4150.

[82] Hirtzel note to Montagu, 4 October 1919, *L/P&S/10*, 4722/18, no. 6203/19; copy in *FO* 371/4183.

Kidston of the Foreign Office, to whom C. C. Garbett (recently of Mesopotamia and now in the India Office) had explained this view, originally at the Foreign Office's request for material with which to counter French attacks, saw it as special pleading; a change must come in the character of Wilson's regime. Young, no friend of Wilson, at least understood the situation; the India Office, he explained to Kidston in October, felt held back by the Foreign Office. Whenever a change was contemplated, the Foreign Office said that the decision of the peace conference could not be prejudiced, when really administrative innovations would not prejudice such a decision. Hardinge tended to agree, for a different reason; Britain's policy could not be declared in public because of the uncertainty, but whether with Arab façade or not, ". . . the control must be British for a long time to come." Curzon disagreed. To him all the evidence suggested that Mesopotamia ". . . has drifted into a semi-Anglo-Indian semi-Military but in any case British gov$^t$."[83] This was only one of a number of Curzon-Hardinge differences, all the more important because in late October Curzon succeeded Balfour as Foreign Secretary and was now in control of the Secretary's speaking tube to the Permanent Under-Secretary (". . . when George blew down Charlie blew up . . . ," as Vansittart put it).[84]

Whatever the Foreign Office views, there were soon indications of more trouble to come. On 19 October Nuri as-Sa'id talked to Young in London. Nuri strongly contended that the Iraqi officers with Faisal had more influence in Iraq than the Foreign Office knew (although the Foreign Office had a fair idea, in fact, through a War Office report on the aims and organization of the three-hundred-odd members of al-'Ahd, called the "Mesopotamian League" in London). The group,

[83] Garbett to Kidston, 7 October, with Kidston minute, 9 October, and Young to Kidston, 14 October 1919, with Hardinge and Curzon minutes, *FO* 371/4183.
[84] Vansittart, *op. cit.*, p. 233.

said Nuri, wanted Britain to live up to its pledge of 1918, and the appointment of one official who subsequently resigned was not what they had in mind. The reception given to Naji Bey as-Suwaidi's proposals had only confirmed the others in their view of Wilson as an enemy who intended no real steps to encourage self-government. Nuri had not been aware of Britain's sanction of the establishment of provincial and divisional councils, and Young, fairly fresh from Mesopotamia himself, was able to enlighten him on that score; but Young still came away from the meeting more than ever convinced that a change was essential and that it would have to be coupled with a declaration that Britain would not directly administer the country.[85]

Criticism, uncertainty, and the necessity of British control until a decision to the contrary was taken all combined to produce some new suggestions. Wilson had outlined an administration of five provinces, each under a commissioner, subdivided into sixteen divisions, with councils at both divisional and provincial level. So far, action had been taken only at the divisional level, said Garbett in memoranda of late October and early November reviewing progress, and Iraqis in Syria saw a vast difference between a British-advised Arab government and a British government with a few Arab officials in advisory positions. If trouble were to be forestalled, a more liberal constitution should be established, Cox should return, and Britain should declare that she would (1) take the mandate, (2) respect the opinions offered in Wilson's earlier poll (a dangerous declaration, under the circumstances), (3) establish a government corresponding to the 1918 declaration, and (4) consult the leaders of Arab opinion in Iraq when framing any permanent constitution. For the time being, the High Commissioner would hold over-all control under the mandate, advised by a

---

[85] Young memorandum, 21 October, on Nuri as-Sa'id conversation; W.O. to F.O., 13 October 1919: *FO* 371/4150; see also Secrétariat-Général, Peace Conference, to Secretary, British delegation, 2 November, enclosing al-'Ahd to Clemenceau, 20 September 1919, *FO* 371/4151. Birdwood, *Nuri*, pp. 118–19.

central council. The basic goal should be to avoid a system in which responsibility was held nominally by Arab ministers and practically by their British advisors—the Egyptian system, in short.[86]

Hirtzel was more cautious. Both Gertrude Bell and Wilson had warned on the ambition—and therefore unreliability—of Faisal's Iraqis, and there were dangers in forcing alien institutions upon Iraq; Britain had, in fact, pledged not to do this. After all, the *native* institutions were tribal system and centralized Turkish bureaucracy. Britain had done well with the former—her strong suit—and while changes had been made in the bureaucracy, notably from a local to a central departmental basis, such changes had been in the direction of efficiency. Wilson, in any case, had declared himself quite willing to make use of able Iraqis if these were available in Syria.[87]

Hirtzel argued that for all his faults Wilson had not received the support he had deserved, and it would be unfortunate if Cox were to be brought back and Wilson removed under a cloud. Wilson had, after all, telegraphed privately to Hirtzel in September that Hirtzel's July statement (an Arab government whether Iraq wanted it or not) was ". . . the first indication I have had as to the significance of self-determination as applied to this country." If the slow but steady construction of a regime based upon the councils was not enough, Wilson would cooperate—he was not Canute to order the waves to stop—but he must be free to give his views.[88]

Hirtzel had concluded his memorandum by agreeing that

[86] Garbett memoranda (B.335 and 336), 28 October and 1 November 1919, *FO* 371/5228; SSI telegram to Wilson, 28 October, and Wilson telegram to SSI, 29 October 1919, produced the information on the number of councils so far established, *FO* 371/4151.

[87] Hirtzel note, 3 November 1919, *FO* 371/5228.

[88] Wilson's private telegram cited by Hirtzel is that of 12 September 1919, *L/P&S/10*, 4722/18, no. 6209/10; a letter of 14 September (quoted) expanded on this theme, *Wilson Papers*, Add. Mss. 52455.

some new steps were necessary and that the creation of a central government, not, if possible, under an Arab amir, would facilitate Iraq's development, but he was obviously concerned lest the Foreign Office allow its views to be overly influenced by the Iraqi officers. The Foreign Office had rather more to worry about, however, including the views of some of Britain's own experts. In November, Lawrence, C. E. Wilson, and Colonel P. C. Joyce (who had been Officer Commanding, Hijaz, and after 1921 was to head the British military mission to Iraq) called on Young and urged upon him the importance of a clearly defined British policy, failing which, they warned, Britain would be thoroughly involved in the resulting upheaval in both Syria and Mesopotamia. But what, asked Kidston understandably, would the policy be? Would Britain fight or assist the concept of Arab unity on which the officers wished a stand to be made? Declarations were no answer when Syria and Palestine remained so uncertain and when Britain seemed to be about to risk Mesopotamian stability for the sake of allowing France into Syria "contrary to the principles of the Peace Conference and the League of Nations." Only Hardinge had an answer, for he had no faith at all in Arab unity: if an Arab amirate was created in Iraq, unity would be forestalled and the Arabs of Mesopotamia satisfied.[89]

For the time being, the only real development was a telegram from Curzon to Cox in Teheran. Curzon outlined the situation, including French insistence on absolute parallelism of the two mandates, and asked how legitimate criticism could be met and the way prepared for constitutional development. Various ways had been suggested: a proposal worked out in London or a commission to Mesopotamia, or asking the advice of local notables, or assurances to the councils that when the mandate

[89] Young memorandum, 12 November 1919, with Kidston (quoted), Tilley (17 November), Hardinge, and Curzon (18 November) minutes, *FO* 371/4184.

was established they would be invited to formulate their own proposals. What did Cox advise? The implication was clear that Cox would be the one to put any proposals into effect.[90]

Wilson, meanwhile, was commenting on a memorandum of Gertrude Bell's. Miss Bell had spent October touring Syria and had reached the conclusion that the Iraqi officers, while possessing little influence in Baghdad, had sound and reasonable views on the future of Mesopotamia under an Arab amir, 'Abdullah by choice. She had rather changed her views since the war's end, but Wilson had not, and he disagreed with the entire proposition that an Arab state would be practicable within a few years.

My observations in this country and elsewhere have forced me to the conviction that this assumption is erroneous, and though I am aware that in holding this view I differ from authorities and observers both at home and abroad who possess a breadth of vision and a wealth of experience to which I can lay no claim . . .

he proceeded to offer his views anyway, probably, as he admitted himself, for the last time.

To begin with, Arab administration would mean disaster for the minorities: Kurds, and Shiite Muslims, and Jews, and Christians. The tribes, too, would surely suffer at the hands of the "effendi class" which would take over. The Arab administration would not be able to control Iraq; Ibn Sa'ud and other leaders would never recognize it. Within a few years the logical result would be the retrogression of the area to Turkey. Wilson's summation was well put but was unlikely to alter home impressions of his attitude:

. . . I beg leave to assure Government that by birth, by training and by temperament, I am in sympathy with a democratic as opposed to

[90] Curzon private telegram to Cox, 14 November 1919, *DBFP*, IV, pp. 531–32; the original (*FO* 371/4185) shows it was drafted after a meeting of the 10th by Young and recast by Curzon. Nevakivi, *Britain, France and the Arab Middle East*, p. 205, prefers to interpret this telegram primarily in the context of the French negotiations.

a bureaucratic conception of Government, and if I find myself unable to advocate the immediate introduction of a logical scheme of Arab Government into Mesopotamia it is because I believe that the results would be the antithesis of a democratic Government and that the creation and maintenance at this stage of an indigenous Arab Government is inconsistent with the changes which we are now endeavouring to introduce into the Governments of India and Egypt, changes the necessity for which I fully recognise and with which I am broadly speaking in sympathy.[91]

While this carefully phrased statement was traveling to London, Wilson returned to his more normal telegraphic style. On 20 November he sent in an optimistic report on improving conditions throughout Iraq; even in Mosul the population was coming to regard the British position as permanent (Wilson's idea of improvement). The Sharifal family was becoming increasingly unpopular, and outside Baghdad the idea of an independent Arab state, which owed such popularity as it had attained ". . . mainly to our own initiative, is fading from the public mind." All "couleur du rose," minuted Kidston, but such optimism had been followed in the past by reports of murdered British officers and wholesale disaffection. Wilson had convinced no one.[92]

On 23 November Cox's reply was received; unfortunately, Cox proved to have no easy answer. Of Curzon's various alternatives, Cox had preferred the last—assurance to the councils of a future voice—but before committing himself he wished to visit Iraq, Kurdistan, and Syria on the way from Persia to London. At the same time Cox added that he had been receiving information regularly on events in Mesopotamia. As far as he could see, the bulk of the population appeared satisfied. Arnold Wilson might have taken heart from Cox's attitude, but Wilson was not told of this exchange until mid-1920. The Foreign Of-

[91] Bell memorandum, 15 November 1919, enclosed in Wilson to SSI, 15 November (B.337, quoted), FO 371/4152. Gertrude Bell's earlier opinions may be found in Burgoyne, op. cit., and Bell, op. cit.
[92] Wilson telegram to SSI, 20 November 1919, and minutes, FO 371/4151.

fice, however, was disappointed. Young minuted, no doubt with some exasperation, that the issue was not the views of the Iraqi tribesmen but the views of the urban and educated or semi-educated classes who must somehow be persuaded to work with Britain. Curzon added only, "Sir P. Cox seems to be out of touch both with us & with Mesopotamia."[93]

The India Office was more enthusiastic, for the councils might be just the place to begin. The difficulty was that the very Iraqis who had created all these problems in the first place were just those unlikely to be nominated by Wilson's administration for positions on those councils. As for Cox's proposed journey, any delay was to be deprecated, and Cox should go at once to Iraq with the title of High Commissioner-Designate. The Foreign Office, a bit concerned about even Cox's attitude, preferred that he visit London to be put in the picture on larger issues and policies.[94]

As usual, no decision was immediately forthcoming. For the moment Wilson occupied himself primarily with throwing the representatives of Faisal's government out of Dair az-Zaur, which town, he had urged in September, should not be handed over to the Arabs, for it would lead to considerable unrest in Iraq.[95] Young in London reached the obvious conclusion: Wilson feared contamination by an Arab state, then intended for Syria, from even such a distance as Dair az-Zaur. After Britain's withdrawal from Syria, an Arab column seized the town on 11 December and Abu Kamal on the 14th. Faisal in Paris repudiated the move and blamed it on the governor of Raqqa (the next major town up the Euphrates, 75 air miles northwest

[93] Cox (Hamadan) private telegram to Curzon, 23 November 1919, with minutes by Young (2 December) and Curzon (about 2–3 December, quoted), *FO* 371/4185; the telegram, but as always not the minutes, is reproduced in *DBFP*, IV, pp. 550–52. F.O. telegram to Cox, 11 June, 1920, *FO* 371/5226, gave Cox approval to show the 1919 exchange to Wilson at that time.

[94] I.O. to F.O., 15 December 1919, and minutes, *FO* 371/4186.

[95] Wilson telegrams to SSI, 23 and 28 September 1919, *FO* 371/4183.

of Dair az-Zaur), one Ramadan ash-Shallash. But Wilson, fearing, like his military colleagues in Iraq, Arab cooperation with the Turkish nationalist movement, which combination could be dangerous in an unoccupied middle ground, had managed to reoccupy Abu Kamal by 21 December. He now argued that while Dair az-Zaur should not be retained in Mesopotamia (his military advisors correctly argued against the longer land frontier this would mean), it should be occupied for the time being in order to forestall anarchy.[96]

The year 1919 thus ended, for Mesopotamia, on a sour note. More than a year had passed since the armistice, a year of argument and few decisions. If anything, Iraq was less settled, less certain of the future than at the end of the war. London, it is true, had some idea of a direction to be followed in constitutional development, presumably under the guidance of Sir Percy Cox, but Wilson had yet to be so informed. So far, Wilson had been unable to keep Faisal's Iraqis at arm's length, but if France occupied the whole of Syria in the wake of British withdrawal those same Iraqis might have nowhere to turn save their own homeland. That this would in fact happen was not definitely clear as yet; the Aleppo-Damascus line was to be handed over to the Arabs, but the French had agreed to this only to the extent to which the Arabs agreed to French occupation—that is to say, not at all. Finally, nothing but the abatement of open hostilities had been achieved in the clash between Husain and Ibn Sa'ud in central Arabia, and that problem too was moving toward a crisis.

In general, the first year of peace for the Middle East was one of search for solutions to the massive problems which followed in the wake of massive victory. The results, so far, had

[96] Gen. Cobbe private telegram to Gen. Sir H. Wilson, 10 March, A. Wilson telegrams to SSI, 12, 14, and 21 December, MacMunn (Commanding, Mesopotamia) telegram to W.O., 15 December 1919, *L/P&S/10*, 5202/18, nos. 6219, 8057, 8110, 8221, 8312/19; Wilson telegrams of 13 and 14 December, with minutes, and Faisal (Paris) to H. Wilson, 18 December 1919, *FO 371/4186*.

been worse than unproductive. Tension, not satisfactory order and stability, was the prevailing atmosphere in the entire sweep of territory from Egypt through the Fertile Crescent and Arabia to Iraq and Kurdistan, and, it might be added, the further arc of Persia, Afghanistan, and India. Even Turkey, which had seemed so seriously defeated, was undergoing a remarkable nationalist development in her own right, strong enough to hamper the achievement of formal peace, at least on Lloyd George's terms. The new year had to bring answers, and indeed it did, but only after Arab fought with Frenchman in Syria and Iraqi clashed with Briton in Mesopotamia.

# VIII

# Revolution, 1920

Blood understood the native mind.
He said: "You must be firm but kind."
A mutiny resulted.
Standing upon a mound,
Blood cast his lethargic eyes around,
And said, "Whatever happens we have got
The Maxim Gun, and they have not."

*Hilaire Belloc*, THE MODERN TRAVELLER

1

If 1919 was a year of unproductive groping for a policy, the
first nine months of 1920 proved beyond any doubt the costs
of confusion. Lloyd George had made a beginning, using what
he considered to be the only possible starting point, the surrender of Syria and Lebanon to France. Such a beginning must
be balanced against his own contributions to the problems of
Anglo-French relations and British Middle Eastern—above all,
Turkish—problems. But Lloyd George's concessions had not
directly affected Arnold Wilson by the new year, and Iraq still
faced the mounting pressures of nationalist sympathies, unsettled frontiers, and continuing debate on the structure of government.

The Mesopotamian situation nevertheless appeared satisfactory. The dispute at Dair az-Zaur was unresolved, but there was no clear evidence that it had significantly affected Iraqi opinion, and it could be put down to Syrian unsettlement, which would no doubt end once the French established their control. Ironically, that French control, while desirable from the Iraqi administrative standpoint and so undesirable to the nationalists, engendered some friendly pro-British feeling within Iraq from the simple contrast between Iraqi stability and Syrian chaos once the French began to push inland. In January, Wilson reported after touring the country that there was considerable support for Britain's regime from council members in locales as widely spread as Basra and Hilla (a divisional center on the Euphrates, 60 miles south of Baghdad). What worried Wilson most, and it was worry enough for him to predict a "breakdown" if it was not repaired in the coming year, was the lack of British officers from home to replace those demobilized or recalled by the Indian administration.[1]

Wilson clearly saw no indigenous alternative to such officers, but in a larger context his fear was that Britain would cut and run, either totally or through the creation of a forced and, to Wilson, artificial Arab government. In late February 1920, for example, the interdepartmental conference in London took a firm decision against railway projects reaching into Kurdistan. The drift of opinion was to leave the area to its own devices, with Young and Curzon the determined advocates of such policy in opposition to Hirtzel. Even Hirtzel admitted privately to Wilson, in another of his prompting letters, that the possibility of withdrawal existed. Britain's great postwar military weakness and the chance of a Labour government in England both had to be considered.[2]

---

[1] Wilson telegram to SSI, 18 January, and Col. Richard Meinertzhagen (C.P.O. to Allenby) telegram to F.O., 13 January 1920, *FO 371/4152* and 4186.

[2] I.D.C.E. 35th minutes, 23 February 1920, *L/P&S/11*, vol. 160, no.

It is in this context that Wilson's persistent arguments against abandonment of Kurdistan must be viewed. Not only was he concerned about the northern frontier, but withdrawal there might be the first step to total withdrawal. There was even something of an implied threat of resignation in his remarks that responsibilities in the Mosul, Sulaimaniya, and intermediate Arbil divisions could not be appreciably reduced without cutting responsibilities totally. Wilson pointed out, with the concurrence of Lieutenant-General Sir George MacMunn (who had assumed command in the spring of 1919), that the three vilayets of Mosul, Baghdad, and Basra were a whole, and the only feasible solution was the use of the armistice line as a boundary. This recommendation could be viewed as a concession, for it set a maximum limit to the Kurdish-inhabited areas to be included in Iraq; but it was not so regarded, since both Wilson and MacMunn were arguing against a General Staff proposal of the late 1919 to restrict British military activity to the south. Officials on the spot, both civilian and military, felt that a partial withdrawal would only increase commitments by leading to great unrest in Iraq.[3]

Much the same sort of argument applied to Dair az-Zaur. Here, too, Wilson insisted on holding on until he received definite orders to the contrary. In late January, Maulud Pasha al-Mukhlis had replaced Ramadan ash-Shallash in charge of the area; Wilson was soon reporting the appearance as far toward the Gulf as 'Amara of Maulud's letters inciting the tribes to

---

2138/20; Hirtzel private to Wilson, 3 February 1920, *Wilson Papers*, Add. Mss. 52455.

[3] Wilson telegram to SSI, 4 February 1920, *L/P&S/10*, 36/19, no. 1124/20; same of 13 February, *ibid.*, 5202/18, no. 1243/20, and *FO* 371/5070. The General Staff had not actually advocated withdrawal, but only discussed it as one way to cut expenses, and, unlike Wilson, the W.O. thought of expenses in terms of internal rather than external enemies. Churchill (W.O.) memorandum, 12 November 1919, enclosing undated General Staff memorandum, received in F.O. 3 May 1920, *FO* 371/5073.

active anti-British rebellion. Wilson argued, not for the first time, that the funds supporting Maulud came essentially from the subsidy Britain paid Faisal. Maulud wrote Wilson on 31 January that Abu Kamal was in the Arab sphere, and if the British failed to withdraw Maulud would no longer restrain the tribes; Wilson replied to this threat that he was there and intended to stay until ordered to leave. The Syrian Arab government was told officially that it would be held responsible for any encroachments on the provisional frontier by anyone under Maulud's orders, and that further payment of subsidy depended upon the government's ability to enforce its orders.[4]

That London had supported Wilson against the Syrian government was still no assurance that a radical solution would not be imposed upon Iraq. One scheme which was beginning to be discussed in earnest appealed to Wilson at once: the assumption by the Royal Air Force of military authority in Iraq, which would provide a means for controlling frontiers and dissident internal areas at relatively low cost. Cost, indeed, was the principal consideration; by February 1920, with the R.A.F. solution still very indefinite, the Cabinet had insisted on halving the £21.5 million estimate for Iraqi expenses for the coming year.[5] It was clear that, if this was not possible, withdrawal would be contemplated. By March the R.A.F. idea had gone far enough for the Air Council to ask for all available information on frontiers and the like so as to be able to work out the details; it was planned to send Air Vice-Marshal Sir W. B. H. Salmond (Air Officer Commanding, Middle East) to study the situation. This was the beginning of a lengthy discussion, tainted with considerable interservice infighting as the entire future of the R.A.F. became caught up in the question; the

[4] Wilson telegrams to SSI, 29 January and 15 February, F.O. telegram to Meinertzhagen, 19 February 1920, *FO* 371/4187 and 5128; F.O. to I.O., 10 March 1920, *L/P&S/10*, 5202/18, no. 1917/20.

[5] Cabinet Financial Committee, 9 February 1920, *CAB* 23/20, appendix to Cabinet 11 (20).

plan would not be implemented until after the period here under consideration.[6]

Meanwhile the general Syrian situation was having a noticeable effect on Baghdad. From London's standpoint Syrian affairs were proceeding smoothly. British forces had been withdrawn as planned by the end of 1919[7] and, in February 1920, Anglo-French conversations were taking place in London on the subject of a possible Allied agreement on the Arab areas even before completion of a Turkish treaty. Syria, Mosul, Kurdistan, and Palestine were all discussed; no formal agreement on policy (excluding the Greenwood-Bérenger oil agreement) resulted, but the discussions were an important preliminary to the decisions soon to be taken at San Remo in a context of improving Anglo-French relations.[8]

To Faisal, back in Syria since January, the situation had a completely different appearance, as indeed it did to Wilson in Baghdad. Unable to sit quietly and await the French, the Amir found the pressures upon him to be so great that he was forced to convoke—or at least approve the convocation of—a Syrian congress, which, reported Allenby, intended to declare complete independence and to crown Faisal king. Faisal knew that if he refused his people would disown him, and he was power-

[6] Wilson telegram to SSI, 4 March, Air Council to I.O., 13 March 1920, *FO* 371/5070; Hirtzel to Hankey, 13 November 1919, mentions the scheme and Wilson's share in supporting it, noting that it had Montagu's backing as well, *FO* 371/4185; on further developments, see W.O. conference minutes, 24 March, and F.O. to Secretary of Air Ministry, 20 April 1920, *FO* 371/5072; and for personal issues and interservice problems, Andrew Boyle, *Trenchard* (N.Y., 1962).

[7] Meinertzhagen to F.O., 13 January 1920, *FO* 371/4186; D.M.I. to F.O., 28 January, Meinertzhagen telegram to F.O., 19 February, and letter, 7 February, Curzon private telegram to Allenby, 22 February 1920, *FO* 371/5032.

[8] Notes on conferences, 10 Downing Street, 17, 18, 20, and 26 February, *DBFP*, VII, pp. 99–119, 153–63, 256–62; the discussions had really begun in December; see Nevakivi, *Britain, France and the Arab Middle East*, pp. 225–32. Curzon private telegram to Allenby, 22 February 1920, outlines the situation, *FO* 371/5032.

less, Allenby said, to restrain nationalist feeling. After discussion with France, the Foreign Office advised Faisal that the Allies would shortly examine the Syrian question at San Remo (which meeting was technically an extension of the Paris conference). They would not make decisions on Syria without consulting him, and therefore he should attend the meeting. On the other hand, grave responsibility would fall on the Arab government if the congress took any action which placed Syria as now constituted in opposition to ". . . the friendly and liberal intentions to which the British and French Governments have given repeated expression." In this issue, at least, the British and French officials were working in rare harmony.[9]

On 8 March, however, Faisal was proclaimed King of Syria by the congress. There was much uncertainty in London on the exact course of events, and even the unsubstantiated suspicion that the French had arranged the whole thing to embarrass Britain. No British representative was actually at the congress, but it was soon realized that, while Faisal was being proclaimed King of Syria, 'Abdullah was similarly being named King of Mesopotamia. Perhaps—but only perhaps—Britain might have taken a softer tone had it not been for Iraq's involvement. As it was, Faisal was told that Britain could not recognize the proceedings of a congress the composition and authority of which were unknown, for only the Allied powers could settle the future of the Arab world. Both France and Britain therefore regarded the proceedings as null and void. Britain added that no body in Damascus could be recognized as authoritative on Mosul or Mesopotamia—but the invitation to Faisal to attend the conference was renewed.[10] Colonel Richard Meinertzhagen, who had succeeded Clayton as Chief Political Officer to

[9] Allenby telegram to F.O., 7 March, F.O. telegram to Allenby, 8 March 1920, ibid.

[10] G.H.Q., Egypt, telegram to W.O., 10 (with minutes) and 12 March, F.O. telegram to Allenby and Curzon to Derby, 13 March 1920, ibid. 'Abdullah, in the Hijaz, denied any complicity, but this was

Allenby, reported that Faisal took the British representations calmly and said he had no intention of dictating to the peace conference. But on 18 March Allenby reported that Faisal would actually be crowned; should the powers continue to regard the congress as illegitimate, war must ensue.[11]

Curzon in London had charge of implementing the basic Anglo-French policy, and he was not to be bullied on this occasion. War, he cabled Allenby on the 19th, was the last thing Britain contemplated, either through her own intervention in Syria or through being dragged in by France. On the other hand, the congress, a self-constituted body with no claim to be representative or authoritative, could not be recognized. The small body of Mesopotamians who happened to be present—here Curzon was relying on *The Times* rather than the scanty information provided by his own officials—must be ignored. There was no objection to Faisal as king if the body which proclaimed him was properly constituted in such a way as not to supersede the peace conference. Allenby wished Faisal to be recognized as head of a confederation to include Syria, Palestine, and Mesopotamia, but how could this be done without discarding the mandate machinery or without treaty sanction? And how would this be applied to Palestine? Finally, what evidence existed to show that Mesopotamia wanted 'Abdullah, considering the results of the 1918-1919 inquiry? The two governments were willing to deal with Faisal at San Remo, and even to recognize him as King of Syria, but only if this title was come by through a normal constitutional process and was pre-

---

not until some time later: Col. Vickery (Jidda) to Cairo, 6 April 1920, *FO* 882/23. In theory, the Congress was composed of delegates who obtained their authority from similar positions held under the Ottomans: Meinertzhagen telegram to F.O., 9 April 1920, *FO* 371/5034.

[11] Meinertzhagen telegrams to F.O., 17 (with Hardinge minute) and 18 March, and Allenby telegram to F.O., 18 March 1920, *FO* 371/5033; Allenby telegram in *DBFP*, XIII, p. 231. On Meinertzhagen, see his *Middle East Diary, 1917–1956* (N.Y., 1960).

ceded by separate agreements with France on Syria-Lebanon and with Britain on Palestine.[12]

There was still Arnold Wilson to be considered. Also on 19 March, Wilson had been told of the proclamation of 'Abdullah and asked, by London, whether there was any reason to suppose that Mesopotamian opinion on a Sharifal ruler had altered since Wilson's earlier investigation. Wilson, in answering this cable, had several other depressing facts in mind. The first was a *fatwa* (juridical opinion) issued by the chief religious leader of Karbala that service under the British administration was unlawful, an ominous portent, which Wilson put down to Syrian nationalist agitation. The second was information that Wilson had received of a new statement by Lloyd George reaffirming the joint declaration of 1918 and that Wilson interpreted as the definite rejection of his own proposals for constitutional development. This development, Wilson had cabled, called for reconsideration of the whole matter; he would be making fresh proposals as soon as he learned of the Turkish peace terms (a reference to the Treaty of Sèvres, which would be formally concluded on 10 August).[13]

News of 'Abdullah's election, therefore, could be calculated to fill Wilson's cup to overflowing—and Wilson had heard of the congress from Cairo. In a telegram of 18 March, which crossed the India Office inquiry, Wilson took the initiative by proclaiming that a "very small minority" of Iraqis in Iraq supported the scheme of the twenty-nine Iraqis who between them, in Damascus and not in Iraq, had decided upon 'Abdullah as King. The India Office's official request for his views gave Wilson the opportunity to make a more detailed statement. He was fully satisfied, he reported on the 20th, that the position

---

[12] See *The Times*, 16 March 1920; clipping with Shuckburgh minute, *L/P&S/10*, 786/19, no. 2096/20. F.O. telegrams to Allenby, 19 and 22 March, Allenby telegram to F.O. and Curzon note, 20 March 1920, *FO* 371/5033–34; telegrams also in *DBFP*, XIII, pp. 231, 233, 235.

[13] SSI telegram to Wilson, 19 March, Wilson telegrams to SSI, 18 and 19 March 1920, *FO* 371/5033 and 5071.

had changed very little in the last year on the issue of an Arab ruler. It was true that general uncertainty had kept alive in some towns the sentiment for an Islamic government, but every indication Wilson had received showed that rule by a son of the Sharif, or by a government based in Syria and owing its inception to the Syrian Baghdadis, would be unpopular. "Its installation would in any case be signal for widespread disturbances which we cannot under present circumstances be sure of suppressing." On the other hand, a legislative council, with the High Commissioner or a local notable as president, and with Arab members in charge of various departments (with British secretaries), ". . . would meet all local ambitions and might possibly work, though country districts are far from ripe for such a change." In other words, the danger was still that of working too fast, and Wilson advised that the earlier error of consulting a population that had no idea of what it wanted should not be repeated. Whatever government Britain intended should obtain its authority from Britain's own initiative. How little this impressed London is shown by Young's minute: Wilson, Young obviously thought, feared for his own job.[14]

The following day, Wilson added some afterthoughts: the very fact that 'Abdullah had been proclaimed for Mesopotamia, and not Faisal for both Syria and Iraq, showed that even the extremists recognized the need for a separate Iraqi administration. No community of Syrian-Iraqi interests existed, and there was little likelihood of Iraq accepting a government dominated by "Syrian politicians." Recognition of the congress's decision would therefore alienate all of Britain's friends in Iraq. The proper answer, he urged, would soon be forthcoming from a committee of (British) Iraqi administrators which Wilson had appointed to study the future constitution.[15]

[14] Wilson telegrams to SSI, 18 and 20 March, with minutes, *FO* 371/5071.
[15] Wilson telegram to SSI, 21 March, and I.O. to F.O., 25 March 1920, supporting Wilson's committee, with minutes, *FO* 371/5033 and 5071.

Some sort of decision was necessary in London on the issue of Mesopotamia. Curzon prepared a statement for Cabinet approval that Britain would accept a mandate, that such a mandate would include Mosul, and that policy would then be to develop an Arab government founded on representative institutions and an Arab administration, including, should Iraq's population change its mind, an Arab ruler, even a Hashimite ruler.[16] Since the statement had not yet been issued, it was not yet passed to Baghdad, but Wilson was told, with accuracy, that the government had rejected any role in Kurdistan other than moral support for independence if it was locally desired. Wilson appealed: this policy, he warned, would in the end be fatal to Mesopotamia through the ill will it would engender "which I am not prepared to facilitate." There was no national movement and no leaders to speak for the Kurds, who asked only the continuation of the present system of control. London must reconsider. Again, afterthoughts followed two days later. The proposed abandonment of the Sulaimaniya and Arbil divisions would give an impetus to pro-Turkish and pro-Bolshevik activities—a new threat Wilson now interjected into the discussion. "Good administration with consequent cheap food for the masses and security of property for all classes is the only bulwark against Bolshevism that I know." [17]

On 25 March, however, Lloyd George outlined for Parliament the policy the Cabinet had approved; the next day the statement was telegraphed to Wilson. Wilson was pleased that the policy of withdrawal to Basra suggested by Asquith, speaking for the opposition, was rejected completely, but he was also concerned about the meaning of the Prime Minister's remarks. He had spoken of Mosul; but did "Mosul" mean "Mosul" as

[16] Cabinet 16 (20), 23 March 1920, *CAB* 23/20; the statement was prepared to answer an anticipated question from Asquith.

[17] SSI telegram to Wilson, 23 March, Wilson telegrams to SSI, 25 and 27 March 1920; see also Wilson telegram to SSI, 5 April, reporting on a trip to Sulaimaniya and the favorable views he found there: all *FO* 371/5068.

administered by Turkey, thus including the Sulaimaniya, Arbil, and Kirkuk areas from which it was proposed to withdraw? Obviously there was still confusion on this issue, and only Curzon seemed to know what he wanted: not a protectorate, nor an area partitioned between Britain and France, nor a fringe of separate states, but an autonomous Kurdistan severed from Turkey. For this purpose the leaders of Kurdistan should be consulted—and here Curzon clearly disregarded Wilson's advice. Unfortunately for Curzon's position, Vice-Admiral Sir J. M. de Robeck, Britain's High Commissioner in Constantinople, whom Curzon tended to consult in preference to Wilson on Kurdish matters, agreed with Wilson that Kurdish independence would be of questionable value and coherent Kurdish public opinion was nonexistent.[18]

But Lloyd George had also said that if Iraq wished an Arab amir, that too might be feasible. Wilson's answer was to report, early in April, that only a handful wished such a ruler, and that news of 'Abdullah's "coronation" was being received with amusement and resentment. Young, however, had been rereading the report on the earlier inquiry and now found that opposition had been aimed at an *uncontrolled* amir. Moreover, Wilson was simply not taking into account the fact that national feeling would grow with the passage of time. The Iraqis in Damascus might not be representative of the current feelings in Mesopotamia, but they did represent the feelings of the future.[19]

Young was again supported by Nuri as-Sa'id, now in London. Nuri had not attended the congress, but he had no difficulty in explaining the factors that had called it into being.

[18] SSI telegram to Wilson, 26 March (see also *The Times* of same date), Wilson telegram to SSI, 28 March 1920, *L/P&S/10*, 36/19, nos. 2476 and 2493/20; Curzon telegram to de Robeck, 26 March, de Robeck telegram to F.O., 29 March 1920, *FO* 371/5067–68; *DBFP*, XIII, pp. 49–50.
[19] Wilson telegram to SSI, 2 April 1920, with Young minute, *FO* 371/5071.

Turkish propaganda, fear of colonization, and the like had all played their roles, but, above all, a regime had been established in Iraq which was not suited to local conditions. Had a national government been established at once the disturbed feelings would not have arisen. Now various Iraqi leaders had given powers of attorney to such men as Faisal, Ja'far al-'Askari, Naji Bey as-Suwaidi (recently governor of Aleppo), Maulud Pasha al-Mukhlis, and Yasin Pasha al-Hashimi (Faisal's Chief of Staff, arrested by Allenby during the British withdrawal from Syria). "The severity of the military administration in Mesopotamia," Nuri continued, "has so far prevented the manifestation of the people's desires in the question of their future and to the casual observer who only skims the surface with unpenetrating eyes the national sentiment does not clearly appear as a factor."[20]

Young, who with Shuckburgh had instituted an inquiry into the election of 'Abdullah and who had asked Nuri to record their private conversation on paper, could only urge the folly of ignoring the leaders mentioned by Nuri. "I have personally no doubt whatever in my mind that people in Mesopotamia itself are afraid to express nationalist views." The way in which Nuri had marshaled his criticisms of Wilson's policy was particularly telling: the administration in Iraq allowed no display of Arab colors, no communication with Syria, no references in the single (government) newspaper to people such as King Husain, no return of the Iraqi officers, and no formation of organizations to discuss the political situation. The apparent calm was deceptive.[21]

Nuri's statements, as interpreted by Young, were reasonable and persuasive, especially since the basic necessity of an Arab

[20] Young minute on conversation with Nuri, 1 April, and note for Curzon, about 3 April, and Nuri to Young (quoted), 5 April 1920, FO 371/5034 and 5226. On arrest of Yasin: Allenby telegram to W.O., 3 January 1930, FO 371/5032.

[21] Young minute (quoted), 7 April, on Nuri letter of 5 April, ibid.

state had already been agreed upon. Whatever happened, Hirtzel once again wrote Wilson, there would be an Arab state; no sham façade, but Arab state. Nor would Kurdistan be included. Facts must be faced.[22] Hirtzel's tone left no margin for doubt, and rightly. There could be no turning back in the light of opposition pressure at home and the approaching meeting at San Remo. At long last, a definite decision had been taken—but in the remaining few days before the meetings a number of details, important enough to affect the basic policy, remained to be worked out.

## 2

Young and Nuri as-Sa'id had given the final nudge to views already held in London that a forward-looking regime had to be introduced in Iraq. Curzon had already moved far in this direction himself since his days as Viceroy of India, and he too had taken to rather strenuous criticism of Wilson, although he respected the Civil Commissioner's force of character. Wilson had views which were now outdated, but he was no bumbler.

Curzon desired two things: a decision on the constitution, along agreed-upon lines, and, more controversial, a revision of the decision on Kurdistan. As he made clear in an interdepartmental meeting on 13 April, Nuri had instilled in him this new train of thought.[23] Curzon now wondered if perhaps it might not be possible to make use of 'Abdullah—and thereby partly appease the demands of the Damascus congress—as ruler of a state in the northern districts of Mesopotamia. Curzon had

[22] Statement by Nuri as-Sa'id, received in F.O. 13 April 1920, *FO* 371/5226; Hirtzel private to Wilson, 6 and 15 April 1920, *Wilson Papers*, Add. Mss. 52455. Wilson's objection to talk of the future, it should be pointed out, did not apply only to nationalists: see D.A. and Q.M.G. to all divisions, 1 April 1920, and other documents in *FO* 371/5074, ordering all ranks not to discuss the future of the country and to insure that no one did so in their presence.

[23] I.D.C.E. 37th minutes, 13 April 1920, *FO* 371/5068.

himself earlier discarded the idea of using 'Abdullah, but this
new plan (it was of course T. E. Lawrence's, warmed over,
but it was newly adopted by Curzon) would satisfy several
criticisms, including that of Arnold Wilson against withdrawal.
The difficulties were twofold: the government had already
decided on withdrawal, and the Iraqis, according to Wilson,
had vetoed the idea of an Arab amir. Curzon did not wish to
hint that the inquiry of 1918 did not represent the feelings of
the country—a remark which implied the contrary—but perhaps opinion had now changed and 'Abdullah would be
accepted.

As for general policy, Curzon pointed out that there had
been two schools of thought all along: the direct rule school of
Wilson and the Native State group of people like Gertrude
Bell. Wilson, Curzon admitted, was a man "of great energy
and power" who had been able to put his views into effect with
involuntary governmental acquiescence. Now the situation
was different, both in the Arab world and at home. The Damascus congress had added another dimension when it proclaimed
'Abdullah king and his younger brother Zaid regent of Iraq
(a subsequent report had added this detail). Even Wilson's administration had altered its tone by appointing a committee to
study constitutional development. Fearing that Wilson would
simply construct a constitution that reflected the results of the
1918 inquiry, the chairman argued that the best policy now
would be to consult the existing councils.

Discussion of a draft statement on the future constitution
followed, with both India Office and Foreign Office providing
their own versions. Garbett of the India Office was, like Curzon, more concerned to establish the basics of an Arab state
for which, as he saw it, a constitution was not really an essential
preliminary. Simply form an Arab cabinet under Cox: that
was his answer. To this Curzon objected, for it would be Egypt
again, with a High Commissioner supervising Arab ministers.
No; the principal issue, as Curzon saw it, was whether the con-

stitution would be formed by consultation with the population or whether the regime would simply impose a "Wilsonian scheme." Since there was no copy available of the instructions given by Wilson to his constitutional committee, it was decided to wait until Wilson furnished the information, while in the meantime Curzon, in consultation with Montagu and the Foreign Office, was to draw up an announcement. When it was ready, Wilson would be sent explicit orders on how to put it into effect.

This assignment proved easier to make than carry out. Curzon's draft stated that His Majesty's Government intended to create "a form of civil administration based upon representative indigenous institutions, which should prepare the way for the creation of an independent Arab State of Irak." The councils had been a step in this direction, and now the British government had ordered the Civil Commissioner to take measures in consultation with those bodies to form proposals for a constitution—in other words, Curzon assumed that the consultation argument had won. On Curzon's draft, Young suggested substituting "support" for "create" (for Britain had already promised not to impose a structure) and specifying that a representative native government would replace the military administration. Curzon overruled both, the latter on the grounds that it was too clear an indication of the unity of Iraq from Mosul to the Gulf.[24]

Precisely such a clause was Montagu's principal goal, however, and the last several days before Curzon's departure for San Remo provided just enough time for an exchange of letters between the secretaries. Montagu threatened to take the issue to the Prime Minister if his clause was not included; Curzon complained that Montagu was making things most difficult on the eve of the conference. To Curzon, intimation of a unified state was not justified unless 'Abdullah proved acceptable to

[24] Curzon note for Young, undated (but 14/15 April), and Young minute, *FO* 371/5226; Young, *op. cit.*, pp. 309–10.

the population, which Curzon doubted. And if Montagu did not agree to Curzon's draft, Curzon himself would take the whole matter to Lloyd George at San Remo, which is precisely what happened.[25]

Not all of Montagu's India Office advisors were as anxious to see a hasty structure established simply—Montagu's main motive—to avoid the humiliation to the Arabs of a "mandate." Hirtzel, in a private letter written with the 13 April meeting fresh in his mind, told Wilson that the India Office political staff was doing everything possible to resist Curzon's inclination toward 'Abdullah, to say nothing of the idea of a separate Kurdistan. Could not Wilson find some member of a loyal local family on the spot to put in for a few years?[26] Hirtzel probably urged his views upon Montagu as well, but Montagu was unlikely to be driven into the anti-'Abdullah camp. On the 16th Montagu met Nuri as-Sa'id for the first time; when told by Nuri that he had not returned to Mesopotamia and could not for so long as the nationalists were likely to be deported for their views, Montagu had to admit that Nuri's attitude was understandable. What did Nuri suggest? Nuri's answer was simple: 'Abdullah was the only hope, for only he could win the cooperation and loyalty of both Sunnite and Shiite.[27]

At San Remo, Curzon won a victory over the absent Montagu, for the Prime Minister approved the Foreign Secretary's version of the drafted announcement. Lloyd George, cabled Curzon to Montagu, strongly objected to any commitment to a single government or kingdom which might be im-

[25] Montagu to Curzon, 15 April, Curzon to Montagu, 16 April 1920, *FO* 371/5226.

[26] Hirtzel private to Wilson, 15 April 1920, *Wilson Papers*, Add. Mss. 52455.

[27] Memorandum on Nuri-Montagu meeting, 16 April 1920, *L/P&S/ 10*, 4722/18, no. 3643/20. It was assumed throughout these conversations, of course, that Faisal would be occupied in Syria and unavailable for Iraq.

possible to realize. Montagu was able to keep discussion alive until early May, but Curzon's draft statement was the one which finally issued.[28] Curzon and Lloyd George, of course, had only discussed the matter in passing, for they had rather more important work to do at San Remo.

On 18 April Lloyd George met with Alexandre Millerand, the new French Premier, to discuss both the Turkish treaty and the assignment of the mandates. There was no disagreement about the basic allotment: Syria and Lebanon to France, Mesopotamia and Palestine to Britain; but there was argument over shares in Iraqi oil. The negotiations completed earlier had never been ratified, and the French saw no obstacle to asking 50 per cent. Lloyd George countered by suggesting that France pay 50 per cent of the administrative costs of Mosul. The end result was largely inevitable: the revival of the Long-Bérenger agreement, now called the Berthelot-Cadman agreement. Essentially, France got her 25 per cent, yielding if necessary 20 per cent (5 per cent of the total shares) to native interests.[29]

On the next day the Council discussed Kurdistan, which it found a harder issue to solve than mandates or oil. Curzon argued that the area should be left to the Turks and not taken up by any power but that the southern Kurds in the Mosul vilayet would have to be incorporated into Mesopotamia; he hoped that eventually they would be able to join forces with their brothers in the north. When a Kurdish state was established, the Kurds under British control would be able to express their preference. The French, not unexpectedly, held to the

[28] Curzon telegram for Montagu, 22 April, SSI telegram to Wilson (including text of declaration), 4 May 1920, ibid., nos. 2225 and 3326/20. Unfortunately, few records of the San Remo conference exist aside from minutes of the actual discussions among the powers, most of which have been published in DBFP, VIII.

[29] Note of conversation, Lloyd George–Millerand, 18 April 1920, DBFP, VIII, pp. 5–10; Berthelot–Cadman agreement, 24 April 1920, L/P&S/10, 2249/15, no. 3674/20.

line that Kurdistan was a matter for Anglo-French discussion
and not the Supreme Council of the conference, and for that
reason no decision was taken immediately.[30]

Temporarily, discussion turned to such subjects as the Hijaz
and Armenia but resulted in no startling confrontations or decisions. Curzon managed to avoid any detailed mention of the
Arab states in the Turkish treaty, pleading, correctly, that the
southern boundaries of Syria and Palestine and Iraq had yet to
be worked out. The decision which was taken, on the 25th, was
to allot the mandates without first concluding a formal treaty
with Turkey, although the treaty would eventually outline
the mandatory areas and responsibilities.[31] It was an important
decision, but many details remained unsettled. The terms of the
mandates had yet to be drawn up; nothing had been done regarding Faisal, although Curzon reported that France apparently would consider him as King of Syria if he recognized the
French role there, a position France had made clear earlier.
Faisal did not attend the conference, and the conference refused to recognize him until he did. In any case, Faisal could
not be recognized in Palestine. One other problem was not
raised, even in discussions of the Hijaz, for the Foreign Office
had decided once again not to suggest Allied recognition of
Britain's Arabian position.[32]

The San Remo conference had ended. France had responsibility for Syria, and Britain for Mesopotamia and Palestine.
Anglo-French agreement, working far more smoothly than a
year earlier, had achieved that much. For Britain, and for Lloyd

[30] Supreme Council meeting (British notes), 19 April 1920 (afternoon session), *DBFP*, VIII, pp. 35–45.

[31] Supreme Council, San Remo, 23 and 25 (morning) April 1920,
*ibid.*, pp. 119–30, 172–84.

[32] Curzon (San Remo) telegrams to F.O. and Allenby, 26 April,
Allenby telegram to F.O. (reporting this information passed to Faisal),
27 April 1920, *FO* 371/5035; Vansittart (Paris) to Curzon, 6 May 1920,
discusses the Arabian chapter, *FO* 371/5244. Mesopotamia, as such, was
not discussed at San Remo.

George, it was a logical step taken in the aftermath of withdrawal from Syria, but it was hardly likely that Faisal or Husain would recognize the new conference decisions. Negotiations, sometimes rather bitter, were not at an end.[33]

If France now had virtually a free hand in Syria, so did Britain in Iraq. Arnold Wilson could be pleased with the result, at least until new orders came from London. So too could Montagu and the India Office, on the Iraqi aspect; but although his staff retained an interest in Iraq, Montagu was rather more concerned with the trend of Turkish affairs and the over-all nature of the Turkish treaty. Since Paris, in fact, Indian representatives had continued to urge clemency for Turkey in the name of Islamic opinion.[34] Montagu was particularly persistent. In late 1919, he had warned the Prime Minister that Indian troops could not be relied upon to enforce a humiliating treaty, and in April 1920 he had demanded the right to memorialize the powers as holder of the Great Seal (for India) from the King and as Plenipotentiary for the Indian government. By that point his days in office were numbered.[35]

By the time of San Remo, Lloyd George had had enough: the British government represented the views of the British government, and Montagu had made use of every opportunity to present the views of his office to other departments of that

[33] Cambon to Curzon, 12 May 1920, discusses the Hijaz protest, *FO* 371/5035.

[34] See, for example, Grant private to Balfour, 7 July, and Balfour private to Grant, 18 August 1919, *Grant Papers;* F.O. to Balfour, 18 August, enclosing draft by Paris delegation, 14 August, and I.O. minutes; Montagu private to Curzon, 28 August 1919, *L/P&S/10,* 4995/19, no. 4995/19.

[35] Montagu private to Lloyd George, 20 August, 8 September, and 13 December 1919, 14 February and 15 April 1920, *Lloyd George Papers,* F/40/2/59–60, 64, and F/40/3/3–4; Montagu to Hankey, 15 and 17 January and 26 February, Hankey to Montagu, 27 February 1920, *FO* 800/157; Montagu to Bonar Law and Bonar Law to Lloyd George, 23 April 1920, *Bonar Law Papers,* 98/9/28 and 101/4/61. Robert Blake, *Unrepentant Tory: The Life and Times of Andrew Bonar Law, 1858– 1923, Prime Minister of the United Kingdom* (N.Y., 1956), pp. 420–21.

government; if anything, he had done so too often. "In fact throughout the Conference," wrote Lloyd George to Montagu, "your attitude has often struck me as being not so much that of a member of the British Cabinet, but of a successor on the thrown [sic] of Aurangzeb!" Montagu would accept the decisions taken or, implicitly, take the consequences. For the moment, Montagu preferred the decisions and remained in office, mainly because of his desire to work on Indian reforms. In May, when the Turks were given the terms of the (Sèvres) treaty, publication of those terms raised no great storm in India —at least immediately—and Montagu's position was further weakened, although when the Khilafat movement began to hit full stride it appeared as if there was something in his arguments.[36]

Montagu's overriding concern for Indian interests was legitimate, considering his position, although an argument might be made against his interpretation of those interests in Turkish affairs. The India Office political staff—above all Hirtzel—still felt a bond with Mesopotamia, but when India discussed Mesopotamia now it was usually because of a clash with Wilson's regime. One sample was an Indian disagreement with Baghdad, beginning in late 1919, over Indian immigration into Iraq. Wilson had in effect installed a passport system which barred such types as small entrepreneurs, agricultural workers, and day laborers who had not actually been hired by the administration; but Baghdad wanted skilled Indian personnel, and India saw such a double-edged policy as decidedly discriminatory.

---

[36] Lloyd George (San Remo) private to Montagu, 25 April (typescript copy; the error is not necessarily the Prime Minister's), and Montagu private to Lloyd George, 29 and 30 April and 3 June 1920, *Lloyd George Papers*, F/40/3/5-8. Montagu's request to be made Viceroy, subsequently withdrawn, could hardly have influenced Lloyd George favorably. Montagu private telegrams to Chelmsford, 1 and 22 January and 27 April, and letter of 20 May, Chelmsford private telegram to Montagu, 3 January, and letter of 26 May 1920, *Chelmsford Papers*. The Turkish treaty terms were made public in mid-May.

The problem was a large one, for Wilson was dealing not only with 1,500 private Indian citizens who had arrived in Iraq since the end of the war but, much more important, with over 50,000 laborers employed by the government. In April 1920 Chelmsford issued an Order in Council which restricted recruitment of Indians for employment in Mesopotamia to government service only, and even this was a concession. The controversy lasted well into 1921 and was further complicated by the fact that Gandhi turned the persuasive powers of his pen to the subject.[37]

The results of these differing attitudes meant that when Britain was assigned the mandate for Mesopotamia in April 1920, and a pro-Arab policy was demanded, neither the Secretary of State for India nor the Viceroy was in a position to defend Iraq's chief administrator with much energy, even had they so desired—and they did not. Wilson, if he maintained his earlier attitudes, was in great jeopardy.

3

From the viewpoint of Baghdad, while the San Remo decision was pleasing the key decisions had already been taken in London. Those decisions, notably that on the constitution, limited Wilson's freedom, but Wilson put his faith in the work of his constitutional committee, which had been working at speed. On 27 April, only a few days after San Remo, he received the committee's report and cabled home its outline.[38] The committee, under the chairmanship of Sir E. Bonham-Carter

[37] Based on *India Home Poli.*, file 51(2) of 1922, particularly Order in Council, 30 April 1920, and references to Gandhi's article, "A Wail from Mesopotamia," in *Young India* (May 1921); and *India Sec. E.* December 1921, 1–79, which covers much of the same ground.

[38] Report of the Bonham–Carter committee, 26 April, and Wilson telegrams to SSI, 27 April (4 of date: nos. 5110–13) 1920, *FO* 371/5226. See also Ireland, *op. cit.*, pp. 200ff.; Wilson, *Mesopotamia*, pp. 242ff.; Marlowe, *op. cit.*, pp. 187ff.

(K.C.M.G., C.I.E., Chief Judicial Secretary) and consisting of Lieutenant-Colonel E. B. Howell (C.S.I., C.I.E., I.C.S., Revenue Secretary), Lieutenant-Colonel F. C. C. Balfour (C.I.E., M.C., Military Governor, Baghdad), Major H. F. M. Tyler (C.I.E., I.C.S., Political Officer, Hilla), and, as secretary, Major R. W. Bullard (C.I.E., Deputy Revenue Secretary), had drawn up a plan in which a two-chamber legislature (Legislative Assembly and Council of State) would control affairs. The Council of State would be the main executive body, composed of some eleven ministers under a president, with membership nominated by the High Commissioner. The president would be Arab, but the ministers, if Arab, would be advised by British secretaries; in any case, the Council would have a British majority, whatever the actual appointments and responsibilities, and the High Commissioner would, further, have veto power over the Council's decisions. The Legislative Assembly would be elected on the basis of communal (religious) representation and would number about fifty (or 1:50,000). Again, the president would be Arab, and the Assembly would have to approve all laws and tax measures passed by the Council of State; but the Council could overrule an Assembly veto.

It was, in short, an Arab façade, and a partial one at that. Wilson, aware that his plan might not find a warm reception, argued in its support, using as weapons the Sunnite-Shiite, tribal, and personnel problems. Mesopotamia, in his mind, could survive only if it remained under British control "for many years to come." His language was a bit unguarded: "There is no difficulty in framing a nonsensical constitution."[39] The real problem was in framing a government which would give power to native elements and yet preserve law and order. More consultation with the population was necessary but could only follow the establishment of the mandate and a period under the provisional constitution as outlined, with foreign affairs

[39] Wilson telegram no. 5111, *ibid.*

and other such key matters under the control of the mandatory power.

It took some time to digest all this, particularly since officials in London were in the process of picking up the threads of other problems after San Remo. Young, as usual, was quick off the mark; the mandate had, after all, been granted, and Wilson was missing this point. Several years of predominantly British government with Arab advice was not enough, although Britain would have to insist that her advice be followed on key matters. Wilson had said that the High Commissioner could decide, at some future date, if an amir was wanted, but again Young returned to the point that the population should decide on this, as on other, questions. To Young, the whole plan was ". . . not an Arab Government at all, and is not likely to become one. Surely the form at any rate of the constitution should be worked out on lines which will eventually develop into an indigenous Government."[40]

On an issue of such magnitude, an interdepartmental meeting was necessary, and it was called for 17 May. In the meantime, Wilson asked on the 8th for permission to frame local announcements according to the Bonham-Carter committee plan and urged London to cancel its order to issue the Curzon draft statement; it was for Britain, as mandatory power, to prescribe the form of government to be adopted, and if London insisted on consulting the councils the extremists would only demand absolute independence again and would threaten violence during the approaching holy month of Ramadan. If Wilson could only be given permission to announce his own proposals in the coming week, he hoped still to have a strong local body of moderate opinion behind him. It was another unfortunate telegram: Wilson had responsibility to the Commander-in-Chief, ". . . in that I could not properly with-

<hr>

[40] Minute by Young, 5 May, on Wilson telegram no. 5113 of 27 April 1920, *FO* 371/5226.

out his approval take action which would imperil his forces and numerous women and children, and lengthen lines of communication in his charge. Procedure of consulting local opinion will have this result." It is hardly necessary to add Young's comment: extremists would have all the more force to their words if they could say Britain was imposing a government upon them, and Young was now nervous that Wilson would take matters into his own hands and publish some communiqué without obtaining prior approval from London.[41]

A series of telegrams from Wilson had prompted this last remark. On 30 April the Civil Commissioner had cabled that continued uncertainty had resulted in increased strength of both pro-'Abdullah and pro-Turkish factions. On 1 May he urged again that the timing of the announcement (his version, not Curzon's) was most important. On the 5th he informed London that Nuri was putting it about that Britain was to establish an Arab government, and Wilson urged that nothing be said to Nuri: "He in no sense represents Mesopotamian interests. . . " Finally, on the 8th, he reported that he had indeed issued a statement of his own, although it referred to Britain's willingness to accept the mandate (news that Wilson would have suppressed had it been possible). The announcement gave a strong indication of British rule for some time to come: reconstruction was required after centuries of misrule; the work could not be done in a day; a civil administration would be established which ". . . will give an ever widening field to native energies." This did not ease Wilson's fears; on the 15th he was warning that, according to his information, 'Abdullah was spending lavish sums on propaganda in Iraq and the Arabs intended to move on Abu Kamal. Even the announcement of a constitution according to the Bonham-Carter committee

[41] Wilson telegrams to SSI, 8 May 1920 (3 of date: nos. 5558–60; no. 5559 quoted), and minutes, *ibid.* (also *L/P&S/10*, 4722/18, nos. 3711, 3684, and 3747/20).

would be insufficient now, for the extremists, "grown fat" on Syrian anarchy, were demanding full independence.[42]

The last point found ready credence in London; Young had said all along that announcement of the Bonham-Carter plan would be useless. The last telegram from Wilson, he minuted, "amounts to a confession of the bankruptcy of our policy in Mesopotamia," and was little more than an appeal for force with which to shore up British control, for Wilson had said that he must have London's support. Yet opinion on solutions was divided; for although Garbett of the India Office had agreed privately with Young's assessment, he had again suggested the return of Cox. Young was not so sure; Cox had his hands full in Persia, and Young not only had doubts about Cox's earlier advice to Curzon but feared that Cox might just ask Wilson to stay on under him. At the moment, moreover, the India Office wished to proceed at once to establish the Council of State and hold elections for the Legislative Assembly, while Young thought a body should be formed to draw up an organic law—that is, he preferred a constitution framed by the population rather than the administration.[43]

On 17 May the interdepartmental committee met, with five India Office representatives to match four from the Foreign Office (but Curzon was in the chair and Young the secretary).

[42] Wilson telegrams to SSI, 30 April, 1, 5 (quoted), and 8 May (no. 5558 quoted) and 15 May 1920 (quoted), *FO* 371/5226. The F.O. was even then still discussing the possible visit of 'Abdullah to London: F.O. telegram to Allenby, 12 May 1920, *L/P&S/10*, 4722/18, no. 3888/20, with hostile I.O. comments. Wilson, in turn, was suggesting the possible visit of the Secretary of State to Iraq, but this, like 'Abdullah's journey, fell through: Wilson private telegram to Montagu, 14 May, and Hirtzel private telegram to Wilson, 19 May 1920, *L/P&S/11*, vol. 173, no. 4027/20. Wilson was at this time engaged in another of those controversies which tended to discredit him, this time over press reports of hangings and the bombing of defenseless villages; see documents in *L/P&S/11*, vol. 168, file 1299/20.

[43] Young minute, 28 May, on Wilson telegram to SSI, 15 May 1920, *FO* 371/5073.

It was clear from the start that Curzon sided with Young, for he began by reviewing the Bonham-Carter scheme and pointing out the fact that it was composed by British officers only (although capable ones) and had taken no evidence. Would not approval of the plan tie Britain's hands just when elasticity was required? And was it fair to the population? Did it fit the terms of the mandate, whatever these would prove to be? To all this Montagu really had no answer, except to say that the mandatory would have to reach agreement with the population. Montagu, too, was alarmed: "If once we started on this line we should never get straight. He regarded Colonel Wilson's ideal as a British-Indian ideal. What he thought we should work to was a native State ideal."

Agreement in principle was not agreement in detail, but from the discussion that followed Curzon concluded that the sense of the meeting was opposition to Wilson's publication of the Bonham-Carter constitution and the conviction that no constitution could issue until the mandate was drafted and sent to the League.[44] It was decided that the India Office would prepare a draft telegram to Wilson corresponding to the meeting's conclusions, and on 20 May Wilson was told by the India Office that announcement of the Bonham-Carter proposals could not now be made, for they "may have to take a different shape"—but, since Wilson had issued his own statement on the mandate, he need not now issue the proclamation drafted by Curzon and approved by Lloyd George. It was an easy way out of a controversy, for Montagu, as has been seen, had objected strenuously to the Foreign Office document. Wilson's own procedure, which might be interpreted as a direct violation of orders, is partly explained by the fact that he issued his declaration on 3 May, and Curzon's pronouncement was only cabled to him on the following day.[45]

On 1 June the conference met again and approved the an-

[44] I.D.C.E. 38th minutes, 17 May 1920, *FO* 371/5226.
[45] I.O. to F.O. and SSI telegram to Wilson, 20 May 1920, *ibid.*

nouncement of Cox's return. On the constitution, however, Curzon still opposed the Bonham-Carter plan, even if applied only temporarily; the regime it outlined might well become stereotyped before an organic law could be framed (as called for in the draft mandate) and put into effect. With this Montagu was in full agreement. No decision was taken on the constitution, but failure to permit the implementation of Wilson's proposals was as good as a formal decision against them.[46]

The committee would have to meet again, for its work on the constitution was uncompleted; but before it could, Wilson again took independent action. A deputation of Baghdadi notables had waited upon him, and Wilson had felt it necessary to voice his regret at the delay in reaching a constitutional settlement and to warn against those urging action by violence. The unfortunate aspect of his statement was his release of an outline of a constitutional structure, which was that of the Bonham-Carter committee's Legislative Assembly, although Wilson spoke in broad terms without actually promising that it would be put into effect.[47] Wilson was no doubt aware that London would object, and strenuously, for he had just been told that precisely such a declaration could not be made. Wilson was governed, however, by local conditions, and local conditions were deteriorating rapidly just as he had predicted. Ramadan and summer had arrived, and revolution was close at hand.

4

The military and financial situation which had been developing throughout the spring had contributed greatly to the dissatisfaction that had caused the decision to replace Wilson immediately. The Treasury was vitally interested in an administration

---

[46] I.D.C.E. 40th minutes, 1 June (and, on mandate discussions, 39th minutes, 26 May 1920), *ibid.*

[47] Wilson telegram to SSI, 2 June 1920, *FO* 371/5227.

that cost over £16 million (and, since revenues were roughly
£4 million, the Treasury paid £12 million), and the War Office
had a similar view, although it estimated costs at £18 million.
Financial and parliamentary pressures had inspired a directive
in April from Winston Churchill at the War Office to
Lieutenant-General Sir Aylmer Haldane, who had replaced
MacMunn in February. Churchill had told Haldane that the
garrison in Iraq must be halved in the coming fiscal year
(March 1920–March 1921). Political decisions must conform
to this directive and, further, all civilian aspects of the administration should be finally transferred out of military hands.
Even the Foreign Office was alarmed at these instructions, for
as Young put it the situation would be most dangerous unless,
by the time of the reductions, Britain had won over the population by "the most liberal measures."[48]

  Churchill complained that the high level of expenditure was
largely due to the urging of political officers who wanted scattered garrisons in remote areas on "various pretexts," with the
result that troops and money enough for a large number of
Indian provinces with millions of inhabitants were used in
Iraq to control ". . . a score of mud villages, sandwiched in between a swampy river and a blistering desert, inhabited by a
few hundred half naked native families, usually starving. . . "[49]
The India Office was duty-bound to answer. A memorandum
by Hirtzel of 22 May admitted the extravagant number of
troops but pointed out in justification that Britain had to
replace the vanished Turkish regime with one at least as good.
Worthless villages were not the point; if Britain did not fill
the vacuum here, somebody else would. Finally, Britain had

---

[48] Churchill telegram to Haldane, 23 April 1920, with minutes by
Young (quoted), Oliphant, and Hardinge, *FO* 371/5073. On Haldane,
see Sir Aylmer Haldane, *A Soldier's Saga: The Autobiography of* . . .
(Edinburgh and London, 1948).

[49] Remarks by Sir G. Barstow (Treasury) in I.D.C.E. (n. 44 above);
Churchill memorandum for Cabinet, 1 May 1920, *Lloyd George Papers,*
F/205/6/1.

undertaken to establish an Arab government; some wished to do this quickly and then cut and run, but such a government would not be popular and would collapse without force with which to defend itself. Hirtzel had an important ally in Milner, the Colonial Secretary, who in a memorandum of the 24th pointed out that Britain had to stay on in Iraq if her position in the Middle East as a whole was considered. He agreed, however, that steps must be taken to deal with the dangers that appeared so threatening there.[50]

On 3 June Wilson telegraphed privately to Hirtzel that the situation in Iraq was worse than at any time since the beginning of the war. Britain's forces were weak and scattered—and the high command was at its remote hill station of Karind (in the Persian Zagros Mountains), while many of his own political officers were tired or away from Iraq on leave. Trouble threatened in the entire Euphrates area, and to Wilson the real cause was the commitment made in the joint declaration of November 1918; the population was unfit to form a government or even to have a voice in the process. Wilson had warned since 1918 of a possible breakdown; he now regarded it as inevitable. Cox's appointment would help, but military action as well would be required when the occasion arose. Officially, Wilson's pessimism was nearly as stark; in another telegram of the same day he added that the only possible procedure was to announce that when the mandate was granted (Wilson still did not grasp this point), a constitutional assembly would immediately be called.[51]

[50] I.O. memorandum, 22 May, drafted by Hirtzel, on Churchill memorandum of 1 May, also in file, *L/P&S/10*, 4722/18, no. 4230/20; Milner memorandum, 24 May 1920, *Milner Papers*, PRO 30/30/20.

[51] Wilson private telegram to Hirtzel and telegram to SSI, 3 June 1920, *L/P&S/10*, 4722/18, nos. 4457 and 4513/20. Karind lies 50 miles east of Khaniqin in the direction of Kermanshah and 150 air miles northeast of Baghdad. The documents do not make clear whether the Persian government was ever asked permission for the establishment of this hill station in Persian territory. The temptation of quoting the following poem on Karind (enclosed in Hirtzel to Chamberlain, 8

Wilson was thus willing to go further than ever before, and the reason for his new attitude was a considerable increase in nationalist pressure which followed both the San Remo decisions and the announcement of the Turkish peace terms. There had even been an attack on Tall 'Afar, 40 miles west of Mosul, and the nationalists with whom Wilson had talked demanded a constitutional convention on an elected basis—and immediately. To Wilson and to Bonham-Carter, this demand was so phrased to permit a body similar to the Syrian congress to meet in order to reject the mandate. Wilson left no doubt of his "I-told-you-so" attitude; such difficulties would not have arisen had he been permitted to announce his own proposals. London's response now was to order Wilson to issue a declaration: Cox would return in the fall and would frame an organic law in consultation with an Arab council of state. To Wilson, this would only mean more disorder; he countered by suggesting a delegation of a few Iraqis to England to discuss the future. Afterward, having gone as far as possible in the direction of conciliation, the Civil Commissioner would be able to take action against the extremists. London also reported that Faisal in Damascus wished to send Nuri to Iraq to discuss frontiers (the attack on Tall 'Afar had apparently been led by Sharifal officers), but Wilson would meet Nuri only at Qa'im, a few miles east of Abu Kamal close to the frontier.[52]

Wilson was obviously worried, and increasingly pessimistic.

---

October 1920, *Chamberlain Papers*, 23/1/14) is too great to resist:
Half a lakh, half a lakh squandered,
Up to the Persian Hills G.H.Q. wandered . . .
Think of the camp they made
Think of the water laid
On, and the golf links made
Think of the bill we paid
Oh, the wild charge they made!
Half a lakh squandered.

[52] Wilson telegrams to SSI, 3, 4, and 7 June, SSI telegram to Wilson, 7 June; Curzon private telegram to Cox, 3 June, and J. A. C. Tilley to Shuckburgh, 8 June 1920, show Cox was told that he would go to Iraq

Troops were in short supply, with only a junior lieutenant-colonel in Baghdad for liaison with the high command. Unless the garrison was kept at current strength for the next two years, no effect could be given to the mandate; also, the areas taken by the Sharifians must be recaptured. Otherwise there was only one alternative: withdrawal from Mesopotamia. If Britain still intended to stay on, it must live up to its pledge to establish a government, a process that must proceed slowly, "regardless of League of Nations," in the development of constitutional and democratic institutions "the application of which to Eastern countries has been attempted of late years with such little degree of success." Half measures would mean only disaster, as France was learning in Syria. But Wilson's increasingly determined tone won only intensified criticism from Young: Wilson totally ignored the third alternative to force or withdrawal, and that was to win over the population. Young continued,

The reason for this is not far to seek. It is because he knows that we cannot obtain the good will of the people without instituting a predominantly Arab government, and this I am perfectly certain Colonel Wilson will use every effort to prevent.

I regard this telegram as tantamount to a resignation and think that it should be accepted as such.[53]

The India Office had little choice save to pass Wilson's remarks on to the War Office. It would seem that 10,000 British and 65,000 Indian troops would be enough, but if they were actually weak and scattered as reported by Wilson, and if outside raids were going to have to be dealt with, perhaps the War Office could ask General Haldane if his troop dispositions were the best under the circumstances. The War Office re-

in the fall: all *FO* 371/5226-7. Wilson telegrams to SSI, 5 (on Tall 'Afar) and 8 (on meeting with Nuri) June 1920, *FO* 371/5129.

[53] Wilson telegram to SSI, 9 June, and Young minute, 16 June 1920, *FO* 371/5227.

acted predictably, replying that Haldane had already been asked and objecting officially to Wilson's remarks. At the same time, however, they telegraphed out to Haldane a series of questions on current troubles, future dangers, and the possible results of a retreat by the forces in both Mosul and Persia to the nearest railhead.[54]

In this quarrel, the Foreign Office sided with the military, for both Young and Hardinge still regarded Wilson as the main problem. The virtual state of war between Baghdad and Damascus, to which Wilson himself had referred, was due, as Young put it, to Wilson's own "implacable hostility to any-thing Sherifian [which] has caused us a great deal of trouble in the past and will cause more in the future"; to which Hardinge added, "The whole situation is too big for Col. Wilson to cope with."[55] Foreign Office officials were particularly un-happy because Iraq had become an issue of public interest. Al-though a regular stream of comments and evaluations had appeared all along, in the latter part of June 1920 a determined attack was mounted in the British press, not only on the policy which had brought the need for suppression of revolt and attacks upon Mesopotamia from the outside, but also upon Wilson as the man responsible for that policy. *The Times* of 15 June is a fair example: the government's statements on Iraq had long been characterized by "evasions, concealments, and half-truths" in the defense of a Civil Commissioner who was trying to Indianize Mesopotamia and whose policy rested upon

---

[54] Wilson private and official telegrams to SSI, 9 June, I.O. to W.O., 10 June, W.O. to I.O., 15 June 1920, *L/P&S/10*, 4722/18, nos. 4513 4593, 4605, and 4679/20; W.O. to I.O., 3 July, I.O. to W.O., 12 July, Wilson private and official telegrams to SSI, 14 July 1920, *L/P&S/11*, vol. 175, nos. 5263 and 5451/20, cover the continued controversy. W.O. questions: W.O. telegram to Haldane, 10 June 1920, *FO 371/5075*.

[55] Wilson telegram to SSI, 8 June 1920, and Young and Hardinge minutes, *FO 371/5129*; Young's attitude toward Wilson makes his *In-dependent Arab* a somewhat dangerous source on this subject as used, for example, by Nevakivi, *Britain, France and the Arab Middle East*, p. 177.

his "dangerous tendency to disregard the broader aspects of Imperial policy. . . " Other articles turned upon the expense and number of troops involved, or Montagu's role, and not unnaturally compared trends in Iraq with the recent horror of Amritsar in India.[56]

It had already been decided in the interdepartmental conference that Cox would return, but the mounting criticism forced a decision at a higher level. At a Cabinet meeting of 17 June, it was agreed that "notwithstanding his great services" Wilson was out and Cox was in. A telegram to Cox was prepared, outlining Wilson's views and the government's criticism of those views and promising that the government would not take a decision on withdrawal from Mesopotamia until Cox had had the opportunity to study the situation there at first hand and to report to London. The following day the ministers further approved as policy a telegram to Baghdad of eleven days earlier announcing Cox's coming arrival in the fall (which Wilson already knew), an organic law within two years, "a predominantly Arab Council of State with an Arab President," and a representative general assembly which would help frame the organic law. But, in issuing this statement, Wilson was also told, "You need not consider yourself tied down to exact form of words." [57]

Wilson released the announcement, but he also released simultaneously his own proclamation, which stated that the government had no intention of withdrawing any of its troops and would maintain a force of all arms with which to fulfill its obligations. For the moment, it was difficult to act with more speed, for Cox had to go to Iraq—where by late June he was consulting with Wilson—and then had to give his own opinions. And,

[56] See The Times, 9, 15 (quoted), 23, 24, and 29 June; Morning Post, 16 and 24 June; Guardian, 24 June; Commons, 23 June; Lords, 24 June 1920. See particularly file of cuttings in FO 371/5226.

[57] Cabinet 53 (20), Appendix II, Conference of Ministers, 17 June, Appendix III, Conference of Ministers, 18 June, and Appendix IV to Appendix III, SSI telegram to Wilson, 7 June 1920, CAB 23/22.

unfortunately, Cox, so long regarded as the answer to all Iraq's problems (except by Young), seemed to share Wilson's views. Wilson reported that the visiting Cox approved all his own announcements and, furthermore, wished to discuss the terms of his own appointment before actually accepting. Both men agreed that the preservation of order was the first essential, and Wilson repeated both his earlier suggestion of an Iraqi delegation to England and the possibility of repressive measures. For himself, Wilson explained that his own announcement on the preservation of order was in answer to the so far indifferent success of attempts to restore order on the upper Euphrates and to the press attacks at home. Time had not permitted reference to London, but Cox had concurred in it, and Wilson claimed, rather obscurely, the authority of a London telegram of 28 November 1918 for his declaration.[58]

London was not satisfied. Not only had Wilson issued his own statement, but it clashed seriously with a government statement in Commons on 28 June that Britain would withdraw when circumstances permitted (Wilson had said no intention to withdraw existed, although he meant in the short run). Moreover, when issuing London's proclamation as ordered, Wilson had removed the key words "predominantly Arab" from before "Council." Wilson subsequently claimed that he felt the words were redundant, for the Bonham-Carter committee had not planned a predominantly British council—which was not only a lame excuse but was not how London had inter-

[58] Wilson telegrams to SSI, 20, 22 (with Young and Hardinge minutes), and 25 June. Wilson's explanation was prompted by an official inquiry (SSI telegram to Wilson, 24 June) and a private telegram from Hirtzel (25 June). The telegram referred to, dated 28 November 1918, simply told the Iraqi administration that its pronouncements should conform to Allied positions; I.O. to F.O., 13 July, and F.O. to I.O., 17 July 1920. All in *FO* 371/5227.

[59] Shuckburgh memorandum, 29 June, discusses the controversy with the government's statement; Wilson's explanation is in Wilson private

preted the Bonham-Carter proposal.[59] Even the India Office
was unconvinced, and in the Foreign Office Wilson had not a
single defender. Ending a series of hostile minutes, Curzon
added: "Personally I would tel[e] & withdraw Sir A. Wilson at
once—but I am afraid that in the absence of Sir P. Cox and until
the arrival of the latter it wl[d] be difficult." The India Office
was warned officially that Wilson should make no more unauthorized declarations.[60]

Meanwhile, Wilson was continuing with the work of dealing
firmly with the discontent. A number of arrests and deporta-
tions were made, which measures, Wilson reported, had given
heart to the moderates. Mosul, too, was given new spirit when
an advance post was established at Tall 'Afar, the raided village.
"We are rapidly drifting in Mesopotamia into a position anal-
ogous to the vicious circle in Ireland," minuted an unappeased
Young, who cited conversations with returned (British) Iraqi
political officers to support his opinion. That there was alarm
in Syria as well was shown by Ja'far Pasha's offer to resign his
post under Faisal and proceed to Baghdad to attempt to remove
misunderstandings through discussion, an offer which received
Allenby's full support.[61] Whether Ja'far's alarm was for stability in Iraq or for the future of the nationalist movement there
is, of course, another question.

Young and Hardinge agreed that no good would result from
the trip so long as Wilson was in control; but it was for Wilson
to decide, and he announced that he would be glad to see Ja'far
—although it would be best if he came by sea and not, as planned, via Tall 'Afar (with prior warning, even that might be

---

telegram to Hirtzel, 27 June 1920: *L/P&S/10*, 4722/18, nos. 5045 and
5104/20.

    [60] F.O. to I.O., 1 July 1920, with Young (28 June), Hardinge, Tilley,
and Curzon (29 June, quoted) minutes on draft, *FO* 371/5227.

    [61] Wilson telegram to SSI, 28 June, with minutes, and Allenby tele-
gram to F.O., 1 July 1920, *ibid.*

possible). Indeed, added Wilson, he had only been awaiting approval of his version of the announcement on Cox and the organic law before informing Damascus that he was inviting selected Baghdadi officers to come and assist in the formation of the electoral law. It was a curious reversal of roles, for Young opposed the visit which Wilson appeared to welcome.[62]

5

A visit by Ja'far was an interesting idea, but before anything could come of it further difficulties had occurred for Wilson and his regime. On 2 July tribes near Rumaitha (on the Hilla canal, east of the Euphrates, and a station on the Basra-Baghdad railway, 200 miles north of Basra, 150 miles south of Baghdad) attacked government buildings there, freeing a shaikh who had been arrested. The railway was cut, and when reinforcements were sent to relieve the town several days later they found the going most difficult. There were a number of casualties, and the reinforcements were themselves cut off. Military authorities were forced to bomb rebel-held areas of the town (the garrison was still holding out), and more troops were ordered held in readiness in India for dispatch to Basra if necessary.[63] The situation was obviously critical; the Foreign Office informed Curzon, attending a meeting of the conference at Spa, adding that more troops hardly seemed the right answer and that Cornwallis of Meinertzhagen's staff should be sent to Baghdad with Nuri and Ja'far and possibly other Syrian Baghdadis. The prior withdrawal of Wilson, "who could not be expected to participate usefully in such a Conference," would be a requirement.

[62] Wilson telegrams to SSI, 20 and 25 June, 2 July and 3 July (with Young minute, 9 July), SSI telegrams to Wilson, 1 and 5 July, F.O. telegram to Allenby, 9 July 1920, *ibid*. Gertrude Bell, in Iraq, had rather mixed views: Burgoyne, *op. cit.*, p. 145.

[63] Wilson telegram to SSI, 4 July, Haldane telegrams to W.O., 7 and 8 July, SSI telegram to Wilson, 8 July 1920, copying telegram to Viceroy of same date, *FO* 371/5227.

Needless to say, it was Young's telegram, with Hardinge's approval.[64]

By the time Curzon received this telegram it was already clear that the relief column was not going to reach Rumaitha; supplies for the beleaguered garrison had to be dropped by air. Wilson explained, meanwhile, that the cause of all this was Bolsheviks, Turks, and Syrians, in that order. When these external factors had been dealt with, Mesopotamia would be calm, for representatives of all three were simply fishing in troubled waters. Part of the problem, Wilson could not avoid adding, was Britain's declarations, ". . . which so widely diverge, if I may be allowed to say so, from realities of life in Mesopotamia, that they find no degree of popular acceptance outside the towns. . ." And if only the military forces had been in better condition . . ."[65]

From London, the entire situation appeared most confused, and there was little choice beyond letting Wilson and General Haldane handle it on the spot. In Syria, Faisal appeared on the point of expulsion at the hands of the French, while Haddad Pasha, his agent in London, was still urging that 'Abdullah be asked to Mesopotamia. The Foreign Office, under the circumstances, ordered that Ja'far's trip be canceled for the time being, and Montagu found himself in the unusual position of arguing against the Foreign Office in favor of the visit to Iraq of an Iraqi nationalist. But to Young, Nuri and Ja'far were "almost our last hope," and they could not be risked with Wilson; ". . . it is more than ever important that we should make a clean sweep of our mistaken methods in Mesopotamia." [66]

[64] F.O. telegram to Curzon (Spa), 10 July 1920, *ibid.*
[65] Haldane telegrams to W.O., 9 and 10 July 1920, *ibid.* Wilson telegram to SSI, 10 July 1920, *L/P&S/10*, 4722/18, no. 5408/20.
[66] Note by General Haddad, received 14 July, Young minute (quoted), 15 July 1920, *FO* 371/5036; I.O. to F.O., 15 July, and Young minute (quoted), 13 July, on undated "Summary of Correspondence" attached to Hardinge private telegram to Curzon, 14 July 1920, *FO* 371/5227.

Only Young appeared to have a clear answer in mind, and this he set out in a memorandum of 18 July written at Curzon's request. The memorandum was long, dealing as it did with causes of the revolt, but the proposed solution was simple: remove Wilson, send in Nuri and Ja'far, establish a Royal Commission to inquire into the administration and sample the views of the population, and, until Cox (or another) could arrive, let Bonham-Carter temporarily be in charge with the help of Cornwallis. In six months, all troops would withdraw to railhead and an Arab state would be established in Mosul. Finally, Britain would announce that it would approve any ruler chosen by a legislative assembly either for the whole of Mesopotamia or for a part of it.[67]

But even had all this been accepted in the Foreign Office, it was not that easy to put the plan into effect, for the revolt was only hitting its peak in late July and August.[68] Virtually the whole of the middle Euphrates area rose against Britain; Samawa below Rumaitha was cut off; intermediate areas, particularly west of the railway around Najaf and Kifl, were out of control, and of three companies of the Third Manchesters sent to hold Kifl, barely half returned to Hilla. Diwaniya, a divisional center, was evacuated. Success of the revolt in the mid-Euphrates led to risings in the lower Euphrates, and by the first week of August, with the whole area in flames, *jihad* had been proclaimed in Karbala. It would not be until October that a number of these towns would be relieved and the revolt put down, and by then Britain would have lost 450 dead and the

[67] Young memorandum, 18 July 1920, *FO* 371/5228.
[68] Details on the revolt are based upon Ireland, *op. cit.*, ch. XIV; Wilson, *Mesopotamia*, ch. XII; Marlowe, *op. cit.*, ch. XI; Lt.-Gen. Sir Aylmer Haldane, *The Insurrection in Mesopotamia, 1920* (Edinburgh, 1922); Burgoyne, *op. cit.*, Chs. XII-XIV; Coke, *The Heart of the Middle East*, pp. 173–93; Loder, *op. cit.*, pp. 87–98; Zeine, *Struggle*, pp. 146–48; Wingate, *Not in the Limelight*, pp. 93–94; Hay, *op. cit.*, pp. 267–68, 349; and, for the most detailed official account, "An Examination of the Causes of the Outbreak in Mesopotamia . . . ," prepared by General Staff, W.O., 26 October 1920 (95 pp.), *WO* 33/969.

same number of missing—with wounded, nearly 2,000 casualties in all.

As if the revolt itself was not enough, the government had to face a growing storm of criticism in press and Parliament. *The Daily Mail*, for example, ran an article on 12 July by Lovat Fraser, a publicist and observer of the Indian scene of some eminence, titled "The War-Mongers," which ran to the tune of "there is nothing in all our history to compare with our folly in Mesopotamia." Parliamentary references compared Amritsar with Iraq or asked with biting sarcasm if the Arabs in revolt knew that British policy was to establish an Arab state. The most damaging attack was a letter of 22 July from T. E. Lawrence to *The Times*. In Iraq, said Lawrence, 450 officers staffed an administration that had been 70 per cent locally run under the Turks; the Arabs had fought for their freedom during the war, and Faisal had managed to maintain his independent state in Syria for two years so far—a period during which virtually nothing had been done in Iraq. The only remedy (as Young had been saying all along) was a radical change: Arabic language in the administration, local levies to replace the military, and so on; within a year Britain would hold as much as she held of Canada or South Africa. It was a bitter and effective attack: "Why should Englishmen (or Indians) have to be killed to make the Arab Government in Mesopotamia . . . ?" [69]

Young might have been expected to sympathize with this view, but he was not one of Lawrence's great admirers either. After all, he pointed out, Faisal's regime had been heavily subsidized by Britain, and it was hardly accurate to predict a withdrawal of British troops in twelve months. "What is wanted is the mean between Lawrentian and Wilsonian ideas." And J. A. C. Tilley added, "With an inclination to Lawrence." Montagu

[69] Collection of clippings of press and Parliamentary remarks, *FO* 371/5227. Lovat Fraser had been editor of *The Times of India;* see his *India Under Curzon and After* (London, 1911). Lawrence's letter of 22 July, which appeared in *The Times* of 23 July, is quoted in Weintraub, *op. cit.,* pp. 78–80, and Garnett, *op. cit.,* pp. 306–8.

in the India Office was similarly critical: the 70 per cent Lawrence had referred to were Sunnite, while the bulk of the population was Shiite—and nothing showed that the 70 per cent was Arab and not Turkish in any case.[70]

Wilson and his administration were saved temporarily by the relief of Rumaitha, and Wilson, reporting hopefully on the event on 21 July, argued that the projected withdrawal from Mosul would sacrifice the entire north—which would seem obvious; it would continue to be necessary not to hold down rebels by force but, as under the Ottomans, to show the minimum of force necessary to secure governmental authority. At the same time, however, the War Office was asking the India Office whether Montagu was really confident ". . . that the local policy pursued by the Political Staff in Mesopotamia is such as to minimise the chance of the repetition of such practical demonstrations of Arab discontent"—Wilson, in other words, ought to be removed.[71]

Montagu retaliated with a memorandum criticizing the Army's lavish expenditure in Iraq: motor cars touring about the country full of officers' wives, and the like. As for the charge (made in public by Lawrence) of "Indianization," Montagu was not certain what that meant, but he assumed the idea was that Iraq was administered like Indian provinces with high taxes and a good deal of unrest. None of this fit the case. For those who had missed earlier memoranda, Montagu outlined the lack of trained officials, the need for replacing the Turkish administration, and the government's policy of using trained Arabs wherever they could be found to be qualified. Taxes, as far as anybody knew, were those of the Turkish regime. The papers had said that Britain extracted £6 million where the Turks had taken only £2.5 million, which was true enough, said the Secre-

[70] Young, Tilley minutes on *The Times,* and Montagu memorandum, all 23 July 1920, *FO* 371/5228.
[71] Wilson telegram to SSI, 21 July 1920, *ibid.*; W.O. to I.O., 22 July 1920, *L/P&S/10*, 4722/18, no. 5679/20.

tary, when prewar figures for the Baghdad vilayet alone were compared with figures for the entire area now under British occupation. Most important, Arnold Wilson and the India Office had several times suggested measures for visiting committees and steps toward Arab administration, but the responsibility for delays in implementation had to be borne primarily by the Foreign Office; and Montagu had at hand the useful example of the Foreign Office veto of Ja'far's visit.[72]

A "series of absurd charges," concluded Curzon, who again gave Young the task of preparing a counterblast. Once more Young took pen in hand, this time to review decisions taken and orders passed to Wilson since early 1919, all demonstrating the basic Foreign Office difficulty in getting the India Office to overrule Wilson's obstructionism—or that of Cox. Young's minute was a useful catalogue of announcements authorized but unissued, issued but unauthorized, and authorized and issued but altered. Wilson, in Young's view, had deliberately changed the constitution London had sanctioned; he had put no time limit on the framing of an organic law (London had called for two years); he had removed "predominantly Arab" from the Council. Montagu blamed the Foreign Office; but since Montagu had all along insisted that Iraq was the India Office's preserve, this was hardly fair.[73]

It was to this level of charge and countercharge, tragically enough, that the key London departments were still reduced, over a year and a half after the end of the war. Meanwhile, both Wilson and Cox, now very much involved, were making suggestions. Wilson was thinking of using Sayyid Talib Pasha, the prewar power in Basra; Talib had now returned to Iraq with Wilson's permission. Cox, while willing to defend Wilson and to point out the special conditions that complicated the Iraqi

[72] Montagu memorandum, 23 July 1920, *FO* 371/5228.
[73] Curzon undated minute for Young (but 27 July) on Montagu memorandum, and Young memorandum, undated (but 29 July 1920), *ibid.*

situation, and to condemn all suggestions of withdrawal from Mosul, would not associate himself with Wilson's regime on points of detail, like Wilson's reported censoring of the text of British Parliamentary debates for Iraqi release. Like Wilson, Cox could offer no hope whatever of an immediate reduction of responsibilities, aside from the hope that perhaps within three years the necessary local security forces would be in existence.[74]

Essentially, however, Cox shared the attitude of London. The Iraqi government must be predominantly Arab—he still used the term "façade"—whatever the price in reduced efficiency. As for a ruler, although the appointment of an amir should be delayed, the conviction was strongly held in London that few observers would believe Iraq to be an Arab state without such a ruler; Cox therefore suggested that there should be for from five to seven years an elected president. This would not bar the solution of an amir in the future. Cox's main reason for this suggestion was his feeling that the introduction of a ruler like 'Abdullah was simply not possible at that time.[75]

Cox also suggested that Wilson be brought back to London for consultation, but both Haldane and Wilson objected. As Wilson put it plainly in a private telegram to Cox (in London), the home authorities already had his view: "govern or go." If there was any doubt, Wilson removed it in this telegram: "An Arab state though not on the lines desired by His Majesty's Government, may yet come, but it will be by revolution and not by evolution." [76] In Wilson's defense it must be said that late July 1920 was hardly the time to withdraw the chief political officer, if only because his subordinates, most of whom re-

---

[74] Wilson telegram to SSI, 25 July 1920, *ibid.*; Cox memorandum, 24 July 1920, *FO* 371/5231. Censorship of Parliamentary debates: Cox private telegram to Wilson, 23 August, Wilson private telegram to Cox, 24 August 1920, *L/P&S/10*, 4722/18, nos. 6326 and 6340/20.

[75] Cox private telegram to Haldane, 27 July 1920, *L/P&S/11*, vol. 175, no. 5845/20.

[76] Wilson private telegram to Cox, 29 July 1920, *ibid.*

mained on in their rather lonely posts, trusted in him to pull
them out when things got really difficult.[77]

Once the revolt appeared to be pushing Britain out of central Iraq, London's conviction that the blame lay with Wilson's
over-all policy seemed vindicated. When a new possibility appeared, officials in London were quick to take advantage of it:
Faisal, driven out of Damascus by the French, had taken refuge
in Palestine and then in Europe and was available for employment. There was some legitimate fear that the expulsion of
Faisal would only mean more problems for Iraq, but here
nevertheless was a chance to prove the superiority of British
methods over French. Such proof was sorely needed. The obvious question was whether Anglo-French relations would
stand the strain if Britain now offered a throne to Faisal. At the
very least, it was clear that Faisal would have to give up all hostility to France in Syria if he was to take up Iraq. In late July
Curzon sounded out Berthelot at Boulogne, making it clear
that Britain could not view the disappearance of Faisal from
the scene with equanimity. It was the opening gun of a lengthy
campaign.[78]

6

It was not surprising that in London Faisal should be thought
of in connection with Iraq. It was surprising, however, that on
31 July Wilson cabled to ask if the government was prepared
to consider Faisal for Iraq. The objections to an amir in Baghdad, he added, had always been based upon the fact that no

[77] See, for example, Hay, op. cit., p. 365, referring to officers who
had died in the north: "All, or nearly all, were inspired in their work
by the great spirit of Sir Arnold Wilson, who showed towards each of
his officers a personal regard and consideration, encouraging them by
his example and advice. . ."

[78] I.O. minutes: Garbett, 26 and 29 July, L. W. Duke, 30 July 1920,
L/P&S/10, 786/19, nos. 5651 and 5841/20; Curzon to Sir G. Grahame
(Paris), 28 July 1920, FO 371/5037.

suitable candidate was available, for Faisal had always been considered as booked for Syria. Wilson had not modified his view on 'Abdullah, but Faisal was a different case. Certainly he had some idea of the practical difficulties of running a state, and Wilson was also aware of the moral effect of such an appointment. The India Office officials must have wondered at Wilson's change of heart, although, taken at face value, the explanation was simple enough—but in any case the Cabinet would have to decide.[79]

The principal problem would be France. This aspect particularly worried the Foreign Office, where the feeling was that negotiation on the mandates and on recognition of British supremacy in Arabia had been going rather well. Caution would be essential. And even if France agreed, and suitable terms were worked out with Faisal, the revolt would still have to be put down, and put down in a situation in which the Cabinet had already decided to halve expenses in the coming year. Yet, as Churchill put it, Britain still was determined "to plough through in that dismal country." [80]

By August continued spread of the revolt had eased enough for the India Office to ask Wilson for a clear explanation of the causes and objectives of the rising. Wilson's answer laid stress on eighteen months of Turkish and Syrian propaganda and cash, at least as principal cause, but claimed that it was only when Britain's military weakness was revealed, as at Dair az-Zaur, that the extremists had concluded that Britain might actually be expelled by direct action. The terms of the Turkish treaty had driven all those with pro-Turkish sympathies into the hostile camp, for it was now said that Britain had an anti-Muslim policy and was growing weaker into the bargain. Fi-

[79] Wilson telegram to SSI, 31 July 1920, FO 371/5038; Montagu memorandum, 2 August 1920, enclosing same for Cabinet, CAB 24/110.

[80] Vansittart (Paris) to Curzon, 2 August 1920, FO 371/5345; Churchill to Lloyd George, 5 and 26 (quoted) August 1920, Lloyd George Papers, F/9/2/37 and 41.

nally, from the local standpoint, the tribes were always anti-government, but in this case they had been led into thinking that *jihad* was involved. Agrarian grievances, such as high taxes, were not the problem; the harvests were good and the burdens light, and if proof were needed, the agitation would not have been so largely confined to the centers of Najaf and Karbala, the Shiite holy cities, were this not the case. Of course the tribes would like to avoid taxation, but that traditional attitude was insufficient to bring revolt unless external factors were added.[81]

A week later, Wilson, as was his custom, added further points, one of which was a new departure. By noting that the tribesmen were aggrieved over the additional burdens placed upon them by their tribal shaikhs, who in turn had been led in this direction by Britain's policy of supporting their authority as against the rank-and-file tribesmen, Wilson was criticizing an aspect of policy very much resembling that followed on the Indian frontier, whose application to Iraq had really not been fully discussed. But there was more, including the postwar inflation, the pressure by the military administration on the natives to perform labor for the repair of the bunds (protective embankments on waterways), the fear of western exploitation, the use of airplanes against dissident elements (a policy that Wilson had supported all along), and a number of other points already raised in earlier correspondence. The result of Arnold Wilson's fourteen numbered points (the satirical parallel was painfully obvious, particularly since one of the points was the statements made by his namesake) was, from his standpoint, a criticism both of British weakness through insufficient severity and of excessive haste in constitutional development. The essence was revealed by Wilson's reference to disagreement on that point at which "a constitutional movement becomes so se-

[81] SSI telegram to Wilson, 2 August 1920, *L/P&S/10*, 4722/18, no. 5869/20; Wilson telegram to SSI, 5 August 1920, *FO* 371/5228.

ditious as to demand or justify repression." The possibility of
regarding this as admission of self-failure was not lost on the
Foreign Office.[82]

Whatever its causes, Wilson and Haldane still had to sup-
press the revolt. After a temporary lull, mid-August witnessed
a number of further flare-ups. On 12 August Leachman was
killed near Falluja (40 miles west of Baghdad), and further
outposts had to be withdrawn, for the death of this able and
strong-willed individual, as Wilson admitted, was a serious
blow to British prestige. By the 16th, Wilson reported that garrisons at Falluja and Ramadi (another 30 miles to the west)
were cut off from Baghdad, and the uproar in the north was so
great that evacuation from Mosul might soon be necessary. The
revolt had moved, said Wilson, from political causes to general
anarchy, and whether Britain went or stayed more troops
would be necessary.[83]

It was inevitable that the renewed outbreak in Iraq would be
paralleled by the criticism at home. "It is odd that we do not
use poison gas on these occasions," wrote T. E. Lawrence in
*The Observer*. *The Daily Herald* and *The Sunday Times* carried lengthy interviews with him, giving him the opportunity
to put forward all his own views and to place blame initially on
"the empty space which divides the Foreign Office from the
India Office," which allowed such a free hand to Arnold Wilson. As for Wilson, he had declared himself a changed man, but
his policy was just the same. Britain, said "T. E.," was worse
than the Turks; the latter had killed an average 200 people in
a year, but Britain had managed to eliminate 10,000 in one summer, and at this rate the population would soon be no more
trouble. Cromer in Egypt had controlled 6,000,000 with 5,000
troops; Wilson could not deal with 3,000,000 with 90,000 men.

    [82] Wilson telegram to SSI, 12 August 1920, *L/P&S/10*, 4722/18, no.
6204/20; see also Wilson private to Hirtzel, 23 August 1920, *Wilson
Papers*, Add. Mss. 52455.
    [83] Wilson telegrams to SSI, 13, 16, and 18 August 1920, *FO* 371/5229.

*The Sunday Times* also carried, in September, a heated exchange between Curzon and Major W. Ormsby-Gore, who had had a role in policy-making (from the London-Cairo side) himself. Ormsby-Gore laid the blame for Wilson's policy squarely on the Eastern Committee—a view that, needless to say, Curzon hardly shared.[84]

R. Marrs, who had served under Wilson and who replaced Garbett when the latter went out to Iraq with Cox, later wrote, "The figure of Col. Wilson with head bloody but unbowed through all this welter of rapine murder and British-press hate will be one of my prized memories." [85] Savage as the attack was, Wilson's removal had already been decided upon before it began; but Cox's appointment was meeting a serious obstacle in General Haldane, who had nothing against Cox but much against the appointment of a High Commissioner who would be superior to the General Officer Commanding. Until the revolt was put down and the situation stabilized, predicted Haldane, Cox's arrival was likely to bring a renewal of the old Cox-Maude difficulties; he advised delay until, perhaps, mid-November. In the Foreign Office some advisors sided with Haldane, feeling that order must be restored first, so that Cox's arrival would not be viewed as an admission of British defeat. Others opposed the doctrine of conquest first, concession second, for, as Tilley remarked, pacification was an argument that appealed particularly to "those who contemplate the permanent annexation of Mesopotamia. . ." Both Hardinge and Curzon agreed, and the policy of Wilson's replacement by Cox

---

[84] *The Observer*, 8 August (quoted), *The Daily Herald*, 9 August, *The Sunday Times*, 22 (quoted) and 29 August and 19 September 1920, *L/P&S/11*, vol. 176, file 6578/20, vol. 177, file 7144/20, and *L/P&S/10*, 4722/18, no. 8230/20. *The Observer*, 8 August, and *The Sunday Times*, 22 August, in Weintraub, *op. cit.*, pp. 92–99. See also Lawrence's "The Changing East," published anonymously in *The Round Table* (September 1920) and reprinted in T. E. Lawrence, *Oriental Assembly* (London, 1939), pp. 71–97.

[85] R. Marrs minute, 6 November 1920, *L/P&S/10*, 4722/18, no. 8230/20.

stood, although Haldane was told that Cox's arrival would in no way interfere with the military operations for which the General was responsible.[86]

Tilley had touched a raw nerve, however. Both Hardinge and Curzon, the two ex-viceroys, would have tried a different policy had there been any chance of success. On a note by Captain I. N. Clayton outlining a discussion with Talib Pasha on how the latter could rule the country himself, particularly if the country was the vilayet of Basra, both officials revealed their nostalgia for the plan of permanent retention of southern Iraq. Curzon wrote, "The strongest opponents of this policy were Lord Cecil and Mr. Montagu who almost fainted at the idea of annexation or a Protectorate and made a fetish of self-determination. I gave Sir P. Cox a strongish hint."[87]

Cox was given more than a hint: he was given two sets of instructions. Both sets had been approved by the Cabinet and were for his general guidance rather than for publication.[88] The more important set of instructions dealt with the problem of an Arab amir, an issue that had to be treated with great delicacy, since France, when directly approached on the possible use of Faisal in Iraq, had clearly indicated that she would regard such a policy as unfriendly. For this reason, and because Cox after all might find that different parts of Iraq required different solutions, it might be necessary to await the development of a consensus in a quieter time while Cox was meanwhile establishing the organic law, a period that should be some two years. The actual instructions required that there be, therefore, a "spontaneous" demand from "a sufficiently representative body of public opinion in Mesopotamia"; also, Faisal would have to approve the mandate terms, which meant in turn that Faisal would have to be contacted and a working agreement negotiated.

[86] Haldane telegram to W.O., 21 August, with minutes, W.O. to F.O., 25 August 1920, *FO* 371/5229.

[87] Clayton note, 22 August 1920, and minutes, *FO* 371/5230.

[88] Cabinet 49 (20), 17 August 1920, *CAB* 23/22.

Britain would have to control foreign affairs, and certainly special administration of the finances would be required. All this, however, was one version of Cox's orders. The other, shorter set made no mention of Faisal but only of an Arab government. It remained, in other words, for Cox to determine the situation in Iraq and for someone else to determine the attitude of Amir Faisal. With these instructions in hand, Cox left London immediately, and by 2 September he was in Egypt, talking to Ja'far, whom he found most pessimistic and convinced that Britain intended in Iraq what France had accomplished in Syria.[89]

Meanwhile, authorities in London were hard at work on a draft mandate for Mesopotamia, work that had been continuing ever since Anglo-French (and interdepartmental) disagreements had been revealed on the subject at Spa. On 3 September an interdepartmental committee outlined a simple statement which corresponded roughly to Cox's instructions, except that the organic law was to be framed in a period not exceeding three years.[90] Discussion of the form of the mandates was to take much time and last well beyond 1921, but it was a subsidiary problem, linking Iraqi affairs with those of Palestine and Syria, and therefore with Anglo-French relations, which should be borne in mind. The India Office had far less responsibility for the actual mandate document than the Foreign Office, and therefore less to do with Cox's instructions: the closer Iraq approached independent standing and the more negotiations involved Faisal and the French, the more Iraq was the responsibility of the Foreign Office. The India Office was still inclined

---

[89] Crowe minute, 10 August, on conversation with French, 8 August 1920, *FO* 371/5039; see British note on conversations, *DBFP*, VIII, pp. 709–22; Appendix I to Cabinet 49 (20), Finance Committee, 12 August 1920, *CAB* 23/22; draft instructions to Cox, 28 August (date printed, four days after Cox's departure), Port Said Consul (from Cox) telegram to F.O. (for SSI), 2 September 1920, *FO* 371/5229.

[90] Drafts of 31 July and 2 August, and various minutes; interdepartmental conference minutes, 3 September 1920: *FO* 371/5245.

to defend Wilson against his attackers, but when Cox departed with the Cabinet's orders events moved out of its hands.[91]

The last problem the India Office faced before Cox took charge was that of the military, for clearly Cox's position would be in jeopardy if Haldane's view of his superior authority until peace was achieved actually prevailed. This was a question of civilian authority rather than of Cox himself, and the India Office could enter the fray with good heart.[92] On 15 September Montagu took the issue, framed in a question on the nature of the statement Cox would issue when he took charge, to the Cabinet. The Cabinet acted quickly, and Montagu's view won for the simple reason that, other things being equal, civilian control offered a better prospect for peace at a time when the British government was privately sounding out the Dominions for contributions of troops to aid the Empire in a time of dire need. India was not asked; she had already complained loudly against the continued drain on her military resources; after all, Britain, not India, received the mandates (and India, it should be recalled, was a member of the League in her own right). The need was for all theaters, not simply Mesopotamia, not even principally Mesopotamia, for by the end of September Wilson was able to report that the worst was over as more troops, cooler weather, and the onset of plowing season all arrived simultaneously. On 4 October Sir Percy Cox formally assumed charge as High Commissioner of Mesopotamia.[93]

Cox's arrival was not an immediate solution to all problems,

[91] See Hirtzel private for Montagu, 13 September, Marrs for Shuckburgh, 19 September, Shuckburgh note, 22 September 1920, *L/P&S/10*, 4722/18, no. 7145/20.

[92] I.O. to W.O., 15 September 1920, *FO* 371/5230.

[93] Cabinet 51 (20), 15 September 1920, *CAB* 23/22; Secretary of Colonies telegrams to Canada, New Zealand, Australia, 18 September 1920—and negative answers—*CAB* 24/111; Wilson telegram to SSI, 22 September, and Cox telegram to SSI, 4 October 1920, *FO* 371/5230. India's views: Viceroy (Army department) telegram to SSI, 3 September 1920, *L/P&S/10*, 4722/18, no. 6081/20.

but he did have clear instructions from home, and those instructions meant a new policy. Wilson had failed, and no matter how much blame must fall on the shoulders of other persons or upon outside events over which Wilson had no control, it remains to be said that a serious and costly rebellion had occurred under his rule. Britain could not afford that rebellion, in the lives or money or good will it cost, at any time; but the harm done was all the more grievous in the postwar era of difficulties. Above all, it could not be afforded in a Middle East where Egypt, Palestine, and Turkey also called for the sort of sacrifice that some were already concluding was no longer justified in a postwar world. On the other hand, in fairness to Wilson, the importance of the extraneous factors cannot be denied. The uncertain future of Kurdistan, the expulsion of Faisal from Syria, the failure for so long to reach a definitive peace with Turkey—and the terms of that peace when it was concluded—all had most assuredly played major roles. Nor had Wilson at any time possessed completely unfettered control of Iraq; unlike Cox after October 1920, Wilson was always subordinate to the military commander with whom he so very obviously had his problems. Wilson's governmental career was over, and he was soon to leave the service—but he had left his mark on the history of Britain's policy in the Middle East.

Finally, it should be clear that for practical purposes Wilson's policy was his own. While he received support from time to time from the India Office, that support was not always the strongest possible, and it was support for Wilson's policy rather than a policy instituted by the India Office itself. India, once the war was over, provided virtually no backing for a regime toward which it had usually little interest and occasionally some hostility. India, therefore, cannot be said to have plagued Britain's Arab policy in Iraq, except as Wilson himself was the product of Indian attitudes and systems of government—India's legacy, as it were, to postwar Middle Eastern policy.

Wilson was a strong man, young and lacking in either the

tact or the experience necessary for a job of such magnitude; he made mistakes on both counts. It is difficult, nevertheless, not to feel some sympathy for a man to whom efficient administration mattered, and who found himself dealing with problems of twentieth-century nationalism that were equally strange to, and no more wisely handled by, many with far wider experience. In another time and place Wilson's name might have been added to the list of benign and serene proconsuls, and John Marlowe has aptly termed his biography of Wilson *Late Victorian*. Another such figure, however, produced from a similar mold, was Sir Percy Cox—and it remained to be seen how he would fare. It remained, too, for Britain to make other decisions: on Ibn Sa'ud, on subsidies, on control of policy—in fact, to apply the principles that had resulted in Wilson's replacement in Iraq to the entire range of problems Britain had to face in the Middle East.

# IX

# Decision and Control, 1920-1921

The Mandatory powers you loose
On us who hold the East in awe,
And cannot find the slightest use
For lesser breeds without the law:
League of the Nations, spare us yet—
Lest we regret, lest we regret.

*Hesketh Pearson, quoting Colin Hurry,*
THINKING IT OVER

In October 1920, Sir Percy Cox was installed in Mesopotamia. His instructions were to arrive at a solution for Iraq which would both appease Arab nationalists and preserve British influence, but he was given wide flexibility as to method. A possible answer, outlined in one version of his instructions, was the utilization of Amir Faisal as King of Iraq. Faisal had been ousted from Syria, he was known through his role in the Arab revolt, he had impressed many during negotiations in Paris and London, and he was experienced in running a government in Damascus. Faisal had been funded by a British subsidy and his regime had collapsed under pressure, but neither fact could be held against him; he was obviously the most favored candidate.

More than Faisal's experience and character worked in his favor. For Britain, there was an intangible but nevertheless real feeling that a debt was still owed to the Hashimite family and to Arab nationalism, and that feeling was as much pragmatic as sympathetic. The chances of Iraq's becoming the stable state that Wilson desired or the Arab state, less efficient perhaps, but presumably as stable, that London desired would be considerably greater if steps could be taken to ward off charges of betrayal. Such steps had to be major ones, for not only Iraq and Syria were involved. There was also the matter of Ibn Sa'ud's pressure upon Husain in the Hijaz.

1

At war's end Ibn Sa'ud could be said to have joined the winning side by his treaty with Britain. On the other hand, his role was most definitely a subsidiary one; Britain's more important alliance with Husain had frustrated some of Ibn Sa'ud's ambitions in the Hijaz. Britain's chosen preference, however, had to be balanced against the pressure of his own supporters, who were less conscious than he of the importance of British relations or the sort of force that could be brought to bear in the unlikely event that Britain determined to use it. Unlike his followers, the Amir had seen the splendors of Basra when it was the principal base for a major campaign.

The year following the armistice had been one of fencing by both Britain and Ibn Sa'ud. The Amir was unwilling to force an open breach of relations, but he was equally unwilling to forgo any opportunity for expansion or trial of strength with Husain's forces. At the same time, British policy-makers were usually conscious of the sheer impossibility of the kind of forceful military intervention in Arabia that might produce a settlement of the rivalry. The result was a series of missions and warnings and pronouncements that steadily decreased in efficacy. London's ardor was also cooled by Husain's apparent lack of cooperation; it was due to him that every attempt at arbitration had failed. Ibn Saʿud's statesmanship was increasingly impressive. It was not yet a question of forsaking Husain, really, but rather a choice of successor. Faisal was still in Syria; ʿAli, the eldest son, was, according to Cheetham, "childish, incompetent, fanatical, and weak"; by October 1919 Cairo decided to back ʿAbdullah when the time came. If Husain intended to refuse to cooperate with Ibn Saʿud's new request for a commission to survey their joint boundary, that time might be at hand.[1]

In late November, a chance to implement this decision was passed over on the grounds that a king with known if irritating faults was better than an unknown quantity. Husain had telegraphed Lloyd George—the vast difference between his style and that of Ibn Saʿud was only too clear—that either a major official came to consult him or he abdicated. He was told that he would soon receive a message which, it was hoped, would satisfy him, but the interdepartmental committee found difficulty in selecting a satisfactory policy favorable to Husain. As Curzon put it, if Ibn Saʿud occupied Khurma permanently, Husain would probably abdicate. If Britain really intended supporting Husain, he would have to be given a few crumbs, such as the ownership of Turaba and Khurma. Philby, who was present and whose faith in Ibn Saʿud was undiminished, merely answered that Ibn Saʿud would then take the whole of the Hijaz. It proved impossible to make a decision—a not unusual result for such meetings—except that Husain would be worked upon with more pressure.[2]

[1] Cheetham to F.O., 16 October, with minutes, I.O. to F.O., 14 November, F.O. to Allenby, 15 November; the Saudi request was made by the Amir's agent, then in London with Ibn Saʿud's son Faisal, note on Curzon conversation with mission representatives, 26 November 1919: *FO* 371/4147.

[2] Husain telegram to Prime Minister, 21 November, F.O. (from

By 1 December a draft message to Husain was finally agreed upon: Britain was unable to see why he refused arbitration when his case was so strong. Britain would not demarcate a frontier, but strongly urged that the King meet Ibn Sa'ud. If such negotiation failed, or if the suggestion was refused, the entire Hijaz might succumb, in which case Britain could hardly give sufficient aid to prevent a catastrophe. This document was passed to Husain, and Allenby was given approval to begin discussions with 'Abdullah in either Cairo or Jidda. In January 1920 Husain indicated that he was willing to meet Ibn Sa'ud.[3]

Meanwhile, a complication ensued from the other side when Arnold Wilson informed London that Ibn Sa'ud had never received the March 1919 dispatch reducing his subsidy, which had been paid at the full rate—£5,000 per month (without Treasury sanction, needless to say).[4] Confusion in communication with central Arabia was pardonable, but the suspicion was soon abroad that Wilson had not overexerted himself in the matter. He had, moreover, written to Ibn Sa'ud in a manner so critical of Faisal in Syria that Allenby when he came to hear of it complained officially; Tilley in the Foreign Office termed Wilson's action "incredible." Wilson was instructed not to en-

---

Prime Minister) telegram to Allenby, 4 December 1919, *ibid.;* I.D.C.E. 33rd minutes, 24 November 1919, *L/P&S/10,* 2182/13, no. 7943/19.

[3] F.O. to C. E. Wilson, 1 December, with earlier drafts, F.O. telegrams to Allenby, 1, 9, and 13 December, Allenby telegrams to F.O., 5 December 1919 and 11 January 1920, *FO* 371/4147.

[4] Wilson telegram to SSI, 12 December 1919, *ibid.;* F.O. to I.O., 27 October, F.O. Financial Dept. memorandum, 25 November 1919, *L/ P&S/10,* 4931/16, no. 6728/19. By March, 1920, Ibn Sa'ud had received £265,000 of which £195,000 was cash, the rest arms and ammunition. Philby was asked what had actually happened and replied that he was going into the country and was working on a book (he was on leave at the time); it is clear from the correspondence that Philby felt aggrieved at the I.O.'s lack of consideration on this issue, and the mistrust shown by its question whether his disbursements were authorized. J. A. Simpson minute, 30 March, I.O. to F.O., 6 April, Garbett to Philby, 11 March, Philby to Garbett, 12 March 1920, *ibid.,* nos. 8059/19 and 1885/20.

courage Ibn Sa'ud in the belief that Faisal's forces were weak.[5] Far more important was Wilson's report that Ibn Sa'ud was himself coming to Bahrain and that he wished to speak to Wilson. The latter was unable to leave Baghdad because of the Syrian frontier situation, but he was sending H. R. P. Dickson from Kuwait and A. P. Trevor, the Deputy Resident. Wilson predicted that Ibn Sa'ud would refuse to travel to Jidda; it was just possible that he would go by sea, or to a meeting at Ta'if. When Dickson's report on his meeting with Ibn Sa'ud at Hofuf arrived, it referred to the Amir's loyalty, the accuracy of his information on events in Syria, and his complaints of divided policy control which led the Arabs to see that they had "two rival cliques of Englishmen" to deal with in an affair such as Turaba. Ibn Sa'ud absolutely refused to meet Husain outside of Najdi territory, and insisted on the validity of his possession of Turaba and Khurma.[6] It was already clear that pressures upon the Amir from his own followers had grown considerably.

Throughout the spring Allenby continued to urge a meeting, since the pilgrimage season was approaching and the Wahhabis, if continually excluded, might well overrun the Hijaz. Nothing Husain had done, said the High Commissioner, justified Britain's abandonment of him—and if Ibn Sa'ud was allowed to conquer the Hijaz, as Wilson seemed to advocate or at least not to fear, Husain would be destroyed and Britain's policy since 1916 would be an admitted failure. Not only would the Arabian balance of power then be destroyed, but the fanatical Wahhabis, held in check by the influence of only one man, would be in power. It was a view with which Young was in full

---

[5] Shuckburgh to Young, 19 January 1920, with Tilley minute, *FO* 371/4147; F.O. to I.O., 23 January and 14 February, I.O. to F.O., 21 February, SSI telegram to Wilson, 4 March 1920, *L/P&S/11*, vol. 166, nos. 626, 842, and 1221/20.

[6] Wilson telegrams to SSI, 24 and 28 January, *FO* 371/4147, and 1 February 1920, *L/P&S/11*, vol. 166, no. 842/20; Dickson to Wilson, 10 February 1920, *L/P&S/10*, 2182/13, no. 2635/20; reported home in Wilson telegram to SSI, 12 February 1920, *FO* 371/5060.

sympathy: Wilson was as wrong about Ibn Sa'ud as about Iraq.[7] Wilson had not advocated a Saudi victory. In fact, he had urged in March that Ibn Rashid be subsidized to the extent of half Ibn Sa'ud's fee, and he was even willing to pay the sum from Iraqi revenues. The suggestion, temporarily tabled pending a review of the entire question of Arabian subsidies, was finally obviated in mid-April when Ibn Rashid's death (an interfamily murder) was confirmed, as his successor was a mere boy of thirteen. Both Wilson and Allenby continued to support friendly relations with Ha'il until the young ruler's representatives negotiated an agreement that in effect put the Jabal Shammar area under Ibn Sa'ud's control.[8]

Schemes for bringing Ibn Sa'ud and Husain together continued to be made. Ibn Sa'ud proved amenable to the suggestion of a meeting in Aden, if someone of the stature of Sir Percy Cox was present as arbiter, but perhaps he was simply aware that Husain was unlikely to agree. By June, in fact, Husain not only had refused to attend any such meeting but had denied that he had ever agreed in principle; further, he had once more resigned (and this time appeared to mean it) when Allenby told him that the dozen each of aircraft and armored cars the

[7] SSI telegram to Wilson, 23 February, Wilson telegram to SSI, 24 February, I.O. to F.O., 6 March, Allenby telegram to F.O., 27 February, with Shuckburgh minute, 8 March 1920, *L/P&S/10*, 2182/13, nos. 1264, 1644, and 1756/20; Wilson telegram to SSI, 15 February, Allenby telegram to F.O., 27 February, I.O. to F.O., 6 March, F.O. to I.O., 16 March, SSI telegram to Wilson, 19 March, Wilson telegram to SSI, 21 March, Allenby telegrams to F.O., 9, 19, and 22 April 1920 (latter with Young minute, 26 April), *FO* 371/5060–61.

[8] Wilson telegram to SSI, 12 March, SSI telegram to Wilson, 26 April, Allenby telegram to F.O., 8 June, with I.O. minutes, and SSI telegram to Wilson, 19 June 1920, *L/P&S/10*, 4929/18, nos. 2000, 3000, and 3161/20; Wilson telegrams to SSI, 2 and 17 April, I.O. to F.O., 9 April 1920, *FO* 371/5061; Philby memorandum (unsolicited), 23 March 1920, suggesting that he be sent to Ibn Sa'ud, *L/P&S/10*, 2182/13, no. 2312/20; Ibn Sa'ud to Bahrain Agent, 25 April 1920, *FO* 371/5062.

King requested would not be supplied.[9] By July Husain complained that his subsidy was no longer being paid. The Foreign Office had approved an emergency £30,000—a far cry from the days of the revolt—but had refused to pay it over (although the money had been sent to Jidda) until the King proved cooperative on another issue. He had refused to sign the Treaty of Versailles because of the discussion of mandates contained in that treaty, and the Foreign Office had concluded that the King's signature was desirable to make the treaty more acceptable generally to Muslim opinion.[10]

In complete contrast, Wilson was recommending an increase in Ibn Sa'ud's subsidy, recognition of his title of "King of Najd," and a visit from Cox on the latter's return from London—all of which would be recompense for Ibn Sa'ud's general attitude of cooperation and at the same time would perhaps ease the Amir's jealousy of Husain. The India Office, leaving the subsidy for later consideration, supported the idea of a visit from Cox. As for the title, Britain could not confer this; but Cox could hint that Ibn Sa'ud could be "Sultan" of Najd by his own action. The Foreign Office agreed, with resignation. "I suppose," minuted Curzon, "all this means that every other Arab chieftain having failed us, we are now going to put all our eggs into Saud's basket. . . . But we must not conceal from ourselves that this means a probable possibly final rupture with Hussein." Cox's visit was sanctioned, with questions of subsidy

[9] Wilson telegram to SSI, 8 June, F.O. telegram to Allenby, 21 June 1920, *L/P&S/10*, 2182/13, nos. 4538 and 4937/20; Young minute, 10 May, on Lawrence proposal, and W.O. to F.O., 9 June 1920, *FO 371/ 5061*; Chelmsford private telegram to Montagu, 24 May 1920, *L/P&S/ 10*, 2182/13, no. 3340/20; I.O. to F.O., 30 June 1920, *FO 371/5062*. See Lawrence's proposal, *The Daily Express*, 28 May 1920 (quoted in Weintraub, *op. cit.*, pp. 66–69).

[10] Allenby telegrams to F.O., 20, 27, and 30 June, F.O. telegram to Allenby, 17 July 1920, *FO 371/5062*; Scott (Alexandria) telegrams to F.O., 9 and 16 August, with minutes on latter, F.O. to Treasury, 19 August, F.O. telegram to Scott, 20 August 1920, *FO 371/5063*.

and Najdi boundaries to be held over until he had a chance to report.[11]

One last attempt at agreement between the two rulers was made when, on a suggestion of Cornwallis, Husain was asked to send Faisal to London to confer. Husain agreed to this, but he was totally unwilling to modify any of his views. And London wanted Faisal to come—but to discuss Mesopotamia, although caution on this was still the order of the day among officials like Hardinge who still failed to see why the Iraqis should desire a Sharifal ruler. Ibn Sa'ud, too, in his discussions with Cox in early October, proved to have altered his hostility to Husain not at all, and to have rather enlarged his own ambitions in the matter of a title—preferring "Sultan of Central Arabia" to "Sultan of Najd and Dependencies," which Cox suggested.[12]

Ibn Sa'ud had, in fact, reached a crisis in his relations with Kuwait, and soon after Cox moved on to Iraq a serious battle occurred near Jahra, 20 miles west of Kuwait, where a Saudi army besieged Salim's forces in the structure subsequently famous in Kuwait as the "Red Fort." Tradition has it that the Wahhabis (not under Ibn Sa'ud's personal command) lost over 800 men in an unsuccessful attempt to scale the walls, making it one of the fiercest battles in modern Arabian history. Both

[11] Wilson telegrams to SSI, 19 and 24 August, I.O. to F.O., 30 August, with minutes (Curzon quoted), Scott telegram to F.O., 1 September, with Clayton, Tilley, Curzon minutes, SSI telegram to Wilson, 4 September 1920, *ibid.;* Wilson telegram to SSI, 10 September, F.O. telegram to Scott, 21 September, Scott telegram to F.O., 30 September 1920, *FO* 371/5064. See also Scott to Curzon, 30 September 1920, and notes, *FO* 371/5065, particularly that of Cornwallis: "King Hussein as a personality is nothing; as a symbol of the Arab Revolt he stands for a good deal in Moslem minds & his disappearance by our agency would not only be a confession of the failure of our whole Arab policy but would be equally seized upon by our ill-wishers as a proof of our cynicism."

[12] SSI telegram to Wilson, 1 October, Husain telegram to Curzon, 5 October, and minutes, Cox telegrams to SSI, 6, 11, and 13 (two of date) October 1920, *F.O.* 371/5065.

sides claimed victory, but the fighting had apparently gone in Kuwait's favor. In the light of this development and Ibn Saʿud's refusal (diplomatically, for reasons of health) to meet Cox again at Bahrain, there was as little chance of his attending a great meeting with a conciliatory attitude as there was for Husain (although the death of Salim in February 1921 permitted subsequent arbitration of the Saudi-Kuwaiti quarrel).[13]

By the end of 1920, then, nothing had been accomplished toward settling the rivalry of Najd and Hijaz. No meeting of principals had taken place or, for that matter, would take place. Husain's relative position had really worsened considerably: Ibn Saʿud had expanded to absorb Jabal Shammar and was pressing hard on the borders of Kuwait, while Husain had not regained Turaba and Khurma, and his relations with Britain were worsening steadily as a result of his refusals to cooperate and his frequent threats of abdication. For the survival of any Hashimite influence, much now depended on negotiations between Britain and Faisal, and those negotiations in turn depended on the nature of the new regime installed in Iraq by Sir Percy Cox in October. Even more, however, the Hashimite role depended upon Britain's attitude to her entire Arab policy, and that policy's control.

2

By the end of the war all major attempts to develop one central control apparatus for Middle Eastern policy had failed. The most promising development had been the appointment of Robert Cecil to a special position in the Foreign Office, but his efforts to create a separate department had run afoul of both

---

[13] Cox telegrams to SSI, 11, 13, and 21 October, 16 November, and 14 December 1920, *L/P&S/10*, 6499/20, nos. 7555, 7620, 7769, 8263, and 8851/20. Kuwaiti memories of the battle of Jahra: ar-Rushaid, *op. cit.*, pp. 227–28; Zahra Freeth (whose father was H. R. P. Dickson), *Kuwait Was My Home* (London, 1956), pp. 94–95; Ralph Hewins, *A Golden Dream: The Miracle of Kuwait* (London, 1963), pp. 182–87.

internal Foreign Office conflicts and India Office obstruction. Even the military were unable to obtain the total control of operational areas they desired; the suggestion of October 1918 that there be one Middle Eastern commander had met with India's unwillingness to sever connections with Iraq so long as India had to provide resources for that theater, and the India Office feared the repercussions of such a development on the Husain-Ibn Sa'ud struggle.[14]

The India Office, above all, presented a problem. That office held persistently to the view that India was the heart of the Empire and vitally interested in areas on her frontiers and in her neighborhood, and it was inconceivable that relations with those areas should be in the sole charge of another department. Shuckburgh, preparing a memorandum on the subject at Montagu's direction shortly after the armistice, could only suggest that a high-level committee of India Office, Foreign Office, and Middle Eastern ministers (assuming the new department ever became a reality) coordinate policy. Cecil, in the midst of his own department-building activities, was rather more concerned with the practical and current problem of obtaining control of Mesopotamian affairs, but again the India Office objected.[15]

The question was raised again in connection with preparations for the peace conference. In one of the last meetings of the Eastern Committee, on 26 December 1918, the width of the gap dividing the departments was again made clear. Both Curzon and Montagu challenged Cecil's claim that the whole of the Arabian Peninsula, and the Persian Gulf as well, would come under the new department. Cecil had to admit that this plan had never been approved in writing, and that it was still

[14] See above, pp. 211–12. General Staff memorandum, 14 October, I.O. memorandum, 25 October 1918, *CAB* 27/35.

[15] Shuckburgh note, 12 November 1918, with Hirtzel, Islington, Montagu, Cecil, and further Montagu minutes, *L/P&S/11*, vol. 141, no. 4988/18.

uncertain whether the new organization would be at ministry level, at least at first. Even then, his own staff was unprepared to assume responsibility for those areas for purposes of the Paris conference. The committee was able to make only one recommendation—the one resulting in its own dissolution.[16]

During the Paris Conference itself, Montagu did his best to maintain separate Indian representation on Turkish peace terms, and it was hardly an auspicious time to recommend to him that India abandon some or all of its interests in the Middle East. On the contrary, India preserved so watchful an eye that Delhi objected to Arnold Wilson's direct communications with London on the policy to be pursued in Muscat, for that area was India's responsibility. It was still accepted, however, that the new department would assume essential authority for such areas as Mesopotamia when the time came, which was not the same as saying that the Foreign Office would hold such authority in the interim. The Foreign Office put up no argument; Curzon too foresaw an eventual Secretary of State for the Middle East.[17]

At Paris it was also clear that the entire question of treaty relations and subsidies in the Arabian Peninsula should be subjected to sweeping review, and a number of suggestions to this effect were made. Allenby, for example, proposed a British mandate for the whole of Arabia, with the Hijaz, 'Asir, Yemen, and Najd each receiving a separate subsidy and with disputed districts apportioned by boundary commission. But no such vast proposal could be entertained unless there was a single controlling body—even granting the (false) assumption that

[16] E.C. 47th minutes, 26 December 1918, and 49th minutes, 7 January 1919, *CAB* 27/24.
[17] Viceroy telegram to SSI, 18 January 1919, *L/P&S/11*, vol. 146, no. 320/19; Shuckburgh for Islington, 4 February, Holderness minute (on Curzon's views), 8 February 1919, *L/P&S/10*, 4722/18, no. 567/19; I.O. to F.O., 11 February 1919, with Young, Kidston, and Cecil minutes, *FO* 371/4148.

Britain desired a mandate for all Arabia—while no single body could assume responsibility until it was clear what that responsibility was going to entail.[18]

It was another of those paradoxical situations to which Middle Eastern affairs seemed so prone. The argument simply went on, and the issue of future control always occupied the background of discussion on any particular area of the Middle East. It was awareness of this problem that prompted Arnold Wilson, when in Europe, to outline his views of what the form of such over-all control should be. To Wilson, the Foreign Office had no administrative experience, and Foreign Office control of Iraq would sever valuable Indian-Iraqi connections. A totally new department would require much added expense, and still that connection would be cut. The same was true if the Colonial Office was made responsible, with the added disadvantage that the Colonial Office was naturally thought, in the public mind, to rule "colonies." The solution: Rename the India Office the "Middle East and India Office," for only the India Office had the men and the experience. This approach was no surprise from Wilson; although circulated to the Cabinet, it received no support. It was not only futile to discuss all this until the conference decided who was going to control what area, but Wilson had stressed exactly that aspect of Iraqi affairs that bothered so many officials—the link with India.[19]

When the conference ended, no solution had been reached, and lines of responsibility were no clearer. When in Parliament the Foreign Office said, in answer to a question, that the Foreign Office decided policy in Iraq in consultation with the Secretary of State for India, Montagu took immediate issue. Baghdad communicated with the India Office, not the Foreign Office,

---

[18] F.O. telegram to Cheetham, 14 March 1919, *FO* 371/4212; Allenby telegram to F.O., 7 April, F.O. telegram to Allenby, 1 May, Paris delegation to F.O., 6 May 1919, *L/P&S/10*, 349/19, nos. 2040 and 2850/19.

[19] Wilson memorandum (B.323), 14 April 1919, with Holderness minute, *L/P&S/11*, vol. 150, no. 1923/19.

and as long as the India Office had the responsibility it should also have the credit. The India Office, in other words, decided in consultation with the Foreign Office, not the other way around.[20] It was exactly the sort of irritable quarrel that made it impossible to make use of the rather opportune moment for change after the signing of the Treaty of Versailles.

There the matter remained, although the latter half of 1919 was not entirely unproductive of suggestions. One such was for the construction of an intelligence-gathering agency, for H. F. Jacob, formerly of Aden and now with the Arab Bureau in Cairo, suggested that a wider, more comprehensive Moslem Bureau be established. Since Jacob was new with Arbur, he perhaps did not know that his proposal was quite similar to one that had been discarded when the Arab Bureau itself was established. The War Office, on the other hand, advocated a central bureau in London, an "Intelligence Service for the Middle East." Both the India Office and the Foreign Office objected, for very similar reasons: the scheme involved the War Office, already too inclined to take at face value pan-Islamic activities which the bureau would study.[21]

Such discussions continued into 1920, when it was reported (in March) that the special Egyptian mission of Lord Milner—to inquire into nationalist disturbances—was on the point of proposing the establishment of a separate High Commissioner for the Middle East, to be located at Cairo, and with a subordinate intelligence officer responsible for the entire area. The Arab Bureau (whose Treasury sanction extended only to 31 July) would serve as a nucleus for this organization. Allenby supported this idea, adding that Aden would then come under complete control of Cairo. But, as with every such proposal,

---

[20] Parliamentary Question, 30 June, with notes for draft answer, and I.O. to F.O., 15 July 1919, *FO* 371/4149.

[21] Arab Bureau special report no. 6, 1 July 1919, *FO* 882/23; W.O. memorandum (B.329), July, with Hirtzel and Shuckburgh minutes, F.O. to I.O., 15 September ,W.O. to F.O., 17 October 1919, *L/P&S/10*, 4744/15, nos. 4865, 5693, and 6843/19.

there was criticism, this time from Young; Baghdad would want more responsibility, too, and he himself was for a "larger London," not a "larger Cairo" or "larger Baghdad." [22]

Not only control of policy and intelligence were involved; financial considerations were also becoming increasingly important in the postwar era. When an interdepartmental conference turned to this issue, it was very clear that contributions, particularly from Iraq and India, depended upon a voice in policy. The India Office knew it would probably have to pay for its interest in the pilgrimage—although it would not admit so in public—but Iraq should also have to make a contribution. The Persian Gulf, a traditional Indian charge for the most part, was also earmarked for control by the High Commissioner in Iraq. India might therefore have said that Iraq would have to pay, but the India Office was rather more concerned to see to it that Iraq did not control the Persian Gulf, particularly as it became less and less likely that Britain would obtain permanent control of Mesopotamia. The actual meeting on the question soon dissolved into a lengthy discussion of the justice of stopping Ibn Sa'ud's subsidy while continuing Husain's, the Treasury strongly objecting to any payment to anybody without prior authorization, for subsidies had a way of going on indefinitely until Treasury sleuths caught wind of them, months after authorization had expired. With conferences dissolving into this kind of squabble, it is not surprising that a decision on this issue as well was put off. [23]

By now, this was the standard pattern: suggestion, discussion, postponement. This time there was valid reason, for the Foreign Office was occupied with San Remo and the hope that

[22] Sir R. Rodd (with Milner mission) private to Hardinge and Allenby private to Hardinge, 3 March, with Young minute, 16 March 1920, *FO* 371/5196. The Milner mission files are in *FO* 848/1–27.

[23] Garbett and Hirtzel notes, 16 April, Garbett note, 20 April, Treasury to F.O., 20 April, I.O. to F.O., 29 April 1920, *L/P&S/10*, 4931/16, nos. 2879 and 3334/20; I.O. memorandum for Cabinet, 13 July 1920, *CAB* 24/110; see also documents at *L/P&S/11*, vol. 146, file 450/19.

perhaps the Allies could be brought to recognize Britain's position in Arabia. So many issues took precedence, however, that it was decided at the last minute (by Curzon and Vansittart) not to bring up Arabia at San Remo but to raise this problem with France later when the parallel structures for the mandates were being worked out, or so Vansittart explained to Young. Unfortunately, the mandate discussions did not prove so harmonious nor so simple, and the matter could not be resolved then either, for France proved unwilling to declare herself to have no desire for political influence in the Hijaz. It was too good an issue not to be used as a pawn in the negotiations—and, after all, France had her own public opinion to consider.[24]

The "Arabian chapter" would have done little for the problem of control save to remove extra-British considerations, but the matter did occupy the Foreign Office for some time, and time was an increasingly scarce commodity. This was not due primarily to Iraq, for when the revolt came it came as a surprise to most. Rather, the principal pressure now was finance. Winston Churchill, whose control of the War Office gave him a vital interest in this matter, was precisely the man to point out the problem. An army of 60,000 men, estimated costs of £18 million a year—yet the War Office had no say in the policy for which the money was spent. The situation would continue so long as there was no central controlling body—meaning a new department of state. He was willing to go even further: the department should be established for the time being in the Colonial Office, best suited for this task of all ministries. There could be only one method of proceeding: count the money available and limit policy accordingly.[25]

Churchill's intervention at Cabinet level in May 1920

[24] Forbes Adam to Tilley, 29 April, with Young minute of 6 May, Vansittart (Paris) to Curzon, 6 May, and enclosures, extract from Vansittart private to Young, 30 April, Vansittart to Young, 21 and 29 June 1920, *FO* 371/5244.

[25] Churchill memorandum, 1 May 1920, *Lloyd George Papers*, F/ 205/6/1.

touched off another round of memoranda, this time, at long last, to result in a decision. On 17 May Young listed once more the varying centers of control and drew the standard conclusions on the makeshift nature of that control. His answer, however—no more surprise than Arnold Wilson's on the other side —was that the Foreign Office should have responsibility. The Foreign Office would in any case have to be responsible for relations with independent Hijaz and Persia, and with France on Syrian problems. Egypt and Palestine were also areas in which other powers were much interested, to say nothing of the responsibility to the League of Nations for mandates.[26]

To the India Office, the Foreign Office was the worst of possible evils, for if any existing department was to take over, the Foreign Office in particular would require total reorganization to enable it to assume such vast administrative responsibilities. The India Office could do it, but India was already a full-time job, and Indian opinion would be unlikely to approve. The Colonial Office, in the view of the India Office, was the only suitable department, provided it was renamed and that the dominions were transferred out of its area of authority. These views were Montagu's own, which he circulated to the Cabinet; he did not say so, but they did not necessarily reflect the views of all his subordinates.[27]

It was now Curzon's turn. In a memorandum of 8 June he agreed on the basic proposition that a new service and a new department should be established, but financial considerations made this inexpedient. The question, therefore, was: Which existing department could best do the job? The India Office itself agreed that it could not; Churchill preferred the Colonial Office, but he must be "very imperfectly acquainted" with Middle Eastern conditions if he thought the population of that

[26] Young note, 17 May 1920, with Tilley, Hurst, Hardinge minutes, *FO* 371/5255.

[27] I.O. memorandum, 1 June, circulated to Cabinet by Montagu, with 2 June 1920 covering note, *CAB* 24/107.

area would be content under Colonial Office administration. Such a solution would be a lethal blow to Egyptian pride, and the mandatory areas would rage. As it was, the Colonial Office now administered only Cyprus in that part of the world, and its administration "has not resulted in anything like the development of the island which its interests and opportunities demand." As for Churchill's criticism of the Foreign Office in Mesopotamia—it was an Indian civil administration, not one run from the Foreign Office. "If I were dispensed altogether to-morrow from having any say in the present or future of these regions, I should breathe a sigh of intense and jubilant relief," a Curzonian way of saying that only the Foreign Office could deal with the League of Nations, Palestine, Egypt, Turkey, Afghanistan, and Persia. The logical, the only, answer was a separate department with a Parliamentary Under-Secretary under the Foreign Office, housed in that office until it could expand to take some of the Colonial Office's rooms. Curzon had the further satisfaction of knowing that the Milner mission had not, as it turned out, actually recommended control of intelligence from Cairo; the field was left clear for London, and a conflict of the Foreign Office with its own subordinates in Cairo was avoided. Curzon's subordinates, however, were under no illusions about what the added responsibility would mean in terms of staff, space, and expertise.[28]

The only party yet to be heard from was India, but India was concerned only in obtaining the reversal of the decision (made originally in 1917) to hand the Persian Gulf to Iraq. On this Wilson agreed with Delhi for once. The Persian Gulf issue was set aside until the larger interdepartmental controversy was settled—but no one knew how or when it would be settled. In mid-August, Curzon circulated a memorandum asking for a

<hr>

[28] Curzon memorandum for Cabinet, 8 June 1920, *CAB* 27/107; Young minute (on Arab Bureau), 12 July 1920, *FO* 371/5196; Young minute, 3 July, Crowe minute, 22 July, and Hardinge minute, *FO* 371/5255.

decision, urging that 1 October, the date on which the Arab Bureau would formally close (having taken some months to wind up its affairs), was the most convenient date for the establishment of (temporary) Foreign Office control—and in favor of such a decision he cited not only earlier arguments but the view of Sir Percy Cox.[29]

As usual, delay was the most convenient answer, with the satisfying excuse that it would be useful to await some indications of the efficacy of Cox's policy. But the delay could not long continue, particularly since Cox had insisted all along that one of the conditions of his acceptance of the High Commissionership was the application of unified control, at ministry or subministry level. Cox very much wished to assure his officers that they would be placed on the strength of the new service which would presumably accompany the establishment of the new department—although Young, as usual, had his doubts, this time about the advisability of accepting without qualification all those men trained by Arnold Wilson in preference to the many (some four hundred) in London who had put their names forward as candidates for Iraqi administrative posts. Cox was also questioning Iraq's contribution to Ibn Sa'ud's subsidy; fully conscious of the need both to economize and to strengthen the Iraqi state structure, he argued that more was to be gained by building up a national force than by buying off potential enemies. He did not, however, wish to end the subsidy altogether.[30]

Once again, subsidies and Cox's staff were linked to the prob-

[29] Viceroy telegram to SSI, 14 July, Wilson telegram to SSI, 17 July 1920, *FO* 371/5270; Chelmsford in Council to Montagu, 29 July, F.O. to I.O., 28 September 1920, *L/P&S/11*, vol. 146, nos. 6460 and 7237/20; Curzon memorandum for Cabinet, 16 August 1920, *FO* 371/5255.

[30] Cox private telegram to Montagu, 3 November, enclosed in I.O. to F.O., 20 November 1920, *ibid.*, and circulated to Cabinet in Montagu memorandum, 18 November 1920, *CAB* 24/115; Cox telegram to SSI, 10 November 1920 (with Young minute of 23 November), *FO* 371/5255; Cox telegram to SSI, 21 November 1920, *L/P&S/10*, 488/20, no. 8305/20.

lem of control. If Iraq was not to pay, for example, who was? In an interdepartmental meeting of 7 December, Montagu argued that certainly India could not be responsible (a view Curzon received with horror; India would not have talked that way when he was Viceroy). Montagu wanted the new department to assume all responsibility for Arabia, and he was admittedly quite willing to differ with the Government of India on this. Hirtzel argued with his own Secretary; while in 1917 the future assumption of Gulf control from Baghdad seemed a good idea, the situation was now much altered. Curzon fully agreed; from his own Indian experience he found it difficult to see how a department based on London could effectively control the scattered chieftains of southeastern Arabia. The meeting, called to deal with subsidies, bogged down on control and got no further on the main issue than general agreement with Young's suggestion that £100,000 should be enough for all Arabian subsidies—but Austen Chamberlain, back in the Government as Chancellor of the Exchequer, insisted still on India's half-share.[31]

These discussions were of minor importance compared to the crisis which arose in mid-December. Churchill had strongly urged a military cutback on financial grounds, and in a request for supplemental funds on the 15th he gave a hint of possible partial British withdrawal from Iraq. Montagu concluded that he and Cox had been betrayed, and in a memorandum for the Cabinet of the following day he asked that the India Office be relieved of responsibility for Iraq. He was prepared to hand over the work to any department the government cared to select. "Even if partial evacuation is decided upon the policy will be so out of harmony with the work which we have been doing, so contrary to the advice that we have given, that it had better be carried out under the auspices of some other Office." By the 22nd, after some discussion of withdrawal had taken

[31] I.D.C.E. 42nd minutes, 7 December 1920, *FO* 371/5065; SSI telegram to Cox, 16 December 1920, *DBFP*, XIII, p. 416.

place, Montagu was even willing to urge that the Foreign Office be given the task. He was reversing his earlier position supporting the Colonial Office because Cox had argued against any step that might be construed as annexation of mandated territory.[32]

But it was not to be the Foreign Office which would take charge. The answer was rather provided by Churchill and the War Office, and the victory went to the Colonial Office—but under Churchill's direction. The reason for the final decision, primarily, was Churchill's argument on Iraqi policy: the alternatives were withdrawal or the creation, at once, of ". . . a Department the Ministerial head of which should be responsible for the policy and for obtaining the money to carry out that policy." In the crucial Cabinet meeting, on the last day of 1920, Curzon argued strenuously, but the decision was taken. Since Parliamentary and other considerations made it impossible at the moment to establish a completely new ministry, some existing body had to take the responsibility, and the majority of the Cabinet opted for the Colonial Office under a new name, something on the order of "Department for Colonies and Mandated Territories." An interdepartmental committee under the Secretary for Colonies (Milner) would work out the details and date of the transfer, with responsibilities to remain as they were in the meantime.[33]

Curzon lost, and the Foreign Office lost (although the staff of that office may well have had fewer regrets than its Secretary). The need for economy and centralization had long been evident, but it had taken Churchill to force the issue. Although the Colonial Office was perhaps the most qualified department —if the least experienced in Middle East affairs—there can be little doubt that personalities played as much of a role in the

---

[32] Montagu memoranda, 16 and 22 December 1920, *CAB* 24/117; Cabinet 69–70 (20), 13 December 1920, *CAB* 23/23.
[33] Cabinet 82 (20), 31 December 1920, *ibid.*

final decision as the relative departmental merits. Lloyd George found both Curzon and Montagu difficult to work with, while Churchill had proven himself a man for difficult tasks for which he might have to take any possible odium and which would keep him fully occupied and away from cabal-making. The decision had been for Milner's Colonial Office, but Milner was obviously close to retirement. His resignation had still not been accepted by Lloyd George, and would not be for some days; apparently when the decision was taken it was not then clear that Churchill himself would take over the Colonial Office, but the evidence cannot be considered conclusive. Churchill's appointment to responsibility for affairs in the most difficult and problematic area at the time, considering the eased demobilization and Russian problems, was a logical counterpart to the decision to give responsibility to the Colonial Office. Now it only remained to determine the policy, beginning in Iraq.[34]

3

In October 1920, when Sir Percy Cox assumed control of Iraq, a new policy was in order; the new policy was Cox himself. Faisal had been mentioned as a ruler, but the actual possibilities of such a solution had yet to be probed and alternatives discarded. All that was really clear was that hope for a pacific and satisfactory solution rested upon Cox, and that, for the moment, at least, the revolt was over.[35] Indeed, argument was still continuing even on the form of the mandatory document, six months after Britain had been assigned mandatory responsibility. When Montagu proposed that Iraq be treated like Egypt, Curzon and Hirtzel, who found much community of interest, pointed out the obvious differences between the two

[34] Gollin, op. cit., p. 597; Virginia Cowles, *Winston Churchill: The Era and the Man* (N.Y., 1956), pp. 230–35.
[35] Haldane telegram to W.O., 17 October 1920, *FO* 371/5231.

areas. Montagu then argued that the formal adoption of the mandate should be delayed pending developments, but his argument was hazy, and even Cox had approved the existing draft—but Montagu was willing to disagree with Cox as he disagreed with India.[36]

Montagu's position was curious, all things considered; he argued that the mandate should be couched only in the vaguest terms and designed to establish an Arab government and relieve Britain of all responsibility as soon as possible. Since no troops and no funds were available, it was very rash to assume an unlimited responsibility. His reference to the impossibility of enforcing the Turkish treaty with Indian troops makes his reasoning a bit clearer, but it was unlikely to persuade either Cox or Hirtzel.[37]

Uncertainty on the form of the mandate did not help Cox's position, nor did the continuing uncertainty of Faisal's status. In the first place, France made it obvious that it considered Faisal unacceptable as ruler of Iraq. Secondly, the acceptability of Faisal to Iraq was unclear—as unclear as the acceptability of the mandate's terms to Faisal. Finally, there was the lesser problem of 'Abdullah, who was upset by the by now obvious substitution of Faisal for himself as principal British candidate for Hashimite ruler of Iraq.[38]

---

[36] Montagu to Curzon, 5 October, Curzon to Montagu, 7 October (with Hirtzel minute), Montagu memoranda for Cabinet, 9 (circulated on the 11th) and 22 October 1920, *L/P&S/10*, 4917/20, no. 7317/20; Montagu to J. T. Davies (Prime Minister's Secretary), 9 October 1920, *Lloyd George Papers*, F/60/3/25; Cabinet 54 (20), 12 October 1920, *CAB* 23/22; Conference of Ministers, 18 October 1920, Appendix to Cabinet 59 (20), *CAB* 23/23; SSI telegram to Cox, 13 October 1920, *FO* 371/5246, with minute by Young: "I can well imagine that the I.O. do not quite see eye to eye with Mr. Montagu on the subject of Mesopotamia."

[37] I.O. to W.O., 12 October, and *The Times*, 14 October 1920, on Cox's farewell speech at Basra for Wilson (clipping with Young minute), *FO* 371/5230.

[38] De Fleuriau to Curzon, 9 October 1920, *FO* 371/5040; Maj. W.

Before these questions could be answered, Cox's assessment of conditions in Iraq had to be considered. Cox had concluded that if a national government was to be established Iraq wished it to be a monarchy under British supervision, although there was disagreement upon the amount of practical participation desired. In the interests of speed, Cox proceeded to establish a Council of State in late October, asking the Naqib of Baghdad, long his own preference, to serve as its president. The Council, which was to advise until elections could select the National Assembly, had some eighteen members, eight of whom were to be ministers controlling various departments with the aid of British secretaries and whose decisions were subject to Cox's veto. All the members selected by Cox were men of prestige, but two appointments were of particular significance: Sayyid Talib Pasha, once ordered to India by Cox himself, became Minister of the Interior, and Ja'far Pasha, whom Cox had talked to in Egypt, was made Minister of Defense (meaning primarily responsibility for organization of the levy force). Cox acted in all this without consulting London on the grounds that the right psychological moment had to be made use of when the Naqib of Baghdad was in an agreeable frame of mind.[39]

Cox had been given flexible instructions, and he could be fairly certain of home approval; London, after all, had never proposed any detailed alternatives. Hirtzel argued strongly that

---

Batten, Acting British Agent, Jidda, report for 10–20 September (on 'Abdullah's attitude), enclosed in Scott to Curzon, 6 October 1920, FO 371/5243.

[39] Cox telegrams to SSI, 26 October 1920 (nos. 12986–7), FO 371/ 5231, and 27 October (that the country be called Iraq, not Mesopotamia), 4 November (that the government negotiate with the mandatory on the war costs and not simply be charged for every establishment taken over), and 6 November (that Arabic should be the only language) 1920, FO 371/5246/47. The appointment of Talib required a rapid editorial change in the published version of Gertrude Bell's report on the civil administration of Mesopotamia, I.O. to F.O., 9 November, F.O. to I.O., 22 November 1922, FO 371/5081.

Cox's action should be approved; and though Montagu was ready to criticize Cox's acting without home approval, the steps taken were announced in Parliament.[40] In Iraq, Gertrude Bell, at least, was ecstatic. No one but Cox, she wrote Hardinge, could have cut through the tangle by establishing a provisional government. Her private view was that the National Assembly, once it met (it never did, as it happened), would almost certainly choose one of the sons of the Sharif—preferably Zaid, "but it is not a matter which we can control." She would probably have welcomed any step by Cox, however, for Miss Bell had broken completely with Wilson before his dismissal. She had changed her view on Arab government over the last several years and wrote, in another letter, that when Wilson left she felt "as if I had stepped out of a nightmare." [41]

By mid-November Cox had met with the Council and had established procedures for handling relations between that body and the High Commissioner's office. The Council would be responsible for actual administration (subject always to Cox's veto), and the ministers would run the departments, but the (British) advisors would be the channel for communication between the ministers and their staffs. Although severely limited in authority, Cox's new administration was at least functioning after its formal installation in November, two years after the end of the war.[42]

[40] Cox telegram to SSI, 13 November 1920, with Hirtzel, Montagu, and further Hirtzel minutes (and cutting of Hansard, 2 November), *L/P&S/10*, 4722/18, nos. 7975 and 8199/20.

[41] Bell private to Hardinge, 8 November 1920, *Hardinge Papers* (Kent County Archives), 29/89; Bell private letter (recipient unidentified), 3 October 1920, Burgoyne, *op. cit.*, p. 169, and pp. 84–87 and 127–41 on her earlier attitude toward Wilson; the change came in the light of personal differences (pp. 167–69) and the rebellion, although she herself (pp. 202–3) saw the key incident as Wilson's failure to reach an accord with the nationalists at his meeting with them in 1919 on his return trip from Paris.

[42] Cox telegrams to SSI of 9, 15, 16, and 22 November 1920, *FO* 371/5231–32; Ireland, *op. cit.*, pp. 277–87; Graves, *Cox*, pp. 266–71; Burgoyne, *op. cit.*, pp. 174–92.

Cox's confidence must have been damaged by a private telegram from Montagu of 1 December. Montagu cited the universal home demand for economy; there would be great problems in obtaining Cabinet support for Mesopotamian policy unless the Secretary could give them "assured prospect of progressive retrenchment." Montagu asked, therefore, for the smallest number of troops with which Iraq could be held, adding that Cox need not fear being irrevocably held to his estimate, but Montagu had to have information on the absolute minimum necessary without which it would be useless to stay in Iraq or to develop an Arab state. In actual fact, a month's discussion had preceded this telegram. On 1 November Churchill, after consultation with Lloyd George, had cabled Haldane privately to ask about the future once the rebel tribes had been disarmed (a process then continuing as far as possible). Indicating his own trend of thought, Churchill had specifically asked whether it was intended once again to spread troops throughout the whole country or whether it might be possible to pacify a smaller area to be used as a base, for the current level of expenditure was most unpopular. Haldane answered only that a general announcement of disarmament would raise difficulties, and, when pressed by Churchill, could only say that the future depended upon the ability of the Arab government to assume responsibility and, specifically, of Arab levies (still in insignificant strength) to control the area.[43]

This was not enough for Churchill. On 1 December he announced to a meeting of ministers that he would be forced in

---

[43] Montagu private telegram to Cox, 1 December 1920, Appendix II to Appendix II to Cabinet 82 (20), *CAB* 23/23; Churchill to Lloyd George, 10 November, enclosing Churchill private telegrams to Haldane, 1 and 8 November, Haldane private telegrams to Churchill, 5 and 9 November 1920, *Lloyd George Papers*, F/9/2/45. Haldane estimated that the effective fighting force of the tribes (not all of whom participated in the rebellion) was over 130,000, with nearly 60,000 modern rifles; after the revolt, over 63,000 rifles were collected, but of these only some 21,000 were modern: *Insurrection*, pp. 124, 298.

the coming week to ask for supplementary estimates of £33-34 million, mainly because of Mesopotamia, and mainly in turn because of the high fees charged by India for the use of its forces. Ireland required a million pounds, the occupation of Constantinople another half-million, a million and a half for Palestine—but Mesopotamia was the real problem. The true cost of dealing with the revolt was painfully obvious; just as clearly, limited occupation was one way to deal with this knotty problem, and the result was the telegram to Cox of the same day asking for the absolute minimum troop strength for 1921-1922.[44]

While Cox contemplated the implications of this request, at home Churchill's viewpoint was supported by General P. de B. Radcliffe, Director of Military Operations, in a memorandum of 7 December which Churchill circulated to the Cabinet.[45] Radcliffe had only to cite the figures: 17,000 British troops, 85,000 Indian troops, total cost over £30 million a year—and that was only £6 million more than the General Staff estimate of normal peacetime Iraqi requirements. The government wished to cut costs, but at the same time it wished not to give up any part of Mesopotamia. The risks in such a policy were great; as it was, disaster had been warded off during the rebellion by the narrowest of margins, and that only "thanks to the energy, courage, and devotion of the British soldier and his Indian comrade." But the heart of Radcliffe's memorandum was a simple question: Why was Britain so determined to remain in Iraq? As he saw it, the reasons were those that had originally prompted the Mesopotamian campaign: oil and control of the Persian Gulf. For these purposes, a lien on Basra and a defended line of Ahwaz (on the Karun River in Persia) to Qurna to

[44] Conference of Ministers, 1 December 1920, Appendix II to Cabinet 82 (20), *CAB* 23/23.
[45] Gen. P. de B. Radcliffe, "The Situation in Mesopotamia," 7 December 1920, with minutes, *FO* 371/5232.

Nasiriya would be quite sufficient and would require only a single division at a cost of £8 million a year.

Whatever the views of India, the General Staff did not contemplate defending India in Iraq. Far better, added Radcliffe—repeating an old argument—to spend the money improving the position on the North-West Frontier. Moreover, the military position in Iraq and on the Persian frontier was basically unsound, as recent events had shown. Next time, there would probably be external aggression as well (a remark aimed at Mustafa Kemal and possible Bolshevik-Turkish cooperation). Since Haldane was under orders to reduce his forces by 1 April to the prerebellion level, the situation would only be that much the worse. But even with reductions, and until good weather permitted withdrawal from Persia and Mosul was evacuated, three divisions and six cavalry regiments would still be needed in Iraq.

Young argued that modern troops would not be invading Iraq, and Radcliffe said nothing about what Britain was to do with the people—Turks or Russians—who would move to occupy the abandoned area; Tilley cited obligations to the Iraqis. But Radcliffe's arguments, and particularly the financial aspect, were persuasive, while Cox was forced to admit that it would not be until the spring of 1923 that he could reduce his forces to one division, and that only if he had 15,000 Indian troops and 5,000 levies and the money to pay them.[46]

On 13 December the Cabinet met twice to consider the whole matter. Cox's estimate for the coming year was less than that of the War Office. (£25 million against £30 million), but both figures were impossible. Churchill therefore argued for withdrawal to a line that would cover Basra only, quoting the General Staff view that Mesopotamia and Persia were "of no importance from the point of view of the defense of India. . ."

[46] Cox private telegram to Montagu, 8 December 1920, *L/P&S/11*, vol. 172, no. 642/21.

Opponents of withdrawal held that the lesser area would cost just as much if attacked, and that a policy of withdrawal would destroy the mandate and the Arab government. In the evening, the Cabinet consulted with Arnold Wilson, now free of responsibilities for Iraq (and soon to accept a position with the Anglo-Persian Oil Company), who maintained that the Arab government was not really the best solution. "He himself, rather as a last resort, had advised a trial of the Emir Feisal . . . ," but Faisal was foreign and Sunnite, and there would be problems. Yet withdrawal would be worse: the end of the mandate and of British prestige, and the necessity for another Mesopotamian campaign to retake the area. "Meanwhile, our national honour would have suffered irreparable damage by our failure to keep our word." But why should the British taxpayer maintain the vast burden of Mesopotamia? Here Wilson had an answer, for the huge potential of Iraq, in irrigation and above all in petroleum, would repay the debt—to say nothing of imperial communications. But the Cabinet was still drifting in the direction of withdrawal, and Haldane was ordered to prepare plans for such an eventuality even though the Cabinet had taken no decision.[47]

Both Cox and Haldane were extremely concerned at what appeared to be Churchill's determination to apply a policy of withdrawal at once. It might be possible in two years, said Cox with Haldane's agreement, but if done now would leave the mandate unfulfilled and an infantile government without means

[47] Cabinet 69–70 (20), 13 December 1920, Cabinet 72 (20), 17 December, and Appendixes I–II, Montagu private telegram to Cox and Churchill private telegram to Haldane, 17 December 1920, *CAB* 23/23. Wilson's version of the meeting: Wilson private to Cox, 21 January 1921, *Wilson Papers*, Add. Mss. 52455. Wilson's subsequent A.P.O.C. employment is discussed in Wilson to Sir F. W. Duke (Permanent Under-Secretary, India Office, since January 1920), 2 February, Montagu note for Duke, 8 February, and *The Times*, 5 March 1921, *L/P&S/11*, vol. 193, no. 762/21. That his new position, in the light of his recent responsibilities in Iraq, might give a harmful impression was obvious both to the I.O. and to *The Times*, but there was no way to stop it.

for defense against a threat from Turkey. Much, of course, depended upon the actual form of government established in Iraq, and rather than answer Cox directly authorities in London returned to that question and to another unanswered question (from Cox, two weeks earlier): What was to be the policy if the approaching elections resulted in the selection of a ruler hostile to British interests? Would he be given a trial and deposed if necessary, or would the election be overruled?[48]

In actual fact, formal elections had not been London's plan; the India Office had rather foreseen another informal poll on the identity of the ruler. Had Cox another alternative in mind? It was clear, in other words, that Britain was not going to be bound by just any popular choice. The Foreign Office in particular was persuaded by Cornwallis's reminder that the Arabs were as determined to establish a national government as Britain was to reduce its garrison, and Britain could not build and run a government counter to the trend of self-determination—a warning that could be interpreted as a fear of a repetition of Wilson's earlier inquiry, but in retrospect seems really to have been designed to insure the selection of Faisal, for he might not be the favored candidate in a popular election.[49]

On the military side, Churchill continued to press toward withdrawal. In a telegram to Haldane on 23 December, he had

[48] Cox private telegram to Montagu, 20 December 1920, *CAB* 24/117; and Cox telegram to SSI, 7 December 1920, *L/P&S/11*, vol. 183, no. 8752/20.

[49] SSI telegram to Cox, 22 December 1920 (Hirtzel draft, modified by Curzon according to Young note to Shuckburgh, 21 December), *ibid.*; F.O. to I.O., 22 December, and Cornwallis minute, 20 December 1920, *FO* 371/5232. Faisal was in London in December, but Iraq was not discussed in detail in his meetings with F.O. personnel: Curzon to Derby, 16 November 1920, *FO* 371/6350; *The Times*, 4 December, clipping with Shuckburgh and Hirtzel minutes, and SSI telegram to Cox, 4 December 1920, *L/P&S/10*, 6513/20, no. 8614/20; see also Nevakivi, *Britain, France and the Arab Middle East*, p. 249. Shuckburgh minute, 23 December, and Hirtzel minute, 27 December, on Marrs note, about 23 December 1920, show lack of information on the negotiations in the I.O.: *L/P&S/10*, 6002/20, no. 8846/20.

outlined the possibility of withdrawal from Mosul even before the coming spring if General Ironside, commanding in Persia, could simultaneously pull his own troops back. "It is understood that the Cabinet regard the necessity for the early reduction of expenditure by the withdrawal of military forces as entirely over-ruling any considerations for the internal security of the country after our troops have left..." As Young minuted, nothing the Cabinet had decided in any way justified this telegram. Crowe added, "It looks as if we were being stampeded into a policy of running away at any price." The India Office agreed, and informed the War Office that Cox would not be similarly informed since the telegram did not correctly interpret the decisions taken. Montagu cabled Cox privately that no doubt the War Office telegram was based solely on military and not political considerations, and Cox's response should be framed in this light. For the Cabinet, Montagu similarly complained that Churchill had been inconsistent with policy. Partial withdrawal was impossible; Britain had pledged the creation of an Arab government, and the alternatives ". . . are, to my mind, *to do this job or to clear out.*" Churchill's policy seemed to be running well ahead of Cabinet-level decisions and aroused the ire of the India Office, the Foreign Office, and the Admiralty (Walter Long of the latter called attention to its interest in Mesopotamian oil—including the oil of Mosul).[50]

By this time Cox had concluded that there was misunderstanding on two counts. The problem of military reductions clearly had to be based upon hypothetical considerations only, for a withdrawal of the nature contemplated would bring, at the least, twelve to fifteen thousand refugees from Mosul with

[50] W.O. telegram to Haldane (quoted), 23 December, with Young and Crowe minutes, I.O. to W.O., 24 December 1920, *FO* 371/5232; Montagu private telegram to Cox, 24 December 1920, *L/P&S/11*, vol. 172, no. 642/21; Montagu memorandum, 22 December, Curzon memorandum, 26 December, and Long memorandum, 24 December 1920, *CAB* 24/117.

which Britain would have to deal. On the issue of government, Cox had thought all along that Britain did not intend to impose a ruler, but would let the population decide. The Assembly would not find it easy to reach a decision, and many would prefer to have the question decided for them. Faisal obviously was the best hope, for he could raise a local army faster than anyone else, and he would satisfy national sentiment sufficiently to permit British military reductions. If the home authorities wanted a decision before the elections, this could be done; if it was to be done, the sooner the better.[51]

In the light of Cox's telegrams and the strong objections to withdrawal at home, the Cabinet decided on 31 December that withdrawal was unacceptable, and that Cox was to press further with his inquiries on the acceptability of Faisal. Cox, however, had decided that further consultation with local notables was undesirable because of the approaching Assembly and that initiative in proposing Faisal must come from London. The High Commissioner therefore suggested that (1) the mandate, in draft form, should be formally and publicly announced, (2) Faisal or one of his brothers should, from Paris or Switzerland, publish telegrams to Nuri and Ja'far saying that since official opposition to his (Faisal's) candidacy had been withdrawn, he therefore offered himself for candidacy; (3) at the same time, he should solicit the Naqib's support, offering him the Prime Ministership, with (4) Talib to continue in the Ministry of the Interior. Talib and the Naqib, thus assuaged (for they were the most likely local candidates in rivalry to Faisal), would (5) then approach Cox to inquire if Faisal had British support, and Cox would reply that Britain offered no serious objection. Faisal would then have the support of the moderate nationalists, and public opinion in general could be sounded to determine if

---

[51] Cox telegram to SSI, 26 December 1920, *FO* 371/6349, and private and official telegrams of 27 December 1920, *L/P&S/11*, vol. 172, no. 642/21.

elections should actually be awaited; at this point, (6) Faisal could arrive in Iraq—but the first reactions should be awaited.[52]

Cornwallis in the Foreign Office, while supporting the end results, objected to Cox's methods, since France was unlikely to abandon her hostility so easily. He suggested that Faisal should be induced, if appointed, to give a satisfactory guarantee on the subject of relations with French Syria, and, presumably, the French should be told about this rather than hear of the whole plan from the press. The Cabinet, meeting on 4 January, postponed a decision on Cox's plan until Curzon could probe the French further.[53]

Postponement may have benefited British policy, but it was no help to Faisal. Faisal was then in London, and news of the Cabinet discussions apparently reached him in rapid order, for on 6 January he wrote to Curzon requesting an interview. It was decided that first Cornwallis would again talk to the Amir about Iraq. In a conversation of the 7th Faisal expressed himself as gratified at the suggestion that he might be a suitable ruler for Iraq; but he refused to put himself forward since 'Abdullah had all along been the Hashimite candidate for that country, and he would not have it said that he had been turned out of one kingdom only to take another from his brother. He was willing only to do everything possible to further 'Abdullah's candidacy. Even if he himself were the candidate, he could not give consent to a mandatory document he had never seen, and he could go to Iraq only with full knowledge of the details of the government to be established there, although he would be willing to make guarantees against anti-French intrigues.[54]

Cornwallis was impressed with Faisal's sincerity and urged that he be chosen in preference to 'Abdullah. Faisal's brotherly

[52] Cabinet 82 (20), 31 December 1920, *CAB* 23/23; Cox telegram to SSI, 2 January 1921, *L/P&S/11*, vol. 183, no. 46/21.

[53] Cox telegram to SSI, 2 January 1921, with Cornwallis and Young minutes, *FO* 371/6349; Cabinet 1 (21), 4 January 1921, *CAB* 23/24.

[54] Faisal to Curzon, 6 January 1921, *FO* 371/6237; Cornwallis note, 8 January 1921 (on conversation with Faisal of 7th), *FO* 371/6349.

concern was commendable, but it was to a certain extent undermined by his willingness to discuss the terms on which he himself would go to Iraq. Faisal was also well aware that Britain was rather disenchanted with his brother, then acting as Husain's Foreign Minister, for 'Abdullah had disappeared from the Hijaz in late October with most of the available funds and had then appeared in Ma'an (in modern-day Jordan, some 60 miles north of 'Aqaba). Britain had no desire fully to occupy the trans-Jordanian area (only a few political officers had been sent as yet), but 'Abdullah's appearance with several hundred men raised the serious danger of an attack on French-held Syria, and, if Britain disclaimed responsibility for the area from which such an attack might be staged, a subsequent French occupation of the trans-Jordan. The crisis passed by the end of December, for 'Abdullah had the shrewdness, apparently, to assess realistically his chances in a foray against Syria; he would be unwise, after all, to move before knowing the outcome of Faisal's London negotiations.[55]

Faisal was in a rather curious position; he had weakened his own strength by supporting 'Abdullah and weakened 'Abdullah by discussing the terms on which he himself would go to Iraq. This was now indicated in a carefully phrased telegram which Curzon and Montagu sent to Cox. Britain would not oppose Faisal if the population desired him, but all appearance of

[55] Scott to F.O., 5 November 1920, FO 371/5243; W.O. to F.O., 22 November, Curzon to Samuel, 30 November 1920, FO 371/5289; Samuel telegrams to F.O., 29 November and 12 and 17 December, F.O. telegrams to Samuel, 19 and 23 December 1920, FO 371/5290; Young memorandum, 29 November 1920, FO 371/6238; Deedes (Jordan) private to Tilley, 19 December 1920, FO 371/6371. The early postwar history of Jordan, which cannot be followed here, may be traced in P. J. Vatikiotis, Politics and the Military in Jordan: A Study of the Arab Legion 1921–1957 (N.Y., 1967); Maj. C. S. Jarvis, Arab Command: The Biography of Lieutenant-Colonel F. W. Peake Pasha, C.M.G., O.B.E. (London, 1942); Sir Alec Seath Kirkbride, A Crackle of Thorns: Experiences in the Middle East (London, 1956); and 'Abdullah, op. cit.

intervention in public opinion or of encouragement of Faisal should be avoided. As an alternative to Cox's plan, London suggested that Faisal might go to Mecca and there announce that Britain did not oppose a Sharifian candidate; 'Abdullah could then put himself forward, and, if rejected, Faisal could replace him—although it had been made quite clear to Faisal that either man would have to approve the mandate and give guarantees regarding the French before ruling Iraq.[56] By this time, however, it was not Montagu who was responsible for Mesopotamian policy, but Winston Churchill.

4

The Cabinet, in December, had authorized Colonial Office control of Middle Eastern policy and appointed a committee to arrange details of transfer. Milner, the originally designated chairman of the committee, had declined the honor; he was to resign in March. The obvious replacement was Churchill and, the day after Milner's formal refusal, he accepted the responsibility. "I feel some misgivings about the political consequences to myself of taking on my shoulders the burden & the odium of the Mesopotamian entanglement . . . ," he wrote Lloyd George, but he did so nevertheless. He did so, however, on the conditions that (1) he had now the authority to give general directions on both civil and military affairs, subject to the Cabinet's general policy; (2) the India Office was to continue in technical administrative responsibility until Churchill could actually take over in the Colonial Office; (3) Churchill would have ultimate responsibility for the committee which would outline details of the transfer of power. Finally, (4) he deemed it necessary to visit Iraq at an early date to make decisions on the spot.[57]

[56] SSI telegram to Cox, 9 January 1921, approval given by Curzon, *L/P&S/11*, vol. 183, no. 9120/20.
[57] Milner private to Lloyd George, 3 January 1921, *Lloyd George*

The Prime Minister agreed to these stipulations; by 8 January, Hankey, for the Cabinet Secretariat, wrote Crowe at the Foreign Office outlining the decision and adding that Sir James Masterson-Smith, Under-Secretary, Ministry of Labour, would chair the committee (again, one of Churchill's suggestions), and that Young would represent the Foreign Office. Young was soon transferred to the Colonial Office staff in charge of the Middle East political section, and although Curzon was sorry to lose him he had little energy left with which to fight any rearguard action on staff changes or areas of responsibility. Austen Chamberlain, who dined with Curzon on the 4th, the day of Milner's retirement, found the Foreign Secretary depressed and disturbed, "uneasy about his position, doubtful of his usefulness & influence—in short very unsettled and wondering whether he could or ought to continue in the Government. I have never before seen him in at all the same mood," he wrote to Bonar Law. Curzon's sympathy for Milner and his sensitivity to Lloyd George's harsh treatment of himself had cut deeply. Chamberlain agreed that some of the Prime Minister's attacks on his own Foreign Secretary had been shocking, and he urged (through Bonar Law) that Curzon's resignation would be fatal to the government, that Lloyd George should be persuaded to treat him more gently.[58]

Thus Churchill assumed control at a moment of serious

---

Papers, F/39/2/37, and Gollin, op. cit., p. 597; Churchill to Lloyd George, 4 January 1921, enclosing note on terms of appointment, Lloyd George Papers, F/9/2/51; the same file includes a one-page draft of the same terms (except the proposed trip to Iraq) given to the Prime Minister on 2 January, obviously anticipating Milner's formal refusal.

[58] Chamberlain private to Bonar Law, 6 January 1921, Bonar Law Papers, 100/1/8; Hankey to Crowe, and Crowe to Curzon, 8 January, Young to Crowe, 11 January, R. C. Lindsay note and Curzon minute, 14 January, Young to Lindsay, 16 February 1921, FO 371/6242. Masterson-Smith, who was to move to the C.O., had been private secretary at the Admiralty for many years, including those when Churchill had been First Lord: Young, op. cit., p. 323.

weakness in the Foreign Office's ability to counterattack on any disputed points. Both Curzon and Montagu had expended their energy in scotching the policy of withdrawal from Iraq; Churchill, although defeated on that issue, was now in full control of policy. The course of events rankled with Curzon— Montagu had for some time been willing to forgo the pleasures of ruling Mesopotamia—but Churchill's position was a strong one in which his freedom of action was bound only by Lloyd George, Percy Cox, and the realities of Iraq.[59]

By 8 January Churchill had reconsidered the idea of traveling to Iraq and wrote Lloyd George that further reflection would be required on the matter. More time was needed, too, before making a definite commitment to Faisal. "I must feel my way and feel sure of my way. I have seen Lawrence and am making certain inquiries." T. E. Lawrence, in other words, had returned, however briefly, to a position of influence in Middle Eastern policy. As for the inquiries to which Churchill referred, he was now initiating a lengthy exchange of views with Cox in Baghdad, who would not accept without discussion Churchill's apparent determination to withdraw from Mosul as soon as possible and to reduce the garrison to the point at which it would be composed only of the R.A.F. and Indian volunteers (with such local levies as could be formed). Cox did not object to the suggestion that 'Abdullah should be given a chance, and only remarked that 'Abdullah's activities in Jordan would probably make him as unacceptable to France as Faisal. The principal requirement was speed whoever was to be chosen.[60]

[59] Compare Vansittart, op. cit., p. 260: "Curzon competed inexplicably with Winston for the load of Palestine, and on both sides officials sent up Christian prayers for the success of the adversary. Fortunately Lloyd George's prejudice against the Foreign Office relieved our anxieties. Winston won. . . "

[60] Churchill to Lloyd George, 8 January 1921, Lloyd George Papers, F/9/2/53; Churchill private telegram to Cox, 10 January, Cox private telegram to I.O. (for Churchill), 13 January 1921, L/P&S/11, vol. 172,

On 15 January, Churchill assumed formal control of Iraq, although he was not yet Colonial Secretary. Cox was told to communicate directly with Churchill and, specifically, to give his views on Faisal. Was he the best man? If Faisal were not available, was 'Abdullah better than any local candidate? "Have you put forward Feisal because you consider taking a long view he is the best man or as a desperate expedient in the hopes of reducing the garrisons quickly?" And, if he really was the best candidate, ". . . can you make sure he is chosen locally?" The more Churchill knew Cox's "true mind," he urged, the sooner a decision could be taken and the means adopted for putting it into effect. Churchill also wished to know the plans for the National Assembly, adding, "Western political methods are not necessarily applicable to the East." [61]

Cox's true mind was that Iraq desired a son of the Sharif, be it Faisal or 'Abdullah. He himself had suggested Faisal because of the latter's war experience and prestige and because his capabilities were greater than those of 'Abdullah. As for elections, these were desirable, but they should follow publication of the mandate. Churchill had already somewhat retreated from his earlier position, and in a telegram which crossed Cox's answer assured the High Commissioner that withdrawal from Mosul was only a last resort, and he had not intended to imply that the idea of a Sharifal ruler had been dropped. But £30 million had been spent in 1920-1921, and £20 million was currently estimated for 1921-1922; Cox's minimum of forces would still cost £12-14 million, and there was no chance of the Cabinet approving such a figure. Churchill's telegram was principally an answer to Cox's of the 15th which had referred to the original

---

nos. 245 and 337/21; Cox telegram to SSI, 11 January 1921, with Young minute, FO 371/6349.

[61] Churchill private telegram to Cox, 15 January 1921, L/P&S/11, vol. 183, no. 380/21; Montagu private telegram to Chelmsford, 15 January 1921, Chelmsford Papers.

terms on which Cox had gone to Iraq and implied possible resignation. To this, Churchill answered,

I have undertaken very reluctantly to face this storm and in the hopes that all British work and sacrifice in Mesopotamia may not be cast away, and I have a right to loyal aid and support from the men on the spot. . . . You would take a great responsibility if before any such decision [on Mosul] had been taken you deprived His Majesty's Government of your local knowledge and influence and thus diminished gravely the chances of a satisfactory solution.[62]

In the light of the Cabinet's decision against withdrawal, Cox was under a misapprehension, and this was now clear to him. He could now proceed with application of the policy as decided, not that this meant an end of all controversy with Churchill.

Masterson-Smith's committee finished its task on the last day of January 1921, and recommended, as expected, that the Colonial Office be responsible for all Middle Eastern Arab areas, with special provision made for the Hijaz and for the Persian Gulf. The former would be under the Foreign Office, and the latter under India, but for both the Colonial Office would have final responsibility; in the case of the Gulf, the Colonial Office would communicate directly with the Resident when necessary. The Colonial Office, to put it another way, would control policy for the entire area, and policy and administration in Iraq, Palestine (and Jordan), and Aden. The decision to leave the Gulf in India's charge was made primarily on financial grounds, rather than because of India's long association with the region. It was simply unnecessarily expensive to create a new structure to replace one already in existence. For the same

[62] Cox private telegram to Churchill and telegram to SSI, 24 January 1921, *L/P&S/11*, vol. 183, no. 520/21; Churchill private telegram to Cox (quoted) and note for Hirtzel, 23 January, Hirtzel for Churchill, 25 January, Cox telegram to SSI, 26 January, Hirtzel for Churchill, 31 January 1921, *ibid.*, vol. 172, nos. 559 and 642/21.

reason, the War Office and Air Ministry would have to control troops in the various areas, as agents of the Colonial Office. The separate commanders would communicate with their departments on matters of administration of their units but would go through the High Commissioners on questions of policy.

The committee had also considered a separate service, but it proved difficult to outline a suitable structure for the whole Arab world; India would remain in the Gulf, for one thing, and the Palestinian service was already well developed. Aden would become part of the Colonial Office service, and Iraqi officials would be in the employ of the Iraqi government. The committee did envisage a cadre of "Arab Political Officers" suitable for service in the Gulf, Aden, and Iraq, but no further immediate steps were taken toward the achievement of this objective. Finally, the new department would be formed in the first instance from officers on loan from other departments, in political-administrative, military, and financial branches, subordinate to an Under-Secretary and Assistant Under-Secretary responsible to the Colonial Secretary. All of this, the committee agreed, could be accomplished by 1 March.[63]

The committee had not drawn conclusions on one further matter of importance: financial costs and contributions. Since the total expense for the Middle East (excluding Egyptian and naval expenses) was running over £46 million, this was no minor matter. Several categories of expenditure were involved, but by far the largest was military: the War Office votes for Mesopotamia and Palestine were, respectively, £33.5 and £8.25 million. Any major cuts would obviously have to come here. There was the further question of India's share of the remaining £4 million, which covered Aden, the Gulf, and the Hijaz. Decisions on subsidies would have to be taken; while Churchill recognized the folly of haggling over a few thousand pounds

[63] Report of interdepartmental committee, circulated to Cabinet by Churchill, 7 February 1921, with Lindsay minute, FO 371/6242.

when millions were involved, the question was an important one.[64]

As Hirtzel argued to Churchill, Britain still wished the other powers to recognize her special position in Arabia. From a moral standpoint, the policy had to be something better than the divide-and-rule of the Turks; subsidies were the easiest form of intervention. Money would keep the Imam from attacking the Aden hinterland; if the Imam was paid, al-Idrisi would have to be paid; if al-Idrisi, then Husain; and so on. Cox argued similarly on Ibn Sa'ud's behalf. Hirtzel therefore urged that subsidies at a level of £100,000 be maintained, as the interdepartmental committee had earlier recommended; further, if a contribution from India was wanted, then India would have to be left some responsibility—an argument for making no radical changes in the administration of the Persian Gulf. Churchill needed little convincing on the matter of subsidies and agreed that they could well be an easier and cheaper answer than soldiers.[65]

Such details, however, could be worked out after the Cabinet had approved the transfer of Arabian affairs to the Colonial Office. Churchill had circulated Masterson-Smith's report on 7 February; on the 8th he cabled Cox that he could not, in view of the approaching Imperial conference, travel to Mesopotamia, but he could and would come to Cairo in early March to confer for a week or so. Cox should come himself, bringing Haldane, Ironside from Persia, and his own principal financial advisor.

[64] I.O. Political Dept. note, 5 February 1921, *L/P&S/11*, vol. 193, no. 583/21.
[65] Hirtzel for Churchill, 5 February, Churchill for Hirtzel, 16 January, and for Hirtzel and Young, 8 February, *L/P&S/10*, 488/20, nos. 695 and 2274/21; Churchill for Hirtzel, 23 January, and Hirtzel minute on Masterson-Smith report, 7 February 1921, *L/P&S/11*, vol. 193, nos. 583 and 768/21; Cox telegram to SSI, 1 February, Young demi-official to Marrs, 5 February, SSI telegram to Cox, 11 February 1921, *FO* 371/6238.

All questions, such as the ruler, the size of the garrison, the boundaries of Iraq, and subsidies, would be discussed, for the new department would have responsibility for all aspects of the Arabian problem. Churchill clearly had no doubts of the outcome of the necessary Cabinet discussion, even though as yet it had only approved transfer of the mandate areas to his authority.[66]

On the 10th, Churchill circulated another memorandum, which requested formal approval both of the committee's report and of the planned conference in Cairo. The Cabinet should indicate for his guidance what they considered a suitable grant-in-aid for 1922-1923 and the subsequent three years, a figure which he advised should be approximately £3 million per year (excluding Palestine). Four days later the Cabinet considered the matter. Curzon, as might be expected, protested that Churchill's outline had gone further than the Cabinet's earlier decisions; he, at least, saw considerable problems that would arise if the Colonial Office was responsible for policies that would affect the Hijaz and the French in Syria, for the Foreign Office could not effectively deal with these areas if another department was making policy. But Churchill's prediction had been accurate, and the Cabinet gave full approval to his proposals, with two stipulations: Churchill was to consult with Curzon to work out an acceptable means for coordinating and controlling Arabian policy, and the Government of India would have the right to express its views on any part of the new policy that affected it. Churchill's trip to Cairo was similarly approved, and he could now begin to plan for a conference, set for less than a month away, which would as far as humanly possible set the lines of Britain's Middle East policy in the postwar era.[67]

[66] SSI (from Churchill) private telegram to Cox, 8 February 1921, *L/P&S/11*, vol. 193, no. 714/21.
[67] Churchill memorandum for Cabinet, 10 February 1921, *CAB* 24/

5

By mid-February, then, the coming meeting at Cairo was definitely accepted. Cox would have preferred Churchill to come to Iraq, but under the circumstances he naturally agreed to make the journey to Egypt, taking Haldane and the others—including Ja'far—in a mission of ten in all. Cox was now dealing with Churchill alone; how little India was involved is clear from Delhi's cable of 15 February pleading for information on the coming conference, of which they assumed the Secretary of State for India would be the chairman.[68]

Montagu was alarmed that India had been given no details on the conference or on the Masterson-Smith report, even though the India Office had so carefully written into the Cabinet's decision a clause safeguarding India's right to comment. India was hastily provided with the information. Some time was to pass before comment could be offered, but just in case Chelmsford made it clear that India objected to paying any share of Arabian subsidies: Britain's Arab policy had already embittered Muslim opinion in India. While India contemplated its full response, the India Office was challenging Churchill's plan for an informal interdepartmental conference under Sir John Shuckburgh (now head of Churchill's Middle Eastern department). As Hirtzel (who stayed with the India Office as Deputy Under-Secretary, a newly created position) put it, the India Office had no wish to be involved if it had neither power nor responsibility. The India Office agreed in the end, but only to

119; Cabinet 7 (21), 14 February 1921, *CAB* 23/24. The Hijaz reservation was of little importance; Churchill had every intention of initiating all policy here: Churchill minute, 19 February, filed with F.O. (Shuckburgh) to Cox, 24 February 1921, Colonial Office files (Public Record Office), *CO* 732/3.

[68] Cox telegrams to SSI, 12 and 14 February 1921, *FO* 371/6242; Viceroy telegram to SSI, 15 February 1921, *L/P&S/11*, vol. 193, no. 768/21.

discuss local and administrative questions relating to the Persian Gulf—and Hirtzel, the India Office representative, could be trusted to avoid entanglements.[69]

Churchill had little time for such minor matters. By 18 February he had prepared an outline of the conference agenda after consultation with both Lawrence and Young. The key issue, that of Iraq's ruler, was not to await the convening of the National Assembly but was to be accomplished via the existing Council of State. Faisal was to be Amir, and Cox was to be asked whether he could secure his election by the Council. At the same time, it was essential to obtain Faisal's prior approval of the draft mandate, on the understanding that once an organic law was established, as the mandate required, Britain would consider any suggestions from the Iraqi government for revision.[70] Already on the 16th T. E. Lawrence, who himself had only just accepted a position as advisor in Churchill's Middle Eastern department, had interviewed Faisal. Apparently for the first time (officially, at any rate), Faisal had been given a hint by his old associate that a reasonable settlement would be reached and had been told of the coming Cairo meeting. The talks with Faisal were hopeful enough, and the choices so limited, that the conference agenda could take the decision for Faisal as granted on the part of the experts who were to assemble in Cairo.[71]

On 26 February the Colonial Office convened its Middle Eastern personnel for a point-by-point discussion of the

[69] Montagu note for Duke, 18 February, and note, 21 February, Hirtzel for Montagu, 21 February, SSI telegram to Viceroy, 18 February 1921, *ibid.*; Viceroy telegram to SSI, 20 February 1921, *CO 732/3*; C.O. to I.O., 22 February, Montagu note, 28 February, I.O. to C.O., 3 March 1921, *L/P&S/11*, vol. 194, no. 1067/21.

[70] Churchill note, 18 February 1921, with Lawrence and Young minutes, *CO 732/4*.

[71] Lawrence memorandum, undated (but 17 February), initialed by Shuckburgh, Churchill, and Curzon, *CO 732/3*; Conference of Ministers, 22 February and 10 March 1921, *DBFP*, XV, pp. 160–66, 396–99; Curzon to Hardinge (Paris), 25 February 1921, *FO 371/6238*.

agenda. These included Shuckburgh, Young, Lawrence, Forbes Adam (another transfer from the Foreign Office), Cornwallis, and various officials not of the permanent London cadre whose expertise was useful: Arnold Wilson, Joyce, Noel of Kurdistan, and R. W. Bullard of Iraq. A number of questions were asked: What if the Iraqi Council objected to Faisal, or Faisal to the terms, or France to the whole idea? But all such worries were brushed away as either unlikely or unimportant. The greatest problem was France; but as Lawrence put it, the French position would be far stronger if they had an alternate proposal, and there was none.[72]

With an agenda—and the policy it outlined—the participants could begin their extended travels. Cox had left Baghdad on the 22nd, leaving Bonham-Carter in charge of a generally quiet situation. His sea voyage gave him time for reflection; from Muscat he advised Churchill that Iraq should control relations with Ibn Sa'ud, and not the Persian Gulf Resident as had been planned. Ibn Sa'ud, Cox felt, would misunderstand, at least at the present time. Cox was still responsible for Kuwait (the rest of the Gulf had passed to Trevor, formerly Deputy Gulf Resident); he argued that he, or whoever was High Commissioner of Iraq, should similarly control relations with central Arabia. The Colonial Office staff cabled its opposition to this idea to Churchill, who had also left London; the Resident, they said, should control all Gulf states and Ibn Sa'ud be dealt with from the Gulf rather than Baghdad.[73]

But it was for Churchill and his advisors to work out such

---

[72] Minutes of conference, 26 February 1921, *CO* 732/3. Lawrence remarked to A. L. Namier that the details were actually worked out at the "Ship Restaurant in Whitehall": A. W. Lawrence, ed., *T. E. Lawrence by His Friends: A New Selection of Memoirs* (N.Y., 1963), p. 186. The structure of the new Middle East section may be traced in *CO* 732/2; it included a staff of fourteen, headed by Shuckburgh as Assistant Under-Secretary, Young as head of the political section, and Meinertzhagen for the military. See Young, *op. cit.*, pp. 324–25; Meinertzhagen, *op. cit.*, pp. 95–99.

[73] Cox telegram to SSI, 22 February, *FO* 371/6349; Cox (Muscat)

details at the conference; on 12 March, the first formal meeting took place of those delegates designated members of the political committee (principally Churchill, Cox, Young, Gertrude Bell, and T. E. Lawrence). The conference itself, the most glittering assembly possible of British Middle Eastern experts, comprised some forty members, some of whom were primarily concerned with financial or military affairs. Among them were Generals Trenchard (Chief of Air Staff), Radcliffe, Ironside, and Haldane; Arnold Wilson, now representing A.P.O.C.; Cornwallis, back in the service of Egypt but brought along by Churchill to consult; Joyce, now advising the Iraqi Ministry of Defense; Ja'far and Sasun Pasha, the Iraqi Minister of Finance; Trevor, from the Gulf; Major-General T. E. Scott, Resident at Aden; Sir Herbert Samuel, High Commissioner of Palestine; Deedes and Peake Pasha from Palestine and Jordan—and no one from India.[74]

The first important issue to be considered was that of Faisal and Iraq. Cox briefed the political committee on his steps to establish a government, the dangers of further delay, and the unsatisfactory nature of other candidates such as the Naqib of Baghdad or Sayyid Talib. To his mind, a son of the Sharif would be popular, provided it was not too obvious that he had been chosen by Britain. The elections would take place shortly, and within six weeks the Assembly would be ready to select a

---

telegram to Secretary of Colonies, 1 March, C.O. telegram to Churchill, 8 March 1921, *CO* 732/1.

[74] Report, Cairo Conference, 11 July 1921, circulated to Cabinet, *CAB* 24/126; various other copies available, including a convenient separately bound copy at *AIR* (Air Ministry files), 8/37. Remarks on the conference, unless otherwise indicated, are based upon this report, which includes, appended, minutes of the various political committee meetings. See also Boyle, *op. cit.*, pp. 378–81; Burgoyne, *op. cit.*, pp. 209–11; Graves, *Cox*, pp. 280–86; S. H. Slater, "Iraq," *Nineteenth Century and After*, 99 (April 1926), 479–94 (Slater also attended the conference as a financial advisor); Aldington, *op. cit.*, pp. 303–7; and Young, *op. cit.*, pp. 325–26.

ruler. Churchill, however, objected to the unique step of an assembly choosing a king by election—although Cox pointed out that the Assembly was designed only to advise on the form of government—and suggested that perhaps a body of a hundred or so notables could be formed, including (this in answer to a question from Gertrude Bell) representatives of the "rebels," which Faisal could then approach.

The following day the political committee hammered out the details of the process by which Faisal would be chosen. Cox produced the timetable. In May (Ramadan), Faisal would arrive in Iraq, "and it was felt that his presence in Irak would have such an inspiring effect upon the majority of the population that there was little fear of any opposition to his candidature." Faisal could not be given guarantees; he must, in the final analysis, take his own chances. In the third meeting, the details were decided. Faisal would telegraph to Nuri (now in Iraq) and Ja'far and other friends that Britain had given its approval of him and that he was now a candidate; Cox would instruct his officers to promote the new policy. It was generally assumed that there would be no need to consult an assembly. Churchill now sent off a telegram to Lloyd George which outlined the decision and urged that the Prime Minister give his approval; once this was done, Faisal would proceed to Mecca. Lloyd George answered that Faisal was certainly acceptable, but that it would be most embarrassing to Anglo-French relations unless his rule was initiated from Iraq—and what of Faisal's insistence that 'Abdullah have first chance?[75]

Churchill had plans for dealing with 'Abdullah, but at the moment he was more concerned with the other side of the Iraqi problem, reduction of the military forces to a tolerable level. He therefore demanded to know from Lloyd George

[75] Churchill private telegram to Lloyd George, 14 March, Lloyd George private telegram to Churchill, 16 March 1921, FO 371/6350; Hankey private to Kerr, 16 March 1921, Lloyd George Papers, F/25/1/16.

whether the Cairo meeting could assume, in discussing Iraqi military forces, that a satisfactory settlement would be reached with the Turkish nationalists and that there would be no danger of Turkish inroads into Mosul. Churchill knew, of course, that no such settlement had been reached, nor could it be guaranteed —but his question forced the Prime Minister to go on record to this effect, thus making it clear that a garrison maintained in Iraq to ward off outside aggression was not Churchill's responsibility.

While awaiting an answer, the political committee at Cairo had gone on to discuss other difficulties, notably Kurdistan. In a meeting on the 15th, at which Noel was brought in to consult, it was clear that there was considerable disagreement on this issue. Cox, who wished to see Kurdistan included in Iraq, had already told his Council of State that he would deal with Kurdistan himself until the Kurds decided—sometime in the coming year—on their own future. Young, among others, opposed this plan, and both he and Noel advised the immediate creation of a Kurdish state; the Kurds would object to Iraqi government authority, and a strong Kurdish state would be a useful counter to any subsequent anti-British feeling in Iraq. Even Lawrence agreed that the Kurds should not come under the Arabs, while Gertrude Bell felt that after six months of stability in Iraq the Kurds would indeed want to come in. Churchill preferred a buffer state—but no solution was adopted except, by default, that of letting matters take their own course, as Cox had suggested. Mosul and Kirkuk, however, would be held, at least until the local levy force planned for those districts came into being. Including this responsibility, and assuming Lloyd George's basic approval, Churchill estimated that by 1922-1923 costs of the garrison could be reduced to £5-6 million, always provided that there was peace with Turkey and that the Arab government was successful.

By this time further details for Faisal had been worked out. Cox would return to Baghdad in April and issue a general amnesty (he had already released some of Wilson's detainees); Faisal would telegraph to his friends; at the same time, 'Abdullah would renounce his candidacy in favor of his brother. Faisal would then tour Iraq, and if all went well it would not be necessary to consult the Assembly; Faisal would dissolve the provisional Council of Ministers and ask the Naqib or someone else to form a cabinet. In a telegram of the 16th, Churchill declared the conference unanimous on this plan and again urged the Prime Minister to give speedy approval, for all the details must be worked out before Cox returned to Iraq. Lloyd George, however, could only give provisional approval to Churchill's various points—and the plans would require more consideration.[76]

Telegrams were now crossing each other, and Churchill was also answering Lloyd George's reservations telegraphed from London on the 16th. The plans for Faisal were not for publication but were rather an indication of the limits within which policy would be framed. All concerned wanted spontaneous selection of Faisal in Iraq, but unless Britain had its mind made up this was unlikely to occur, given the possible number of candidates. Cox and Gertrude Bell were convinced that the plan would work—as convinced as they were that Faisal was the best of the Sharifians—"But this will be partly because the mere fact that we have allowed him to return will universally be interpreted as if it were a coupon election candidature." Anything less might well lead to an incoherent verdict by a small minority in favor of an unsuitable candidate. As for 'Abdullah's priority, the conference members felt that this no longer represented the true situation. As a final argument, Churchill added that all his proposals hung together, and once they were approved further steps would be forthcoming, including a guar-

[76] Churchill private telegram to Lloyd George, 16 March 1921, *FO* 371/6350; Lloyd George private telegram to Churchill, 18 March 1921, *Lloyd George Papers*, F/25/1/18, and other documents in that file.

antee to France. "I do hope you will give me personally the support to which I am entitled in a task which I certainly have not sought." [77]

There were indeed reservations on the plan, even in Churchill's own Middle Eastern staff in London. Shuckburgh was convinced that France would believe that Britain had arranged Faisal's selection, and equally convinced that France would not be far wrong. But there seemed little choice: Churchill made this as clear as possible in a telegram of the 21st, designed for circulation to the Cabinet prior to its meeting of the 22nd. When the Cabinet did meet, it approved the entire scheme, provided Faisal agreed to the mandate and promised not to use his position for anti-French intrigues. When Faisal had announced himself from Mecca, Britain could communicate with the French. Churchill agreed, and suggested that Lawrence telegraph privately to Faisal to start him on his road to Mecca. By the 24th, Lawrence's message had been passed to the Amir, who promised to leave as soon as possible. On 31 March he paid his farewell visit to the Foreign Office and began a journey that finally brought him to Baghdad as King of Iraq. [78]

A number of problems remained, particularly one on which the Cabinet expressed quite determined reservations in its meeting of the 22nd. This concerned the future of Trans-Jordan and of 'Abdullah. One way of dealing with any embarrassing claims by Faisal's brother, and at the same time forestalling his capacity for making trouble with the French, was to make him head of a separate statelet in that area, a solution which would

[77] Churchill private telegram to Lloyd George, 18 March 1921, *FO* 371/6350.

[78] Shuckburgh memorandum, 19 March 1921 (citing his department's view), *Lloyd George Papers*, F/9/3/16; Churchill private telegrams to Lloyd George, 21 and 23 (latter enclosing Lawrence's message) March, Lloyd George private telegram to Churchill, 22 March 1921, *FO* 371/6350; Cabinet 14 (21), 22 March 1921, *CAB* 23/24; F.O. to C.O., 6 April 1921, *FO* 371/6239.

have the further advantage of removing the Trans-Jordanian area from official Palestine and therefore from the area to which the Balfour Declaration applied. Sir Herbert Samuel, Palestine's High Commissioner, objected at Cairo to this solution, for 'Abdullah in Trans-Jordan could still jeopardize the stability of both Palestine and Syria and therefore of Anglo-French relations as well. Anti-Zionist agitation, raids into Palestine: Samuel could foresee only trouble. But once again, there seemed no alternative. Britain could not support Faisal in Iraq and oppose 'Abdullah in Trans-Jordan. Only the good will of the Hashimite family as a whole could bring a pacific, cheap solution. In any case the specter of having to drive 'Abdullah out of Amman with force in order to impose another solution for Trans-Jordan was hardly appealing, and political officers with experience in the area suggested that this might not even be possible.

The Cabinet, however, was worried; if the establishment of one Sharifian state on the frontiers of Syria would make the French nervous, what would be their view of two? They would naturally see this as an assault upon their position, plotted by Britain. The necessity of another British military commitment to police the area, the small size of the future kingdom, the possibility that 'Abdullah himself might object—there were too many difficulties. Churchill had an answer to every criticism. 'Abdullah might indeed see the area as too small; all that was wanted was his acceptance of an Arab governor (not necessarily himself) for the area. A small British force would be necessary for the establishment of stability; but for the future reduction of forces already in Palestine, Trans-Jordanian stability was requisite. For France, law and order in Jordan would be far more advantageous than disorder.[79]

[79] 'Abdullah arrived in Amman on 2 March: Samuel telegram to C.O., 8 March 1921, *FO* 371/6371; Jordanian developments may be followed in this file. Cabinet nervousness mentioned in Lloyd George private telegram to Churchill, 22 March (and see Churchill private

As planned earlier, Churchill now moved from Cairo to Jerusalem for conversations with Samuel and 'Abdullah in order to work out a solution, despite the Cabinet's misgivings. In fact, a settlement was not reached in Jerusalem; 'Abdullah was told the British plan, but he had his own reservations on such topics as British support for King Husain against Ibn Sa'ud and, more important, Britain's policy toward the Jews in Palestine proper. His own solution—an Arab governor for the whole of Palestine and Trans-Jordan—was clearly unacceptable, but Churchill made it clear that Britain would make a separate administrative area of Trans-Jordan, and 'Abdullah, admitting that the idea was interesting, promised to think it over and consult his father and brother. Since 'Abdullah had indicated to Churchill his lack of desire to press his claim to Iraq under the circumstances, it seemed likely that he would accept the Trans-Jordanian position when the terms could be worked out.

Churchill's work was done, as far as could be. He could return to London with considerable satisfaction, for while massive problems remained the basic answer—Faisal in Iraq, 'Abdullah in Trans-Jordan—had been reached. The precise form of the two governmental structures had yet to be worked out, and Faisal's agreement to the mandate obtained—but these are subsequent stories. Further intensive debate was to take place on the development of Iraqi oil, the return of the by now homeless Iraqi officers (most of whom were repatriated finally at British expense), or India's contribution to Middle Eastern expenses. And the whole solution rested on two basic hypotheses, both as yet untested: Faisal's suitability to Iraq and a satisfactory peace with Turkey. There were many dark days ahead, and Churchill would even return to discussion of the advisability of resigning the mandates and quitting Iraq and Palestine as

telegram to Lloyd George, 23 March), *FO* 371/6350. Jerusalem discussions noted below are appended to Cairo Conference report, n. 74 above.

a result of problems with Turkey, the United States, and the League of Nations.[80]

But policy-making is a continuous process, and the Cairo meeting had marked a watershed in that process as far as Middle Eastern policy was concerned. It was the end of years of debate and controversy and confusion, as it was the beginning of years of debate and controversy and confusion. It was also the start of an Arab state system, disunited, subordinate to different mandatory powers, and faced with serious problems of economies, frontiers, minorities, and political groups. Still, it was a state system, and, for better or worse, that system still survives, half a century after the meeting of the "Forty Thieves" [81] at Cairo in March of 1921.

[80] Churchill to Lloyd George, 2 June 1921, *Lloyd George Papers*, F/9/3/48.

[81] The term is attributed to Churchill himself: Boyle, *op. cit.*, p. 382.

# X

# Conclusion: India and Britain's Arab Policy, 1914–1921

Do you remember Coko Ffoulkes,
Flossie St. Vincent and Bimbo Stookes,
Twirly Rogers and Bushy Ames?
They all of them had such expressive names,
And Monkey Trotter in guardsman's rig
Doing a rather suggestive jig . . .

The men we loved have all passed on
Like the world we knew they are dead and gone.

*S. Wilson, quoted by R. Fulford
in Simon Nowell-Smith,* EDWARDIAN ENGLAND

1

The preceding pages have reviewed the role of India, directly and indirectly, in the formation of Britain's policy toward the Arab Middle East in the era of World War I. That there was considerable Indian influence upon that policy cannot be denied, although it came as often in matters of minor importance as in statements of high policy. But it is the collective, total effect that requires some final remark.

In the first place, the attitudes of the Indian government, its subordinate officials, and the India Office considerably handicapped Britain in the extent to which aid could be furnished to the Arab movement, and, more important, in the extent to which pledges on the future could be made to that movement. Indian limitations applied to the suggested use of troops in the Hijaz (an issue on which the Indian authorities had strong allies in Cairo and London) or to prisoners of war or pan-Islamic agents or activities on the Red Sea coast. Those same limitations restricted public statements on policy toward Arabia. Most important of all, they applied to privately given pledges. The reservation of Mesopotamia for Britain made by McMahon to King Husain was the direct result of Indian intervention, and it is hard not to conclude that that single reservation might well have been the central Anglo-Arab issue in the unlikely possibility of Franco-Arab understanding on the one hand and Zionist-Arab agreement on the other. Fortunately, perhaps, for India and for Iraq, those issues took precedence. In part, India's intervention, it is true, was based upon a misconception: the conviction that Cairo wished to establish a large, unified, pan-Arab state—which was far from the truth. That Indian intervention was based upon a false premise made it no less effective.

The justification of India's concern was partly historical, in the sense of her long-standing role in the Persian Gulf and in Aden. It was also the product of her own venture in Mesopotamia. That venture was entered into with a certain amount of unwillingness at first, and without adequate preparations, as the subsequent military disaster made perfectly clear. When the opportunity for advance came, however, India made use of it; in any case, whatever qualms there may have been about the capture of Baghdad there were none about the future possession of Basra. In fairness to India it must be kept in mind that there was no Arab revolt in Iraq, and that British forces had always to be wary in their dealings with the inhabitants. Whether a different policy from the start might have created a different environment is not the point; given the existing situation, and Indian methods, which could not be changed overnight, the course of the war in Iraq was considerably different than in the Hijaz or Palestine or Syria.

There was, too, another justification for India's attitude from the standpoint of Indian internal affairs. Again, rightly or wrongly, the Indian authorities were consistently nervous about the effect of the war against the Ottoman Empire upon the opinion of Indian Muslims. This consideration was of far more importance for such issues as Rabigh or the Caliphate than for Mesopotamia. India's administration, after all, was charged with responsibility for administering India—efficiently, quietly, and as cheaply as possible—and the more the outside world was allowed to impinge upon Indian affairs the less possible such administration became. India, in short, objected to the impact of the war as much as those responsible for conducting the war objected to Indian internal conditions determining the nature of that wartime leadership.

Second, because India was part of the Empire and governed by Imperial servants, there was far slower development in India and in subordinate Iraq of recognition of the inevitability of nationalist pressures—and far less of the inevitability of their long-range victory. Officials in London, outlining concessions in postwar Iraq or Egypt or even India, might admit—or, conversely, block their minds to—the inevitable final result of independence. India's rulers, however, had a greater vested interest in the results, and more direct contact with the meaning, of such developments. Few kept pace even with authorities in London, much less with extremist nationalist opinion in Iraq or India. It was not that Empire was "good" and nationalism "bad"; people like Arnold Wilson rather felt that efficient, benign government was of far more benefit to the people than anarchical independence. Enlightened paternalism was slower to die in India, and so were its corollaries of protected frontiers, dangers from Russia, and the like. Briefly, tenuously, India's rulers dreamed of an Empire within an Empire: India with its satellites in Mesopotamia or East Africa. There were good arguments: Was India to sacrifice so much blood and treasure in her far-flung campaigns for no return? Other countries, other sections of Britain's Empire, had similar aims, some of which were achieved; that India's were not made them no less important in their time and place.

Third, in a more specific context, India's role hampered more than relations with the Arabs. The long-held conviction that Basra, as a minimum, should become part of India's empire seriously limited the flexibility with which Britain could fend off the claims to Ottoman spoils of her Allies—meaning, for the Arab world, France. So long as Britain continued to hold and to desire to keep on holding Basra and southern Iraq, to say nothing of Mosul and the north, so long was her position extremely weak from which to attempt to deny Syria to France. India was not solely responsible for visions of British-held Basra, but India's relations with Iraq had been of importance in the campaign in the first instance, and her military failures made it all the more difficult to yield up the area without compensation. To put it another way, so long as Britain held Iraq, France would demand Syria, over and above the other pressures that propelled France toward that area. And so long as the two powers divided the area, there could be no Arab unity.

The fourth point concerns Mesopotamia itself. After 1916, London conducted the campaign in Mesopotamia, but by 1916 it was already too late to change the nature of the administrative structure there without the sort of wholesale replacement of personnel that was never seriously discussed. India was soon removed from direct conduct of Iraqi affairs, although it kept a role in the Persian Gulf, and India was to have occasion for viewing the regime in Baghdad as hostile, just as London did.

Conclusion                                          479

But India lived on in Iraq not only through the intermediary administrative role of the India Office but also in the attitude and outlook of Sir Percy Cox and to a much more marked extent of Sir Arnold Wilson: good government for, but not necessarily by, the people. Wilson was of the clay of the great proconsuls of British Imperial history, if a bit flawed in the final casting—or, more charitably, given far too much responsibility when still without the requisite experience. In the end Wilson had to be removed, and Cox, more experienced, more amenable, returned to introduce a different policy. Wilson's approach, whatever its several merits and whatever outside problems with which he had to deal, had ended in bloody rebellion.

Although the struggle over administrative policy in Mesopotamia only further complicated problems which were hardly of Arnold Wilson's making—delay in the Turkish treaty and uncertainty in neighboring Syria—the general desire for a British presence in Iraq made a considerable contribution to both those issues. Arnold Wilson's views also made a direct contribution to Britain's policy problems on such questions as Kurdistan, future Syrian boundaries, the attitude toward Britain of Faisal's closest advisors, and, more obviously, the constitutional structure of Iraq. When the British government collectively decided that Mosul would be included in Iraq, that decision insured once and for all that France would be confirmed in Syria, for earlier errors of judgment, however understandable, had assigned Mosul to France, and recognition in Syria was the French price for yielding Mosul. Insofar as long-range Indian influence, or Arnold Wilson's views, contributed to the delay of the Mesopotamian settlement, then to that extent were India, and Wilson, responsible for the incongruity of a grandiose declaration of Iraqi liberation, made in Baghdad in 1917, and the spectacle of murdered political officers and besieged garrisons three years later.

Fifth, Britain's relations with postwar Turkey were influenced by India through the instrumentality of Delhi's view of

Indian public opinion and Montagu's interpretation of his own responsibilities. There can be no question of the significance of the Khilafat movement for internal Indian politics, as a review of the literature on the subject will make clear. The role of that pressure upon British policy is less clear, particularly in the light of Lloyd George's inclination to disregard such considerations while in search of his own vision of Turkey's future, but it has not been possible to treat this subject in a work focused upon Arab rather than Turkish policy.

The last point concerns the question of control. Without the perpetual struggle with India over the host of issues ranging from the Red Sea through Arabia into Mesopotamia and Turkey, there could not have occurred the perpetual struggle throughout the years treated here to establish the one central authority that could find some operative principle of policy and then decide the policy in the light of that principle. What was the principle (or principles) upon which Britain acted? To ask such a question is far too often to assume the existence of a clear-cut answer. The historian who studies the day-to-day operation of a foreign policy is likely to conclude that diplomats, like other men, often act on a day-to-day basis according to vague, perhaps unverbalized generalities. The gap between generalizations and specific decisions is often so wide as to be unbridgeable. Mark Sykes had self-determination before his eyes, but Mark Sykes had great difficulty—as much as President Woodrow Wilson—in harmonizing that principle with the details of racial, linguistic, and ethnic complexity in the Middle East.

Others may simply have seen "Empire" as desirable, and wished to see it expand, develop resource potentials in neighboring areas, and certainly protect communications routes and military flank positions. Oil, irrigation, Indian colonization, anti-Bolshevism, pro- or anti-Arab nationalism: all of these motivated individuals; and those wishing to understand a government's foreign policy can never forget that policy is made by individuals, and that individuals can act from motives of personal ambition, or spite, or even—most horrifying of all to those who like diplomatic history in neat packages—from confusion of mind.

Beyond the direct effects, however, there is one further conclusion to be made. It is sometimes said—this author has said so himself—that the era of Lord Curzon, which ended in India in 1905, was the last in which India pursued a separate foreign policy of its own, often at the cost of the policy desired by the technically superior officials in London. On the whole, that conclusion is justified, but only if exception is made for the years covered in this study. So complex, so unusual, were the conditions accompanying World War I, that several centers of policy-making developed. Consideration has been given here to Cairo, Delhi, and Baghdad—but the point is that India was one of those centers. While steps introduced in 1916 began to reduce India's recovered role, it was not until 1921 that the end of the process was reached, and even then not all the effects were finished. As a separate center of policy formation, India had a different viewpoint, a viewpoint, for example, which looked first to Ibn Sa'ud and only second to King Husain, within the framework of the Arabian Peninsula. It was a matter of principle: Should such an area be treated as a native Indian state complex, with Britain dealing with existing regimes as it found them (al-Idrisi, the Imam of Yemen, Ibn Rashid) and letting the area work out its own fortunes in all matters save those directly concerning Britain? Or should Britain deal with the area in the wider framework of an over-all policy for the future Arab world? The latter view, tenuously held by Cairo and London, gradually emerged supreme, but India had the satisfaction of knowing that in the long run Ibn Sa'ud was the strongest runner in a confusing race, a race in which India had managed to back more than one contestant.

Should Britain then have supported Ibn Sa'ud and not King Husain? There can be, of course, no answer, since the question raises the possibility of no Arab revolt, no Hashimite rulers, perhaps even no Arab policy. The historian who attempts to create as accurate as possible a description of a policy, the varying motives that prompted that policy, and the individual responsibility for its application, all from documentary evidence, is on dangerous ground if he raises such a wide-ranging hypothesis, the answer to which includes so many unknown quantities. It is enough if this work has served to show that the role of India, broadly defined, was significant—more significant, perhaps, than has been realized—in Britain's relations with the Arab world during a crucial period.

2

It is not possible in a work such as this to give full value to the individual personalities of the men (and Gertrude Bell) who were responsible for the events it describes. Many, indeed, are the subject of biographical or autobiographical works—and occasionally, as with T. E. Lawrence, the subject of a vast body of literature. Lawrence, Arnold Wilson, Young, Philby, Bell, Meinertzhagen, Storrs, Haldane, MacMunn, Townshend, and a few others have written their own accounts. Cox, Montagu, Wingate, Allenby, and such obvious figures as Lloyd George and Curzon, to mention but a few, have been the subject of one or more biographies. Some of these persons finished in high places; while there is no need to recount the subsequent history of Churchill or Curzon or T. E. Lawrence, some remark is in order on the lesser-known figures.[1]

From the India Office, and India, Montagu did resign in 1922 and died only two years later. Sir John Shuckburgh became,

---

[1] Remarks in this section are based upon the works cited in the Bibliography section on "Biography and Memoirs" and information culled from the Foreign Office List, the India Office List, the *Dictionary of National Biography*, and general works treating post-1921 Iraq and Saudi Arabia, particularly Birdwood, *Nuri*, and Longrigg, *'Iraq 1900–1950*.

after transfer to the Colonial Office in 1921, Under-Secretary from 1932 to 1943; he was appointed Governor of Nigeria in 1939 (but did not assume the post because of the war). Hirtzel was Permanent Under-Secretary from 1924 until his retirement in 1930. Sir Denys de Samouriez Bray was Foreign Secretary of India, 1923-1930, and Indian delegate to the League, 1932-1935; Garbett was Civil Secretary in Iraq, 1920-1922, and ended his career in Indian provincial administration. Cox stayed on as High Commissioner in Iraq until 1923; he died in 1937 at the age of seventy-three after a career that had been exceptional among some exceptional men and that made him Major-General Sir Percy Cox, G.C.M.G., G.C.I.E., K.C.S.I. Arnold Wilson, on the other hand, fared well with A.P.O.C. and after 1933 was a Conservative Member of Parliament; he became "missing believed killed" as an R.A.F. gunner over France in 1940 (surely the only gunner with a name preceded by "Sir" and followed by K.C.I.E., C.S.I., C.M.G., D.S.O., M.P.). Wilson's writing was prolific, and some of his work, notably *The Persian Gulf*, of permanent value.[2] Yet, somehow, Wilson never fulfilled the promise he displayed as a young political officer in Persia, the Gulf, and Iraq. If Curzon never lived down being Viceroy of India, Wilson never lived down being Civil Commissioner of Iraq.

From Cairo, not all of those concerned did so well. McMahon never again held high position after his removal in 1916; he died in 1949 after an active life concerned mainly with Masonic and Y.M.C.A. activities. Ironically, he might have held office again if Britain had participated in the King-Crane Commission, for McMahon was to be a principal British delegate. Allenby remained High Commissioner of Egypt until 1924; he died at the age of seventy-five in 1936 as Viscount Allenby of

---

[2] Sir Arnold T. Wilson, *The Persian Gulf: An Historical Sketch from the Earliest Times to the Beginning of the Twentieth Century* (London, 1928). A bibliography of Wilson's works may be found in Marlowe, *op. cit.*, pp. 399–406.

Megiddo and Felixstowe, with a Parliamentary gift of £50,000 to his credit. Wingate, like McMahon, lived on for many years (to 1953) but did not again occupy high office. When he died, he was Colonel Commandant of the Royal Artillery and active in affairs of the British Legion, the Royal National Life-Boat Institution, and the Royal African Society, and Baronet of Dunbar and Port Sudan, G.C.B., G.C.V.O., G.B.E., K.C.M.G., D.S.O. Storrs became military governor of Jerusalem (later civil governor), and Governor of Cyprus (1926-1932) and of Northern Rhodesia (1932-1934); he died in 1955. Clayton returned to service with the Egyptian government, was appointed High Commissioner of Iraq in 1929, and died the same year. Cornwallis for many years was an advisor to King Faisal of Iraq, and was Britain's Ambassador to that country during World War II (1941-1945). C. E. Wilson died in 1938. Hogarth returned to his profession of archaeology as keeper of the Ashmolean Museum, Oxford, until his death in 1927.

From the Foreign Office, Hardinge's last post ended with his retirement as Ambassador to France in 1923. Crowe and Vansittart were both successors to Hardinge as Permanent Under-Secretary; Young, however, stayed with the Colonial Office, serving in Gibraltar and Iraq, and from 1932 onward was Governor successively of Nyasaland, Northern Rhodesia, and Trinidad and Tobago, twice standing unsuccessfully for Parliament; he died in 1950. Robert Cecil, Viscount Cecil of Chelwood, died in 1958 after a succession of government posts—but his major concern was the League of Nations, for which work he received the Nobel Peace Prize in 1937.

King Faisal I of Iraq died in 1933; King 'Abdullah of Jordan was assassinated in 1951; King Husain of the Hijaz died in exile in 1931; King 'Ali of the Hijaz, briefly Husain's successor in Jidda in 1925, similarly died in exile in 1935. The family history was a glorious one—but the glory had a habit of turning to tragedy. Al-Idrisi, ruler of 'Asir, died in 1923; his successor was unable to preserve the integrity of 'Asir, and it was absorbed

by Ibn Sa'ud. 'Abd al-'Aziz ibn Sa'ud died in 1953, but not before he had been proclaimed King of the Hijaz (1926), King of
the Hijaz and Najd (1927), and King of Saudi Arabia (1932).
In Iraq, both Ja'far and Nuri lived on to serve and to control
the Iraqi government for many years, but both ended in tragedy: Ja'far was killed in a coup d'état in October 1936, and
Nuri in the bloody events of 1958. Sayyid Talib, once virtual
ruler of Basra, then pensioner of the Indian government, then
Minister of the Interior in Iraq, ended his career through opposition to Faisal: he was exiled in the early days of the new
regime, passed through Ceylon, appeared in Italy and Amman,
and finally died in Munich in 1929 after a decade of wan-
dering.[3]

For some, indeed, a tragic ending. But many were inspired
by the highest motives, most were sincere, all were human. It
was the conflict of these individuals, each in the pursuit of his
own ambitions and his view of his country's or dynasty's ambitions, that determined the history discussed in these pages.
Treachery, betrayal, double-dealing—such charges are often
levied at many of those mentioned in this list. Without question,
such things do and did exist—but those who make such charges
should bear in mind that people in positions of official power,
particularly those raised in Victorianism and trained in Indian
paternalism, came to realize that deceit has a way of having unfortunate consequences, and that the repercussions of policy applied in all sincerity are often damaging enough. It was not, in
the final analysis, deliberate deception that underlay Britain's
problems in the Middle East, but the unforeseen and unplanned
contradictions arising from unexpected pressures in a new
world—and the imperfection of man.

[3] Ceylon telegram to High Commissioner, Egypt, 2 March 1922;
High Commissioner, Baghdad, telegram to High Commissioner, Egypt,
22 September 1924; Acting Consul-General, Munich, to F.O., 18 June
1929: *FO* 141/607.

# Bibliography

## MANUSCRIPT COLLECTIONS

### OFFICIAL CORRESPONDENCE

Great Britain
  Public Record Office, London
    Air Ministry files, series 8 (Chief of Air Staff). 1916–1921.
    Cabinet files, series 1 (Committee of Imperial Defence, Misc. Records), 17 (C.I.D., Correspondence and Misc. Papers), 19 (War Cabinet; Mesopotamian Commission), 21 (Cabinet registered files), 22 (War Council: Dardanelles and War Committees), 23–24 (Cabinet minutes and memoranda), 25 (Supreme War Council, 1917–1919), 27 (Cabinet Committees), 28 (War Cabinet: allied conferences), 29 (Preparations for Peace), 44–45 (Cabinet Historical Section: compilations, official histories, correspondence). 1914–1922.
    Colonial Office files, series 730 (Iraq), 732 (Middle East). 1920–1922.
    Foreign Office files, series 141 (Egypt, Embassy archives), 371 (post-1905), 608 (Peace Conference), 686 (Jidda Agency archives), 794 (Private office archives), 848 (Egypt, Milner mission files), 882 (Arab Bureau archives). 1914–1921.
    War Office files, series 33 (Misc. reports), 106 (Directorate of Military Operations and Intelligence: papers). 1914–1921.
  Commonwealth Relations Office: India Office Records, London
    Political Department, Political and Secret Subject files (L/P&S/10), Regular Series files (L/P&S/11), and Persian Gulf Territories archives (R/15). 1914–1922.
  Ministry of Power, Records Department, London
    Petroleum Executive files. 1917–1921.
India
  National Archives of India, New Delhi

Home Department Proceedings. Political files, 1914–1922.
Foreign Department Proceedings. Secret External and War files. 1914–1922

PRIVATE CORRESPONDENCE

Beaverbrook Library, London
The Private Papers of the Rt. Hon. Andrew Bonar Law, M.P., P.C.
The Private Papers of David, Earl Lloyd George of Dwyfor, O.M., P.C.
Bodleian Library, Oxford
The Private Papers of Alfred, Lord Milner.
The Private Papers of Lord Oxford and Asquith.
British Museum, London
The Balfour Papers. The Papers of Arthur James Balfour, 1st Earl of Balfour. Add. Mss. 49683–49962.
The Cecil Papers. The Correspondence and Papers of Lord Edgar Algernon Robert Cecil, Viscount Cecil of Chelwood, Add. Mss. 51071–51204.
The Correspondence between Gen. Sir Archibald James Murray, G.C.M.G., and Sir William Robert Robertson, G.C.B., 1916–1917. Add. Mss. 52461–52463.
The Wilson Papers. The Correspondence and Papers of Lt.-Col. Sir Arnold Talbot Wilson, K.C.I.E. Add. Mss. 52455–52459.
Cambridge University Library
The Papers of Charles, Baron Hardinge of Penshurst.
India Office Library, London
The Papers of Frederic John Napier Thesiger, 1st Viscount Chelmsford.
The Papers of Sir Arthur Hamilton Grant.
The Papers of the Hon. Edwin Samuel Montagu.
The Papers of Rufus Daniel Isaacs, 1st Marquess of Reading.
The Papers of Freeman Freeman-Thomas, 1st Marquess of Willingdon.
Kent County Archives, Maidstone
The Papers of Charles, Baron Hardinge of Penshurst.
Public Record Office, London
The Private Papers of Lord Balfour (*FO* 800).
The Private Papers of Lord Robert Cecil (*FO* 800).
The Private Papers of Lord Curzon (*FO* 800).
The Private Papers of Sir Edward Grey (*FO* 800).
The Private Papers of Lord Kitchener (*PRO* 30/57).
The Private Papers of Alfred, Lord Milner (*PRO* 30/30).
The Private Papers of Sir Arthur Nicolson (*FO* 800).
The Private Papers of Sir Mark Sykes (*FO* 800).
St. Antony's College, Oxford (Middle East Centre)
The Private Papers of Sir D. G. Hogarth.

The Private Papers of Sir Herbert Samuel (reproductions).
The Private Papers of Sir Mark Sykes (reproductions).
University of Birmingham Library
The Papers of Sir Austen Chamberlain.
University of Durham Library (Oriental Section)
The Papers of Brig.-Gen. Sir Gilbert Clayton.
The Papers of Gen. Sir Reginald Wingate.

PUBLISHED DOCUMENTS

Great Britain
Admiralty. Naval Intelligence Division. Geographical Handbook
Series. *Iraq and the Persian Gulf*; *Palestine and Transjordan*; *Syria*;
and *Western Arabia and the Red Sea*. Oxford: Oxford University
Press for H.M.S.O., 1943–1946.
Committee of Imperial Defence. Historical Section. *History of the
Great War Based on Official Documents.*
*The Campaign in Mesopotamia, 1914–1918.* Compiled by Brig.-
Gen. F. J. Moberley. London: H.M.S.O., 1923–1927. 4 vols.
*Naval Operations.* Compiled by Sir Julian S. Corbett. London:
Longmans, Green, 1920–1928. 5 vols. in 9.
Foreign Office.
*British Documents on the Origins of the War, 1898–1914*, ed. by
G. P. Gooch and Harold Temperley. Vol. X, part II. London:
H.M.S.O., 1938.
*Documents on British Foreign Policy, 1919–1939*, ed. by Rohan
Butler, J. P. T. Bury, and E. L. Woodward. First series, vols.
I–XV. London: H.M.S.O., 1947–1967.
Historical Section. *Peace Handbooks*. Vol. XI: "Turkey in Asia,"
nos. 61 (Arabia) and 63 (Mesopotamia); Vol. XIII: "Persian
Gulf, French and Portuguese Possessions," no. 76 (Persian Gulf).
London: H.M.S.O., 1920.
Parliament. *Parliamentary Debates* and *British and Foreign State
Papers*. London: H.M.S.O., 1914–1921.
Hurewitz, J. C., ed. *Diplomacy in the Near and Middle East: A Docu-
mentary Record.* Vol. II: 1914–1956. Princeton, N.J.; D. Van
Nostrand, 1956.
Iraq
British Occupation Administration. *The Arab of Mesopotamia.* Basra:
Superintendent, Government Press, n.d.
India
Foreign and Political Department. *A Collection of Treaties, Engage-
ments and Sanads Relating to India and Neighbouring Countries.*
Compiled by C. U. Aitchison. Vol. XI. Delhi: Manager of Pub-
lications, 5th ed., 1933.
*The Last Week of War in Mesopotamia.* Delhi: Superintendent,
Government Press of India, 1919.

United States
    Department of State. *Papers Relating to the Foreign Relations of the
    United States. The Paris Peace Conference, 1919.* Washington,
    D.C.: U.S.G.P.O., 1942–1947. 13 vols.
Smith, Harvey H., et al., eds. *Area Handbook for Iraq.* Washington,
    D.C.: U.S.G.P.O., 1969.

### BIOGRAPHIES AND MEMOIRS

Abdullah ibn Hussein. *Memoirs of King Abdullah of Transjordan,* ed.
    by Philip Graves. Trans. from the Arabic. N.Y.: Philosophical Li-
    brary, 1950.
Addison, Rt. Hon. Christopher. *Politics from Within: 1911–1918. In-
    cluding Some Records of a Great National Effort.* London: Herbert
    Jenkins, 1924. 2 vols.
Aldington, Richard. *Lawrence of Arabia: A Biographical Enquiry.* Chi-
    cago: Henry Regnery, 1955.
Arfa, Gen. Hassan. *Under Five Shahs.* N.Y.: William Morrow, 1965.
Arthur, Sir George. *Life of Lord Kitchener.* Vol. III. N.Y.: Macmillan,
    1920.
Barber, Maj. Charles H. *Besieged in Kut and After.* Edinburgh and
    London: William Blackwood, 1917.
Barker, A. J. *Townshend of Kut: A Biography of Major-General Sir
    Charles Townshend, K.C.B., D.S.O.* London: Cassell, 1967.
Barrow, Gen. Sir George. *The Life of General Sir Charles Carmichael
    Monro, Bart., G.C.B., G.C.S.I., G.C.M.G.* London: Hutchinson, 1931.
Beaverbrook, Lord. *Men and Power, 1917–1918.* N.Y.: Duell, Sloan,
    Pearce, 1956.
———. *Politicians and the War, 1914–1916.* London: Thornton Butter-
    worth, 1928.
Belhaven, Lord. *The Uneven Road.* London, John Murray, 1955.
Bell, Lady, ed. *The Letters of Gertrude Bell.* London: Ernest Benn,
    1927. 2 vols.
Bentwich, Norman and Helen. *Mandate Memories, 1918–1948.* N.Y.:
    Schocken, 1965.
Birch-Reynardson, Capt. H. *Mesopotamia 1914–15: Extracts from a
    Regimental Officer's Diary.* London: Andrew Melrose, 1919.
Birdwood, Field Marshal Lord, of Anzac and Totnes. *Khaki and Gown:
    An Autobiography.* London: Ward, Lock, 1941.
———. *Nuri as-Said: A Study in Arab Leadership.* London: Cassell, 1959.
Birkenhead, Rt. Hon. the Earl of. *Contemporary Personalities.* London:
    Cassell, 1924.
"Black Tab." *On the Road to Kut: A Soldier's Story of the Mesopo-
    tamian Campaign.* London: Hutchinson, 1917.
Blake, Robert. *Unrepentant Tory: The Life and Times of Andrew*

*Bonar Law, 1858–1923, Prime Minister of the United Kingdom.* N.Y.: St. Martin's, 1956.

Bodley, Ronald, and Lorna Hearst. *Gertrude Bell.* N.Y.: Macmillan, 1940.

Bolitho, Hector. *James Lyle Mackay, First Earl of Inchcape.* London: John Murray, 1936.

Bonham-Carter, Victor. *The Strategy of Victory, 1914–1918: The Life and Times of the Master Strategist of World War I: Field-Marshal Sir William Robertson.* N.Y.: Holt, Rinehart, Winston, 1964. [English title: *Soldier True.*]

Boyle, Andrew. *Trenchard.* N.Y.: Norton, 1962.

Bray, Maj. N. N. E. *Paladin of Arabia: The Biography of Brevet Lieut.-Colonel G. E. Leachman, C.I.E., D.S.O., of the Royal Sussex Regiment.* London: John Heritage, Unicorn Press, 1936.

———. *Shifting Sands.* London: Unicorn Press, 1934.

Brémond, Général E. *Le Hedjaz dans la guerre mondiale.* Paris: Payot, 1931.

Buchan, John. *Mountain Meadow.* Intro. by Howard Swiggett. Boston: Houghton Mifflin, 1941.

Buchanan, Sir George. *The Tragedy of Mesopotamia.* London: William Blackwood, 1938.

Burgoyne, Elizabeth. *Gertrude Bell, from Her Personal Papers, 1914–1926.* London: Ernest Benn, 1961.

Callwell, Maj.-Gen. Sir C. E. *Field-Marshal Sir Henry Wilson, Bart., G.C.B., D.S.O., His Life and Diaries.* N.Y.: Scribners, 1927. 2 vols.

———. *The Life of Sir Stanley Maude, Lieutenant-General, K.C.B., C.M.G., D.S.O.* London: Constable, 1920.

Collier, Basil. *Brasshat: A Biography of Field-Marshal Sir Henry Wilson.* London: Secker & Warburg, 1961.

Colvin, Ian. *The Life of Lord Carson.* Vol. III. N.Y.: Macmillan, 1937.

Cowles, Virginia. *Winston Churchill: The Era and the Man.* N.Y.: Grosset and Dunlap, 1956.

de Gaury, Gerald. *Three Kings in Baghdad, 1921–1958.* London: Hutchinson, 1961.

Dugdale, Blanche E. C. *Arthur James Balfour, First Earl of Balfour, K.G., O.M., F.R.S., etc.* Vol. II. N.Y.: Putnam, 1937.

Dunsterville, Maj.-Gen. L. C. *The Adventures of Dunsterforce.* N.Y.: Longmans, Green, 1920.

———. *Stalky's Reminiscences.* London: Jonathan Cape, 1928.

Edmonds, C. J. *Kurds, Turks, and Arabs: Politics, Travel and Research in North-Eastern Iraq, 1919–1925.* London: Oxford University Press, 1957.

Edmonds, Charles. *T. E. Lawrence.* London: Peter Davies, 1935.

Egan, Eleanor Franklin. *The War in the Cradle of the World: Mesopotamia.* N.Y.: Harper, 1918.

Freeth, Zahra. *Kuwait Was My Home*. London: Allen & Unwin, 1956.

Gardner, Brian. *Allenby*. London: Cassell, 1965.

Garnett, David, ed. *The Letters of T. E. Lawrence*. N.Y.: Doubleday, Doran, 1939.

Gollin, A. M. *Proconsul in Politics: A Study of Lord Milner in Opposition and in Power*. N.Y.: Macmillan, 1964.

Graves, Philip. *The Life of Sir Percy Cox*. London: Hutchinson, 1941.

Graves, Robert. *Lawrence and the Arabs*. London: Jonathan Cape, 1927.

———, and B. H. Liddell Hart, eds. *T. E. Lawrence to His Biographers*. Garden City, N.Y.: Doubleday, 1963.

Grey of Fallodon, Viscount. *Twenty-Five Years, 1892–1916*. N.Y.: Stokes, 1925. 2 vols.

Gulbenkian, Nubar. *Portrait in Oil: The Autobiography of . . .* N.Y.: Simon & Schuster, 1965.

Haldane, Lt.-Gen. Sir Aylmer L. *The Insurrection in Mesopotamia, 1920*. Edinburgh: William Blackwood, 1922.

———. *A Soldier's Saga: The Autobiography of . . .* Edinburgh and London: William Blackwood, 1948.

Hancock, W. K. *Smuts: The Sanguine Years, 1870–1919*. Cambridge: Cambridge University Press, 1962.

———, and Jean van der Poel, eds. *Selections from the Smuts Papers*. Vols. III–IV (1910–1919). Cambridge: Cambridge University Press, 1966.

Hankey, Lord. *The Supreme Command, 1914–1918*. London: Allen & Unwin, 1961. 2 vols.

Hardinge of Penshurst, Lord. *My Indian Years, 1910–1916: The Reminiscences of . . .* London: John Murray, 1948.

———. *Old Diplomacy: The Reminiscences of . . .* London: John Murray, 1947.

Hay, W. R. *Two Years in Kurdistan. Experiences of a Political Officer, 1918–1920*. London: Sedgwick & Jackson, 1921.

Herbert, Aubrey. *Ben Kendim: A Record of Eastern Travel*, ed. by Desmond MacCarthy. 2nd ed. N.Y.: Putnam, 1925.

[———.] *Mons, Anzac and Kut, by an M.P.* London: Edward Arnold, 1919.

Jarvis, Maj. C. S. *Arab Command: The Biography of Lieutenant-Colonel F. W. Peake Pasha, C.M.G., O.B.E.* London: Hutchinson, 1942.

Jenkins, Roy. *Asquith*. London: Collins, 1964.

Kirkbride, Sir Alec Seath. *A Crackle of Thorns: Experiences in the Middle East*. London: John Murray, 1956.

Knightley, Phillip, and Colin Simpson. *The Secret Lives of Lawrence of Arabia*. London: Nelson, 1969.

Lawrence, A. W., ed. *T. E. Lawrence by His Friends: A New Selection of Memoirs*. N.Y.: McGraw Hill, 1963 (orig. publ., 1937).

Lawrence, T. E. *Oriental Assembly*. London: Williams & Norgate, 1939.

———. *Secret Despatches from Arabia by* . . . London: Golden Cockerel Press, [1939].

———. *Seven Pillars of Wisdom: A Triumph*. Garden City, N.Y.: Doubleday, Doran, 1936.

Leslie, Shane. *Mark Sykes: His Life and Letters*. London: Cassell, 1923.

Liddell Hart, B. H. *"T. E. Lawrence" in Arabia and After*. 2nd ed. London: Jonathan Cape, 1935.

Lloyd George, David. *Memoirs of the Peace Conference*. New Haven, Conn.: Yale University Press, 1939. 2 vols. [English title: *The Truth About the Peace Treaties*.]

———. *War Memoirs of* . . . Boston: Little, Brown, 1933–1937. 6 vols.

Long, P. W. *Other Ranks of Kut*. London: Williams & Norgate, 1938.

Lyell, Thomas. *The Ins and Outs of Mesopotamia*. London: A. M. Philpot, 1923.

MacMunn, Lt.-Gen. Sir George. *Behind the Scenes in Many Wars: Being the Military Reminiscences of* . . . London: John Murray, 1930.

Magnus, Philip. *Kitchener:Portrait of an Imperialist*. N.Y.: Dutton, 1959.

Marlowe, John. *Late Victorian: The Life of Sir Arnold Talbot Wilson, K.C.I.E., C.S.I., C.M.G., D.S.O., M.P.* London: Cresset, 1967.

Marshall, Lt.-Gen. Sir William. *Memories of Four Fronts*. London: Ernest Benn, 1929.

Meinertzhagen, Col. Richard. *Middle East Diary, 1917–1956*. N.Y.: Thomas Yoseloff, 1960.

Menzies, Mrs. Stuart. *Sir Stanley Maude and Other Memories*. London: Herbert Jenkins, 1920.

Molesworth, Lt.-Gen. G. N. *Curfew on Olympus*. N.Y.: Asia Publishing House, 1965.

Mousa, Suleiman. *T. E. Lawrence: An Arab View*. Trans. by Albert Butros. London: Oxford University Press, 1966.

Mousley, Capt. E. O. *The Secrets of a Kuttite: An Authentic Story of Kut, Adventures in Captivity and Stamboul Intrigue*. London: John Lane, The Bodley Head, 1922.

Murphy, Lt.-Col. C. C. R. *Soldiers of the Prophet*. London: John Hogg, 1921.

Nicolson, Harold. *Curzon: The Last Phase, 1919–1925: A Study in Post-War Diplomacy*. London: Constable, 1934

———. *Peacemaking, 1919*. N.Y.: Grosset & Dunlap, 1965.

Nogales, Rafael de. *Four Years Beneath the Crescent*. Trans. from the Spanish by Muna Lee. N.Y.: Scribners, 1926.

O'Dwyer, Sir Michael. *India as I Knew It, 1885–1925*. London: Constable, 1925.

O'Moore Creagh, Gen. Sir. *Autobiography*. London: Hutchinson, [1924].

Oxford and Asquith, Earl of. *Memories and Reflections, 1852–1927.* Vol. II. Boston: Little, Brown, 1928.

Pearson, Hesketh. *Hesketh Pearson by Himself.* N.Y.: Harper, 1965.

———. *Thinking It Over: The Reminiscences of . . .* N.Y.: Harper, 1938.

Petrie, Sir Charles. *The Chamberlain Tradition.* N.Y.: Stokes, 1938.

———. *The Life and Letters of the Right Hon. Sir Austen Chamberlain, K.G., P.C., M.P.* Vol. II. London: Cassell, 1940.

Philby, H. St. J. B. *Arabia of the Wahhabis.* London: Constable, 1928.

———. *Arabian Days: An Autobiography.* London: Robert Hale, 1948.

———. *The Heart of Arabia: A Record of Travel.* N.Y.: Putnam, 1923. 2 vols.

Presland, John [Gladys Skelton]. *Deedes Bey: A Study of Sir Wyndham Deedes, 1883–1923.* London: Macmillan, 1942.

Repington, Lt.-Col. C. à Court. *The First World War, 1914–1918: Personal Experiences of . . .* London: Constable, 1920. 2 vols.

Robertson, Field Marshal Sir William. *From Private to Field-Marshal.* Boston: Houghton Mifflin, 1921.

———. *Soldiers and Statesmen, 1914–1918.* N.Y.: Scribners, 1926. 2 vols.

Ronaldshay, The Rt. Hon., the Earl of. *The Life of Lord Curzon: Being the Authorized Biography of George Nathaniel, Marquess Curzon of Kedleston, K.G.* Vol. III. N.Y.: Boni & Liveright, [1928].

Sandes, Maj. E. W. C. *In Kut and Captivity with the Sixth Indian Division.* London: John Murray, 1919.

Sherson, Erroll. *Townshend of Chitral and Kut.* London: Heinemann, 1928.

Skrine, Sir Clarmont. *World War in Iran.* London: Constable, 1962.

Slim, Field Marshal Sir William. *Unofficial History.* N.Y.: David McKay, 1962.

Smith, Janet Adam. *John Buchan: A Biography.* London: Rupert Hart-Davis, 1965.

Smith-Dorrien, Gen. Sir Horace. *Memories of Forty-Eight Years' Service.* N.Y.: Dutton, 1925.

Spender, J. A., and Cyril Asquith. *Life of Herbert Henry Asquith, Lord Oxford and Asquith.* Vol. II. London: Hutchinson, 1932.

Stirling, Lt.-Col. W. F. *Safety Last.* London: Hollis & Carter, 1953.

Storrs, Sir Ronald. *Memoirs.* N.Y.: Putnam, 1937. [English title: *Orientations.*]

Sykes, Christopher. *Wassmuss, "The German Lawrence".* London: Longmans, Green, 1936.

Symes, Sir Stewart. *Tour of Duty.* London: Collins, 1946.

Thompson, Edward. *These Men, Thy Friends.* N.Y.: Harcourt, Brace, 1928.

Townshend, Maj.-Gen. Charles Vere Ferrers. *My Campaign.* N.Y.: James McCann, 1920. 2 vols.

Vansittart, Lord. *The Mist Procession: The Autobiography of . . .* London: Hutchinson, 1958.

Waley, S. D. *Edwin Montagu: A Memoir and an Account of His Visits to India.* N.Y.: Asia Publishing House, 1964.

Weintraub, Stanley and Rodelle, eds. *Evolution of a Revolt: Early Postwar Writings of T. E. Lawrence.* University Park, Pa.: Pennsylvania State University Press, 1968.

Wester Wemyss, Lady. *The Life and Letters of Lord Wester Wemyss, G.C.B., C.M.G., M.V.O., Admiral of the Fleet.* London: Eyre & Spottiswoode, 1935.

Wilson, Lt.-Col. Sir Arnold T. *Loyalties, Mesopotamia, 1914–1917: A Personal and Historical Record.* London: Oxford University Press, 1930.

———. *Mesopotamia 1917–1920: A Clash of Loyalties. A Personal and Historical Record.* London: Oxford University Press, 1931.

Wingate, Sir Ronald. *Not in the Limelight.* London: Hutchinson, 1959.

———. *Wingate of the Sudan: The Life and Times of General Sir Reginald Wingate, Maker of the Anglo-Egyptian Sudan.* London: John Murray, 1955.

Wrench, John Evelyn. *Alfred Lord Milner: The Man of No Illusions, 1854–1925.* London: Eyre & Spottiswoode, 1958.

Young, Maj. Sir Hubert. *The Independent Arab.* London: John Murray, 1933.

## SPECIAL ARTICLES

Beatson, F. C. "Mesopotamia, I: The Recent Military Policy of the Government of India," *Nineteenth Century and After,* 82 (July–December 1917, 260–75.

Busch, Briton C. "Britain and the Status of Kuwayt, 1894–99," *Middle East Journal,* 21 (Spring 1967), 187–98.

Carruthers, Douglas. "Captain Shakespear's Last Journey," *Geographical Journal,* 59 (May–June 1922), 321–34, 401–17.

Chesney, G. M. "The Mesopotamian Breakdown," *Fortnightly Review,* 108 (1917), 34–44.

Cotes, Everard. "Mesopotamia, II: The Tragedy of an Impossible System," *Nineteenth Century and After,* 82 (July–December 1917), 272–82.

De Novo, John A. "The Movement for an Aggressive American Oil Policy Abroad, 1918–1920," *American Historical Review,* 61:4 (July 1956), 854–76.

Earle, E. M. "The Turkish Petroleum Company: A Study in Oleaginous Diplomacy," *Political Science Quarterly,* 39 (June 1924), 265–79.

Edmonds, C. J. "Gertrude Bell in the Near and Middle East," *Journal of the Royal Central Asian Society,* 56 (October 1969), 229–44.

Evans, Maj. R. "The Strategy of the Campaign in Mesopotamia, 1914–1918," *Journal of the Royal United Service Institution,* 68 (1923), 254–69.

Falls, Cyril. "The Army," *Edwardian England, 1901–1914,* ed. Simon Nowell-Smith. London: Oxford University Press, 1964. Pp. 517–44.

Forbes, Rosita. "A Visit to the Idrisi Territory in Asir and Yemen," *Geographical Journal,* 62 (September 1923), 271–78.

Fraser, Lovat. "Problems of Indian Administration," *Edinburgh Review,* 227 (January 1918), 166–87.

———. "The Responsibility for Baghdad," *Edinburgh Review,* 226 (October 1917), 396–406.

[Garbett, C. C.] "Turkish Rule and British Administration in Mesopotamia," *Quarterly Review,* 232 (October 1919), 401–23.

Haig, Sir Wolseley. "The Indian Army, 1858–1918," *The Cambridge History of the British Empire,* vol. V: *The Indian Empire 1858–1918,* ed. H. H. Dodwell. Cambridge: Cambridge University Press, 1932. Pp. 395–402.

Harrison, Austin. "Mesopotamias," *English Review,* 25 (1917), 175–79.

Hogarth, D. G. "Present Discontents in the Near and Middle East," *Quarterly Review,* 234 (April 1920), 411–23.

Hovannisian, Richard. "The Allies and Armenia, 1915–18," *Journal of Contemporary History,* 3 (January 1968), 145–68.

Hurwitz, Samuel J. "Winston S. Churchill," *Some Modern Historians of Britain: Essays in Honor of R. L. Schuyler,* ed. Herman Ausubel, et al. N.Y.: Dryden Press, 1951. Pp. 306–24.

Kedourie, Elie. "Cairo and Khartoum on the Arab Question 1915–18," *Historical Journal,* 7:2 (1964), 280–97.

Khadduri, Majid. " 'Azīz 'Ali al-Miṣrī and the Arab Nationalist Movement," *Middle Eastern Affairs,* No. 4 (St. Antony's Papers, No. 17), ed. Albert Hourani. Oxford: Oxford University Press, 1965. Pp. 140–63.

Klieman, Aaron S. "Britain's War Aims in the Middle East in 1915," *Journal of Contemporary History,* 3 (July 1968), 237–52.

Kurat, Y. T. "How Turkey Drifted into World War I," *Studies in International History: Essays Presented to W. Norton Medlicott, Stevenson Professor of International History in the University of London,* ed. K. Bourne and D. C. Watt. Hamden, Conn.: Archon Books, 1967. Pp. 291–315.

Marmorstein, Emile. "A Note on 'Damascus, Homs, Hama and Aleppo,' " *Middle Eastern Affairs,* No. 2 (St. Antony's Papers, No. 11), ed. Albert Hourani. London: Chatto & Windus, 1961. Pp. 161–65.

Maurice, Maj.-Gen. Sir Frederick. "The Campaign in Palestine and Egypt, 1914–1918 . . . ," *Army Quarterly,* 18 (1929), 21.

———. "The Eastern and Western Controversy," *Contemporary Review,* 114 (July–December 1918), 623–30.

"Mesopotamia," *Blackwood's,* 200 (1916), 796–813.

Morison, Sir Theodore. "A Colony for India," *Nineteenth Century and After,* 84 (July–December 1918), 430–41.

"Musings Without Method," *Blackwood's,* 202 (1917), 265–79.

Nevakivi, Jukka. "Lord Kitchener and the Partition of the Ottoman

Empire, 1915–1916," *Studies in International History: Essays Presented to W. Norton Medlicott, Stevenson Professor of International History in the University of London*, ed. K. Bourne and D. C. Watt. Hamden, Conn.: Archon Books, 1967. Pp. 316–29.

Ormsby-Gore, The Hon. W. "Great Britain, Mesopotamia and the Arabs," *Nineteenth Century and After*, 88 (July–December 1920), 225–38.

————. "The Organization of British Responsibilities in the Middle East," *Journal of the Central Asian Society*, 6:3–4 (1919), 83–105.

Sheppard, Capt. E. W. "Some Military Aspects of the Mesopotamian Problem," *Journal of the Central Asian Society*, 8:1 (1921), 13–28.

Slater, S. H. "Iraq," *Nineteenth Century and After*, 99 (April 1926), 479–94.

Sydenham of Combe, Lord. "The Future of India, I: India as a Colonising Power," *Nineteenth Century and After*, 84 (July–December 1918), 762–70.

Taylor, A. B. "The River Tigris from the Sea to Baghdad," *Journal of the Central Asian Society*, 4:3 (1917), 72–90.

Tibawi, A. L. "Syria in the McMahon Correspondence: Fresh Evidence from the British Foreign Office Records," *Mid-East Forum* (Beirut), 42:4 (1966), 5–32.

————. "T. E. Lawrence, Faisal and Weizmann: The 1919 Attempt to Secure an Arab Balfour Declaration," *Journal of the Royal Central Asian Society*, 56 (June 1969), 156–63.
*Contemporary History*, 3 (October 1968), 89–107.

Tinker, Hugh. "India in the First World War and After," *Journal of Contemporary History*, 3 (October 1968), 89–107.

Usher, Capt. H. B. "Mesopotamia's Claim on Britain," *Contemporary Review*, 120 (July–December 1921), 332–38.

Willcocks, Sir William. "Two and a Half Years in Mesopotamia," *Blackwood's*, 199 (1915), 304–23.

Wilson, Lt.-Col. Sir Arnold. "Mesopotamia, 1914–1921," *Journal of the Central Asian Society*, 8:3 (1921), 144–61.

Woodhouse, Henry. "American Oil Claims in Turkey," *Current History*, 15 (March 1922), 953–59.

Yate, A. C. "Baghdad and Gaza—and After," *Nineteenth Century and After*, 82 (July–December 1917), 1276–86.

————. "Britain's Buffer States in the East," *Journal of the Central Asian Society*, 5:1 (1918), 3–23.


## MONOGRAPHS AND GENERAL WORKS

Adamec, Ludwig W. *Afghanistan 1900–1923: A Diplomatic History.* Berkeley, Calif.: University of California Press, 1967.

Anderson, M. S. *The Eastern Question, 1774–1923: A Study in International Relations.* London: Macmillan, 1966.

Antonius, George. *The Arab Awakening: The Story of the Arab National Movement*. London: Hamish Hamilton, 1938.

Arfa, Hassan. *The Kurds: An Historical and Political Study*. London: Oxford University Press, 1966.

Austin, Brig.-Gen. H. H. *The Baqubah Refugee Camp: An Account of Work on Behalf of the Persecuted Assyrian Christians*. London: Faith Press, 1920.

Avery, Peter. *Modern Iran*. London: Ernest Benn, 1965.

Aziz, K. K. *The Making of Pakistan: A Study in Nationalism*. London: Chatto & Windus, 1967.

Barker, A. J. *The Neglected War: Mesopotamia 1914–1918*. London: Faber & Faber, 1967. (Revised American edition: *The Bastard War: The Mesopotamian Campaign of 1914–1918*. N.Y., Dial Press, 1967.)

Barnett, Correlli. *The Swordbearers: Supreme Command in the First World War*. N.Y.: William Morrow, 1964.

Browne, Brig. J. Gilbert. *The Iraq Levies, 1915–1932*. London: Royal United Service Institution, 1932.

Burne, Lt.-Col. A. H. *Mesopotamia, the Last Phase*. Aldershot: Gale & Polden, 1936.

Busch, Briton C. *Britain and the Persian Gulf, 1894–1914*. Berkeley, Calif.: University of California Press, 1967.

Candler, Edmund. *The Long Road to Baghdad*. London: Cassell, 1919. 2 vols.

Churchill, Rt. Hon. Winston S. *The Unknown War: The Eastern Front*. N.Y.: Scribners, 1931.

———. *The World Crisis*. London: Thornton Butterworth, 1923–1929. 5 vols.

Coke, Richard. *The Heart of the Middle East*. London: Thornton Butterworth, 1925.

Collins, Doreen. *Aspects of British Politics, 1904–1919*. Oxford: Pergamon Press, 1965.

Connell, John [Robertson, John H.] *The "Office": The Story of the British Foreign Office, 1919–1951*. N.Y.: St. Martin's, 1958.

Cumming, Henry H. *Franco-British Rivalry in the Post-War Near East: The Decline of French Influence*. London: Oxford University Press, 1938.

Dane, Edmund. *British Campaigns in the Nearer East, 1914–1918, from the Outbreak of War with Turkey to the Armistice*. London: Hodder & Stoughton, 1919. 2 vols.

Dickson, H. R. P. *Kuwait and Her Neighbours*. London: Allen & Unwin, 1956.

Edmonds, Brig.-Gen. Sir James E. *A Short History of World War I*. London: Oxford University Press, 1951.

Ellis, C. H. *The British Intervention in Transcaspia, 1918–1919*. Berkeley, Calif.: University of California Press, 1963.

Ellison, Lt.-Gen. Sir Gerald. *The Perils of Amateur Strategy as Exemplified by the Attack on the Dardanelles Fortress in 1915.* London: Longmans, Green, 1926.

Evans, Laurence. *United States Policy and the Partition of Turkey, 1914–1924.* Baltimore: Johns Hopkins University Press, 1965.

Falls, Cyril. *The Great War.* N.Y.: Capricorn, 1961.

Fraser, Lovat. *India Under Curzon and After.* London: Heinemann, 1911.

Gidney, James B. *A Mandate for Armenia.* Kent, Ohio: Kent State University Press, 1967.

Gopal, Ram. *Indian Muslims: A Political History (1858–1947).* N.Y.: Asia Publishing House, 1959.

Gottlieb, W. W. *Studies in Secret Diplomacy During the First World War.* London: Allen & Unwin, 1957.

Guinn, Paul. *British Strategy and Politics, 1914 to 1918.* Oxford: Clarendon Press, 1965.

Hankey, Lord. *Government Control in War.* Cambridge: Cambridge University Press, 1945.

Hewins, Ralph. *A Golden Dream: The Miracle of Kuwait.* London: W. H. Allen, 1963.

Higgins, Trumbull. *Winston Churchill and the Dardanelles: A Dialogue in Ends and Means.* N.Y.: Macmillan, 1963.

Holt, P. M. *Egypt and the Fertile Crescent, 1516–1922: A Political History.* Ithaca, N.Y.: Cornell University Press, 1966.

Hourani, Albert. *Arabic Thought in the Liberal Age, 1798–1939.* London: Oxford University Press, 1962.

Hovannisian, Richard G. *Armenia on the Road to Independence, 1918.* Berkeley, Calif.: University of California Press, 1967.

Howard, Harry N. *The Partition of Turkey: A Diplomatic History, 1913–1923.* N.Y.: Howard Fertig, 1966 [1931].

———. *The King-Crane Commission: An American Inquiry in the Middle East,* Beirut: Khayat's, 1963.

Ireland, Philip Willard. *'Iraq: A Study in Political Development.* London: Jonathan Cape, 1937.

Jacob, Harold F. *Kings of Arabia: The Rise and Set of the Turkish Sovranty in the Arabian Peninsula.* London: Mills & Boon, 1923.

James, Robert Rhodes. *Gallipoli.* N.Y.: Macmillan, 1965.

Jung, Eugène. *La Révolte arabe.* Paris: Colbert, 1924–1925. 2 vols.

Kazemzadeh, Firuz. *The Struggle for Transcaucasia (1917–1921).* N.Y.: Philosophical Library, 1951.

Kearsey, A. *A Study of the Strategy and Tactics of the Mesopotamian Campaign, 1914–1917, up to and including the Capture and Consolidation of Baghdad, April, 1917, Illustrating the Principles of War.* Aldershot: Gale & Polden, n.d.

Kedourie, Elie. *England and the Middle East: The Destruction of the Ottoman Empire, 1914–1921.* London: Bowes & Bowes, 1956.

Khadduri, Majid. *Independent Iraq, 1932–1958: A Study in Iraqi Politics.* 2nd ed. London: Oxford University Press, 1960.

Kimche, Jon. *The Unromantics: The Great Powers and the Balfour Declaration.* London: Weidenfeld & Nicolson, 1968.

Liddell Hart, Capt. B. H. *The Real War, 1914–1918.* Boston: Little, Brown, 1930.

——. *The War in Outline, 1914–1918.* N.Y.: Random House, 1936.

Loder, J. de V. *The Truth about Mesopotamia, Palestine, and Syria.* London: Allen & Unwin, 1923.

Longrigg, Stephen Hemsley. *Syria and Lebanon under French Mandate.* London: Oxford University Press, 1958.

——. *'Iraq 1900 to 1950: A Political, Social, and Economic History.* 2nd ed. London: Oxford University Press, 1956.

Louis, William Roger. *Great Britain and Germany's Lost Colonies, 1914–1919.* Oxford. Clarendon Press, 1967.

Main, Ernest. *Iraq from Mandate to Independence.* London: Allen & Unwin, 1935.

al-Marayati, Abid A. *A Diplomatic History of Modern Iraq.* N.Y.: Robert Speller, 1961.

Marder, Arthur J. *From the Dreadnought to Scapa Flow: The Royal Navy in the Fisher Era, 1904–1919.* Vols. I–III. London: Oxford University Press, 1961–1966.

Masani, R. P. *Britain in India: An Account of British Rule in the Indian Subcontinent.* Bombay: John Brown, Oxford University Press, 1960.

Maurice, Maj.-Gen. Sir F. *British Strategy: A Study of the Application of the Principles of War.* London: Constable, 1929.

Mehrotra, S. R. *India and the Commonwealth, 1885–1929.* N.Y.: Praeger, 1965.

Monroe, Elizabeth. *Britain's Moment in the Middle East, 1914–1956.* London: Methuen, 1965.

Neave, Dorina L. *Remembering Kut: "Lest We Forget".* London: Arthur Baker, 1937.

Nevakivi, Jukka. *Britain, France and the Arab Middle East, 1914–1920.* London: University of London, Athlone Press, 1969.

Parfit, Joseph T. *Marvellous Mesopotamia: The World's Wonderland.* London: S. W. Partridge, [1920].

——. *Mesopotamia: The Key to the Future.* London: Hodder & Stoughton, 1917.

Philby, H. St. J. B. *Arabian Jubilee.* N.Y.: John Day, 1953.

——. *Sa'udi Arabia.* N.Y.: Praeger, 1955.

ar-Rushaid, Abdul 'Azīz. *Ta'rīkh al-Kuwait* [History of Kuwait]. Beirut: Dār maktabat al-Hayāt, n.d.

Schwadran, Benjamin. *The Middle East, Oil, and the Great Powers, 1959.* 2nd ed. N.Y.: Council for Middle Eastern Affairs Press, 1959.

Seaman, L. C. B. *Post-Victorian Britain, 1902–1951.* London: Methuen, 1967.

Stein, Leonard. *The Balfour Declaration.* N.Y.: Simon & Schuster, 1961.

Sykes, Christopher. *Two Studies in Virtue.* N.Y.: Knopf, 1953.

Thomas, Hugh. *The Story of Sandhurst.* London: Hutchinson, 1961.

Thornton, A. P. *The Imperial Idea and Its Enemies: A Study in British Power.* Garden City, N.Y.: Doubleday, 1968 [1959].

Trumpener, Ulrich. *Germany and the Ottoman Empire, 1914–1918.* Princeton, N.J.: Princeton University Press, 1968.

Vatikiotis, P. J. *Politics and the Military in Jordan: A Study of the Arab Legion, 1921–1957.* N.Y.: Praeger, 1967.

Wilson, Sir Arnold T. *Persia.* N.Y.: Scribners, 1933.

———. *The Persian Gulf: An Historical Sketch from the Earliest Times to the Beginning of the Twentieth Century.* London: Allen & Unwin, 1928.

Wilson, Trevor. *The Downfall of the Liberal Party, 1914–1935.* Ithaca, N.Y.: Cornell University Press, 1966.

Winder, R. Bayly. *Saudi Arabia in the Nineteenth Century.* N.Y.: St. Martin's, 1965.

Woodward, Sir Llewellyn. *Great Britain and the War of 1914–1918.* London: Methuen, 1967.

Zeine, Zeine N. *Arab-Turkish Relations and the Emergence of Arab Nationalism.* Beirut: Khayat's, 1958.

———. *The Struggle for Arab Independence: Western Diplomacy and the Rise and Fall of Faisal's Kingdom in Syria.* Beirut: Khayat's, 1960.

Ziadeh, N. A. *Sanūsīya. A Study of a Revivalist Movement in Islam.* Leiden: E. J. Brill, 1958.

# Index

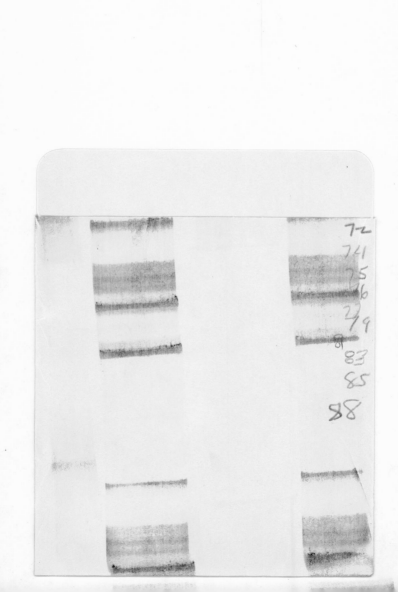